We read, at first, Tennyson's Idyls, *with profound recognition of the finely elaborated execution, and also of the inward perfection of* vacancy, – *and, to say truth, with considerable impatience at being treated so very like infants, though the lollipops were so superlative. We gladly changed for one Emerson's* English Traits; *and read that, with increasing and ever increasing satisfaction every evening; blessing Heaven that there were still Books for grown-up people too! That truly is a Book all full of thoughts like winged arrows [...].*

Thomas Carlyle (1867)

Contents of Cabinet

Emerson's English Traits
and the
Natural History of Metaphor

David LaRocca

B L O O M S B U R Y

NEW YORK • LONDON • NEW DELHI • SYDNEY

Bloomsbury Academic

An imprint of Bloomsbury Publishing Inc

1385 Broadway	50 Bedford Square
New York	London
NY 10018	WC1B 3DP
USA	UK

www.bloomsbury.com

Bloomsbury is a registered trade mark of Bloomsbury Publishing Plc

First published 2013

© David LaRocca, 2013

Library of Congress Cataloging-in-Publication Data
A catalog record for this title is available from the Library of Congress.

ISBN: PB: 978-1-4411-6140-6
HB: 978-1-4411-9317-9
ePub: 978-1-4411-3702-9
ePDF: 978-1-4411-7561-8

Typeset by Fakenham Prepress Solutions, Fakenham, Norfolk NR21 8NN
Printed and bound in the United States of America

*A Florilegium
of Varied Specimens and Propitious Excerpts
from Transcendental Biology
and
Related Fields of Inquiry,
Selected,
Arranged and Presented
by
David LaRocca, B.A. ΦBκ, M.A., M.T.S., Ph.D.*

in memoriam
Earl Charles LaRocca
1921–2010
filius est pars patris

That is, here, to make from a volume, approximately, more or less, a flower, to extract a flower, to mount it, or rather to have it mount itself, bring itself to light. [...]

Metaphor in the text of philosophy. [... I]s there metaphor in the text of philosophy? [...] The question demands a book.[1]

[1] Jacques Derrida, 'White Mythology: Metaphor in the Text of Philosophy', *Margins of Philosophy*, tr. Alan Bass (Chicago: The University of Chicago Press, 1982), 209.

Solertia et Labore – Ingenuity and Labor
Socordiam Lvimvs – Atone for Indifference

* * *

[Detail from the Frontispiece of]

CHARLES BUTLER's *The Feminine Monarchie*;
or, a Treatise Concerning Bees, and the Due Ordering of Them:
Wherein
The truth found out by experience and diligent observation,
discovereth the idle and fond conceipts,
which many have written anent this subiect.
Printed at Oxford, 1609.

[In the 1623 edition Butler amended the subtitle to read]

or, The Historie of Bees, SHEWING Their admirable Nature, and Properties,
Their Generation, and Colonies, Their Government, Loyaltie, Art, Industrie, Enemies,
Warres, Magnanimitie, & c. TOGETHER with the right ordering of them
from time to time: *And the sweet profit arising thereof.*

Contents

Prefatory Notes

1. LUDWIG WITTGENSTEIN, *Philosophical Investigations*
   What we are supplying are really remarks on the natural history of human beings; we are not contributing curiosities however, but observations which no one has doubted, but which have escaped remark only because they are always before our eyes.[1]

   D. Q. MCINERNY, *Being Logical*
   [... R]eaders might be put off by what they perceive to be an emphasis upon the obvious. I do, in fact, place a good deal of stress on the obvious in this book, and that is quite deliberate. In logic, as in life, it is the obvious that most often bears emphasizing, because it so easily escapes our notice.[2]

   RALPH WALDO EMERSON, 'Spiritual Laws'
   No man can learn what he has not preparation for learning, however near to his eyes is the object.[3]

2. WITTGENSTEIN, *Philosophical Investigations*
   The work of the philosopher consists in assembling reminders for a particular purpose.[4]

   EMERSON, 'The American Scholar'
   He plies the slow, unhonoured, and unpaid task of observation.[5]

3. MCINERNY, *Being Logical*
   We do not really understand our own ideas if we suppose them to be self-generating, that is, not owing their existence to extramental realities.[6]

   FRIEDRICH NIETZSCHE, *Twilight of the Idols*, '"Reason" in Philosophy'
   [... T]he higher ground is not *permitted* to grow out of the lower, is not *permitted* to have grown at all. [...]
      Moral: everything of the first rank has to be *causa sui*. Origination from something else counts as an objection that casts doubt on the value of what has thus originated. All the supreme values are of the first rank, all the highest concepts, what *is*, the unconditioned, the good, the true, the perfect – all this cannot have become, and *must* consequently be *causa sui*.[7]

4. GERTRUDE STEIN, *Narration*
   After all anybody is as their land and air is. [...] It is that which makes them and the arts they make and the work they do and the way they eat and the way they drink and they way they learn and everything.[8]

5. VIRGIL, *Georgics*
   And so that we can learn from known signs about these matters – [...].[9]

Introduction: Some Traits of *English Traits*

1.   ON 6 AUGUST 1856 RALPH WALDO EMERSON published *English Traits*, a book that is distinctive – an anomaly, an uncharacteristic hybrid, a unique specimen – when compared with works in the established pedigree of his prior writing, and perhaps as a consequence the book has become, in one well-informed estimation, 'the most overlooked text in Emerson's corpus'.[1] *English Traits* is a work about the interaction between a concept and a country – about how we know a place by a name, and understand its people by their characteristics. Since Emerson was most interested in answering the question 'Why England is England?' his attention is most overtly directed to an analysis of the traits of the English people as they are manifest in the cultural, institutional, intellectual and physical attributes of the land and its generations of inhabitants.[2] What made these vital and delicate natures? Was it the air? Was it the sea – both as the limit of land and as an invitation to the uncharted beyond the shore? Was it the parentage? Emerson asks in staccato about the conditions and forces that created these people. In *English Traits* he formalizes his long-running taxonomic diagnostic of the English by reference to and description of the race's features and tendencies – and the land, founders, descendants and culture that define them. Building on earlier essays and lectures – indeed, works written before he even made his inaugural visit to the island in 1833 – in this late, amalgamated volume, Emerson offers a multiform treatise that incorporates passages that are philosophical, psychological, sociological, anthropological, literary, religious, journalistic and teeming with a biological history of a country and its citizens – while also book-ending those varied interventions with autobiographical reflections befitting a travel narrative. In characterizing his own vision for the new work on England, Emerson remarked to Henry David Thoreau: 'I am ambitious to write something which all can read, like *Robinson Crusoe*'.[3]

Despite his continual reflection on England – beginning in the 1830s, a decade that included his first visit there at a time of much-needed vocational discernment – Emerson had deferred for decades the creation of a book on the subject. Furthermore, in the meantime, he had written nothing comparable that addressed his homeland, such as *American Traits* – though it may be contended that, in posterity, most if not all of his other published writing and lectures ably and appropriately fit under such a broad but descriptive title. And even as he was invited by his friend and admirer Alexander Ireland to return to England to give a series of lectures beginning in 1847, it took many years – almost an additional decade – for a finished work on the English to appear by Emerson's hand. Why the work gestated in Emerson for so long is as intriguing as why the work looks and sounds the way it does – that is, so divergent from the writing that made him internationally famous and his style sufficiently well-known to be at once humbly imitated and humorously parodied.

The long period of scholarly development cannot be attributed to a novel mode of composition. In writing about the English Emerson employs methods familiar to the generation of his other, earlier work, drawing widely from his private journals written during his two voyages to the island in 1832–3 and 1847–8, and from letters he sent to friends and family. This kind of adaptation – from one genre of writing to another – was common very early on in his writing career, when for example his sermons became the backdrop for, or at least informed the structure of, his public lectures and published essays. Later, private journal entries would be excerpted for the purposes of public discourse, sometimes with minimal emendation. *English Traits* sustains this lifelong method and presses it forward to encompass even more genres of writing. Depending on where one reads, it is natural history; social history; cultural criticism; race theory; memoir; travelogue; political analysis; literary theory; literary criticism; art criticism; political theory; racial theory; foray into the psychology of temperament; physiology of blood and brain; anthropology; archaeology; civics; rhetoric; architectural history; educational analysis; clerical commentary; critique of business, markets and finance; moral philosophy; philosophy of technology; meditation on controversial topics of the day, such as aid to the poor; declaration of humanitarian allegiances; diplomatic brief; open letter; confession; narrative of an adventure; – and there's a speech added to the end! The book, such as it is, is presented as a unified work, despite its varied styles, sub-topics and forms. While there is much in the work that is reminiscent of Emerson's thinking, before and after 1856, the book does appear as a kind of genetic deviation: it is Emerson's effort to create an extended work on a single topic – something different than a book of essays, or a collection of lectures. Consequently the 19 chapters of the book should not be treated like discrete and independent creations but as parts of an expertly curated collection of remarks that add up to a definitive – hard won, deeply informed – statement on the English by the writer who Walt Whitman claimed was 'the finest critic of our land' – the leading American intellectual of the age.[4]

* * *

AS A READER of Washington Irving's *Sketch Book* (1820) Emerson may have gleaned the possibility of creating his own hybrid work of travel literature. When more than two decades later Emerson read Charles Dickens' *American Notes for Circulation* (1842), he commented in his journal that the work – written after Dickens' first of two visits to America – is marked by the 'the broadest caricature', and for his own sake seemed at once to remember and feel admonished by its author that 'monstrous exaggeration is an easy secret of romance.'[5] Emerson grants that Dickens' book 'answers its end very well, which plainly was to make a readable book, nothing more. Truth is not his object for a single instant, but merely to make good points in a lively sequence, and he proceeds very well. As an account of America it is not to be considered for a moment: it is too short, too narrow, too superficial, and too ignorant, too slight, and too fabulous, and the man totally unequal to the work'. (Despite being profoundly unsettled by America and disappointed by Americans, Dickens appears to have been sufficiently pleased with his New England experience that he concedes 'If I were a Bostonian, I think I would be a Transcendentalist'.[6] Dickens did not meet Emerson until 25 April 1848 at a dinner given in London by John Forster; when Dickens presented the inaugural reading of his American tour in Boston on 2 December 1867, Emerson was in the audience.) Emerson can be said to have created in *English Traits* a work that is fairer and more factually accurate than *American Notes*; whether this changes what claims for truth it might make about its subject becomes part of our interest in the ambitions of its form and content. The particular hybridity of Emerson's book provides a context for asking about the purpose and value of ethnographic description and national history as offered by outsiders and foreigners. If works of criticism that caricature can humble or insult a host nation, perhaps even celebrating hubristically their 'monstrous' attributes of atrophy or distension, Emerson's *English Traits* presents an alternative shape and tone. While Emerson's judgement of England is often personal – indeed he begins in the vein of memoir and travel reminiscence – it is neither offered to reinforce his private opinions and anxieties nor motivated by a desire to find evidence to support pre-established prejudices. Unlike an instrumental sort of critic who collects facts and assembles anecdotes to substantiate prognostications, Emerson proceeds in a fashion that harmonizes both literary and scientific sensibilities: he seeks to describe a way of approaching relationships between things, and to fathom the significance of those points of resemblance and difference. Hence the crucial role that metaphor plays in his analysis, for it is precisely by reference to those points of similarity or dissimilarity that the description becomes conceptually resonant and intellectually commanding. An empirical encounter, for Emerson, is not meant to stand as a proof of his opinion but as a point of departure from it. In this way intuition and induction coalesce as a hybridized mode of cultural critique. Though Emerson may have chosen to address a single topic, his critique does not provide a single theory of the English, still less a personally motivated thesis about them, but instead offers a kaleidoscopic, interdisciplinary account of their features and attributes.

In considering the range of Emerson's reading in travel literature prior to the publication of *English Traits* – for example, in the years between his first and second voyages to England, Emerson read in Frances Trollope's *Domestic Manners of Americans* (1832) and James Fenimore Cooper's *Gleanings in Europe: England* (1837) – Philip Nicoloff notes in *Emerson on Race and History: An Examination of* English Traits (1961):

> While it may be too much to say that *English Traits* by itself terminated the period of criminative travel literature (Washington Irving, Bayard Taylor, Frederick Law Olmsted, Margaret Fuller, and others were significant contributors here) this was the first book-length study of England by an American which combined depth of perception with a complete freedom from sycophancy or petulance. Emerson more successfully than any of the others held aloof not only from the points of international controversy, but also from the personal bias which had cramped so much of the earlier literature of English travel.[7]

Emerson's aloofness, though, should not be mistaken for a kind of neglect of the 'points of international controversy' that were overwhelmingly evident in day-to-day life, among them, and principally, the persistence of chattel slavery on American soil. Emerson is decidedly aware of the existence and endurance of slavery in the United States, defined and defended as it was by laws and statutes; it is a point of discomposing shame and paralyzing confusion for his sense of American judgement. Moncure Daniel Conway declares 'Emerson was the first American scholar to cast a dart at Slavery', and emphasizes how, in 1831 and 1832, the Reverend Emerson – many years before he would himself publically and tenaciously declaim the institution – 'admitted an abolitionist to lecture on the subject in his church, and in the following year another was invited to his pulpit'.[8] In 1841 Emerson's considered remarks on the prospects of man as a reformer of his world – its nature, its citizens – found him nonchalantly excoriate 'the ordinary abominations of slavery', and write with punning critique of 'the blacker traits' that distort the dignity of man's mind and morals – traits that he hopes 'are exceptions denounced and unshared by all reputable men', a class in which he manifestly counts himself a member.[9] Emerson's early support for abolition later gave way to his own articulated agitation and direct remonstrations, as for example, in his heraldic and chastising anniversary speech 'An Address ... on ... the Emancipation of the Negroes of the British West Indies' (1844). As part of his entreaty to the political order that ruled the Union, Emerson asked: 'let not this stain attach, let not this misery accumulate any longer'. And he cites the 'bright example of England' as evidence for a 'moral revolution' that American imagination and will can yet manifest for itself.[10] Even as Emerson was citing England as a beacon for ethical reasoning, his arguments against slavery as a phenomenon were non-nationalistic. He did not believe that the English GENIUS for liberty was a proprietary trait of their race, but a shared feature of a rational species – that slavery was, quite clearly, something that could be legislated against. As Joseph Blau has written, Emerson 'saw the slavery question as a political question as the great philosophers have always seen politics, as an aspect of man's quest for the fulfilment of humanity. His was a transcendental politics that could be carried on only by transcendental politicians – in the language of Plato, by philosopher-kings, 'who can open their eyes wider than to a nationality, namely, to considerations of benefit to the human race, can act in the interest of civilization'.[11] Emerson's capacity to address the charged and churning political crisis of his day – in the terms of transcendental politics – appears underwritten, even occasioned, by his less obviously relevant transcendental biology. A closer look will show that a faith in the coherence and continuity of moral and physical law, for instance, will justify and expedite a political statement about the corrupt, depraved status of chattel slavery.

In *English Traits* Emerson might be said to address slavery obliquely – by trans-forming the overtly stated, provocatively tautological, inquiry 'Why England is England?' into a subversive investigation: why America is itself and not England? Or more in the terms and questions that parallel Emerson's leading interests in the book: why have the children of a liberty-loving, -granting, and -defending people persisted in depriving freedom to their fellow man? Is that fellow man not a man? Why have conspiring Americans debased themselves in the passage of a 'quadruped law' (namely, the Fugitive Slave Law of 1850) that confirms their moral weakness and blindness to viable claims of liberty and equality? If Emerson spends more time in

English Traits focused on the effects of expansive historical forces and the varieties of biological determinism than he does lining up definitive arguments to support his already highly developed and publically articulated negative declamation of slavery, it is not because he fails to see their influence on those who hold the whip and the key to the chains.

Given the timing of the book's appearance – 1856 – the assigned and coalescing topic of TRAITS stands out both for its political and ethical significance and for its scientific prominence. Somewhat unassumingly, this is a book about race published in the decade preceding the American Civil War. It is also a book that dwells on the nature of blood and descent in the years of Charles Lyell's pre-eminence just before Charles Darwin's burst of conceptual innovation reshaped the modern view of human evolutionary development. It is, in less direct ways, a book about America and its promise and failings as the child of the then world-dominating empire. England was, for Emerson, an aboriginal place – where his family (all the way back, at least, to Peter Waldo and the Waldensians) descended from the Saxons, and later emigrated to the shores of a new England where William Emerson, the esteemed preacher of Concord, Massachusetts, would stand witness to the first day of the American Revolution: the British and Continental forces spilling first blood there before him, at the edge of his yard on the Concord River, by the North Bridge. It is blood – with its connotations of DISSENT (in political terms) and DESCENT (in biological ones) – that reveals the sanguineous bond that Emerson possesses with the England of his ancestors, and with the breach that would make America, and Emerson, something else – something other than England, something after it. Acknowledging descent reinforces the reality of biological continuity (it makes the child aware of its parents and ancestral influences), but contesting that constitutional force through dissent invites the denial of descent, otherwise rendered as the myth or delusion of being self-made.

In mid-nineteenth century thinking the meaning of 'trait' is charged by the radical controversies surrounding notions of aristocracy and heredity, and the indefatigable fact of chattel slavery. Like those inherited institutions, the term 'trait' is increasingly unmoored – denaturalized, glossed more as a trope than a literal referent – by the investigations of the natural sciences emerging in their modern forms. The very implication of the term 'trait' into the discourse Emerson engages and develops – in racial theory, in national and personal identity, but also more generally addressing the definition and meaning of the human and the natural – bears special mention since the word is itself a metaphor of a rich and peculiar type. Metaphor, as such, is understood as a correlation of elements, usually as some variant on a part/whole relationship or an association that binds disparate things together through an actual or assumed commonality of features. A reliable account of metaphor will include a sense for the way one thing (a word, a sign, an image) can stand for something else. The metaphor is a mark that represents or relates other, unseen characteristics. In the metaphor of trait we seem to approach some sort of primordial or archaic origin of MARK-MAKING as a method for creating or understanding identity and order in complex systems.[12] The basic, root or founding images that substantiate the meaning of TRAIT draw etymologically from *tractus* in Latin and *traict* or *tret* from the archaic French. The Latin links the image to inscription, drawing and draughting, while the French registers the gradual abstraction of the word to include 'stroke, touch, line' (while retaining a sense of the 'draught'). Reading in the entry for trait in the *Oxford English Dictionary* (OED), terminological descent can be traced in the cascading variations on the meaning of the word, here selected and abbreviated:

3. That which is drawn; a line, streak, stripe.
4. A stroke made with a pen or pencil; a short line.
   b. something penned; a line, passage, or piece of writing.
5. A line or lineament of the face; a feature.
   b. of a thing.
   c. a 'touch' of some quality.
6. A particular feature of mind or character; a distinguishing quality; a characteristic.[13]

A line of Emerson's from 'Behavior' is cited in the *OED* as an exemplary illustration of the meaning of 5a.: 'A man finds room in the few square inches of the face for the traits of all his ancestors'.[14] As one reads further through the series of definitions, the intensifying specificity of the term 'trait' – and its more specialized, abstracted and metaphorized uses – raises questions not just about the evolution of linguistic and semiotic attributes, but even more immediately and viscerally, how the application of a word in a new context can transform both the word and the condition of its usage.

The foregoing quick etymological sketch is intended to highlight the mark-making nature of 'trait', and also to emphasize how the term meaningfully reflects – in essence, enacts or performs – the central transformation of mark-making into the kind of representation we call metaphor. Now, with a perhaps more animated, multivalent notion of 'trait' in mind – as a kind of mark or trace that registers a distinctive, often distinguishing feature – we are led, as it were naturally, to questions about how metaphor (in general) and a trait (more specifically) alters and enriches our capacities for representativeness and representation. As Emerson's work is cited by the *OED* as a representative source for the meaning of 'trait' – confirming that he has used the term so well that his writing (his *tractus*, his *traict*) contributes to our better understanding of the very *definition* of the word – there is reason to anticipate his expertise with the term, its meaning and its radiating intellectual force and metaphorical impact in *English Traits*. Emerson's chosen title, then, anticipates the richness and variety of his investigations, and in the wake of a brief etymological inquiry, prompts a reader either familiar with or new to *English Traits* to ask: What is the relation between individual traits and the features or signs of a race? Can one read a species from a specimen?[15] Is the individual anomalous or representative? Can we predict a child's form and character by reference to its parents, or search the countenance and disposition of a child to discern its progenitors? Does the individual's body (or face, as Emerson writes above) speak solely for itself? Or does it exhibit itself emblematically, as Emerson contends in the exemplary line from 'Behavior', as an enduring display of perspicuous traits – tracts, traces, touches – that exceeds its limited boundaries in time and place?

Emerson's book title as featured in the title of the present book is intentionally left without its customary formatting in italics as a way of graphically suggesting how my interest in Emerson's book (namely, *English Traits*) is also motivated by an interest in *Emerson's* English traits. This doubleness – of the 1856 book whose subject is traits, and the traits of the author who wrote it – attests to the peculiar way in which a writer implicates himself – literally, letter-ally – word by word in the constitution of his sentences, the lines that define his speech and his intellectual identity. The doubleness is further reflected in the image on this book's cover – in the Rorschachesque rendering of Great Britain according to its nineteenth century boundaries: a double-image that invites consideration of the nation's relation to itself (a split personality?, of two minds?, with genuine histories and fabricated ones?); of England's effects when mirrored in its descendants (is America a copy of England, its inversion or some mutated form?); of England's status as a real place and as a concept or ideal. ENGLISH TRAITS is written once in this book's title, as it was for Emerson in 1856, but stands as a double, available to readers under different aspects.

2.   Considering the vast amount of criticism addressed to the expanse of Emerson's oeuvre – especially writing and lectures that appear between *Nature* (1836) and *The Conduct of Life* (1860) – there remains, despite a few significant studies, a comparative dearth of critical literature on *English Traits*. (In the present manuscript, as elsewhere, Emerson's first book *Nature* is to be distinguished from the essay of the same name published in 1844 as Chapter VI in *Essays, Second Series*). As mentioned at the outset, Cornel West has claimed that *English Traits* is 'the most overlooked text in Emerson's corpus'.[16] Yet there is an enviable power and intellectual precision in the few works that have taken up a robust and extended engagement with Emerson's only book on a single topic. Just as I do not aim in this book to analyze every line of *English Traits* or attempt a comprehensive theory of the work, I will not rehearse all of the insights by scholars who have written compellingly about it.[17] Rather I would prefer to acknowledge specific aspects and angles of their readerly achievements as a means of emphasizing a few ways in which their researches aid the present investigation and, I hope, are complemented by it.

Emerson lived through a very dynamic period of transformation in conceptual thinking – especially as it was expressed scientifically. His formative and most productive years lie between the heights of Immanuel Kant's 'Critical' or Transcendental philosophy and the broader movement of German Romanticism it inspired (including its effects among English writers), and the impact of Darwinian theory as it commenced formally in 1859 upon the publication of *The Origin of Species*. In so far as Emerson was interested in, and even kept pace with, advances in science (mostly as it was conducted in Europe), he was part of the generation that struggled to define or redefine the meaning of literature and philosophy. Was modern natural science merely a re-named version of (ancient) natural philosophy, or was it something altogether distinct – itself a kind of superseded or evolutionarily more sophisticated species of what had been known as the arts of observation, description, argumentation and experimentation since at least Aristotle? The question is answered for Emerson, in part, by his adoption of NATURAL HISTORY as the primary metaphor that underwrites most, if not all of his work. Such a broad and emphatic claim finds company with Elizabeth Dant's more conscribed focus on the metaphor of the 'cabinet of natural history', which she argues is 'both the dominant symbol' and an 'ordering principle for Emerson's thought and writing'.[18] Emerson perceived a continuity in nature – from the laws of science to the laws of mind – so, for him, 'natural history' should pertain as aptly to physical phenomena as to mental and moral phenomena; the cabinets of natural history, by extension, reflect both the effort to harmonize those relationships (as a curator does) and to create the conditions for further insight because of new perceptions and encounters with them (as the cabinets embody). Natural history is then not just an area of inquiry but the very condition for thinking.

Friedrich Nietzsche, a loyal, lifelong reader of Emerson's work, explored a variation on the connection between science and ethics in a chapter entitled 'Natural History of Morals' in *Beyond Good and Evil* (1886); there he took up an analysis of the pervasive ways in which metaphors – and their legacy in language, behaviour and beliefs – have contributed to the development and stratification of moral thought, often in troubling manifestations.[19] He notes how even 'the term "science of morals" is much too arrogant considering what it designates;' that we should therefore cease to be too literal about the study, and should, in turn, 'prepare a *typology* of morals' that 'attempts to present vividly some of the more frequent and recurring forms of such living crystallizations'; how, owing to an age that 'mixes races [...] human beings have in their bodies the heritage of multiple origins [...]'; how European civilization is overrun by a 'herd animal morality'.[20] Nietzsche's lively metaphor-laden assessment of the moribund state of contemporary moral philosophy is complemented, in part, by his awareness of dominant (and dominating) metaphors in the history and 'science' of ethics, and his willingness to employ new, countermanding tropes. Nietzsche's vigorous critique *and* application of metaphor illustrates how any analysis of the metaphors that define moral expression will involve the introduction of new metaphors, or new readings of old metaphors. Hence Nietzsche's natural history of morals continually requires an interrogation of the philological in order to say something defensible about the logical. His methodology – in his words, 'to collect material, to conceptualize and arrange', to create a typology of morals – is a deep grammar.[21] More than a half-century earlier, in 'The Uses of Natural History' (1833), Emerson recognized the revelatory powers of metaphors, especially those habitually derived from the phenomena studied in science and natural history; furthermore, he postulated that if we study nature and language in tandem, we are poised to elucidate perhaps unexpected ethical content: 'The whole of Nature is a metaphor or image of the human Mind. The laws of moral nature answer to those of matter as face to face in a glass'.[22] Emerson included these same lines a few years later in Chapter IV ('Language') of his first book, *Nature*, where he added: 'The axioms of physics translate the laws of ethics'. And in a sermon written a few years earlier, Emerson said: 'There is nothing in external nature but is an emblem, a hiero-glyphic of some thing in us'.[23]

And yet Emerson had so deeply absorbed and integrated the scientific thinking of his day that, as Laura Dassow Walls notes in *Emerson's Life in Science: The Culture of*

Truth (2003), when he 'came to read Darwin, which he did in 1860, he saw nothing he had not seen before – a fact that reveals little about Darwin and a great deal about Emerson.'[24] Even the poetic epigraph to *Nature*, technically among the first published words of his career, finds Emerson anticipating and enacting the dominant conceptual shift of his generation: 'And, striving to be man, the worm / Mounts through all the spires of form'. As the Emerson acolyte Moncure Daniel Conway wrote in his autobiography: '[W]e who studied him were building our faith on evolution before Darwin came to prove our foundations strictly scientific.'[25] Evolutionary thinking, even its pre-Darwinian formulations as Emerson read them in Louis Agassiz, Robert Chambers, Georges Cuvier, Michael Faraday, Charles Lyell, Jean-Baptiste de Lamarck, Richard Owen, Adam Sedgwick, John Tyndall and others, possessed the fundamental elements that excited his thought and framed his outlook, namely, that creation was neither static nor hierarchical – especially as those terms were understood religiously to mean divinely ordained and evaluatively ranked. (And as Emerson read widely in the science of his day, Darwin read Emerson – finding his way to the essay 'Nature' in 1844). In Conway's biography *Emerson at Home and Abroad* – a work that is prone to hagiographic excess but written with such candour and heartfelt sincerity that we learn from his personal intimacy with Emerson and easily forgive the occasional encumbrances of his adoration – he assures the reader that Emerson 'could not prove it, but it was perfectly clear to him that the method of nature is evolution, and it organized the basis of his every statement.'[26] Conway then quotes from Emerson's August 1841 address to the Literary Society of Waterville College, 'The Method of Nature':

> We can point nowhere to anything final; but tendency appears on all hands: planet, system, constellation, total Nature is growing like a field of maize in July; is becoming somewhat else; is in rapid metamorphosis. The embryo does not more strive to be man than yonder burr of light we call a nebula tends to be a ring, a comet, a globe, and a parent of new stars.[27]

Emerson habituates the latest science to his existential outlook, finding in the influence of scientific learning a credible analogy to account for continuity and difference. Lecturing 'On the Relation of Man to the Globe', just after returning to America from his first visit to Europe – and numerous conversations with its leading scientists – he deduces: 'that, from times incalculably remote, there has been a progressive preparation for him [man]; an effort (as physiologists say,) to produce him; the meaner creatures, the primeval sauri, containing the elements of his structure and pointing at it from every side [.... H]is limbs are only a more exquisite organization – say rather the finish – of the rudimental forms that have been already sweeping the sea and creeping in the mud: the brother of his hand is even now cleaving the Arctic Sea in the fin of the whale, and innumerable ages since was pawing the marsh in the flipper of the saurian.'[28] The word 'progressive' may suggest that the later forms are better than the earlier, 'meaner' ones, but Emerson aims to dismiss the notion that 'a more exquisite organization' is only possible *because of* the 'rudimental forms'. In 'Works and Days' he perceives the contours of development, the latency and therefore presence of the 'higher' (or later) in the initial stages: how 'the secular, refined, composite anatomy of man, which all strata go to form, which the prior races, from infusory and saurian, existed to ripen'.[29] A claim defending the superiority of the higher/later forms misses the underlying CONTINUITY of all forms. Emerson asks rhetorically: 'Why should we fear to be crushed by savage elements, we who are made up of the same elements?'[30] Yet such fear may simply reflect the awe we experience when perceiving familiarity and continuity in seemingly disparate, foreign elements, as when 'we detect the brother of the human Hand in the fin of the whale & the flipper of the saurus'.[31] In the year Darwin read Emerson, 1844, more than 15 years before the publication of *The Origin of Species*, Emerson read Robert Chambers' *Vestiges of the Natural History of Creation*, which he found contained 'the most plausible and comprehensive view of evolution that [he] had ever encountered. But so familiar was this way of thought by then', notes Joseph Warren Beach, 'that it caused him neither shock nor excitement'.[32]

In 1858, the year before Darwin's epoch-shaping work was published, Emerson spoke in terms that anticipate Darwin's sense of evolution, and its implications for religion, science and literature in the lecture 'The Natural Method of Mental Philosophy':

> You do not degrade man by saying, Spirit is only finer body; nor exalt him by saying Matter is phenomenal merely. [...] You will observe that it makes no difference herein whether you call yourself materialist or spiritualist. If there be but one substance or reality, and that is body, and it has the quality of creating the sublime astronomy, of converting itself into brain, and geometry, and reason; if it can reason in Newton, and sing in Homer and Shakespeare, and love and serve as saints and angels, then I have no objection to transfer to body all my wonder and allegiance.[33]

Since, as Harold Fromm has noted, 'the laws of nature and the laws of thought were the same' for Emerson, there is no cause to distinguish between granite and oyster or between Newton and Shakespeare.[34] We are comprised of continuities that reach out in all directions. Science, literature, religion and philosophy are interpenetrating phenomena that yield different glimpses of the shared laws that animate and define them.

3.   The apprehension of evolutionary ideas in Emerson's pre-Darwinian thinking continually comes in for assessment among his inheritors – and variously, in moods of doubt and confirmation. Among the contemporary critics who have taken great pains to evaluate the role of science generally in Emerson's thinking, and more specifically his intellectual sympathy for evolutionary accounts, consider not just the aforementioned scholarship by Philip Nicoloff and Laura Dassow Walls, but also well-known and influential work by Barbara Packer, David Robinson and Robert D. Richardson, and book-length studies such as Lee Rust Brown's *The Emerson Museum: Practical Romanticism and the Pursuit of the Whole* (1997), Eduardo Cadava's *Emerson and the Climates of History* (1997), Eric Wilson's *Emerson's Sublime Science* (1999), Peter Obuchoswki's *Emerson and Science: Goethe, Monism, and the Search for Unity*

(2005), Christopher Windolph's *Emerson's Nonlinear Nature* (2007), David Greenham's *Emerson's Transatlantic Romanticism* (2012) and Daniel Koch's *Ralph Waldo Emerson in Europe: Class, Race, and Revolution in the Making of an American Thinker* (2012).[35] Looking to early occasions of scholarly reception, we find Harry Hayden Clark's 'Emerson and Science' (1931), Bliss Perry's *Emerson Today* (1931) and Ralph Rusk's *The Life of Ralph Waldo Emerson* (1949).[36] A common feature of the analysis underway in all these works – though with varying degrees of emphasis and expansiveness – involves speculation about Emerson's apprehension of science, and his capacity to be affected by its theories and methods. Among the nineteenth-century critics, John Jay Chapman recorded his dubiousness in 1898, and without finding fault with Emerson per se, nevertheless stated: 'He lived too early and at too great a distance from the forum of European thought to absorb the ideas of evolution and give place to them in his philosophy. Evolution does not graft well upon the Platonic Idealism, nor are physiology and the kindred sciences sympathetic'.[37] Within a few years of Chapman's remarks, Charles William Eliot, then President of Harvard University, countered such a sentiment: 'It is interesting to-day, after all the long discussion of the doctrine of evolution, to see how the much earlier conceptions of Emerson match the thoughts of the latest exponents of the philosophic results of evolution'.[38] And a similarly corroborative reading prevailed decades later when, in 1926, Lewis Mumford wrote: 'Emerson was a Darwinist before the Origin of Species was published, because he was familiar with the investigations which were linking together the chain of organic continuity, and he was ready to follow the facts wherever they would lead him'.[39] This quick chronology of contended interpretations may suggest that the further away one gets from Emerson and Darwin the more similar they seem. Is the similarity, if recognized, boldly evident or do we need to squint to see it?

4.   Ludwig Wittgenstein, like Emerson, spent time among the gardens and galleries of natural history. And like Emerson, because of these hours of study and contemplation, Wittgenstein was moved to new thoughts about structure and relationship, form and variation. When visiting Maurice Drury in Dublin, Wittgenstein perambulated the National Botanic Gardens at Glasnevin and marvelled at what he saw in the zoological holdings in nearby Phoenix Park.[40] To extend his opportunities for regular and extended visitation, Drury even made it possible for Wittgenstein to become a member of the Royal Zoological Society. At this time, according to biographer Ray Monk, Wittgenstein was struggling to 'expose the barrenness and confusion of "the philosopher's search for generality"'.[41] Generality in the context of natural history amounted to homogeneity, and during his walks and meals taken at nearby cafes, Wittgenstein became preoccupied by the analogy between natural forms and the forms of language – namely, that they both were better understood by their specificity, and this was illuminated by highlighting variety and noting differences. As Monk recounts in his coruscating biography, *Ludwig Wittgenstein: The Duty of Genius*:

> His concern was to stress life's irreducible variety. The pleasure he derived from walking in the Zoological Gardens had much to do with his admiration for the

immense variety of flowers, shrubs and trees and the multitude of different species of birds, reptiles and animals. A theory which attempted to impose a single scheme upon all this diversity was, predictably, anathema to him. Darwin had to be wrong: his theory 'hasn't the necessary multiplicity'.[42]

Wittgenstein related to Drury that he considered using a line from *King Lear* as an epigraph to the *Philosophical Investigations*: 'I'll teach you differences'.[43] As the Earl of Kent addressed Lear so Wittgenstein told Drury, 'Hegel seems to me to be always wanting to say that things which look different are really the same, whereas my interest is in showing that things which look the same are really different'.[44] Emerson, like Carl Linnaeus, believed that cabinet- and composition-making, that the order and organization of gardens, may be motivated by finding similarity but that such resemblances – naturally, logically – create the conditions for recognizing and for learning the differences that obtain by proximity.[45] 'Not only resemblances exist in things whose analogy is obvious', Emerson writes in *Nature*, 'but also in objects wherein there is great superficial unlikeness'.[46] In this respect, Wittgenstein (in an anti-Darwinian mood) and Emerson (in a pre-Darwinian mode) both appreciated how the radical abundance of natural forms encouraged the observation of variations – subtle and otherwise – and that for philosophical thought, and any movement in the natural history of intellect, differences matter. The proliferation of forms of life, each apparent for differences between one and another, is mirrored in the fecundity of language.

5.   The foregoing, varied estimations of Emerson's capacity for evolutionary thinking – whether he anticipated it or integrated it – are bound up with accounts of Emerson's methodology: what it was and what it entailed. Contemporaries such as Orestes Augustus Brownson – cutting against the grain of Emerson's own appreciation for the differences that become discernable because of overt similarities noted just above – described how '[h]is power of detecting the identical in the diverse, the analogous in the dissimilar, the uniform in the manifold, the permanent in the transitory, is remarkable, and unsurpassed in any writer of our acquaintance. He is ever surprising us by unexpected resemblances. To him all things are the same. In all this he is right'.[47] Another contemporary, William Henry Channing noted that Emerson 'has a quick eye for analogies, and finds in all nature symbols of spiritual facts'.[48] In the same generation, Amos Bronson Alcott said of Emerson's work: 'Living for composition as few authors can, and holding company, studies, sleep, exercise, affairs subservient to thought, his products are gathered as they ripen, and stored in his commonplaces; the contents transcribed at intervals, and classified. The order of ideas, of imagination, is observed in the arrangement, not that of logical sequence'.[49] The attention to arrangement gives rise, as Alcott adds in an eruption of glee, to 'endless time in the composition. Jewels all! separate stars. You may have them in a galaxy, if you like, or view them separate and apart'.[50] The composition is of a particular sort, one that Augustine Birrell described, while sustaining Alcott's interstellar proportions: 'He likes things on a large scale – he is fond of ethnical remarks and typical persons. Notwithstanding his habit of introducing the names of common things into his discourses and poetry ("Hay, corn,

roots, hemp, flax, apples, wool, and wood", is a line from one his poems), his familiarity therewith is evidently not great. "Take care, papa", cried his little son, seeing him at work with his spade, "you will dig your leg".[51] Theodore Parker also recognized this penchant for individuation and identifying in Emerson's prose:

> His marked love of individuality appears in his style. His thoughts are seldom vague, all is distinct; the outlines are sharply drawn, things are always discrete from one another. He loves to particularize. He talks not of flowers, but of the violet, the clover, the cowslip and anemone; not of birds, but the nuthatch, and the wren; not of insects, but of the Volvex Globator; not of men and maids, but of Adam, John, and Jane. Things are kept from things, each surrounded by its own atmosphere. This gives great distinctness and animation to his works, though latterly he seems to imitate himself a little in this respect.[52]

Re-read Parker's lines while replacing 'Emerson' with the 'naturalist' and the two figures overlay without overlap; the appeal to the specific as a representative of a class or species – to give it a name, or to call it by its given name – is a hallmark of science, the proper work of the field researcher and thereafter of the museum curator.

In Emerson's hand, these signs and strokes become literary as well. It can be noted as a mark of Emerson's perception of natural science's blooming advances in the 1830s that he chose to appropriate its methods and moods, its habits and hypotheses, for his own intellectual mission. Natural science was open to all explorers and adventurers, but Emerson had a different ambition for it – not literal science but literary science. In his phrase: a natural history of intellect. And such work required agents who would study and profess it, who would act as perceivers and proclaimers of this science, or as Emerson wrote in his journal in the early 1840s – in terms that would later appear in the lecture 'Prospects' (first delivered in 1842) and 'The Scholar' (a composite of work from myriad early addresses, delivered at The University of Virginia in 1876) – and find translation, and acknowledgment, in Nietzsche's own profession of the gay science:

> In every week there is some hour when I read my commission in every cipher of nature, and know that I was made for another office, a professor of the Joyous Science, a detector & delineator of occult harmonies & unpublished beauties, a herald of civility, nobility, learning, & wisdom; an affirmer of the One Law [...].[53]

At the beginning of the twentieth century John Dewey, aware of distorting opinions of Emerson's methodology, felt the need to defend Emerson's proclivity to adduce names, types, signs and symbols: 'As for those who contemn Emerson for superficial pedantry because of the strings of names he is wont to flash like beads before our eyes, they but voice their own pedantry, not seeing, in their literalness, that all such things are with Emerson symbols of various uses administered to the common soul'.[54] Concurrently with Dewey, William James characterized his appreciation for this naming, listing and arranging aspect of the prose: 'Emerson's drastic perception of differences kept him at the opposite pole from this weakness. After you have seen men a few times, he could say, you find most of them as alike as their barns and pantries, and soon as musty and as dreary. Never was such a fastidious lover of significance and distinction, and never an eye so keen for their discovery. [...] He could perceive the full squalor of the individual fact, but he could also see the transfiguration.'[55]

George Santayana said of Emerson that 'he took a curious and smiling interest in the discoveries of natural science and in the material progress of the age. But he could go no farther.'[56] Lewis Mumford, contrariwise, suggested the nature of Emerson's intellectual advance given his social milieu: 'Emerson's uniqueness, for his time, consists in the fact that he appreciated not merely the factual data of science, and the instrumental truth of scientific investigation: he also recognized the formative role of ideas, and he saw the importance of "dialectic" in placing new patterns before the mind which did not exist, ready-made, in the order of Nature. "All the facts of the animal economy, sex, nutriment, gestation, birth, growth, are symbols of the passage of the world into the soul of man, to suffer there a change, and reappear a new and higher fact".'[57] Mumford's selected quotation – 'symbols of the passage of the world into the soul of man' – reminds his readers that science was an ally for understanding the continuities that philosophers have been writing about for millennia. For instance, Emerson said early on, in the chapter on 'Beauty' in *Nature*: 'For although the works of nature are innumerable and all different, the result or the expression of them all is similar and simple. Nature is a sea of forms radically alike and even unique. A leaf, a sunbeam, a landscape, the ocean, make an analogous impression on the mind.'[58] And with more compression, Emerson noted a year later in 'The American Scholar' that 'science is nothing but the finding of analogy'.[59] When Charles Ives paraphrased Emerson – 'Nature loves analogy and hates repetition' – he glossed the aphorism by saying 'Botany reveals evolution, not permanence'.[60] And as nature loves analogies, so must its agents: 'Man is an analogist. He cannot help seeing every thing under its relation to all other things & to himself. The most conspicuous example of this habit of mind is his naming the Deity Father.'[61] Keeping consistent with his extensive optical tropes, Emerson extrapolates so that not just seeing but consciousness itself sees and seeks analogy: 'All thinking is analogizing, and it is the use of life to learn metonymy'.[62] Emerson would even analogize the language in which he composed his perception of resemblances, as when he wrote: 'I like gardens and nurseries. Give me initiative, spermatic, prophesying, man-making words'.[63] We are directed to notice the resemblance between vines and veins, especially as they correspond with lines of prose, the circuitry of sentences: 'Cut these words and they would bleed; they are vascular and alive'.[64]

Emerson's methodology – drafting the powers of natural science into the reserves of his literary art – enriches our understanding of comparison (as act and as art) through composition. The intellectual potential and potency of arrangement was evident to Emerson very early: 'I remember when I was a boy walking along the river, how the colours and shapes of shells used to enchant me. I would collect handfuls of them and put them in my pockets. When I got home I could find nothing of what I had collected: nothing but wretched snails' shells. From this I learnt that composition and context are more important than the beauty of individual forms. On the shore they lay *in solidarity* with the sky and the sea'.[65] Comparison of objects in their living contexts, doubtless an obvious and essential part of the natural scientist's work, is weaved into the art of finding conceptual resemblances – noting similarities by virtue of proximate differences. 'Emerson was so afraid of the letter that killeth', wrote John Jay Chapman, 'that he would hardly trust his words to print. He was assured there was no such thing as literal truth, but only literal falsehood. He therefore resorted to metaphors which could by no chance be taken literally. And he has probably succeeded in leaving a body of work which cannot be made to operate to any other end than that for which he designed it. If this be true, he has accomplished the inconceivable feat of eluding misconception. If it be true, he stands alone in the history of teachers; he has circumvented fate, he has left an unmixed blessing behind him'.[66] Yet it is precisely Emerson's use of metaphors – his resistance to the literal – that at once enhances and enlarges his texts and opens them to varied readings; metaphors demand interpretation and thus continually invite and risk being misconstrued.

In the summer of 1841, Emerson wrote in his journal a passage that consolidates the above remarks on his relation to evolutionary thinking, the appropriated (and transformed) methodologies of natural science, and the perception of continuities between mind and matter:

> The metamorphosis of Nature shows itself in nothing more than this, that there is no word in our language that cannot become typical to us of Nature by giving it emphasis. The world is a Dancer; it is a Rosary; it is a Torrent; it is a Boat; a Mist; a Spider's Snare; it is what you will; and the metaphor will hold, and it will give the imagination keen pleasure. Swifter than light the world converts itself into that thing you name, and all things find their right place under this new and capricious classification. [...] Call it a blossom, a rod, a wreath of parsley, a tamarisk-crown, a cock, a sparrow, the ear instantly hears and the spirit leaps to the trope. [...] I think we may easily see how mere lists of words should be suggestive to a highly imaginative and excited mind.[67]

6.   Thinking further in Laura Dassow Walls' *Emerson's Life in the Sciences: The Culture of Truth*, there are several parallels between her remarks on Emerson's understanding of metaphor and the core preoccupations of the present investigation. Walls ably defines what might be described, after Emerson, as the 'master-tones' – the dominant conceptual, thematic and schematic elements – that underwrite Emerson's clever and persistent transformation of natural scientific discourse and methodology into tropes and narratives that suit his own literary and philosophical purposes.[68] As Walls writes: 'By this metaphoric transference, the key working concepts of nineteenth-century science – polarity, magnetism, Newtonian optics, chemical affinity, electrical circulation, the balance of nature, progressive development, geologically deep time, anatomical correlation of parts, physical geography – became so much a part of Emerson's familiar, accepted and unquestioned working vocabulary that they dropped virtually out of view'.[69] That is, these metaphors – and I add to this crucial list, attention to those tropes drawn from the breadth of the biological sciences and proto-psychology, among other fields – are so pervasive, so apparent and so integrated into the conceptual workings of his writing that we by and large have ceased to see them

as imported from the discourses of natural science. Once it is pointed out, however, as Walls' book demonstrates – and as we see also in Eduardo Cadava's eloquent and inventive readings in *Emerson and the Climates of History* – the prevalence of natural scientific metaphor is so obvious that one may feel immediately compelled – especially 'a highly imaginative and excited mind' – to undertake a reconsideration of the full extent of Emerson's oeuvre in the light of this correspondence.

Walls traces a change in the dominant metaphor that organized scientific investigation, an alternation that was occurring in the wider cultural and intellectual context of Emerson's day, namely, 'from "mechanism" to "organicism"'.[70] As Walls describes it: 'This shift confirmed and intensified the moral dimension of natural law by relocating its power from external force to internal suasion. That is, *natural* law acted not by exercising legislative command from without but by organizing irresistibly from within [...]'.[71] Emerson's conscious apprehension of organicism's conceptual implications – later complicated and enriched by robust evolutionary theories – proved an attractive field from which to undertake his own research and writing. 'Emerson became interested in science', as Walls points out, 'less as a practice than as a discourse, not as a way of doing so much as a way of thinking, seeing, and talking'.[72] And yet, Emerson's understanding of scientific practice contributes meaningfully to the way his own project remains incomplete; like a scientist, Emerson's work is always provisional, always as he might say, undertaken in a spirit of onwardness. Or as Walls suggests: 'The very failure of Emerson's persistent but uncompleted work on a "Natural History of the Intellect", which was to have applied the method of science to the study of the mind, suggests that Emerson's engagement with science was, from first to last, not an escape into complacent certainty or unthinking optimism but a fiercely sustained campaign to read order into a universe that persistently threatened to fly apart'.[73]

As one example of a metaphor borrowed from the sciences, the notion of 'natural law' became bound up with Emerson's account of moral law. Contrary to many popular accounts, Emerson's understanding of Nature was neither sentimental nor Romantic, but rational *and* religious ('In the woods', he wrote in *Nature*, 'we return to reason and faith'.)[74] Walls develops this reading with evidence that Emerson analogized natural law with moral law, a potent transference that 'attributes the regularities of nature to an act of legislation [...]'; and so 'this metaphor allows the natural, social and spiritual worlds to merge, an elision basic to Emerson's enterprise'.[75] Consequently, Walls writes, 'since laws encode action in language, the fundamental metaphor of law unites the realms of natural science, cultural politics, *and* social discourse into one broad front, the "one culture" of Anglo-Euro-America before America's Civil War and the post-Darwinian debates'.[76] When John Jay Chapman encountered this multiform, ameliorating feature of Emerson's work, he wrote in the final years of the nineteenth century:

> The fancy that the good, the true, the beautiful, – all things of which we instinctively approve, – are somehow connected together and are really one thing; that our appreciation of them is in its essence the recognition of a law; that this law, in fact all law and the very idea of law, is a mere subjective experience; and that hence any external sequence which we coordinate and name, like the law of gravity, is

really intimately connected with our moral nature, – this fancy has probably some basis of truth. Emerson adopted it as a corner-stone of his thought.[77]

Emerson wrote in his journal: 'I fear the progress of Metaphysical philosophy may be found in nothing else than the progressive introduction of apposite metaphors'.[78] That is, metaphysical philosophy had settled on this achievement and not sought to go beyond it. 'The point of Emerson's turn to science', Walls emphasizes, 'was precisely to get *beyond* the mere succession of apposite metaphors [...]. Emerson unceasingly poured the universe through bits of itself, until the point was clearly to arrive at no one triumphant solvent metaphor but at the metaphorical relationship itself'.[79] One of the things that language users are customarily prone to forget – for language works best when it ramparts fade, and its powers are employed as if unconsciously – is that the use of metaphors consists primarily in an activity of relations and relationships. The art of metaphor is fundamentally an effort to understand the nature of a thing or concept better by virtue of its relationship to the qualities of another, different, often very dissimilar thing. Walls, and others such as Donald Pease, have noticed that Emerson isolates the very power of metaphorizing – its capacity to elicit an attention to space, type and relation – to register an insight about related phenomena.[80] As a result, Emerson analogizes our experience of metaphor to frame an understanding of moral law; the two phenomena are perhaps uncannily coordinate. From Emerson's perspective, Walls suggests that 'moral laws are the laws that govern not things but the relations between things, and moral knowledge is relational knowledge, subsisting in that space or interaction or convergence *between* subject and object'. For Emerson, 'Metaphor became a way to dissolve the objects of knowledge into relational, or moral, knowledge – the true knowledge of which they are merely the vehicle'.[81] Walls poetically distills this distinctive insight: 'Like the press of wings against the wind, truth is not an essence but a relationship between bodied beings'.[82]

In the essay 'Nature' (1844) Emerson used metaphors, analogies and ready-to-hand scientific knowledge to state an underlying feature of transcendental philosophy:

> Nature is the incarnation of a thought, and turns to a thought again, as ice becomes water and gas. The world is mind precipitated, and the volatile essence is forever escaping again into the state of free thought. Hence the virtue and pungency of the influence on the mind of natural objects, whether inorganic or organized. Man imprisoned, man crystallized, man vegetative, speaks to man impersonated. That power which does not respect quantity, which makes the whole and the particle its equal channel, delegates its smile to the morning, and distils its essence into every drop of rain. Every moment instructs, and every object: for wisdom is infused into every form. It has been poured into us as blood; it convulsed us as pain; it slid into us as pleasure; it enveloped us in dull, melancholy days, or in days of cheerful labor; we did not guess its essence until after a long time.[83]

Nearly a decade earlier, in the 'Language' chapter of *Nature* (1836), Emerson collated scientific metaphor with moral meaning, and in that context depicted how language hosts – as cipher – the truths of natural objects and natural phenomena, and illuminates the continuity of natural science (the 'technical use' of tropes) with the ethical dimensions of culture.

> The world is emblematic. Parts of speech are metaphors, because the whole of nature is a metaphor of the human mind. The laws of moral nature answer to those of matter as face to face in a glass. 'The visible world and the relation of its parts, is the dial plate of the invisible'. The axioms of physics translate the laws of ethics. Thus, 'the whole is greater than its part;' 'reaction is equal to action;' 'the smallest weight may be made to lift the greatest, the difference of weight being compensated by time;' and many the like propositions, which have an ethical as well as physical sense. These propositions have a much more extensive and universal sense when applied to human life, than when confined to technical use.[84]

7.   The notion of laws for non-physical phenomena continues to appear, despite the trend of dominance by natural scientific discourse (and its concentration on material facts), for example, in Michel Foucault's *The Order of Things: An Archaeology of the Human Sciences* (1971), where, in a chapter on 'Classifying', he asks a rhetorical question Emerson would have found familiar and expected – a question that presumes the pertinence of analogizing nature and morals: 'since it had proved possible, by means of experimentation and theory, to analyze the laws of movement or those governing the reflection of light beams, was it not normal to seek, by means of experiments, observations, or calculations, the laws that might govern the more complex by adjacent realm of living beings?'[85] Emerson's transcendental biology – and the natural history of intellect it contributes to – depends on this recognition of adjacency and permeability. Likewise, according to Foucault, the possibility of taxonomy requires that 'nature must be truly continuous, and in all its plenitude. Where language required the similarity of impressions, classification requires the principle of the smallest possible difference between things'.[86] And the agent of language's application, in this context, is the naturalist. 'As Linnaeus says', writes Foucault, 'the naturalist – whom he calls *Historiens naturalis* – "distinguishes the parts of natural bodies with his eyes, describes them appropriately according to their number, form, position, and proportion, and he names them"'.[87] The naturalist's task of observing, classifying and naming merely, or rather substantively, reflects the work of natural history more generally. Foucault adduces a remarkable series of definitions that accommodate the richness and vitality of the undertaking:

> Natural history is contemporaneous with language: it is on the same level as the spontaneous play that analyses representations in the memory, determines their common elements, establishes signs upon the basis of those elements, and finally imposes names. Classification and speech have their place of origin in the same space that representation opens up within itself because it is consecrated to time, to memory, to reflection, to continuity.[88]

> Natural history has as a condition of its possibility the common affinity of things and language with representation.[89]

Natural history [...] is the space opened up in representation by analysis which is anticipating the possibility of naming.[90]

Natural history [...] resides in its entirety in the area of language, since it is essentially a concerted use of names and since its ultimate aim is to give things their true denomination.[91]

Natural history is nothing more than the nomination of the visible.[92]

Foucault's own analogical work – 'the archaeology of the human sciences' – so-named in the subtitle of his book, parallels Emerson's transcendental biology and natural history of intellect in so far as Foucault recognizes how once 'signs were [...] part of things themselves' whereas now, since the seventeenth century, 'they become modes of representation'.[93] And thus if, as Emerson contends, names are things 'very readily transferable to that or this', then the naturalist is charged with constituting the world for our perception – showing that naming is a form of generation, perhaps akin to divination. Even as we realize names are superficial assignations, we see how they are also, despite our shift to modernity, substantial – as if they were not just transferable representations but the things themselves. 'By limiting and filtering the visible', writes Foucault, 'structure enables it to be transcribed into language. It permits the visibility of the animal or plant to pass over in its entirety into the discourse that receives it. And ultimately, perhaps, it may manage to reconstitute itself in visible form by means of words, as with the botanical calligrams dreams of by of Linnaeus'.[94] What Foucault says of plants, by way of Linnaeus, we may say of Emerson's project: that he studies nameable features, and aims to find definitions for them; that he invents categories to assess the traits by which one can judge a culture and its people; that he characterizes and classifies them – occasioning points of difference, seeking similarity – to the end of knowing them, for better or worse, according to the shape-giving powers of language. Foucault's account of natural history, when coupled with the course of our reading in Emerson, provokes an awareness of the creative and constitutive side of observation. If it has already become standard to acknowledge the subjectivity inherent in observation, perhaps it remains strange to recall how that subjectivity is creative, or at least co-creative, as well; and as observation seeks expression, language becomes a medium for human consciousness to mediate between natural facts and the mental perception or sensation of those rough realities. In his seasons of disciplined awareness of natural phenomena, Thoreau observed: 'Facts collected by a poet are set down at last as winged seeds of truth [...]. O may my words be verdurous & sempiternal as the hills. Facts fall from the poetic observer as ripe seeds'.[95] Or as Foucault, after Linnaeus, put its tersely – 'The plant is thus engraved in the material of the language into which it has been transposed'.[96] – and with more elaboration:

Things and words are very strictly interwoven: nature is posited only through the grid of denominations, and – though without such names it would remain mute and invisible – it glimmers far off beyond them, continuously present on the far side of this grid, which nevertheless presents it to our knowledge and renders it visible only when wholly spanned by language.[97]

8.   French biologist Joseph Pitton de Tournefort (1656–1708), who first articulated an account of *genus* as a method for naming and classifying plants, wrote at the outset of his *Éléments de Botanique, ou Méthode pour reconnaître les Plantes* (1694):

> To know plants is to know with precision the names that have been given to them in relation to the structure of some of their parts. [...] The idea of the character that essentially distinguishes plants from one another ought to invariably to be one with the name of each plant.[98]

An analogist caught up in the unexpected associations of the 'character' of plants and the character or characteristics of persons, might wish to rewrite the sentence trading out the name 'plants', so it reads:

> To know persons is to know with precision the names that have been given to them in relation to the structure of some of their parts. [...] The idea of the character that essentially distinguishes persons from one another ought to invariably to be one with the name of each person.

In *English Traits* Emerson undertakes a study in this mode of name-giving or name-granting – an activity in the service of finding, and making, distinctions based on observations of observable characteristics, and inspired by speculations of what is unseen but perceived to be justifiably relevant. In this respect Emerson appears to have taken up what Foucault will call the System (as opposed to the Method) for such naming. Instead of 'making total comparisons' (as with the Method), Emerson selected 'a finite and relatively limited group of characteristics, whose variations and constants may be studied in any individual entity that presents itself' – a hallmark of the System.[99] Consequently, any particular Englishman might become the basis upon which to make inductive generalizations about the Saxon race; such generalizations as we find them in *English Traits* occur under chapter titles that both acknowledge the limitedness of topics under investigation (Land, Race, Manners, Truth, Character, Aristocracy, Universities, Religion, Literature, The 'Times', Stonehenge, etc.) and for the richness of associations intimated by these topics, extend a seemingly endless radiating effect. 'For the systematician', writes Foucault, 'continuity consists only of the unbroken juxtaposition of the different regions that can be clearly distinguished by means of characters'.[100] Thus Emerson's approach is not totalizing but intentionally partial – meant to be representative in his sense of that term, supporting the notion that a man can speak of mankind for mankind, that a man can represent himself at the same time that he is a figure of a race or type. From the individual we find, by degrees, the genus; from the specimen the species is made and revealed.

9.   In his 1857 essay 'Nature's Greatness in Small Things', Charles Dickens offered a useful analogue to Emerson's outlook when he wrote:

> Thus, beyond and above the law of design in creation, stands the law of unity of type, and unity of structure. No function so various, no labours so rude, so elaborate, so dissimilar, but this cell can build up the instrument, and this model

prescribes the limits of its shape. Through all creation the microscope detects the handwriting of power and of ordnance. It has become the instrument of a new revelation in science, and speaks clearly to the soul as to the mind of man.[101]

10.   Richard Owen, whom Emerson met on his second visit to England in 1848, personally offered Emerson a tour of the Hunterian Museum in London (as well as guided his visit to the art studio of Romantic landscape painter J. M. W. Turner). At the time of their visit, Owen had been a professor in the Royal College of Surgeons (to which the Hunterian belonged) for over a decade, and in that time had contributed significantly to the cataloguing of its vast number of diverse specimens; such work required innovation in terms of order, organization, relationship and display. In his work as biologist, comparative anatomist and paleontologist, Owen postulated a theory of anatomy for idealists, which he called 'transcendental biology', and which I contend usefully names the studies that occupied Emerson and his contemporaries before the advent of Darwinian evolution. The term wears on its surface a hybrid quality that allows both scientist and philosopher to use the idea for his or her own purposes; and depending on its use and context, we see how one of the words becomes metaphorical. Thus, for the scientist 'transcendental' is a metaphor, while 'biology' is not; for the philosopher, 'biology' is a metaphor, while 'transcendental' is not.

In his 1837 *Hunterian Lectures in Comparative Anatomy*, Owen acknowledged the influence of German philosophy in his scientific thinking. Interpreting this crucial pedigree of influence, Phillip R. Sloan points out that at the end of Kant's *Critique of Pure Reason*, 'physiology is contrasted with transcendental philosophy. The latter deals generally with the conditions of the possibility of objects in general. Physiology deals with nature'.[102] Sloan highlights the metaphorical quality of the term by noting that 'although the "transcendental" meaning of "Physiology" would have little concrete relation to the kinds of inquiry of interest to medical men and anatomists, the "immanent" meaning could be directly related to these inquiries – as an inquiry concerned with the physiological laws and forces between bodies'.[103]

Crucially, in my estimation, transcendental biology includes an awareness of something that will be scientifically demonstrated with Darwin, namely, the deployment of morphological evidence to support a more fully developed evolutionary perspective. Historian of biology and evolutionary thought Peter J. Bowler expertly defines the relationship this way:

> Traditionally, morphologists looked for the archetype, or most basic structure, of each group. But for the evolutionist, the idealized archetype became the real, common ancestor from which the group had diverged. This placed more constraints on the hypothetical reconstructions because the ancestor had to be visualized as an actual creature with its own adaptations. The transformations which led from the common ancestor to its various descendants also had to be plausible in terms of the pressures of adaptation and internal coherence. More excitingly, where the archetypes of the major groups were seen as completely isolated from one another, evolutionism implied that transitions between them had to be possible. Wherever possible, fossils

would be used to throw light on these ancient transformations, but even where fossils were not available anatomy and embryology would fill in the gaps.[104]

Morphological study, championed principally by Thomas Henry Huxley (whom Emerson met in London in 1873), made the study of animals and fossils in the laboratory something that transformed biogeography, and the way archaeologists traced and understood the adaptive implications of the physical specimens and their respective locations.[105] Darwin's account of his visit to the passage of Cordillera – between Valparaiso and Mendoza, Chile – while still travelling with the *Beagle*, offers an indication of how these early speculations ultimately give way to a more mature evolutionary theory.

> The lofty mountains, their summits marked with a few patches of snow, stood well separated from each other; the valleys being filled up with an immense thickness of stratified alluvium. I may here briefly remark, without detailing the reasons on which the opinion is grounded, that in all probability this matter was accumulated at the bottoms of deep arms of the sea, which running from the inland basins, penetrated to the axis of the Cordillera – in a similar manner to what now happens in the southern part of this same great range. This fact, in itself most curious, as preserving a record of a very ancient state of things, possesses a high theoretical interest, when considered in relation to the kind of elevation by which the preset great altitude of these mountains has been attained.
>
> [...] Even at the very crest of the Peuquenes [mountains], at the height of 13,210 feet, and above it, the black clay-slate contained numerous marine remains, amongst which a gryphæa is the most abundant, likewise shells, resembling turritellæ, and an ammonite. It is an old story, but not the less wonderful, to hear of shells, which formerly were crawling about at the bottom of the sea, being now elevated nearly 14,000 feet above sea level.[106]

11.   Emerson does not appear to align himself with either Kant or Owen's teleological view of nature; in fact, the term 'teleology' does not appear anywhere in his collected works. If natural phenomena are said to reach specific outcomes, these ends or consequences should not be assumed necessary. In this respect Emerson's transcendental biology would be at home in Darwin's theory of natural selection, since neither presume a preordained destiny. In 1844 Emerson inflected his transcendental biology in a register that aligns more with Darwin's arguments than Owen's postulates:

> The ancients, struck with this irreducibleness of the elements of human life to calculation, exalted Chance into a divinity, but that is to stay too long at the spark, – which glitters truly at one point, – but the universe is warm with the latency of the same fire. The miracle of life which will not be expounded, but will remain a miracle, introduces a new element. In the growth of the embryo, Sir Everard Home, I think, noticed that the evolution was not from one central point, but co-active from three or more points. Life has no memory. That which proceeds in succession might be remembered, but that which is coexistent, or ejaculated from a deeper cause, as yet far from being conscious, knows not its own tendency.[107]

Emerson joins his analysis of cosmic history to human development as the passage continues:

> So is it with us, now skeptical, or without unity, because immersed in forms and effects all seeming to be of equal yet hostile value, and now religious, whilst in the reception of spiritual law. Bear with these distractions, with this coetaneous growth of the parts: they will one day be *members*, and obey one will. On that one will, on that secret cause, they nail our attention and hope. Life is hereby melted into an expectation or a religion. Underneath the inharmonious and trivial particulars, is a musical perfection, the Ideal journeying always with us, the heaven without rent or seam. Do but observe the mode of our illumination. When I converse with a profound mind, or if at any time being alone I have good thoughts, I do not at once arrive at satisfactions, as when, being thirsty, I drink water, or go to the fire, being cold: no! but I am at first apprised of my vicinity to a new and excellent region of life. By persisting to read or to think, this region gives further sign of itself, as it were in flashes of light, in sudden discoveries of its profound beauty and repose, as if the clouds that covered it parted at intervals, and showed the approaching traveller the inland mountains, with the tranquil eternal meadows spread at their base, whereon flocks graze, and shepherds pipe and dance. But every insight from this realm of thought is felt as initial, and promises a sequel. I do not make it; I arrive there, and behold what was there already. I make! O no! I clap my hands in infantine joy and amazement, before the first opening to me of this august magnificence, old with the love and homage of innumerable ages, young with the life of life, the sunbright Mecca of the desert. And what a future it opens![108]

Instead of teleology, then, what seems more plausibly linked to Emerson's version of transcendental biology is Owen's appreciation for the interaction of forces, as Sloan says, which allow Owen to 'retain his physiological and functional perspective, appealing to the explanatory role of vital forces in the development both of the individual and the species. The archetype concept Owen would develop in detail after 1845 presented this concept both as a transcendental organizational plan and as an immanent law, manifested in the action of causal forces acting dialectically with matter to bring about an increase of organization.'[109] For Emerson an 'increase of organization' – such as it is expressed in the human mind – need not prove that such a development was predetermined, but only lends further evidence to the 'latency of the same fire.'[110] As he says in *The Conduct of Life*, we perceive 'that Law rules throughout existence, a Law which is not intelligent but intelligence; – not personal nor impersonal – it disdains words and passes understanding; it dissolves persons; it vivifies nature.'[111]

When I refer to TRANSCENDENTAL BIOLOGY in the context of Emerson's writing, I mean then to emphasize the ways in which he recognized the significance of evolutionary theory for an understanding of the laws of nature and of thought. Very often Emerson's expression of transcendental biology is found in a literary-philosophical engagement with the metaphors of science and natural history. We find this abundantly evident in *English Traits* but also in works by writers he read, admired and emulated, among them Goethe, Coleridge, Carlyle and Schiller, who postulated and enacted some of the promising parallels between the sciences of laws and letters. The tandem name transcendental biology should not incite the charge of pseudo-science since Emerson was not a physical or experimental scientist. Rather Emerson's application or analogizing of scientific thinking, methods, models and tropes, to the exploration of literary and philosophical expression, can be treated as a sign of his conviction that a proper account of the natural world would naturally invite comparison with the qualities of mind, morals and sentiment.

12.   Emerson cites Robert Knox in *English Traits* as one of the sources that informs his thinking on race theory. In a distinguished assessment of the impact Knox's work had on Emerson's personal and political feelings about the notion of racial purity, Cornel West has emphasized that Emerson's 'rejection of [Robert] Knox's theory of racial physiological incompatibility (hence rigid racial boundaries) and approval of racial "mixing" make Emerson a rather liberal "racist".[112] In 1850, six years before Emerson's book appears, Knox published *The Races of Men: A Fragment* in which he writes with some circumspection about the applicability of his postulates: 'I speak from extremely limited experience', he confides.[113] While race theory in the mid-nineteenth century may be characterized, or even caricatured, as a perpetual debate on the essential or innate characteristics of men (such as found in blood that would draw continuities between men (and perhaps even more controversially link man irrevocably to 'lower' forms), or turning the other way – define and separate races), consider both Knox's intimations of the deeper sanguinity between life forms, and of the superficial features that appear to confirm differences between types of men:

> Let it be remembered, however, after all, it is to the exterior we must look for the more remarkable characteristics of animals; it is it alone which nature loves to decorate and to vary: the interior organs of animals, not far removed from each other, vary but little. To this fact I shall advert more particularly in the lecture on transcendental anatomy, the internal structures of animals present details which we read imperfectly, connected as they are, on the one hand, with mechanical arrangements, and on the other with the primitive laws of creation.[114]

Knox's 'transcendental anatomy' is equivalent to the more widely-used term comparative anatomy, though Knox's version usefully sustains the philosophical – and also literary and poetical – nature of his investigation. Georges Cuvier's comparative anatomy is meant to confer a greater degree of assurances in its scientific, empirical credibility, while Knox contends that his practice is fundamentally an art of reading, and at that, a reading of topical features. The account of 'exterior' characteristics must be read, then, in the light of Knox's suppositions about the interior of humans, namely, that, as he says: 'to me the unity of man appears evident'.[115] Physiology suggests continuities between races and species, while physiognomy suggests breaks and breaches. Conduct post-mortems on men to see the anonymity of guts, and feel vindicated that the body's interior proves membership in a nameless fraternity.

Knox translates his scientific–poetic speculations into potential political agitation when he alludes to the possibility that non-Anglo Saxons deserve 'equal rights and privileges'. He points out with nervous exasperation: 'What a field of extermination lies before the Saxon Celtic and Sarmatian races!' And adds genuinely, but with a sense of defeat:

> I venture to recommend the honest ones [among British philanthropists – that is, 'philanthropists' in the etymological sense] – to try their strength in a practical measure. Let them demand for the natives of Hindostan, of Ceylon, or even of the Cape or New Zealand, the privileges and rights wholly and fairly of Britons; I predict a refusal on the part of the Colonial-office. The office will appoint you as many aborigines protectors as you like – that is, spies; but the extension of equal rights and privileges to all colours is quite another question.[116]

13.   If transcendental biology is an idealist anatomy, then, in the light of science since Darwin, we are prompted to consider whether Emerson's analogizing leaves his philosophy imperiled by its attachment to a science that has been eclipsed. Laura Dassow Walls worries that Emerson's understanding of the 'laws of science' could not anticipate the shift from 'constitutive' to 'descriptive' definition in present day science.[117] Despite Emerson's dedicated use of scientific metaphors, his version of transcendental biology does not lead him to transcendentalism realism. Rather, it seems that 'the more he learns of natural history', Joseph Warren Beach wrote, 'the more certain he is that it is all a projection of the mind, an expression of the inherent moral purposes of the universe which is found in the human spirit'.[118] Harold Fromm echoes Beach's sentiment by saying that 'Emerson was so disposed to see the laws of nature as intrinsically ethical that he took for granted that ethical concepts were embedded' in nature.[119] Beach concludes that Emerson 'never glimpsed the idea that ethical concepts may be themselves the product of evolution'.[120]

In an early 1835 letter to Lydia Jackson, written before they were married, Emerson confided: 'Still I am a poet in the sense of a perceiver & dear lover of the harmonies that are in the soul & in matter, & specially of the correspondences between these & those'.[121] This pre-*Nature* private, epistolary confession signals a range of sentiments that will be formalized in the years following: 'Particular natural facts are signs of particular spiritual facts'; 'The Transcendentalist adopts the whole connection of spiritual doctrine'; and 'Nature is transcendental'.[122] But as a perceiver of continuities and connections, as someone marshaling his resources to distinguish between the 'true and the false subjective', as F. O. Matthiessen clarifies, Emerson was '[…] occupied with consciousness, not with self-consciousness. He wanted to study the laws of the mind, what he called throughout life the natural history of the intellect, but he always felt a repugnance to self-centred introversion'.[123] He eschewed solipsism and skepticism, in part, by appealing to the enduring continuousness of creation – that 'the inmost in due time becomes the outmost', and so identity, law and truth were superabundant and available to anyone who wished to see them.[124]

14.   Emerson, 'Education' (1863–4)

> We learn nothing rightly until we learn the symbolical character of life. Day creeps after day, each full of facts, dull, strange, despised things, that we cannot enough

despise – call heavy, prosaic and desert. The time we seek to kill: the attention it is elegant to divert from things around us. And presently the aroused intellect finds gold and gems in one of those scorned facts – then finds that the day of facts is a rock of diamonds; that a fact is an Epiphany of God.[125]

15.   The aroused intellect discovers that '[e]very new relation is a new world'.[126] By drawing on Emerson's own strategies of transcendental biology, I aim to indicate that his methods of analogizing – of making connections, of seeing correspondences, of tracing relations – remain highly pertinent to our present condition, and may inform a tremendous range of contemporary assessment of metaphor usage. In particular, there are reasons to dwell at the intersection of literary-philosophical uses of metaphor and the moral implications of that employment; making those reasons explicit without didacticism and pedanticism is part of the methodology, and hope, that informs this undertaking. My efforts for the present study, then, are focused primarily on both the nature – and natural history – of metaphor, and the implications of scientific metaphors for ethical understanding. Even as Walls, Beach and Fromm contribute to our ongoing appraisal of Emerson's sense of the relationship between morals and metaphors, it is precisely because we live in an age of science that vastly supersedes Emerson's that the idealist implications of transcendental biology are, in fact, of far *greater* relevance to us than they could have been to Emerson. Given that our contemporary situation assumes the reality (or at least well-founded plausibility) of quantum theory, relativity, micro- and nano-computing, computational biochemistry, epigenetics, nuclear astrophysics and artificial intelligence, what could a 'natural history of intellect' possibly mean for us? Can it be anything more than a part of intellectual history – or, perhaps a 'museum-interest', as D. H. Lawrence once derisively conjectured about Emerson's relevance?[127] 'We must therefore', as Santayana admonished, 'distinguish sharply the transcendental grammar of the intellect, which is significant and potentially correct, from the various transcendental systems of the universe, which are chimeras'.[128] Emerson's natural history of intellect should be counted a member of the former sort, not the latter: seen as early as *Nature*, it is a semiology, a logic, a grammar, an archaeology of knowledge, a classifying and cabinet-making enterprise of embodied perception and spirit.

In what I have written and assembled thus far, and in what follows, I employ what might be described analogically as conceptual and textual parataxis, namely, the use of arrangement, juxtaposition and commentary to identify a bona fide connection or to support an implied one. In writing and speaking, parataxis is often defined by the grammatical form of the coordinating conjunction, and the method employed here is very much aimed at suggesting consecutiveness in thinking, onwardness through relationship and ordering; in this way, the work is also similar to montage technique in film. Paratactic and montage techniques are commonly suggestive (rather than declarative and definitive), letting the mind of the reader/observer blend or fuse according to his or her own categories of judgement; this is something I have intentionally cultivated given the complexity of the collected specimens of text here presented, arranged and commented on. While I have endeavoured to contribute worthwhile criticism (in the guise of the 'expert'), I have also followed after moments of literary and philosophical resemblance that might be noticed by the novice who has wandered into the laboratory of an unknown science, or stumbled upon a collection of unlabelled objects. Coupling these kinds of engagement – placing them side by side – I have striven to illuminate the allusive as much as to make sense of the explicit; very little of that work has felt readily apparent, but almost of all it feels generative. In response to these scenarios of investigation into myriad texts and specimens, I mostly intervene to add connective tissues of commentary, but at other times I select, orient and arrange materials to marvel merely at their relation – to avail the reader of what happens when they are made proximate, introduced as company.

16.   George Santayana, 'The Genteel Tradition in American Philosophy' (1911)

Emerson was particularly ingenious and clear-sighted in feeling the spiritual uses of fellowship with the elements.[129]

But he coveted truth; and he returned to experience, to history, to poetry, to the natural science of his day, for new starting-points and hints toward fresh transcendental musings.

To covet the truth is a very distinguished passion. Every philosopher says he is pursuing the truth, but this is seldom the case. As Bertrand Russell has observed, one reason why philosophers often fail to reach the truth is that they often do not desire to reach it. Those who are genuinely concerned in discovering what happens to be true are rather the men of science, the naturalists, the historians; and ordinarily they discover it, according to their lights. The truths they find are never complete, and are not always important; but they are integral parts of the truth, facts and circumstances that help to fill in the picture, and that no later interpretation can invalidate or afford to contradict.[130]

Santayana means to conclude that Emerson – in his love of truth, and his methods for discerning it – is closer in spirit and outlook to natural scientists than professional philosophers, the latter of whom are 'usually only scholastics', 'absorbed in defending some vested illusion or some eloquent idea'. Professional philosophers 'do not covet truth, but victory and dispelling of their own doubts'.[131] When Richard Rorty addressed the genteel tradition of Santayana's attention, he noted how the 'tradition claimed that one could take both scientific truth and religious truth with full seriousness and weave them together into something new – transcendental philosophy – which was higher than science, purer than religion, and truer than both'.[132]

17.   As Laura Otis notes at the outset of her anthology of selected works in literature and science in the nineteenth century, there was a tremendous permeability between the two fields, the 'two commingled', 'science was in effect a variety of literature', and the same subjects – including the nature of origins, individuality, and the human – 'occupied both scientific and literary writers'.[133] It is reported that in 1833 William Whewell recommended that the appellation 'scientist' be used to describe what had

previously – indeed, since antiquity – been understood to be the work of 'natural philosophers'.[134] Interestingly, though, as Otis points out, the nineteenth century scientist started off by trading on the credibility of the literary and philosophical tradition. She writes: 'To win the confidence of educated readers, nineteenth century scientists made frequent references to the fiction and poetry of the day and to that of earlier generations. By doing so, they declared an affinity, sometimes of thought but more often of culture, with respected authors and, indirectly, with their readers'.[135] The pendulum also swung in the other direction, and we find literary writers reaching out to the qualities, methods and principles of science. Otis illustrates the point this way: 'Novelists of the period were greatly concerned with facts. Many, like George Eliot, performed careful research in order to make their works not just credible but historically accurate'.[136] Thus as 'science gained prestige, literary writers in turn gained credibility by incorporating the voices of scientists' and employing scientific 'styles and use of evidence', as we see, for example, in Edgar Allan Poe and Mark Twain.[137] Just as the notion of transcendental biology courts the hybridization of philosophy and science, we find scientists such as Jean-Baptiste de Lamarck writing a work entitled *Zoological Philosophy* (1809) where 'philosophy' modifies and buoys the credentials of the descriptive scientific sub-discipline. Sometimes, though, the confluence of the literary and scientific modes of writing caused anxiety for authors: Charles Darwin, notably, 'worried that his writing sounded too literary and feared that his metaphors would lead readers astray'.[138] And yet, while his writing may have *sounded* too literary, it is worth emphasizing that the literary nature of his scientific theorizing was part of his achievement, as Otis remarks, 'Like the philology and literature of his day, Darwin's writing reflects the assumption that origins establish identity, yet conveys a strong conviction that 'origins' are fictions'.[139] Emerson, especially in *English Traits*, may be usefully regarded as the literary-philosophical converse of Darwin: for he may have worried that his writing sounded too scientific *unless* a reader recognized the degree to which the scientific claims he adduced are not facts but interpretations, not realities but imaginative incarnations – as when he writes of tenuous distinctions between races, and the 'frail boundaries' that divide them. It is 'easy to add to the counteracting forces to race', Emerson writes in the chapter 'Race', so we should be circumspect about any science that takes its observations and descriptions (again, so often achieved through dynamic use of metaphors) for natural facts:

> These limitations of the formidable doctrine of race suggest others which threaten to undermine it, as not sufficiently based. The fixity or inconvertibleness of races as we see them, is a weak argument for the eternity of these frail boundaries, since all our historical period is a point to the duration in which nature has wrought. Any the least and solitariest fact in our natural history, such as the melioration of fruits and of animal stocks, has the worth of a *power* in the opportunity of geologic periods. Moreover, though we flatter the self-love of men and nations by the legend of pure races, all our experience is of the gradation and resolution of races, and strange resemblances meet us every where. It need not puzzle us [...] that the barriers of races are not so firm, but that some spray sprinkles us from the antidiluvian seas.[140]

18.　Whewell's and Lamarck's awareness of the interpenetration of philosophical and scientific thinking draws attention not just to methods (e.g., observation, description, theorizing, collection of specimens), but also to the shared fact that both philosophy and science (even if understood as distinct enterprises) share the need to be expressed in language – and thus rely on metaphor for the achievement of explanation and insight. Otis points us to the contemporary theorist, Gillian Beer, who has pushed our understanding of this shared fact to a new degree of sophistication:

> Scientists knew that like literary writers, they relied heavily on imagination. Only a comparison of the unknown with the known can create new forms of under-standing, so that metaphor plays a key role in original thought. As Gillian Beer has observed, scientific writing is most like fiction when it is struggling to say something new, at which time it relies heavily upon comparisons. Metaphor, in Beer's words, 'can allow insight without consequences'. Whether studying physical or biological events, scientists depicted the world imaginatively so that they could draw inferences about invisible phenomena based on observable effects. Picturing the unknown, they acted like novelists or poets, inviting readers to imagine hidden worlds.[141]

Metaphor is fundamentally a mode of comparison by reference to shared qualities; it is an activity that uses analogy to elucidate common traits. As 'literary writers, who for centuries had told their stories in the cultural language of biblical tales, were able to challenge accepted views of human nature by interweaving traditional stories with new narratives made available by science', Emerson participates in this practice of poetizing scientific models, theories and results through a similar form of analo-gizing.[142] Importantly, the metaphors shared by literary and scientific writers were not static but constantly under negotiation and re-definition, in terms of usefulness, meaning and ethical significance: 'As writers confronted the problem', Otis continues, 'they imitated each other's ways of describing it, experimenting with one another's metaphors while defending their own moral interpretations of the world around them'.[143] Such experimentation with the moral nature of metaphors is one of the most prominent – and innovative – aspects of *English Traits*, and lies at the core of my inves-tigation in this book. If every word, or nearly every word, is a metaphor, and language is continually in a process of being inherited and transformed through its use, then every metaphor we use seems to demand a kind of radical self-consciousness and a continual re-interpretation in the light of its application and context. Such awareness may take the form of postmodern deconstructive analysis; for Emerson it is exercised in a mode of ethnographic study that analogizes scientific and linguistic procedures for an understanding of national and racial characteristics, and more profoundly, of the existential predicates we use to describe humans.

19.　As readers come to consciousness about the use of metaphors and analogies, it becomes increasingly clear that scientific work trades on the poetic power of the relationships it finds in language and image; meanwhile, poetry draws its capacity for affect and summons its reserves of potency from the empirical phenomena that form the basis of scientific investigation. As M. H. Abrams reminds us in his enduring study of poetry from the first four decades of the nineteenth century – *The Mirror and the Lamp: Romantic Theory and the Critical Tradition* (1953): 'Critical thinking, like that in all areas of human interest, has been in considerable part thinking in parallels, and critical argument has to that extent been an argument from analogy'.[144] What Abrams says of his own work I should like to adopt and apply here, if I may respectfully hazard this parallel: namely that 'the bringing of submerged analogies into the open puts certain old facts into a new and, it seems to me, a revealing perspective. [...] I have tried to use whatever ways [of approaching the history of criticism that] seemed most pertinent, and to restrict the analysis of basic metaphors to problems in which this approach promised genuine illumination'.[145] This kind of 'illumination' (noting Abrams' use of a metaphor to describe his ambition) can be traced in his account of how a change in metaphor either accompanies or provokes – and is an 'integral part' of – 'a corresponding change in popular epistemology'.[146] Because, for Emerson, the laws of mind and the laws of science are coordinate, the transformation of metaphor usage must also entail changes in our *moral* understanding. The use of tropes and analogies does not, for him, merely link the poetic arts with scientific methods, but binds them meaningfully to similar consequences. The selection, arrangement and aptness of metaphor is thus a matter of both truth and right.

20.   There is a robust, highly nuanced, and lengthy critical discourse about the meaning and nature of metaphor and metonymy reaching from Aristotle to Max Black, and more recently from Donald Davidson and David Lodge to Bernard Harrison and Hugh Bredin. While classical authors, following Aristotle, tended to see metonymy (μετωνυμία, a change in name) as a subset of metaphor, contemporary authors have argued for a clear division between the two, noting in particular how they serve different purposes and achieve dissimilar results. David Lodge has offered a careful analysis of Roman Jakobson's essay 'Two Aspects of Language and Two Types of Aphasic Disturbances' (1956) in which he links Jakobson's achievement to every-thing from the filmic nature of realistic fiction (such as in George Eliot) to the theories of cinematic montage espoused by Sergei Eisenstein. Lodge's prodigious accumulation of examples – and analogies between media – though should not overshadow the fundamental claims of his analysis. For instance, following Jakobson, Lodge writes that 'metaphor is substitution based on a certain kind of similarity'.[147] Yet, in order to have cognitive effect that 'similarity' must at the same time be predicated on difference, or on what Stephen Ullmann calls a 'feeling of disparity', or relatedly what Gillian Beer describes as a perception of 'abrupt shifts of scale'.[148] In order to perceive the lines of connection and affinity – say that airplanes and birds both have wings – we must also be struck by the enormous differences between these two entities of flight.

Lodge, tracing Jakobson, tells us that 'metaphor and metonymy are *opposed*, because [they are] generated according to opposite principles'.[149] Namely the principles of selection and combination: 'Metaphor', Lodge writes, 'belongs to the selection axis of language; metonymy and synecdoche belong to the combination axis of language'.[150] While Lodge broadly investigates the implications of this claim in *The Modes of Modern Writing: Metaphor, Metonymy, and the Typology of Modern Literature* (1977), I mean to signal its pertinence for an appreciation of Emerson's vigorous use of metaphor and metonymy in *English Traits*, and indeed throughout his writing. Hewing closely to the contours Darwinian evolutionary theory, it may be surprising to see the close parallel between a description of metaphor and metonymy as principles, respectively, of selection and combination. After all, selection – natural selection – is the core of modern evolutionary thought, and combination is the effective mode through which selection finds its expression. Speaking euphemistically, the 'combination' of parents makes the child; the combination of DNA through selection is the ground of new life forms; as if anticipating the implications of genetic structure in the form of the double-helix, Emerson writes: 'There is no thread that is not a twist of these two strands'.[151] Likewise, selection and combination define the work of the ethnographer, anthropologist, archaeologist, linguist and natural scientist as they conduct their studies; record data; create log books; develop taxonomies; draft charts and indexes; build libraries and cabinets; and invent and invest the categories of description. Natural evolutionary phenomena – such as the creation and development of life – are as defined by selection and combination as is the record we make and keep of those phenomena.

In the lecture 'The Relation of Intellect to Natural Science', which Emerson delivered in London in 1848 as the second in his series *Mind and Manners of the Nineteenth Century*, he draws from experiences he had on his first visit to Europe in 1833:

> If we go through the British Museum, or the *Jardin des Plantes* in Paris, or any cabinet where is some representation of all the kingdoms of nature, we are surprised with occult sympathies, and feel as if looking at our own bone and flesh through colouring and distorting lenses. [...]
>
> I see the same fact everywhere. The chemist has a frightful intimacy with the secret architecture of bodies; as the fisherman follows the fish, because *he* was *fish*; so the chemist divines the way of alkali, because he was alkali.
>
> As we cannot go into the Zoological Museum without feeling our family ties, and every rhomb, and vesicle, and spicule claiming old acquaintance, so neither can a tender Soul stand under the starry heaven, and explore the solar and stellar arrangements, without the wish to mix with them by knowledge. If men are analagons of acids and salts, and of beast and bird, so are they geometric laws, and of astronomic galaxies.[152]

In this passage, as is a hallmark of his work, Emerson deploys metaphor and metonymy even as he is commenting on their very definition. The notion that man is an analogon of *anything* – that he bears a relation or sympathy to other apparently dissimilar forms of life – is at once an announcement of a belief and a kind of intellectual defence by enacting its significance. Or as Bernard Harrison has said in 'The Truth about Metaphor:' 'What we need, perhaps, if we are to begin to understand metaphor, is not a theory of metaphorical *meaning*, but an account of what it is to *assert* metaphorically: an account, that is, which would operate at the level of the sentence rather than at that of the word'.[153] While Emerson's work is replete with striking and enduring metaphors, it is not merely their presence – as lively and inventive entertainments – that mark his philosophical contribution, but rather the continuous, intentional display of those metaphors assertorically, in the flow of his sentences. Stanley Cavell has written that the sentence is Emerson's proper mental and metaphysical milieu; it is the space in which his speech takes its form: 'essentially every Emersonian sentence [...] can be taken as the topic of the essay in which it finds itself', or as Cavell later glosses this idea – 'any sentence of an Emerson paragraph, or essay, may be taken to be the topic sentence'.[154] Every line of Emerson's prose, Cavell continues, 'every sentence of his writing', manifests a 'continuous resistance to dictation, an aversiveness to conformity, not an acceptance but an exploration of, or experimenting with, the conditions and contradictions of speech'.[155] Emerson, then, does not dwell on the de-contextualized trope, but continually employs it in context – in the sentence – in what could be called the habitat of its sense. Literary invention can often be marked by the sophistication of its metaphor – say as in Shakespeare or Proust – but with Emerson, the analogizing act transforms an interest in an isolated image or figure into a deeper perception of relation and connection. As Donald Davidson states in 'What Metaphors Mean', 'A picture is not worth a thousand words, or any other number. Words are the wrong currency to exchange for a picture'.[156] And that act of analogizing in the context of a sentence further illustrates how the singular word (or image) is transfigured by its association with another word (or image), and thereby makes an argument assertorically from allusion.

In 'Roman Jakobson on Metaphor and Metonymy', Hugh Bredin, writing about the same texts that drew Lodge's attention, makes a promising distinction between metaphor and metonymy – a distinction that seems especially elucidating for a consideration of metaphor's function in Emerson's usage.

> A metaphor is understood by virtue of its own semantic structure; if it asserts a similarity between things [...] this is something that may strike us for the first time, but which is none the less intelligible for that. But if I use the metonymic 'crown' or 'sceptre' for the institution of monarchy, the auditor must *already know* of the close connection between those objects and the institution. If he does not, he will fail to understand. Metaphor creates a knowledge of the relation between its objects; metonymy presupposes that knowledge.[157]

We need not take Bredin's definition as an exhaustive account but rather may adopt it as an illustrative description of the difference between metaphor and metonymy, one that reminds – or for some, perhaps suggests for the first time – that the effective use of metaphor is a creative act. Consequently, metaphor use should be thought of as a function of a writer's intellect, will and imagination, while also leaving space for acknowledging the unintentional and unconscious ways in which metaphors come to prominence in a writer's prose. And while it may be intuitive to link the creative contributions of poets who use, and rely heavily on, metaphor; it may not be obvious that philosophers and scientists are as dependent on metaphor as poets – and thus, necessarily, as involved and invested in creating knowledge.

21.   In *Emerson's Liberalism* (2009) Neal Dolan's primary task is the articulation and defence of a view of Emerson 'as a preacher of liberal culture'.[158] One of Dolan's finest and most worthy contributions to contemporary scholarship is his corrective to the notion of Emerson as a protopragmatist: 'Against the antifoundationalist misreading', Dolan writes, 'I argue that Emerson's work, both as a whole and in its details, is structured by an Enlightenment-Platonic hierarchy of values in which experience, observation and independent critical reason are given preference over authority and tradition as guides to basic truths about the world'.[159] Dolan's substantive critique may find a proper antagonist in Cornel West's 'The Emersonian Prehistory of American Pragmatism' where he contends that Emerson '*evades* modern philosophy; that is, he ingeniously and skillfully refuses [...] its search for foundations'.[160] Meanwhile Dolan can find company for his critique in Stanley Cavell's rhetorically titled 'What's the Use of Calling Emerson a Pragmatist?' where Cavell wishes to 'suspend applause – doubtless more a transcendentalist than a pragmatist gesture on my part – for ideas that seem to be gaining prominence [...], according to which Emerson is to be understood as a protopragmatist [...].[161]

As part of the 'Enlightenment-Platonic' outlook, Dolan maintains that Emerson applied its conceptions, values and methods to his own work, including the project that culminated in *English Traits*:

> For two hundred years New England ministers had drawn upon the enormous symbolic resources of the Bible to inspire the members of their congregations with such Christian values as awe before God, charity to their neighbors, and faith in the next life. Emerson drew on what he saw as the no less potent symbolism of nature, history, and the marketplace to inspire the citizens of his young nation with liberal values such as rational wonder at the cosmos, disciplined work in pursuit of property, a critical attitude toward tradition, suspicion of government, and respect for natural rights, especially the core right to liberty.[162]

Emerson's use of symbolism to express and defend liberal values is a practice, Dolan claims, that permeates Emerson's writing. In fact, while *English Traits* appears fairly late in Emerson's publishing career – in 1856 when he is 53 – Emerson's thinking on the subject can be traced to a lecture series given before the publication of his first book *Nature*, 20 years earlier. To illustrate Emerson's extended meditation, consider the titles of lectures presented in 1835, 'Permanent Traits of the English National Genius' and in 1843, 'Genius of the Anglo-Saxon Race'. As Dolan reminds us, in these lectures 'Emerson directly anticipates several of the major themes of *English Traits*'.[163] Philip Nicoloff, in his historically rich and serviceable Introduction to the *English Traits* volume of *The Collected Works of Ralph Waldo Emerson*, adds further detail about the earlier work written in the years after Emerson's first visit to England: for the lecture series on English literature, given in 1835, Emerson drew considerably from Sharon Turner's *The History of the Anglo-Saxons* and James Mackintosh's *History of the Revolution in England*. Nicoloff attests: 'Subsequently Emerson's five-part lecture series on New England in 1843 might be seen as a conscious response to both Turner and Mackintosh'.[164] Nicoloff directs us to the uncanny ways in which the titles of many of these lectures from the 1830s and 1840s are adopted in *English Traits*: in the 1843 lecture ('Genius of the Anglo-Saxon Race') we find titles or topics such as Trade, Manners, Literature, Religion, and Results; from the highly developed and regularly revised lecture 'England' (1848–1852) there are sequential remarks on Land, Race, Manners, Cockayne, Aristocracy, Education and, again, Literature.[165] In Nicoloff's account 'in both models the discussion would begin with biological traits and conclude with the condition of the spirit'.[166] Dolan says the chapters of *English Traits* divide into 'two general categories' – Chapters IV through X consider 'an extensive set of characteristics that have been conducive to English success' (viz., Race, Ability, Manners, Truth, Character, Cockayne and Wealth); – Chapters XI through XV focus on institutions (viz., Aristocracy, Universities, Religion, Literature and The 'Times').[167]

In Dolan's accentuation of Emerson's use of symbolism and Nicoloff's attention to the genealogy of Emerson's writing about the English, *English Traits* itself becomes a work full of characteristics inherited from predecessors. The 1856 book is so much the child and inheritor of Emerson's reading and prose deliberations from the preceding 20 years.

22.   A sketch of the structure and prominent shifts in content in *English Traits* might be profitably, or at least suggestively, rendered this way: Chapters I–II, memoir and travelogue; Chapters III–XV, characteristics of England and the English (in Chapter III, the first after the autobiographical opening pair of chapters, Emerson addresses the place ('Land') and in Chapter IV its people ('Race'), while in Chapters IV–XV he evaluates the phenomena that abide on that land, and are the effects of its inhabitants); Chapters XVI ('Stonehenge') and XVII ('Personal') include acknowledgments, and a return to memoir; and Chapter XVIII ('Result'), which is akin to a report card, features a series of valuations or estimations of the English. The titles of Chapters VI ('Manners') and VIII ('Character') replicate essay names from *Essays, Second Series* (1844); Chapter X ('Wealth') is the title of a chapter that will appear in *The Conduct of Life* (1860); and Chapter XI ('Aristocracy') shares its name with a lecture Emerson delivered in London, 1848. The resonance and resilience of these topics suggests their prominence in Emerson's thought before, during and after the composition of *English Traits*.

The final chapter, 'Speech at Manchester', Emerson wrote before he set foot on the island in 1847 and yet he says in the speech – even in the wake of his arrival and the experience of significant travel that might augment or countermand his remarks – that like a robust specimen the speech succeeds in 'fitly expressing the feeling with which I entered England, and which agrees well enough with the more deliberate results of better acquaintance recorded in the foregoing pages'.[168] At this moment in 1856, or at the time he finalized the speech in 1847 before disembarking, Emerson seems to suggest that the traits of the English were something he gleaned rather well, even sufficiently, on his first visit in 1833, or that they might even be discerned *a priori* – but from what? Books of history read with interest in his Concord study on the Cambridge Turnpike? Reports given by English friends visiting in New England? From a sense, if one is a descendent, of the features and content one's own English-derived blood?

'But I have known all these persons already', confides Emerson, 'When I was at home, they were as near to me as they are to you'.[169] Emerson, in short, did not require vast, ready-to-hand empirical evidence from his most recent visit to generate meaningful, penetrating remarks about English characters and constitutions; he could find his sources from a wide span of time and in disparate locations (books, anecdotes, arcane or neglected or outmoded scientific studies, histories, biographies, maps, charts, newspaper reports, letters, pictures and sketches, sculpted busts, the invention of machines, ship design and other feats of engineering, models of architecture, train schedules, sartorial details and so on). Even if exceptions and counter-examples were presented to Emerson in Manchester – cited as objections to his claims and account – they would themselves become part of his consideration of the English: why the insistence on verification and consistency, the desire for specific incarnation over the trends of types and classes? For Emerson, traits are multivalent phenomena that express themselves at varying levels, at differing times, in myriad forms and circumstances. One cannot predict or anticipate the provocative features that will stimulate a thought, or given rise to an impression.

England might be a land that supports the Saxon seed and also allows for its able dispersal into other soils and climates. The Englishman who moves to Boston, New York or San Francisco would be very much himself; and if he sired children, perhaps they would not be Americans first but Englishmen and -women in an American context. Perhaps such a potentiality is a consequence of Emerson's loaded inflection of the tropes at hand, for instance, when he speaks of the English as possessing 'the imperial trait' – a image that accords with his sentiment from the penultimate chapter about 'that puissant nationality'.[170] It is this trait – and 'the moral peculiarity of the Saxon race' – that 'lures a solitary American in the woods with the wish to see England'.[171] He speaks as if addressing the island as it comes into view (say, as a ship approaching him instead of him aboard a ship approaching the island), Emerson exclaims: 'See this, I say. All hail! mother of nations, mother of heroes'. At the end of the speech, which is only a few pages from the end of the book and hence is positioned for summoning conclusive remarks, Emerson writes of the context in which the English live – 'from which my forefathers came'. England was for them:

> [...] no lotus-garden, no paradise of serene sky and roses and music and merriment all the year round, no, but a cold foggy mournful country, where nothing grew well in the open air, but robust men and virtuous women, and these of a wonderful fibre and endurance; that their best parts were slowly revealed; their virtues did not come out until they quarreled: they did not strike twelve the first time; good lovers, good haters, and you could know little about them till you had seen them long, and little good of them till you had seen them in action; that in prosperity they were moody and dumpish, but in adversity they were grand.[172]

Emerson analogizes this 'British island' as a ship that has returned '[...] with torn sheets and battered sides, stript of her banners, but having ridden out the storm [...]' – 'with the infirmities of a thousand years gathering around her' – and yet as 'not dispirited, not weak'.[173] Perhaps drawing from his own experience in the 'cold foggy' homeland, he wonders if England 'sees a little better in a cloudy day', and remains possessed of a 'secret vigor'.[174] 'So be it! so let it be!' he cheers. But in the very last line of *English Traits* he seems acquiescent, and not mournful, that the imperial trait may diminish, that its secret vigour may fade, and he would then have to revise down any estimate of endless English dominance. Knowing his own and his country's status as the proper offspring of this island, an option presents itself: the heirs will be inheritors, the children will be invigorated as the parents face debility.

> If it be not so, if the courage of England goes with the chances of a commercial crisis, I will go back to the capes of Massachusetts, and my own Indian stream, and say to my countrymen, the old race are all gone, and the elasticity and hope of mankind must henceforth remain on the Alleghany ranges, or nowhere.

Such would be a report to a new world – 'the old races are all gone' – perhaps belatedly stated in 1856 as much as it was predictive.

Chapter XVI, 'Stonehenge', is principally a reminiscence of travelling to the ancient site with 'my friend Mr C'. – that is, Carlyle – and more than half of Chapter XVII, 'Personal', is dedicated to Wordsworth – to his works, and as a man. 'We found Mr Wordsworth asleep on the sofa'.[175] In Emerson's walking with Carlyle in the out of doors, and on his follow-up visit to Wordsworth in 1848, *English Traits* in this very late stage loops back to the autobiographical mode of Chapter I where Emerson began with notes on his first encounter with Carlyle on the hills of Craigenputtock and with Wordsworth at Rydal Mount. Emerson's inclusion of everyday details along with high-minded literary criticism – from his host's napping, curmudgeonly complaining and keeping a 'modest household' to his acknowledgment of Tennyson's 'right poetic genius' – sustains Wordsworth's sentiment, which he confirms for his guest: '[…] but then you know the matter always comes out of the manner'.[176] In the first edition of *English Traits*, Emerson notes Wordsworth's generalization that 'No Scotchman, he said, can write English'.[177] But when he came to record Wordsworth's acerbic summation of his friend, Mr C., in particular his capacity to write – Emerson is at pains to minimize the insult, replacing 'Carlyle' with three asterisks: 'nor can * * *, who is a pest to the English tongue'.[178] In much of the rest of their conversation, Emerson and Wordsworth discussed their views on 'English national character', which illumined a point of interest for Emerson: namely, Wordsworth's claim that if Plato's *Republic* were a new book it would find no readers in England because '[…] we have embodied it all'.[179] If the judgement be apt and accurate, Emerson could not but be both admiring and confounded that such a remark was made with 'that complacency which never deserts a true-born Englishman'.[180] But it is a complacency informed by the representative nature of English traits – that they are both literal and symbolic phenomena.

Chapter XVIII, 'Result', begins with a conclusion – 'England is the best of all actual nations' – and the chapter more broadly could be treated as the conclusion of Emerson's cultural anthropology, his work as a naturalist of intellect in England, because it complicates the apparent baldness and boldness (and perhaps self-admitted emptiness) of his claim. He confides without shame or regret: 'What we must say about a nation is a superficial dealing with symptoms'.[181] Thus Emerson – and we – are privy only to the forms and effects of man and nature as they are observable at a given time. Much like any remarks on or theories of race, Emerson's notes on English culture must be superficial, tentative, experimental, revisable. After all, how many essential traits and characteristics can one perceive (or be assured of) from two fast-moving tours through a foreign nation? How many eternal proclamations could be made under touristic conditions? (Emerson acknowledges as much in the opening line of the previous chapter, where he attests to the pace of change in his chosen subjects – namely, the English and their land: 'In these comments on an old journey now revised after seven busy years have much changed men and things in England [...]'.[182] Perhaps Emerson's acknowledgment of his elusive, ever-evolving subjects can be generalized to *any* effort to catalogue the traits of race – that no matter how long and carefully studied, our observations in the field, or even in the laboratory and library, will yield nothing more than temporary speculations, 'superficial dealing with symptoms'. It could be said that evolutionary process is, by nature, a perpetual re-writing, an ongoing negotiation of biological inscription owing to the interaction between traits and their circumstances.

23.   If Emerson's consciousness was oriented to, as Dolan conjectures, the 'symbolism of nature, history, and the marketplace', these were – in the decades leading up to the publication of his book on England – bound up with the cultural transformation of the meaning and status of race in America and England.[183] Emerson celebrated William Wilberforce's moral victory of emancipation in the British West Indies with a speech given in 1844, and thereafter continued to read in a range of racial theory and historiography, including works by Johann Gottfried von Herder, Victor Cousin, Robert Chambers, Jean Baptiste Van Mons and Johann Stilo, among others.[184] Emerson's reading in science was at once deep and diverse:

> He became to a greater or lesser extent acquainted with the craniometry of Blumenbach, the environmental theories of [Richard] Owen, the radical constitutional determinism of Robert Knox, the facial geometry of Lavater, the brain studies of Cabanis, the materialistic neurology of Gall and Spurzheim, the statistical studies of Quentelet ('these adamantine bandages'), and, quite likely (through Oliver Wendell Holmes and [Louis] Agassiz), the osteological work of the American Samuel Morton.[185]

Emerson's early declaration of support for the emancipation of slaves importantly informs his decades of reading in racial theory. And even though, as Nicoloff and Len Gougeon have described in their scrupulously well-researched studies, respectively, *Emerson on Race and History: An Examination of* English Traits (1961) and *Virtue's Hero: Emerson, Antislavery, and Reform* (1990), Emerson critically considered the possibility of racial determinism, and summarily dismissed it.[186] One of the many salient insights of Gougeon's book – supported by extensive documentation from Emerson's private and public writing – shows the extent to which biographers distorted Emerson's thinking on topics pertaining to race theory and consequently sullied his intellectual and social legacy as an active, even militant, reformer. Partly the distortions and 'significant inconsistency' stemmed from the absence of original works of protest: 'antislavery addresses from 1837, 1845, 1846, and 1849 were either lost or destroyed'.[187] Such omissions of source materials were coupled with and exacerbated by the effects of 'biographical selectivity' – the degree to which biographers shape a portrait based on their own ideas and interests, sometimes, perhaps more than we should like to admit or believe, instead of those that truly preoccupied and defined their subject.[188] Robert Habich expertly explores and exhaustively studies the phenomena of biographical creation – and mutation – in his accomplished *Building Their Own Waldos: Emerson's First Biographers and the Politics of Life-Writing in the Gilded Age* (2011). In Oliver Wendell Holmes' influential and popular biography of Emerson, published the year after Emerson's death, for example, Holmes appears to have portrayed Emerson 'in the light of his own conservative image and likeness', according to Gougeon.[189] When offering a biographical memorial for friend Theodore Parker, Emerson confided: 'I have the feeling […] that biography is at [the biographer's] own expense. He furnishes not only the facts but the report. I mean all biography is autobiography. It is only what he tells of himself that comes to be known and believed'.[190] Because of the publication of extensive source materials in *The Journals and Miscellaneous Notebooks* and *Emerson's Antislavery Writings*, and a continual re-engagement with these widely available works, such as in *A Political Companion to Ralph Waldo Emerson* and the aforementioned *Building Their Own Waldos*, biographical omission and distortion can be better and more quickly identified.[191] Owing to the availability of these primary texts, recent decades have witnessed a vigorous critical reassessment and reversal of claims that Emerson 'successively withdrew' from social reform over time.[192] Consequently, momentum has shifted in the critical literature toward actively dissolving the deleterious myth of Emerson's apolitical indifference to social crisis. The robust integration of work that registers Emerson's outrage and disappointment in the political thinking of his day, especially as leaders and the law were informed by pernicious racial definitions, also, not incidentally, prompts a renewal and revision of our understanding of individualism as a concept and as an activity.

When Nicoloff assesses Emerson's appraisal of racial forms, types and divisions, he also confirms both Emerson's dismissal of fixed boundaries and his commitment to the fluidity of racial constitution. 'In the opening argument of his chapter "Race", the fourth in *English Traits*', Nicoloff contends that 'Emerson presented one of the more liberal and perceptive statements on the question of race to be written by a layman in the middle of the nineteenth century. Without at any point denying the unique importance of the "kind" of men which formed a nation, he had reduced to confusion the glib doctrine of permanent racial distinctions'.[193]

Dolan offers revitalizing support for Nicoloff and Gougeon's already well-defended claims for Emerson's skepticism about racial difference and fixity: 'For one, Emerson casts serious doubt on the possibility of isolating race from the large multitude of factors that combine to shape the character and long-term destiny of any group of people. An almost immeasurable array of geographical, social, cultural, economic and institutional influences, he points out, play a decisive role: 'Civilization is a re-agent, and eats away the old traits'.[194] And as Emerson continues in the chapter 'Race':

> Though we flatter the self-love of men and nations by the legend of pure races, all our experience is of the gradation and resolution of races, and strange resemblances meet us everywhere. It need not puzzle us that Malay and Papuan, Celt and Roman, Saxon and Tartar should mix, when we see the rudiments of tiger and baboon in our human form, and know that the barriers of races are not so firm, but that some spray sprinkles us from the antediluvian seas'.[195]

While this sentiment lends weight to Emerson's faith in the continuity and permeability of races, Dolan adds another valence to the positive implications of miscegenation – 'Emerson credits English success not to racial purity but to promiscuous hybridity'.[196] – and adduces these passages from the chapter on 'Race' for textual support:

> The English composite character betrays a mixed origin. Every thing English is a fusion of distant and antagonistic elements. The language is mixed; the names of men are of different nations, – three languages, three or four nations.[197]

> On the whole, it is not so much a history of one or of certain tribes of Saxons, Jutes, or Frisians, coming from one place, and genetically identical, as it is an anthology of temperaments out of them all.[198]

> The best nations are those most widely related; and navigation, as effecting a world-wide mixture, is the most potent advancer of nations.[199]

As Nicoloff and Gougeon before him, Dolan finds ample textual evidence to support Emerson's 'decisive rejection of racial purism', so, Dolan asks, 'Why does Emerson use racial or even national categories at all?'[200] Dolan is attentive throughout *Emerson's Liberalism* to the 'symbolism' of Emerson's writing generally, and how more particularly *English Traits* 'demonstrates Emerson's urbanity with response to his own categories and names the kind of symbolic cultural work that will be performed by the putatively empirical-historical sketch provided by *English Traits*' – qualities illustrated by Emerson's remarks such as: 'Though, I doubt not, the nobles of both tribes [viz., the Normans and Saxons], and the workers of both, yet we are forced to use the names a little mythically [...]'.[201] Dolan glosses Emerson's crucial meta-critical self-awareness with a useful elaboration on Emerson's application of racial symbolism:

> Myths, whatever other purposes they may also serve, tend to provide the societies to which they belong with an orientation to the long past – to distant, often sacred, origins. [...] Emerson writes about English 'traits' and 'Saxon' virtues in *English Traits* because he wants to secure the deep roots, however mythical, of an Anglo-American commitment to freedom that he worries may be wavering under the increasing pressure of the Southern 'slave power' in the United States of the 1850s.[202]

Emerson's awareness of the potency of symbolic and mythical sign-systems conspicuously informs his use of metaphor in *English Traits*. One reason may be the virtue of indirectness, the capacity of metaphor to possess multiple meanings and frame associations, and even to destabilize them. While the linguistic and ideological destabilization inherent in metaphor usage can often give rise to an ambiguity that some writers find debilitating – and some critics fault for being impressionistic, inconsistent or illogical – it should be considered highly advantageous to write with the aid of prominent, enduring, culturally resonant metaphors if one is discussing the core problem of the age, which in Emerson's case, at least, included the persistence of slavery and the sense of America's delayed creation of great works of art and literature – a lacuna, of course, that was beginning to be ameliorated by the efforts of Emerson and his contemporaries during the very decade he composed *English Traits*. As 'a preacher of liberal culture', in Dolan's phrase, Emerson was all too aware of both the rhetorical effect of speech – its tropes, tones, and the temperament of the speaker – and the delicacy of political and intellectual claims made from the authority of religion or science.[203] Emerson directed himself to the task of poetizing natural history, of finding abiding and essential lessons in the course of human descent – including the history of linguistic dissent. If these inherited and interpreted images could be applied – by politicians and statesmen, for example – to the apparently intractable problem of slavery, Emerson would welcome the company.

24.   In her seminal book *Darwin's Plots: Evolutionary Narrative in Darwin, George Eliot and Nineteenth Century Fiction* (1983), Gillian Beer addresses the phenomenon of Charles Darwin as a writer. In a second edition (2000), she clarifies the intentions of the first: 'This book does not imply that Darwin's work is "fiction", as some puzzled readers at first assumed. It argues that how Darwin said things was a crucial part of his struggle to think things, not a layer that can be skimmed off without loss'.[204] Beer notes how *The Origin of Species*, for example, was 'partly the outcome of Darwin's struggle to find a language to think in. He was working in a milieu where natural theology had set the terms for natural historians.[205] Attending to the function of metaphor in the work of science, Beer 'shows how his non-technical language (which may indeed have imagined a technical readership) allowed a wide public to read his work and appropriate his terms to a variety of meanings (Nature, race, man, struggle, fit, and family would be examples of story-generating words)'.[206] Metaphors, then, cannot be 'skimmed off' or otherwise separated from the texts that contain them because, as Beer argues, 'narrative and argument share methods'.[207]

The use of metaphor in science, as in literature, is not frivolous or extraneous but part and parcel of the undertaking – 'a means both of initiating and of controlling novelty'.[208] And unlike other forms of explanation, such as an inventory of traits or a taxonomy of features, metaphors can sustain an array of applications by diverse writers in varied circumstances. While this openness may suggest imprecision, it also evidently creates the space for necessary invention – the work of the imagination coming into contact with the empirical world. As Beer notes:

> Darwin himself saw that taxonomies always cause trouble with boundaries, that they draw on prior assumptions, that their values tend to form an evidential circle about what matters for categorization. Darwin never doubts the world is real. But

he does doubt our categories for understanding it and indeed questions, while he shares, the categorizing zeal of human beings. That unsteadying of plot allows him to continue to generate new debate and insight in an extraordinary variety of fields.[209]

Darwin, like many scientists of his generation, drew heavily from the 'metaphors, myths, and narrative patterns', as Beer puts it, in work by non-scientists.[210] She reminds us that 'the one book [Darwin] never left behind during his expeditions from the *Beagle*' was *The Poetical Works of John Milton*.[211] The image of Darwin with Milton under his arm is itself a metaphor! And it is a dynamic, suggestive one. The lines of affinity between the poetical and scientific mind, between the religious and rational temperament were coextensive in the nineteenth century; a fact appreciated differently depending on where one stood. While John Herschel declaimed Darwin's theory as the 'law of higgledy-piggledy', he was expressing an anxiety about the unknown impli-cations, we might say, of Darwin's metaphors.[212] The tropes were themselves generative – and as Beer says, the 'unused, or uncontrolled, elements in metaphors such as "the struggle for existence", take on a life of their own. They surpass their status in the text and generate further ideas and ideologies.'[213] Consider the impact of metaphors that appear to both captivate and motivate a range of human endeavours and disciplines: Founding Fathers for American history; for economics, Adam Smith's invisible hand (mentioned only twice in *The Wealth of Nations*); and back to Darwin, the descent of man for biology and anthropology. Beer assesses the function of metaphor use in science and literature: 'Symbol and metaphor, as opposed to analysis, can allow insight without consequences because perceptions are not stablised and categorised. They allow us fleetingly to inhabit contradictory experience without moralising it'.[214] I should add that it appears that metaphor's fucundity – its overflowing, almost promis-cuously generating influence on thinking – is the condition for analysis. Beer's book is evidence of this self-reflexivity: scholarship devoted to tracing the proliferating effects of metaphor use develops in that process a remarkable new approach to our thinking about how essential metaphor is to our thinking and theorizing. And of course, the 'fleeting' quality of metaphor use can demand a great deal of time. Even when the 'unexamined and diminished use' of a given metaphor leaves us at risk for being or becoming blind to it, its potency merely lies dormant – awaiting a new reader. We might consider that metaphor use – and sometimes neglect – assures our investigation will never reach its end, never conclude in the form of definitive analysis or fixed taxonomies. 'Metaphor is never fully stable', as Beer says, 'it initiates new meaning but not permanent meaning'.[215] Metaphor animates our thinking, keeps it vital and moving. Coursing through language, metaphor is the lifeblood of thought.

25.   George Levine, who was like me and many others 'humbled and exhilarated' by *Darwin's Plots*, notes in his own innovative yet still Beer-indebted work, *Darwin and the Novelists: Patterns of Science in Victorian Fiction* (1988), that 'Whatever his presentation, the theory was only possible because Darwin had seized it imaginatively before he could prove it inductively. He had the power to imagine what wasn't there

and what could never be seen, and he used analogies and metaphors with subtlety and profusion as his imagination actually defied the experience that Baconian theory privileged'.[216] One of the signal contributions of Levine's approach to the language of science and literature in the nineteenth century is his emphasis on analyzing works by authors who – unlike in Beer's study – did not read Darwin, 'writers who were probably not directly "influenced" by scientific writing'.[217] Indeed, it was Beer who prompted Levine's path when she wrote 'Ideas pass more rapidly into the state of assumptions when they are *unread*'.[218] Levine does not conduct a study of influence, but as he describes it, a practice of reading literature in which he finds the authors involved in the 'absorption and testing of Darwinian ideas and attitudes (even when the writers are not thinking of them as Darwinian)'.[219] In this way Levine attunes us to methods that befit a *literary* investigation in place of a literal (or sign-tracing) approach. Given the literal nature of genetics – the way traits are indeed lettered – there is much to recommend Levine's attempt to fathom what exceeds that kind of inscription; for example, how we are transformed by letters (in language and blood) that elide the strict determinations of grammar and genetics. Levine's own metaphors – especially 'absorption' with its connotation of passive osmosis – frame a lively and provocative study of a writer or artist's capacity to internalize and innovate ideas that he does not, as it were, *know*.

26.   Robert William Mackay, *The Progress of the Intellect* (1850)

A remnant of the mythical lurks in the very sanctuary of science. Forms or theories ever fall short of nature, though they are ever tending to reach a position above nature, and may often be found to include more than the maker of them at the time knew.[220]

27.   Immanuel Kant, *Critique of Judgment* (1790)

Hence, where an author owes a product to his genius, he does not himself know how the ideas for it have entered into his head, nor has he it in his power to invent the like at pleasure, or methodically, and communicate the same to others in such precepts as would put them in a position to produce similar products.[221]

28.   The First Epistle of John

But if we walk in the light, as he is in the light, we have fellowship one with another, and the blood of Jesus Christ his Son cleanseth us from all sin.[222]

29.   Emerson, 'The Sovereignty of Ethics' (1878)

Then up comes a man with a text of I John v.7, or a knotty sentence from St Paul, which he considers as the axe at the root of your tree. You cannot bring yourself to care for it. You say: 'Cut away; my tree is Ygdrasil – the tree of life'. […] Let him know by your security that your conviction is clear and sufficient, and if he were Paul himself, you also are here, and with your Creator.[223]

30. Carlyle, 'The Hero as Divinity' (1841)

> I like, too, that representation [the Norse] have of the Tree of Igdrasil. All Life
> is figured by them as a Tree. Igdrasil, the Ash-tree of Existence, has its roots
> deep-down in the kingdoms of Hela or Death; its trunk reaches up heaven-high,
> spreads its boughs over the whole Universe: it is the Tree of Existence.[224]

31. While some words and phrases announce their metaphorical status directly
(e.g. light, blood, sin, tree (root, trunk, bough), family tree, tree of knowledge of good
and evil, tree of life, tree of liberty), others – perhaps for the frequency of use, or the
indirectness of their allusions – may cease to appear metaphorical, or may need to be
pointed out as such. A couple of examples from Darwin's *The Origin of Species* should
suffice to both amplify the subtitle of the present work – with its mention of 'varieties'
and invocation of 'transcendental biology' – and, more broadly, address the work of
metaphor in philosophy, literature, religion and science (especially as Emerson interpreted the presence of tropes and symbols in these multiform fields of human inquiry
and expression).

> How will the struggle for existence [...] act in regard to variation? Can the
> principle of selection, which we have seen is so potent in the hands of man, apply
> in nature? I think we shall see that it can act most effectually. [...] Can it, then,
> be thought improbable, seeing that variations useful to man have undoubtedly
> occurred, that other variations useful in some way to each being in the great
> and complex battle of life, should sometimes occur in the course of thousands of
> generations? [...] On the other hand, we may feel sure that any variation in the
> least degree injurious would be rigidly destroyed. This preservation of favourable
> variations and the rejection of injurious variations, I call Natural Selection.[225]

Even as Darwin himself worried that his work sounded too literary, his prose remains
a touchstone – almost a cliché – of modern scientific thinking. Yet consider how the
words he uses – 'struggle', 'act', 'selection', 'useful', 'battle', 'injurious' and 'preservation'
– are boldly metaphorical. At the outset of the passage above, Darwin introduces an
analogy: trading the nature of selection in man (by his 'hands' no less, where choice is
illustrated by a manipulation of the world) to the notion of selection in or by nature
(nature, therein, taking on consciousness, or a capacity to perceive and choose). With
the metaphor in mind – of intention, of nature, of choice, indeed, of the hand of man
– we are not far from thinking that Natural Selection is a scientific analogy for God.

Darwin, to his credit, is both aware of his metaphor usage and to the ways his
analogies summon forms of thinking familiar to his audience, such as the existence
and agency of a divine creator. 'I should premise that I use the term Struggle for
Existence', he writes, 'in a large and metaphorical sense'. And when he finds his account
searching for 'transitional grades' – namely, the specimens and species that create
continuity for descent – he confesses his own doubts about the way our language, our
way of describing phenomena, can interrupt what must be a rather simple and logical
consequence of given conditions. Here he addresses the evolution of the eye:

He who will go thus far, if he find on finishing this treatise [viz., *The Origin of Species*] that large bodies of facts, otherwise inexplicable, can be explained by the theory of descent, ought not to hesitate to go further, and to admit that a structure even as perfect as the eye of an eagle might be formed by natural selection, although in this case he does not know any of the transitional grades. His reason ought to conquer his imagination; though I have felt the difficulty far too keenly to be surprised at any degree of hesitation in extending the principle of natural selection to such startling lengths.[226]

32.   In *Emerson on Race and History: An Examination of* English Traits (1961), a careful, thorough, multi-layered investigation, and one of the most in-depth and capacious studies of *English Traits*, Philip Nicoloff relates that his book began as a dissertation written under famed Emerson scholar Ralph Rusk. And it appears both pertinent to the conditions of the work's generation and to its subject (*English Traits* being a work that also took Emerson a long time to complete) that Nicoloff prefaces his book by saying 'A special statement of gratitude must be reserved for my wife, Marguerite McInerney Nicoloff. She bore Lee, Paul, Elizabeth, Ann and Martha while I was laboring with my single and less lovely child'.[227] The acknowledgment is both fitting and tragic, for what doctoral student cum professional academic, who has spent months, years, maybe a decade or more, writing does not feel humbled by the pace of life – and production – beyond the limits of his desk? And moreover, what man who laboured to create by his own hands a work of lasting power and dignity has not been awestruck by the infinitely more dynamic figure and features of his child? Nicoloff's acknowledgment of gratitude places the achievement of his work (whatever its quality and effect) in relation to the existence and development of his children; it also can meaningfully orient a reader of *English Traits* to that work's core preoccupation with the nature – limits and meaning – of descent. When DESCENT in its Darwinian sense came up against ASCENT in its Christological sense, the nineteenth century thinker was pushed to ask whether existence is meliorating (evolving into forms more finely suited to conditions) or deteriorating (atrophying progressively from an originally perfect beginning).

While Nicoloff ably traces the scientific sources that inform Emerson's understanding of descent and ascent, I should like to add a complementary attention to the metaphorical means by which the issue or question of, as it is called, 'amelioration', is handled. Nicoloff, as other scholars have corroborated, notes that Emerson was a close reader of Robert Chambers' *Vestiges of the Natural History of Creation* – a reading that occurs in the mid-1840s, in the wake of the publication of *Essays, Second Series* (1844), and ahead of his second trip to England (1847–8). In that work Chambers writes:

The different mental characters of individuals may be presumed from analogy to depend on the same law of development which we have seen determining forms of being and the mental characters of particular species. This we may conceive as carrying forward the intellectual powers and moral dispositions of some to a high pitch, repressing those of others at a moderate amount, and thus producing all the varieties which we see in our fellow-creatures.[228]

The development of individuals, by this account, is subject to the same sorts of environmental considerations as the species encounters; Chambers' specimens – as individuals and as groups – are informed and affected by empirical circumstances. 'The menagerie, or forms and powers of the spine, is a book of Fate', Emerson writes in the eponymous essay from 1860: 'Ask Spurzheim, ask the doctors, ask Quentelet if temperaments decide nothing? – or if there be anything they do not decide?'[229] If Emerson 'could give his full assent' to Chambers' view of biological determinism, he also, as Nicoloff says, 'found for the first time in Chambers a convincing account of a mechanism of ascent'.[230] This mechanism is given the name 'arrested and progressive development', or 'ameliorative evolution'. And Nicoloff describes it as 'the poetic key to all contemporary natural science'.[231]

It is precisely in the invitation to think about Emerson's adoption of Chambers' work as a 'poetic key' that we are poised to appreciate the sophistication of the tropes used to give credence to the theories of natural science that so excited Emerson and his contemporaries. The metaphors of ascent/descent (as well as assent/dissent) are part of a system of orientation and directionality, and for that reason suggest that one is in a position – an originary locus – from which to address the movement or spectrum of development. Are we 'lower forms' (having 'fallen' from God) or are we the pinnacle of creation (having descended from that divine source)? In our distance from a divine origin are we deteriorating? Could that deterioration itself suggest that we are in the process of becoming reconciled to the source again, as particles re-combined or re-absorbed? The cycles inherent to a Plotinian worldview stand in the shadow of such questions, and yet they are also very much at the centre of the inquiries of nineteenth century science. What are the effects of combination (in the form of a species, specimen and the process of speciation), transformation (as we find in mutation) or disintegration (through extinction)? In the *Vestiges of the Natural History of Creation*, Chambers writes:

> It is only in recent times that physiologists have observed that each animal passes, in the course of its germinal history, through a series of changes resembling the *permanent forms* of the various orders of animals inferior to it in the scale. [...] Nor is man himself exempt from this law. His firm form is that which is permanent in the animalcule. The organization gradually passes through conditions generally resembling a fish, a reptile, a bird, and the lower mammalia, before it attains its specific maturity. At one of the last stages of his foetal career, he exhibits an intermaxillary bone, which is characteristic of the perfect ape; this is suppressed, and he may then be said to take leave of the simial type, and become a true human creature.[232]

That a human child, in its foetal form, once resembled a fish or a bird in a similar stage of development – 'that man carried both in his embryological and in his matured form rudiments of the lower animals' – was a source of great intellectual satisfaction to Emerson precisely because this image 'offered evidence of the ameliorative program' that he believed was present throughout the vastly elongated time scales confirmed by geologists. As Nicoloff describes Chambers' theory in the terms Emerson came to understand them: 'the higher orders of life were potential in the embryos of all species. The level of organization which a particular embryo reached at maturation was dependent upon how much of its latency of development had been arrested or freed. The arresting (or permissive) force which determined both the rate and direction of development was the natural environment in which the parent animal and its progenitors had lived since the origin of organic life'.[233] With Chambers' view of evolution understood as a release of potential – displacing or complicating Lamarck's transmutational claims – Emerson could describe evolution (with a metaphor fitting the continuity of such 'release' through successive births) as an 'unswaddling', and therefore, as Nicoloff writes, 'not as an arbitrary and meandering ascent'.[234]

Still, the unfolding or unswaddling of forms – given the tropes in play – suggests either that we are ascending to some more perfect future form (as human consciousness, for example, appears to be an advance on the 'mind' of the amoeba), or that we are descending – step by step, or form by form, progressively – in the ways Darwin describes, toward eventual and assured extinction (entropy and nonexistence apparently being the ultimate aim of our varied and complex energies). Nicoloff helpfully consolidates a lesson on this point:

> Chambers' theory permitted a reconciliation of the 'scientific or skeptical' view of man as having evolved from the 'animalcule savage' of the waterdrop with the 'believer's' or 'poet's' view that man had descended from some purer and superior race. The question which Emerson had posed to himself in 1843 – 'that point of imperfection which we occupy – is it on the way *up* or *down*?' – could thus be answered with a kind of double affirmative. Man was at once in a state of arrestment from the potential perfection which his nature embodied, and in a state of radical development from the primordial elastic sack with which life had begun. The answer to the question 'whether the trilobites, or whether the gods are our ancestors', was simply that both were, depending on whether one chose to view man according to the perspective of time or according to the perspective of law. According to either view there was a single life type and a single evolutional series.[235]

33.   In evolutionary terms descent is presented as a 'progression' from primitive to ever more elegant, sophisticated and 'higher' forms; hence the confusion that descent is really more like ascent. While some nineteenth-century cultural anthropologists and social theorists deployed the TREE OF LIFE schema as an explanatory icon or metaphor for the superiority of later forms, the metaphor itself reinforces continuity and connection between generations and types – thereby retaining the notion, troubling to some, that the higher form remains bound to the lower form in so far as something of the vestigial type persists in the higher.[236]

By contrast, the tropes that dominate conceptions of social class structure – of course, conceptions interlinked with undeniably empirical cultural practice – presume fixed categories of *separation* that arrive in tandem with a hierarchy. That evolutionary scientists were contemporaneously innovating 'class' theory as a function of how to organize data and structure evidence – in terms of classification – lies beside any consideration of the evolving concepts of political class in late modernity. Class structure, as inherited in the nineteenth century, reinforces a clear designation of the HIGHER form, say, aristocrats and intelligentsia; so that the UPPER – of the upper class – becomes a metaphor for more wealth, property and education, and other forms of power. In this image of class there is no indication that the higher/upper forms descend (much less ascend) from the lower class. These two levels appear to exist independently and in exclusive parallel – and decidedly without connection or inter-directional movement. Consequently, there is a potent disanalogy between evolutionary tropes for the purposes of explaining the transmission of traits from 'lower' to 'higher' forms and those metaphors that might be usefully applied to an understanding of the inheritance of social characteristics among individuals and the classes they inhabit.

While the TREE OF LIFE metaphor (so dominant in Darwinian theory as a graphic of the DESCENT of hominid forms and kinds) reinforces how species are biologically linked, the difficulty (or even possibility) of social movement from the lower class to the higher class reveals how a gap between the two realms was historically prominent, a feature that would find its way figuratively into the daily lives on both sides of the divide (for example, in the upstairs/downstairs scenarios of aristocrats and their servants). The very idea of a 'middle' class – much less its historical development from existing norms – seems, in retrospect, the most plausible response to the division: namely, the creation of a new HYBRID class to occupy the gap between the lower and higher, a class with the apparent dignity and vitality of the labouring class coupled with the apparent prestige and comfort of the elite. Prior to the existence of a robust middle class, however, when there was movement between classes it would, by and large, appear to point only in one direction. For the wealthy, the spectre of impoverishment may have been largely a threat, and yet it was sufficiently pronounced to encourage financial, legal, social, political and other institutional bulwarks to minimize its occurrence and extent. By contrast there was less chance of suddenly and accidentally becoming wealthy, educated and powerful; instead 'upward mobility' would become a phenomenon for generations to struggle with as they attempted to 'emerge' slowly 'out of' the lower class – as if making the transition from sea to land, from troglodytes to *homo sapiens*. While the lower class is open to all, the upper class is structured to resist permeability by lower forms of life. And when the aristocracy begins to 'share' its privileges (education, capital, etc.), as it was in the nineteenth century, the cessation of its quarantine led progressively to its ongoing dissolution. One cannot adopt pedigree, the emergent classes learn, the way one can over time acquire tuition, property and political influence.

Emerson is sensible to the commonly unacknowledged fact that the definition of class in mid-nineteenth century England is contingent, the arbitrary (if intentional) invention of historical actors: 'The nearer we look', he writes in a chapter on 'Ability' in *English Traits*, 'the more artificial is their social system. Their law is a network of fictions. Their property, a scrip or certificate of right to interest on money that no man ever saw. Their social classes are made by statute. Their rations of power and representation are historical and legal'.[237] In 'Aristocracy', Emerson assesses how these artifices and fictions, these invisible forms and invented statutes shape everyday life: 'The upper classes have only birth, say the people here, and not thoughts. Yes, but they have manners, and, it is wonderful, how much talent runs into manners: – nowhere and never so much as in England. They have the sense of superiority, the absence of all the ambitious effort which disgusts in the aspiring classes, a pure tone of thought and feeling […]'.[238] As one might say of their tea, Emerson says the English are 'in all things, very much steeped in their temperament' – and for him it is little shock to discover that such enrichment of the upper classes should highlight the impurity and meanness of the lower.[239] Nevertheless, the dissolution of aristocrat forms – such as the 'perishing of heraldry' – signal how the 'privileges of nobility are passing to the middle class'.[240] And yet, by the time they pass, 'the badge is discredited, and the titles of lordship' become 'musty and cumbersome'.[241] Perhaps most innovatively, however, Emerson notes that 'an untitled nobility' – or newly emergent middle class – 'possess all the power without the inconveniences that belong to rank'.[242] Emerson was present for and aware of the radical and rapid emergence of this new hybrid species: the bourgeoisie.

In sections of his *Evolution: The History of an Idea* (1984) devoted to 'Evolution and Race' and 'Social Darwinism', Peter J. Bowler makes clear how the widespread use of the above metaphors – tree of life, struggle, ascent/descent, upper/lower, sophisticated/primitive – is at once prominent and also confused in cultural and scientific history. For example, while the metaphor of Darwinian 'struggle' dominated discussions about the possibility of individual (as well as class and race) change, Lamarckism was more suited to supporting a theory of cultural transformation, both for individuals and classes. As Bowler writes: 'Lamarckism required one to believe that individuals are not totally constrained by their biological inheritance. For new characters to be acquired and transmitted, inheritance had to be "soft" enough to allow for some modification. But natural selection included no such requirement: heredity could be "hard" in the sense that it allowed no room for individual modifications, and still evolution would occur because only the fit individuals would transmit their rigidly defined characters'.[243] Bowler's emphasis of these additional metaphors – soft and hard – offers additional validation for the dynamic, but often misleading, conceptual frameworks for applying evolutionary theories to social, class and individual development.

34. Harriet Ritvo, *The Platypus and the Mermaid and Other Figments of the Classifying Imagination* (1997):

> The existence of hybrids or mongrels or crosses thus emphasized the existence of boundaries between groups and simultaneously obliterated them. The intensity of the aversion provoked by mixed creatures suggested the importance of the divisions thus called into question, whether they were zoological or political, agricultural or social. Often, indeed, that aversion could not be adequately expressed with the conventional rhetoric of purity and contamination; it required, in addition, the heightened register reserved for abominations. This language emphasized the extent to which hybrids violated the order of nature, an order designed, it was

variously alleged, precisely to 'avoid filling the world with monsters'; to maintain 'Distinction in her [nature's] Work' lest 'a Line of Connection be drawn [...] uniting the Elephant and the Mouse'; or to prevent, as Lyell put it, 'the successive degeneracy, rather than the perfectibility [...], of certain classes of organic beings'. Yet as this rhetoric of repulsion emphasized the transgressive nature of hybrids, it also signaled their attractiveness. Border violations were appealing as well as threatening.[244]

35.   In *Darwin and the Linguistic Image: Language, Race, and Natural Theology in the Nineteenth Century* (1999), the historian Stephen G. Alter has provided a noteworthy contribution to the analysis of metaphors and other image-systems in the work of natural science, especially as such science was conducted in the nineteenth century. Alter's inquiry emphasizes the way evolutionary theory was analogized to understand – or explain – philology, or in today's parlance, linguistics. There was an interest in how language evolves – in a perceived similarity 'between the transmutation of biological species and the 'evolution' of languages' – as if the existential forms and mechanisms of change in language are similar to what we infer or observe in biology.[245] Alter points to the 'integrative thinking among intellectuals of the Victorian era', – 'not only how linguists looked at Darwinism but, more especially, how and why scientific thinkers took an interest in the quintessentially humanistic subject of the history of language'.[246] Likewise in the present study, centred on *English Traits* but radiating into historically relevant texts (as Emerson's work also does), we find a shared interest in the literary or linguistic image as a means – among poets, scientists, critics and curators – for consolidating, articulating and disseminating meaning. The image was, in some cases, used as a surrogate for empirical data, or as a model for organizing it; the image often brought with it a long history of associations that would serve to amplify and support a claim, or dismiss an erred or archaic theory. As Alter notes, 'a number of language-based disciplines adopted a comparative research method and produced a genealogical arrangement of their data, thereby mirroring the Darwinian tree of life'.[247] As Ernst Haeckel drew the tree-like 'General Morphology of Organisms' in an eponymous book from 1866, and featured a branching 'Pedigree of the Twelve Species of Men' in *The History of Creation* (1868), a few years later he sketched an arborescent 'Pedigree of Indo-Germanic Languages' – with Indo-Germanic as the originary seed or sprout.[248] Alter speculates usefully on the way fields of evolutionary theory and linguistics borrow from one another:

> Every age, perhaps, has its special predilections with regard to this kind of cross-disciplinary affinity, its couplings of different phenomena that mutually resonate nonetheless. These seemingly natural metaphors – half-conscious bonds of logic among distinct fields of knowledge – draw upon the aesthetic sensibility of a given time and place: they ground the communicative strategies and plausibility structures of science in juxtapositions that are as much imaginative as they are cognitive. Study of the illustrative figures used in past scientific discourse thus affords insight into larger habits of interdisciplinary transfer, a topic having as much intellectual-historical import as the study of scientific findings themselves.[249]

The 'bonds of logic' between different fields, one should add, involve not just 'aesthetic sensibility' but ethical judgement as well. In fact as aspects of value theory it is striking how intimately bound together are aesthetic and moral judgement – and metaphors often provide bold evidence for this coagulation. In other words the choice of a metaphor may be part of generational predilections (such as ours with the dominance of viral, virtual, electronic and digital metaphors), but the choice also carries with (and within) it rich networks of meaning, definition and association. As Alter notes: 'In all use of analogy and metaphor, it is difference that allows one to really see; the other provides the ground of contrast that makes perception possible'.[250] The productivity of the metaphor, then, will likely depend on the richness of its existing relationships; these 'half-conscious bonds of logic' are always situated in an aesthetic and ethical context. 'Darwin's analogies with linguistic phenomena', Alter says, 'fit into this same general category' – namely, 'comparisons bridging distant conceptual boundaries' – 'for those images represented nature through a quintessentially socio-cultural realm. By extension, the analogy included as well the human family's racial divisions, for language and ethnos had traditionally been paired with each other as covariants in human history'.[251] When Darwin analogized philology with biological descent, he, along with many other scientific thinkers, implicated language use with racial qualities – an analogy that disturbs the logic of the system, and introduces a troubling conjecture. While Darwin's analogy may have been based on an attractive metaphor of coextension, the aesthetic coherence of the image was compromised by an ethical lapse. Of course, experimentation is by definition fraught with the uncertainty of outcomes. We cannot and should not fault scientists for their use of analogy and metaphor, but we can take care to study the implications – aesthetic as well as ethical – when they do.

36.   The elegance of a chosen metaphor – its simplicity, its sense of fit with one's theories, and its capacity to explain them – may have the unintended consequence of limiting, reducing or even confusing readers. Darwin's reference to a tree as an explanatory trope, and his use of an illustration to that effect in *The Origin of Species*, may obscure or overshadow the vast range of competing, even contradictory metaphors in the book. Gillian Beer usefully complicates our inheritance of Darwin's most prominent trope when she writes:

> The polysemism of metaphor means that it is hard to control its implications: it may be argued, for example, that Darwin's metaphor of the tree is a formal analogy whose function is purely diagrammatic, describing a shape not an experience. Its initial value for Darwin lay undoubtedly in the fact that the diagram *declared* itself as a tree, rather than being foreknowingly designed to represent a tree-like shape for descent. On the page, however, it could as well be interpreted by the eye as shrub, branching coral, or seaweed. But Darwin saw not only the explanatory but the mythic potentiality of this diagram, its congruity with past orders of descent, and extended these in a form which is experimental rather than formal [...].[252]

Beer's shrewdly observed remark also serves as a general admonition for the interpretation of metaphors. Context may delimit the purview of a trope's interpretive instability, but as this case shows volatility remains – especially when the author integrates images that may be difficult to harmonize, and for that reason (perhaps inadvertently) creates a competition between metaphors, and even a struggle for interpretive domination between readings of a single trope. With Darwin's tree metaphor in mind, consider this passage from *The Origin of Species*:

> We can see clearly how it is that all living and extinct forms can be grouped together in one great system; and how the several members of each class are connected together by the most complex and radiating lines of affinities. We shall never, probably, disentangle the inextricable web of affinities between the members of any one class; but when we have a distinct object in view, and do not look to some unknown plan of creation, we may hope to make sure but slow progress.[253]

Does a tree function like a web? Or is Darwin aiming to highlight certain attributes of a tree (to the exclusion of others) that are compatible with the features of a web? In an earlier passage in *The Origin of Species* Darwin notes that 'the several subordinate groups in any class cannot be ranked in a single file, but seem rather to be clustered round points'.[254] This description displaces the prominence of hierarchy so visible in trees, and thus a notion of descent – as a progressive hierarchy of incrementally higher forms – will be challenged by the placement of lateral points or the characteristics inherit to a web. '[P]lants and animals, most remote in the scale of nature', Darwin writes, 'are bound together by a web of complex relations'.[255] The variable and consequential effects a single conspicuous trope can have on our interpretation of a text, such as Darwin's landmark work, should reinforce the general significance of Beer's analysis of metaphor use. Her treatment should indicate a need for synoptical criticism of tropes, where a reader becomes simultaneously aware of both a metaphor's distinctive representative qualities and its membership in an integrative system of other signs.

37.   In private journal entries as well as public lectures, Emerson characterized his semiology. In a journal passage he sketched the follow syllogism: 'Man puts things in a row / Things belong in a row / The showing of the true row is Science'.[256] The compactness of expression is developed more fully in 'Humanity of Science', a lecture he gave in 1836 and returned to in 1847 to revise for presentation during his second tour of England. The lecture begins: 'It is the perpetual effort of the mind to seek relations between the multitude of facts under its eye, by means of which it can reduce them to some order'.[257] The mind's work involves a 'perpetual comparison of objects to find resemblances', which is the method of Classification, 'one of the main actions of the intellect'.[258] And yet, as Emerson articulates in this long-considered lecture:

> There is great difference between men in this habit or power of classifying. Some men united things by their superficial resemblances, as if you should arrange a company by the color of their dress, or by their size, or complexion. Others by occult resemblances, which is the habit of wit; others by intrinsic likeness, which

is Science. The great moments of scientific history, have been the perception of these relations.[259]

All three phases or types of classification, however, rely on metaphors and imagistic description. For this reason superficial resemblance may be informative and eluci- datory even if scientifically unfounded; in fact, the surface may, paradoxically be the very space where hidden structures and linkages reveal themselves – if we have eyes to see them. 'This act of classifying is attended with pleasure, as it is a sort of unlocking the spiritual sight'.[260] And it is quite plausible that a scientist might pass through these evolutionary stages – from superficial to occult to intrinsic – as he or she conducts research and experimentation. In 'Demonology', presented in 1839 and carried into his 'Natural History of Intellect' lectures at Harvard in 1871, Emerson postulated that 'the universe is pervaded with secret analogies that tie together its remotest parts' – analogies that are perhaps as profitably transformed by the poet's eye as through the application of scientific theories and instruments.[261] Emerson concludes the chapter 'Language' in *Nature* by saying that when a 'doctrine is abstruse […] we must summon the aid of subtler and more vital expositors to make it plain'.[262] As the agents who undertake readings of natural order and form – who translate natural signs, who make them legible and intelligible – the poet and the naturalist merge: 'A life in harmony with nature, the love of truth and of virtue, will purge the eyes to understand her text. By degrees we may come to know the primitive sense of the permanent objects of nature, so that the world shall be to us an open book, and every form significant of its hidden life and final cause'.[263]

In his journals, in the months leading up to delivering 'Humanity of Science', Emerson noted: 'Man is an analogist. He cannot help seeing every thing under its relation to all other things & to himself'.[264] As an analogist, Emerson claims '[i]t is the constant tendency of the mind to Unify all it beholds, or to reduce the remotest facts to a single law. Hence all endeavors at classification. […] There is a tendency in the mind to separate particulars & in magnifying them to lose sight of the connexion of the object with the Whole. Hence all false views, Sects'.[265] In 'Humanity of Science' – first presented in late 1836 and recovered for his lectures in England in 1848 – we find the translation of these private insights into public expression: 'The first process of thought in examining a new object is to compare it with known objects and refer it to a class. The mind is reluctant to make many classes or to suppose many causes. This reduction to a few laws, to one law, is not a choice of the individual. It is the tyrannical instinct of mind'.[266]

A few years later, in the labouratory of his notebook, Emerson parallels man's habitual analogizing to constitutional facts about man himself: 'a man is a compendium of nature, an indomitable savage. Take the smoothest curled courtier in London or Paris; […] he has a physique which […] is directly related there amid essences & billets doux to Himmaleh mountain chains, wild cedar swamps, & interior fires, the molten core of the globe'.[267] Likewise, 'a leaf is a compend of Nature, and Nature a colossal leaf'.[268] In 'Poetry and Imagination', once again Emerson moves his private reflection to the lecture hall:

For the value of a trope is that the hearer is one: and indeed Nature itself is a vast trope, and all particular natures are tropes. As the bird alights on the bough, then plunges into the air again, so the thoughts of God pause but for a moment in any form. All thinking is analogizing, and it is the use of life to learn metonymy. The endless passing of one element into new forms, the incessant metamorphosis, explains the rank which the imagination holds in our catalogue of mental powers. The imagination is the reader of these forms. The poet accounts all productions and changes of Nature as the nouns of language, uses them representatively, too well pleased with their ulterior to value much their primary meaning. Every new object so seen gives a shock of agreeable surprise.[269]

38.   British writer Harold Laski once wrote in a Foreword to Alexis de Tocqueville's *Democracy in America* (Vol. I 1835 and Vol. II 1840) that 'It is, perhaps, the greatest work ever written on one country by the citizen of another'.[270] With quite a bit more qualification, Howard Mumford Jones claimed in his Introduction to *English Traits* that 'no better book by an American about Victorian England (or rather Great Britain at mid-century) has ever been written'.[271] After Nathanial Hawthorne travelled in England reading *English Traits* he wrote a letter to Emerson appraising the book by conjecturing that it 'undoubtedly' offered 'the truest pages that have yet been written' about England – and added, apparently in a mood of shared Americanness: 'I am afraid it will please the English only too well; for you give them credit for the possession, in very large measure, of all the qualities that they value, or pride themselves upon; and they never will comprehend that what you deny is far greater and higher than what you concede'.[272] John Jay Chapman said that in *English Traits* Emerson had created the 'ruddiest book he ever wrote. It is a hymn to force, honesty, and physical well-being [...]'.[273] Other American contemporaries, many of them close friends and intellectual accomplices, recognized in *English Traits* both Emerson's literary achievement and his capacity for incisive cultural criticism, as Amos Bronson Alcott put it:

> [...] I may say that his book of 'Traits' deserves to be honored as one in which England, Old and New, may take honest pride, as being the liveliest portraiture of British genius and accomplishments, – a book, like Tacitus, to be quoted as a masterpiece of historical painting, and perpetuating the New Englander's fame with that of his race. 'Tis a victory of eyes over hands, a triumph of ideas. Nor, in my judgment, has there been for some time any criticism of a people so character-istic and complete. It remains for him to do like justice to New England.[274]

When he reflected on *English Traits*, Theodore Parker emphasized Emerson's decisively expressed and ineluctable Americanness, that the 'victory of the eyes', in Alcott's phrase, could not be helped:

> Now and then he wanders off to other lands, reports that he has seen, but it is always an American report of what an American eye saw. Even Mr Emerson's recent exaggerated praise of England is such a panegyric as none but an American could bestow.

We know an American artist who is full of American scenery. He makes good drawings of Tivoli and Subiaco, but, to colour them, he dips his pencil in the tints of the American heaven, and over his olive trees and sempervines, his asses and his priests, he sheds the light only of his native sky. So is it with Mr Emerson. Given him the range of the globe, it is still an American who travels.[275]

Parker's reading subtly illuminates a double sense of Emerson's remarks as being 'always an American report' – that is, a report of a foreign culture coloured and shaped by 'what an American eye saw', but also – even more strikingly – a report on America. That is, *English Traits* does in turns, time and again, lend itself to being what Alcott so eagerly encouraged from his neighbour, namely, a portrait that does 'justice to New England' by means of creating a photographic negative of Old England. Naturally, though almost imperceptibly – because of its pervasiveness, line by line – the commentary on England in *English Traits* cannot help but take as its standard reference the America whence the American undertakes his critique.

Even before returning to Chelsea to find his copy of *English Traits* awaiting him, Thomas Carlyle wrote to his American friend: '[...] let all England understand (as some choice portion of England will) that there has not been a man talking about us these very many years whose words are worth the least attention in comparison'.[276] When Carlyle wrote to Emerson to register his impression of the new work, he said 'Such books do not turn up often in the decade, in the century. In fact I believe it to be worth all the Books ever written by New England upon Old. Franklin might have written such a thing (in his own way); no other since! We do very well with it here, and the wise part of us *best*'.[277] When Carlyle re-read *English Traits* more than a decade later, his laudatory estimation of the work was solidly preserved: it is 'a Book all full of thoughts like winged arrows' – a work for 'grown-up people'.[278]

Among the English intelligentsia that Emerson admired and favoured with his strong support, Walter Savage Landor stood out; he was, for example, the subject of a near-hagiographic portrait Emerson published in *The Dial* (1841). So when Emerson referred to his May 1833 meeting with Landor in the opening chapter of *English Traits*, Landor's outsized fury at the representation of their 23-year-old conversation seems, then as now, at once anomalous in the history of the book's reception by others and at odds with the spirit in which it was written. Landor, known for an unpredictable temperament – Samuel Arthur Jones described him as 'imperial, imperious, impetuous, and irascible' – was greatly agitated not so much by reading Emerson's opinions on the English, as by fielding Emerson's remarks on Landor's opinions.[279] Within months of the appearance of *English Traits*, Landor drafted a lengthy open letter that he had published in Bath in which he effectively conducts a line-by-line re-reading of Emerson's account of their discussion at Landor's Villa Gherardesca in Fiesole, when the host was 45 years old and Emerson had just turned 30. A contemporary critic from the *Athenaeum* in London contextualized the nature of Landor's open letter by noting how 'a prick rouses a war-horse' – and though Emerson 'touched Mr Landor with his lance [, … t]he hurt was not serious – a touch-and-go that scarce drew blood'.[280] Landor's response to Emerson's reminiscence is both fascinating and alarming – at once captivating because it suggests how differently two people can remember and recount the 'same' experience, and troubling for the way it illustrates how vanity can interfere with one's capacity to read what others write about you. Landor seems injured, and perhaps temperamentally prone to rant – especially when he felt himself misunderstood or misremembered. Yet even as Landor reproaches Emerson for saying he 'undervalued Socrates', Landor takes a moment to agree with Emerson's estimation that he is a similar sort of victim: 'I make no complaint of what is stated [...] that "Landor is strangely undervalued in England". I have heard it before, but I never have taken the trouble to ascertain it'.[281] Samuel Arthur Jones, an Englishman who wrote an Introduction to an 1895 edition featuring the letter, comes to Emerson's defence by contending that 'the chapter in *English Traits* that gave offence was simply an inadvertence, – the one instance in which [Emerson's] consummate tact gave a furtive nod, as even Homer has done', and added by way of remembering Emerson's long-standing promotion of the writer that 'we are content to leave the *Dial* paper on Walter Savage Landor to more than offset the trifling inadvertence of the initial chapter of the *English Traits*'.[282]

In his assessment of the broader critical reception of *English Traits*, Nicoloff writes that the work was 'widely reviewed in Great Britain – perhaps more widely than any of Emerson's other books had been – and with a diversity of response that defies easy generalization'.[283] One response, printed in *The Rambler* suggested that despite its title the book appeared 'to glorify America through England'.[284] While the comment may intend to suggest the author's effort to cloak his vanity or national pride, it prompts a more searching question about the status of America in *English Traits*. Because it is so apparent – 'implicitly evident' as Dolan says – it may go without much notice but every line of *English Traits*, as Theodore Parker alluded to above, is written by an American, and so the work – despite a conspicuous lack of explicit mention of America – is composed from an American point of view, and with America as the principle node of reference and comparison.

When Matthew Arnold, himself in a mood of comparison, took up an assessment of *English Traits* for his audience, he noted:

> Some people will tell you that Emerson's poetry, indeed, is too abstract, and his philosophy too vague, but that his best work is his *English Traits*. The *English Traits* are beyond question very pleasant reading. It is easy to praise them, easy to commend the author of them. But I insist on always trying Emerson's work by the highest standards, and compared with the work of the excellent markers and recorders of the traits of human life, – of writers like Montaigne, La Bruyère, Addison, – the *English Traits* will not stand the comparison. Emerson's observation has not the disinterested quality of the observation of these masters.[285]

The reason Arnold gives for *English Traits* failing to be 'a work of perfection in its kind' owes to this want of disinterestedness, a trait, we could say, that earlier Alcott and Parker both recognized – but with pleasure and praise. It is precisely in Emerson's partiality – his American outlook, his very transfiguration of the Old English in his New English frame – that gives his book vitality, character and purpose. But Arnold, either on his own reading or perhaps echoing disparagers, finds Emerson's (self-described) 'persistent optimism' a liability in the art of culture critique.[286] 'The kind of work attempted in the *English Traits* [...]', Arnold concludes, 'is work which cannot be done perfectly with a bias such as that given by Emerson's optimism [...]'.[287] For some readers, Arnold's epithet may be treated, inversely – and more generously, as a synonym of a certain American outlook: either something Emerson's cultivated, or possessed naturally, as one of his American traits. Arnold's English skepticism makes an American wonder about the degree to which optimism is not personal – not an affectation of Emerson's bias – but an impersonal or generic (which insinuates a genetic) feature of the people who grow on or out of American soil, each of whom may be capable, as Parker suggested, of shedding 'the light only of his native sky'.[288]

Just a few years before publishing *English Traits*, Emerson wrote 'The Anglo-American' (1852) a kind of compare-and-contrast lecture of the English and the American in the light of Emerson's latest trip into the Midwest, and with his most recent visit to England still in recent memory. The lecture was as well-received in Williamsburg Brooklyn and New York as in Concord and Boston, and narrates Emerson's travels in Rochester, Cincinnati and St Louis, among other places west of the Alleghenies. The lecture begins with an attempt to define an American trait – 'a national trait' – that pervades the land. For Emerson it is marked by a new relation to pace and interval: 'Everything in America is at a rapid rate', he begins, keeping his prose in a rhythm that matches his subject – 'speedy', 'quick', 'restless', even at times, 'hasty'.[289] He offers an illustrative vignette of a university founded at Rochester, admires the promise of St Louis for its confluence of rivers, and ends with a glittering fantasia of California's symbolic significance for the nation ('The wild, exuberant tone of society in California is only an exaggeration of the uniform present condition in America [...]'.)[290]

Despite a declaration that reads more as description – 'we are forced, therefore, to make our own precedents' – Emerson's investigation weaves in strands of interest in England and Europe, each time hinting at or querying after the differences that present themselves in the new conditions we have grown accustomed to calling the New World – more generally America, and more proximately, New England.[291] 'The English slow, sure finish has changed into the irresistibility of the American. [...] Nature in this climate, ardent, rushing up, after a shower, into a mat of vegetation. Nature goes into the genius, as well as into the cucumbers [...]'.[292] Emerson addresses the 'leading features of national character', and how they make men productive but also exhausted and uncertain. He traces the social and spiritual effects of agriculture, livestock and the telegraph – 'the poetic wires' – in 'this age of tools'.[293] While he worries that for many a dedication to the land leaves insufficient time for letters, arts and sciences, he implicates his own interests and talents in this moment of praise by contrast with the English:

> [... H]e has chambers opened in his mind which the English have not. He is intellectual and speculative, an abstractionist. He has solitude of mind and fruitful dreams. See what good readers of dreamy Germans we are – books which the English cannot bear.[294]

Among the several traits that recommend the American, Emerson recurs to the benefit of his adaptability to new conditions and his perception of their uses. The Anglo-American 'has wonderful powers of absorption and appropriating'. 'He is a good combiner'.[295] Emerson's profound appreciation for these skills links at once to his experience of their effects in science and in the literary arts. Combination aids invention, and after the fact, it reveals its sources and affiliations. One can trace the evolution of an idea's transmission into culture as much as the variable designs of plow and sickle. Put them into an aggregate form – a collection or taxonomy – and find new points of difference and similarity. The Victoria and Albert Museum's attention to textile and foundry reveals the mysterious and unfolding patterns of nature observed under an alternate lens at the Museum of Natural History.

Even with an abundance of notes on England, it is not surprising that Emerson considered at one point including 'The Anglo-American' in the book that would become *English Traits* as a way of having his remarks on England find their associations 'with the parallelisms on this continent'.[296] But how much more intriguing – in terms of narrative, topic and rhetorical effect – to leave out a more explicit engagement with America between the covers of *English Traits*. By not quarantining his reflections on America in a clearly defined chapter, Emerson invites his readers – on both sides of the Atlantic – to read every line twice, once for its resonance in an English ear, another for the way an American ear interprets the sonic register. That the sound *English Traits* makes, line after line, may be heard differently by these two audiences – and what those differences portend for the contested continuity of these peoples – is among the most novel and arresting characteristics of the work itself.

Thus, while there is praise for the quality of *English Traits*, along with some negative criticism, what seems most compelling from a contemporary vantage is the dynamic between the book's author, his objects of interest and his various methods of inquiry: the foreign citizen embedded in a new region, perhaps drawn and repelled by it, but ultimately emerging from the encounter with some kind of report. There is a deeply anthropological and ethnological strain to this undertaking, where the foreigner feels confident enough to judge what is happening in a non-native place, and moreover poised to draw general, though pointed, observations based on personal anecdote and private sensibilities. As Hugo Münsterberg wrote in his *American Traits from the Point of View of a German* (1901): 'If I saw America with the eyes of an American I should hardly hope to notice features which possibly my neighbours overlook. It is the contrast which brings out the lines, and that fact alone excuses my speaking to Americans on American subjects after so short a period of acquaintance; had I waited longer I should have seen my surroundings more nearly with American eyes and should have perceived less the characteristic differences'.[297] For Münsterberg, aspects of the ignorance and unfamiliarity of the foreigner provide the conditions for special powers of observation. One wonders if the same applies to the critics who review books written by such observers; if it does, we have more reason to take seriously the dialogue of criticism from both sides of the Atlantic. American reviewers such as Parke Godwin described *English Traits* as 'racy, idiomatic, sinewy', and Noah Porter, Jr noted how Emerson joined together 'at once the widest range, and the most microscopic delicacy of intellectual vision'.[298] Such impressions capture Emerson's skill as an observer who can link a range of discourses, histories, and conventions in such a way that the normal feels natural, and the foreign seems familiar – even surprising assertions arrive with credibility and depth. 'We seem to have heard every sentence before', wrote a British commentator for the *Westminster Review*, 'and yet to find every sentence new. We know it all, and yet we like to read it. It could not have been done better'.[299]

In Tocqueville the conceit of a writer-off-native-grounds lends weight and perspective to chapters with titles that suggest answers to questions, such as 'Why the Americans Show More Aptitude and Taste for General Ideas than Their English Fathers', or – in an effort to contrast his native countrymen with these foreign counterparts – 'Why the Americans Have Never Been as Passionate as the French for General Ideas in Political Matters'.[300] Tocqueville's comparativist approach presumes that the differences that lead to these judgements derive from national characteristics instead of something that supervenes over, say, Western democracies or Industrial nations. Howard Mumford Jones notes that 'If Tocqueville analyzed democracy in America as a lesson to the French, Emerson analyzed a limited monarchy, product of centuries of tradition, as a lesson to the United States. If [Emerson] did not make the lesson explicit, it was because he found the problem of analysis so absorbing he could not work out the problem of comparison'.[301] Or rather it may be that Emerson did not appoint himself the task of such comparativist work in *English Traits* because he imagined it was work for readers to do – since 'The America Scholar', 'The Young American' and 'The Anglo-American', among other such work of cultural critique would position readers to judge the relationship between the traits and characteristics of the English and their American counterparts – and Emerson's assessment of their features and fortunes; but a thoroughgoing compare-and-contrast of nations and their citizens was not a project Emerson overtly or systematically attempted to undertake in *English Traits*.

Two decades before *English Traits* was published, as early as 1835, and less than a half-century after the United States Constitution was ratified, Tocqueville already sensed a *bona fide* nationalist quality in the people who populated America, and he was at pains to articulate a definition of the American character and its qualities (especially as contrasted with the French). Comprised of many races, and many ethnicities – from Scotland to the Sudan – there were, he noted, myriad attributes (despite overt differences) that nevertheless distinguished the Americans from their British and European counterparts, not least of which were the conditions of the nation's founding and the effects it had on the comportment and outlook of its citizens. Emerson, following a comparable interest in the English, was intrigued by the conditions of England's beginning and development. 'A child of the nineteenth century', Jones remarks, Emerson 'tends to seek the genetic explanation, to go back in time to origins, to trace development and disuse, insisting that the power of Britain can be understood best in a temporal context'.[302] Thus, if Emerson occasionally draws from the methods of the historian, journalist and sociologist, like Tocqueville, he is more attracted to the explanatory tools of the anthropologist, geologist and biologist. The long history of

England, contrasted with America's nascent development, called for an appreciation of the elongated and dispersed effects of land, island, migration, war, ancestry, names, race, class and forms of government on a people shaped by millennia of influences; the natural scientific modes of inquiry fitted Emerson's temporally extended investigation as they naturally invited and involved the consideration of deep time and the 'deep traits of race'.[303] Meanwhile, in Emerson's lifetime there were many who still possessed a living memory of America's founding. Perhaps Tocqueville's perception of a nationalist identity in America bespeaks the tenacity a new country's citizens must show if they would be counted more than a seasonal presence; the identities of ancient nations, by contrast, do not appear to need such jealous guarding and cultivation.

Emerson did not set out for England in the early 1830s with the intention of writing a book about the country – its history, land, people, institutions; and even after his first visit he did not esteem his reflections on the culture worthy of developing into book form. By the time he did write such a book, however, after his second voyage, he remained clear that it would not be a touristic account of sites; at the opening of *English Traits* he modestly remarked: 'On looking over the diary of my journey in 1833, I find nothing to publish in my memoranda of visits to places'.[304] Emerson did not aim to achieve deductions or make generalizations based on empirical encounters, or first-hand reminiscences. *English Traits* would be no *Baedekers*. But there is reason, Emerson thought, to describe a few encounters with persons, for these living representatives embody the long history of the race – its manners, moods, forms and characteristics – and as such one may reasonably hope to glean some measure of insight about the natural and social history of the island from those inhabitants who persist within its watery boundaries.

Arriving in 1833 as an unknown, unpublished ex-minister, Emerson's brave intent was to introduce himself to the literary and philosophical heroes that still lived on the island – principally Samuel Taylor Coleridge, William Wordsworth, Walter Savage Landor, Thomas De Quincey, and 'the latest and strongest contributor to the critical journals' (such as the *Edinburgh Review*), Thomas Carlyle. And of these meetings, Emerson drew portraits from notes and memories that register the necessary disappointments young scholars undergo when seeking to find the greatness of works in the people who wrote them. Yet even in maturity Emerson counters with the discovery of occasions when 'I have, however, found writers superior to their books'.[305] Though Emerson may not have felt convinced of the worth or interest of his reflections on the places he visited, perhaps naturally as a consequence of his interest in persons, he blends biography with cultural anthropology. Thus, while walking with Carlyle among the celebrated ruins at Stonehenge, Emerson cannot help but explore the mythic significance of the ancient, cryptic site. For Emerson, to be sure, Carlyle is the tourist attraction, but in thinking with Carlyle, while walking with him, Emerson – as is commonly found in *English Traits* – finds occasion to speak beyond persons because he is speaking with them.

When Emerson returned to England in 1847, by that time a celebrated American man of letters, among the most well-known writers in the world, he was charged with the task of giving a series of lectures in various industrial cities in the Midlands.

While on his second visit, he wrote a series of six lectures entitled *Mind and Manners of the Nineteenth Century*, and presented them before members of the Literary and Scientific Institution in Portman Square in London, June 1848 – upon returning to England after having spent a few weeks in Revolutionary Paris with the companionship of poet Arthur Hugh Clough, and likely finding himself in the crowd with Charles Baudelaire, though unaware of him. Moreover, in addition to the *Mind and Manners* series, Emerson delivered 64 lectures between November 1847 and February 1848 in 25 cities and towns in England and Scotland.[306] But it was only upon returning home to Concord, and over the course of the next 8 years – while continuing to read on his subject, sorting notes taken while abroad and gathering new ones from his study, and culling materials from the lecture series noted above – that he found the direction and inspiration to compose *English Traits*. Unlike Tocqueville, Emerson saw the book as a personal project – frankly admitting his individual investment in the topic; it begins, as mentioned, with two chapters of autobiographical prose. While there is a clear sense that Emerson wanted to make claims about England that would extend beyond his own private experience, the tone of the book suggests that he is aware that everything he says is opinion, if informed speculation (after all, during the 1840s Emerson conducted a deep and wide course of reading in British history). Being personally motivated does not, in Emerson's field of reference, make his claims less qualified for universality and truth. Rather, the difference noted here is meant to highlight the contrast between a Tocquevillian judgement based on empirical observation and an Emersonian judgement – a form of interpretation that acknowledges the necessary and important contribution of one's individual perspective, as it were, without proof or evidence. That is to say, much of the composition of *English Traits* derives from Emerson's study in Concord – where travel notes were synthesized with reading in work by others – and not strictly from writing in the field; unlike a travel writer who seeks up-to-the-minute accuracy for his guide book, Emerson addressed how contemporary life in England reflected or embodied its ancient past and lengthy social evolution. For Emerson, the nation – like the many histories written about it – was a field of signs that could be read, discerned and subsequently employed for the kind of prose he wanted to represent his impressions of the island and its people; yet, like Tocqueville, Emerson's approach was adopted as a way to demonstrate innovative methods of social-scientific analysis. Still, Emerson's variant of Tocquevillian comparativism shows, in particular, how reading cultural history can be aligned with natural history – how the interaction between the two becomes a means for understanding continuities, deviations and anomalies, such as we find in children and other kinds of descendants.

39.   More than a century before Tocqueville arrived on American shores to undertake a foreigner's study of a foreign land, Francois-Marie Arouet, better known by his assumed name, Voltaire, composed letters 'on the English nation' to his friend, Nicolas Thiriot (Thieriot or Tiriot). Thiriot, who was the correspondent on this epistolary form of cultural criticism, prefaced the collection that was written between 1728 and 1731: 'The present Work appears with Confidence in the Kingdom that gave Birth to

it', emphasizing that Voltaire wrote these letters while living among the English, mostly in London.[307] Speaking in the third person, Thiriot conscribes the nature and limits of that work, a 'correspondence' that excludes his contribution, even if it owes him the proximate cause of its existence:

> [T]hese letters were not design'd for the Public. They are the Result of the Author's Complacency and Friendship for Mr *Thiriot*, who had desir'd him, during his Stay in *England*, to favour him with such Remarks as he might make on the Manners and Customs of the *British* Nation. 'Tis well known that in a Correspondence of this kind, the most just and regular Writer does not propose to observe any Method. Mr de *Voltaire* in all Probability follow'd no other Rule in the Choice of his Subjects than his particular Taste, or perhaps the Queries of his Friend.[308]

Voltaire directs his attention to a range of pertinent topics, including ecclesiastical history, government, science and philosophy (with remarks on Bacon, Locke, DesCartes and Newton), literature (Shakespeare) and poetry (Pope). When Voltaire goes in for comparing the French and English, as Tocqueville will later do with the French and American, Voltaire notes with characteristically grave humour:

> The *English* generally think, and Learning is had in greater Honour among them than in our Country; an Advantage that results naturally from the Form of their Government. [… E]very Man has the Liberty of publishing his Thoughts with regard to publick Affairs; which shews, that all the People in general are indispensibly oblig'd to cultivate their Understandings.[309]

More than a century later, Emerson described a similar trait in the English cultivation of mental life, a characteristic supported and enlarged by the British love of liberty and freedoms secured by the arrangement of political order:

> They have assimilating force, since they are imitated by their foreign subjects; and they are still aggressive and propagandist, enlarging the dominion of their arts and liberty. Their laws are hospitable, and slavery does not exist under them. What oppression exists is incidental and temporary; their success is not sudden or fortunate, but they have maintained constancy and self-equality for many ages.[310]

40.   George Santayana, another foreigner writing in a non-native land, used the word 'genteel' to describe Emerson's (and Poe's and Hawthorne's) method of reading:

> They could not retail the genteel tradition; they were too keen, too perceptive, and too independent for that. But life offered them little digestible material, nor were they naturally voracious. They were fastidious, and under the circumstances they were starved. Emerson, to be sure, fed on books. There was a great catholicity in his reading; and he showed a fine tact in his comments, and in his way of appropriating what he read. But he read transcendentally, not historically, to learn what he himself felt, not what others might have felt before him. And to feed on books, for a philosopher or a poet, is still to starve.[311]

Consider how the reading (or critical) methods of Tocqueville and Emerson are rather more idiosyncratic than scientific, more reflective of their talents for discerning associations and differences in temperament than deducing neutral or empirical facts. There is a sense in *Democracy in America* and *English Traits* that the authors are learning about themselves, as Santayana puts it, in the course of their investigations, and that, in important ways, is among the primary gifts of these works – such as they present models of (and variations on) self-analysis enlarged to sufficient size for national or international, or least transatlantic, critique. (For chronological reference, Tocqueville had already published *Democracy in America* [volume I in 1835 and volume II in 1840] when he met Emerson in Revolutionary Paris in 1848 – after Emerson had presented the bulk of his lectures on his second tour of England and several years before publishing *English Traits*.) Emerson had shown in *Representative Men* (1850), in those same years preceding the appearance of *English Traits*, that he was not just comfortable with but a defender of connections made between specific men and general modes of life. Each of his chapters in that book reflects his predilection for the representative quality of individual humans. For example, the way a single man can stand for a whole category – in short, can, at his best, stand for himself; or, in the present case, perhaps, demonstrate the way a single man can epitomize a whole nation – embody and exemplify its most notable and defining characteristics. Tocqueville and Emerson, from this view, are both ambassadors from their respective countries, representatives to the task of critiquing their self-appointed foreign charges. Both writers invigorate the notion that a domestic view of domestic life may miss a lot, and that by virtue of having foreign eyes directed and foreign ears attuned to a new land much that has become invisible or silent through familiarity can be seen and heard. We are not quite ourselves until some foreign critic finds a way to articulate our fitness and faults.

41.   More often than not in *English Traits* Emerson's comments on England and the English race are praiseworthy rather than critical; and even his criticisms have a way of reflecting his awe and admiration for achievements that remain part of an ongoing, usually skeptical, inquiry of the modern mind – colonialization, capitalism, industrialization. How can it be, then, that the American writer of the nineteenth century most acclaimed for his contribution to the project of establishing an American thinking, who, after returning from his first voyage abroad to Europe and England celebrated the consummation of rebellion and revolution, who was an unflinching advocate of severing ties and dissolving bonds with the Old World, be here – in *English Traits* – published some 20 years after the appearance of his seminal *Nature*, found writing an Anglophilic tract that not only heralds the power of the English race but also insists that America is its proper and actual heir? Did Emerson have a change of heart some time between departing Liverpool in 1833 and arriving there again in 1847? Or does the shift in treatment or understanding, instead, highlight a different reading of the same facts and propositions? Howard Mumford Jones reflected on the contrast in Emerson's prose and outlook on England before landing in the British Isles in 1833 and after writing *English Traits* in the wake of his second voyage there:

Emerson was an idealist, but he was also a hardheaded Yankee, and he was never more Yankee than when writing *English Traits*, the tone of which is so radically different from that, say, of *Nature* that if, a thousand years from now, both books were dug up and the name of the author had disappeared, a cautious scholar of the thirty-first century would scarcely dare assign them to the same pen.[312]

In the lecture 'The Naturalist', read to the Boston Natural History Society on 7 May 1834, Emerson wrote in a mood that anticipates the tone of *Nature*, informed by his first-hand experience of England the year before:

Imitation is the vice eminently of our times, of our literature, of our manners and social action. All American manners, language, and writing are derivative. We do not write facts, but we wish to state facts after the English manner. It is at once our strength and weakness that there is an immense floating diction from which always we draw, to which by the ear we always seek to accommodate our expression.

It is the tax we pay for the splendid inheritance of the English literature. We are exonerated by the sea and the revolution from the national debt but we pay this which is rather the worst part. Time will certainly cure us, probably through the prevalence of a bad party ignorant of all literature and of all but selfish, gross pursuits. But a better cure would be in the study of Natural History.[313]

How astonishing, even unintuitive, to be led to this conclusion – that the study of Natural History is a cure to our habits of imitation – even with the hint of the title and the topic of the lecture. Emerson continues: 'Imitation is a servile copying of what is capricious as if it were permanent forms of Nature. The study of things leads us back to Truth, to the great Network of organized beings made of our own flesh and blood with kindred functions and related organs and one Cause'.[314] The 'one Cause' is God or Providence rendered in the language of the naturalist, and the effect of the translation – despite initial appearances – liberates the thinker from a dependence on origins or the privileging of first things (such as parents, such as England). The one Cause pervades the entire 'great Network', not just some part or portion of it. Later in the lecture Emerson says 'This passion, the enthusiasm for nature, the love of the Whole, has burned in the breasts of the Fathers of Science. It was the ever present aim of Newton, of Linnaeus, of Davy, of Cuvier, to ascend from nomenclature to classification; from arbitrary to natural classes; from natural classes to primary laws; from these, in an ever narrowing circle, to approach the elemental law, the *causa causans*, the supernatural force'.[315]

In 'Genius' (1839) Emerson described genius as possessing a 'sight' that is 'piercing and pauses not like other men's at the surface of the fact, but looks through it for the causal thought. [...] There is at the surface infinite variety of things. At the centre, there is simplicity and unity of cause'.[316] In the following passage, Emerson appears to join some of these Plotinian aspects of unity-in-being together with a Calvinist sensitivity to origins – and in so doing transforms the sin of origins into the sin of surfaces.

Our eye rests on the multiplicity of the details and does not pierce to the simplicity and grandeur of the Cause. Yet as soon as we do enter into the causes we sympathize with it; we see that it is aloof from everything artificial, low, and old: that it is pure and fresh as childhood and morning: its words and works affirm their own right to exist: in short, that it is allied to God. [...] The work of genius implies and is a species of worship of the supreme Being [...].[317]

Emerson affirms that since genius is allied with the 'simplicity and grandeur of the Cause' genius possesses the 'dignity of its origin' – and as such 'the work of genius is not perishable.'[318] The language of 'The Naturalist' and 'Genius' finds its more familiar form in *Nature* and 'Self-Reliance', but it is illuminating to see in these earlier lectures the residual influence of metaphysical and theological thinking on Emerson's conceptual scheme – especially the value-laden contrast between the 'artificial, low, and old' aspects of life amid surfaces and the 'pure and fresh' attributes of simplicity and unity. Even as late at 1837, Emerson described the 'flimsy & unclean precinct of my body.'[319] In 'Circles', Emerson tersely poetizes the contrast: 'I am God in nature; I am a weed by the wall.'[320] In time the traces of existential depravity will be nearly burnished away by the perception of cosmic continuity; the high and low, clean and soiled, sacred and profane, divine and ordinary will coalesce.

What a reader likely will find in Emerson from early to late is not so much an ambivalence about the nature of inheritance, or what Harold Bloom calls influence, but a determined effort to come to terms with its presence. And this struggle seldom culminates in consistent or definitive conclusions, but rather something more like a series of moods that disclose a crucial aspect of the phenomenon. For instance, figured as an awareness and anxiety owing to what Stanley Cavell has described as 'America's having come late into the world', we must contend with 'the fatedness to quotation.'[321] Living belatedly – as children, as descendants, as heirs – necessarily implies our relation to, and reliance on, what preceded us. Call them parents or father lands or mother tongues (such as we learn from reading Thoreau's chapter on 'Reading' in *Walden, or, Life in the Woods*). Cornel West contextualizes Emerson's contingent location and orientation around the time of 'The American Scholar': 'For too long the identity of the country lagged behind its independence from Britain. This lag reinforced a cultural dependence, intellectual parasitism, and national inferiority complex vis-à-vis older European countries.'[322] Given the grounds of this circumstance, by the mere accident of living in this place at this time, Emerson wants to understand both how one comes to be (existentially) and how one comes to be oneself and not someone else (in terms of identity and expression). The existential-aspect highlights the continuity of forms – for example, how the moral law pervades nature; how we are 'the channel through which heaven flows to earth' – in short, 'God in distribution.'[323] By contrast, or at least in tension, is the identity-aspect where we 'wish to be recognized as individuals', retain a desire of a 'lower strain' – a perception of hierarchy and difference recurring in his use of this phrase in 'Self-Reliance' – and are preoccupied with the nature of influence (what appears in Emerson under the names imitation and quotation, or becomes transformed under the names GENIUS and ORIGINALITY).[324] Thus, what Bloom calls an anxiety of influence, and what could also be understood as an anxiety of inheritance, resides in the space of astriction or conflict between these two aspects.

Harold Bloom, in fact, describes the 'great triad of "The Divinity School Address", "The American Scholar", and "Self-Reliance"' as 'anti-influence oration-essays'. And he notes that Emerson's should be 'called the only poetic influence that counsels against itself, and against the idea of influence'.[325] The problem of Emerson's 'conflicting ideas of influence', according to Bloom can be traced to the manner in which Emerson simultaneously heralded a 'Dionysian influx, yet [...] preached an Apollonian Self-Reliance while fearing the very individuation it would bring'.[326] Addressing the young members of the Phi Beta Kappa society in 1837, Emerson declared: 'Genius is always sufficiently the enemy of genius by over-influence'.[327] Two years later he noted in his journal: 'It is the necessity of my nature to shed all influences'.[328] This is why Bloom will conclude that Emerson's 'best lesson is that all true subjectivity is a high but difficult achievement, while supposed objectivity is merely the failure of having become an amalgam of other selves and opinions'.[329]

If we can say that Emerson was, in the late 1830s and early 1840s, insisting without pause or apology on an American thinking that does not just subvert or convert an English and European ancestry but somehow – more radically – comes into being through some act of self-creation or by means of an appeal to a source beneath the surfaces (namely, as genius intimates), then in *English Traits*, written in the late 1840s and early 1850s, we can, with a surfeit of evidence stand ready for a different assessment: America is a child after all. Between his first and second voyages to England, had Emerson gone from testifying to and defending a fantasy of terrestrially causeless or existentially originless America (owing to an appeal to the one Cause that displaces superficial differences), to some years later deciding that his country was very much a descendent of England? Was *Representative Men* a first sign of his gradual restoration of a European pantheon (Shakespeare is the only featured Englishman) – a book in which he appears to overtly displace worthy American candidates, among them Franklin, Jefferson, Washington and a handful of other prominent but dead Americans, not to mention the range of choices among his living contemporaries?

In *Nature*, 'The American Scholar', and *Essays, First Series*, Emerson writes as if offering a hermeneutic gloss on the existential effects of conception by means of linguistic utterance – 'In the beginning was the word'. The Declaration of Independence would be understood as a confirmation that America had words enough to give birth to itself, to fulfil its title as a New England of a New World – yet somehow at the same time exist without an origin, without an evolution, without a pedigree, without a need to acknowledge its parent(s), and its dependencies. Oliver Wendell Holmes described 'The American Scholar' as 'our intellectual Declaration of Independence', perhaps inadvertently reminding us that such an act – or idea, or myth – always involves a relation: that one becomes independent *from* prior forms and models, parents and pedigrees. In 'Man the Reformer', Emerson relayed to his audience the news that, for each of them, 'nothing is left [...] but to begin the world anew', quickly remonstrating those who would plead a pardon from the duty: 'We are all implicated, of course, in this charge'.[330] George Herbert Mead said the 'romantic discovery of a self' by Emerson, and his Concord contemporaries, manifested in the broader fact of how 'the

American became self-conscious in his belief that he had broken with the structure of European society. He felt himself to be hostile to the society from which his culture sprang'.[331] Cornel West describes this phenomenon as 'the Emersonian refusal of "being fathered" – of being curtailed by any set of antecedent conditions or restrained circumstances'.[332] 'There are new lands, new men, new thoughts. Let us demand our own works and laws and worship', Emerson wrote in *Nature*.[333] Still, as accentuated, one must declare independence from something; the new depends on a contrast and distinction from what preceded it – even in matters of 'insight' and 'revelation' (terms that, again, appear in the opening salvo of *Nature*). So we are reminded that, for example, being one's own origin and having, say, 'an original relation' are different in kind. By 1860, in the wake of *English Traits*, with a new or renewed sense of English influence and America's tangible continuity with its parent country, Emerson appears to rethink the lesson of 'the great Network' and the figurative role of a *causa causans*.

> Our life is consentaneous and far-related. This knot of nature is so well tied, that nobody was ever cunning enough to find the two ends. Nature is intricate, overlapped, interweaved, and endless. [...] But where shall we find the first atom in this house of man, which is all consent, inosculation, and balance of parts?[334]

The 'floating diction' of 1834 returns in 1860 in the more virulent form of influence Emerson calls 'irresistible dictation'.[335] We do not draw so much as are drawn. The cultural process of imitation would appear to be no match for the biological process of replication – fate in its genetic sense. The organic bond between parent and child is not a matter of choice, but a function of the natural order – 'intricate, overlapped, interweaved, and endless'.

42.   Cornel West accentuates that 'Emerson's first noteworthy attempt to come to terms with history, circumstances, or fate occurs not in *The Conduct of Life* (1860) in which his classic "Fate" appears, but rather in *English Traits* (1856)'.[336] Part of Emerson's coming to terms involves – or more suggestively, implicates – the readers of *English Traits*, who must come to terms with Emerson's reading of English traits. As a reader of *English Traits*, West isolates a crucial concern about the interaction between fate and freedom as it is informed by race, and more particularly how race may breach away from its effect on individual identity and underwrite new and expansive powers for the state: 'What I am suggesting is that Emerson's conception of the worth and dignity of human personality is racially circumscribed; that race is central to his understanding of the historical circumstances which shape human personality; and that this understanding can easily serve as a defence of Anglo-Saxon imperialist domination of non-European lands and peoples. In this way, Emerson's reflections on race are neither extraneous nor superfluous in his thought. Rather, they are the pillar for his later turn toward history, circumstance, fate, and limitation'.[337] West's claims need to be digested slowly, and supplemented by the inclusion of related inquires about the way race informs the traits of writing, concepts, personal identity (and personality) and nations. If *English Traits* is a biography of a nation, is it hagiographic? If 'all biography is autobiography' as Emerson says, is *English Traits*

his self-portrait under various guises?[338] How much, for instance, of West's characterization of Emerson's political orientation translates to the mainstream of Englishmen in Emerson's own day: 'Emerson is neither a liberal nor a conservative and certainly not a socialist or even civic republican. Rather, he is a petit bourgeois libertarian, with at times anarchist tendencies and limited yet genuine democratic sentiments'.[339]

43.   Questions beget questions. Each instance of asking gestures toward new gestations of thought, prompts inquiry, which in turn promotes the development of a new valence of insight – or, almost as appealingly, points to where darkness and obscurity remain. Concomitantly, any effort to conduct a meaningful inquest into *English Traits* will reveal the many ways the book changes owing to the reader's interests, frames of reference, temperament and accumulated store of tropes. Some of these angles of reading may be reflected in the following entries – sections 44 to 55, below – most of them asking or implying questions that, for the most part, are meant to coalescence elements from what has already been said, and to sanction and inform the investigation that follows thereafter.

44.   What is the scientific and political significance of *English Traits* as it appears in 1856 – in England, on the eve of Darwin's confessions of a new faith in the natural basis of life (a life, for example, deprived of belief in miracles), and in America, in the midst of an uncivil debate that will lead to a Civil War? These are years before Abraham Lincoln's Emancipation Proclamation – an executive order made first as a threat and then as a tactic to preserve the Union – which took effect at the beginning of 1863, followed by further force of political will and moral imagination by the passage of the Thirteenth Amendment in 1865. With Darwin's *The Origin of Species* (1859) and the political consequences of the Civil War – both involving radical redefinitions of what it means to be human, and to be a man before men – a new era begins: one that seeks the unfettered liberation of science from unchecked superstition, and the legalized assurance of civil liberties; an era that reforms the language and landscape for how we understand race and blood.

45.   During the 1840s and 1850s Emerson spoke publicly to the question of race in America, specifically, to the question of American slavery. In 1844, he said before a live audience: 'The blood is moral: the blood is anti-slavery: it runs cold in the veins: the stomach rises with disgust, and curses slavery' ('An Address ... on ... the Emancipation of the Negroes in the British West Indies'). In that address Emerson is at pains to make explicit 'the civility of no race can be perfect whilst another race is degraded'. Why does not that institution – American chattel slavery – come under extended and explicit attack in *English Traits*? Emerson lauds the English for freeing its slaves and points to the British largesse on this matter as a moral directive for America to follow. And yet, in the chapter 'Truth', Emerson mocks the English for 'extraordinary delusions' in politics, such as the belief that they 'are at the bottom of the agitation of slavery, in American politics'.[340] As Emerson said in the Address, more than a decade before *English Traits*, perhaps the existence of representative men – of

any race – is sufficient for the advocacy of their position. 'When at last in a race, a new principle appears, an idea, – *that* conserves it; ideas only save races'. And it is man who has ideas, and 'carries in his bosom an indispensible element of a new and coming civilization'.

> So now, the arrival in the world of such men as Toussaint, and the Haytian heroes, or of the leaders of their race in Barbadoes and Jamaica, outweighs in good omen all the English and American humanity. The anti-slavery of the whole world, is dust in the balance before this, – is a poor squeamishness and nervousness: the might and the right are here: here is the anti-slave: he is man: and if you have man, black or white is an insignificance. The intellect, – that is miraculous! Who has it, has the talisman: his skin and bones, though they were of the color of night, are transparent, and the ever-lasting stars shine through, with attractive beams.[341]

46.   In the context of ongoing American slavery any invocation of individual 'possession' takes on a haunting valence, especially if that notion includes self-possession. Perhaps it is precisely English materialism – founded on the rights of private property – that gave that nation the logical grounds upon which to emancipate, letting the moral reasons follow after. In England 'property has reached an ideal perfection. It is felt and treated as the national life-blood'.[342] This 'blood' must be indifferent to those who live by it. Still, Emerson remains ambivalent about the strict continuity of old and new England: 'Whatever surly sweetness possession can give, is tested in England to the dregs. Vested rights are awful things, and absolute possession gives the smallest freeholder identity of interest with the duke'.[343] One distinction between parent and child, here figured as related countries, appears to be England's rigorous and exhaustive commitment to materialism (expressed almost sublimely in its laws that are 'framed to give property the securest possible basis'), while America – certainly enamored with the prospects for the transformation of material life – shows evidence of a robust (but distorting) faith in the significance of imagination and (self-) invention, or less generously, a willingness to indulge in delusions about endogenous creation, native power, perception of right and moral elevation. Partly the difference between these two lands is owing to, or is illuminated by, England's status as an achieved nation, while the America of the 1840s and 1850s is still in the paroxysm of adolescence – not yet achieved, not yet itself; no longer possessed by England, not yet self-possessed.

47.   The lectures Emerson wrote while in England, toward the end of his time abroad in 1848, are known as *Mind and Manners of the Nineteenth Century*. What is the significance of the title's distinction or conjunction? Is this association of 'mind and manners' between thought and action, ideas and behaviour, mind and body, concept and performance, privately held principle and publicly derived custom? Or is it not aimed at underscoring difference at all but rather emphasizing the concatenation of coextensive phenomena; an interdependence that reveals itself when we live under images – pictures – that frame their enmeshed affiliation? If human nature is given *and* mutable, if blood is brute and intelligent, then we are victims of fate while also beings its creators.

48.   Emerson became familiar with pre-Darwinian theory as he found it in work by Charles Lyell, Georges Cuvier, Jean-Baptiste de Lamarck, Jean Baptiste Joseph Fourier, Louis Agassiz, John Tyndall, Adam Sedgwick, Robert Chambers, John Herschel, William Hooker, Robert Brown, Michael Faraday, Richard Owen and of course, Goethe, whom he read in German. How does Emerson, who died the week after Darwin, sustain the influence of the science he read prior to *The Origin of Species*?

Given his wide-ranging reading in science – as well as literature, philosophy and religion – it is not surprising that Emerson was sensible to ways in which these FIELDS (noting this as an anachronism) of inquiry, explanation and description overlapped and were mutually reinforcing, and led to his appropriation and application of 'natural history' as analogue to the study of mind. Emerson called his art and mode of research a Natural History of Intellect, and he regarded the project as 'the chief task of his life', in the estimation of his friend, literary executor and biographer, James Elliot Cabot.[344] Even in the early 1830s, when he was in the throes of a severe vocational crisis, Emerson would not renounce his interest in philosophy, literature and religion for training in, say, comparative anatomy, physics or chemistry. Rather, he meant the analogy seriously but metaphorically. He would, it seems, find correspondences and relations, combinations and taxonomies, catalogues and characteristics, varieties and variations in the firmament of his philosophical, literary and religious investigations that would amount to a Natural History of Reason, as he sometimes referred to it. The writer and thinker we know as Emerson – whose reputation has itself evolved over the years from appellations such as sage, essayist, aphorist, poet and philosopher – knew himself as this kind of scientist of the mind. Not a psychology, Emerson's science of mind is closer to a philosophy of mind, or a kind of metaphysical and moral understanding of physics and the physical world. In his essay 'Nature' (1844), Emerson's remarks reflect his study:

> Now we learn what patient periods must round themselves before the rock is formed, then before the rock is broken, and the first lichen race has disintegrated the thinnest external plate into soil, and opened the door for the remote Flora, Fauna, Ceres, and Pomona, to come in. How far off yet is the trilobite! how far the quadruped! how inconceivably remote is man! All duly arrive, and then race after race of men. It is a long way from granite to the oyster; farther yet to Plato, and the preaching of the immortality of the soul. Yet all must come, as surely as the first atom has two sides.[345]

A decade later – with his second voyage to England elapsed, and in the time just prior to the publication of *English Traits* – Emerson considered some consequences of Faraday's theories in 'Poetry and Imagination' (1854):

> The ends of all are moral, and therefore the beginnings are such. Thin or solid, everything is in flight. I believed this conviction makes the charm of chemistry, – that we have the same avoirdupois matter in an alembic, without a vestige of the old form; and in animal transformation not less, as in grub and fly, in egg and bird, in embryo and man; everything undressing and stealing away from its old into new form, and nothing fast but those invisible cords which we call laws, on which all is strung.[346]

And presumably, following this logic, the space between beginning and end is moral, and thus everything is moral.

49.   *English Traits* appears 23 years after Emerson's first voyage to England, and eight years after his second. Are these Englands the same in his mind? Do the nation's characteristics change during these years, or rather is Emerson's perception of them altered?

50.   Is *English Traits* mainly of interest and importance owing to Emerson's unique/ anachronistic/unconventional/singular methods of accounting for his topic? Is the work's composition, and not its content, what arouses curiosity? To what degree does style and structure inform the matter of this mature but anomalous book? If *English Traits* was the most reviewed work of Emerson's career, who now – American, English or other audience – reaches for the book; and how does such a reader understand the work as he or she adopts and addresses it? Does *English Traits* remain, as it was for Carlyle, 'a Book all full of thoughts like winged arrows?' – a quiver of collected lines that are velocious and graceful, may land with accuracy and precision, yet may also be dangerous? Is a contemporary attraction to the work found in assessing one or more aspects of Emerson's historical consciousness, literary achievement, political and rhetorical savvy, philosophical acumen, confessional insight or scientific theorizing – and might that interest also involve a fascination with the perceived lapses, inconsistencies, conflicts and liabilities of the text?

51.   Can the achievement of *English Traits* – its metaphors, associations, combinations and methods – transfer intelligibly and intuitively to the present – that is, become pertinent for contemporary readers? The idea, then, is not what one thinks *Emerson* thought he accomplished in *English Traits* but what, in the course of composing that volume, he *did* accomplish for his country and the thinking he was, perhaps to his surprise and occasional chagrin, continuing to help found and develop. Can a contemporary reader take away more than just an appreciation for the novelty of his style, the richness of his examples and allusions, and the interdisciplinary inventiveness of his methodology?

52.   What is the most intelligent way to understand America in terms of English descent? Is America a (rogue) child? Is America the manifestation of English genius/ temperament/constitution? Who are America's parents? Is it parentless? Who are its founders? Does America become itself by denying its founders – by orphaning itself, by becoming a foundling? As Stanley Cavell has written: 'Is it conceivable that we are all foundlings?'[347]

Emerson, 'Cockayne'

> Strange, that the solid truth–speaking Briton should derive from an impostor [viz., 'Saint George of England, patron of chivalry, emblem of victory and civility, and the pride of the best blood of the modern world'.]. Strange, that the New

World should have no better luck, – that broad America must wear the name of a thief. Amerigo Vespucci, the pickle-dealer at Seville, who went out, in 1499, a subaltern with Hojeda, and whose highest naval rank was boatswain's mate in an expedition that never sailed, managed in this lying world to supplant Columbus, and baptize half the earth with his own dishonest name. Thus nobody can throw stones. We are equally badly off in our founders; and the false pickle-dealer is an offset to the false bacon-seller.[348]

Stanley Cavell, *Emerson's Transcendental Etudes*

Since both Milton and Columbus appear among the many sequences of names recited in the essay ['Experience'], I would like to take it as uncontroversial that the expulsion from Eden is something being invoked as a place lost, and hence that existing in the world is discovered as being thrown for a loss; and uncontroversial that finding a new America in the West while being, or because, lost, is remembering or repeating something Columbus did, repeating it otherwise than in *Nature*.[349]

Emerson, *Journals* (1836)

Out of Druids & Berserkirs were Alfred & Shakspear made.[350]

53.   Is *English Traits* a private family history in the guise of a general cultural critique where Emerson is looking to England as if to find his ancestors – tracing, perhaps, a line of pedigree and descent that began with Peter Waldo and the Waldensians?

54.   What is the relationship between genesis, generation, genealogy, genes, genus and genius? And how do their common and evident etymological features inform, or transform, an understanding of progenitors and progeny, the exogenous and endogenous, agency and miscegenation? Etymologies are genealogies; they encode the lines of language and disseminate the allusions they contain.

55.   What would it mean to re-read *English Traits* accounting for 'traits' differently – say according to categories and tropes that are present but are not brought under scrutiny by Emerson? Part of the project would be to consider whether *English Traits* invites an analysis of the legible elements on the surface of the text – that remain apparent but largely unacknowledged – an analysis that comes to life when certain patterns, pathways and partnerships are noted. And what if the ambition to read the alleged meaning was facilitated by mixing his congregation of ideas from *English Traits* with the vast resources of his other writing so that different things come into view when passages are arranged in a different order. And perhaps even more intriguingly, when fugitive thoughts are recovered and concealed remarks elucidated, because Emerson's writing is placed beside writing by others?

I

More Prone to Melancholy

1. Robert Burton, the English bibliophile and resident of Christ Church, Oxford, whom Emerson refers to in *English Traits*, published *The Anatomy of Melancholy* in 1621 under a pseudonym: Democritus Junior. Unlike Michel de Montaigne's *Essays*, which were read closely by Burton either in French or in the 1603 Florio translation that Shakespeare relied on, Burton's self-described 'antic' and 'insolent' deployment of pseudonymous authorship in *The Anatomy* is worthy of considerable attention, for among other reasons: to consider the author's self-awareness of being an 'artificer' behind the name (even after he publishes future versions under his given surname); and that he writes a book-length preface introducing his reasons for believing himself a rightful heir of Democritus (c. 460–370 BCE). Emerson conjectured that 'many men can write better under a mask than for themselves' – that the 'device of ascribing their own sentence to an imaginary person' lends it a consequence – a 'weight' – otherwise unrealized.[1] In this way authorial creation happens by proxy: the writer names the parent of the work phantasmagorically – as if such writing needed something more than the author to achieve its manifestation. If we understand that Burton wants to be, as it were, a son of Democritus, and that his desire (and his adopted name) stems from feeling sired by the ancient Greek philosopher (or his writing, and the philosophical temperament it embodies), then we witness yet another form of how authors birth their works, how in this case men give birth to one another: from one text to another, by an elective procreation. Burton's book – the material site of his life as Democritus Junior – becomes the proper child of what posterity has inherited from fragmentary aphorisms, sideways rumors in myriad ancient documents. Yet, while the meaning of Burton's pseudonymity elicits new directions in our thinking about names and naming, books and the creation of books (as much as the (creation of the) men who write them), it is to the subject and methodology of *The Anatomy of Melancholy* that we now turn.

Ostensibly about melancholy, Burton claims through quotation of another: '*Invenies, hominem pagina nostra sapit*. My subject is of man and humankind'.[2] As such, one can only imagine what kind of method must be employed to account for everything that is human. Burton's approach is encyclopedic, quixotic, anecdotal and possessed of the spirit of the *florilegium* (a fuller account of which follows below in Chapter V). He casts disparate elements together to see how they relate to one another, where many varied things find a common home under a single topic; and isolates a thing to study it with a series of different lenses, where an isolated atom (to draw from the core of Democritus' teaching) stands for an apparent miscellany. The scale of the investigation continually shifts from the microscopic to the everyday to the macroscopic. Burton is an aggressive assembler hoping that the apposition of exhaustively gathered elements amounts to something more than a very long book. Of the origins and development of his self-ascribed and -inscribed undertaking, he says that he had a 'want of good method', and yet he very ably reveals the intimacy of his subject and his method.

> [...] I had a great desire (not able to attain to a superficial skill in any) to have some smattering in all, to be *aliquis in omnibus, nullus in singulis* [a somebody in general knowledge, a nobody in any one subject], which Plato commends, out of him Lipsius approves and furthers, 'as fit to be imprinted in all curious wits, not to be a slave of one science, or dwell altogether in one subject, as most do, but to rove abroad, *centum puer artium* [one who can turn his hand to anything], to have an oar in every man's boat, to taste of every dish, and sip of every cup', which, saith Montaigne, was well performed by Aristotle and his learned countryman Andrian Turnebus. This roving humour (though not with like success) I have ever had, and like a ranging spaniel, that barks at every bird he sees, leaving his game, I have followed all, saving that which I should, and may justly complain, and truly, *qui ubique est, nusquam est* [he who is everywhere is nowhere], which Gesner did in modesty, that I have read many books, but to little purpose, for want of good method; I have confusedly tumbled over divers authors in our libraries, with small profit for want of art, order, memory, judgment.[3]

We can enjoy the humour of this passage – and indeed Burton's 'roving humour' – yet not be distracted by his false modesty from seeing his talent for collecting specimens and assembling them. All those days of careful reading in libraries leave him with a notebook full of quotations. What can he do with them? And so again we see, as Emerson did, 'how much finer things are in composition than alone. 'Tis wise in man to make Cabinets'.[4] And what are books, in part, if not cabinets for words, sentences, paragraphs that have been intentionally and artfully composed, gathered, sequenced and otherwise curated? How much finer *words* are in composition than alone, we might say, to emphasize the double sense of 'composition' in Emerson's journal jotting – where the work of writing is placed in partnership with the work of curating. Burton's book-as-cabinet reflects the reading of a 'ranging spaniel', barking with salivating delight at the tantalizing morsels that tease him forward in the pages he turns.[5] He collects quotations as a dog collects bones and birds. The parallel is apt since any person driven by such an obsessive passion will wonder what to make of his or her collection. Is it enough to collect? But then for Burton collecting involves complex arrangement, penetrating knowledge of his sources (along with their literary and philosophical contexts and histories; and familiarity with their home languages), and a sensitivity to the contribution such sources make to the unfolding – a flower-like disclosure befitting the original etymology of anthology – he aims to accomplish synthetically in the defence and explication of his theories of melancholy. Is the collector's contribution, then, one of selection, ordering, deletion and emphasis? For Burton, as a reader of his own work, the opus can seem a private enterprise reflecting his effort to address his own melancholic temperament; is *The Anatomy of Melancholy* another inflection of autobiography – a self-generated biography of one's body, moods and reading list?[6]

In his study (at once a place and a mode of attention), he seems to discover how new thoughts can emerge by the apposition of old ones, perhaps even lines and sentiments that are not one's own. He is treated to some palliative effect not just by the wisdom compacted in discrete lines of prose but by the energies of interaction unleashed when they are placed side by side. This is the catalytic effect of composition, even if the composition is achieved principally from quotations. Thomas Warton, author of the poem *The Pleasures of Melancholy* (1747), wrote about Burton's achievement in *The Anatomy*: 'the author's variety of learning, his quotations from rare and curious books, his pedantry sparkling with rude wit and shapeless elegance […] have rendered it a repertory of amusement and information'.[7] For Burton, the *act* of collecting remarks on melancholy – sourcing them and arranging them – was part and parcel of addressing his affliction. We find in Burton's case industry as antidote to distemper.

> If any man except against the matter or manner of treating of this my subject, and will demand a reason of it, I can allege more than one. I write of melancholy, by being busy to avoid melancholy. There is no greater cause of melancholy than idleness, 'no better cure than business', as Rhasis holds: and howbeit *stultus labor est ineptiarum*, to be busy in toys is to small purpose, yet hear that divine Seneca, better *aliud agere quam nihil*, better do to no end than nothing. I writ therefore, and busied myself in this playing labour, *otiosaque diligentia ut vitarem torporem feriandi* [to escape the ennui of idleness by a leisurely kind of employment], with Vectius in Macrobius, *atque otium in utile verterem negotium* [and so turn leisure to good account]. […]
>
> To this end I write, like them, saith Lucian, that 'recite to trees, and declaim to pillars for want of auditors': as Paulus Ægineta ingenuously confesseth, 'not that anything was unknown or omitted, but to exercise myself', which course if some took, I think would be good for their bodies, and much better for their souls. […] When I first took this task in hand, *et quod ait ille, impellente genio negotium suscepi* [and, as he saith, I undertook the work from some inner impulse], this I aimed at, *vel ut lenirem animum scribendo*, [or] to ease my mind my writing; for I had *gravidum cor, fœdum caput*, a kind of imposthume in my head, which I was very desirous to be unladen of, and could imagine no fitter evacuation than this. […] I was not a little offended with this malady, shall I say my mistress Melancholy, my Egeria, or my *malus genius* [evil genius]? and for that cause, as he that is stung with a scorpion, I would expel *clavum clavo* [a nail with a nail], comfort one sorrow with another, idleness with idleness, *ut ex vipera theriacum* [as an antidote out of a serpent's venom], make an antidote out of that which was the prime cause of my disease. [… T]o do myself good I turned over such physicians as our libraries would afford […].[8]

With the aid of physicians such as Seneca and Montaigne, Burton became his own diagnostician, medical and otherwise. And like Montaigne, who quoted extensively from Seneca and other ancient sources and sages, Burton's method – his 'melancholizing,' as he called it[9] – is kindred to the author of the *Essays*: not motivated by a desire to generate fixed and final definitions but rather moved to create a community of texts around a topic – to surround an idea with wise perspectives; to quote artfully; to illuminate by proximity, apposition and refraction; to enrich our view of things prismatically; to create from diverse parts an entire world of interest. As he liked to say of his approach, Burton 'anatomized' a condition that afflicted him as well as the ancients, and he figured so also clung to his contemporary audience and would abide into posterity. He self-diagnosed a purulent infection, what he called melancholy (or 'a kind of imposthume in my head'), and felt it like a pus in his brain, something he had to purge from his system.[10] He learned that by exercising – keeping busy, moving his mind to the *cause* of his malady – he could exorcise its symptoms. Looking at the gargantuan size of Burton's book, we might reasonably infer that he suffered an abundance of melancholy. The final book, then, held in hand, feels like an externalization – an expression – of his malady, a preserved synecdoche of his somatic condition.

2. Emerson, 'Personal'

> In speaking of I know not what style, [Wordworth] said [to Emerson], 'to be sure, it was the manner, but then you know the matter always comes out of the manner'.[11]

3. Walter Benjamin, 'Unpacking My Library: A Talk about Book Collecting'

> For such a man is speaking to you, and on closer scrutiny he proves to be speaking only about himself. [... W]hat I am really concerned with is giving you some insight into the relationship of a book collector to his possessions [in a library], into collecting rather than a collection. [...] For what else is this collection but a disorder to which habit has accommodated itself to such an extent that it can appear as order? [...] And indeed, if there is a counterpart to the confusion of a library, it is the order of its catalogue.
>
> Thus there is in the life of a collector a dialectical tension between the poles of disorder and order. [...] The most profound enchantment for the collector is the locking of individual items within a magic circle in which they are fixed as the final thrill, the thrill of acquisition, passes over them. [... F]or a true collector the whole background of an item adds up to a magic encyclopedia whose quintessence is the fate of his object. In this circumscribed area, then, it may be surmised how the great physiognomists – and collectors are the physiognomists of the world of objects – turn into interpreters of fate. [...]
>
> For him, not only books but also copies of books have fates. And in this sense, the most important fate of a copy is its encounter with him, with his own collection. I am not exaggerating when I say that to a true collector the acquisition of an old book is its rebirth.[12]

4. Wittgenstein, *Philosophical Investigations*

> Though – one would like to say – every word has a different character in different contexts, at the same time there is *one* character it always has: a single physiognomy. It looks at us. – But a face in a painting looks at us too.[13]

The familiar physiognomy of a word, the feeling that it has taken up its meaning into itself, that it is an actual likeness of its meaning – there could be human beings to whom all this was alien. (They would not have an attachment to their words.) – And how are these feelings manifested among us? – By the way we choose and value words.[14]

5. It is important to recognize how Burton, like Montaigne (who died when Burton was 15 years old), takes on his French counterpart's inescapable attention to the human body, in particular, his own – especially in so far as his body was the context and condition of his mind. Montaigne called what he wrote *les essais* – an *essai* being a kind of trial, test or attempt; and as one might expect, the word is the basis for the English 'assay'. Montaigne's experimentation led him to the same conclusion that Burton reached a few decades later, namely, that writing about oneself – what is in oneself, though not necessarily as oneself – is a way to understand what is happening for others, and in the world at large. A private or spiritual investigation will contribute to greater humility and empathy for how, as Emerson said, 'the inmost in due time becomes the outmost'; 'Every man is an inlet to the same and to all of the same'.[15] In another context, the word *essai* was used in France to describe the work of miners: those who by means of conspicuous trials dig deeply for rare and precious materials. After he has retrieved the special, sought after elements, a miner might test their composition in order to assess content and value. Composition and quality is determined by a careful and rigorous interrogation. Similarly, Montaigne believed that there is no distinction between his investigation of ideas and his inquiry into himself. While Burton (quoting from Martialis) declares at the outset of *The Anatomy* that his subject is 'of man and humankind', Montaigne delimits the purview of his undertaking: 'I am myself the matter of my book'.[16] And yet Montaigne's, and later Emerson's, sense of the representative quality of his insights lends credence to the notion that all readers will benefit from his private essaying.

Montaigne's view of writing makes his assay into the self appear like a form of excavation that is conducted, line by line, as an act of reading in and through an embodied but also spiritual condition. His work is at once invasive and introspective. He digs deeply, but into himself. And for that individuated inquiry, to understand better the human – how this particular specimen of the race relates to and resounds with the rest of its creatures. Such exploration and experimentation, though, also resembles a form of anatomizing – as if Montaigne were operating on himself. Since he does not seek to repair, as in surgery, but to find discrete parts and understand their relationships, such working on oneself can seem strangely cadaverous. And yet since such inward looking does not culminate in the dissection and dissolution of a body but yields the creation of another body – his essays – the trial he undergoes also seems like a form of impregnation. Through his writing Montaigne's gestation of mind yields not a baby, but a book. Of course, it is a book that is animated and individuated. In his journal Emerson remarked: 'Let us answer a book of ink with a book of flesh & blood'.[17] When describing Montaigne's work in particular, Emerson pronounced his impression that the *Essays* had achieved an answer to the book of ink: 'Cut these words and they would bleed; they are vascular and alive'.[18] In *Biographia Literaria*, Coleridge noted of William Lisle Bowles' work: 'The poems themselves assume the properties of flesh and blood'.[19] John Jay Chapman said of Emerson: 'His style is American, and beats with the pulse of the climate. He is the only writer we have had who writes as he speaks, who makes no literary parade, has no pretensions of any sort. He is the only writer we have had who has wholly subdued his vehicle to his temperament. It is impossible to name his style without naming his character: they are one thing'.[20]

In his essay 'Montaigne; or, the Skeptic', the fourth chapter in *Representative Men*, Emerson means to align Montaigne's achievement (as the inclusive disjunction of the title suggests) with a proper thinking about reason and faith, belief and doubt, and the vicissitudes of fate as they are informed by responses from the history of skepticism. A crucial turn in his eclectic intellectual history of the skeptic's philosophical stance comes when Emerson situates Montaigne's thinking in his body – the only place human thinking will ever know itself as human. Though we should be convinced that our mind is the site and sire of our reason, there is another anatomical part that upbraids our confidence: namely, our guts.

> There is the power of moods, each setting at nought all but its own tissue of facts and beliefs. There is the power of complexions, obviously modifying the dispositions and sentiments. The beliefs and unbeliefs appear to be structural; and as soon as each man attains the poise and vivacity which allow the whole machinery to play, he will not need extreme examples, but will rapidly alternate all opinions in his own life. [...] Are the opinions of a man on right and wrong, on fate and causation, at the mercy of a broken sleep or an indigestion? Is his belief in God and Duty no deeper than a stomach evidence? And what guaranty for the permanence of his opinions?
>
> [...] What front can we make against these unavoidable, victorious, maleficent forces? What can I do against the influence of Race, in my history? What can I do against hereditary and constitutional habits; against scrofula, lymph, impotence? against climate, against barbarism, in my country? I can reason down or deny every thing, except this perpetual Belly: feed he must and will, and I cannot make him respectable.[21]

Do we have reasons for thinking what we believe above diet and digestion? The skeptic worries, assuredly, that we are too much framed by our existence to be its best accomplice. In this way Montaigne's skepticism, and Emerson's reading of it, remembers the body as a kind of critique or constraint of reason. When we are forgetful of our embodied compromise, we suffer life's illusions – including the faith that events do more than 'leave us exactly where they found us'.[22] Emerson suggests that the only means of abating skepticism is 'in the moral sentiment, which never forfeits its supremacy. All moods may be safely tried, and their weight allowed to all objections: the moral sentiment as easily outweighs them all, as any one. This is the drop which balances the sea'.[23] The counter-acting, directed force of moral sentiment is underwritten by a faith that 'the world is saturated with deity and with law'.[24] From this vantage, we can better behold and confront the 'miscellany of facts' and the very real influence of our stomachal desideratum and the many ways we are 'sopped and drugged'.[25] Emerson's reading of Montaigne was an education in this conciliation to our condition: 'If we compute it in time, we may, in fifty years, have half a dozen reasonable hours'.[26] Montaigne's writing is both the location of his private philosophical investigations and their distillate. The essays are both the 50 years and the half-dozen hours. The point is process, and the process will find its expression.

Colin Burrow has suggested that Montaigne's work 'should be thought of as belonging to a form of discourse which is more or less unnameable (unless one names it the essay), in which what is said is much less significant that the process by which it is said, and in which the movement of the mind matters more than the propositions that are advanced'.[27] As a result, the interest we have in Montaigne may be more likely found in a fascination with his moods and habits of thinking than in any system or theory he might propose. Montaigne exhibits his talent by revealing, as Burrow says, his private dispositions rather than formal propositions. For Montaigne, 'writing about and exploring or refining beliefs' is the principal undertaking of the work: 'the process of writing and arguing is what thinking is; it is not concluding' on some fixed precept or set of rules. Reflecting on his countryman's achievement, Maurice Merleau-Ponty wrote that Montaigne did not pursue or revel in 'self-satisfied understanding', but placed 'a consciousness astonished at itself at the core of human existence'.[28] Montaigne's genuine wonder about his mind's capacity to reflect – including its strange power to consider its own embodied place in the world – generated a kind of thinking that did not demand 'starting from the beginning', for instance, by seeking origins or foundations or fundamental principles, but a 'thinking onwards and backwards'.[29]

Emerson described how a person's 'onward thinking leads him into the truth' by a process of engagement with the world – not strictly by imposition or force but also by an awareness of flow and permeability.[30] Nearly two decades later Emerson wrote: 'To this streaming or flowing belongs the beauty that all circular movement has; as the circulation of waters, the circulation of the blood, the periodical motion of planets, the annual wave of vegetation, the action and reaction of nature', and we might add: the circulation of ideas from one human to another. And 'if we follow it out, this demand in our thought for an ever onward action is the argument for the immortality' of beauty.[31] Or as Montaigne said: 'Everyday I spend time reading my authors, not caring about their learning, looking not for their subject matter, but how they handle it'.[32] Montaigne, like Emerson, is captivated by how the writer undergoes his trial (*essai*) of onward thinking, revealing with each sentence new circuitries of his mind, and more likely, new aspects of his mood.

Robert Burton shared this spirit of onward action as a form of circulating, since above all, he was an anatomist, someone who parsed the widely complex pathways of veins and connecting muscle tissues in order to understand better how things flow and hold together. He saw how philosophy, such as Montaigne's, is enfleshed, how thoughts are always embodied. As such, an investigation of ideas requires the sensitivity of a surgeon. The subtitle on the frontispiece of the 1628 edition of *The Anatomy of Melancholy* reads: 'What it is, with all the kinds, causes, symptoms, prognostickes & severall cures of it, in three Partitions, with their severall sections, members & subsections. Philosophically Medicinally Historically opened & cut up'.[33] Burton entered the Bodleian Library at Oxford as if it were a surgery hall, a place of bodies to be vented, studied, healed and perhaps modified or extracted from. While spending time in these bodies of work, he began to collect what amounted to two millennia of apothegms from these many sources, an aggregation which in turn enabled him to create, he presumed, a solider body – that is, with finer circulation and more pronounced strength. Each excised element represented some aspect of the long history of human scholarship in matters of melancholy and, naturally due to the way bodily networks are connected, to a wider experience known to 'man and humankind'.

6.   At this point an odd and salient convergence of etymologies comes to light, namely between the words ESSAY and TRAIT. Montaigne's essays are understood to be trials, but also, more obviously, more colloquially, simply pieces of writing. In sixteenth-century France, when Montaigne was writing, a *traite* was an arrow, or some form of projectile. Simultaneously in England, 'trait' was being used to describe not only arrows but lines and streaks (that is, pathways an arrow might take). 'Trait' also referenced 'something penned', for example, a 'line' of prose; and, a line or lineament of the face, and so a particular feature of a person's physiognomy, but also, and still further, features such as emotional and mental characteristics. 'An Englishman will pick out a dissenter by his manners[,]' writes Emerson in 'Race'; 'Trades and professions carve their own lines on face and form'.[34] Essays and traits are considerably similar in so far as we regard them as forms of writing that reveal their authors; essays and traits are written in prose but they can also be written in the blood. For Montaigne, his essays were embodied, fleshy, and as Emerson put it 'vascular and alive'. For the renaissance anatomist, traits are discernable in a human face, and in a mood or temperament; for the modern-day physiologist and biochemist, traits are written in a genetic alphabet circulating through the body.

7.   Emerson, *Journals* (1842)

> Calvinism seems complexional merely; as Gam[aliel] Bradford [1795–1839, superintendent of Massachusetts General Hospital] said, 'The Calvinists have the liver complaint: the Unitarians have not'.[35]

8.   Emerson, 'Experience' (1844)

> What cheer can the religious sentiment yield, when that is suspected to be secretly dependent on the seasons of the year, and the state of the blood? I knew a witty physician who found the creed in the biliary duct, and used to affirm that if there was disease in the liver, the man became a Calvinist, and if that organ was sound, he became a Unitarian. Very mortifying is the reluctant experience that some unfriendly excess or imbecility neutralizes the promise of genius.[36]

9.   The doctrine of the four temperaments or humours (viz., sanguine, choleric, phlegmatic and melancholic) finds a parallel in the four cardinal virtues (viz., justice, prudence, fortitude and temperance) – not to say that a particular humour corresponds to the

expression or deficit of a given virtue, but rather to note how Aristotle, in his *Nicomachean Ethics*, describes the temperate or self-restrained (*sôphrona*) person as one who is *eukratês* – that is, 'well-mixed'. Making evident his study of these ancient theories and prognostications, Emerson glosses in the following passage from 'Fate' (1860) how temperament – especially if 'unmixed' – surreptitiously constrains the liberties of minds and manners:

> Read the description in medical books of the four temperaments, and you will think you are reading your own thoughts which you had not yet told. Find the part which black eyes, and which blue eyes, play severally in the company. How shall a man escape from his ancestors, or draw off from his veins the black drop which he drew from his father's or his mother's life? It often appears in a family, as if all the qualities of the progenitors were potted in several jars, – some ruling quality in each son or daughter of the house, – and sometimes the unmixed temperament, the rank unmitigated elixir, the family vice, is drawn off in a separate individual, and the others are proportionally relieved. We sometimes see a change of expression in our companion, and say, his father, or his mother, comes to the windows of his eyes, and sometimes a remote relative. In different hours, a man represents each of several of his ancestors, as if there were seven or eight of us rolled up in each man's skin, – seven or eight ancestors at least, – and they constitute the variety of notes for that new piece of music which his life is. At the corner of the street, you read the possibility of each passenger, in the facial angle, in the complexion, in the depth of his eye. His parentage determines it. Men are what their mothers made them. You may as well ask a loom which weaves huckaback, why it does not make cashmere, as expect poetry from this engineer, or a chemical discovery from that jobber. Ask the digger in the ditch to explain Newton's laws: the fine organs of his brain have been pinched by overwork and squalid poverty from father to son, for a hundred years. When each comes forth from his mother's womb, the gate of gifts closes behind him. Let him value his hands and feet, he has but one pair. So he has but one future, and that is already predetermined in his lobes, and described in that little fatty face, pig-eye, and squat form. All the privilege and all the legislation of the world cannot meddle or help to make a poet or a prince of him.[37]

10. Emerson, 'Literary Ethics' (1838)

> Ask not, Of what use is a scholarship that systematically retreats? or, Who is the better for the philosopher who conceals his accomplishments, and hides his thoughts from the waiting world? Hides his thoughts! Hide the sun and moon. Thought is all light, and publishes itself to the universe. It will speak, though you were dumb, by its own miraculous organ. It will flow out of your actions, your manners, and your face.[38]

11. Emerson, 'Spiritual Laws' (1841)

> A man passes for that he is worth. What he is engraves itself on his face, on his form, on his fortunes, in letters of light. Concealment avails him nothing; boasting

nothing. There is confession in the glances of our eyes; in our smiles; in saluta-
tions; and the grasp of hands.[39]

12.   Emerson, 'Worship' (1860)

If the artist succor his flagging spirits by opium or wine, his work will characterize
itself as the effect of opium or wine. If you make a picture or a statue, it sets the
beholder in that state of mind you had, when you made it. If you spend for show, on
building, or gardening, or on pictures, or on equipages, it will so appear. We are all
physiognomists and penetrators of character, and things themselves are detective.[40]

13.   Emerson quoted from Montaigne's 'Of Physiognomy' – the penultimate chapter
of the *Essays* – in a collection Emerson developed for more than a decade, which he
called *Encyclopedia* (1824–36), a compendium that Ralph H. Orth notes 'provided
many of the quotations for the early lectures, *Nature*, and the opening essays of *Essays,
First Series*'.[41] In a chapter that follows 'Of Cripples', we discover Montaigne's qualified
commitment to the art of reading the countenances of others, and his reticence about
gaining prophesy from an analysis of their physiognomies:

The face is a weak guarantee; yet it deserves some consideration. And if I had to
whip the wicker, I would do so more severely to those who belied and betrayed
the promises that nature had implanted on their brows; I would punish malice
more harshly when it was hidden under a kindly appearance. It seems as if some
faces are lucky, others unlucky. And I think there is some art to distinguishing the
kindly faces from the simple, the severe from the rough, the malicious from the
gloomy, the disdainful from the melancholy, and other such adjacent qualities.
There are beauties not only proud but bitter; others are sweet, and even beyond
that, insipid. As for prognosticating future events from them, those are matters
that I leave undecided.[42]

14.   John Webster, *The Dutchess of Malfi* (1612–3)

FERDINAND
May be some oblique character in your face
Made him suspect you.

BOSOLA   Doth he study physiognomy?
There's no more credit to be given to the face
Than to a sick man's urine, which some call
The physician's whore, because she cozens him.[43]

15.   Pliny the Elder, *Natural History* (c. 77–9 CE)

Although our faces or features contain ten or so characteristics, no two faces
exist among all the thousands of human beings that cannot be differentiated – a
situation that no form of art could aspire to achieve.[44]

16.   George Combe, *Elements of Phrenology* (1824)

The Phrenologist compares cerebral development with the manifestations of mental power, for the purpose of discovering the functions of the brain, and the organs of the mind; and this method of investigation is conform to the principles of the inductive philosophy, and free from the objections attending the anatomical and metaphysical modes of research.[45]

17.   Johann Gaspar Spurzheim, *Phrenology in Connection with the Study of Physiognomy* (1826)

It will be sufficient for my purpose merely to mention the error committed by those writers who, after [literary critic Joseph de] La Porte, [artist Charles] Lebrun, and others, compare the human face with that of certain animals. These comparisons, like fortune-telling and chiromancy, or the interpretation of moral dispositions from the form of the hand, are to be classed among the aberrations of the human understanding.

Innumerable observations have proved, that the affective and intellectual faculties, as innate dispositions, are manifested by various parts of the brain. Hence the physiognomical signs of these faculties are to be sought for in the size and organic constitution of cerebral parts.[46]

18.   Herman Melville, *Moby-Dick*, 'The Prairie' (1851)

Physiognomy, like every other human science, is but a passing fable.[47]

19.   Emerson, 'Domestic Life' (1859)

The physiognomy and phrenology of to-day are rash and mechanical systems enough, but they rest on everlasting foundations. We are sure that the sacred form of man is not seen in these whimsical, pitiful and sinister masks (masks which we wear and which we meet), these bloated and shriveled bodies, bald heads, short winds, puny and precarious healths and early deaths. We live ruins amidst ruins.[48]

20.   Emerson, *Journals* (1838)

Lidian wonders what the phrenologists would pronounce on little Waldo's head. I reply, that, his head pronounces upon phrenology.[49]

21.   Nietzsche, *Beyond Good and Evil*, 'The Free Spirit' (1886)

Even if *language*, here as elsewhere, will not get over its awkwardness, and will continue to talk of opposites where there are only degrees and many subtleties of gradation; even if the inveterate Tartuffery of morals, which now belongs to our unconquerable 'flesh and blood', infects the words even of those of us who know better – here and there we understand it and laugh at the way in which precisely science at its best seeks most to keep us in this *simplified*, thoroughly artificial, suitably constructed and suitably falsified world.[50]

Shouldn't philosophers be permitted to rise above faith in grammar?[51]

Nietzsche points to the complexity masked by our techniques and technologies of simplification. We are used to a scientific or mathematical reduction and therefore miss – or more perniciously, choose to dismiss or neglect – the continuity persisting in the facts and things and thoughts of experience. The dissected heart gives up the secrets of valve and ventricle, aorta and artery, but the mystery of its lost pulse, and of why and how it came to beat in the first place, remains.

> What is most difficult to render from one language into another is the *tempo* of its style, which has its basis in the character of the race, or to speak more physiologically, in the average *tempo* of its metabolism.[52]

22.   Notebook *ED* – 'England' – is a 'retrospective reordering of materials concerning Emerson's first and second visits to England' conducted in 1852–3 meant to gather characteristics that he found of particular dominance among the English, and aimed at finding an arrangement of such features under a specific topic. Among the topically ordered reflections, Emerson wrote: '*Traits*. Melancholy cleaves to the Saxon mind as closely as to the tones of an Aeolian harp.'[53] This perceived intimacy is later reflected in *English Traits* where Emerson suggests that, in his estimation, the English are prone to a 'natural melancholy', and are 'very much steeped in their temperament.'[54] And he elaborates on the observation:

> Their habits and instincts cleave to nature. They are of the earth, earthy; and of the sea, as the sea-kinds, attached to it for what it yields them, and not from any sentiment. They are full of course strength, rude exercise, butcher's meat, and sound sleep; and suspect any poetic insinuation or any hint for the conduct of life which reflects on this animal existence, as if somebody were fumbling at the umbilical cord and might stop their supplies.[55]

It is curious that 'cleaving' can mean either to adhere strongly to something or to split and sever from something. Emerson, using the first sense of the word in both instances above, points out the way in which the English seem to grow naturally out of the land they inhabit, and live naturally according to its limits and requirements. They are distinctly natural or native, we might say, appearing to give the impression that they were always on that island. Melancholy makes the English at once very comfortable in their own opinions, and yet or perhaps for that reason often at odds with the temperaments of the non-English. 'The Saxon melancholy', writes Emerson, 'in the vulgar rich and poor appears as gushes of ill-humour, which every check exasperates into sarcasm and vituperation.'[56] In short, feeling at home in themselves, on their land, they speak their minds. Others may find this natural confidence as an affront, a presumption of right; but it is only, we are meant to believe, an expression of their consanguinity with place. Part of the offence, then, derives from one's own alienation – and, by contrast, the way the English appeared attached to the world naturally; and 'not from any sentiment' or some other form of passing emotion or fickle election. 'They do not wear their heart in their sleeve for daws to peck at'.[57] There is a habit of knowing how to have a conversation that respects the parties involved and of abiding by standards of decorum, but the instinct is, nevertheless, to an unguarded frankness. Where the English are sincere, the Americans are sentimental. Perhaps this is why Emerson believes that the English are 'cheerful and contented' when compared with Americans who are 'much more prone to melancholy'.[58]

23.   Emerson, 'Works and Days' (1857)

> Man flatters himself that his command over Nature must increase. Things begin to obey him. We are to have the balloon yet, and the next war will be fought in the air. We may yet find a rose-water that will wash the negro white. He sees the skull of the English race changing from its Saxon type under the exigencies of American life.[59]

24.   Americans are 'more prone to melancholy' because they do not inhabit a place they can take for granted. The country does not seem settled or founded in a way that affords anything but contingent faith in its existence – a faith that requires vigilant renewal and reaffirmation. And the attendant pressure of human freedom such faith implies – the burden to create something, continually – can overwhelm, leaving Americans tormented and disoriented by the radical variability that surrounds them, and is perpetually felt under foot. The New World was regarded by many early settlers as an 'errand into the wilderness', yet by the time the Constitutional Convention occurred we could be assured of our orientation within this expansive, unknown field of experimentation. American democracy was a wilderness by another name, a space at once encountered and created. In an afterword to Mark Twain's *The Innocents Abroad, or, The New Pilgrim's Progress*, Leslie Fiedler wrote:

> We have always been aware that ours is a country which has had to be invented as well as discovered: invented even before its discovery (as Atlantis, Ultima Thule, a Western World beyond waves), and re-invented again and again both by the European imagination – from, say, Chateaubriand to D. H. Lawrence or Graham Greene – and by the deep fantasy of its own people, once these existed in fact. Europeans, however, begin always with their own world, the Old World, as *given*; and define the New World in contrast to it, as nature versus culture, the naïve versus the sophisticated, the primitive versus the artificial. We Americans, on the other hand, are plagued by the need to invent a mythological version of Europe first, something against which we can define ourselves; since for us neither the Old nor the New World seem ever given, and we tend to see ourselves not directly but reflexively: as the Other's Other. Only when the two worlds become one, as they seem now on the verge of doing, will Europeans and Americans alike be delivered from the obligation of writing 'travel books' about each other, i.e., books whose chief point is to define our archetypal differences and prepare for our historical assimilation.[60]

The peculiar logic of creating a place such as America requires that, as Fiedler provocatively and poignantly puts it, we invent a place before we discover it; in other words, that we found the country in order to find it. And yet we still do not have our bearings. Such orientation is not something the country, as it has been made, is capable of offering its citizens. What the country provides instead is an alternative to the static and settled: rather than feeling naturally at home in America – as if an umbilical cord were tied between a citizen and the very earth that bears the name she named herself after; in calling oneself 'American', one will have to feel naturally at home with oneself, that is, become a companion to the experiment of which one is a part, a neighbour to its aspirations. The result is a citizenry compelled to conduct a continual self-investigation and self-invention in the context of the nation's ongoing tumult. This means neighbouring as negotiation, as an unending process of invention and discovery. And it commonly entails living as if one had no roots. For some it means changing one's name or one's affiliations, or moving from one coast to another or from sea to mountain, city to country. Other times rootlessness announces or provides the conditions for recognizing that merit can supervene upon inheritance and tradition; detachment is a liability until it is the basis for experimentation. All the time, this unmoored status shows that we live in a country without a foundation but instead with a set of principles and values that by their very definition, paradoxically, are adaptable to evolving purposes: 'life, liberty, and the pursuit of happiness' are values for a people who cannot not expect a bequest of good fortune but may – if naïvely – anticipate the emerging conditions for making it oneself.

25.   In 2004 there was an exhibition of William Eggleston's photography entitled 'Los Alamos' at the Louisiana art museum in Humlebaek, near Copenhagen, Denmark. The Danish curator of the exhibit wrote an introduction that included the following observation:

> To be an American was simply to make tracks through the trackless, to take up the struggle with the wilderness. This drive, this fundamental notion, still plays a central role for modern Americans. No other people dislocate themselves with such serenity from the familiar and move hundreds or thousands of miles away to educate themselves, work, or simply start afresh.

26.   Harold Bloom, 'Mr America' (1984)

> I think Emerson remains *the* American theoretician of power – be it political, literary, spiritual, economic – because he took the risk of exalting transition from one activity or state of mind or kind of spiritual being to another, for its own sake. American restlessness, which has been pervasive ever since, puts all stable relationships or occupations at a relatively lower estimate, because they lack the element of risk.[61]

27.   Where Leslie Fiedler described American suffering from an apparent need to mythologize – to deny its origins and promote its capacity to found/find itself – the

Danish curator described Americans as moving about with 'serenity'. Which is it? Are we still troubled by our relationship to Europe: its parentage, its history, its rootedness – and our childlike rebellion against it, our youth? Have we not yet transformed the liabilities of immaturity to our advantage? Are we at last comfortable with our status as a culture of experimentation, movement and rootlessness, always poised to 'make tracks'? Emerson said that 'this one fact the world hates, that the soul *becomes*' – 'Life only avails, not the having lived. Power ceases in the instant of repose; it resides in the moment of transition from a past to a new state, in the shooting of a gulf, in the darting to an aim'.[62] Is 'American restlessness', as Bloom phrased it, a legacy of Emerson's praise of transition?[63] After all, power does not reside in the new state but in the transition to it – in becoming – hence the need for, or abiding fact of, continuous movement. Does the rebellion against becoming find its expression in an American perpetual motion? Replies to these questions depend on one's understanding of or belief in origins. If we need to know origins in order to go on with confidence from them, then we are bound to look back to Europe continually, and therein compromise our sense of independence from that place (given that independence is also a value we appear to privilege). If Americans are, as the Danish curator seems to think we are, liberated from our reliance on origins, a culture comfortable with continual self-initiated dislocation, then we are discharged from the duty of looking back to Europe, ambivalently or otherwise. In 1836 Emerson suggested in bold terms that Americans shift from a reliance on origins to a skepticism about their role in our development; the passage has been so frequently quoted, however, that it has become an origin unto itself – and thus can be a challenge to re-read with fresh eyes:

> Our age is retrospective. It builds the sepulchres of the fathers. It writes biographies, histories, and criticism. The foregoing generations beheld God and nature face to face; we, through their eyes. Why should not we also enjoy an original relation to the universe? Why should not we have a poetry and philosophy of insight and not of tradition, and a religion by revelation to us, and not the history of theirs? Embosomed for a season in nature, whose floods of life stream around and through us, and invite us by the powers they supply, to action proportioned to nature, why should we grope among the dry bones of the past, or put the living generation into masquerade out of its faded wardrobe? The sun shines to-day also. There is more wool and flax in the fields. There are new lands, new men, new thoughts. Let us demand our own works and laws and worship.[64]

An 'original relation' is not one that requires origins – just the opposite: it inculcates a belief that one can be one's own beginning. 'New lands, new men, new thoughts' should not be equipped with old, inherited eyes, but accompanied by a sense that they are seeing things – not necessarily for the first time – but for themselves. Such newness however leaves us with a different form of anxiety. Where once we were nervous because of Europe's imposing history we are now nervous because we have no one to rely upon but ourselves. How can we trust what we see? How can we resist using the old models and metaphors as a means for understanding ourselves? What ensues from these agitated questions is a different kind of pathology: call it the anxiety of living without origins. The anxiety derives from a faith in the new mythology of origin-lessness, a new reality custom-made for a people who believe it needs to continually begin anew, for those who are consumed by the pressure to invent and re-invent and discover themselves. Such creative activity requires a strain not unlike the incubation of pregnancy and the subsequent pain required for the deliverance of new life, and so we find anxious people labouring for a term and then giving birth to themselves. They are thinking onwardly, seeking a next self, endlessly.

In the wake of Fiedler's remarks, and Emerson's injunction in *Nature* and found elsewhere (such as in 'The American Scholar'), we have inherited a problem about creating original work, being original, and having an original relation; as such we are called upon to ask: Have we solved nothing but simply replaced one complicated picture with its converse (say aristocracy for democracy, forsaking the role of nativity for the unsteady promise of an ongoing errand)? Is discovering or inventing, finding or founding oneself even possible? Is it based on an irrational belief or hope that equates originality with goodness, and derivativeness (or being caused or following after) with badness? In a word, can the subsequent be consequent? Is the American melancholic because of her freedom and opportunities, or melancholic because every attempt she makes to capitalize on them is, at last, derivative? Does one's concern with origins – being original, or achieving an original relation – have to do with feeling caused, and hence under the control of something beyond one's power (nature, gods, necessity, randomness)? Does this concern turn to melancholy – a sense of futility and despair? Is the move to self-creation, self-control, self-reliance, to the original (or as Emerson also says, Aboriginal) self, beginning with Socrates, an attempt to become one's own cause? Would being self-caused cure melancholy or perhaps create yet another dire condition: paralysis in the face of radical freedom? But then that is a self-appointed American condition, is it not? Or is it?

When the American creates perhaps she feels it is never a truly novel creation but always a form of quotation. Instead of believing 'The sun shines to-day also', the American suspects that 'There is nothing new under the sun'. Though Emerson admonitions us to have an original relation, he does not suppose that even the most seminal minds were not themselves deeply indebted to the ideas and influence of others.

> Plato, too, like every great man, consumed his own times. [... H]is contempo-raries tax him with plagiarism. But the inventor only knows how to borrow. [...]
> When we are praising Plato, it seems we are praising quotations from Solon and Sophron and Philolaus. Be it so. Every book is a quotation; and every house is a quotation out of all forests and mines and stone quarries; and every man is a quotation from all his ancestors.[65]

We are then bound to quote – directly or in paraphrase – what has gone before us, whether it be a passage of prose, or a parent. Such continuity is inescapable. Perhaps then the question of our nervousness about origins has more to do with an attitude – either anxious or accepting – about the meaning of this condition. Do Americans recognize in themselves the 'serenity' the Danish curator observed in them?

28. Nietzsche, *Human, All Too Human*, 'The Wanderer and His Shadow' (1880)

> *How one tries to improve bad arguments.* Some people throw a bit of their person-
> ality after their bad arguments, as if that might straighten their paths and turn
> them into right and good argument – just as a man in a bowling alley, after he has
> let go of the ball, still tries to direct it with gestures.[66]

29. Emerson claims that 'The Englishman speaks with all his body. His elocution is
stomachic, – as the American's is labial'.[67] The Englishman speaks with his manners; in
his fashion – by the cut of his jacket and with his whiskers; in the rhythm of his gait
upon leather-soled steps on Jermyn Street and Savile Row. 'An Englishman walks in a
pouring rain, swinging his closed umbrella like a walking stick; wears a wig, or a shawl
or a saddle, or stands on his head, and no remark is made. And as he has been doing
this for several generations, it is now in the blood'.[68] Bodily gestures and habits of action
camouflage the degree to which they are expressions of unseen forces; instead of the
superficial chatter of gossip – the labial arts – these deeper traits are outward manifestations of inner conditions, traits that lay dormant until a situation arises to invite
their disclosure; once confirmed to be Lamarckian-style speculations, perhaps without
ground, they find new experimenters and advocates in the emerging science of epigenetics. As it is with the English so too with human behaviour in general, as Emerson
writes: 'Manners are partly factitious, but, mainly, there must be capacity for culture in
the blood. Else all culture is vain. The obstinate prejudice in favor of blood, which lies
at the base of the feudal and monarchical fabrics of the old world, has some reason in
common experience. Every man, – mathematician, artist, soldier or merchant, – looks
with confidence for some traits and talents in his own child'.[69] America was founded
in opposition to the 'obstinate prejudice in favor of blood'. The founding documents
of the country, pages full of upbraid and reprimand, were belted across the Atlantic to
a bewildered king: listing grievances, noting insults and declaring independence from
the English cause in its most literal sense – namely, the blood-based rule of a single
man, the power written into the aristocratic lineage. The new mythology of EQUALITY
among men in America (admitting that while it was a category quickly heralded at the
country's founding, it was scandalously delayed in being applied equally to all human
life on the continent) entailed a disregard for appeals to blood – much less the even
higher cause of divinity – as a reason for belief, a cause for action, or an authority to
uphold power or prestige. In short, the myth implied that merit primarily – or even
more fantastically, alone – would be the new measure. Self-summoned, self-applied
talent would sire the new classes of political leaders, scientists, merchants, artists and
scholars. One could still assume that manners are factitious yet could not cite their
artificial quality as a reason to dismiss them; rather their contingent and adaptable
use could be heralded, as Emma Lazarus' did in 'The New Colossus', as a fundamental
component of the new articles of American faith: 'Give me your tired, your poor / Your
huddled masses yearning to breathe free'. Lazarus wrote retrospectively, though, of her
country's capacities, since by 1883 that yearning was expressing itself in the context
of the expanding marketplace of liberal society. Those masses – once huddled by the

tyrannies of aristocracy, pedigree and political disenfranchisement – were becoming the energized masses dispersing to all corners of the continent.

And yet 'common experience' has confirmed the 'obstinate prejudice in favor of blood'. Ironical facts show that as some Founding Fathers were bringing America into being as a civilization based on the liberty of human beings, they went home to be served by slaves. The New and Old Worlds were fighting it out on American soil even after Evacuation Day. And still are. After the discovery of the double-helix and in the wake of the mapped human genome, there has been a swelling crescendo of consensus about the undeniable influence of our genes – an influence that is measured along a spectrum from slight to severe. At frequent intervals reports are published with scientific evidence that suggests new ways that manners are not at all factitious, and that the 'capacity for culture in the blood' is enormous. The notion of self-creation – whether that means denying the motherland or displacing the influence of one's parents – seems a naïve, sentimental myth, a bit of brash propaganda used to stimulate a difficult and fragile political, social, and artistic experiment.

The consolation for those who have waged honourably to defend the equality of humans, when aristocracy and feudalism insisted violently otherwise, is that the 'capacity for culture' is in all blood. Not least, one might note, that as death is said to be a great equalizer – so is birth; every child on earth is born by the circumstances of creation and consciousness. No man is above or below this level, and as such equality – of blood at birth – is an observable fact. Relatedly, as Emerson observed, or contended, in 'The Over-Soul' (1841), 'And this because the heart in thee is the heart of all; not a valve, not a wall, not an intersection is there anywhere in nature, but one blood rolls uninterruptedly an endless circulation through all men, as the water of the globe is all one sea, and truly seen is one'.[70] We die as equals and are born as equals, so to presume inequality for the span of life in-between is an effect of political grammar, and of the distorting powers of wealth.

The differences we seem to identify in cultures – in strains of aptitude and ranges of temperament, between styles of life and systems of thinking – manifest themselves as clusters of traits. Such coalescence is to be expected, as Darwin observed, since natural selection manifests types that reflect genetic 'capacity' in the blood. The differences between humans that have had the most political significance relate to the phenotype: skin colour, physiognomy and other physical characteristics; yet these contested traits reflect natural processes of genetic and environmental adaptation and therefore should not be cited as evidence for political differences. When Emerson writes of a 'capacity for culture in the blood' the emphasis is on mood, temperament and methodology. He is not lobbying for a distinction in genotype that would make one race politically distinct from another, but instead promoting sensitivity to the phenotype of localized communities. We can grant all human beings equal rights without insisting that all human beings are created equally; universal human rights, for example, is a homogeneity of regard not rank. Historically, the overt or observable differences between humans, skin colour principal among them, led to the presumption of different legal and moral statuses; hence different skin tones entailed different political states, different rights – all antagonisms where there should have been accord. While

Emerson advocated publicly for the emancipation of black Africans in America, he did not want to exaggerate the scope of his claim. It is one thing to say that all men will have liberty and equality under the law, it is quite another to say that such shared political status entails the dissolution of remaining physical and metaphysical differences. The notion of 'culture' in the blood is meant to resonate as a scientific claim about how individuals – with their undeniable, ineluctable and highly evolved traits – develop uncommon attributes, aspects of a distinct organism that when brought together politically may constitute a shared form of life: a community, a world. But is the claim scientific, or is the notion of culture in the blood a metaphor masquerading as science: intended to unsettle our largely inherited understanding of inheritance and acquisition?

30. Emerson invokes Lamarckism – the inheritance of acquired characteristics – as an explanatory analogy for cultural and racial theory, perhaps because this pre-Darwinian approach is itself more suited to our experience of non-biological traits. Jean-Baptiste de Lamarck, who was contemptuous of the new chemistry espoused by the likes of Antoine Lavoisier, proposed in his *Zoological Philosophy* (1809) notions such as *le pouvoir de la vie* ('the complexifying force') and *l'influence des circonstances* ('the adaptive force') that may be said to align better with cultural and political rather than biological or genetic theory, especially regarding the transmission or dissemination of traits. If while reading the 'laws' Lamarck describes for the adaptive force, reproduced below, one understands the idea of 'organ' symbolically – as a sign of cultural, social, political, artistic, linguistic, etc., but also emotional and cognitive traits and habits – then the proposal suddenly seems much more sound, even survivable in the wake of Darwinian theory and modern genetics.

> First Law: In every animal which has not passed the limit of its development, a more frequent and continuous use of any organ gradually strengthens, develops and enlarges that organ, and gives it a power proportional to the length of time it has been so used; while the permanent disuse of any organ imperceptibly weakens and deteriorates it, and progressively diminishes its functional capacity, until it finally disappears.

> Second Law: All the acquisitions or losses wrought by nature on individuals, through the influence of the environment in which their race has long been placed, and hence through the influence of the predominant use or permanent disuse of any organ; all these are preserved by reproduction to the new individuals which arise, provided that the acquired modifications are common to both sexes, or at least to the individuals which produce the young.

Yet even as a memetic theorist may draw profitably from Lamarckism to reinforce an account of the transmission of cultural traits – using this 'science' analogically – there are times when Emerson appears to press the analogy the other way: as if he were making the transmission of cultural phenomena into a metaphor that *science* could adopt, and perhaps in time literalize by empirical and testable means. For example,

Emerson seems to find some credence in the idea not just that biological traits are 'in the blood', as science would confirm, but that presumably non-biological traits can achieve passage through the same organic mechanism. Emerson might describe those traits in terms such as temperament or constitution, which themselves are prone to empirical vagueness; hence the need for treating them initially as tropes. At present, while we may be able to note a visible or congenital biological characteristic found in a child befitting an alliance with that perceived in a parent, it would be beyond the limits of scientific evidence to predict the range of less demonstrable, but no less dominant, inherited traits. Or rather, for now, such prediction would be described in the language Emerson uses for non-scientific discourse: 'As yet we have nothing but tendency and indication'.[71]

Emerson grants that 'it is a medical fact that the children of the blind see'.[72] But there is more than one way to go blind – among them accident, disease, and congenital aberration. While Lamarckism may not yet be promising for predictions about the inheritance of characteristics acquired during one's lifetime, it may yet inform our thinking about the things we carry in us (genotypically) despite what happens to us (phenotypically). Emerson suggests that such biological baggage may include not just overt physical traits but mercurial emotional ones as well. As Montaigne, Burton and others attuned to the influence of the humours and the radiating consequences of moods have written, there is good reason and some evidence to think that a child will manifest traits that we might presume are individually and accidentally acquired but in fact persist from generation to generation. Emerson draws two lines of thinking together when he remarks that as we see how a child biologically 'blends in his face the faces of both parents', so we also 'see that things wear different names and faces, but belong to one family'.[73] We can identify mother and father in the countenance of their child, but may want to go further – namely, to consider the predictive power of that face: 'What pretty oracles nature yields us on this text in the face and behavior of children, babes, and even brutes!'[74] Children are not delivered as neutral material but already deeply informed by constitutional, fatal, conditions: 'When we look in their faces we are disconcerted'.[75]

As evolutionary science Lamarckism was eclipsed by Darwinian theory, but read through Emerson's conceptual adaptation, Lamarckism can seem both intellectually inviting and with certain qualifications, scientifically plausible. The effect of Emerson's gloss on the notion of blood's possession of traits neither confirms a wholesale embrace of Lamarckism nor does it sidestep the controversies Lamarck's propositions create for the dominant Darwinian strain of evolutionary theory, but rather it invigorates our own hermeneutics of metaphor usage. What is it that we think we mean when we say 'in the blood' – and why not imagine, Emerson invites us to consider, that something like moods and ideas, as much as visible characteristics, might pass without detection, silently, through this clandestine stream and only later encounter conditions that invite emergence into the phenomenal realm? Likewise, the very conditions for stating – or proving scientifically – what is given and what is acquired, what is caused and what is created, are shifting. The angle at which mechanical gears are toothed is helical, culminating in a fixed and forceful conjunction of parts; meanwhile, strands of DNA dance in helical rotation, aiming but occasionally erring in replication. For some time now, the two frames of reference – the biological and the cultural – seem themselves to be irrevocably entwined, as if coiled in a helical embrace.

31.   GENOTYPE, *n.* (γένος, *genos*, race or clan; *typus*, type)

1. The genetic makeup, as distinguished from the physical appearance, of an organism or a group of organisms.
2. The combination of alleles located on homologous chromosomes that determines a specific characteristic or trait.

PHENOTYPE, *n.* (πηαινω, *phaino*, to show; *typus*, type)

1. a. The observable physical or biochemical characteristics of an organism, as determined by both genetic makeup and environmental influences.
   b. The expression of a specific trait, such as stature or blood type, based on genetic and environmental influences.
2. An individual or group of organisms exhibiting a particular phenotype.[76]

32.   Emerson, 'Race'

> Men hear gladly of the power of blood or race. Every body likes to know that his advantages cannot be attributed to air, soil, sea, or to local wealth, as mines and quarries, nor to laws and traditions, nor to fortune, but to superior brain, as it makes the praise more personal to him. […]
> The fixity or inconvertibleness of races as we see them, is a weak argument for the eternity of these frail boundaries, since all our historical period is a point to the duration in which nature has wrought. Any the least and solitariest fact in our natural history, such as the melioration of fruits and of animal stocks, has the worth of a *power* in the opportunity of geologic periods.[77]

33.   Some clinical psychiatrists now argue that there may be biological material worth describing as American DNA.[78] The claim is based on neurochemical research and the idea that America is populated by immigrants who appear to have a higher rate of 'exploratory and novelty seeking D4-7 allele' in the dopamine receptor system of the brain.[79] The neuropsychiatrists advancing this theory suggest that the concentration of such genes contributes to an 'American temperament'.[80] It is acknowledged, however, that other countries with large populations of immigrants, such as Canada and New Zealand, reveal similar dispositional attributes. If hosting or welcoming immigrants is not a trait exclusive to America, then the notion of 'American' DNA as such is a metonym for an assembly of dominant phenotypical traits that may already be biologically encoded and perhaps selected as a function of immigrancy. One could then put aside that Canada and New Zealand did not fight wars of independence from British rule, and remain in many substantive ways, colonies of the empire. If the observable features of the Canadian and Kiwi sub-type correspond to specific genotypical traits, then the 'American temperament' is a condition – a sort of transnational existential predicate. A nation comprised of immigrants, despite differences in

points of origin and variations in race, who share this gene are drawn into a unified sub-type. Answering the question how one becomes an American may be answered simply by coming to America – since the movement itself is a form of selection, a means of aggregating a specific constitutional feature. Yet the intrigue of the scientific proposal at hand suggests that the notion of AMERICAN, in this neurochemical and genetic context, could be a name for a global trait – a synonym, metonym, synecdoche or pseudonym for the D4-7 allele. And so it would follow that people who possess this gene yet do not live in America are, nevertheless, American in a biological sense. According to this research, once immigrants – by and large a self-selecting group – gathered in America there developed a higher concentration of people with the D4-7 allele. Consequently, American DNA or an American temperament would cease to be a function of race (or *a* race), but strictly a matter of blood. The presence of the trait would not, or not any longer, require inhabiting America since it would seem America – in the form of this genetic feature and temperamental disposition – already inhabits the carrier wherever he or she resides.

34.   Abundant scholarly attention has been paid to the effect Emerson's treatment of self-reliance has had on American and, more broadly, global culture. Customarily his writing is invoked to support and even legitimate an extreme and austere individualism; as if the meaning and significance of self-reliance bore an analytic relation to individualism. Yet, individualism – as a political or social creed – need not make any appeal to self-reliance; they are distinct phenomena, and in certain cases antagonistic concepts. Still, there are critics who have tried to broker a useful relationship between them – while correcting abundant and persisting popular caricatures; Joseph Blau, for instance, argued that Emerson's transcendentalist individualism founded on self-reliance is crucial to social and political philosophy, and even the emergence of altruism.[81]

Regardless of one's critical stance on the conceptual relationship between self-reliance and individualism, however, Emerson's work (and Thoreau's) is often invoked in the course of considering the history of American rebellion and conformity. In Emerson the prospect of acquiescence or disobedience is frequently depicted as a struggle between individual conscience or genius and social forces – the 'joint-stock company' of civilization.[82] Instead of treating Emerson's intuitionist gloss on the nature of genius as evidence of a latent selfishness or a justified narcissism, what if it were brought into conversation with contemporary research in neuroscience, for instance, where 'findings indicate that the tendency to conform one's values to those expressed by other people has an anatomical correlate in the human brain'? As the authors of the study 'Structure of Orbitofrontal Cortex Predicts Social Influence' summarize in the journal *Current Biology*:

> Some people conform more than others. Across different contexts, this tendency is a fairy stable trait. This stability suggests that the tendency to conform might have an anatomical correlate. Values that one associates with available options, from foods to political candidates, help to guide choices and behaviour. These values can often be updated by the expressed preferences of other people as

much as by independent experience. In this correspondence, we report a linear relationship between grey matter volume (GM) in a region of lateral orbitofrontal cortex ($IOFC_{GM}$) and the tendency to shift reported desire for objects toward values expressed by other people. This effect was found in precisely the same region in each brain hemisphere.[83]

35. Emerson believed that the English are 'bound in character', and that 'every [English] man carries the English system in his brain'.[84] The English system, then, is a sort trait that all Englishmen share, despite their rank and relation to one another. This common element obtains equally and consequently connects them one to the other. As a person cannot be more equally inhabited by the trait, it does not make sense to speak of being more or less English; and yet in England, as in America, the possession of a right or trait does not equalize. The common fact is possession – that the feature abides in all – not that the possession confers prestige, power or privilege.

As there is for the American strain, perhaps there is an equivalent genetic explanation for the English temperament, maybe a gene or allele that reflects a people who evolve on islands, and who feel rooted enough in their land that they can explore the world and even colonize it (while remaining very much themselves); Gertrude Stein said: 'I do know about English literature that it has been determined by the fact that England is an island […]'.[85] Emerson has more to say about other aspects of such a distinguishable temperament:

> Nature makes nothing in vain, and this little superfluity of self-regard in the English brain, is one of the secrets of their power and history. For, it sets every man on being and doing what he really is and can. It takes away a dodging, skulking, secondary air, and encourages a frank and manly bearing, so that each man makes the most of himself, and loses no opportunity for want of pushing. A man's personal defects will commonly have with the rest of the world, precisely that importance which they have to himself. If he makes light of them, so will other men. We all find in these a convenient meter of character, since a little man would be ruined by the vexation.[86]

It is not that the English are more or less practical than Americans, or that they are any less aware – or transgressive – of their limits. It is, perhaps, rather that 'the English brain' can perceive more deeply into its past and does not feel compelled to rally and rage against it. The American brain, on the other hand, has to consider its fresh independence and youth as a nation, and so it is continually studying its limits to see whether they are fixed, or how fixed they are. The American ceaselessly renegotiates her status, and her self-regard. She may ask prospectively: 'If all this is invented, and I am among the inventions – a self-made man – then why can't I do things differently? Differently from what, and why differently at all? If the American is not "bound in character" the way the English appear to be, then there is nothing "natural" that I have to answer to or fight against. And If I am my own origin, my value is perpetually endogenous, and I can – or is it should? – live after my own evolving judgements and self-sanctioned criteria'. She may stumble upon faulty notions of self-creation, originality, personal identity and land in the compromised and unflattering position of the rugged individualist – a distorted and dangerous figuration. Yet she may also moderate the promptings of vanity and raw, untutored confidence to appreciate the instructive, constructive interactions between inner and outer forces. As Emerson knows whatever freedoms one perceives, one is also always hemmed in by the 'irresistible' dictations of blood and circumstance – the parts that come together, with more or less elegance, to frame and form one's existence.

36.   Montaigne, 'Of Friendship'

> And in Truth, what are these Things I scribble, other than *Grotesques*, and monstrous Bodies, made of different Parts, without any certain Figure, or any other than accidental Order, Coherence, or Proportion?[87]

37.   Coleridge, *Biographia Literaria*

> The fairest part of the most beautiful body will appear deformed and monstrous, if dissevered from its place in the organic whole.[88]

38.   The English character according to Emerson expresses animal and brutal qualities, yet at other times is gentle and tender. These are not contradictions but observations of different moods, of life under different casts of mind. And moods so often seem to reflect one's conditions and conditioning. *The Strange Case of Dr Jekyll and Mr Hyde* (1886) by Robert Louis Stevenson takes this view to an extreme – in some respects literalizing the impression of inner contrasts and conflicts – and generates a story suitable to a number of pathologies that plague humans, including dissociative identity disorder. Yet the story need not be read as a fictionalized account of some neurochemical ailment; it can also be understood as a modern myth of anxiety over personal identity and culpability. If we are all to some degree of two minds, possessed of a double-consciousness, or suspect we possess a personality that splits or otherwise opposes itself, we live frightened by our radical transformations from one mood to another. For matters of self-interest as well as culpability for one's action, one wants to know not just what one is doing but *who* is doing what. Am I me? Or in a question that reflects a concern for the implications of mind-body dualism, Stanley Cavell asks in *The Claim of Reason*, 'Am I, or am I in, my body?'[89] *Dr Jekyll and Mr Hyde* narrates a mind-mind dualism in which there is a debate over the nature of cognitive residency or ownership in a body. One becomes, as it were, other to oneself – and thus a problem to oneself as another would be. One's skepticism of one's own mind – one's right mind, or not being of two minds – is further complicated by Stevenson's attention to the effect of psycho-pharmacology. The ingestion and effect of mind-alternating – or human nature-transforming – substances alludes to millennia-old beliefs that evil is *in* man or can be attributed to man, for instance, that some moral toxin has been implicated and can and should be expunged. Stevenson's story takes for granted that evil is already a part or a potential of the human constitution, something

apparent at its origin, like sin. Under the spell of this myth we may believe we are whole, yet tainted; party to something that – or someone who – is not one's own, not recognizable as oneself.

Generated from Mary Shelley's *Frankenstein; or the Modern Prometheus* (1818) comes another version of a modern myth that suggests we are men of parts, and that the origin of those parts matters. The condition of being a unity-made-from-fragments prompts the anxiety of being a person who is created as a direct quotation from allocations and aspects of others. *Frankenstein* is, notably, a parable of being unoriginal – or worse still, of being derived from the unhandsome portions of others. The monster is literally a man composed of other men: a body made from the bodies of others; as such the monster's existence is purely one of quotation. The anxiety erupts, for us, the story's readers, when we ask whether such derivation suggests – by analogy – that one's identity is fundamentally plagiarized; that the monster is a quotation and construction from the morally depraved seems as terrifying as the realization that he is not wholly himself – and not even partly so. Instead the *impression* of his wholeness derives strictly from the assemblage of parts that originated with others, as others.

What is the status of a body made up of foreign and unfamiliar body parts? The uses or habits of literary quotation suggest that drawing bits from other bodies can yield a new work that earns an individual a defensible identity of one's own. In Shelley's narrative that assembled body is a monster. What then are our books? What then are we? – since we too are bodies made from parts and quotations of other bodies, call them parents. As children, are we literary innovations from known origins, or do we remain literal compilations of the selected and sewn/sown; are we works of inspired genius or lackluster imitation? 'She has her mother's eyes'. 'She is the very image of her father'. Like the modern Prometheus we are born of invention: our production happening in a moment of conception, a different kind of stitching together of materials. The particularity of that material – DNA – assures that we are differently formed from all others, but is that also to say de-formed? 'The man', writes Emerson, 'is physically as well as metaphysically a thing of shreds and patches, borrowed unequally from good and bad ancestors, and a misfit from the start'.[90] The abnormal is the natural.

39. Writers might worry that what holds for the creation of people holds for the creation of books. Is monstrousness – as a result of quotation – what writing becomes, especially writing *about* writing? Is all secondary literature monstrous? Does it not extract fractions and features from old bodies in order to make new bodies? Every set of quotation marks is another act of slicing, patching and stitching – of fabricating a new entity from existing elements. Depending on one's view of books – as living organisms or as pulseless repositories – this is either a form of surgery or autopsy; is the writer a healer or an anatomist? Or perhaps writing is by nature something else: a practice of cannibalism where quotation is form of feeding on another body – drawing sustenance from the very lines of life one extracts and digests. Augustine once confessed how he fed upon – and was nourished by – the words of God.

40. Melville, *Mardi and a Voyage Thither* (1849)

> But as for that Babbalanja of ours, he must needs go and lunch by himself, and, like a cannibal, feed upon an author; though in other respects he was not so partial to bones.[91]

41. One could hope to create a book naturally, according to the logic of nature. The work would not be an artificial assembly of scraps and shreds, but a natural unity – something put together so well that its seams do not show. And not just a unity unto itself – a totality of balanced and functional parts – but also an entity living in continuous connection with its creator. After Emerson visited Carlyle in Scotland, on the American's first visit abroad, Carlyle wrote not long after to reassure his guest – who impressed him so deeply of America's talent and promise – that despite the wide ocean and a revolution of independence within the living memory of their contemporaries, Emerson and Carlyle were compatriots:

> And so here, looking over the water, let me repeat once more what I believe is already dimly the sentiment of all Englishmen. Cisoceanic and Transoceanic, that we and you are not two countries, and cannot for the life of us be; but only two *parishes* of one country, with such wholesome parish hospitalities, and dirty temporary parish feuds, as we see: both of which brave parishes *Vivant! vivant!*[92]

Yet if despite Carlyle's enthusiasm, and the romance of his hyperbole directed at flattering and endearing his American friend (or it is brother? or son?) to him, we consider that America is, after all, separate, a distinct land – and nation – unto itself, then we might find that a good book would be recognized as a good child is recognized, as something that is well-bred. And so instead of denying the reality of cold ocean water and bloody battles, England might do better to claim New England as its second edition – an improved or improvised version? a version with fewer errata? an offspring without unflattering mutation? – all the while drawing attention to the enduring vitality of the parental stock and admirable variation of its traits. A few years later, in 1838, Carlyle returned to the same subject, and offered what amounts to an acknowledgment of England's child, America: 'that Transoceanic England, New and improved Edition of England.'[93]

The writer likewise trains himself in the art of conception, gestation, maturation, labour and tuition. The writer is the parent of his words. So if the writer steals his words – does not learn to quote well, to honour or transform his sources (as Montaigne says of his own practice: 'disguising and altering it for a new service'[94]) – then his book, his child, is not his own; the writer discovers to his shame and chagrin that he has claimed paternity for another's child. His plagiarism entails infidelity, and his rude quotation engenders illegitimacy. 'We naturalists', writes Montaigne, 'judge that the honor of invention is greatly and incomparably preferable to the honor of quotation.'[95]

Emerson's gloss on the distinction between invention and allegation comes in his lecture on 'Quotation and Originality' (1868) where he describes the eponymous pair as coordinate enterprises – the one needing the other: 'in proportion to the spontaneous power should be the assimilating power' (a line of his own that Emerson fittingly quotes from his own work: first in resemblance to the 'assimilating force' of *English Traits*, then in a strict transcription from 'Culture' (1860), and again relies upon it in 1873, having recently returned from Egypt and his third and last visit to England, when offering an 'Address at the Opening of the Concord Free Public Library'.)[96] When quoting from others – from their experience – we are to be wary of living as 'exiles', 'foreigners', 'our body borrowed, like a beggar's dinner', with feeble claim to the merits of our own expressivity.[97] 'Quotation confesses inferiority' only when it disenfranchises genuine action, only when it eclipses one's faith in making it.[98] Vanity interrupts our proper acknowledgment of sources so that 'our very abstaining to repeat and credit the fine remark of our friend is thievish'.[99] Plagiarism is piratical; imitation with acknowledgment is artistic. Better then to quote with humility and discernment – drawing the best work of others into the frame of one's best efforts to render the same. When achieved, the identity of the creator may diminish beside the insight and provocation of the work. 'If an author give us just distinctions, inspiring lessons, or imaginative poetry, it is not so important to us whose they are. If we are fired and guided by these, we know him as a benefactor, and shall return to him as long as he serves us so well'.[100] Composition of 'new' work would always be understood as a collaboration – where borrowing and 'vast mental indebtedness' is expected as part of one's bid for intellectual honesty.[101]

II

With Muffins and Not the Promise of Muffins

1.   Pliny the Elder, *Natural History* (c. 77–9 CE)

Trees were the temples of the gods, and, following old established ritual, country places now dedicate an outstandingly tall tree to a god. Even images of shining gold and ivory are worshipped less by us than forests and their silence.[1]

2.   Thomas Carlyle, 'The Hero as Poet' (1841)

It is all a Tree: circulation of sap and influences, mutual communication of every minutest leaf with the lowest talon of a root, with every other greatest and minutest portion of the whole.[2]

3.   In the age of mechanical reproduction, which the English helped inaugurate, they shifted, according to Emerson, from a natural approach to mind and matter to something inorganic.

The artificial succor which marks all English performance, appears in letters also: much of their aesthetic production is antiquarian and manufactured. [...]
   The bias of the Englishmen to practical skill has reacted on the national mind. They are incapable of an inutility, and respect the five mechanic powers even in their song. The voice of their modern muse has a slight hint of the steam-whistle, and the poem is created as an ornament and finish of their monarchy. [...] They are with difficulty ideal; they are the most conditioned men, as if, having the best conditions, they could not bring themselves to forfeit them. Every one of them is a thousand years old, and lives by his memory: and when you say this, they accept it as praise.[3]

So they are not yet machines, but something much further along than anything in a state of nature. When writing about *English Traits* in the essay 'Society and Authenticity', Lionel Trilling noted how 'the belief that the organic is the chief criterion of what is authentic in art and life continues, it need hardly be said, to have great force with us'. The feeling that there is 'something intervening between man and his own organic endowment is a powerful element in the modern consciousness', and yet, Trilling suggests, we should consider how this 'inhuman force' is 'more terrible than any that Emerson imagined'.[4]
   Emerson says 'England is a garden', that sort of tended space that is between the natural and the manufactured – or rather is an instantiated attempt to summon the

forces of nature by the directing mind and trained hands of the horticulturalist.[5] It would be fitting then to name the English themselves as living things that grow in a garden, a people-as-plant whose development is treated with the utmost attention – by parents, schools, governments, and the effects of shared customs and habits surviving through consistent, loyal application based on an ancient culture with a long memory. The Englishman is, then, not a wild forest varietal, but a topiary. He is the 'most conditioned' plant, of a shape and design that only human intervention could achieve.[6] A man shaped by men provides another reading of the notion of self-cultivation – for what is an individual, under these conditions, according to these terms, but a creature who sees to his own formation? Still, the influence is not solely endogenous, but one factor among the wider social and environmental effects each man, each plant, registers in his character.

When Emerson was travelling in Wiltshire with Carlyle, Emerson was asked by a host about the American landscape, and replied:

> [I]n America, lies nature sleeping, over-growing, almost conscious, too much by half for man in the picture, and so giving a certain *tristesse* [melancholy], like the rank vegetation of swamps and forests seen at night, steeped in dews and rains, which it loves; and on it man seems not able to make much impression. There, in that great sloven continent, in high Alleghany pastures, in the sea-wide, sky-skirted prairie, still sleeps and murmurs and hides the great mother, long since driven away from the trim hedge-rows and over-cultivated garden of England. And, in England, I am quite too sensible of this.[7]

At Stonehenge the English conscientiousness about its long history of cultivation – in matters of both agriculture and anthropos-culture – seems confirmed by 'the wide margin given in this crowded isle to this primeval temple', 'the old egg out of which all their ecclesiastical structures and history had proceeded'.[8] The continuity of roots is as palpable to the British mind as the flowing of blood from generation to generation. These images afford an Englishman to act as if he were a thousand years old; gardens and hereditary titles are outward signs that confirm the conceit. The English are deeply rooted creatures, heavily invested in their land, in their island, aware of the burdens and rewards of pedigree, and the challenge of inheriting such a culture in the punctuated but nevertheless continuous flow of generations. Emerson's description of English serfs as 'attached to the soil' seems apropos of such rootedness and immobility[9]; the farmer's labour on the field is akin to the seed's labour to give rise to new vegetation, or as Virgil wrote in the *Georgics*: 'the genius of the soil claims its place, its vigor and color and its natural power for supporting plants'.[10] Yet the English university is perhaps the place, above all, except maybe the seminary, where men are constrained, clipped, nipped, shaped, given nutriment and generally formed by their grounding conditions – noting also how the ongoing use of the term 'form' in English schools (to mean a group or cohort of students) engenders a complementary reading of the stages in the process of education understood as the fashioning of pupils, as the cultivation of plants. We refer to the college or university as an *alma mater* – that other conditioning agent, who mothered us, who gave us shape and form. The image of an Englishman as a topiary gives a whole new sense to the idea of the 'cultivated person'.[11]

[The English] parry earnest speech with banter and levity; they laugh you down, or they change the subject. 'The fact is', say they over their wine, 'all that about liberty, and so forth, is gone by; it won't do any longer'. The practical and comfortable oppress them with inexorable claims, and the smallest fraction of power remains for heroism and poetry. No poet dares murmur of beauty out of the precinct of his rhymes. No priest dares hint at a Providence which does not respect English utility. The island is a roaring volcano of fate, of material values, of tariffs, and laws of repression, glutted markets and low prices.

In the absence of the highest aims, of the pure love of knowledge, and the surrender to nature, there is the suppression of the imagination, the priapism of the senses and the understanding; we have the factitious instead of the natural; tasteless expense, arts of comfort, and the rewarding as an illustrious inventor whosoever will contrive one impediment more to interpose between the man and his objects.

Thus poetry is degraded, and made ornamental. […] We want the miraculous; the beauty which we can manufacture at no mill, – can give no account of. […] The English have lost sight of the fact that poetry exists to speak the spiritual law, and that no wealth of description or of fancy is yet essentially new, and out of the limits of prose, until this condition is reached.[12]

Who then still speaks about liberty and lives after it: without so much conditioning, without becoming ornamental? It is the American, not as topiary, but as weed: adaptable, able to grow most anywhere, wild in the wilderness (not in a garden), spreading, sprawling, seemingly unstoppable, not always particularly beautiful or elegant – and all these attributes on native as well as foreign soil? Americans live in a boundless, perpetually 'new, yet unapproachable America' in the West, to the west of England. America is not a garden but a mythological frontier forever receding at the horizon, whereas the English live on an island, every square inch of which has been tended to for ages, yielding settled pathways and historic gardens. The English are made from their land. Thus when the English colonize, the limits of the island must extend ever outward from the motherland, the source that sustains and nourishes its people while half-a-world away. By contrast, for Americans, the land is a proxy for an idea, and as such the American can grow ably wherever – in whatever soil – the idea thrives. English colonialism, by necessity, is material and political in ways that American colonialism is – if also material and political – a decidedly conceptual intervention on foreign land.

4. J. Hector St John de Crevecoeur, *Letters from American Farmer*, 'What Is an American' (1782)

In this great American asylum, the poor of Europe have by some means met together […]. Everything has tended to regenerate them; new laws, new mode of living, a new social system; here they are become men: in Europe they were as so many useless plants, wanting vegetative mould, and refreshing showers; they withered, and were mowed down by want, hunger, and war; but now by the power of transplantation, like all other plants they have taken root and flourished![13]

Men are like plants; the goodness and flavour of the fruit proceeds from the peculiar soil and exposition in which they grow. We are nothing but what we derive from the air we breathe, the climate we inhabit, the government we obey, the system of religion we profess, and the nature of our employment.[14]

Every industrious European who transports himself here, may be compared to a sprout growing at the foot of a great tree; it enjoys and draws but a little portion of sap; wrench it from the parent roots, transplant it, and it will become a tree bearing fruit also.[15]

5.   John Stuart Mill, *On Liberty* (1859)

Human nature is not a machine to be built after a model, and set to do exactly the work prescribed for it, but a tree, which requires to grow and develop itself on all sides, according to the tendency of inward forces which make it a living thing.[16]

Many persons, no doubt, sincerely think that human beings thus cramped and dwarfed, are as their Maker designed them to be; just as many have thought that trees are a much finer thing when clipped into pollards, or cut out into figures of animals, than as nature made them.[17]

Persons of genius, it is true, are, and are always likely to be, a small minority, but in order to have them, it is necessary to preserve the soil in which they grow.[18]

6.   Coleridge, *Biographia Literaria* (1817)

The highest perfection of natural philosophy would consist in the perfect spiritu-alization of all the laws of nature into laws of intuition and intellect. [...] The theory of natural philosophy would then be completed, when all nature was demonstrated to be identical in essence with that, which in its highest known power exists in man as intelligence and self-consciousness.[19]

7.   In 1826 Emerson read enthusiastically in Sampson Reed's *Observations on the Growth of the Mind*, a book that appeared the same year and runs in a breathless pace, without chapters or even section breaks. As a fitting reflection of Reed's claims for the continuity of man, law, nature and God, the book exhales in one long breath. Emerson did not temper his esteem when he wrote that it is 'one of the best books I ever saw' and 'the best thing since Plato of Plato's kind'.[20] The book's impact on Emerson's awareness of the metaphors of natural history in the burgeoning science and philosophy of mental phenomena is apparent in Emerson's writing in the decade leading up to and culminating in the publication of *Nature* – a kind of sibling volume to Reed's exuberant Swedenborgian vision of the unity of consciousness with what normally seems distinct from it – and as late as his lectures *Mind and Manners of the Nineteenth Century* presented in England more than a decade later.

Trees, flowers, vines and other plants; fruit, seeds, soil and germs, are among the tropes that predominate in Reed's cosmology, metaphysics and philosophy of mind. As Reed's book title suggests, this is a work undertaken in the spirit of a natural scientist: observations will be made. The title stands in strict and striking parallel to Emerson's chosen name for his project: Reed's observations of mind become, for Emerson, an inquiry into the natural history of intellect. These tandem undertakings require a sensitivity to the analogies deployed to account for the relationship between natural 'growth' (or development) and the qualities of mental phenomena. As Reed says:

> The mind must grow, not from external accretion, but from an internal principle. Much may be done by others in aid of its development; but in all that is done it should not be forgotten that, even from its earliest infancy, it possesses a character and a principle of freedom, which *should be* respected, and *cannot* be destroyed. Its peculiar propensities may be discerned, and proper nutriment and culture supplied; but the infant plant, not less than the aged tree, must be permitted, with its own organs of absorption, to separate that which is peculiarly adapted to itself; otherwise it will be cast off as a foreign substance, or produce nothing but rottenness and deformity.[21]

The analogical relationship between the mind and empirical science is further reinforced when Reed adds:

> The science of the mind itself will be the effect of its own development. This is merely an attendant consciousness, which the mind possesses, of the growth of its own powers; and therefore, it would seem, need not be made a distinct object of study. Thus the power of reason may be imperceptibly developed by the study of the demonstrative sciences.[22]

Or glossed further by Reed: 'The science of the mind, then, will be the effect of all the other sciences'.[23] For Reed, whose very name seems to imply that he is a plant among men, the human mind is 'planted in nature by its heavenly Father' and is 'designed to enter into matter, and detect knowledge, for its own purposes of growth and nutrition'.[24] In other words the development of the natural sciences is the logical consequence of the development of the human mind since it is 'the continual endeavor of Providence' that 'the natural sciences should be the spontaneous production of the human mind'.[25] The laws of the mind are discovered to be the laws of nature outside the mind because the two phenomena are continuous. Furthermore, as we find in Emerson, Reed turns the claim of mind 'implanted' in nature into a conjecture about the fitness of mental capacities to discern moral truth: 'The natural world was precisely and perfectly adapted to invigorate and strengthen the intellectual and moral man'.[26]

There is also a social and cultural aspect of the relationship of individuals to their environments, which Laura Dassow Walls highlights by emphasizing the significance of the analogy between horticulture and 'self-culture' – the latter being 'a figure that united Romanticism's "touchstone" metaphor, organicism, with the traditional American and Unitarian conception of the individual as a growing plant'.[27] Walls' sensitivity to the nineteenth century meaning of 'culture' amplifies the resonance of education as enrichment, of the mind as 'both the process and the result'.[28] The Germans Emerson read, such as Goethe, described it as *bildung*: a continual process of self-development by means of an interaction between the outer and the inner, between the world and the content of consciousness. As Walls says: 'The notion of culture as a process of continual growth held together the culture of truth'.[29] And like scientific inquiry that is always ongoing, 'growth' for the individual was a moral ideal – 'effective because it was ever approached but never reached'.[30] (Stanley Cavell has written definitively of this phenomenon under the name 'moral perfectionism'.[31]) Of the parallel between man and plant, Walls notes how an individual was 'forever in a state of education, the "self-cultivation" or "educing" of the soul's various hidden faculties and capacities by experience in the outer world'.[32] In an ideal scenario, 'the culture of truth thus bound the individual to society by the reciprocal action of self-culture. Each individual would grow and strengthen by assimilating ever more of the social landscape to his own interests, needs, and desires; society would grow and strengthen by assimilating ever more individuals to the collective agreement'.[33] Like plant and soil (coupled with light, air and water), this interaction of parts – and interdependency of forms and transformations – is sustained in the metaphor of metamorphosis, another concept that finds its origins in botanical tropes and models reaching back to antiquity and renewed by European humanism and romanticism. When writing of Goethe, Emerson evaluates how, in the application of the botanical sciences to the study of moral philosophy, his German mentor shows 'that every part of a plant is only a transformed leaf to meet a new condition; and, by varying conditions, a leaf may be converted into any other organ, and any other organ into a leaf'.[34] And it was in the work of Sampson Reed that Emerson found an heir of Goethe's botanical analogizing, and a new point of reference for thinking about the relationship between the laws of nature and the laws of mind.

When Emerson presented 'The Powers and Laws of Thought' in England in 1848 – the inaugural lecture in the series *Mind and Manners of the Nineteenth Century*, given before members of the Literary and Scientific Institution in London – Reed's work of more than 20 years earlier seems an undeniable and affecting palimpsest:

> The idea of vegetation is irresistible in considering mental activity. Man seems a higher plant. What happens here in mankind is matched by what happens out there in the history of grass and wheat. This curious resemblance repeats, in the mental function, the germination, growth, state of melioration, crossings, blight, parasites, and in short all the accidents of the plant. Under every leaf if the bud of a new leaf, and not less under every thought is a newer thought. The plant absorbs much nourishment from the ground in order to repair its own waste by exhalation, and keep itself good. Increase its food and it becomes fertile. The mind is first only receptive. Surcharge it with thoughts in which it delights and it becomes active. The moment a man begins not to be convinced, that moment he begins to convince.[35]

And elsewhere in the same lecture Emerson adduces aspects and definitions of mind befitting Reed's analysis:

We can trace three descents, shall I say, from the mind into nature, assuming identity as the base.

1. Truths as thoughts become perceptions of mind.
2. What is a truth in his mind is a power in nature.

Whilst the man of ideas converses with truths as thoughts, they exist also as plastic forces, as the soul of a man, the soul of a plant, the genius or constitution of any part of nature, which makes it what it is. Like a fragment of ice in the sea, so man exists in the firmament of truth which made him. He is a thought embodied, and the world of thought exists around him for element. [...]

But of those elemental organic thoughts which we involuntarily express in the mould of our features, in the tendency of our characters, there is no measure known to us. [...]

And as we distinguished truths first, as thoughts when they were perceptions of the mind, and second, as species in nature, so third, we see them as powers self-organized into the talents of men: Insight, Memory, Imagination.[36]

8. In *The Mirror and the Lamp*, M. H. Abrams shows that the perception of a meaningful analogical relationship between the plant and the mind was present almost a half-century before Sampson Reed's *Observations* in J. G. Herder's essay 'On the Knowing and Feeling of the Human Soul' (1778). And while acknowledging that this essay 'must be accounted a turning point in the history of ideas', Abrams usefully traces the idea to even earlier sources:

To the elementaristic and mechanical explanation of nature and man, body and mind, Herder vehemently opposed views woven out of Leibniz's monadology, Shaftesbury's pantheism, and biological science, especially Albrecht Haller's theory that the essential aspect of living organisms is its *Reizbarkeit* – its power to respond to external stimuli by a self-contradiction or expansion. Herder's essays thus heralds the age of biologism: the area of the most exciting and seminal discoveries having shifted from physical science to the science of life, biology has begun to replace Cartesian and Newtonian mechanics as the great source of concepts which, migrating into other provinces, were modifying the general character of ideation.[37]

From the growing influence of biologism Abrams deduces a crucial effect of natural metaphors on the theories of mental phenomena: 'It hardly needs to be said', he affirms, 'how strongly a mode of thinking patterned on a growing plant fostered the genetic habit of mind. From this point of view, to understand anything is to know how it is has come about'.[38] The very notion of 'origin' is altered when the trope shifts from divination to dirt, from an unknown cosmic force beyond comprehension to the humble – but no less awe-inspiring – forms of vegetal life. Yet even as the plant, vine and tree have roots, we do not find the 'source' of its life by looking at the tips of its roots. Origin then cannot properly mean a place of beginning – or genesis – but something more like a space of continual change. As Abrams continues: 'Much that has hitherto been conceived as Being is now see as itself a Becoming – the universe itself is a process, and God's creation is a continuant. Change, instead of a meaningless Heracleitean flux, is conceived to be the orderly emergence of inner forms, and is held to constitute the very essence of things; and the ancient distrust of mutability is annulled'.[39]

9.   J. G. Herder, 'On the Knowing and Feeling of the Human Soul'

> The deeper anyone descends into himself, into the construction and source of his noblest thoughts, the more will he cover his eyes and feet and say: 'What I am, that I have become. Like a tree have I grown: the germ was there; but air, earth, and all the elements, which I did not myself provide, had to make their contribution to form the germ, the fruit, the tree'.[40]

10.   In between Herder and Reed we find Coleridge inheriting and institutionalizing the new biologism, grafting as it were the sights and insights of horticultural science onto the shoots of poetic form, or as he writes: 'Events and images, the lively and spirit-stirring machinery of the external world, are like light, and air, and moisture, to the seed of the Mind, which would else rot and perish. In all processes of mental evolution the objects of the senses must stimulate the Mind; and the Mind must in turn assimilate and digest the food which it thus receives from without'.[41] In *The Statesman's Manual* (1816), Coleridge consolidates the image of plant with that of mind to effect a compelling portrait of their shared traits:

> Lo! – with the rising sun it commences its outward life and enters into open communion with all the elements, at once assimilating them to itself and to each other. At the same moment it strikes its roots and unfolds its leaves, absorbs and respires, steams forth its cooling vapour and finer fragrance, and breathes a repairing spirit, at once the food and tone of the atmosphere, into the atmosphere that feeds *it*. Lo! – at the touch of light how it returns an air akin to light, and yet with the same pulse effectuates its own secret growth, still contracting to fix what expanding it had refined.[42]

11.   England is a place of distinctive topographical features and atmospheric qualities, yet many of them coordinate with the attributes of any island: limited raw material, precious soil and the dominance of climatic influences. Still, this island – among all islands – appears to have generated, or attracted, a people who work the land with uncanny fortitude and efficiency. Did the land breed men adapted to its conditions, or did the men shape the land to suit their already abiding nature? If the latter then the English offer a recent illustration of the cultural aspect of natural selection.

> I know not from which of the tribes and temperaments that went to the composition of the people this tenacity was supplied, but they clinch every nail they drive. They have no running for luck, and no immoderate speed. [...] At Rogers's mills, in Sheffield, where I was shown the process of making a razor and a penknife, I

was told there is no luck in making good steel; that they make no mistakes, every blade in the hundred and in the thousand is good. And that is the characteristic of all their work, – no more is attempted than is done.[43]

The English success in manufacturing and markets led to a transformation in the style of production. Hand-craft became machine-craft. And quantities of material passing through a given factory overwhelmed any human sense of the time-tables and conditions of natural and artisanal production. Emerson wrote of the 'violence of artificial legislation' that threatens the great benefit of wealth generated by that very system.

> Such a wealth has England earned, ever new, bounteous, and augmenting. But the question recurs, does she take the step beyond, namely, to the wise use, in view of the supreme wealth of nations? [...] At present, she does not rule her wealth. She is simply a good England, but no divinity, or wise and instructed soul. She too is in the stream of fate, one victim more in a common catastrophe.[44]

The English exhibit a different kind of labour, not of natural birthing but rather of artificial production. And why not? Natural, that is body-driven, labour on such an island might yield a stone hut and a fence to manage the flock but mechanical labour makes many things of greater use in application than in discovery. Emerson marvels how the inventions of various instruments have come to 'perform the labour of the world'.[45] Artificial creation has shown its promise by feeding the hungry, sheltering the cold and freeing humans from tasks they disparage – turning them out to settle other deficiencies. We are certainly apprised of the 'violence' of such harsh and degrading work, but we are also, it appears, reconciled to withstand it given the benefits we so eagerly and easily transform from luxuries to necessities. The English found a way to liberate themselves from the fate of their limitations in geography, material and population. Acting as their own advocates in the organization, use and maintenance of the world, they innovated what we all take for granted: the degree to which we can make our own conditions for creation. In this world, man and woman alike can labour and give birth. And a cold, damp, North Sea island can become one of the primary sources of global production. If it is a turbine and not a womb we do not seem to mind any longer.

> A proof of the energy of the British people is the highly artificial construction of the whole fabric. The climate and geography, I said, were factitious, as if the hands of man had arranged the conditions. The same character pervades the whole kingdom. Bacon said, 'Rome was a state not subject to paradoxes;' but England subsists by antagonisms and contradictions. The foundations of its greatness are the rolling waves; and, from first to last, it is a museum of anomalies. This foggy and rainy country furnishes the world with astronomical observations. Its short rivers do not afford waterpower, but the land shakes under the thunder of the mills. There is no gold mine of any importance, but there is more gold in England than in all other countries. It is too far north for the culture of the vine, but the wines of all countries are in its docks. [...] The native cattle are extinct, but the island is full of artificial breeds. [...] The rivers, lakes and ponds, too much fished, or obstructed by factories, are artificially filled with the eggs of salmon, turbot and herring. [...]

> By cylindrical tiles, and guttapercha tubes, five millions of acres of bad land
> have been drained and put on equality with the best, for rape-culture and grass.
> [...] The latest step was to call in the aid of steam to agriculture. Steam is almost
> an Englishman. I do not know but they will send him to Parliament, next, to make
> laws. [...] Artificial aids of all kinds are cheaper than the natural resources. No
> man can afford to walk, when the parliamentary-train carries him for a penny a
> mile.[46]

The English and American alike have only compounded the 'antagonisms and contradictions' of artificial legislation: from nuclear fusion to the mapping of the human
genome, from solar power to computational power, we are daily supported (and also
accosted) by the things and means we have created. The office worker looks out to a
family of trees, hears birds on branches, welcomes the warm impression of the sun's
rays on his cheek, and wonders longingly about the genius of those creations, which
lay as far behind any human effort as they do behind the thick pane of glass that
separates him from their habitat, once his own primordial context. We are the benefi-
ciaries of the 'well-husbanded forces', and also their victims.[47] Elastic desire, and an
ongoing history of almost always trailing its expansion, leaves us melancholic amidst
the opportunities for health, safety, and riches.

> The English muse loves the farmland, the lane, and market. [...] For, the
> Englishman has accurate perceptions; takes hold of things by the right end, and
> there is no slipperiness in his grasp. He loves the axe, the spade, the oar, the gun,
> the steampipe: he has built the engine he uses. He is materialist, economical,
> mercantile. He must be treated with sincerity and reality, with muffins, and not
> the promise of muffins. [...] When he is intellectual, and a poet or a philosopher,
> he carries the same hard truth and the same keen machinery into the mental
> sphere.[48]

Yet there is ample ingenuity left to develop in matters of distribution and the expansion
of conditions to other lands. And while there is much pleasure and power to be had
in the artificial legislation of the world, there is also a demand to manage that estate, a
care that may sit or settle beyond our capacities – if only because we can never see too
far past our present circumstances and state of being. When the world is meaningful
only for its material nature what becomes of spiritual facts? While Emerson marvels
at the English talent for industry and utility he exempts himself from their labour.

> I know that the world I converse with in the city and in the farms, is not the world
> I *think*. I observe that difference and shall observe it. One day, I shall know the
> value and law of this discrepance. But I have not found that much was gained by
> manipular attempts to realize the world of thought. Many eager persons succes-
> sively make an experiment in this way, and make themselves ridiculous.[49]

Emerson is on guard to avoid 'a paltry empiricism' that would turn him away from
spirit, thought, and private revelations.[50] He is not against experimentalism – on
the contrary, he describes himself as 'experimenter', an 'endless seeker' – but he is

suspicious of instrumentalism, where a thing derives all its meaning by reference to its use or purpose.[51] Emerson's experimentalism yields a different outcome, one might even call it a methodology peculiar to American thinking: 'The true romance which the world exists to realize, will be the transformation of genius into practical power'.[52] This is an organic vision of experimentation where the conditions and the causes for creation are endogenous. Americans express themselves outwardly from within. The English, by contrast, reflect an artificial system in which they are caused, conditioned and created by outward circumstances; that they shape natural and material forces to their will is a savvy and skilled response to an exogenous environment. For the English practical power is transformed into genius.

12.   Voltaire, *Letters Concerning the English Nation*

The *English* have so great a Veneration for exalted Talents, that a Man of Merit in their Country is always sure of making his Fortune. [...] The Picture of the prime Minister hangs over the Chimney of his own Closet, but I have seen that of Mr [Alexander] *Pope* in twenty Noblemens Houses.[53]

III

The Lively Traits of Criticism

1. Emerson, *Journals* (1847)

> All biography auto-biography. [...] I notice that the biography of each noted individual is really at last communicated by himself. The lively traits of criticism on his works are all confessions made by him from time to time among his friends & remembered & printed.[1]

We display our traits in writing as we do in various thoughts and actions. '[... H]unters, farmers, grooms, and butchers [...] express their affection in their choice of life, and not in their choice of words'.[2] We all 'write' in some form or another: 'We are symbols, and inhabit symbols; workmen, work, tools, words and things, birth and death, all are emblems'.[3] Expertise in a given area of life is a matter of knowing a grammar. Such knowledge requires a sensitivity to the tools, their uses and the context of both.

2. Emerson, 'History' (1841)

> We are always coming up with the emphatic facts of history in our private experience, and verifying them here. All history becomes subjective; in other words, there is properly no history; only biography.[4]

Nietzsche, *Human, All Too Human* (1878)

> *Life as the product of life.* However far man may extend himself with his knowledge, however objective he may appear to himself – ultimately he reaps nothing but his own biography.[5]

If history is better understood as biography, and biography is, in fact, autobiography, then individual life is self-same with what we know as history. We are not a part of history so much as its scribes, and we do not write history through research, discovery and exposition – but through the blunt, ceaseless continuity of the moment-to-moment. History is not verified, an achievement of empirical facts that align, but an ongoing fleshy experiment, as Emerson writes:

> The true poem is the poet's mind; the true ship is the ship-builder. In the man, could we lay him open, we should see the reason for the last flourish and tendril of his work; as every spine and tint in the sea-shell pre-exist in the secreting organs of the fish. The whole of heraldry and of chivalry is in courtesy. A man of fine

manners shall pronounce your name with all the ornament that titles of nobility could ever add. […]

In like manner, all public facts are to be individualized, all private facts are to be generalized. Then at once History becomes fluid and true, and Biography deep and sublime. […]

He finds that the poet was no odd fellow who described strange and impossible situations, but that universal man wrote by his pen a confession true for one and true for all. His own secret biography he finds in lines wonderfully intelligible to him, dotted down before he was born.[6]

3.   William James, *Pragmatism: A New Name for Some Old Ways of Thinking*

The history of philosophy is to a great extent that of a certain clash of human temperaments. […] Of whatever temperament a professional philosopher is, he tries, when philosophizing, to sink the fact of his temperament. Temperament is no conventionally recognized reason, so he urges impersonal reasons only for his conclusions.[7]

4.   David Hume, *A Treatise of Human Nature*

The generosity, or baseness of our temper, our meekness or cruelty, our courage or pusillanimity, influence the fictions of the imagination with the most unbounded liberty, and discover themselves in the most glaring colors.[8]

5.   Ludwig Wittgenstein

It is sometimes said that a man's philosophy is a matter of temperament, and there is something in this. A preference for certain similes could be called a matter of temperament and it underlies far more disagreements than you might think.[9]

6.   Carl Jung, 'Letter to Arnold Künzli'

Philosophy still has to learn that it is made by human beings and depends to an alarming degree on their psychic constitution. […] There is no thinking qua thinking, at times it is a pisspot of unconscious devils, just like any other function that lays claim to hegemony. Often what is thought is less important than who thinks it.[10]

7.   Emerson, 'Behavior'

A main fact in the history of manners is the wonderful expressiveness of the human body. If it were made of glass, or of air, and the thoughts were written on steel tablets within, it could not publish more truly its meaning than now. Wise men read very sharply all your private history in your look and gait and behavior. The whole economy of nature is bent on expression. The tell-tale body is all tongues. Men are like Geneva watches with crystal faces which expose the whole movement. They carry the liquor of life flowing up and down in these beautiful bottles, and announcing to the curious how it is with them. The face and eyes reveal what the spirit is doing, how old it is, what aims it has. The eyes indicate the antiquity of the soul, or, through how many forms it has already ascended. It almost violates the proprieties, if we say above the breath here, what the confessing eyes do not hesitate to utter to every street passenger.[11]

8.   Johann Gottlieb Fichte, *The Science of Knowledge*

What sort of philosophy one chooses depends, therefore, on what sort of man one is; for a philosophical system is not a dead piece of furniture that we accept or reject as we wish; it is rather a thing animated by the soul of the person who holds it.[12]

9.   Ferdinand C. S. Schiller, *Our Human Truths*

Philosophy, then, will have the duty of tracing out the consequences of personality in all our knowledge. Now as regards the philosophies, this task is easy enough: they all testify aloud to the often highly romantic personality of their makers, and the more original they are, the plainer it is that this is what has determined their every detail.[13]

10.   Nietzsche, *Beyond Good and Evil*, 'On the Prejudices of Philosophers'

Gradually it has become clear to me what every great philosophy so far has been: namely, the personal confession of its author and a kind of involuntary and unconscious memoir; also that the moral (or immoral) intentions in every philosophy constituted the real germ of life from which the whole plant had grown. [...] In the philosopher there is nothing whatsoever that is impersonal.[14]

11.   Miguel de Unamuno, *The Tragic Sense of Life*

In most of the histories of philosophy that I know, philosophic systems are presented to us as if growing out of one another spontaneously, and their authors, the philosophers, appear only as mere pretexts. This inner biography of the philosophers, of the men who philosophized, occupies only a secondary place. And yet it is precisely this inner biography that explains for us most things.[15]

12.   John Oulton Wisdom, *The Metamorphosis of Philosophy*

The statements of a speculative philosopher do not directly express facts about the universe but symptomatically express facts about himself – they form his unconscious autobiography.[16]

13.   When we write things down, in words, such work is said to be recognized for its VOICE – an unexpected feature of a silent medium. Stanley Cavell has addressed

the presence of voice in the work of philosophy, noting for instance that his essay 'What's the Use of Calling Emerson a Pragmatist?' is a 'brief gloss' on the observation that 'in philosophy it is the sound which makes all the difference'.[17] The voice or sound of writing is a figure of speech meant, in this context, to emphasize the personal or particular nature of human utterance. And as we can make a generic language into individual expression by means of selection, emphasis and grammatical arrangement, so the generic language of genetic material (ATCG) creates a specific, individuated genomic trace. Writing, like genetic replication, is a form of creation. In the chapter on 'Ability' in *English Traits*, Emerson quotes from seventeenth-century naval commander, diplomat and physicist, Sir Kenelm Digby's *Of Bodies and Souls*:

> [S]yllogisms do breed or rather are all the variety of a man's life. They are the steps by which we walk in all our businesses. Man, as he is man, does nothing else but weave such chains. [...] This linked sequel of simple discourses, the art, the cause, the rule, the bounds, and the model of it.[18]

Syllogisms breed the way humans do, and the way writing does: by means of sharing and combination – the commingling of grammar and logic. A syllogism is a mode of reasoning in which we draw a conclusion from premises. The premises share a common term that does not show up in the conclusion; it is the connection that makes the outcome possible. One proposition is drawn with another, and by virtue of their receptivity to one another – in the form of this middle term – they generate something that makes a claim about the world. Such claims are made by syllogistic conclusions as by books and children.

Thus the panic associated with what Aristotle called the enthymeme, namely, an argument in which a premise is not stated. Logicians point out the enthymeme as indicative of fallacious reasoning, as leading us to thoughts that may be unsupportable. Keeping with Digby's image, though, we see another peculiarity of the enthymeme: it is unnatural. Syllogisms cannot breed, nor can we take steps in our reasoning, if they are missing the thing necessary for generation. In order to create there must be a contribution and interaction of the elements involved – genes, proteins, premises, words. We would neither expect water to form if two hydrogen atoms were not combined with an oxygen atom, nor would we believe that a woman could conceive with an egg alone. It is a merit of the English, Emerson believes, that they are aware of the natural logic of the syllogism, and have found the means of employing it to tremendous material and intellectual effect:

> Their practical vision is spacious, and they can hold many threads without entangling them. All the steps they orderly take; but with the high logic of never confounding the minor and major proposition; keeping their eye on their aim, in all the complicity and delay incident to their several series of means they employ. There is room in their minds for this and that, – a science of degrees.[19]

Such methodology follows 'the sequence of nature', and along with the English 'faith in causation, and their realistic logic or coupling of means to ends [has] given them the leadership of the modern world', alleges Emerson.[20] 'By their steady combinations they succeed'.[21] Bees and silkworms labour constantly to produce honey and silk. The ancient skills of the apiarist and the five millennia of sericulture offer a tutorial on how creation follows from a marriage of materials (land, leaves, nectar, pollen, soil, genes, blood) and the labour required to realize the product. 'A manufacturer sits down to dinner in a suit of clothes which was wool on a sheep's back at sunrise'.[22] The English genius, then, is displayed in generation: namely, the exercise of artful and productive combinations that follow the lines of logic and nature; their culture is a testament to Digby's notion that 'Syllogisms do breed'.

14. GENIUS derives from the Latin *gignere*, to create or beget, an etymology that was an offspring of the Greek γιγνεσθαι, to be born, come into being. Some further selected etymologies and definitions – other linguistic kith and kin – for the word are found in the *OED*:

1. With reference to the classical pagan belief: The tutelary god or attendant spirit allotted to every person at his birth, to govern his fortunes and determine his character, and finally to conduct him out of the world; also, the tutelary and controlling spirit similarly connected with a place, an institution, etc.
    b. After Lat. use: This spirit viewed as propitiated by festivities; hence, one's appetite.
    c. *(A person's) good, evil genius*: the two mutually opposed spirits (in Christian language *angels*) by whom every person was supposed to be attended throughout his life. Hence applied *transf.* to a person who powerfully influences for good or evil the character, conduct, or fortunes of another.
    d. In astrological use the word survived, with some notion of its original sense, passing into a symbolical expression for the combination of sidereal influences represented in a person's horoscope.
    e. The quasi-mythological personification of something immaterial (e.g., of virtue, a custom, an institution), esp. as portrayed in painting or sculpture. Hence *transf.* a person or thing fit to be taken as an embodied type of (some abstract idea). [...]

2. A demon or spiritual being in general. Now chiefly in pl. *genii* (the sing. being usually replaced by Genie), as a rendering of Arab *jinn*, the collective name of a class of spirits (some good, some evil) supposed to interfere powerfully in human affairs.

3. Of persons: Characteristic disposition; inclination; bent, turn, or temper of mind.
    b. With reference to a nation, age, etc.: Prevalent feeling, opinion, sentiment, or taste; distinctive character, or spirit.
    c. Of language, law, or institution: Prevailing character or spirit, general drift, characteristic method or procedure.
    d. With reference to a place: The body of associations connected with, or inspirations that may be derived from it.

e. Of material things, diseases, etc.: The natural character, inherent constitution or tendency.

4. Natural ability or capacity; quality of mind; the special endowments which fit a man for his peculiar work.

5. Native intellectual power of an exalted type, such as is attributed to those who are esteemed greatest in any department of art, speculation, or practice; instinctive and extraordinary capacity for imaginative creation, original thought, invention, or discovery. Often contrasted with *talent*.

This sense, which belongs also to F. *génie*, Ger. *genie*, appears to have been developed in the 18ᵗʰ c. (It is not recognized in Johnson's Dictionary.)[23]

15.   Emerson, *Journals* (1841)

Away with your prismatics, I want a spermatic book. Plato, Plotinus, & Plutarch are such.[24]

16.   Purity in ideas, or in stock, is not the source of power. 'Mixture is the secret of the English island'.[25] And not just in the aggregation of physical material but in the matter of literature as well. The English possess what Emerson calls a 'mental materialism', which is characterized as 'common sense inspired'.[26] The brilliance and fecundity of the English mind is attributed to the rare synthesis of unique traits: 'In their dialect, the male principle is Saxon; the female, the Latin; and they are combined in every discourse'. Further along these lines: 'Shakespeare is the perfect example' of 'the union of Saxon precision and oriental soaring'.[27]

17.   Another way of understanding combination is by way of correspondence or comparison – namely, through analogy. The English had many 'disciples of Plato' who excelled at being 'cognizant of resemblances' – among them: 'More, Hooker, Bacon, Sidney, Lord Brooke, Herbert, Browne, Donne, Spenser, Chapman, Milton, Crashaw, Norris, Cudworth, Berkeley and Jeremy Taylor'.[28] Emerson cannot account for the 'genesis' or 'diffusion' of this trait, but it 'seems an affair of race, or of meta-chemistry; – the vital point being, – how far the sense of unity, or instinct of seeking resemblances, predominated'.[29] Analogical thinking puts things in apposition, places them side by side, trades terms from one scene to an often foreign correlate, but in such a way that shared features or overt differences become both evident and interesting: making each aspect more revealing of its common nature and its points of divergence, and occasionally intimating some feature that exceeds both sameness and difference – some third, hybridized form that eludes its grounding in two stable referents (whether they are parents or not). In this way analogy can be used to establish the conditions for creation. Emerson, even more staunchly, predicts: 'Whoever discredits analogy, and requires heaps of facts, before any theories can be attempted, has no poetic power, and nothing original or beautiful will be produced by him'.[30] In other words the connections that are made, or the resemblances noted, by the analogists, perhaps in the absence of

facts, are creative acts, ones that often yield unconventional, unfamiliar, even jarring accounts of value and action, and occasionally summon forth new beings we must contend with – not just scientific theories but also novels, poems, plays and works in the pitch of philosophy. The analogist may act according to an unspecified instinct instead of in proportion to the justified dictates of explicit evidence; his talent lies, in many cases, in seeing anew what lies in front of us. The method for such revelation – and revaluation – is comprised of noting various features and forms that exist in different realms of life – often at a far remove from one another, as the micro- and macroscopic continually appear as sibling realms. When his work is done well we are convinced of the relationship between things that had previously left their connection undisclosed.

18.   David Hume advocated a strict empiricism for which he claimed all ideas are derived from sense experience, or as he says, 'But though our thought seems to possess this unbounded liberty, we shall find, upon a nearer examination, that it is really confined within very narrow limits, and that all this creative power of the mind amounts to no more than the faculty of compounding, transposing, augmenting, or diminishing the materials afforded us by the senses and experience'.[31] The analogist employs 'compounding, transposing, augmenting, or diminishing' in every act of judgement. Hume, of course controversially, points out how far this métier can take the analogist: 'Even those ideas, which, at first view, seem the most wide of this origin, are found, upon a nearer scrutiny, to be derived from it. The idea of God, as meaning an infinitely intelligent, wise and good Being, arises from reflecting on the operations of our own mind, and augmenting, without limit, those qualities of goodness and wisdom'. For the skeptics of this claim, that is, for the faithful, Hume soberly attests: 'We may prosecute this enquiry to what length we please; where we shall always find, that every idea which we examine is copied from a similar impression'. Hume, of course also controversially, reports this finding as an achievement of his philosophical system – an insight worthy of praise, not scandal.

Whether a reader takes Hume's pronouncement, now several centuries old, as an incitement or merely a well-worn insight that transformed Western thinking about the nature of religious concepts (and the very real phenomena they were believed to reference), it remains worth dwelling on the way his account of how we form and inform our ideas requires an analogical movement or description. GOD is a hypertrophic abstraction derived from rudimentary sensuous and immediate experience. Adopted in a certain mood, say that of a German Romantic or an American Transcendentalist, Hume's account gives credence to an exalted intimacy between Nature and God.

In a chapter entitled 'Language' in *Nature* Emerson wrote: 'There seems to be a necessity in spirit to manifest itself in material forms; and day and night, river and storm, beast and bird, acid and alkali, pre-exist in necessary Ideas in the mind of God, and are what they are by virtue of preceding affections, in the world of spirit. A Fact is the end or last issue of spirit. The visible creation is the terminus or the circumference of the invisible world'.[32] He then went on to quote a Continental thinker on the subject: 'Material objects', said a French philosopher, 'are necessarily kinds of *scoriae* of the substantial thoughts of the Creator, which must always preserve an exact relation to their first origin; in other words, visible nature must have a spiritual and moral side'.[33] Emerson quotes from Guillaume Oegger (c.1790–1853), a linguist and Swedenborgian, having read his work – *The True Messiah; or the Old and New Testaments, Examined According to the Principles of the Language of Nature* – in Elizabeth Palmer Peabody's manuscript translation from the French. While Emerson and Oegger share an outlook that emphasizes the continuity between the mental and material, they both employ a range of metaphors that represent that relationship differently: in Emerson, 'terminus' and 'circumference'; in Oegger, 'origin' and 'side'. These spatial images are meant to enhance, not distract from, a theory of intimacy among mental, moral and material phenomena. The material world and moral action are unmistakably, on this view, *ex*-pressions of God.

A little later in *Nature*, in a chapter entitled 'Idealism', Emerson uses Humean terminology, but his gloss on the Scottish philosopher's work registers a different understanding of his postulation, or perhaps threat, of skepticism: 'It is a sufficient account of that Appearance we call the World, that God will teach a human mind, and so makes it the receiver of a certain number of congruent sensations, which we call sun and moon, man and woman, house and trade. In my utter impotence to test the authenticity of the report of my senses, to know whether the impressions they make on me correspond with outlying objects, what difference does it make, whether Orion is up there in heaven, or some god paints the image in the firmament of the soul?'[34] Though Emerson says 'I cannot try the accuracy of my senses', he does not believe 'the Ideal theory' culminates in 'burlesque'. And he adds 'we resist with indignation any hint that nature is more short-lived or mutable than spirit'.[35] For Emerson, it is precisely when thought commences – perhaps granting Hume's narrative of the origins of the idea of God as an analogical extrapolation from empirically-, sensuously-based input – that 'this despotism of the senses' diminishes. The very act of analogizing – find grounds for similarities and differences in mental, moral and material phenomena – seems completely befitting a position that cannot distinguish or separate the triad, but is continually enriched by a perception of its striking affiliations: 'If the Reason be stimulated to more earnest vision, outlines and surfaces become transparent, and are no longer seen; causes and spirits are seen through them'.[36]

Emerson's remarks would appear to sustain Baruch Spinoza's neutral monism in which he described a single substance that possessed mind and 'extension' (matter). Spinoza's contribution to the postulation that God and Nature are unified is usually expressed in his phrase *Deus sive Natura*. Such a formulation renders a de-personalized divinity that does not preside over so much as pervade existence. God simply is what is. And mind and body are necessarily part of that totality. With the inclusive disjunction 'or' (*sive*), Spinoza transformed an analogy between two aspects of experience – God, Nature – into a single, continuous phenomenon.

19.   Melville, *Moby-Dick*, 'The Sphinx'

> O Nature, and O soul of man! how far beyond all utterance are your linked analogies! Not the smallest atom stirs or lives on matter, but has its cunning duplicate in mind.[37]

Moby-Dick; or, The Whale is a Cabinet of Natural History as composed by a writer of fiction. Melville is an inspired analogist who finds connections and affiliations, and his dislocations and disanalogies inform just as well. But then these achievements may leave us forgetful of the kind of work *Moby-Dick* is. I once witnessed a room full of loquacious professors of nineteenth-century American history, literature and philosophy fall mute at the claim 'No great novel, no great work of literature was ever produced by the Transcendentalists'. Silence. And thereafter more silence – and not awkward of embarrassed silence. Neither a conjecture nor an objection stammered out. I was sufficiently disoriented and intimidated by the silence that I remained mute as well; I did not then hazard a recommendation so I now aim to amend my reticence by saying that Aye, it is *Moby-Dick* that is America's most representative work of Transcendentalist literature in the nineteenth century. Is a reminder all that we need, or must more be said – to qualify or otherwise defend the claim? Melville takes as native and necessary that his literary-philosophical excursion must be conducted by Transcendental means and methods. Perhaps it is Melville's peerless enactment of literature that leaves one forgetful of its singular presence; *Moby-Dick* is so much itself that it appears to transcend itself; it is at once representative of the form (a novel form of the novel?) and a provocation to the possibilities of imaginative literature as we know it – or forget – it.

When Orion published its abridged *Moby-Dick in Half the Time* (2007) the editor cut out 'the lengthy descriptions of whaling history and of whales, some philosophical observations, a number of other digressions and reflections'.[38] What then is left? 'The main narrative line' and 'the ongoing graphic narrative'. In other words the anonymous editor de-transcendentalized *Moby-Dick* in order to serve up a story. What was cut out, flensed and hoisted overboard was thereafter artfully edited by Damion Searls into a book of its own, *; or The Whale* (2009).[39] Searls' book though is not so much a cabinet as a bin of unwanted remainders. This repository of discards and fragments, bits of prose made from severed whale flesh, is defined strictly and solely in terms of its apparent fatness – that which was deemed to interrupt the meat of the story. This surplus of philosophical lard was cut out, pushed overboard, having been judged at odds with the possibility of narrative flow. The reader of *; or The Whale* wonders whether these eliminated parts (as it were, the transcendental elements of *Moby-Dick*) survive the rupture from their native context: do the remnants retain their transcendental credentials in this bin of a book?

20.   Emerson converted from preacher to naturalist. Not quite from a man of God to man of science, but rather, into a man of God in Nature. Approaching 30, he revealed this new, hybridized identity by moving from a controversy over the Eucharist – as seen in his inflammatory sermon 'The Lord's Supper' (1832) followed soon after by his personally life-altering letter of resignation to the Second Church in Boston – to a perception of the natural connectedness of things. His complaint over abiding by the ceremony of the Eucharist resists the privileging of origins in favour of the warranting of elective affinities. We should not presume to say how something began, and still less to derive authority from its antecedents. Instead we should say how we stand

in relation to the ritual, and rely on our own sense of what draws or repels us: 'If I believed [celebrating the Eucharist] was enjoined by Jesus on his disciples, and that he even contemplated making permanent this mode of commemoration, [...] and yet on trial it was disagreeable to my own feelings, I should not adopt it'.[40] Emerson writes of Jesus as a person and accordingly addresses him as one would a fellow man, and not as a mendicant at the feet of an indifferent deity: 'I will love him as a glorious friend, after the free way of friendship, and not pay him a stiff sign of respect, as men do those whom they fear'.[41] A few years later, when he writes in his first book *Nature* about his aspiration for human experience, he does not command us to seek origins but encourages the pursuit and possession of 'an original relation'.[42] Such a distinction reflects his understanding of the difference between feeling obliged to expiate our origins (be they from God or parent), and having the desire to express freely one's wonder about how one is tied into an astonishingly complex existential circumstance that does not yield an easy perception of cause or origin.

The exaltation Emerson feels standing before the Cabinets of Natural History in Paris reflects his awe in the face of specimens that resist a search for origins at every turn, but reinforce his perception of alliances that exist, undeniably, between him and the wider order of things:

> The universe is a more amazing puzzle than ever, as you glance along this bewildering series of animated forms, – the hazy butterflies, the carved shells, the birds, beasts, fishes, insects, snakes, and the upheaving principle of life everywhere incipient, in the very rock aping organized forms. Not a form so grotesque, so savage, nor so beautiful but is an expression of some property inherent in man the observer, – an occult relation between the very scorpions and man. I feel the centipede in me, – cayman, carp, eagle, and fox. I am moved by strange sympathies.[43]

We seem equipped, almost preternaturally, to inquire after origins, perhaps because we maintain a hunch that knowing how something came into being would mean knowing what something is. Emerson's revelation in Paris suggested that our primary interest should not be in things themselves, still less their origins, but in how they are related to one another. Our instinct to define a thing by means of its origins can be replaced by an interest in knowing what something is by reference to its context and connections – namely by studying the nature of the relationships that surround us in all directions. An elaborated project of 'a professor of the Joyous Science' – charged and charmed by his elective mission – would doubtless include the perception of all variations of the 'occult' encountered and pervading his work: the occult harmonies, sympathies, symmetries, powers, facts, mutual attractions, resemblances and relations.[44] The natural scientist of the intellect, then, is also intuitive – able, even eager, to avail himself of what is observable and yet may remain unseen by 'manipular attempts to control the world of thought', by a 'paltry empiricism'.[45]

Emerson's shift in consciousness – that would take him gradually from the fixed preacher's pulpit to the peripatetic and agnostic lecture circuit – was not a short-lived protest or a blunt experiment but a permanent transition that he tracked outwardly and inwardly for the rest of his intellectual life. As he toured the Cabinets of Natural

History on the eve of his thirtieth birthday, making notes toward a new model for his thinking, likewise some 40 years later, nearing 70 years old, preparing to embark on his final voyage to Europe (and his first to the Near East), he writes in his journal from Naushon Island:

> I thought today, in these rare seaside woods, that if absolute leisure were offered me, I should run to the College or the Scientific school which offered best lectures on Geology, chemistry, Minerals, Botany, & seek to make the alphabets of those sciences clear to me. How could leisure or labor be better employed. 'Tis never late to learn them, and every secret opened goes to authorize our aesthetics. Cato learned Greek at eighty years, but these are older bibles & oracles than Greek.[46]

For Emerson, apprehending the relations between things requires tremendous availability to the world of sensuous experience. One has to be in a position to be affected in order to see connections, to be 'moved by strange sympathies'.

> So the great man, that is, the man most imbued with the spirit of the time, is the impressionable man, – of a fibre irritable and delicate, like iodine to light. He feels the infinitesimal attractions. His mind is righter than others, because he yields to a current so feeble as can be felt only by a needle delicately poised.[47]

Being sensible to the presence of signs and sensations does not require direct apprehension but an awareness of oblique suggestions, often coded in analogies between mental and physical life, the human and non-human: As Emerson notes in 'Poetry and Imagination': 'A happy symbol is a sort of evidence that your thought is just. I had rather have a good symbol of my thought, or a good analogy, than the suffrage of Kant or Plato. If you agree with me, or if Locke or Montesquieu agree, I may yet be wrong; but if the elm-tree thinks the same thing, if running water, if burning coal, if crystals, if alkalies, in their several fashions say what I say, it must be true. Thus a good symbol is the best argument, and is a missionary to persuade thousands'.[48] Likewise, if linguistic expression would share the animating force of the figures it represents, it too must speak with images and signs, pictures and resemblances. Emerson continues in the same lecture:

> Conversation is not permitted without tropes; nothing but great weight in things can afford a quite literal speech. It is ever enlivened by inversion and trope. God himself does not speak prose, but communicates with us by hints, omens, inference and dark resemblances in objects lying all around us. [...] The impressions on the imagination make the great days of life: the book, the landscape or the personality which did not stay on the surface of the eye or ear but penetrated to the inward sense, agitates us, and is not forgotten. Walking, working or talking, the sole question is how many strokes are drawn quite through from matter to spirit; for whenever you enunciate a natural law you discover that you have enunciated a law of the mind.[49]

21.   In the years between studying at Harvard Divinity School and publishing *Nature* and reliably thereafter, Emerson read John F. W. Herschel's *A Preliminary Discourse on*

the Study of Natural Philosophy (1831) and confided in a letter to his brother, William: Herschel's 'General Nature and Advantages of the Study of the Physical Sciences' (the title of Part I of *A Preliminary Discourse*) is 'a noble work enough to tempt a man to leave all duties to find out natural science. When I am a man I will have an observatory & telescope & a laboratory'.[50] In *A Preliminary Discourse* Herschel develops a conception of inductive reasoning – the means and method by which one's experience of observable phenomena can become the basis for the development and defence of theory beyond the bounds of empirical record:

> [F]rom what has been said, it appears that induction may be carried on in two different ways, – either by the simple juxta-position and comparison of ascertained classes, and marking their agreements and disagreements; or by considering the individuals of a class, and casting about, as it were, to find in what particular they all agree, besides that which serves as their principle of classification. Either of these methods may be put in practice, as one or the other may afford facilities in any case; but it will naturally happen that, where facts are numerous, well observed, and methodically arranged, the former will be more applicable than in the contrary case: the one is better adapted to the maturity, the other to the infancy of science: the one employs, as an engine, the division of labor; the other mainly relies on individual penetration, and requires a union of many branches of knowledge in one person.[51]

Herschel's book appeared in *The Cabinet of Natural Philosophy* – part of a unique series with the parent name *The Cabinet Cyclopedia* (1829–1846) – edited or rather, as it says on a title page, 'conducted by' the Rev. Dionysius Lardner, LLD, FRS., L & E, MRIA, FLS, FZS, Hon FCPS, M Ast S & c & c. His titles alone form a collection for the cabinet! Lardner notes that he had help in his voluminous endeavour – that his series is 'Assisted by Eminent Literary and Scientific Men'. Herschel contributed his *Discourse* as one of the 133 volumes in the series. But there were also eminent women 'assisting' him. Mary Shelley, author of *Frankenstein* – a story about a monster who is himself a collection or cabinet composed of parts from other bodies – contributed five volumes of biographical writing to Lardner's *Cabinet*. Her contributions were entitled, following intimations of Plutarch and Vasari, *Lives of the Most Eminent Literary and Scientific Men*. She wrote about men from the fourteenth to the eighteenth centuries in Italy (two volumes), Spain and Portugal (one volume) and France (two volumes). Shelley's skill at fashioning the lives of these many dozens of men – installing them ably in Lardner's *Cabinet* – comes with her attendant innovation of feminist historiography. These are not, then, lives re-told but lives made anew in the eyes of a woman who possessed both the philosophical acumen and the literary finesse to give them life. In her hands, and from her perspective, these were not Frankenstein monsters but men given back to history after being transformed by a woman. In Shelley's assessment of their characters and characteristics these figures were restored to posture and poise.

22. Those who make the present world and its connections their business Emerson calls thinkers, or MAN THINKING. This office is distinguished from the work of

scholars. Thinkers 'live and act'; they are involved in the world; they develop a process not a system; they speak what they think instead of citing the authority of what others have thought; they do not seek origins as a means of explanation but use ordinary words to account for the world as they find it, or (in what may amount to the same thing) to propose a new vision of the world. For a thinker, every thing is present, is at hand and accessible, which is not to say that such availability makes for effortless articulation. Just the contrary – the appeal to origins is facile: history, books, names, and the authority of others excuse us from thinking. That is why Emerson admonishes us to 'speak in hard words'.[52] Hard in the double sense: words are hard to use, and hard to understand. And so we are not surprised to learn that thinking is 'the hardest task in the world'.[53]

> We must respect Fate as natural history, but there is more than natural history. For who and what is this criticism that pries into the matter? Man is not order of nature, sack and sack, belly and members, link in a chain, nor any ignominious baggage, but a stupendous antagonism, a dragging together of the poles of the Universe.[54]

We cannot know a thing by knowing how it was caused. Thinking then is a 'stupendous antagonism', an evolving perspicacity of the ways things are related to one another – as sibling phenomena, as neighbours.[55] More formally, we may simply call this investigation CRITICISM. Thinkers write, speak, and act in a way that creates by means of connections not causes; by relying on affiliations not origins. A created thing – whether it be a body or a book, something written in words or in the blood – will continually avail itself to our perception of its place in a system and so express the 'lively traits of criticism' that identify us, one from the other, even while binding us inexorably, one to the other.[56]

IV

The Cabman is Phrenologist So Far

Picture Thinking

1.   Human knowledge driven by sentimentality is precarious and vulnerable, and prone to obfuscation and distortion. Despite this danger, our metaphors continually reinforce the sentimentality of picture thinking. Picturing something can mean creating a limited impression of it – often static, linear and two-dimensional; this holds for linguistic inscriptions as well as photographs and drawings. The allure of pictures (as image or text) is regularly found in the stillness, composition and permanency they suggest to us as an alternative to the movement, disorientation, and ephemerality of the life that creates them. Books can outlast their authors. While we might use a picture to temporarily hold a thought, we more commonly allow the picture to absorb the thought – and to become its enduring representative. Not surprisingly we begin to think that we learn something from the picture itself instead of from the concept it was made to refer to. The picture becomes the world we think of when we think of the thing it represents. And there is a tendency – from the inked lines of handwritten correspondence to the faded snapshot and the home movie – to allow, indulge and encourage an emotional bond that stimulates our sentimentality about pictures, including the metaphors – or picture language – we use.

Our metaphors about origins, for example, are deeply imbued with nostalgia. In our pictures, purity has a high value. So does causelessness. And originlessness. As we think about birth and race our pictures reinforce habits that equate originality with goodness and purity with virtue. Purity is a metaphor – a picture that holds us captive, along with our metaphors of sin and origin. Yet we clarify our sense of discrepancy and confusion by drawing distinctions between pictures and things; for example, by noting that race is a metaphor, whereas species is a real, material fact. ENGLISH TRAITS are metaphors. They are culturally-, aesthetically-, temperamentally-inflected inventions. Such traits reflect beliefs and interpretations, not facts. With this in mind, we recognize how countries, peoples and individuals are ruled, guided and inspired by different metaphors. On this reading, PURE is not a scientific description or an empirical state of affairs; it is a philosophical, religious, literary and cultural metaphor. In other words, science does not say sin. For science, miscegenation is a metaphor because distinct races (of the same species) can procreate. The interest for science is not in keeping something pure, but in studying how breeding leads to mutations that, depending on conditions, thrive or perish. For science, power is generated by natural selection: through mixing and mutation species create new candidates who may excel or falter. But in philosophy and religion, power is generated by developing, defending or revising the definitions of metaphors. The blood is moral (ethics), beautiful (aesthetics), right (law), ordered (logic) and true (epistemology) – as a reflection of our pictures, and our respective esteem or denigration for them. The differences we see among races, cultures and countries accord with our generation of images – the pictures we create to formalize our ideas. Even geographies become iconographic, allowing and inviting us to equate a shape (e.g. the British Isles or the continental United States) with a people or an idea. As we are said to live in a post-national and post-racial age – when power can no longer be a matter of naturally occurring differences immanent within topography and blood – we are even more dependent on the way our ideas derive from our picturing of them, our figuration of them in language. Following this trajectory, our inheritance of metaphors suggests that it will continually be one of our greatest sources of power and also of conflict. Geographers and philosophers have debated the 'cognitive geometry of war', the way the physical shape of territories affects the fate of nations: a country's fortunes may rest, for example, with whether a border is 'bona fide' (a naturally occurring mountain range, river or sea) or imposed by fiat – such as with a negotiated or declared boundary between states.[1] Emerson writes, in 'Compensation', of the 'influences of climate and soil in political history'.[2] A militarily- or politically-sanctioned line can be argued over – fought over – in a way that the Andes and Alps, Rhine and Rio Grande cannot. The line or border is a picture – a cognitive affect – not an object; it is an idea that gives conceptual shape to nations, and thereafter contributes to the conditions of nationalism, for good or ill. Change the shape of a country and the idea of the nation also changes.

Correspondingly, if we esteem a picture of origins, this image necessarily implicates a demand to search for them; the search is apparently requisite, for when have origins been postulated that have not also, at the same time, been sought? Compelled by that need to search, a need we have invented it seems by picturing things, we seek or develop criteria for what something *is* in order to know what it means or how we should value it. Usually, quite clumsily, we use some physical thing (terrestrial features such as mountains and seas, skin colour, DNA) to define a metaphysical idea (nation, race, self) or a moral principle (freedom, equality, conscience). Metaphors comprise the liminal space of contact between idea and material fact. And as metaphors are structurally adaptable, ever changing according to context and description – caught up in the exigencies of moral, political, and philosophical debate – any pursuit of a final, fixed identity or essence for them is bound to involve a search for something that cannot be found. There are no origins for metaphors, only an endless series of histories, etymologies and explanations (such as we find in Nietzsche's 'On the Truth and Lies in a Nonmoral Sense'[3]). We call the gentleman Sir, and when he has a child, Sire.

2.   Often we use a group of metaphors to create stories and narratives. Depending on the selection, order and assigned emphasis of the pictures, the story can vary widely, be put to different, even competing purposes. The lesson can be turned from one side

to another, inverted. Perhaps we can see how conspiracy theory is a mode of using evidence (in the form of salient metaphors) to generate rogue histories in the empty spaces, ruptures and interruptions between things. Such theorizing about absences, in turn, leaves us worrying about how something was caused – where it began. When there is an apparent lack of connection between parts, the conspiracy theorist promotes an alternative account of facts and events that imposes a bond – something to satisfy a desire to perceive continuity and causation. Creating such theories or stories often requires eliding a premise or two, often leaving us – or rather prompting us – to fill in a conclusion that is merely implied.

Our thinking about origins – in philosophy, religion, politics, sometimes even science – is similar to theorizing conspiracies: we have a number of facts (that we are born, that we suffer, that we die), and then because we have so many pictures at our disposal, and are empowered to fashion more of them (cognitively, linguistically, imagistically), we create stories to explain or give meaning to the facts (e.g., by saying that we *have* an origin, that our suffering is a function of the *corrupted nature* of our origin, that we die because we are not able to *overcome* the nature of our origin).

3.   Wittgenstein, *Philosophical Investigations*

> A *picture* held us captive. And we could not get outside it, for it lay in our language and language seemed to repeat it to us inexorably.[4]

4.   Nietzsche ironically praised an advance in moral philosophy where, after thousands of years, 'it is no longer the consequences but the origin of an action that one allows to decide its value.'[5] The unnamed hero of the reversal is Immanuel Kant, who gave a definitive reason to believe that consequences conferred no moral value to an action. Despite the develoment, Nietzsche says, we became merely captivated by 'a calamitous new superstition': 'the origin of an action was interpreted in the most definite sense as the origin in an *intention*; one came to agree that the value of an action lay in the value of the intention'. Nietzsche points to the need for a further advance in values, namely, an advance to an 'extra-moral' understanding of action: 'After all, today at least we immoralists have the suspicion that the decisive value of an action lies precisely in what is *unintentional* in it'. One is tempted to gloss this by saying that the 'decisive value' of an action would lie, therefore, in what is *unoriginal* in it. Who then will assume the task of 'that long secret work which has been saved up for the finest and most honest, also the most malicious, consciences of today'? Namely, who will take up the work of defining value beyond 'the morality of intentions'? To move past intentions, though, one must revitalize – revaluate – what we mean by origins. While Kant's deontology shifted the onus of moral value from consequences to intentions, he still held fast to origins. The next moral philosophers will have to innovate new pictures for their thinking: either re-conceiving the meaning of origins (perhaps rendering them strictly figurative), or divorcing the concept once and for all from moral science.

Seeing Connections

5.   Emerson, *Journals*

> How much finer things are in composition than alone. 'Tis wise in man to make Cabinets.[6]

Things are better in composition, and combination, than alone because we see how they are related. Aspects dawn.

An alternative to the search for origins, with its attendant pursuit of criteria and essences, is the development of a perspective that enables us to SEE THINGS AS. In terms of ascription, we find what a thing means and how to value it based on how it is related to other things. The project involves a change in perception, attitude, approach, method and requires a non-reductive spirit of investigation.

Aspect seeing may be regarded as a kind of literary looking: observing the ways in which the world shifts before our eyes, resembles one thing then another.[7] The switch of aspects, then, does not correspond to an actual change in objects but registers one's inhabitation in the world of sign and symbol; as such these encounters do not reflect literal transformations but perceptual revisions – re-seeings – of phenomena. Seeing aspects is a process in which the terrestrial interacts with the cognitive terrain of accumulated metaphors. '[… W]e do not see directly, but mediately', writes Emerson, that is through the gauze of representation that *figures* reality – in the present study, metaphors – and enables its uncanny movements.[8]

The methods of philosophical investigation, then, would involve collecting, combining, comparing, arranging and cataloguing metaphors – in the tradition of the *florilegium* – in order to curate a cabinet: to see if new relations, new aspects dawn for our understanding. Perhaps the insight that comes to light reflects some new aspect of our condition, a condition that is so dependent on metaphors. Such work would always remain provisional, never reach some final state, never achieve the status of a theory; it would require an ongoing, vigilant practice of 'assembling reminders' in order to see how things are related, and how we use pictures for thinking.[9]

Event and Character

6.   As we experience the manner in which our physical constitution is continuous with mental experience and behaviour, it would seem our interior lives – thoughts, emotions, intentions – are evident on the very surface of our skin, in the squint of our eyes, in our posture. How we read each other with such facility! And at that 'the gross lines are legible to the dull: the cabman is phrenologist so far: he looks in your face to see if his shilling is sure'.[10] Does this reading cause us chagrin? Are deep forces and recessed features in fact that transparent? 'Does the reading of history make us fatalists? What courage does not the opposite opinion show! A little whim of will to be free gallantly contending against the universe of chemistry'.[11] What then is the

relationship between inner and outer lives, the silent coursings of the brain and the boisterous prating on the streets?

In 'Fate' (1860) Emerson lets his protracted reading of natural history come to the surface of his thinking about how a person experiences life – makes it, is made by it. As he says, the 'adaptation is not capricious' for 'the correlation by which planets subside and crystallize, then animate beasts and men, will not stop, but will work into finer particulars, and from finer to finest'.[12] In other words, no one gets out of here alive. Or rather living is a process of continual interaction of forces – sometimes appearing to create, other times to destroy. Here we find 'the secret of the world', 'the tie between person and event. Person makes event, and event person'.[13] As William James noted in 'The Present Dilemma in Philosophy', the initial lecture in *Pragmatism: A New Name for Some Old Ways of Thinking* (1907), there is an unwillingness – a seemingly conscious resistance atop a deeply unconscious aversion – to confirm the man and his peculiar temperament in the ideas he expresses:

> There arises thus a certain insincerity in our philosophical discussions: the potentest of all our premises is never mentioned. [...] What the system pretends to be is a picture of the great universe of God. What it is – and oh so flagrantly! – is the revelation of how intensely odd the personal flavor of some fellow creature is.[14]

Because of such 'insincerity' a man is befuddled by what seems the incongruity between his desires and his satisfactions, the inconsistency of his will applied to the world beyond him. Emerson reworks the logic of 'our philosophical discussions':

> He thinks his fate alien because the copula is hidden. But the soul contains the event that shall befall it, for the event is only the actualization of its thoughts; and what we pray to ourselves for is always granted. The event is the print of your form. It fits you like your skin. What each does is proper to him. Events are the children of his body and mind.[15]

In the epistle of Paul to the Galatians, we read about these 'children' – our deeds:

> Be not deceived; God is not mocked: for whatsoever a man soweth, that shall he also reap. For he that soweth to his flesh shall of the flesh reap corruption; but he that soweth to the Spirit shall of the Spirit reap life everlasting. And let us not be weary in well doing: for in due season we shall reap, if we faint not.[16]

The presumption here does not seem superstitious, but logical. And it is especially poignant that 'well doing' would exhaust us sufficiently to threaten our collapse. 'Nature magically suits the man to his fortunes, by making these the fruit of his character. [...] Events grow on the same stem with persons; are sub-persons'.[17] For this reason, 'a man will see his character emitted in the events that seem to meet, but which exude from and accompany him. Events expand with character'.[18] Events are the children of thought, as history is the 'action and reaction' of Nature and Thought.[19] Does Emerson give too much over to intention? Who can say what one precisely wants, much less claim credit for actualizing those desires? Emerson does not give anything, for it is already given: constitutionally, fatally. Intention is an epiphenomenon of the interaction between Nature and Thought. Our consciousness is a bystander to super-vening powers. If we are humbled by the news, we need not whimper and flee, but respect what right we do have: to look, to find the sublime contours of fit, and the unexpected correspondences that obtain in all directions.

> Hence in each town there is some man who is, in his brain and performance, an explanation of the tillage, production, factories, banks, churches, ways of living, and society, of that town. If you do not chance to meet him, all that you see will leave you a little puzzled: if you see him, it will become plain. We know in Massachusetts who built New Bedford, who built Lynn, Lowell, Lawrence, Clinton, Fitchburg, Holyoke, Portland, and many another noisy mart. Each of these men, if they were transparent, would seem to you not so much men, as walking cities, and, wherever you put them, they would build one. [...] What is the city in which we sit here, but an aggregate of incongruous materials, which have obeyed the will of some man?'[20]

The city is an artifact of the man and mind who built it, a text that lies before us, beneath the *flaneur's* feet, inviting a reading and a reception, as if the man himself had come for supper. Decades earlier, just returned from his inaugural trip to Europe and England, Emerson asked in his first book: 'What is a farm but a mute gospel?'[21] The soil and the brow's sweat are so many 'sacred emblems' that give call and cause for reading.[22] The farmer works the land with his hands so pervasively that his produce embodies his qualities as a man. We buy his beets and bread because we admire his posture, and the way he keeps his horses. With the cabman's glance, we look into his eyes and can taste the fresh corn.

7.   Emerson, 'Perpetual Forces' (1862)

> That band which ties [laws] together is unity, is universal good, saturating all with one being and aim, so that each translates the other, is only the same spirit applied to new departments. Things are saturated with the moral law. There is no escape from it. Violets and grass preach it; rain and snow, wind and tides, every change, every cause in Nature is nothing but a disguised missionary.[23]

8.   As fitness and finesse are reflected in the events we emanate, so are the defects. In 1824 Georg Möller published *An Essay on the Origin and Progress of Gothic Architecture Traced in and Deduced from the Ancient Edifices of Germany with References to Those of England* where, according to Emerson, he 'taught that the building which was fitted accurately to answer its end, would turn out to be beautiful, though beauty had not been intended'.[24] At the end of the nineteenth century, architect Louis Sullivan wrote *The Tall Office Building Artistically Considered* (1896) in which he echoed a sentiment of American sculptor Horatio Greenough (whom Emerson met in Florence in 1833), and sustained Möller's account with the terse phrase 'form ever follows function'. By the early twentieth century the original sense of the description was put to use by architectural and artistic modernists who concluded that it entailed the criminal

use of ornamentation. Sullivan's notion, like Greenough's and Emerson's, implies rather the elegance of a good fit. Ornament does not threaten; instead imbalance, the indecorous and the disjointed do. And in human affairs, the lack of fit – the maladaptation – candidly reveals one's own defects and liabilities. In the wake of Möller's essay, Emerson notes:

> I find the like unity in human structures rather virulent and pervasive; that a crudity in the blood will appear in the argument; a hump in the shoulder will appear in the speech and handiwork. If his mind could be seen, the hump would be seen. If a man has a seesaw in his voice, it will run into his sentences, into his poem, into the structure of his fable, into his speculation, into his charity. And as every man is hunted by his own daemon, vexed by his own disease, this checks all his activity.[25]

In the course of these proceedings, thus far and to come, I open the doors of some cabinets of natural history, explore the contents of drawers and vials, point to many pinned specimens, and try to present evidence that prompts us to take seriously the moral qualities of metaphors. We find these signs, symbols and emblems inherent in the language we speak and write, inescapable as the fate of human embodiment. Though we would work in vain to rid our language of these signs – a foolish errand since, as Nietzsche and others have reminded us, language itself is comprised of lively tropes – we should accept as compensation a perspicuous view of their shifting relationships. Not glad of the situation, we can at least be aware of it: 'If the Universe have these savage accidents, our atoms are as savage in resistance.'[26] As we learn in the laboratory: 'A tube made of a film of glass can resist the shock of the ocean, if filled with the same water.'[27] Language is malleable, seemingly endlessly convertible (a hint of the freedom it allows), and yet it is the soup and circumstance we inhabit, our 'limit' as Wittgenstein poetically observed. Hunted and vexed by our condition, Emerson suggests we are at last better for our perception of the translations and transmissions we manifest – in words, in pictures, in blood – many of them made more perspicuous by the symbols we employ to add grace and elegance to an otherwise cumbersome and tedious affair. Since 'relation and connection are not somewhere and sometimes, but everywhere and always', we are made to acknowledge them.[28] The examination of metaphors – as the site of those relations and connections – seems a fitting place to train our attention. If we are so many children of thought's universe, we are also ineluctably our own inheritance in blood and in language.

V

The Florilegium and the Cabinets of Natural History

1. Pliny the Elder, *Natural History* (c. 77–9 CE)

The nature of living creatures in the world is as important as the study of almost any other field, even though the human mind is not able to pursue all aspects of the subject. Pride of place will rightly be given to one for whose benefit Nature appears to have created everything else. Her very many gifts, however, are bestowed at a cruel price, so that we cannot confidently say whether she is a good parent to mankind or a harsh stepmother.[1]

2. Thomas Carlyle, *Sartor Resartus: The Life and Opinions of Herr Diogenes Teufelsdröckh* (1833–4)

More especially it may now be declared that Professor Teufelsdröckh's acquirements, patience of research, philosophic and even poetic vigor, are here made indisputably manifest; and unhappily no less his prolixity and tortuosity and manifold ineptitude; that, on the whole, as in opening new mine-shafts is not unreasonable, there is much rubbish in his Book, though likewise specimens of almost invaluable ore. A paramount popularity in England we cannot promise him. [...] Considered as an Author, Herr Teufelsdröckh has one scarcely pardonable fault, doubtless his worst: an almost total want of arrangement.[2]

3. Arthur Hugh Clough, Letter to Emerson (12 September 1856)

My dear Emerson,
    Your copy of the English Traits has just reached me – I am very glad to have it, for it is a far prettier book than Mr Routledge's – not to mention any other considerations. [...] I was not quite prepared [to] find your experiences defined into what may be called a series of lectures – but I do not know that I have to find any fault with the arrangement [...].[3]

4. Aristotle is known for developing the idea of the ENTHYMEME, which forms the core of his theory about rhetorical exposition. The basic idea being that the writer *leaves out* something crucial on the way to the conclusion he wishes his audience to arrive at; a crucial premise is intentionally, strategically, left unsaid. Surprisingly, the form is quite effective because it puts the pressure of interpretation on the reader, and

much less so on the writer (though the writer must have a skill for knowing what should remain unmentioned). The reader has the difficult task of discerning what is missing and understanding how that absence relates to the things that are said. (Emerson has written wistfully about a consequence of our Aristotelian legacy: 'There is something of poverty in our criticism. [...] 'Tis the good reader that makes the good book'.)[4] Sentences or propositions, which together participate to form arguments, in this view, can seem like puzzles, like flakes and fragments strewn about, lacking a coherent intimation of how they might, or do, go together. And even when there is a cursory sense of sequence there are often difficulties in making convincing connections among various and diverse parts.

English Traits is not organized around a central thesis. It proceeds as a series of comments on a range of sub-topics held together by reference to the title's main topic – as a melittologist comments on a genus through an analysis of a species of bees; or an arborist notes the attributes of fir specimens. The criticism in Emerson's book scales down further and further so that the paragraphs and sentences of a given chapter are coordinated and given direction, more or less, by reference to the chapter's title (a sub-topic) – as notes on bee wings or fir leaves are meant to add useful detail to an appreciation of the workings of their respective organisms, and the relationships between them. The smaller details are meant to inform in their own right, but also no doubt to shed light on the grander scheme. Given the complexity and reciprocity of such observations, there is often a great deal of movement between sentences – from one issue to another – and frequently an even greater degree of conceptual mobility from one paragraph to another. The prose therefore seldom reflects a desire to create a syllogism; that is, a form of deductive reasoning that requires a conclusion be reached based on the stated propositions or premises. As Aristotle says, the enthymeme differs from the dialectical syllogism 'for one must draw its conclusions from not too remote premises and not from all ones'.[5] The enthymemetic form of Emerson's prose suggests that connections can be made not just between the explicit statements at hand but also throughout the book, and beyond it. In other words, if something like a syllogism can be presented, it is something the reader will have to fashion from Emerson's sentences, and then go about defending on his or her own terms. As a collection of remarks, rather than an argument with rigidly defined conclusions, *English Traits* is more a point of departure for thinking about the topics and sub-topics Emerson addresses than a destination, a source of answers about them, or a set of rules for defining them. The book is a field guide scripted from first-hand observations, exploratory conversations, and extensive reading.

The sentences and paragraphs in *English Traits* can sometimes resemble a series of photographic snapshots or postcards – things that can be shuffled, with new narratives and accounts given each time, new things noticed, other things forgotten. One can, for example, imagine reading the chapters in reverse order, or simply out of order, without losing a sense of momentum; the energy of the prose moves in many directions without summoning competing or cancelling forces. Reading this way one is reminded that a photographic album, which seems to have the power of a coherent and chronological story, is only an assembly of fragments. The art – along with ideas and narratives

– becomes evident in the assembly; insight appears in the manner of apposition just as the impact of a given comment derives from its specific position in the series of other sentences. This is the suggestive power of montage, where what something is takes on new significance depending on what it is placed beside. Montage can announce itself as such, or may be fashioned to hide its fragmentary nature. A reader of books, as a moviegoer, is better entertained when he does not notice seams in the work; the goal of masterful Hollywood filmmaking is strictly devoted to this achievement, to making the signs of editing – signs of construction, interference, fabrication – disappear. But all works are aggregations with fissures and cracks, lesions and caesurae, ruptures and ellisions. Who makes the connections? What holds the estate of gathered ideas – sentences, film sequences – together? 'I know better than to claim any completeness for my picture', said Emerson of his writing, 'I am a fragment, and this is a fragment of me'.[6] The remark ranges over Emerson's work generally but seems especially apt for *English Traits* since the work is – however artfully and eloquently brought together – fundamentally a pastiche, a collage of myriad parts and portions. Even with the richness of Emerson's prose each element of it often appears to suggest what is not there – to reinforce the collection's incompleteness. Putting the animal's tooth on display only animates our sense of what is not presented: the rest of the body hovers ghostlike around the suggestive bicuspid. Emerson's awareness of lacunae and lapses, along with his appreciation for those intervals and absences, is shared by Aristotle in his cognisance of the conceptual effects of the enthymeme. From Emerson's understanding of the fragment, and Aristotle's of the enthymeme, one suspects that explanation is not, or is not wholly, logical, but psychological: human perception heals the spaces and distortions, as when the brain brings two inverted perceptions of the eyes together and upright to form a harmonious, three-dimensional semblance of what lies ahead.

5.   Emerson kept a journal that developed into an archive of notes, quotations and reflections. His first biographer, James Elliot Cabot said these notes formed mines in which Emerson 'quarried'. Emerson described the entries as his 'savings bank', which he would then draw from when he needed a line or passage for a lecture or essay. Searching through the extensive indices and cross-indices he had created for the journal, he would retrieve a parcel of prose from this or that volume. In this way, an essay became an association of disparate remarks written sometimes years apart, even at the remove of decades. If the essay felt coherent, if it appeared to lack seams and feature compatible tones of voice, then we can credit Emerson with a talent for soldering without detection. He was an exemplary editor. For *English Traits* Emerson used these familiar methods of cut and paste, borrow and blend, selection, revision and arrangement. The book is – by sentence, by paragraph, by chapter – a work of art and intellect formed from divergent sources. The constitution of the book illustrates its topic: by means of associating individually distinct elements – here sentences carry traits instead of blood, or we might say, convey the letters that comprise a kind of conceptual DNA – a body coalesces, the body of a book instead of a human body.

Emerson's curation of remarks in *English Traits* reveals a similarity to the way Ludwig Wittgenstein, in his *Philosophical Investigations*, spoke of writing a series of thoughts that should come together in a 'natural order', one subject leading to another, each question prompting a subsequent one. A sudden change in topic or direction, however, should not undermine the progression of ideas since such movement can be rhizomatic as well as linear; and so the philosopher gives credence to his own, and presumably his reader's, exploration away from an apparent order, origin, or pattern (hence the earlier notion that Emerson's fragments might find a new logic according to a different sequencing, very much like Wittgenstein's description of his work as an 'album'). In the *Philosophical Investigations* thoughts are held together by assignment number; and the sentences that fall under it often reflect Wittgenstein's wide-ranging philosophical interests, and his willingness to experiment with different points of view, frequently by virtue of introducing alternate voices into his text. The book is filled with more than the sound of Wittgenstein's narration; it contains a community of inquirers asking questions and offering replies; this multivocality gives the impression of many projects simultaneously underway. In his Preface to the work Wittgenstein said:

> I have written down all these thoughts as *remarks*, short paragraphs, of which there is sometimes a fairly long chain about the same subject, while I sometimes make a sudden change, jumping from one topic to another. [...] The essential thing was that the thoughts should proceed from one subject to another in a natural order and without breaks. [...]
>
> The same or almost the same points were always being approached afresh from different directions. [...] Thus this book is really only an album.[7]

Wittgenstein's says his remarks should proceed in a 'natural order', and elsewhere in the book he says 'What we are supplying are really remarks on the natural history of human beings; we are not contributing curiosities, however, but observations which no one has doubted, but which have escaped remark only because they are always before our eyes'.[8] Given the context – and his choice of metaphors – Wittgenstein is quick to point out (in case it was not already sufficiently obvious) that his remarks are not trivialities in a curiosity cabinet but part of the work philosophers do, namely, 'assembling reminders for a particular purpose'.[9] In what follows I will say more about how Wittgenstein's various descriptions of his work – as remarks, as an album, as a natural history of human beings, as a collection according with a natural order – may be pertinent to Emerson's *English Traits*, a book that should be included as part of Emerson's unfolding project, the NATURAL HISTORY OF INTELLECT.

6.   In the summer of 1833, while travelling alone in Paris, Emerson visited the Muséum National d'Histoire Naturelle and the specimen collections at the Jardin des Plantes. It was a transformative experience for the 30-year-old widower and ex-minister. Reflecting on his time there he confided to his journal a new sense of perspective and enthusiasm:

> The limits of the possible are enlarged, & the real is stranger than the imaginary. [...] Here we are impressed with the inexhaustible riches of nature. The Universe is a more amazing puzzle than ever as you glance along this bewildering series of

animate forms. [...] I am moved by strange sympathies, I say continually 'I will be a naturalist'.[10]

Emerson followed his nascent desire, only he pursued it the way a man trained in theology and the history of philosophy would do so, by proposing what he called a 'natural history of intellect'. This project began at once and in earnest upon his return to American with lectures such as 'The Uses of Natural History' (1833–5), 'Humanity of Science' (1836–48), the book *Nature* (1836), and then continued steadily in his wide-ranging, multi-disciplinary investigations for the remainder of his intellectual life, culminating nearly four decades after the visit to the Jardin in his Harvard lectures of 1871 on the 'Natural History of Intellect'.

In the essay 'Intellect' (1844) Emerson describes the eponymous term as that which 'lies behind genius, which is intellect constructive', as 'the simple power anterior to all action or construction'.[11] The intellect is a raw force – 'spontaneous in every expansion' – so it is by means of genius, or the conscious mind, that we begin to account for our human experiences. A natural history of intellect then would involve understanding how the mind is constructive, for example, how it organizes experience according to topics, or as Immanuel Kant had earlier suggested in the *Critique of Pure Reason*, categories.

While in London in 1848 Emerson delivered a series of lectures entitled *Mind and Manners of the Nineteenth Century*. The title of the lecture series refracts *Men and Manners in America* (1833), a work by Emerson's friend Thomas Hamilton (brother of the Sir William Hamilton mentioned in 'Experience'), a work of criticism by a Scotsman who visited America. Hamilton, who is depicted in the first chapter of *English Traits* as having harsh things to say about American journalists and congressmen alike, composed this two-volume work as a frank narrative, regularly taking pains to describe some aspect of the 'misery' of travelling in America in 1830.[12] A self-proclaimed man of 'pure breeding', Hamilton – born in Italy and educated in Scotland – is scandalized by the democratic nature of the country and the hypocrisy it manifests: 'There is a large body of landed proprietors, who are men of education and comparative refinement; and who, though publicly advocating the broadest principles of democracy, are in private life aristocratic and exclusive. Like the Virginians, they are of blood purely English, and disposed to relinquish no claim, which a descent from several generations of respectable ancestors can be understood to confer'.[13] Hamilton's partiality – his preference for English men and manners – announces itself in the temper of his often-caustic appraisal of the young democracy. Hamilton's travelogue suggests the perhaps unconscious way in which a writer may assume, even enmesh, the identity of a nation with his own private constitution. Such self-appointed representative force – where, for example, a critic that sets out to speak as an Englishman ends up speaking for England – complicates ethnographic literature. In *Mind and Manners of the Nineteenth Century*, Emerson, unlike Hamilton, has digested his experience of nationalities and races, customs and countenances, to make room for a different sort of registration of traits. Variation is not a point of irritation for Emerson but of interest – and admiration. And the radical contrasts and convergences made evident by first-hand transatlantic experience become the conditions for critical assessment of the wider innovations of nineteenth century thinking. And so from the particularities of Hamilton's itinerary we move to the inaugural essay of Emerson's lectures series, 'The Powers and Laws of Thought'.

Back in America Emerson used a revised version of the essay to lead off a new series entitled 'Laws of the Intellect'. And a year after that Emerson revised the essay once again, and with that new version concluded a series he called 'Natural History of Intellect'. Emerson was deeply invested in this lecture, as testified by his attentive and ongoing revisions, but it is the tone of the essay that reveals just how close this material is to the core of his thinking. Emerson sounds like he did years earlier, during his formative encounter with the leading edge of natural science in Paris: enlivened by a perception of unity pervading mental, moral and material phenomena, inspired by the idea of applying natural history to a philosophy of mind, and stimulated by the emerging community of scientists at work on new models for understanding the world. Listening to 'Richard Owen's masterly enumeration of the parts and laws of the human body, or Michael Faraday's explanation of magnetic powers, or the botantist's description', Emerson thought: 'could not a similar enumeration be made of the laws and powers of the Intellect [...]? Why not? These powers and laws are also facts in Natural History'.[14]

Emerson wanted to be a naturalist – metaphorically or analogically. His intimate and transfiguring hours at the Jardin des Plantes led him to wonder whether there was a continuum between the world of animals, plants and physical forces and the world of thought. Should not mind come under the laws that govern the world? If so, is not the philosopher at work on the same project as the botantist, biologist, geologist, chemist, physicist and physiologist? A continuity appeared to Emerson between these fields of inquiry – and prevailed in shaping his work as a natural scientist of intellect: he was, like Wittgenstein, offering 'remarks on the natural history of human beings', remarks that should follow a 'natural order'. And like Wittgenstein, Emerson did not propose theses but instead assembled 'reminders' – often of what lay before our eyes and yet remained unseen.[15]

7. Wittgenstein said that his collected remarks known as the *Philosophical Investigations* should be treated as an 'album' of 'sketches'.[16] In tandem the metaphors connote an idea of a keeping a register or log-book such as a natural scientist might keep when making observations in the field; and creating or keeping an album also alludes to a practice of collection, arrangement and editorial commentary. Because Wittgenstein emphasized that his remarks are part of a natural history and follow a natural order, we are not at risk for misconstruing 'album' to mean a haphazard collection of fragments put together in a random order. Wittgenstein related in the preface that he wanted to write a book but 'my thoughts were soon crippled if I tried to force them on in any single direction against their natural inclination'. So the *Philosophical Investigations* is an album where the contestedly fragmentary nature of the work is countered by the author's belief that he has arranged his thoughts in a special order, or more precisely that the thoughts have arranged themselves according

to 'their natural inclination' – compelling readers 'to travel over a wide field of thought' and 'criss-cross in every direction'.[17] Wittgenstein did not intend for the book to 'spare other people the trouble of thinking' but hoped rather it would 'stimulate someone to thoughts of his own'.[18] We are left to wonder the degree to which the arrangement of his remarks – the natural order in which he placed them – affected the chances for his readers to be productively agitated and unsettled by his sketches.

Epigrammatic sentences and numbered paragraphs, such as those contained in the *Philosophical Investigations*, are not novelties of twentieth century philosophy. The art of collecting remarks, if not always according to a natural order or inclination, reaches back to antiquity. Some of the fragmentary nature of work by Heraclitus is due simply to the suspected loss of material, but with writers such as Diogenes Laertius or Seneca, and later Epictetus and Marcus Aurelius, there is sufficient extant work for us to see that the writers meant to collect fragments into books or albums.[19] And there are many thinkers between Aurelius and Wittgenstein who adopted the form – among them Montaigne, Burton, Bacon, Pascal, Emerson, of course, and Nietzsche. More recently Barthes, Blanchot, Adorno and Baudrillard continued in this vein of creating books as collections of remarks, quotations, letters, notes, apothegms and essays.

8.   In 1647 the English poet Christopher Harvey wrote *The Synagogue, or, the Shadow of the Temple* in which he spoke of 'the florilegia of celestiall storyes'. A *florilegium* is a compound word derived from flower (*flos*) and the Latin root for gathering or collecting (*legere*); it is a literal rendering of the Greek word for ANTHOLOGY (*anthos* meaning flower; ἄνθος). The word can refer, quite literally, to a 'collection of flowers', such as a botanist might compile; but in the eighteenth century it became understood to mean a collection of the 'flowers of literature'. In this way, the anthology of literature was a kind of bouquet, a gathering of the finest specimens from the field. When Emerson compiled a book of poems entitled *Parnassus* (1875), giving his book the name of the famed Greek mountain home to poetry and literature, he acted as an anthologist and created a florilegy; he proclaimed his ambition to collect 'gems of pure lustre' that are often left out of the best of comparable volumes. Many of these 'voluminous octovos', he noted, 'have the same fault of too much mass and too little genius'.[20] It could be said that Wittgenstein's book is also a florilegy since he himself describes it as the 'precipitate of philosophical investigations which have occupied me for the last sixteen years'. Wittgenstein does not claim that he has gathered the finest versions of his thoughts, just ones that are 'tolerable' and not 'badly drawn'.[21] Emerson said of his own 'album', created from many years of jottings: 'I am aware that no two readers would make the same selection'.[22] And so, paradoxically, any album-maker and florilegist will have to consider how much value is contributed to a final collection by what is intentionally left out of it.

When Emerson visited the Muséum National d'Histoire Naturelle he was peering into multiple and richly populated Cabinets of Natural History. Each large case was filled with carefully preserved and displayed specimens from around the world – insects, fish, mammals, plants and fossils of extinct species. Like a manifest – a comprehensive document of a ship's contents – each cabinet contained representatives of a genus or species that was labelled with a tag to announce what category the specimen belonged to, where it originated from, what traits defined and distinguished it. This kind of scientific labelling privileges the importance of identity, source and relationship. When reading a book instead of a taxonomical label, we are still met with a desire for footnotes and bibliographies – a wish that reflects a reader's interest in the identity and source of the thoughts, or what is said – or supposed – to have influenced the thoughts. These kinds of notes, we presume, record the origins and development of a scholar's thinking. Often however the link between a source text and a commentary is missing or mysterious; as readers we may simply not be able to discern how a writer moved from a source to its purported effects; likewise, even a writer may be unable to testify to the pedigree of his or her prose – the sites and sources of influence may fade while their results remain observable, identifiable and tangible in writing. Sometimes though explanatory and bibliographic annotations function similarly to the labels and notes in the Cabinet of Natural History: they orient us to a more specific text or context. And while the footnote or label may suggest where something is from or how it evolved, putting many specimens together – in composition – may yield the best chances for investigative insight. A linear map of a species' evolution – from this earlier form of life to that latter incarnation – may not be nearly as interesting as a holistic map of many contemporaneous species brought into concert. In Emerson's day the emerging field of comparative anatomy was based on this premise. In his journal, on one of his visits to the collection, Emerson wrote: 'How much finer things are in composition than alone. 'Tis wise in man to make Cabinets'.[23] It is not just labelling an item (giving a manifest of its origins and pedigree) that orients us, but also the way items are collected and arranged. What gets selected? How is it placed in relation to some other constituent? Why is this specimen placed next to that one? What more or less can be said about how that relationship affects all the various elements under consideration – for example, does it inadvertently or propitiously emphasize what was absented? How can the fragments that are featured be held together by means of an organizing principle, category of experience or common trait? These are questions asked by anyone who is involved in creating albums, among them the anthologist, archivist, collector, cataloguer, curator, editor, librarian, biologist, anatomist, florilegist and philosopher.

9.   The anthologist's work is formidable and no less than Robert Burton – whose *The Anatomy of Melancholy* may be regarded as one of the most exhaustive, learned and interpolated florilegy ever composed – wrote with hope that the 'flowers' he had selected would suffice: 'I have done my endeavour. Besides, I dwell not in this study, *Non his sulcos ducimus, non hoc pulvere desudamus*, [I am not driving a furrow here, this is not my field of labor], I am but a smatterer, I confess, a stranger, here and there I pull a flower; I do easily grant, if a rigid censurer should criticise on this which I have writ, he should not find three sole faults [...] but three hundred'.[24] 'As a good housewife', Burton writes:

> [...] out of divers fleeces weaves one piece of cloth, a bee gathers wax and honey
> out of many flowers, and makes a new bundle of all, *Floriferis ut apes in saltibus*

omnia libani [as bees in flowery glades sip from each cup], I have laboriously collected this cento out of divers writers. [...] I cite and quote mine authors [...]; and what Varro, *lib. 3 de re rust.*, speaks of bees, *minime maleficæ nullius opus vellicantes faciunt deterius* [they do little harm, and damage no one in extracting honey], I can say of myself, Whom have I injured? The matter is theirs most part, and yet mine, *apparet unde sumptum sit* [it is plain whence it was taken] (which Seneca approves), *aliud tamen quam unde sumptum sit apparet*, [yet it becomes something different in its new setting].[25]

Burton's relation to texts written by others, like a bee to a flower's pollen and nectar, requires that he 'incorporate, digest, and assimilate' what he reads. As Augustine drew nutriment from scripture, so Burton says: 'I do *concoquere quod hausi* [assimilate what I have swallowed]'.[26] For the florilegist then a source text is transformed by what is extracted from it; subsequently the adapted or converted material may be of further interest in how it is arranged in some new context, placed alongside some other specimen. Burton nonironically quotes from others to describe what he brings to the creation of a collection: 'I make them pay tribute to set out this my *Macaronicon*, the method only is mine own; I must usurp that of Wecker *e Ter., nihil dictum quod non dictum prius, methodus sola artificem ostendit*, we can say nothing but what has been said, the composition and method is ours only, and shows a scholar'.[27] As it was for Emerson standing before the cabinets in Paris, so it is for Burton in his Oxford libraries: the work of composition is the heart of the endeavour.

As Burton describes his scholarship as an art drawn from 'that which I have stolen from others, *Dicitque mihi mea pagina, fur es* [my page cries out to me, You are a thief], he postulates that this stealing, this kind of selection, is generative: 'As apothecaries we make new mixtures every day, pour out of one vessel into another; [...] we skim off the cream of other men's wits, pick the choice flowers of their tilled gardens to set out our own sterile plots'.[28] When considering Plato's outsized influence on the history of philosophy, Emerson underscores how Plato may have been better than others in masking, making anonymous or otherwise internalizing his sources, since we are in the habit of attributing his ideas to him and not to those from whom he read.[29] Burton, by contrast, makes the citation of his authors and sources a principal methodological feature of his *Macaronicon* – a repetition of acknowledgment to others that we can read as a sign of his humility as a CREATOR and his indifference to the accumulation of literary celebrity. While Plato makes 'great havoc [...] among our originalities', Emerson says we should remember that 'the inventor only knows how to borrow;'

And society is glad to forget the innumerable laborers who ministered to this architect, and reserves all its gratitude for him. When we are praising Plato, it seems we are praising quotations from Solon, and Sophron, and Philolaus. Be it so. Every book is a quotation; and every house is a quotation out of all forests, and mines, and stone quarries; and every man is a quotation from all his ancestors. And this grasping inventor puts all nations under contribution.[30]

Looking back to the lines quoted above from Wittgenstein, now in the light of Burton, Emerson and Plato, et al., we find that the florilegist is involved in – perhaps unintentionally caught up in – the project of supplying 'remarks on the natural history of human beings'.[31] These are not 'curiosities' – such as one might place in a carefully arranged cabinet only then to be ignored or lost sight of – but 'observations which no one has doubted', observations that have 'escaped remark only because they are always before our eyes'.[32] Remarks, in this mood, are reminders – *hypomnemata* (υπομνηματα) – that continually need to be said, extracted, re-placed and read again.[33] We do not measure the anthologist's talent by the degree to which he writes new prose but by the artistry and insight he makes evident through his selection and placement of existing materials, and his commentary on them. The new work stands as a natural history of the florilegist's personal history of incorporation, digestion and assimilation. Like the bee's labour, this scholarly work should yield some testament full of flavour and use – a sweet and serviceable product. In reading a *florilegium* – from *The Anatomy of Melancholy* to *English Traits* to the *Philosophical Investigations* – readers want to know what the author sought to remind them of: especially those elements that we are continuously faced with but fail to see.

10.   Emerson once wrote despairingly in his journal that 'facts in thousands of the most interesting character are slipping by me every day unobserved, for I see not their bearing, I see not their connexion, I see not what they prove. By & by I shall mourn in ashes their irreparable loss'.[34] In *Biographia Literaria* Coleridge wrote: 'I began to ask myself; is a system of philosophy, as different from mere history and historic classification, possible? If possible, what are its necessary conditions? I was for a while disposed to answer the first question in the negative, and to admit that the sole practicable employment for the human mind was to observe, to collect, and to classify'.[35] Philosophy in this Coleridgean mode would be conducted as a kind natural scientific enterprise – stemming Emerson's fear of remaining insensible to the 'connexion' between things, and motivated by description rather than explanation, arrangement rather than speculative judgement. Philosophy would be a curatorial activity: sorting, sifting, above all, as Ray Monk has said of the proper work of philosophical biography, and what Wittgenstein describes for his own work, finding conditions for 'the understanding that consists in seeing connections' – and in seeing those connections clearly. Monk notes: 'this is explicitly contrasted with *theoretical* understanding'. Motivated by this spirit, Monk describes how 'the form Wittgenstein's later work takes is not to advance a thesis and then to defend it against possible objections, but rather to say, 'Look at things this way'.[36]

Yet for Coleridge a danger lurks in the misapplication of his intuition about philosophical enterprise. As he writes a few chapters later, 'the worst and widest impediment still remains'.

> It is the predominance of a popular philosophy, at once the counterfeit and the mortal enemy of all true and manly metaphysical research. It is that corruption, introduced by certain immethodical aphorising eclectics, who, dismissing not

only all system, but all logical connection, pick and choose whatever is most plausible and showy; who select, whatever words can have some semblance of sense attached to them without the least expenditure of thought; in short whatever may enable men to talk of what they do not understand, with a careful avoidance of every thing that might awaken them to a moment's suspicion of their ignorance. This alas! is an irremediable disease, for it brings with it, not so much an indisposition to any particular system, but an utter loss of taste and faculty for all system and for all philosophy. Like echoes that beget each other amongst the mountains, the praise or blame of such men rolls in volleys long after the report from the original blunderbuss.[37]

The author of the present work (or a text similarly constructed) will surely wonder whether the fragments gathered between its covers confirm him to be an 'immethodical aphorisming eclectic'. Yet it should not be a protest to suggest the presence of system and logical connection in the manner of selection and arrangement. (Or perhaps it would serve better to say, as Wittgenstein did, that a certain 'natural order' obtains from the 'natural inclination' of the selections – 'my thoughts were soon crippled if I tried to force them on in any single direction against their natural inclination'.[38]) If one adopts an inductive methodology the approach is no less honest in its aspiration for insight. The assembled entries should of their own power commend reasons to take them seriously as the connections between them prompt readerly reflection. By their very association the remarks eschew one's fear that they are incidental and contingent – mere 'curiosities'; they earn their own credibility through a palpable relational energy – as if the force of magnetisms were generated by proximity, which they are; as if repulsions become pronounced for intimacy, which they must. These remarks are attracted to one another! They announce their natural affinities. If by chance a specimen remains singular, aloof, unmoved, such a one may yet prompt reflection for its lack of fit, its failure to stir.

11.   Melville, *Moby-Dick*, EXTRACTS (Supplied by a Sub-Sub-Librarian)

It will be seen that this mere painstaking burrower and grub-worm of a poor devil of a Sub-Sub appears to have gone through the long Vaticans and street-stalls of the earth, picking up whatever random allusions to whales he could anyways find in any book whatsoever, sacred or profane. Therefore you must not, in every case at least, take the higgledy-piggledy whale statements, however authentic, in these extracts, for veritable gospel cetology. Far from it. As touching the ancient authors generally, as well as the poets here appearing, these extracts are solely valuable or entertaining, as affording a glancing bird's eye view of what has been promiscuously said, thought, fancied, and sung of Leviathan, by many nations and generations, including our own.

So fare thee well, poor devil of a Sub-Sub, whose commentator I am. Thou belongest to that hopeless, sallow tribe which no wine of this world will ever warm; and for whom even Pale Sherry would be too rosy-strong; but with whom one sometimes loves to sit, and feel poor-devilish, too; and grow convivial upon tears;

and say to them bluntly, with full eyes and empty glasses, and in not altogether unpleasant sadness – Give it up, Sub-Subs! For by how much more pains ye take to please the world, by so much the more shall ye for ever go thankless! Would that I could clear out Hampton Court and the Tuileries for ye! But gulp down your tears and hie aloft to the royal-mast with your hearts; for your friends who have gone before are clearing out the seven-storied heavens, and making refugees of long pampered Gabriel, Michael, and Raphael, against your coming. Here ye strike but splintered hearts together – there, ye shall strike unsplinterable glasses![39]

Within 200 words of the commencement of Herman Melville's *Moby-Dick; or, The Whale* the reader encounters a veritable library of 'extracts' on the whale. Running briskly from Genesis to Darwin's *Voyage of a Naturalist* with stops in Montaigne's *Apology for Raimond Sebond*, *Hamlet* and Bunyan's *The Pilgrim's Progress*, the narrator warns the reader that he must 'not, in every case at least, take the higgledy-piggledy whale statements, however authentic, in these extracts, for veritable gospel cetology'. The reader of the present volume – defined as it is by a healthy compendium of extracts – should likewise proceed without the presumption of receiving a gospel on metaphor or the uses of metaphor in Emerson and other authors. Rather, as a kind of Sub-Sub librarian with a philosophical bent, my work is akin to the florilegist's who collates, combines, collects and composes according to the features, patterns and affinities that seem apparent yet can hardly be claimed definitive. By the evidence of this presentation can I displace the notion that I am a 'mere painstaking burrower and grub-worm of a poor devil of a Sub-Sub' who 'appears to have gone through the long Vaticans and street-stalls of the earth, picking up whatever random allusions to whales' – in this case metaphors of a certain kind – 'he could anyways find in any book whatsoever, sacred or profane'? While it may be true that I belong to a 'hopeless, sallow tribe', that by 'how much more pains ye take to please the world, by so much the more shall ye for ever go thankless!', I have laboured to make the allusions coalesce, to give the extracts a sense of sequentiality (and consequentiality), at times a logic even, and to that end to create for the reader an experience that is not at all 'random' but quite studied and deliberate – as if an effect of (in Wittgenstein's terms) a 'natural order' or 'natural inclination'. While I should wish these extracts are 'valuable or entertaining', I also do hope – countering the anonymous, disparaging commentary on the appointed author, his tribe, and perhaps himself – that the proffered *florilegium* affords more than 'a glancing bird's eye view of what has been promiscuously said, thought, fancied, and sung of' metaphors 'by many nations and generations, including our own'. I have the ambition, perhaps necessary for any Sub-Sub of a phlegmatic disposition – who aspires to the truths of the melancholic – that the collection, for all its odds and ends, nevertheless coheres and issues forth satisfactions.

12.   Antedating Christopher Harvey's work by a few centuries was the fourteenth-century book-form known as *zibaldone*, or 'hodgepodge book'. The *zibaldone* was written in a vernacular language, and was said – by one of its most celebrated creators, Giovanni Rucellai – to be 'a salad of many herbs'.[40] The paleographer Armando

Petrucci has accounted for the 'astonishing variety of poetic and prose texts' contained in the *zibaldone*.[41] Written in cursive script, the *zibaldone* contained literary texts as well as devotional, technical and documentary writing, often mixed together without a pre-established plan or set of categories. Passages from Dante Alighieri, Francesco Petrarca (Petrarch) and Giovanni Boccaccio – the primary sources of Florentine vernacular prose and poetry – would be pushed up against a list of fiscal accounts, information about the currency markets, tables of weights and measures, laws and legal formulas, abstracts of important arguments, reference materials, proverbs, prayers, local remedies for medical ailments, culinary recipes and include drawings and sketches. A salad is a very different sort of collection than a cabinet, and among the innovations of the *zibaldone* – reflecting the wider availability of paper – is the very practice of binding together a mixed collection of disparate kinds of knowledge and information. The *zibaldone* brings to light the emerging potential of books to collect miscellany and hints at the nascent science of encyclopedia-making, a tradition that becomes increasingly ordered, rigorous and systematic – and which arguably achieves its printed apotheosis in Diderot and D'Alembert's eighteenth-century *Encyclopédie* (1751–72), the first full title of which read:

> *Encyclopédie, ou Dictionnaire raisonné des sciences, des arts et des métiers, par une société de gens de lettres, mis en ordre par M. Diderot de l'Académie des Sciences et Belles-Lettres de Prusse, et quant à la partie mathématique, par M. d'Alembert de l'Académie royale des Sciences de Paris, de celle de Prusse et de la Société royale de Londres* [Encyclopedia: or a Systematic Dictionary of the Sciences, Arts, and Crafts, by a Company of Men of Letters, arranged by M. Diderot of the Academy of Sciences and Belles-lettres of Prussia: as to the Mathematical Portion, arranged by M. d'Alembert of the Royal Academy of Sciences of Paris, to the Academy of Sciences in Prussia and to the Royal Society of London].

13.   The *zibaldone* and *florilegium* lead to another touchstone in the development of forms that aggregate literary flowers or herbs: the so-called COMMONPLACE BOOK. Commonplace in this context does not mean ordinary, but derives from the Latin *locus communis* and the Greek τόποσ κοινόσ (*topos koinos*). The book in this sense was a common or shared space in which to collect a variety of texts. The form was widely adopted in the seventeenth century and the methodology for keeping and reading commonplace books became part of the curriculum at Oxford. As D. Graham Burnett writes of the phenomenon: 'It hails from a world that still recognized 'commonplace' as a common verb, and meant by it the act of reading for, pulling out, copying down and endlessly managing the best bits of all one's books. [...] This body of practices – techniques for indexing, strategies for note taking, mechanisms for the maintenance of prosthetic memories [...] amounted to an elaborate tactical convergence between the art of reading and the art of writing.'[42]

When John Locke published *An Essay Concerning Human Understanding* (1690), he added his notes on strategies for indexing entries in commonplace books, thereby shifting the nature of these collections away from mere aggregating or listing and toward the explication of thematic design – the latter being especially advantageous when seeking to efficiently retrieve the passages one desires on a specific topic. In *Letters on Study*, Locke remarked:

> Nothing can contribute more to obviate the inconvenience and difficulties attending a vacant or wandering mind, than the arrangement and regular disposal of our thoughts in a well ordered and copious Common Place-Book; which, by readily suggesting a number and variety of pertinent ideas on every interesting occasion, must operate to banish or suppress such intruding notions as are foreign to the purpose, and to fix the attention on the desired object of contemplation.[43]

Other writers who were dedicated to the practice of commonplacing, as it was called, yet applied a range of methods and styles to their particular practice of the art, include Montaigne, Bacon (who titled his book of private notes, *The Promus of Formularies and Elegancies*, c. 1594), Milton, Coleridge, Thomas Hardy, Mark Twain and E. M. Forster. Thomas Jefferson, who kept both literary (1762–7) and legal (1758–72) commonplace books of his own, consulted Sir John Randolph's commonplace book published in London entitled *A Brief Method of the Law, Being an Exact Alphabetical Disposition of All the Heads Necessary for a Perfect Common-Place. Useful to all Students and Professors of the Law; Much Wanted, and Earnestly Desired* (1680).

At Harvard in the early nineteenth century it was common to learn commonplacing methods, and both Emerson and Thoreau were avid users of the form. Emerson began keeping a private journal while still a student at Harvard, and these earliest volumes bear a strong resemblance to commonplace books, filled as they were with a range of materials – not just personal reflections, but treasured quotations, drawings in his own hand, and miscellaneous gleanings from other texts. As Emerson continued to keep a journal into maturity, the sophistication of his indexing methods kept apace. By the time he was writing his public essays and lectures, he was continually mining his journals for passages. To find the passages, Emerson employed a highly complicated conceptual indexing scheme that involved cross-referencing. When he wanted to locate passages he had written on a designated topic – again, thinking back to the origins of this practice in finding a common place, *locus communis*, or τόποσ κοινόσ – Emerson would consult the index that would in turn lead him to the appropriate location. The rigor and elegance of his system functioned as a self-created, highly customized concordance, which enabled rapid access to sources that stimulated, reinforced or inspired writing – sources that could have eluded reclamation at a crucial moment of composition, been easily lost or otherwise obscured by poor organization. In Emerson's hands, the highly orchestrated and arranged commonplace book is very far from the *zibaldone's* mixed salad.

In 1845 Emerson wrote in his journal about the difference between the mere custody of information and the agitating promise of catching sight of its auspicious relationships: 'For the best part, I repeat, of every mind is not that which he knows, but that which hovers in gleams, suggestions, tantalizingly unpossessed before him. His firm recorded knowledge soon loses all interest for him. But this dancing chorus of thoughts & hopes is the quarry of his future, is his possibility [...]'.[44] The commonplace book, for Emerson, then, is not a repository of finished thoughts, whether his own or others', but an atmosphere in which to think. Possessing an idea does not come from jotting it down under some heading but from perceiving its connection to other terms and fields, concepts and features – and by means of that perspicuity, going on from it – for 'it is not instruction, but provocation, that I can receive from another soul'.[45]

14.   Michael Ondaatje, *The English Patient*

Hana listened as the Englishman turned the pages of his commonplace book and read the information glued in from other books – about great maps lost in the bonfires and the burning of Plato's statue, whose marble exfoliated in the heat, the cracks across wisdom like precise reports across the valley as Poliziano stood on the grass hills smelling the future. [...]

Now, months later in the Villa San Girolamo, in the hill town north of Florence, in the arbour room that is his bedroom, he reposes like the sculpture of the dead knight in Ravenna. He speaks in fragments about oasis towns, the later Medicis, the prose style of Kipling, the woman who bit into his flesh. And in his commonplace book, his 1890 edition of Herodotus' *Histories*, are other fragments – maps, diary entries, writing in many languages, paragraphs cut out of other books. All that is missing is his own name. There is still no clue to who he actually is, nameless, without rank or battalion or squadron. The references in his book are all pre-war, the deserts of Egypt and Libya in the 1930s, interspersed with references to cave art or gallery art or journal notes in his own small handwriting.[46]

In the 1890 edition of the *Histories* that the nameless and amnesiac Count Almásy uses as a commonplace book, we find that Herodotus himself seems to describe his mission and his art as motivated by a desire to remember, written in the third person:

This is the Showing forth of the Inquiry of Herodotus of Halicarnassos, to the end that neither the deeds of men may be forgotten by lapse of time, nor the works great and marvelous, which have been produced some by Hellens and some by Barbarians, may lose their renown; and especially that the causes may be remembered for which these waged war with one another.[47]

15.   The commonplace books were an important repository for individual learning since they both registered personal tastes in literature and ideas, and also served as an aid to the memory of what was collected. Sir John Randolph begins his commonplace book with a preface 'To the Reader' that aligns the practice with mnemonics and the preservation of memory:

How absolutely necessary, and of what great use and benefit a COMMONPLACE is in all Sciences whatsoever, there is none that does pretend to any Study or Letters, but sufficiently knows: and how many have made it their particular Business to give us Tractates and Books of Directions only for it, in every Science, is a clear Indication. That no great matters can be done without it. It is impossible to bear all one reads in the Head, without having one thing to justle out another; and we have not always the command of our Memory, when most we stand in need of its assistance, it is treacherous, and very apt to deceive.[48]

The commonplace book is, we might say, a form of idealized and externalized memory: the very embodiment of what one might hope to remember clearly and precisely. But then one needs to remember what one wants to remember! When the body of organized prose is read as a map, as a *topos* from which one seeks orientation to find what one is looking for (or learns what one should be searching for), then we glimpse the ways in which the book functions as both repository and prompt. The commonplace book has to be created but once created it possesses an independent power of rigid and loyal preservation that one can only wish one's memory was unfailingly capable of achieving. Randolph's point about memory remains an essential part of the 'use and benefit' offered by a commonplace book, and also helpfully coordinates the art of commonplacing with the ancient Greek practice of writing *hypomnemata* (ὑπομνήματα) or aids for remembrance. Wittgenstein's understanding of his remarks as 'reminders' is a fitting modern legacy of the ancient philosophical practice.[49]

Plato acknowledged writing as a kind artificial memory, and imagined that the technology should be used to help students develop their reasoning skills. As the etymology of the word suggests, *hypomnemata* involve principles focused on creating strong associations between things read and things written – a power evident in the mere transcription of prose, which later may manifest in one's memory and other habits of mind and action. As Foucault said when considering the purposes of the ancient practice: *hypomnemata* 'must be re-read from time to time so as to reactualize their contents'.[50]

Pierre Hadot, who is among those who have done much to reinvigorate our sense of and appreciation for the ancient practice of *hypomnemata*, sees how keeping an assiduous set of notes, often written on a daily basis, is both an aid to memory and a guide to action.[51] Most importantly, this mode of collecting should support and improve one's sense of *prosoche*: 'attention to oneself and vigilance at every instant'.[52] *Hypomnemata* create the occasion to thoughtfully consider or reconsider one's place in the world; they function as a resource to which one may repair for guidance or remembrance about one's position. The logic of *prosoche* is present in Hadot's assessment of Socratic *eros* and irony: 'a divided consciousness, passionately aware that it is not what it ought to be'.[53] The ancients who preached the importance of *prosoche* emphasized how 'self-consciousness is, first and foremost, a moral consciousness', and consequently how continuous self-attention presupposes 'the practice of examining one's conscience'.[54] In this ancient context, the memory aid was also a moral aid; the reminders – themselves organized around *topoi* – gave ethical direction to diligent readers. Hadot describes the positive effects of *prosoche* as including the development of 'techniques of introspection', for example, 'an extraordinary finesse in the examination of conscience and spiritual discernment'.[55]

A practice of *prosoche* on these terms helps one see, at least, that one cannot take stock of oneself – judge oneself, as if from on high. Instead a writer or note-taker is only in a position to set down reminders to be taken up again and again, perpetually and vigilantly. The title given to the notes Marcus Aurelius composed in the second century is almost universally translated as *The Meditations*. Consequently, his book of fragments has become part of the expansive category of autobiographical writing (including confessions, memoirs, journals, diaries and epistolary prose). Yet the translation is misleading, with the result that we are unable to appreciate the kind of writing Aurelius composed. Hadot offers a corrective in translating Aurelius' work as *Exhortations to Himself*.[56] The revised translation effectively counters the notion that Aurelius might be writing down notes *about* himself as if from a distant or distinct vantage (that is not always already from his point of view), and moreover that such remarks might be intended for posterity – for us, his readers. The work, according to Hadot's remedial retitling, should be regarded as a collection of notes meant strictly to aid Aurelius and him alone in keeping attention on his practice of *prosoche*. Aurelian *hypomnemata* are wholly different from autobiography. They are not aimed at describing a narrative of one's life, but rather are directed to the task of creating the conditions that make life possible.

While we may claim for *florilegia*, *zibaldoni*, commonplace books and *hypomnemata* distinctive purposes and contexts, there are some points of resemblance: each of these independent forms, for example, alters the practice of collection and composition into a means for remembering. Though users deploy a wide range of organizational strategies (from the *zibaldone*, in which there is almost none at all, to Emerson's commonplace books cross-referenced with exacting rigor), there appears to be a common effort to ward off the threat of forgetting – and the pain forgetting causes, whether when searching for the *mot juste*, the passage that best illustrates one's point, or, in the case of the English Patient, one's very own name. For Count Almásy, his copy of Herodotus – his commonplace book – became his memory, the traces and texts that suggested the *topoi* of his mind and the nature of his identity.

16.   Georges Cuvier was responsible for the design of the Cabinet of Comparative Anatomy situated on the ground floor of the Muséum National d'Histoire Naturelle, part of the complex that included the Jardin des Plantes. As Emerson studied these collections he began to see, as Lee Rust Brown describes in *The Emerson Museum: Practical Romanticism and the Pursuit of the Whole* (1997), 'how the naturalist had begun by methodically choosing and abstracting such invariable affinities to form a higher classification; then how the naturalist had repeated the operation of selection and abstraction to form even higher classifications'.[57] The cabinets as Emerson encountered them were not just offering specimens to admire but intentional arrangements of those specimens to guide a visitor to think about biological classification and connection in very expansive ways by means of reference to these highly specific, individuated samples. 'Preserved specimens from the order', as Brown notes, 'were juxtaposed, in families, in the glass-doored armoires that lined the walls of the Cabinet; thus the visitor could see the obvious affinities between, say, an armadillo and a pangolin. But the Cabinet also brought the invisible natural order into conceptual visibility by another, higher juxtaposition'.[58] Cuvier's cabinets were not full of disparate

curiosities but rather astonishingly connected, coextensive, familial specimens. Emerson recognized the collections in these armoires – and indeed, among and between the cabinets – for the way that concepts and qualities, designs and attributes supervened on the actual, individual creatures. Immediate, approachable instances of taxidermy inform any speculation on the meaning of taxonomy. One stands before a cabinet of amphibians scientifically and artfully arranged and suddenly the notion that an animal evolved out of the water and onto land – or conversely, into the water from the land – is not speculative, still less preposterous, but evident.

17.   In thinking about Emerson at the Jardins des Plantes, and in the light of Lee Rust Brown's book just noted, Stanley Cavell writes: 'I might formulate the image Brown constructs {of Emerson finding in the Cabinets 'an image of what he wanted his writing to be'} as one in which Emerson sees that his words may become specimens of a totality of significance arrived at otherwise than by a system (philosophical or scientific [or narrative?]), of which Emerson felt incapable'.[59]

The pertinence of Cavell's description in part lies in the way it reminds us of Emerson's ongoing vocational crises – particularly acute during his first visit to Europe and Great Britain in 1833, that is, in the wake of resigning the only profession he was trained for and had executed with success, if also with profound misgivings. One important way to read the tone of Emerson's declaration 'I will be a naturalist' is simply that he is gratified to have found a way of adequately and accurately describing what it is that he is. He is not, for example, any longer a minister – though he continues to minister *ex situ* upon returning from Europe. And likely fearing what it is he might have to do vocationally when he returns to Boston, claiming the mantle of naturalist is a relief: the kind of relief one feels when one finds the right name for something, and in this case, for oneself.

Now, in the light of Cavell's remark, the adoption of a vocation as naturalist is not straight or literal, but an emblem or analogue for Emerson of a kind of thinking that is collected or combined in one's words – how one chooses them and arranges them. Cavell notes that Brown's 'formulation leaves deliberately open [...] whether Emerson's "words" refers to single words, to sentences, to paragraphs, or to essays'.[60] More pressing though is Cavell's speculation about how 'the philosophical interest of collecting' is bound up with 'its comparable connection with the concept of philosophical writing, particularly in the cases of Emerson and Wittgenstein'.[61]

It is worth emphasizing that Emerson does not write, as is sometimes paraphrased, 'How much finer things are in *combination* than alone', but in 'composition' than alone; the solecism is understandable, even welcome, given that composition involves combination. Furthermore, the reader will hear the double sense of COMPOSITION – with its shared attributes of the author's labour and of the work that issues from it. Emerson is not captivated by the mere putting together of things (an unstudied accretion), but quite differently, he is intrigued by the art and methods of collecting and displaying common or shared elements (such as solitary words) in order to generate an apprehension of something profoundly more auspicious than a mere vocabulary – namely, words correlated in such a way (namely as sentences) that they reveal or stand for ideas. In Emerson's hands this notion of collecting first takes the form of a sentence, then – as Cavell indicates – by degrees, the paragraph, and in the course of composing a sequence of paragraphs, the essay. 'Implicitly', Cavell notes, 'everything about Emerson's practice as a writer bespeaks this sense of aggregation and juxtaposition'.[62] While studying Cuvier's cabinets, Emerson discovers a scientific analogue for his literary-philosophical ambitions: as the sentence is a living entity of its own, the essay will become a cabinet of organisms – not merely poised to display eloquence but to provoke a clearer sense of the ideas that animate those lines (sentences, paragraphs, essays) comprised of well-chosen, well-placed words. Turning back to Brown's account of the cabinets, we can apprehend and appreciate why a writer of Emerson's temperament and vision would be interested in collecting-as-composition when understood as a mode or model for philosophical writing:

> The primary aim of juxtaposing specimens behind the glass was to clarify their classification to the viewer; the mere curiousness of the exotic specimens was tangential to this aim. The spectator managed to 'see' the classification not simply by looking at the specimens themselves but by looking, as it were, *through* them to the higher idea that contained them. There was always, in other words, an element of conceptual depth to the pagelike exhibition arrangements. The classification was the point: it lay on an invisible plane 'behind' or 'before' examples of its elements.[63]

Brown's analysis isolates some of the correspondences that obtain between Emerson's writing and the image of the cabinet, but there are also points of dissimilarity worth noting. Emerson's cabinet is not populated, for example, by the taxidermic and ossified but rather by live specimens: his sentences pulse with vitality, achieving and retaining their own distinctive rhythms while also admitting sanguineous relations to the lines that surround them. These are living entities with the power to procreate new forms; in this way composition (in one sense) begets composition (in the other sense). Consequently, the image of collecting-as-composition elicits a significant disanalogy with literal cabinets.

Meanwhile, from another frame of reference, Emerson's prose finds an analogue with cabinets in so far as associations are made with the manner by which he selects, arranges, pins and permanently fixes his sentences to the page. From this angle, Emerson's collection is no menagerie or zoo (of fertile specimens at work on new compositions). Elizabeth A. Dant has argued that the cabinet of natural history is 'both the dominant symbol' and an 'ordering principle for Emerson's thought and writing'.[64] While maintaining an interest in the more literal points of resemblance between a cabinet of natural history and Emerson's essay-as-cabinet, Dant emphasizes the 'odd twin features of Emerson's prose: its diffuseness and its insularity', features that in turn may provide 'an understanding of the assumptions governing the enclosed world of Emerson's essays'.[65] If Emerson's writing is enclosed and insular (like a cabinet), it is also – as a cabinet masterfully collected – capable of inciting and inspiring the perception of similarity and differences between cabinets (from essay to essay, from author to author and from text to world). Therefore the cabinets of Emerson's writing – lectures, essays, addresses, journal entries, letters – appear both as self-contained collections (worthy of our consideration within their bounds) *and* as possessed of seemingly endless relevance and reference to the world beyond their limits.

Such a clarifying gloss – highlighting how variously a single metaphor can be interpreted – should offer another reminder that metaphors, more generally, cannot graft all their features, associations and allusions into new contexts of application. As inherently unsettled and incomplete, metaphors themselves add life to language. But that life can be unruly and impel readers to emphasize qualities that diminish or even contradict the lesson at hand. Thus a metaphor is a collection unto itself, a collection that churns its contents from one context to another. Consequently, each metaphor – and each instance of its invocation – has to be defined and qualified with points of similarity noted and exceptions mentioned. The multiple and varied meanings of a given metaphor steadily compete for our attention, and in that struggle for recognition and usefulness seem to mimic the structure of natural selection. As it is for a species subject to natural selection, a metaphor's fate is beyond prediction since our ignorance of future conditions leaves us unable to say which inflections of a trope will successfully adapt – that is, continually captivate our interest and maintain their descriptive usefulness.

18.   Another way to describe the analytical or structural nature of *English Traits* is to read it as an inductive argument. The claims in such arguments make a specific point – often limited in scope, sometimes accented by anecdote or personal experience; then from this delimited position, a wider, more general conclusion or moral can be drawn out. (Contrariwise, a deductive argument begins with general claims and narrows down to a discrete, curtailed conclusion.) In *English Traits*, as in much of his other writing, Emerson seldom argues deductively – and when he does (as in the opening lines of the chapter 'Language' in *Nature*), the syllogistic presentation may become part of the critique, prompting a reader to a new degree of consciousness about the created nature of Emerson's text. More commonly we find Emerson presenting his thoughts as a series of meditations on topics that lead outward to other topics – ever reaching and radiating to other realms and topics. Part of that expansive and experimental work involves using terms not just for themselves but also for their allusions, their inherited connotations; for example, when Emerson employs the word TRANSCENDENTAL he assumes his reader will be aware of Kant's Transcendental philosophy and Coleridge's interpretation and translation of the concept, and he uses these associations to enrich his deliberate selection and application of the word.

In *English Traits* Emerson admits an appropriate degree of self-awareness about his accession of scientific methodology and terminology into his discourse. 'We must use the popular category', he writes, 'as we do by the Linnaean classification, for convenience, and not as exact and final. Otherwise, we are presently confounded, when the best settled traits of one race are claimed by some new ethnologist as precisely characteristic of the rival tribe'.[66] Since 'good or bad are but names very readily transferable to that or this', the argument is all in the arrangement of particulars.[67] Such a lesson is as readily apparent in Cicero's rhetoric as in contemporary jurisprudence, and it is a formidable reminder for any literary investigation of scientific thinking.

An inductive method of argument is enhanced by a careful and artful use of metaphor because metaphors by nature offer particular representation for general conditions, or (as with metonyms) highlight a part/whole relationship. Metaphor usage then is highly complementary to induction. Consider an instance in which a word ('absorbed') is applied to an object or state of affairs that is not literally the case ('the death left him absorbed by grief'). Likewise a metaphor may be an image that is symbolic for, or a part of, some larger, abstract phenomenon, such as with a metonym ('He believed the hole in his heart would never heal'). Strangely, some may say sadly, or at least confusingly, vernacular speech commonly inverts this logical order and insists that these metaphorical phenomena are LITERALLY the case; increasingly this has become something of an infelicitous trend. The appeal to the literal should not be dismissed as merely a function of hyperbole, since it is not a matter of exaggeration (by degrees), but rather conceptual exchange (a demonstrated trade in category); to say something is literally the case does not reinforce any measure of the figurative or connotative, but asserts their opposites. Perhaps reaching for the literal – and here such reaching is intentionally deployed figuratively – reflects an emerging anxiety about the status of the VIRTUAL, and its apparently ever-widening scope. Then it would be precisely this anxiety – coupled with skepticism about what is not, or is no longer literally the case – that confirms a speaker's desire to counteract the virtual with an affirmation of how things are – or are felt – to be really or ACTUALLY happening in the world. Not in virtual reality, but in actual reality. Literally.

Metaphors are, by nature, the kinds of representations that capture the qualitative and 'gradal' aspects of symbolic thought, in opposition to the 'sortal'; they are, consequently, more given to interpretive ambiguity, but also – for the same reason – cognitive richness.[68] One can, for example, revise the above examples by modulating the metaphor's allusions ('Despite the ongoing reassurance of friends, grief clung to him') or the metonym's nuance ('The void in his heart will be filled by new love'). That such examples may seem sentimental and cliché, given to euphemism ('time heals' and the like), and even unpoetically rendered, should not distract us from noting the convulsive and mobilizing nature of metaphors, attributes that makes them so effective for inductive reasoning.

The Greek root of the word METAPHOR is *metaphora*, meaning to transfer. In modern-day Greece public buses are called λεωφορείο, a word that discloses a common root with metaphor and suggests how metaphors might be thought of as a form of (conceptual) transportation – as an energizing force, as a means of getting from one place in thought to another. Even the word metaphor can be used as a metaphor! The English word TROPE derives similarly from a Greek word suggesting movement or motion: *trephein* (τρεπειν) to turn – as in a turn of phrase; in an etymological sense, figurative speech invites repositioning, substitution and association. In 'The Poet', Emerson parallels the insight and the etymology when he writes: 'All language is vehicular and transitive, and is good, as ferries and horses are, for conveyance, not as farms and houses are, for homestead'.[69] Just as the bus – or ferry or horse – creates a kind of continuity between one place and another, so metaphors reinforce analogical thinking, since metaphors frame our concepts in terms of connections and relationships, and the movement that defines them. Or to keep with the same metaphor: metaphors suggest intersections and pathways, points of convergence and transference for conceptual movement. They are used to elucidate similarities between things based on shared qualities, and also to frame differences; through an act of substitution they can illuminate something otherwise obscured by literal description. And crucially, metaphors can move us emotionally as well as propel us intellectually and imaginatively.

A modern-day Greek moving or transport vehicle might have Metaphora embossed on its sides, again, in an uncanny way, literalizing what we do with metaphors linguistically and representationally all the time. 'Thinking of one thing in terms of another' is a primary function of metaphors in human language and expression, and consequently implicates us, as David Punter has noted, in an ongoing 'process of translation'.[70] When we feel constrained to express something difficult, for example, a profound emotion or an inchoate idea, we often resort to metaphors because they expand the limits set by language used referentially or literally. Remarkably, that movement – or translation – to the figurative, or symbolic, helps us better understand the actual qualities of the literal experience, for example, someone's heartache over a loss. 'A mourner will try in vain to explain the extent of his bereavement better than to say a *chasm* is opened in society', wrote Emerson in his journal.[71] The metaphor, in such a case, gives us an insight into the interior, non-literal experience of another person: how he perceives this brute fact at a given moment. In this way, the metaphor enables him to transport himself out of the confines of literalism and transfer us by means of a translation into an intimacy with his inner life – what might be understood as the creation of a kind of literary contact with the emotional truths that elude direct description.

Just as using a metaphor (or metonym) can involve making a connection between a specific phenomenon (this mourner's pain) and a wider one (the loss of a beloved for a community), so inductive reasoning begins with the particulars, and suggests – on the basis of relationships and connections – something larger, more general and universal. When the man tells us of his private experience in the wake of his loss, we may be startled to discover that we too have had a sensation that felt akin to 'a hole in the heart'. Suddenly the private experience of one person connects analogically to the private experience of others – by means of the transfer device known as a metaphor (or metonym) – and the larger community of mourners, of people generally, is poised to say something more meaningful about genuinely shared human experiences. In these instances metaphor usage can seem an antidote to skepticism and alienation – a profound effect for a common linguistic habit to perpetually hold in reserve.

Metaphor may avail a certain kind of unexpected perception; in some cases a penetrating insight into the deeper or more abiding truth of a text, a situation or a set of relations. It is pertinent to our inheritance of metaphor as an art of image-making and image-using how William Whewell has noted in *The Philosophy of the Inductive Sciences* (1840), that the Greek etymology of aesthetics (αισθανεσθαι) means to perceive. If an aesthetics of metaphor would allow us to perceive valuations of the beautiful in tropes, so would an ethics of metaphor enable a view of the moral nature of symbolic language. Metaphor, like myth, is an unusually plenitudinous site from which to elucidate a general theory of value – both aesthetic and ethical – for a given culture or subculture. Since there is no way to elide metaphor use in language, we are perpetually presented with its power to encode meaning and value. Consequently the study of metaphors appears to be both endless and endlessly informative.

In *English Traits* Emerson often deploys metaphors as a means of examining ethical problems, claims and meanings. His use of metaphors enables him to speak openly about a number of volatile and controversial topics (parents and progeny, nationality, empire, power, race) without concomitantly incurring the danger of being too direct or too literal. Ethical beliefs are scrutinized without the sense that Emerson is moralizing. Instead of factionalizing and alienating, his use of metaphors stimulates philosophical thinking principally because the imagery extends the limits of the issue (pushing the particular into the general, analogizing concrete instances of a species with the nature of a genus); by contrast, one could say the political use of metaphors is often directed to constraining or fixing parameters – or as Carl Schmitt has remarked, politics is primarily the act of defining the enemy in contradistinction to the friend[72]; enemy and friend are, in turn, metaphors that call out for use by politicians and for criticism by political theorists. In Emerson's case tropes can effectively disturb settled definitions, opinions and sometimes, quite unexpectedly, complicate one's own understanding of metaphor and one's capacity to use it. Sometimes the indirectness of Emerson's critique by means of metaphor leaves open the extent to which the metaphor itself, and not the thing it refers to, is implicated in the ethical problem.

Part of the work Emerson undertakes in *English Traits*, and much of the account that is underway here, concerns the extent and variety of effects the use of metaphors can have on self-understanding and the wider context of communities of individuals trying to make themselves intelligible to one another. It is one thing to employ a metaphor to talk about an ethical crisis; it is quite another issue when the metaphor itself contributes to moral turbulence, making its very presence morally suspect. Emerson's writing on England's TRAITS, among the many other tropes in his book, brings attention to the moral use of metaphor (for there are others, such as the aesthetic). Emerson's investigation, perhaps inadvertently, makes manifest some of the confusions, contradictions, conflicts and errors in judgement related to metaphor usage more generally, especially when that application generates problems it was meant to describe – and perhaps, more ambitiously, to explain or resolve. Emerson's robust catalogue of metaphors goes some way toward showing how we understand, define and judge ourselves (and others) through our uses of metaphors; and his work incites us to ask whether we wish to maintain or reform our usage, perhaps especially when we are describing other people and their habits of mind and action. Metaphors often do more than merely or neutrally present an insubstantial vision of our ethical nature; more often they reveal and reinforce that vision, making it possible, with however much difficulty, to offer an account of ourselves and our perceptions of others.

In much of *English Traits* there is a sense that one metaphor leads to another – after a fashion similar to Wittgenstein's 'natural order' – and as such that many diverse things share common characteristics and possess familiar relationships. Apparent continuity or consecutiveness may yield an intellectual and emotional insight (a perception of 'strange sympathies', as Emerson noted at the Jardin[73]), yet if the terms of this advancement are treated as fixed such assumed ossification may lead to the impression that metaphors are not just word-images that get us from A to B but *are* A and B. While the transfer from one place to another reflects the process of learning how things are related to one another, the relationship itself – as formalized or figured temporarily by the trope – can obscure the most salient aspects of the participating elements. Instead of being tools for improved intelligibility, metaphors become the very categories of experience; they cease to be shorthand for complex expression, or a means of indirect communication, and instead become essentialized, over-determined figures – clichés – that tempt our dismissal of them, and consequently endanger the chances for a critical evaluation of ethical terms such tropes might imply. *English Traits* is by contrast, beginning with its title and throughout its series of chapters, a text in which Emerson both enacts and complicates our use of metaphors and our understanding of them.

Like a good preacher sensitive to the power of allegory and image, and like a good naturalist aware that the methods of science are truly pictures of procedures, Emerson's *English Traits* is a Cabinet of Metaphors, often morally-laden metaphors. When a reader encounters this collection she might say, as Emerson did before the Cabinets of Natural History: 'The limits of the possible are enlarged, & the real is stranger than the imaginary. [...] Here we are impressed with the inexhaustible riches of nature. The Universe is a more amazing puzzle than ever as you glance along this bewildering series of animate forms'.[74] Emerson's specimens are tropes; his science is their arrangement under topics, giving them order where there once seemed only randomness. He labels his specimens – his metaphors – for our consideration, then leaves the reader to determine how all these remarkable things might be connected, and what the significance of those relationships might be. We are left to make inferences, and to follow after our impressions by employing an inductive method of reasoning. If we are adept at making such inferences, 'the limits of the possible' will be enlarged as the metaphors carry us into new realms of thinking, orient us to new forms of moral knowledge.

19.   Carlyle, Emerson, Nietzsche and Wittgenstein articulated their concerns over our forgetfulness about metaphors – their heritage as linguistic phenomena, their variety of uses, their variable capacities for representation, and their prodigality as sites of interpretation:

Carlyle, *Sartor Resartus* (1833–4)

[W]hat is Man himself, and his whole terrestrial Life, but an Emblem; a Clothing or visible Garment for that divine ME of his, cast hither, like a light-particle, down from Heaven? Thus is he said to be clothed with a Body.
   Language is called the Garment of Thought: however, it should rather be, Language is the Flesh-Garment, the Body, of Thought. I said that Imagination

wove this Flesh-Garment; and does not she? Metaphors are her stuff: examine Language; what, if you except some few primitive elements (of natural sound), what is it all but Metaphors, recognised as such, or no longer recognised; still fluid and florid, or now solid-grown and colourless? If those same primitive elements are the osseous fixtures in the Flesh-Garment, Language, – then are Metaphors its muscles and tissues and living integuments. An unmetaphorical style you shall in vain seek for: is not your very *Attention* a *Stretching-to*?[75]

Emerson, 'The Poet' (1844)

For though the origin of most of our words is forgotten, each word was first a stroke of genius, and obtained currency, because for the moment it symbolized the world to the first speaker and to the hearer. The etymologist finds the deadest word to have been once a brilliant picture. Language is fossil poetry. As the limestone of the continent consists of infinite masses of the shells of animalcules, so language is made up of images, or tropes, which now, in their secondary use, have long ceased to remind us of their poetic origin.[76]

Nietzsche, 'On the Truth and Lies in a Nonmoral Sense' (1873)

What then is truth? A movable host of metaphors, metonymies, and anthropo-morphisms: in short, a sum of human relations which have been poetically and rhetorically intensified, transferred, and embellished, and which, after long usage, seem to a people to be fixed, canonical, and binding. Truths are illusions which we have forgotten are illusions; they are metaphors that have become worn out and have been drained of sensuous force, coins which have lost their embossing and are now considered as metal and no longer as coins.[77]

Wittgenstein, *Philosophical Investigations* (1953)

A simile that has been absorbed into the form of our language produces a false appearance, and this disquiets us. 'But *this* isn't how it is!' – we say. 'Yet *this* is how it has to *be!*'[78]

(*Tractatus Logico-Philosophicus*, 4.5): 'The general form of propositions is: This is how things are'. – That is the kind of proposition that one repeats to oneself countless times. One thinks that one is tracing the outline of the thing's nature over and over again, and one is merely tracing round the frame through which we look at it.[79]

A *picture* held us captive. And we could not get outside it, for it lay in our language and language seemed to repeat it to us inexorably.[80]

20.   These collected remarks by Carlyle, Emerson, Nietzsche and Wittgenstein notwithstanding, many philosophers employ metaphors in their work while forgetting the nature of these representations, believing or simply taking for granted that the proxy *is* the thing. What seems at first like literariness (to them, to us) becomes in time literalness; we are then encumbered by the rigidity of the literal, and the intimation

that potentially dangerous effects must follow – as if a range of terrors and losses (racism and war, alienation and broken hearts) were all traceable to the troubled use and misunderstanding of metaphors.

Metaphors employed in philosophical works can often become concentrates of undeveloped and unexplored meaning. In the midst of a rigorously defiant critical inquiry a writer may unconsciously replicate inherited, ready-to-hand metaphors – at times appearing to passively absorb the figurative language of the texts under scrutiny, and thereafter (unwittingly?) redeploying it, as if the author were an agent in a trance. Whenever a metaphor is used, however, one must grant without complaint that some things are assumed, left unsaid or unarticulated; even a self-conscious critic cannot exhaust the range of allusions the metaphor implies. In this way metaphors function as enthymemes, leaving aside important propositions, suppressing or concealing premises (intentionally and not), thereby rendering a given philosophical syllogism more suggestive of truth than possessive of it. Metaphors are in many cases, in philosophical writing as elsewhere, used commonly enough to become cliché – an achievement, one might say, since that pervasiveness reflects the usefulness of the image, but also a success that carries with it a defeat. Ubiquity inures our perception of the obvious and the obscure. In the prominent status that defines cliché lurks the danger of the metaphor's overt and tacit meanings: as a cliché possesses both apparent and deeper truths it is commonplace that both sorts of truths can remain hidden in plain sight.

Even as the use of metaphor may conceal important meanings, its deployment in philosophy also improves the richness and variety of human expression, creating new opportunities for interpretation and insight. While this is an obvious good, perhaps the primary good in literature, does it make sense for philosophy? Should not philosophy be the careful analysis of these concentrates – offering an ongoing inquiry into the ethics, aesthetics, logic and epistemology of metaphor? Should not philosophy seek clarity where literature creates and thrives in density, ambiguity and mystification, in the play of allusion and allegory? Should not philosophy – especially value theory – involve the practice of analyzing our metaphors? ('Metaphor in the text of philosophy [...I]s there metaphor in the text of philosophy? [...] The question demands a book.')[81] What if it were a given that philosophers cared for the use of their metaphors, and made that care explicit in the analysis of the ideas that depend on them? Would that signal the point, as Stanley Cavell asked in the concluding question of *The Claim of Reason*, where philosophy might 'become literature' – and cease to know itself as philosophy?[82] If theories of action and belief depend on metaphors then it matters greatly which metaphors are deployed and how they are defined. 'Shall I say', Emerson asked in 'The Relation of Intellect to Natural Science', 'that the world may be reeled off from any one of its laws like a ball of yarn; that a chemist can explain by his analogies the process of the Intellect; the physician from his; the geometer, and the mechanician, respectively from theirs?'[83]

Consider the example of purity metaphors in the history of philosophy, and how the tacit but ubiquitous presence of these signs influenced centuries of thinking and belief from clergy to common men – and consequently also shaped the actions of leaders and their armies, contributed to the shaping of nations and the characteristics of their citizens. Until metaphors of organic or evolutionally thinking began emerging in the eighteenth century, gaining strength and plausibility through scientific investigations, purity was among the dominant metaphorical reference points in Christian doctrine, especially in Calvinism and Catholicism. Conspicuously in Goethe, then in Carlyle, Emerson, John Stuart Mill (whose *On Liberty* appears in 1859, the same year as *The Origin of Species*) and others, organic metaphors displace purity metaphors – giving rise to an implicit critique of the distortion purity metaphors create in human understanding. Though compelling in their emotive effects – because they terrify in their presumed or promised consequences – purity metaphors are largely, but meaningfully, rhetorical since purity does not make logical sense either for fleshy humans or for a transcendental godhead. Still, as Cavell has noted: 'It is perhaps a mark of the seriousness of philosophizing to be forced to come to some understanding with philosophy's impure craving for purity'.[84] Part of that understanding and that seriousness may require giving up on purity metaphors. Evolutionary metaphors, to cite one alternative, suggest that humans are not tainted but trained (pruned like so many topiaries), or allowed to grow wild – constrained mainly by the shaping forces of self-trust and intuition. In the light of these evolutionary symbols, race and culture are no longer matters of purity in descent, but of acculturation and development, of accidental and intentional commingling. Blood, families, races and cultures are forever and everywhere mixed. Purity metaphors then are of philosophical interest not because they possess truth but rather because they represent dubious philosophical commitments.

Metaphor use, like most linguistic practice, is not surprisingly highly correlated with one's education and experience, both of which are comprised of the specific range and inflection of one's particular cultural formation. Metaphors, like jokes and fairy tales, are provincial in time and space; they are embodied. Consequently a person's use of metaphor reflects a great deal about that person's intellectual, psychological, social and emotional environment. This claim and myriad illustrations of it are provided by George Lakoff and Mark Johnson in their *Philosophy in the Flesh: The Embodied Mind and Its Challenge to Western Thought* (1999). In their capacious taxonomy of tropes, Lakoff and Johnson remind us how a person's philosophical thinking is embedded in the metaphors he or she deploys, often perhaps unconsciously. Many times it seems that metaphor usage is largely unintentional or arbitrary, a function of the texts one draws from to defend a theory or to define a point. At times a philosopher can seem to merely sustain an inherited metaphor – acting like a bee pollinating a dominating flower species; at other times a philosopher may be innovating a new (modified? mutated?) metaphor based on analogies that emerge from a specific temporal and cultural context, for example, where we find early modern philosophers writing about clocks the way the ancient Greeks invoked wax.

Lakoff and Johnson discuss the prevalence of metaphor in philosophy, and the way metaphor guides and shapes the contours of our thinking and the content of our values.

In asking philosophical questions, we use a reason shaped by the body, a cognitive unconscious to which we have no direct access, and metaphorical thought of which we are largely unaware. The fact that abstract thought is mostly metaphorical means that answers to philosophical questions have always been, and always will be, mostly metaphorical. In itself, that is neither good nor bad. It is simply a fact about the capacities of the human mind. But it has major consequences for every aspect of philosophy. Metaphorical thought is the principal tool that makes philosophical insight possible and that constrains the forms that philosophy can take.[85]

In the light of such claims, a reading of *English Traits* would appear to benefit considerably from an attention to the way its author's thinking is informed by his chosen (and accidentally, unintentionally and involuntarily used) metaphors. Conversely a reader may be poised for new insights by positing how the use of those metaphors derives naturally and consequently from the life of the writer. Lakoff and Johnson's research and postulations, for instance, reinforce the extent to which a person's philosophical thinking is embedded in metaphor, and how the selected metaphors that define such thinking emerge from lived experience – from proximate cultural influences and prominent intellectual examples. Why does Carlyle dwell on the sartorial arts, Foucault on archaeology, Emerson on climatology, Mill on arboriculture or Nietzsche on genealogy? Because each metaphor is constitutive of their thinking, not a superficial label applied to its surface; the allied discipline from which analogies are drawn underwrites the transition to a new context and application. To begin understanding a philosopher's metaphors entails the beginning of understanding his philosophical ideas.

21.   In his eulogy for Thoreau, printed in *The Atlantic Monthly* (1862), Emerson writes of how his friend's study of nature was not as one of 'these young scholars' referenced in the poem 'Blight' (1847), 'who invade our hills, / Bold as the engineer who fells the wood, / And travelling often in the cut he makes. / Love not the flower they pluck, and know it not, / And all their botany is Latin names'.[86] Rather, Thoreau was implicated in nature without perceptible seam. For him, self-reflection and the surface of the pond, keeping a journal or accounting for the harvest, were continuous activities.

> His interest in the flower or the bird lay very deep in his mind, was connected with Nature, – and the meaning of Nature was never attempted to be defined by him. He would not offer a memoir of his observations to the Natural History Society. 'Why should I? To detach the description from its connections in my mind would make it no longer true or valuable to me: and they do not wish what belongs to it'. His power of observation seemed to indicate additional senses. He saw as with microscope, heard as with ear-trumpet, and his memory was a photographic register of all he saw and heard. And yet none knew better than he that it is not the fact that imports, but the impression or effect of the fact on your mind. Every fact lay in glory in his mind, a type of the order and beauty of the whole.
>
> His determination on Natural History was organic. He confessed that he sometimes felt like a hound or a panther, and, if born among Indians, would have been a fell hunter. But, restrained by his Massachusetts culture he played out the game in this mild form of botany and ichthyology. His intimacy with animals

suggested what Thomas Fuller records of Butler the apiologist, that 'either he had told the bees things or the bees had told him'.[87]

The Butler here analogized, Charles Butler – one of Robert Burton's English contemporaries at Oxford – composed a work on bees and beekeeping entitled *The Feminine Monarchie* with the 1609 subtitle: *or, a Treatise Concerning Bees, and the Due Ordering of Them: Wherein the truth found out by experience and diligent observation, discovereth the idle and fond conceipts, which many have written anent this subiect.*[88] In the 1623 edition, Butler amended the subtitle to read with more taxonomical explicitness: *or, The Historie of Bees, shewing their admirable Nature, and Properties, Their Generation, and Colonies, Their Government, Loyaltie, Art, Industrie, Enemies, Warres, Magnanimitie, & c. together with the right ordering of them from time to time: And the sweet profit arising thereof.*[89] Butler's book is said by him to be 'found out' (1609) or 'written out' (1623) by experience. Butler's approach, like Thoreau's, was immersive and observational: it did not frame nature by definitions but encouraged the description of first-hand encounters with it, in it, as it; occasionally those honest and disciplined reflections contributed to the stock of scientific, philosophical and even political knowledge. Yet despite, in Emerson's word, the 'organic' nature of Thoreau's natural scientific observations, that he could not 'detach the description from its connections in my mind', Thoreau's work, like Emerson's, was pervaded by metaphor's perpetual presence – the pond, the bean-field, the village, brute neighbours, winter animals; each and all was both itself and a representative for reflection on correlates in religion, philosophy and history. Likewise for Butler the bees were always both fascinating in their own right and revelatory – by analogy – for the human community. Thomas Fuller, author of the *History of the Worthies of England* (1662), praised Butler for discerning 'the state mysteries' of the bees' commonwealth; and Butler himself suggested that insight gleaned from studying bees might be translated analogically back to the operations of mankind – that nature is not a foreign tutor full of rare and impertinent mysteries but a guide of refined and fitting tuition. Should we avail ourselves of its lessons we would be rewarded with a 'sweet profit' more than honey.

22.   Virgil, *Georgics* (c. 29 BCE)

The wonder-stirring drama of a tiny state,
its great-hearted leaders and the entire species' habits
and pursuits and swarms and battles – of these I shall tell you.
Trivial the work, but hardly trivial the glory if
unlucky powers so permit and Apollo heeds one's prayers. [...]

Having followed these signs and these habits, some say
that bees own a share of the divine soul and drink in
the ether of space; for god invests everything –
earth and the tracts of the sea and deepest heaven;
from him, flocks, herds, men, all species of wild animals –
each one gains for itself at birth its little life;

doubtless, afterward, all return to him and, released, are
made new; death has no place but, alive, they fly up, each
to be counted as a star and ascend into heaven above. [...]

Here, a sudden omen, plain to see, almost incredible
to tell: out of the putrefying guts, out
of the bellies and burst sides, bees, buzzing, swarming,
then streaming upward into huge clouds till they join in a tree-
top and hang in a great ball from a bending branch.[90]

23.   In the inaugural essay of *Essays, First Series* Emerson takes history for his subject. But where Herodotus wrote of the dynastic history of Persian kings, conducted an 'inquiry' (ἱστορία) into the events and causes of Greco-Persian conflict, Emerson reconceives history – the presentation of facts, the shape of narratives, the nature of characters – as biography. In other words, the activity of historical description is coterminous with the authorship of history. The historical text registers the traits and temperament of the historian – a person who creates biographies of experience (including his own) where we are used to thinking of realities. 'We are always coming up with the emphatic facts of history in our private experience', Emerson writes, 'and verifying them here. All history becomes subjective; in other words, there is properly no history; only biography.'[91] There is then no objective account only embodied perspective that treats 'facts as symbols'.[92]

> The true poem is the poet's mind; the true ship is the ship-builder. In the man, could we lay him open, we should see the reason for the last flourish and tendril of his work; as every spine and tint in the sea-shell pre-exist in the secreting organs of the fish. The whole of heraldry and of chivalry is in courtesy. A man of fine manners shall pronounce your name with all the ornament that titles of nobility could ever add.'[93]
>
> In like manner, all public facts are to be individualized, all private facts are to be generalized. Then at once History becomes fluid and true, and Biography deep and sublime.[94]
>
> He finds that the poet was no odd fellow who described strange and impossible situations, but that universal man wrote by his pen a confession true for one and true for all. His own secret biography he finds in lines wonderfully intelligible to him, dotted down before he was born.[95]

24.   Combination and admixture are ways to despoil the possibility of pure states; another that Emerson is fond of he calls COMPOSITION. Such methods undermine the claims – often superstitions – of parties and persons who would use purity as an argument or a form of proof. In the Fall of 1845, more than a decade before *English Traits* was published, Emerson wrote in his journal about the Native Americans – not the aboriginal people of North America but the seafaring immigrant tribes crowding the shores and estuaries of the New World, introducing a brute, almost ungodly element into the Providential American experiment:

I hate the narrowness of the Native American Party. It is the dog in the manger.
It is precisely opposite to all the dictates of love & magnanimity: & therefore, of
course, opposite true wisdom. It is the result of science that the highest simplicity
of structure is produced, not by few elements, but by the highest complexity. Man
is the most composite of all creatures, the wheel-insect, *volvox globator*, is at the
beginning. Well, as in the old burning of the Temple at Corinth, by the melting
& intermixture of silver & gold & other metals, a new compound more precious
than any, called the Corinthian Brass, was formed so in this Continent, – asylum
of all nations, the energy of Irish, Germans, Swedes, Poles, & the Cossacks, &
all European tribes, – of Africans, & of Polynesians, will construct a new race, a
new religion, a new State, a new literature, which will be as vigorous as the new
Europe which came out of the smelting pot of the Dark Ages, or that which earlier
emerged from the Pelasgic & Etruscan barbarism.

La Nature aime les croisements. [Nature loves cross-breedings.][96]

The following year, in a subsequent journal, Emerson added another variation on
Charles Fourier's sentiment:

Nature loves to cross her stocks. A pure blood, Bramin on Bramin, marrying in
& in, soon becomes puny & wears out. Some strong Cain son, some black blood
must renew & refresh the paler veins of Seth.[97]

In 'Works and Days', a lecture given in 1857 and included as the second lecture in
the *Natural Method of Mental Philosophy* the following year, Emerson, invoking
Hesiod's ancient text, comments on the labour, instruments and the international
intercourse of men. And here Fourier's *La Nature aime les croisements* finds another
context:

Our selfishness would have held slaves, or would have excluded from a quarter
of the planet all that are not born on the soil of that quarter. Our politics are
disgusting; but what can they help or hinder when from time to time the primal
instincts are impressed on masses of mankind, when the nations are in exodus
and flux? Nature loves to cross her stocks, – and German, Chinese, Turk, Russ and
Kanaka were putting out to sea, and intermarrying race with race; and commerce
took the hint, and ships were built capacious enough to carry the people of a
county.[98]

When speaking in England in 1848 as part of a series entitled *Mind and Manners of the
Nineteenth Century*, Emerson gave a lecture – 'Powers and Laws of Thought' – which
would later be revised and included in the *Natural History of Intellect*. Fourier's remark
about combination appears in this context as well:

The botanist discovered long ago that Nature loves mixtures, and that nothing
grows well on the crab-stock, but the blood of two trees being mixed a new and
excellent fruit is produced. And not less in human history aboriginal races are
incapable of improvement; the dull, melancholy Pelasgi arrive at no civility until

the Phoenicians and Ionians come in. The Briton, the Pict, is nothing until the Roman, the Saxon, the Norman, arrives.[99]

25. As things are better in combination, so Emerson claims that things are better understood in composition – through juxtaposition, arrangement, association and analogy; not unlike the realities created in film, which rely on the artful use of montage. Similarly, Emerson focuses not strictly on objects, but also on the relations between objects – on the negative spaces that surround them, the contexts and contrasts that provide the conditions for their perception as objects. As a naturalist would, Emerson builds a cabinet that will house a collection of apparently disparate elements. Yet the cumulative effect of reading in his cabinet called *English Traits* – as one might study a box of carefully arranged bees, beetles or shells – is a novel account of the English in the nineteenth century. Because of Emerson's taxonomy of terms and tropes we can see better, with more clarity and depth of insight, the interaction and mutual influence of language and culture.

In the lecture 'The Relation of Intellect to Natural Science', Emerson asks himself: 'What is the interest in tropes and symbols to men? I think it is that; unexpected relationship. Each remote part corresponds to each other, can represent the other; because all spring from one root'.[100] One can only encounter an 'unexpected relationship' if one puts things in relation, or becomes cognizant of the way they have already been arranged (by history, by culture, by the agents of language in books and speech). Creating a cabinet is one such methodology of active relationship-making: one must collect, order, orient, place, display and label. Insights about individual elements will likely derive from the consideration of elements – near and far. Sometimes a striking contrast may emphasize a crucial similarity, and it is just as possible that a shared feature can stimulate an unexpected perception of the uniquely or distinctively different qualities of an object.

Though it may not seem it, the work of the present collection is meant to be a deliberate enterprise for considering, and reconsidering, some of the connections between the various parts and elements in *English Traits*; while inspired by disparate energies and influences, much effort has been applied to facilitate a coherent investigation. Still, the bold pedigrees of source materials are often sufficiently pronounced to retain their features despite attempts at grafting and mating them. As such, odds bits stick out; vestigial remnants remain; points of resemblance may be chronicled without also revealing – or justifying a claim to – influence.

Each of the chapters in this *florilegium* are meant to trace some dominant lines of inquiry in Emerson's cabinet, in *English Traits* and elsewhere. From these perceived webby relations, qualities may be discerned that obtain independently and between constituents in the collection; and yet connections may not be apparent. Either way there is interest is why some relationships seem elucidatory and others vague, why some moments of apposition cheer and still others confound. Lines from *English Traits* become text-specimens intentionally stationed, and noted for their points of difference or resemblance to one another – or simply left side by side to disclose their affinities. The nature of such a methodology demands that associations between elements cannot be exhaustively rendered; this is both requisite and welcome – allowing the reader the chance to discover if these comminglings are sterile or productive, leading outward to other text-specimens. I must hope, or as Ishmael says in *Moby-Dick*, 'be content to produce the desired impression by separate citations of items, practically or reliably known to me as a whaleman; and from these citations, I take it – the conclusion aimed at will naturally follow of itself'.[101] I do not take this sense of consequence nonchalantly but rather with an interest in the sort of thing Emerson reported when visiting the Jardin des Plantes: an unexpected glimpse of relations that are both contingent and necessary. The individual specimen represents its species, and then shocks with its suggestion of sinuous connection to life forms higher and lower, parallel and ancillary.

While Emerson postulates what a natural history of intellect means in *Mind and Manners of the Nineteenth Century* and the *Natural Method of Natural Philosophy*, it is in *English Traits* that he seems to be conducting such a natural history. His book, written after many years of travelling and reading, laboured note-taking and common-placing, researching and reconnoitering and lecture writing, reflects his effort to reveal his broad topic – the traits of the English. Navigating diverse genres, incorporating disparate texts and tropes, Emerson presents his findings as a literary and philosophical cabinet. As it is in the field, one sees a thousand particular beetles before beginning to understand what the representative might signify about the species. So with the English, Emerson draws together his specimens, inspects them, and hypothesizes on their meanings and relations – and leaves abundant space for speculations to come. Given the nature of his enterprise, and his distinctive methods for conducting it, one may not be altogether surprised that his cabinet should, once assembled and presented, prompt our renewed interest in the moral significance of his metaphors and the people they are said to represent. After all, *English Traits* is neither scripture nor instruction manual, but rather a site of experimentation.

26.   The Natural History of Metaphor might be regarded as subset of the Natural History of Intellect. Conducting the inquiry into Emerson's use of metaphor in *English Traits* I find myself adapting his methodology, or what I understand it to be at this stage. In part he invokes natural history as a meaningful picture of the kind of work one might conduct on one's ideas, and the wide spectrum of their cultural and linguistic effects when they are embodied in language – and imaged as tropes, figures, signs and symbols. From Emerson's labours in *English Traits*, and many other books and fragments written by him and others, I have built a cabinet of metaphors – most of the metaphors bearing some identifying or explicating label, others left to speak for themselves, or awaiting intelligibility from their placement in the collection. I recognize – even emphasize – that a cabinet of metaphors and a natural history of metaphor are themselves metaphors! These images carry with them associations that are felicitous as well as unproductive. There are compelling analogical relations and there are moments that lack fit. Surprisingly, though, the judgement of what is promising and propitious changes in the course of selection and commentary; a neglected sample may become the prized centrepiece of new thinking on a subject.

In speaking of a natural history of metaphor – in Emerson and elsewhere – I mean to reflect an interest in and an investigation into how metaphor has been used. If I were being literal I might call this some variant of linguistic ethnology or research in cultural anthropology, much less philosophical inquiry. The analogy with natural history, then, should suggest how metaphors live, evolve, and then decay to oblivion or ossify to unique effect. 'Language is fossil poetry', Emerson reminds us reflexively – using a metaphor to comment on the nature of language.[102] Much of the overlap between the metaphor of natural history and the work of the present book appears in the way a collection or cabinet of dead things – fossils, taxidermy, artifacts – reframes and reorients living things – communication, concept formation, notions of value. Just as natural history is an ongoing, live experiment, so this present cabinet is provisional, subject to rearrangement, re-description (new labels inscribed for well-known parts of the collection, etc.) and re-evaluation. As old metaphors change and new metaphors emerge, the contents of the cabinet must also undergo rethinking and reordering. New relationships appear while old resonances fade.

As noted at the outset, I do not offer an exhaustive historical, literary or philo-sophical context for Emerson's remarks in *English Traits*; this has been done very ably by many of the diligent, informed scholars whose work I have relied on and integrated into the present work. But then an inquiry into metaphor – as a linguistic and philo-sophical phenomenon – is not part-for-part identical with an inquiry into *English Traits*; they are complementary endeavours, each amplifying qualities of the other. Where Emerson characterized some features and attributes, histories and gardens, architecture and literature, railroads and naval science to form a picture of the English (an admittedly partial, subjective portrait 'now revised after seven busy years'[103]), my inquiry looks intently at the very nature of those representations. Consequently the present collection will necessarily conform more to the style and form of the compendium, and take seriously the qualities of such work: 'a concise, yet compre-hensive compilation of a body of knowledge', often concerning 'some delimited field of human interest or endeavor'. Loyal to the roots of its Latin name – *compenso* meaning to weigh together or balance – a natural history of metaphor will aim to evaluate the credentials and credibility of the compiled specimens, and interrogate the elucida-tions made possible from their relationships. Because it is exploratory and speculative rather than deductive and definitive, this work invites the pursuit of allusive, anecdotal and affective aspects of Emerson's prose – the way it makes possible thinking on certain topics, and renews thinking on other issues. A collection of such remarks forms a report on these encounters and interactions, sometimes producing odd effects and artifacts – perhaps ones that are inadvertently against the grain of the thinking that spurred them on. A natural history of metaphor implies a need to conduct an inquiry somewhat obliquely, to seek – and sometimes interpolate – connections and refractions in the esoteric and idiosyncratic, since a direct encounter often leaves us where it found us. But then the unsettled qualities of these associations and relation-ships constitute the point of such inquiry. Metaphor after all is meant to carry us from one place to another – to move us.

27. As Eduardo Cadava sees Emerson with 'a tendency to render political and historical issues in climatological and meterological terms', I see him – especially in *English Traits* – with an inclination to represent biological and racial topics through genealogical tropes.[104] I find Emerson engaging 'the ideologeme of nature' from another angle. The ideologeme, according to Frederic Jameson, is 'the smallest intelligible unit of the essentially antagonistic collective discourses of social classes'.[105] That smallest intelligible unit appears to be, in the present case, the metaphor. Yet even as each metaphor is identified in its particularity, much intellectual reward comes from discovering the metaphor's conceptual depth and in discerning the metaphor's relationship to realms beyond its immediate specificity.

One of those radiating features of *English Traits* – and of Emerson's use of metaphors therein – includes the consideration of the autobiographical nature of the work: how his metaphors are related to his experiences, and by extension, more generally – how one's selection and use of tropes is in itself an indication of the traits of thought. The present work is no different, of course, and the metaphors that I choose to focus on, and the connections I see between Emerson's work and the work of others – connections that are often contingent, arbitrary, but nevertheless on occasion apparent – derive admittedly from my own experiences, my own encounters with texts, my own implication in the language I use. My remarks and reflections are not strictly or literally autobiographical, yet the connections I make must be understood as informed by the embodied circumstance of language: as such these amalgamations necessarily reflect and reveal something highly particular and partial about me as an author, biographer, compiler, curator, reader and florilegist. But this is not a confession. Rather, as Walter Kaufmann has written of Nietzsche's work, there is in every reader an occasion to be 'prompted by personal experience' to see a connection, to draw a line of relationship.[106] Emerson too is embodied and embedded in his culture and time, inspired and constrained by his use of language, and shaped by his reading and other influences – cultural and natural. Such particularity is not a deficit or defect, a liability to one's pursuit of clear thinking and brave experimentation; just the opposite. And here the autobiographical reality of one's reading – that it must always derive from this particular point of view – reinforces the stakes for articulating and assessing the moral implications of metaphor use. For Emerson intellect is in metaphor.

If the elements of the present *florilegium* are arranged well, or well enough, if the assembly suggests profitable connections and relationships, then the work itself should be prismatic. As the Stranger from Elea says in Plato's *Sophist*: '[A]ny light, whether dim or bright, thrown upon the one will illuminate the other to an equal degree, and if, on the other hand, we cannot get sight of either, at any rate we will make the best we can of it under these conditions and force a passage through the argument with both elbows at once'.[107] Hold the book in a certain way and you can see through it to other texts. Ideally those other texts in turn illuminate *English Traits*. 'That is, here', as Derrida wrote at the beginning of 'White Mythology: Metaphor in the Text of Philosophy': 'to make from a volume, approximately, more or less, a flower, to extract a flower, to mount it, or rather to have it mount itself, bring itself to light. [...]'[108]

VI

Founding Thoughts

1. Ralph Waldo Emerson, 'Land'

    The American is only the continuation of the English genius into new conditions, more or less propitious.[1]

2. For 164 years after its sole printing in Boston in 1773, the book that exerted the most influence on the founding thinkers of the American republic – John Locke's *Second Treatise on Government* (1689) – was not reprinted in the United States.[2] Locke was provoked to write the work in part by the appearance of a posthumous treatise arguing for the absolute authority of monarchs; Locke's *First Treatise* was a substantial attack on the idea as represented by Robert Filmer and carried the unvarnished subtitle 'The False Principles and Foundations of Sir Robert Filmer, and his Followers, are Detected and Overthrown'. In 1680 Filmer's *Patriarcha, or the Natural Power of Kings* was published in England, albeit decades after the author's death. Filmer's argument was in keeping with several of his earlier works, including *The Necessity of the Absolute Power of the Kings* (1648). Filmer believed that the basis for monarchical power lay in the direct, unbroken descent of rulers all the way back to Adam. Yes that Adam. And it was only through total commitment to the divine right of blood inheritance that anything like meaningful authority over men could be achieved and defended.

    Filmer's Adamite rendering of authority drew its logical force from an analogy with the role and position of the father in a family, at least as they were understood in Biblical terms. In chapter 1 of *Patriarcha* entitled 'That the First Kings Were Fathers of Families', Filmer characterizes the relationship between the ancient state of society and the present one:

    > I see not then how the Children of *Adam,* or of any man else can be free from subjection to their *Parents*: And this subjection of Children being the Fountain of all *Regal Authority,* by the Ordination of God himself; It follows, that Civil Power, not only in general is by Divine Institution, but even the Assignment of it Specifically to the eldest Parents, which quite takes away that New and Common distinction which refers only Power Universal and Absolute to God; but Power Respective in regard of the Special Form of Government to the Choice of the people.[3]

    While Filmer's thesis had its supporters (and surprisingly not solely from the monarchy), it also appeared in the late-seventeenth century – a time of great religious, political and legal foment – at which point it was almost immediately taken up by James Tyrell, Algernon Sidney and John Locke as a warranted site for attack. Filmer's posthumous work stirred a tremendous intellectual counter-movement, a rebellion against the central metaphor and attempted analogy at the heart of *Patriarcha*. The title of Tyrell's work bears the most blatant inversion of Filmer's work: *Patriacha Non Monarcha (The Patriarch Unmonarched)*. In his *Discourses Concerning Government* (1680), Sidney mounted a chapter-by-chapter, section-by-section, refutation of Filmer's book, and called him out, line by line, in order to challenge the beliefs that underwrite any faith in the divine right of kings:

> If he say true, there is but one government in the world that can have anything of justice in it: and those who have hitherto been esteemed the best and wisest of men, for having constituted commonwealths or kingdoms; and taken much pains so to proportion the powers of several magistracies, that they might all concur in procuring the publick good; or so to divide the powers between the magistrates and people, that a well-regulated harmony might be preserved in the whole, were the most unjust and foolish of all men. They were not builders, but overthrowers of governments: Their business was to set up aristocratical, democratical or mixed governments, in opposition to that monarchy which by the immutable laws of God and nature is imposed upon mankind; or presumptuously to put shackles upon the monarch, who by the same laws is to be absolute and uncontrolled: They were rebellious and disobedient sons, who rose up against their father; and not only refused to hearken to his voice, but made him bend to their will.[4]

Filmer would find in John Locke another 'rebellious and disobedient son' who composed his own radical refutation of *Patriarcha* in his *First Treatise on Government* (1689), a negative critique of Filmer's core thesis. In his *Second Treatise on Government*, Locke developed a positive argument for the nature of civil society in the absence of an absolute monarch:

> The law, that was to govern Adam, was the same that was to govern all his posterity, the law of reason. But his offspring having another way of entrance into the world, different from him, by a natural birth, that produced them ignorant and without the use of reason, they were not presently under that law; for nobody can be under a law, which is not promulgated to him; and this law being promulgated or made known by reason only, he that is not come to the use of his reason, cannot be said to be under this law; and Adam's children, being not presently as soon as born, under this law of reason, were not presently free: for law, in its true notion, is not so much the limitation, as the direction of a free and intelligent agent to his proper interest, and prescribes no farther than is for the general good of those under that law: could they be happier without it, the law, as a useless thing, would of itself vanish; and that ill deserves the name of confinement which hedges us in only from bogs and precipices. So that, however it may be mistaken, the end of law is not to abolish or restrain, but to preserve and enlarge freedom: for in all the states of created beings capable of laws, 'where there is no law, there is no

freedom;' for liberty is to be free from restraint and violence from others; which cannot be where there is not law: but freedom is not, as we are told, 'a liberty for every man to do what he lists:' (for who could be free, when every other man's humour might domineer over him?) but a liberty to dispose, and order as he lists, his person, actions, possessions, and his whole property, within the allowance of those laws under which he is, and therein not to be subject to the arbitrary will of another, but freely follow his own.[5]

Inspired or unnerved by Filmer, the Tyrell-Sidney-Locke triad refutation did not just stimulate a negative reaction to the proposition that the king deserves unquestioned authority over all subjects – as a father was assumed to hold over his children. Their work also contributed to the foundation of late colonial thinking in North America where the likes of Thomas Jefferson, Benjamin Franklin, John Adams, James Madison, Alexander Hamilton and George Washington were discovering their admiration for the work through increasingly outward, political applications of it. These 'rebellious and disobedient sons' wrote to their king, articulated a challenge to his sovereign authority, and pronounced a new phase in the order of the human family. The father was no longer king; the king was no longer father.

Locke's *Second Treatise on Government* was not reprinted in America for 164 years after its founding because the work was regarded as best suited to the commencement of revolutions, and the establishment of a new civil, anti-monarchical government, but not advantageous to a Constitution or legislature that were in place. Locke's treatise agitated a generation to rewrite the relationship between children and parents, to reconfigure the power colonies might claim from the sovereigns who were presumed to rule them. Once these children matured, parental dictates and decrees no longer seemed fixed and absolute but instead appeared open to revision, redaction and other modes of political transformation. Yet when an alternative government was settled on the shores of the Hudson and Potomac, the new founding fathers should not want to publish anew the ideas that inspired the deterioration of parental power.

3.   In 1768 Silas Downer, a Rhode Island lawyer gave a speech entitled 'A Son of Liberty' on the occasion of planting a so-called 'Tree of Liberty'. The traditions associated with this commemorative act 'went back to the days before the Norman conquest of Britain, when Saxon clans would assemble for town meetings under a large tree. Saxons had continued this tradition under Norman rule in remembrance of their lost liberty, and their descendants continued the tradition as a sign of their willingness to defend their chartered rights'.[6] Downer addressed his audience as 'Dearly beloved Countrymen', and argued against a British rule that would tax the colonies without granting them equal representation under the law: 'King's subjects shall not be governed by laws, in the making of which they had no share'.[7] Downer had an explanation for how Great Britain felt entitled to this privilege: 'This claim of the commons to a sovereignty over it, is founded by them on their being the *Mother Country*'. Making reference to the symbolic significance of the early planting of liberty trees, and extending the logic of a mother country having a claim to the jurisdiction

of its child colonies, Downer said: 'by the best account, *Britain* was people from *Gaul*, now called *France*, wherefore according to their principles the parliaments of *France* have a right to govern them'.[8] Downer neatly and unequivocally summoned his outrage at the obvious inconsistency of this unenforced idea: 'If this doctrine of the maternal authority of one country over another be a little examined, it will be found to be the greatest absurdity that ever entered into the head of a politician'.[9] Downer concluded his critique with the hope that 'in the future the *Mother Country* will not be so frequently in our mouths, as they are only sounds without meaning'.[10] This 'son of liberty' was not at all pleased with the authority his 'mother country' assumed. If he was going to be ruled over, he wanted a chance to CREATE that rule, and not have the conditions of his creation – his tethering to a sovereign mother who issues decrees – dictated to him. Laws that constrained him, or left him free, would be drawn in part by his own design, and given by his own consent. The idea of a Republic fashioned by a governing people within it – a democracy – was being heralded within earshot of the Crown's authority. 'Let us act prudently, peaceably, firmly, and jointly', Downer counseled, 'Let us break off all trade and commerce with a people who would enslave us, as the only means to prevent our ruin'.[11] It is some measure of the stakes involved that Silas Downer could claim it prudent and peaceable to say: 'We will be freemen, or we will die'.[12]

4.   On 12 September 1835 in Concord, Massachusetts, on the bicentennial anniversary of the incorporation of the town, Emerson gave a public lecture entitled 'Historical Discourse', in which he quoted from the Town Records (of Concord) a statement of public union dated 24 January 1774:

> We cannot possibly view with indifference the past and present obstinate endeavors of the enemies of this, as well as the mother country, to rob us of those rights, that are the distinguished glory and felicity of this land; rights, that we are obliged to no power, under heaven, for the enjoyment of; as they are the fruit of the heroic enterprises of the first settlers of these American colonies.[13]

5.   Silas Downer, again:

> Our fathers fought and found freedom in the wilderness; they clothed themselves with the skins of wild beasts, and lodged under trees among bushes; but in that state they were happy because they were free.[14]

6.   On 10 January 1776 the Englishman Thomas Paine, having resided in the British colonies in America for only two years, published what proved to be one of the most incendiary and influential pamphlets in support of separation from the British Empire. In *Common Sense* he claimed that 'Now is the seed-time of continental union, faith, and honor'.[15] Paine wished to address the 'connection and dependence' on Great Britain with recourse to 'the principles of nature and common sense, to see what we have to trust to, if separated, and what we are to expect, if dependent'.[16] He began:

I have heard it asserted by some, that as America has flourished under her former connection with Great Britain, the same connection is necessary towards her future happiness, and will always have the same effect. Nothing can be more fallacious than this kind of argument. We may as well assert that because a child has thrived upon milk, that it is never to have meat, or that the first twenty years of our lives is to become a precedent for the next twenty. [...]

But Britain is the parent country, say some. Then the more shame upon her conduct. Even brutes do not devour their young, nor savages make war upon their families; wherefore, the assertion, if true, turns to her reproach; but it happens not to be true, or only partly so, and the phrase *parent* or *mother country* hath been jesuitically adopted by the king and his parasites, with a low papistical design of gaining an unfair bias on the credulous weakness of our minds. Europe, and not England, is the parent country of America. This new world hath been the asylum for the persecuted lovers of civil and religious liberty from *every part* of Europe.[17]

Paine, like Downer, resented the idea that England was a 'mother country' to America, or that the King was America's father. With invective interlaced with Biblical references Paine said: 'I rejected the hardened, sullen-tempered Pharaoh of England for ever; and disdain the wretch, that with the pretended title of FATHER OF HIS PEOPLE can unfeelingly hear of their slaughter, and composedly sleep with their blood upon his soul'.[18] If he truly were the father, then it would be his blood that he sheds in harming his child.

7.   By the summer of 1776 the Declaration of Independence was drafted and prepared for submission to the courts of England. In the final two paragraphs of the document, following the extensive list of alleged wrongs against the Colonies by the present sovereign, King George, the familial nature of the connection between Britain and America remains the principal image used to represent the crown's logic and to refute its authority:

Nor have We been wanting in attention to our British brethren. We have warned them from time to time of attempts by their legislature to extend an unwarrantable jurisdiction over us. We have reminded them of the circumstances of our emigration and settlement here. We have appealed to their native justice and magnanimity, and we have conjured them by the ties of our common kindred to disavow these ursurpations, which would inevitably interrupt our connections and correspondence. They too have been deaf to the voice of justice and of consanguinity. We must, therefore, acquiesce in the necessity, which denounces our Separation, and hold them, as we hold the rest of mankind, Enemies in War, in Peace Friends.

We, therefore, the Representatives of the United States of America, in General Congress Assembled, appealing to the Supreme Judge of the world for the rectitude of our intentions, do, in the Name and by Authority of the good People of these Colonies, solemnly publish and declare That these United Colonies are, and of Right ought to be Free and Independent States; that they are Absolved from all Allegiance to the British Crown, and that all political connection between them and the State of Great Britain is and ought to be totally dissolved [...].[19]

8.   Just as the language of the Declaration of Independence shifts from that of the intimate, family-inflected 'brethren' to that of the more distant, more elective 'Friends', so in the Articles of Confederation (drafted in 1778 in order to create a confederation of the States in America), the relationship between sovereign States of the Union was understood as a choice, and not an inheritance.

> Article III. The said States hereby severally enter into a firm league of friendship with each other, for their common defence, the security of their Liberties, and their mutual and general welfare, binding themselves to assist each other, against all force, offered to, or attacks made upon them, or any of them, on account of religion, sovereignty, trade, or any other pretence whatever.[20]

9.   Does the language of the Declaration of Independence figure the beginning of a revolution or a secession? Conditions were not turning back, in the sense of reverting or being restored to some earlier state of affairs; rather these agents were inaugurating a new circumstance by means of a withdrawal, or severance, from a pre-existing association or bond. The American Revolution may be better understood as an American Evolution: a movement onward, into new conditions.

The relationship between a child and his parents is different from the relationship between a married couple. The tie of marriage can be cut by a word, by a perform- ative utterance, by a decree of divorce, but afterwards we do not use the same word to describe the divorcee's status: the husband, for instance, does not return to bachelorhood (at least not nominally) since the marriage has changed him, his capacity to be named and described, the kinds of relationships that once obtained and now have been cancelled. Just as the marriage vows – legally and divinely – commenced a new metaphysical situation, so a divorce renders them void. But the husband and wife, now unbound from each other, do not walk away unmarked, even if they are legally free of one another. The child is in a different position, however: no matter what the child does in relation to his parents, he remains – forever, ineluctably – their child. Divorcing oneself from one's parents is an image poorly borrowed from our thinking about marriage, a realm of human association that does not share the same logical and physiological characteristics. A marriage is, even if arranged, even if 'in the stars', always an elective union. A decision is made to create this bond, to generate it from law and language, to sanction a reality by declaring it. But the child's relation to his parents is born in the blood and can never be extracted or de-created. A child is bred and as such is inherently bound to his parents; for better or worse, he can do nothing to change the fact of this perpetual continuity. A marriage is a union sanctified under law and God, and at its best is (also) a harmony of the mind and heart's true dictates. But a child is an effect of a physical, biological union. The child is the harmony of the parents' DNA. Like the structure of the double-helix, the child is coiled together irrevocably with the parents who caused the child's creation.

If America is the child of England, then maybe there is no way to enact anything more than a *declaration* of independence – that is, a public, ratified and ultimately legislated pronouncement that the associations between a parent (sovereign) and child (colony) no longer obtain. The parent would then have no legal jurisdiction over its offspring. But as the case of a child divorcing his parents shows, even in the space of legal or political freedom, no matter how forcefully stated and stipulated, the child is still through and through physically bound to his parents – if for no other reason than he is constituted by them, by means of the chemicals and characteristics of their blood.

10.   America is said to have Founding Fathers. How do we mean this? Why do we mean this? Perhaps we believe that, as colonies, America was born of the 'mother country', a child of Great Britain, but that men – men of words, say – sired the country through the writing of a constitution. Or rather, the re-writing of a constitution: shifting from a bond of blood, to a bond of grammar. Henceforth the language of freedom from a parent would be written in declarative sentences instead of passively received through the inheritance of blood. A Founding Father, instead of a divinely ordained monarch dependent on the fate of blood flowing without interruption from generation to generation, would parent freedom. Perhaps having many such Fathers encourages citizens to disperse and deflect the habit of seeking a single sire (and therefore disentangle paternity from legitimacy), and concomitantly reinforces a democratic imagination antagonizes the fate of having parents by means of language – by the composition of new constitutions.

11.   In 1847 when Emerson was considering a return to England – to give lectures prompted by the invitation of his friend and admirer Alexander Ireland – Carlyle wrote with a reassuring reminder to his far-off friend, coaxing him back, that the voyage should be undertaken. Though Carlyle was from Scotland, and at that point in his life Emerson had only spent a few months in England, Carlyle wrote with enthusiasm and conviction:

> And in short, for the truth must be told, London is properly your Mother City too,
> – verily you have about as much to do with it, in spite of Polk and Q. Victory, as
> I had! And you ought to come and look at it, beyond doubt; and say to this land,
> 'Old Mother, how are you getting on at all?' To which the Mother will answer,
> 'Thankee, young son, and you?' – in a way useful to both parties! That is truth.[21]

12.   Ferdinand C. S. Schiller, *Must Philosophers Disagree?* (1934)

> Actually every philosophy was the offspring, the legitimate offspring, of an
> idiosyncrasy, and the history and psychology of its author had far more to do with
> its development than *der Gang der Sache selbst* [the course of the thing itself].
> [...] The naïve student insists on viewing the system from the outside, as a logical
> structure, and not as a psychological process extending over a lifetime. And he
> thereby throws away, or loses, the key to understanding.[22]

13.   Hannah Arendt, *On Revolution* (1963)

It was only in the course of the eighteenth-century that men began to be aware that a new beginning could be a political phenomenon, that it could be the result of what men had done and what they could consciously set out to do. From then on, a 'new continent' and a 'new man' rising from it were no longer needed to instill hope for a new order of things.[23]

14.   Colonial America was, then, the place in history where men realized that they could give birth to something – even to themselves! Writing was used to consciously create something: a land CONCEIVED in liberty. In the case of the Founding Fathers, language was used to form a new conception of a nation, a people and the ideas that rule them.

15.   Stanley Cavell, *Emerson's Transcendental Etudes*

I seem to myself obedient to [Emerson's] 'Experience' in taking the essay's idea of itself as pregnant to be declared in the passages that relate the son now dead to the writer-father's body: 'When I receive a new gift, I do not macerate my body to make the account square, for if I should die I could not make the account square'; and 'Something which I fancied was a part of me, which could not be torn away without tearing me, nor enlarged without enriching me, falls off from me and leaves no scar'. These passages are a man's effort to imagine – to fancy – giving birth.[24]

16.   In colonial America, being a Founding Father meant being a Founding Thinker. To father a nation required thinking – and writing – it into existence. It is not from the commingling of a man and a woman that America's constitution was formed but through the cross-pollination of ideas and ideologies. Thomas Jefferson is said to have remarked upon his composition – the Declaration of Independence – that it was 'the expression of the American mind'.[25] No doubt the mind that by and large crafted the work was his. And yet we know that Jefferson drew from and adapted many ideas from Aristotle, Seneca, Montesquieu and Locke – certainly not American minds. Maybe then Jefferson's use of Greek, Roman, French and English thought was part of his contribution; his manner of blending these eclectic sources enabled him to issue something novel, something blended and not pure, something apart from the ancients and the Europeans, something American. Men give birth then by conceiving ideas and writing them down as constitutions.

17.   Thomas Carlyle, 'The Hero as Divinity'

His blood made the Sea; his flesh was the Land, the Rocks his bones [...]. Untamed Thought, great, giantlike, enormous; – to be tamed in due time into the compact greatness, not giantlike, but godlike and stronger than gianthood, of the Shakespeares, the Goethes! – Spiritually as well as bodily these men are our progenitors.[26]

18.   In 'Literary Ethics' (1838), presented nine days after the Address to the Divinity School at Harvard, Emerson wrote of the intellectual fathers of the Western mind and its letters, and positioned himself in relation to their achievement – and the terrible specter of their imagined nonexistence:

> If you would know the power of character, see how much you would impoverish the world, if you could take clean out of history the lives of Milton, Shakspeare, and Plato, – these three, and cause them not to be. See you not, how much less the power of man would be? I console myself in the poverty of my thoughts; in the paucity of great men, in the malignity and dulness of the nations, by falling back on these sublime recollections, and seeing what the prolific soul could beget on actual nature; – seeing that Plato was, and Shakspeare, and Milton, – three irrefragable facts. Then I dare; I also will essay to be. The humblest, the most hopeless, in view of these radiant facts, may now theorize and hope. In spite of all the rueful abortions that squeak and gibber in the street, in spite of slumber and guilt, in spite of the army, the bar-room, and the jail, *have been* these glorious manifestations of the mind; and I will thank my great brothers so truly for the admonition of their being, as to endeavor also to be just and brave, to aspire and to speak. Plotinus too, and Spinoza, and the immortal bards of philosophy, – that which they have written out with patient courage, makes me bold. No more will I dismiss, with haste, the visions which flash and sparkle across my sky; but observe them, approach them, domesticate them, brood on them, and draw out of the past, genuine life for the present hour.[27]

Three irrefragable and radiant fathers, we might also say – fathers who show us 'what the prolific soul could beget on actual nature'. As readers we cannot contest the generativity of their writing – how their works and thoughts also beget so much of ours, even if borrowed as in quotation. Emerson declared he 'also will essay to be' and therein by contrast not be, nor give birth to, 'all the rueful abortions that squeak and gibber in the street'. The essay, writes William H. Gass, is 'simply a watchful form', 'halfway between sermon and story, the essay interests itself in the narration of ideas – in their *unfolding* [...]'.[28] Gass' emphasis prompts our thinking about the variations of unfolding in essay-writing that make it both a watchful form and a constitutive one. UNFOLDING is one way of describing the creation of prose, the development of ideas, and it is also an apt image of the cell dividing again and again into its own life-form. In the biological process of mitosis a 'parent' cell splits into two or more 'daughter' cells, which in turn can further divide; just before the division, the parent cell undergoes DNA replication, a process that allows the genome to pass into the daughter cells. The writer, the essayist – the one who essays to be – will be a father to himself, give birth to a 'glorious manifestation' of his own, even as – in essaying – he will create the conditions for readers to found or manifest themselves on their own terms. But these are men we speak of – men of letters – and yet they appear to create new life. Are these elocutions meant to be analogical ejaculations? As if the ear were egg and all that is needed for independent life to grow is a session of listening.

Within the year in which he presented the above remarks to an audience of men at Dartmouth College, Emerson wrote in his journal:

> There is no history. There is only biography. The attempt to perpetuate, to fix a thought or principle, fails continually. You can only live for yourself; your action is good only whilst it is alive, – whilst it is in you. The awkward imitation of it by your child or your disciple is not a repetition of it, is not the same thing, but another thing. The new individual must work out the whole problem of science, letters and theology for himself; can owe his fathers nothing. There is no history; only biography.[29]

William H. Gass, commenting on this journal passage, writes: '*To owe our father nothing* ... it is the impossible idea of this nation, still a child of Europe'.[30] Melville once wrote in a letter, after hearing Emerson speak: 'The truth is that we are all sons, grandsons, or nephews or great-nephews of those who go before us. No one is his own sire'.[31] Earlier in his essay Gass remarked: 'Emerson himself did not sprout from his native soil like the local corn, for he was full of Old World inclinations; he was the Old World gone to seed'.[32] The temptation to follow after the analogies of male pregnancy are here truncated by Emerson, Melville and Gass; the life-giving energy is not just something given or spilled, but also something necessarily contained. One is sired but one must also sire oneself – as one must write one's own books if even from quotations. An extreme case makes the point: Pierre Menard's *Quixote* is, despite its repetition of father-Cervantes' words, written in Menard's own hand. And Borges provocatively suggests, or more accurately the narrator of 'Pierre Menard, Author of the *Quixote*', intriguingly notes: 'Menard's fragmentary *Quixote* is more subtle than Cervantes' – and thus Menard's version may mark an improvement over the original.[33] Yet the narrator's sense of the difference between Cervantes' work and Menard's re-inscription of that source indicates that while the texts may be isomorphic they are not, paradoxically, identical: 'It is a revelation to compare the *Don Quixote* of Pierre Menard with that of Miguel de Cervantes' – and though the excerpted lines are the same, the narrator relates: 'The contrast in styles is equally striking'.[34] Still, this analogue from literature does not register the human difference, namely, that we are – each of us – composed of a unique sequence of letters: hence generation can never mean a strict or literal repetition. For this reason the human is fundamentally a literary phenomenon. One can hardly fathom a more elegant response to the question of individual identity than genetic distinction as the condition of existence. Each human person is not a replicated product but a novel invention.

New life will be self-actualizing, asexual, rhizomatic – after it has received its genetic conception (while, of course, not forgetting but perhaps suspending for the time being the knowledge that half a child's genetic material is provided by the mother – a fact that becomes temporarily obscured or displaced by tracing the father-metaphor from the journal passage). Owing the father is not so much a debt as a gift, offered once and thereafter forever unrepayable. In time the father-as-origin becomes an influence under other names and forms – as parent, mentor, friend, teacher, Nature, Church, State, Europe, England, America, Harvard, Books and History. These are now the obliging forces of moral and intellectual instruction, and the child or pupil passing through them, contending with them, is no longer a legitimate offspring or proper heir – certainly not a perfect repetition of the father, or these fathers – rather, something wholly different, all his own. The child, like his biological father, has the whole burden upon him and cannot take over his father's life or identity as he would accept the family business, as he would passively assume a surname or heraldry – as if skipping the necessary step of making his life his own, from within. If there are similarities these are known by comparison, by drawing connections: 'Nature loves analogies, but not repetitions'.[35] Thus the difficult conclusion 'can owe his fathers nothing' does not mean he should not want to, but that he cannot. It is 'the impossible idea' only in so far as the analogy is taken straight, that is as heterosexual. The father – the fatherland – may appear to have rendered a bequest, conscribed the terms of an inheritance, but it is only an initial condition for the child's independence – his thinking, his own generative powers.

The loss of debt to the father goes hand-in-hand with the notion that individuals are, and must be, fathering themselves into existence. Now deemed 'part or particle of God' there is no need for an appeal to origins either to claim salvation or to accept damnation. The gradual displacement of a Calvinist faith in human depravity – that sin is real and ineluctable – takes with it the father-as-cause. The child is not the father's in the way we thought he or she was; and the child certainly neither comes laced and lined with sin from the father nor with a demand to atone for the father's life – its facts and infractions. In this post-Calvinist American mood, the nodes of genesis, generation, and genius all appear endogenous – because 'the inmost in due time becomes the outmost'.[36] One makes oneself as much as one saves oneself; these are the movements of containment and germination as well as the conditions for expression and expiration.

Re-reading Gass' metaphoric phrase – that Emerson was 'the Old World gone to seed' – has at least two further fascinating senses: first, that the plant is allowed to reach a state where its power can become experimental – roaming – subject to hungry birds, diverse soils and unpredictable winds; and secondly, that this allowance or lack of constraint, is a function of being uncultured – we might say, untutored or otherwise abandoned by the father. The seedling, in this sense, is a foundling. The nineteenth century, and its preceding century, was much consumed with the notion of self-culture [*bildung*] so this phenomenon cannot be strictly deemed an Emersonian event. And yet, in the light of what Gass writes about the journal passage – 'Here he is already halfway to the hall. And what the hall holds. Emersons' – a reader may be shocked to think that Emerson's prose is perhaps especially affecting to the fatherless, to any of those readers who have suffered a crisis of the father.[37]

If one is fathered well – though used to the agricultural notion of husbanded – raised from seed to sapling (or sibling), perhaps one has no need of Emerson. Does the variable status of one's own father define whether Emerson is or is not a worthy tutor? Is this difference in fathers why Nietzsche adores Emerson and the likes of John Updike do not?[38] Are we given an unexpected clue to the reader's sense of being cultivated or cultured by a father – his forces husbanded by the father – by virtue of the reader's literary taste? If Emerson's is prose for the fatherless – or perhaps more perversely, those who wish to be fatherless, who wish to 'owe our fathers nothing' – then it is prose once and always for Americans, a people perpetually caught in the tension between being created and creating anew. 'This one fact the world hates, that the soul becomes', – a hatred that abides in the crisis of the father: that one is created by him and not entirely created by him.[39] And it is by virtue of becoming that, according to Emerson, we have any hope for antagonizing necessity, for summoning power – since 'Power ceases in the instant of repose; it resides in the moment of transition from a past to a new state'.[40] We are then best understood as fathered and also fathering ourselves since seeds are subject to a continuum of fates – from being cultured by knowing, tender hands to being strewn haphazardly, and left to fend for themselves.

19.   When Frederick Douglass came to speak before the Carlisle School for Indians in 1872 his reflections on 'Self-Made Men' were not just informed by Emerson's account of representative men but transformed by Douglass' status as an ex-slave and further affected by the constituency he addressed. Now an emancipated citizen of the United States, Douglass spoke before an audience representing the indigenous inhabitants of North America. These earlier Americans neither struggled with a relation to the mother or father country (as whites did) nor contended with the legacy of chattel slavery (as blacks had to), but instead reflected on a history in which they were variously killed, dispossessed and quarantined in the course of European (then American) expansionism from the East, and into the West. As the audience listened to the celebrated orator and abolitionist articulate his gloss on being 'self-made', how did this culture's narratives, associations and tropes of the term inform its listening? Was the notion of *causa sui* – independent self-creation – just another peculiarity of the Caucasian race, a concept now co-opted and rendered anew by a prominent African-American statesmen? If the African slave had been forcibly exiled from his mother- or fatherland – and often literally stripped from his mother and father – the Native American had been displaced or decimated on the continuous soil of North America. Why would either of these figures – ex-slave and Indian – meeting in 1872 want to invest in the notion that they are – could have been, or could be – self-made? For the aboriginal peoples no ocean was crossed and yet the places of origin were disestablished, destroyed, denied. Was Douglass' appropriation of self-making a way, perhaps, of fathoming a strategy for re-founding, for creating new origins, and for doing so by means of a free will beyond the reach of political definitions and racial categories? The self-made man would not be slave or ex-slave, Indian or white, but HUMAN. Douglass addressed this line of thinking in forms of paradox and double-entendre:

> I have by implication admitted that work alone is not the only explanation of self-made men, or of the secret of success. Industry, to be sure, is the superficial and visible cause of success, but what is the cause of industry? In the answer to this question one element is easily pointed out, and that element is necessity. Thackeray very wisely remarks that, 'All men are about as lazy as they can afford

to be'. Men cannot be depended upon to work when they are asked to work for nothing. They are not only as lazy as they can afford to be, but I have found many who were a great deal more so. We all hate the taskmaster, but all men, however industrious, are either lured or lashed through the world, and we should be a lazy, good for-nothing set, if we were not so lured and lashed.

Necessity is not only the mother of invention, but the mainspring of exertion. The presence of some urgent, pinching, imperious necessity, will often not only sting a man into marvelous exertion, but into a sense of the possession, within himself, of powers and resources which else had slumbered on through a long life, unknown to himself and never suspected by others. A man never knows the strength of his grip till life and limb depend upon it. Something is likely to be done when something must be done.[41]

All men 'are either lured or lashed', 'All men are about as lazy as they can afford to be' – these exclusive, provocative generalizations – stated and quoted – are meant, it seems, to recover the human circumstance that we share: necessity afflicts us all, and Douglass urges, it can become the condition for freedom, creativity and self-emancipation. Limitation can stoke the 'sense of the possession, within himself, of the powers and resources which else had slumbered'. Slumbering seems a peculiar – philosophically sanitized – euphemism for the kinds of necessity slaves and Indians encountered. And while Douglass admits that men are not strictly or literally 'self-made' – 'Properly speaking, there are in the world no such men as self-made men'[42] – he appears to lend reinforcement to the paltry theories of 'rugged individualism' that were popularized in this era of Horatio Alger's *Ragged Dick*, published in 1868. Consider how Douglass, despite his acknowledgment of necessity, and the influences that shape men, defends a logic for the 'self-made' that demands a faith in spontaneous, endogenous creation.

Self-made men are the men who, under peculiar difficulties and without the ordinary helps of favoring circumstances, have attained knowledge, usefulness, power and position and have learned from themselves the best uses to which life can be put in this world, in the exercises of these uses to build up worthy character. They are the men who owe little or nothing to birth, relationship, friendly surroundings; to wealth inherited or to early approved means of education; who are what they are, without the aid of any of the favoring conditions by which other men usually rise in the world and achieve great results. In fact they are the men who are not brought up but who are obliged to come up, not only without the voluntary assistance or friendly co-operation of society, but often in open and derisive defiance of all the efforts of society and the tendency of circumstances to repress, retard and keep them down. They are the men who, in a world of schools, academies, colleges and other institutions of learning, are often compelled by unfriendly circumstances to acquire their education elsewhere and, amidst unfavorable conditions, to hew out for themselves a way to success, and thus to become the architects of their own good fortunes. They are in a peculiar sense, indebted to themselves for themselves.[43]

By this point in his lecture Douglass has noted that 'self-made' as a 'term implies an individual independence of the past and present which can never exist',[44] and yet as he defines the notion, it involves independence from conditions – necessities, limits, constraints – that he seems focused on suppressing or denying. The self-made, he contends, have arrived 'motherless and fatherless'.[45] And yet it would be of considerable consequence to any American in 1872, much less in 1862 (the year preceding the Emancipation Proclamation), if he were the son of a slave or the daughter of a delegate to Congress, a European immigrant or a member of the Cherokee or Choctaw tribes. With the shared history of the preceding decades – the Indian Removal Act, the agitation for abolition, the Civil War, the government-sponsored war against native peoples of the West – present in the living memory of the appointed speaker and his audience, Douglass said of America:

> But here, wealth and greatness are forced by no such capricious and arbitrary power. Equality of rights brings equality of positions and dignities. Here society very properly saves itself the trouble of looking up a man's kinsfolks in order to determine his grade in life and the measure of respect due him. It cares very little who was his father or grandfather. The boast of the Jews, 'We have Abraham for our father', has no practical significance here. He who demands consideration on the strength of a reputation of a dead father, is, properly enough, rewarded with derision. We have no reverence to throw away in this wise.[46]

In the next phase of his speech, Douglass takes this comment on anonymous fathers – and American society's apparent lack of care for pedigree – and gives them proper names. Even though Douglass was an adolescent when John Quincy Adams presided as the sixth President of the United States – son of the Second President, John Adams – Douglass pressed his point despite ready-to-hand realities to the contrary. His idealism, or bracketing, should perhaps be taken up as a mark of his hopefulness for democracy – its promise and process – the way it preserves a space for fantasies of freedoms conceived and yet unrealized:

> The sons of illustrious men are put upon trial like the sons of common people. They must prove themselves real CLAYS, WEBSTERS and LINCOLNS, if they would attract to themselves the cordial respect and admiration generally awarded to their brilliant fathers. There is, here, no law of entail or primogeniture. [...]
>
> I would not assume that we are entirely devoid of affection for families and for great names. We have this feeling, but it is a feeling qualified and limited by the popular thought; a thought which springs from the heart of free institutions and is destined to grow stronger the longer these institutions shall endure. George Washington, Jr., or Andrew Jackson, Jr., stand no better chance of being future Presidents than do the sons of Smith or Jones, or the sons of anybody else.[47]

The individual – a figure heralded at the dawn of the republic – is given new powers of independence in this latest phase of the country's maturation: 'With equal suffrage in our hands, we are beyond the power of families, nationalities or races', writes Douglass.[48] Emancipation has not only granted literal freedoms – those essential rights necessary for equal citizenship that, he contends, shift our focus from the races of men to 'an equal chance in the race of life' – but, in Douglass' view, it has also transfigured the metaphysical bonds of man-to-man and man-to-family.

'We ask not for his lineage,
We ask not for his name;
If manliness be in his heart,
He noble birth may claim.
We ask not from what land he came.
Nor where his youth was nursed;
If pure the stream, it matters not
The spot from whence it burst'.[49]

20.   These several lines of thinking about father and fatherland, mother and motherland – and perhaps most unsettling, the uncaused 'motherless and fatherless' – naturally antagonize what has been said about the degree to which we are strictly the children of parents – are sired, fathered, mothered, parented, raised from seedling to sapling, and moreover bound in overt and covert ways to parents – from countenance to the constitution of blood. A whole thinking about traits – full of claims and contradictions, innovations and lapses – is held up anew for comment and question; and by implication, the metaphors that carry and display these features draw our continued, considered attention. This complicated, often warped and disjointed, narrative of the use and influence of metaphors need not be dismissed or derided for its discrepancies: rather its contours and cleave-points can be read as complementary, soliciting attention yet again to the pliability of metaphor – its uncanny adaptability to varied contexts.

21.   Virgil, *Georgics* (c. 29 BCE)

So, you who work the land, learn the right way to grow according
to genus and tame wild fruits with your cultivation.
Don't let you fields lie fallow. [...]

Trees that volunteer, lifting their branches into the light
are barren, it's true, but they spring up abundant and strong,
for they grow in soil fertile by nature. Yet these, too,
if you make grafts and or transplant them to deep-dug trenches,
will shed their wildness and, tended with due care,
will bend to your bidding with little delay.[50]

22.   Thomas Jefferson, like other founders, was a gardener, and so tropes of generation, cultivation, inheritance and constitution are profitably considered in the context of this terrestrial practice – full as it is of compelling images of new life, responsiveness to conditions, and growth. As Andrea Wulf writes in *Founding Gardeners: The*

Revolutionary Generation, Nature, and the Shaping of the American Nation (2011): 'The founding fathers' passion for nature, plants, gardens and agriculture is woven deeply into the fabric of America and aligned with their political thought, both reflecting and influencing it. In fact, I believe, it is impossible to understand the making of America without looking at the founding fathers as farmers and gardeners'.[51] Wulf's analysis of gardens at Washington's Mount Vernon, Jefferson's Monticello, Madison's Montpelier, and Adams' farm in Peacefield, as well as Franklin's expansive interest in horticulture, gives credence to her claim. For the Founders, botany, gardening and the life of plants become the source of metaphors that inform political speech, political theory, the administration of government and the values and virtues proposed for the new nation. Are America's citizens, to borrow Jefferson's words, capable of 'spontaneous growth' on their new and native soil, or must they be 'cultivated' by governments, foreign and domestic?[52] In what sense is a man like a plant – and in what ways different?

As it was with Downer's description of the 'The Tree of Liberty', so for Washington and his accomplices, Wulf notes: 'trees were both a glorious expression of America's beauty and a political trope [...] and when Washington described his lack of funds to pay his soldiers as "an Ax at the Tree of our Safety Interest & Liberty", he used trees as metaphors in the struggle for independence'.[53] When Jefferson and Adams visit The Leasowes together, near Birmingham England, Wulf claims the pastoral scene 'was a metaphor for a republican and simple way of life, influenced by the writings of Homer and Virgil, for whom working the soil was a model of republican virtue'[54]; both men drew from their tour of the English countryside as they planned and planted their American gardens, and it appears, devised the terms and conditions in which to express their political ideas and aspirations. In the time leading up to the Constitutional Convention of 1787, Jefferson, Wulf recounts, 'had consulted [...] John Bartram's travel journal and Humphry Marshall's recently published *Arbustrum Americanum: The American Grove*, the first botanical book about America's plants to be written by an American and published in the United States'.[55] Bartram, a friend of Franklin's, was an American farmer and plant collector, who regularly sent new plant specimens from America to England, and avidly requested novel English varieties be sent to the colonies. The correspondence in seeds transformed the composition of both American and English gardens. The exchange contributed to the range of plants, trees and vines that the Founders and other political writers became familiar with as they planted their gardens and created the conditions for new ideas to take root.

23.   Emerson's sense of England as a garden – as a land (and island) with conditions fit for bountiful (even excessive) production from successful types – is reflected, or paralleled, in his invocation of Cockayne as an analogue or synonym for England. *The Land of Cockaygne* – part of a suite of poems written in or near Kildare by Franciscans in an Irish dialect of Middle English and traced to a manuscript from the 1330s – is a satire of a community of profligate monks living in a place of plenty, Cockaygne. The monks are restive and disobedient, seemingly overwhelmed by their virility. If they act against the laws of God they are loyal to the native powers of their blood – their capacity to seed the soil – as in this stanza from *The Land of Cockaygne*:

The monke that wol be stalun gode
And kan set-a-right is hode,
He schal hab, withoute danger,
Twelve wiues euche yere.

The monk that can be a good stallion
And knows where to put his hood,
He can easily have, without danger,
Twelve wives each year.[56]

24.   In America, 'the whole generative force of nature', as Thomas Jefferson remarked in *Notes on the State of Virginia* is similarly a fact and feature of this new land – a garden in need of tending and tilling, as its men ('cultivators of the earth') are to find responsibilities in siring and sowing.[57] With his attention to conditions, terms and abiding features, the '*State*' of his book's title may be read as a pun – not just the terrestrial limits of the land called Virginia but the very nature of its qualities and attributes. A pun that highlights doubleness, a point of resemblance, a likely or evident analogy and is apparent also in Jefferson's own alternating status between farmer and statesman. Jefferson blends his interest and expertise as a gardener and his skills as a politician to reflect on the conditions for productivity not just in the fields but in Virginia and the country more generally: how to avoid war, stimulate trade and protect freedom.

> To this estimate of our abilities, let me add a word as to the application of them, if, when cleared of the present contest, and of the debts with which that will charge us, we come to measure force hereafter with any European power. Such events are devoutly to be deprecated. Young as we are, and with such a country before us to fill with people and with happiness, we should point in that direction the whole generative force of nature, wasting none of it in efforts of mutual destruction. It should be our endeavor to cultivate the peace and friendship of every nation, even of that which has injured us most, when we shall have carried our point against her. Our interest will be to throw open the doors of commerce, and to knock off all its shackles, giving perfect freedom to all persons for the vent of whatever they may chose to bring into our ports, and asking the same in theirs. [...] This I hope will be our wisdom. And, perhaps, to remove as much as possible the occasions of making war, it might be better for us to abandon the ocean altogether, that being the element whereon we shall be principally exposed to jostle with other nations: to leave to others to bring what we shall want, and to carry what we can spare. This would make us invulnerable to Europe, by offering none of our property to their prize, and would turn all our citizens to the cultivation of the earth; and, I repeat it again, cultivators of the earth are the most virtuous and independent citizens.[58]

25.   As Jefferson addressed the conditions for a country as a garden, as a land of plenty, so Abraham Lincoln attuned us to the terms on which the nation was founded:

Four score and seven years ago our fathers brought forth on this continent, a new nation, conceived in Liberty, and dedicated to the proposition that all men are created equal.

Now we are engaged in a great civil war, testing whether that nation, or any nation so conceived and so dedicated, can long endure. [...]

It is rather for us to be here dedicated to the great task remaining before us – that from these honored dead we take increased devotion to that cause for which they gave the last full measure of devotion – that we highly resolve that these dead shall not have died in vain – that this nation, under God, shall have a new birth of freedom – and that government of the people, by the people, for the people, shall not perish from the earth.[59]

On 19 November 1863 Abraham Lincoln spoke these words on ground being consecrated that day as a Civil War cemetery in Gettysburg, Pennsylvania. During the battle that was fought there only a few months earlier, nearly 51,000 soldiers died in combat over the course of three days. (By comparison 58,000 American soldiers were killed in action during the entire war in Vietnam, from 1961–75). Lincoln reminds the audience – the divided nation – that America was 'conceived in liberty', and that the only appropriate memorial for the dead is a 'new birth of freedom'. With the surrender of the Confederate Army on 9 April 1865, the nation was legally re-united; Lincoln was shot to death within the week. Given these grave, poignant, unprecedented circumstances, Lincoln's memorial could be said to have preceded his demise.

Lincoln might have inaugurated a 'rebirth' of freedom, but he chose instead to proclaim 'a new birth', which leaves us with the sense that America was not being reconceived, but conceived anew in liberty. Rebirth and new birth are not synonymous since properly or literally speaking there is no such thing as a new birth (in the sense of being born again), while there can be a rebirth – such as a *renaissance* – that warrants the impression of a reclamation, revision or reconceptualization that draws from a prior model and adds to it or reforms it. A new birth encodes a redundancy (for all births are by definition new) and orients us to the establishment of new origins – a clean slate, a pure beginning, starting over – whereas, by contrast, a rebirth-as-renaissance offers a new reading based on what is extant.

On 22 September 1862, Lincoln issued the first part of the Emancipation Proclamation, which would legally go into effect on 1 January 1863. He said 'I do order and declare that all persons held as slaves within said designated States, and parts of States, are, and henceforward shall be free'.[60] This statement was made as part of an executive order by a President of the United States during wartime; its content was neither a law ratified by Congress, nor an edict that made ex-slaves instantaneously into free citizens of the republic.

At the time of America's founding the freedom of slaves was neither declared nor enacted. For a constituency determined to establish a formal separation from the colonial empire that ruled it, and as consequence of that breach to found a nation conceived in liberty, the founders nevertheless neglected to secure the rights and freedoms of the many people it had taken or inherited dominion over. Despite its bold rejection of the parent country, the founders remained loyal to increasingly retrograde moral readings of race; Americans, it would seem, had not yet had their own thoughts on the subject of human equality. And like the Founding Fathers whose 'declaration' did not secure independence but rather proclaimed it as a political and moral exigency, Lincoln's proclamation – echoing the founders' authority, but narrowing it from a 'we' to his own, individual, Presidential, 'I do order and declare' – gave words for the shape of freedom to come, words that would become legitimated as law by Congress in the Thirteenth Amendment, adopted in December 1865. Lincoln's genius – and his gift, in multiple senses – was to recognize that a grammar for personal freedom needed to be provided (though prescribed mainly as an agent to preserve the Union), just as the founders knew that a grammar for independence, or national sovereignty, needed to be set out. These are fathered freedoms for fathered lands.

Emerson was immediately cognizant of Lincoln's achievement – both politically and morally, and spoke publically of his praise and admiration in the same month Lincoln made his executive decree. In a lecture given in September 1862, three months before the 'poetic act' would take effect, Emerson addressed an audience in Boston:

> The President by this act has paroled all the slaves in America; they will no more fight against us: and it relieves our race once for all of its crime and false position. The first condition of success is secured in putting ourselves right. We have recovered ourselves from our false position, and planted ourselves on a law of Nature.[61]

As on other occasions, Emerson equivocates the laws of nature and the moral law – agitating his audience to admit that these distinct forms, despite appearances, constitute an ineluctable unity. Provincial habits and the power of faction reinforce an abiding, even aggressive faith in difference, but Lincoln's bold performative utterance brought the particular into communion with the general, made a single man's idea representative of man's idea at large:

> These are the jets of thought into affairs, when, roused by danger or inspired by genius, the political leaders of the day break the else insurmountable routine of class and local legislation, and take a step forward into the direction of catholic and universal interests. Every step in the history of political liberty is a sally of the human mind into the untried Future, and has the interest of genius, and is fruitful in heroic anecdotes. Liberty is a slow fruit.[62]

When Emerson, like many of his countrymen and the international community, was shocked by Lincoln's assassination – 'Old as history is, and manifold as are its tragedies, I doubt if any death has caused so much pain to mankind as this has caused, or will cause, on its announcement'[63] – he eulogized the slain emancipator, caretaker and cultivator of the 'slow fruit' of freedom by saying:

> There is a serene Providence [...] which [...] thrusts aside enemy and obstruction, crushes everything immoral as inhuman, and obtains the ultimate triumph of the best race by sacrifice of everything which resists the moral laws of the world. It

makes its own instruments, creates the man for the time, trains him in poverty, inspires his genius, arms him for his task.[64]

And so Lincoln – 'thoroughly American, had never crossed the sea, had never been spoiled by English insularity or French dissipation; a quite native, aboriginal man, as an acorn from the oak; no aping of foreigners, no frivolous accomplishments [...]' – had a genius for recognizing the relationship between 'a law of Nature' and 'the moral laws of the world'.[65] And if he was, in this sense, a transcendentalist, Lincoln was also empowered to translate its abstractions for the benefit of all Americans, and by extension provide a model for liberty among humankind. 'The virtues of a good magistrate', Emerson observed, 'undo a world of mischief'.[66] That is, if those inherent capacities are given expression; if the discernment of moral and natural laws are not sequestered owing to fear and embarrassment but earn their application in the world. With Lincoln, we find a blend of intellectual perspicuity and practical force, patient reflection and courageous demand; and for those combinations Emerson concluded, '[r]arely was a man so fitted to the event'. 'He is the true history of the American people in his time'.[67]

When it was founded as a nation apart from Europe, at odds with England, the 'truths' that were held 'to be self-evident' – principal among them 'that all men are created equal, that they are endowed by their Creator with certain unalienable Rights' – were not applied to the chattel slave population of the United States.[68] Much later, when Lincoln intervened to preserve the Union the founders created, nearly a century after the first stirrings of the American Revolution, he was not re-issuing what the Founding Fathers had declared for the Caucasian race (namely, a distinction drawn between the English and the American, the imperial force and the rebellion one); he was conceiving anew what freedom could mean for the human citizens of America. Though his primary goal was the preservation of the Union – and, as he told Horace Greeley in 1862, 'If I could save the Union without freeing any slave I would do it' – he was, nevertheless, serving as midwife to a new (or rather long dismissed) idea of freedom by first proclaiming – and thereafter facilitating the legislation of – the truth that 'all men are created equal'.[69] If Lincoln is seen as a midwife – an image that harkens back to Socrates' use of maeutic metaphor to picture his role as a thinker who aided *anamnesis* (ἀνάμνησις, recollection or reminiscence) for others, helping them draw out ideas they already knew, or that lay within, still unconceived – he might also be regarded as pregnant with the thought of freedom and equality on these new terms. In either case (and perhaps both – since one may be a midwife to one's own ideas as well as ideas from others that remain latent within), he recognized these conceptions as a possibility for himself, in others and for the greater benefit of the nation. And so he laboured, and he laboured beside the labourers of such thoughts, coaching and coaxing these ideas into existence. It was not an easy labour: the declaration of independence for people of African descent entailed the comingling or coupling of natural law and political action; and it involved a nuanced distinction between the brute laws of nature and the sober humanism of natural law. If not created equally, then made equal by law, before the law. As such Lincoln's proclamation was a novel conception for America, and an overdue birth of freedom. That the Union's preservation should be tied to the legislation of freedom for all men seems at once an irony and fitting testament to the legacy of men who father nations – or act as the midwives of their actualization – of men who create freedom as if from their speech and their pens – by means of grammar and ink.

26.   Emerson's oration to the graduates at Harvard College in 1837 is at once a commencement, a proclamation, a declaration and an inauguration since he calls forth – on this land – a solicitation for a making and a thinking that is creative, not derivative. As the lecture self-reflexively produces an example of the very thing it seeks to inspire in others, 'The American Scholar' echoes the seminal, enacting speech of the American founders:

> Our day of dependence, our long apprenticeship to the learning of other lands, draws to a close. The millions, that around us are rushing into life, cannot always been fed on the sere remains of foreign harvests.[70]

> Mr President [of Harvard College] and Gentlemen [of the Phi Beta Kappa Society], this confidence in the unsearched might of man belongs, by all motives, by all prophecy, by all preparation, to the American Scholar. We have listened too long to the courtly muses of Europe.[71]

In 'The Young American', a lecture presented to the Mercantile Library Association years later, in early 1844, Emerson remains committed to the need for thinking on American terrain on American terms.

> Gentlemen [of the Mercantile Library Association]: It is remarkable, that our people have their intellectual culture from one country, and their duties from another. This false state of things is newly in a way to be corrected. America is beginning to assert itself to the senses and to the imagination of her children, and Europe is receding in the same degree.[72]

It is part of Emerson's legacy – both in the popular imagination and in fact – that he is known for being critical of an American dependence on European letters, manners and morals. After all, it was upon returning to America from Europe, after a nine-month gestation period, that Emerson asked in his first book *Nature* (1836): 'Why should not we also enjoy an original relation to the universe?'[73] It is as much worth dwelling on the postulation of an ORIGINAL relation as it is worth considering the pleasure one is said to enjoy when having such a relation. Partly this involves pointing to the obvious but easily overlooked fact that Emerson does not promote a relation to an *origin*, but a conscientiousness about the nature of orientation: how one stands in the world, how one looks at it. Emerson continued with a clarifying question: 'Why should not we have a poetry and philosophy of insight and not of tradition, and a religion by revelation to us, and not the history of theirs?'[74] The us and them in this scene of inquiry – we Americans and they, the English or Europeans – reflects Emerson's Revolutionary credentials, his ongoing awareness of the divorce that was meant to break the New World from the Old. In these and similar episodes of reaffirmation of America's difference – and its value – we may take note of what might be called the anxiety of inheritance embedded in his claims; either this anxiety is a condition he shares with his fellow Americans or it is a condition he expects them to share with him. One manifestation of the concern centres on the belief that one is both capable and duty-bound to do, create, or think something that responds to these favored (American) conditions, and at the same time merits comparison with the best of other civilizations. The eroding culture and the emerging one come in for legitimate assessment. Emerson imagines that 'thus far' Americans have been on 'holiday' when it comes to the task of expression on their own terms, because they seem to be 'a people too busy to give to letters any more'.[75] In the 1830s and early 1840s Emerson is asking what Americans have done – in literature, in philosophy, in the arts generally – to 'fill the postponed expectation of the world with something better than the exertions of mechanical skill'.[76] He feels a certain vacancy, almost a poverty of thinking, in America.

Emerson, 'The Young American' (1844)

> In America, we have hitherto little to boast in this kind [of European excellence in public gardens, civic architecture, and other arts]. The cities drain the country of the best part of its population: the flower of the youth, of both sexes, goes into the towns, and the country is cultivated by a so much inferior class. The land, – travel a whole day together, – looks poverty-stricken, and the buildings plain and poor. In Europe, where society has an aristocratic structure, the land is full of men of the best stock, and the best culture, whose interest and pride it is to remain half the year on their estates, and to fill them with every convenience and ornament.[77]

Stanley Cavell, 'Declining Decline' (1989)

> Poverty as a condition of philosophy is hardly a new idea. Emerson deploys it as an idea specifically of America's deprivations, its bleakness and distance from Europe's achievements, as constituting America's necessity, and its opportunity, for finding itself. [...] Others take Emerson to advise America to ignore Europe; to me his practice means that part of the task of discovering philosophy in America is discovering terms in which it is given to us to inherit the philosophy of Europe.[78]

Alexis de Tocqueville, *Democracy in America* (1840)

> I think that there is not, in the civilized world, a country where philosophy is paid less attention than in the United States.
> The Americans have no philosophic school which is their own, and they pay very little mind to those which divide Europe; they scarcely know their names.[79]

VII

A Child of the Saxon Race

1. Emerson acknowledged that 'race works immortally to keep its own', meaning that there are strong forces conspiring within our bodily constitutions that make us who we are.[1] And as Cornel West has written: 'For Emerson, to grapple with the constraints on human power, vision, and newness is to understand first and foremost the role of race in history'.[2] Yet Emerson at times seems to qualify this by suggesting that history is akin to fate while civilization antagonizes them both. Race, as a type of fate, is 'resisted by other forces', principally 'civilization', which Emerson describes in chemical terms as a 're-agent', or solvent. Civilization is said to 'eat away the old traits'.[3] For it is in civilization that we learn, among other things, the construction of race as a concept; we recognize the ways in which race is a NAMED phenomenon – even as we admit that it is also, more structurally, an inherited one.

The English, however, maintain habits of civilization that appear to reinforce rather than resist, or dissolve the traits that distinguish them. 'The English lords', says Emerson, 'do not call their lands after their own names, but call themselves after their lands; as if the man represented the country that bred him; and they rightly wear the token of the glebe [i.e., land] that gave them birth; suggesting that the tie is not cut [...]'.[4] The bond between the Englishman and his land reflects that '[t]heir habits and instincts cleave to nature'.[5] Emerson describes them being 'attached' to land – and sea – for the good it gives them, and says the English 'suspect' any attempt to question this tie, 'as if somebody were fumbling at the umbilical cord and might stop their supplies'.[6] Cornel West asserts that, for Emerson, if race is antagonized or resisted by civilization it remains – as the English appear to treat it – a fundamental part of one's temporal and physical context, an elemental factor in defining one's identity both as an individual and as a member of a race, or a class of persons that share blood, such as a family: '[...] Emerson's conception of the worth and dignity of human personality is racially circumscribed; [and] race is central to his understanding of the historical circumstances which shape human personality'.[7]

2. Emerson arrived alone in Old England from the forests of New England to live, for a time, on 'the British island from which my forefathers came'.[8] Giving a speech in Manchester in 1848 Emerson told his audience 'That which lures a solitary American in the woods with the wish to see England, is the moral peculiarity of the Saxon race', and to perceive 'the imperial trait' that 'lies at the foundation of that aristocratic character, which certainly wanders into strange vagaries, so that its origin is often lost sight of'.[9] By 'peculiarity' he means a perversion that demonstrates uniqueness. And

when he speaks of that trait as 'imperial', we should take it in a double sense – referring both to its dominance and premier status in the system of traits that govern the English constitution, and to the way that inner force manifests itself outwardly, on the global scale as imperial British influence in the form of colonialism. And though the evidences of English imperialism are pervasive – especially so in nineteenth century America – Emerson is keen to consider the land and traditions that give rise to this trait with its attendant 'moral peculiarity'.

And as we might conjecture for most traits, moral and otherwise, Emerson says of the imperial trait that 'its origin is often lost sight of'.[10] Thus when Emerson reflects on travelling to the place of his forefathers, and salutes his Manchester audience with 'All hail! mother of nations', the English listeners – as much as the Americans who will later read the respectful, though somewhat servile salutation in *English Traits* – must marvel that they are at once 'born in the soil' and unable to trace origins owing to 'strange vagaries'.[11] Such is the myth and mystery of origins: that we are all, decidedly even defiantly, born but appear incapable of precisely tracing whence we came. A mother, surely. A mother country, perhaps. But then if 'born in the soil' or born from blood what connects the land and its people? Is it – has it always been and will it always be – the language that cites those sources, that describes the traits and traces of blood? The origins, if there are any, and if they are at all interesting, will not so much be found in the dirt and debris of culture, but in the etymologies and grammar of description. We can see – or say – that America is the child of England, that Old England gave birth to New England, but these are themselves 'strange vagaries' of language, metaphors that heighten the intrigue of origin and descent even while further obscuring their meanings.

VIII

Living Without a Cause

1. Ludwig Wittgenstein, *On Certainty*

It is so difficult to find the beginning. Or better: it is difficult to begin at the beginning. And not try to go further back.[1]

2. Virgil, *Georgics*

Earth swells moistly and begs for bursting seed.
Then Sky, all-powerful father, descends to the womb
of his fertile spouse with inseminating rain and, uniting
his strength with her strong body, nourishes all they conceive.[2]

3. In the gospel of John, the Word causes the beginning. Or better: the beginning is a word, and the word is God. God is said to be The Father of Earth and Heaven so if 'all things were made by Him; and without Him was not any thing made that was made', are we not given an image of a man giving birth?[3] We have no organic precedent for this among *homo sapiens*, so it is an image of faith or allegory; it is a creation myth or an account of extramental realities that exceed human comprehension. Yet drawing from empirical instances we can fathom a sort of asexual creation, perhaps logically antedated by an immaculate conception. Does God, the Father, inseminate himself – after Virgil – 'often without any coupling, pregnant by the wind (oh, strange to relate)'?[4] The Word (*logos*, λόγος) of God, or as God, is understood in this ancient context as the creative force, or divine order according to which things come into being. In America the Word was given by Thomas Jefferson and other Founding Fathers; pronouncing the Declaration of Independence initiated a new beginning. Saying words created new things – a nation, a people, an idea of the nation and the people.

4. In the mid-twentieth century, British philosopher J. L. Austin elucidated some of the ways in which we can, or should say, that words do things: 'It was for too long the assumption of philosophers that the business of a 'statement' can only be to 'describe' some state of affairs [...]'.[5] The assumption is countered, it would seem, in myriad examples – from the Gospels of the New Testament to the charters of the Founding Fathers – where 'the uttering of the sentence is, or is a part of, the doing of an action, which again would not normally be described as saying something'.[6] Austin called such declarations 'performatives', and his account, in part, pointed out how words do things.[7] Such word-actions appear to have a causative power (in Austin's examples,

with the taking of wedding vows, the making of promises), and thus it should follow that we can also speak of performatives as creative.

5.   There are many conceptions of America: thinking that creates ideas that define the sort of place it is, or that conjecture what kind of power – political, philosophical, personal – it possesses and makes possible. One conception of the nation emphasizes its attraction to immigrants; how it is a land that people come to. The idea is provocative in so far as it may also apply to the native born: that they are not yet arrived in the nation until – born unto it – until they have become aware of their own status as immigrants. Rather than being a member of the lineage-based Daughters of the Revolution – a group that requires siring by Founding Fathers as the criterion for inclusion – the immigrant arrives without genetic claim. The immigrant can make, or mark, his transition away from a native land by taking on citizenship. We describe this in creative, constitutional, performative terms: he pledges allegiance to the country and thereby *becomes* an American.

> I hereby declare, on oath, that I absolutely and entirely renounce and abjure all allegiance and fidelity to any foreign prince, potentate, state or sovereignty, of whom or which I have heretofore been a subject or citizen; that I will support and defend the Constitution and laws of the United States of America against all enemies, foreign and domestic; that I will bear true faith and allegiance to the same; that I will bear arms on behalf of the United States when required by the law; that I will perform noncombatant service in the armed forces of the United States when required by the law; that I will perform work of national importance under civilian direction when required by the law; and that I take this obligation freely without any mental reservation or purpose of evasion; so help me God.[8]

This oath is a performative that shed origins. After 'all allegiance and fidelity' is 'absolutely and entirely renounce[d]', the citizen is reborn under a new creed, able to claim equal membership in a community founded without inherited, hierarchical power. By pronouncement the speaker is incorporated, 'naturalized'. No longer a subject who is subject to aristocratic rule, the immigrant – now citizen – pledges a faith that not only generates a new status with a new set of commitments, but also liberates him from the sanctions and sins of the mother- or fatherland.

6.   Brother Lawrence, *The Practice of the Presence of God*

> That all possible kinds of mortification, if they were void of the love of GOD, could not efface a single sin. That we ought, without anxiety, to expect the pardon of our sins from the blood of JESUS CHRIST, only endeavoring to love Him with all our hearts.[9]

7.   St Francis of Assisi, *Letter to All the Friars*

> I also beseech in the Lord all my brothers who are and shall be and desire to be priests of the Most High that, when they wish to celebrate Mass, being pure, they offer the true Sacrifice of the Body and Blood of our Lord Jesus Christ purely, with

reverence, with a holy and clean intention, not for any earthly thing or fear or for the love of any man, as it were pleasing men.[10]

8.   Sophocles, *Oedipus the King*

OEDIPUS   What is the rite of purification? How shall it be done?
CREON   By banishing a man, or expiation of blood by blood [...].[11]

9.   If the immigrant is banished, or exiles himself, to America – and discovers in this new land that the claims of the old do not survive – what bonds preside instead? Does not the vision (or expectation) of America without heredity and heraldry, and only government-granted and self-appointed election, mean there is no blood to expiate? If America was founded on an idea and not by the transmission of the blood among kings, queens and their kin, then is the American a fantasy of a bloodless body? Namely one that is not constrained by lineage, descent and aristocracy but only his own imagination and will – again, a self-made man, a *causa sui*, a motherless and fatherless foundling?[12] No matter where one comes from, in America one is invited to exist as if free from origins and causes. The American lives a myth of being originless, a myth that appears to announce human nervousness about the possibility of freedom. Fearing the logical consequences of causation – determinism, fate, necessity – a new story is told: one where the citizen is empowered to begin from his own volition, the nation comes into being by decree. A written charter or a spoken act of declaration is taken to confirm one's freedom from origins; by being able to begin again, one no longer begins at the beginning but at some further point.

Yet there is blood in American origins. Paradoxically, its founding and re-founding wars were fought for imagined bloodlessness by the shedding of blood – first to free itself from aristocratic Britain in the Revolutionary War, then to free itself from itself in the Civil War – declaring, at last, freedom for all. And freedom from all blood for all. America's occasional blood-letting seems to activate, or re-activate, the conviction that blood does not matter.

It has been very advantageous, perhaps essential, to American identity that it is allowed to have a faith in this myth. Being originless, in this sense, becomes the condition for social, artistic and political adaptability. Anyone can be born an American; it is not a privilege of select breeding; and many can be naturalized as Americans – drawn into the nation bloodlessly, without recourse to the exile's origins. Nationalism, in turn, is heterogeneous; and every American can make his or her own myth of America because there is no hereditary origin to refer to. Without blood-relations to remind citizens of their inclusion or exclusion from a family, they are freed to write their own stories and histories – or to rewrite them. The ending changes the beginning, again and again; each day gives new depth and orientation to the days that precede it.

With no origin, all points in the network can be claimed as the centre. Or as so many people have, one may move to a central city, such as New York, where the abundant proliferation of difference has the effect of creating anonymity; the anonymity in turn may become the condition for one's rebirth or re-description.

New York, in E. B. White's description, 'is peculiarly constructed to absorb almost anything that comes along'.[13] Since the city defeats the effects any single personality can have on the place, New York is as uniquely welcoming upon one's arrival as it is indifferent upon one's leave-taking. The city's vast infrastructure encourages arterial in-goings and out-goings, enabling and encouraging a permeable flow and a perpetual transformation of the city's citizens, contents and constitution. Every morning a new aggregation of New Yorkers awakens; today's arrangement reflects yesterday's attrition from death, bad luck, lost desire and the allure or demand to emigrate to other places, and accounts for the new day's births and other arrivals. The city's vast system of diverse, churning elements reinforces the originlessness of its members. As a city that is made of and proud of its immigrants, and continually renewed by their arrival from all directions, being from New York is not as meaningful as it might be in another city; and similarly, being from somewhere other than New York is certainly not a mark of shame – it is a sign of verve, ambition and a willingness to rethink and re-make one's identity.

The very notion of NATIVE is proudly, almost defiantly, under negotiation in New York since it is a city that can shift one's attention from where one is *from* to where one *lives*. As Emerson was sailing east to America in 1833, returning from Europe and England, he wrote in his journal 'I […] wish I knew where & how I ought to live'.[14] It is a desire that deflects an interest in origins in favor of an inquiry into becoming, or as Emerson will ask in 1844, 'Where do we find ourselves?'[15] – a question of literal and existential orientation that New York endlessly invites in its inhabitants. Yet the finding is not a discovery but a creation that derives from an intellectual and emotional initiative – as Nietzsche intimates in his response to the question: 'We have never sought ourselves – how could it happen that we should ever *find* ourselves?'[16] The year after 'Experience' appeared, Thoreau addressed Emerson's question in *Walden*, taking a queue from the woods and wilderness when he wrote: 'Not till we are lost, in other words, not till we have lost the world, do we begin to find ourselves, and realize where we are and the infinite extent of our relations'.[17] While Thoreau's context suggests that lostness is something that happens to us, or can happen to us (only then becoming the condition for finding or creating), Jonathan Franzen proposes that it is also something one can actualize. In his essay 'First City' Franzen writes: 'There's no better way of rejecting where you came from, no plainer declaration of an intention to reinvent yourself, than moving to New York; I speak from experience'.[18] And yet going to the woods, or moving to the city are choices – willful enterprises in which one proposes to get lost in order to be found. Still, Franzen's notions of rejection and reinvention should be described with humour, for the immigrant to New York will be ineluctably marked as such – as an 'endless seeker', in Emerson's phrase.[19] Becoming a New Yorker (or the correlated enterprise, becoming an American) could be understood as a perpetual undertaking of the immigrant resident – a project of self-formation or -reformation that recedes as one attempts to approach it, that remains elusive and unfinished, like the city itself.

Being born in New York suggests an aspect or element of aristocratic birth: that no matter what the immigrant does in his life, there will never be a claim to New

York as his origin. He will never inhabit a metaphysic residency in the city. Such a permanent immigrancy, by contrast, makes the mere fact of one's birth in New York a kind of heredity – a matter of one's blood. Yet while being born in New York may be a conspicuous example – part of the lore of the city (including its appeals from the perspective and authority of the native), and inform the rhetoric of becoming a New Yorker – all this can be said about being born anywhere. The presumption that a New York birth confers a trait unavailable to the immigrant, to be sure, is part of the mythic definition of the city; the grandness – even incomprehensibility – of the place perhaps invites an appeal to residency or a claim from nativity as an edge in understanding, as some form of possession. Yet whether one is born in New York or Nacogdoches, Nairobi or Nagasaki, Nantes or Niagara Falls, this habit of marking the place of birth as a constitutionally significant – and unchangeable – fact reinforces the valuation of origins. The size and scope of the farm or remote wilderness can be just as affecting as the vaunted metropolis for the privileging of place. As the Lord and Lady are created by birth and remain Lord and Lady for life – retaining their heraldry as a matter of an aristocratic claim – so every birth in every blood is bound to its particular site of birth. Move away, change a name, and one is still from this place and no other. For better or worse, or just indifferently, and however contingently, one is marked for life by the land that hosted the occasion of one's birth.

10.   In the chapter on 'Land' in *English Traits*, Emerson offers a portrait of the ambivalent American mind at the middle of his century: a mind at once preoccupied with the formidable reality of British history and influence, and the antagonizing force and fact of an emerging American prominence.

> In all that is done or begun by the Americans towards right thinking or practice, we are met by a civilization already settled and overpowering. The culture of the day, the thoughts and aims of men, are English thoughts and aims. A nation considerable for a thousand years since Egbert, it has, in the last centuries, obtained the ascendant, and stamped the knowledge, activity, and power of mankind with its impress. Those who resist it do not feel it or obey it less.[20]

Emerson appears to be describing the English impress – or impression – as a form of that 'irresistible dictation' he will write about in *The Conduct of Life*.[21] Even if we should want to define ourselves outside of the English orbit, or claim that our ideas or land is not infiltrated with the English style, we will find that 'England has inoculated all nations with her civilization, intelligence, and tastes; and, to resist the tyranny and prepossession of the British element, a serious man must aid himself […] if only by means of the very impatience which English forms are sure to awaken in independent minds'.[22] A serious man himself, Emerson early on in his own literary and philosophical career felt the 'impatience' England can stimulate, and returned from his early-1830s travels provoked to find or invent new forms. Now in middle age, Emerson speculates on a kind of Gibbon-like future for the British 'as some signs portend that [London] has reached its highest point'.[23] And he adds more generally: 'It is observed' – he does not mention by whom, perhaps it is his own observation made anonymous – 'that the English interest us a little less within a few years; and hence the impression that the British power has culminated, is in solstice, or already declining'.[24]

As it is a great risk to emigrate from one's homeland, in effect enacting a kind of judgement that a breach is necessary (while also showing that it is possible), the immigrant to America is given a context in which to rethink, among other national affects and influences, the English impression. For some, America became the home of the brave, a broad platform for those who would leave the motherland and subvert inherited traces for more general, transnational values. 'Perhaps the ocean serves', Emerson conjectures, 'as a galvanic battery to distribute acids at one pole, and alkalies at the other. So England tends to accumulate her liberals in America, and her conservatives at London'.[25] America appears to enlist the vital energies of the globe's inhabitants that would conjecture an identity beyond inheritance, who could fathom the counteracting forces of free expression and experimentation. If this is or was an American condition – one is tempted to say it has become an American trait – it is no longer a phenomenon confined to its home terrain. Americanism has been adopted and incorporated across international borders, and adapted to serve the local constituencies. Coming to America may no longer require emigrating from some other nation.

11.   Does declaring independence from one's parent country – either in active revolt or in mere preference for another land – make one an orphan? Do the seditious revolutionary and the immigrant 'yearning to breathe free' make orphans of themselves? America's welcome to 'huddled masses' is not an invitation to accept something that is given, but a disclosure that confirms the conditions for making something that is not. The Statue of Liberty – a beacon to the immigrant – can be taken as a sign of the freedoms that await: first, a freedom from the past, history, political ties and allegiances, religion, parents, old names, family traits and native lands; and, secondly, a freedom to create a new life by means of one's own hands, heart and mind. Here the myth of making oneself an orphan – where the parents are disowned, lost or forgotten – is paired with the myth of being self-made.

While it is often read otherwise, when Emerson writes 'I shun father and mother and wife and brother, when my genius calls me', he acknowledges the existence of parents and siblings, and even the elective covenant of marriage; the movement to shun or turn away – to abandon – is a confession of having an origin (and similarly rigid affiliations such as wedlock).[26] Responding to origins, in this way, Emerson confirms the child's weddedness to the world not his separation from it. Parents and children use the fact of their connection differently, at different times – sometimes to broker deeper intimacy, sometimes to leverage wider estrangement. Either way the bond between parent and child, like that between nation and native citizen, creates unique conditions for the struggle of identity, freedom and power.

12.   When Emerson writes of parents and nations-as-parents, he seems to speak to an audience of children, but then we are all children of parents and the subjects of nations. Thus his audience is assured, and especially so if it includes children who are

exiles and immigrants, foundlings and orphans, or anyone at odds with conventional theories of origins:

> All things are dissolved to their centre by their cause, and, in the universal miracle, petty and particular miracles disappear. If, therefore, a man claims to know and speak of God, and carries you backward to the phraseology of some old mouldered nation in another country, in another world, believe him not. Is the acorn better than the oak which is its fulness and completion? Is the parent better than the child into whom he has cast his ripened being? Whence, then, this worship of the past? The centuries are conspirators against the sanity and authority of the soul. Time and space are but physiological colors which the eye makes, but the soul is light; where it is, is day; where it was, is night; and history is an impertinence and an injury, if it be any thing more than a cheerful apologue or parable of my being and becoming.[27]

The following remarks from 'Education' were among those Emerson delivered at Waterville College (Maine), Dartmouth College (New Hampshire) and Middlebury College (Vermont), among other places. These are so many words to parents, disclosures about the genuine nature of their children:

> I call our system a system of despair, and I find all the correction, all the revolution that is needed and that the best spirits of this age promise, in one word, in Hope. Nature, when she sends a new mind into the world, fills it beforehand with a desire for that which she wishes it to know and do. Let us wait and see what is this new creation, of what new organ the great Spirit had need when it incarnated this new Will. A new Adam in the garden, he is to name all the beasts in the field, all the gods in the sky. And jealous provision seems to have been made in his constitution that you shall not invade and contaminate him with the worn weeds of your language and opinions. The charm of life is this variety of genius, these contrasts and flavors by which Heaven has modulated the identity of truth, and there is a perpetual hankering to violate this individuality, to warp his ways of thinking and behavior to resemble or reflect your thinking and behavior. A low self-love in the parent desires that his child should repeat his character and fortune; an expectation which the child, if justice is done him, will nobly disappoint.[28]

Emerson refracts Plato's theory of *anamnesis* when he writes of Nature 'sending' a soul into the world already knowing what it wishes to know. It is the parents' duty to clear the way for this inrush, or when appropriate to present obstructions (provocations in Emerson's language), so that children may avail themselves of these new things (the new mind, the new creation, the new organ, the new Will, the new Adam). Emerson's parable of a continually refreshed Garden of Eden, with new Adams, and one presumes new Eves, arriving daily, introduces the logical possibility of contamination. The new is the pure, on some readings; for others the new must always derive from sources and causes – defilements all. Traditions and habits and the status quo are positioned to 'violate' this sacred estate. Notice how Emerson connects genius with 'the identity of truth'. This subtle collusion concedes a great deal of what lies behind Emerson's belief in the power and form of individuals. GENIUS is his preferred term, really more of a synonym, for soul, spirit, conscience and the Socratic idea of the *daimon*. It is the quality of a person that makes him who he is. One's genius is the individual manifestation of truth. Genius, in this sense, may not be contaminated by influencing agents since it is impervious – itself a pure node of influence – the site upon which *anamnesis* finds its expression.

13.   If parentless, is one never born in America but always reborn, or even born unborn (that is, alive but without a cause)? Is speaking of such things speaking of monsters and miracles?

We might say that America is a place where a certain kind of fate is made, not strictly inherited. If blood no longer matters – if its matter is no longer an issue for one's identity and worth – then blood is also no way to explain one's self; instead of recourse to parentage and homeland, a person can only point to his thoughts and actions. While daunting, this is the ideal proposed in shifting from aristocracy to meritocracy – where equality and freedom are taken for granted as the rights of all men, but the honours of excellence are bestowed only upon those who manifest thought and action worthy of such attention. By contrast, equality and freedom are not rewards for thought and action, they are its conditions. As fate would have it, though, constraints – the forms of 'irresistible dictation' that everywhere surround us and encode us – are also, arguably, the finer accomplices of thought and action.[29] The amalgamated ideal, then, would have us free enough to find our limits, and sufficiently equal to discover our difference.

14.   Emerson admired the Englishmen he met on his trips, and believed they held an enviable position: somehow as a private citizenry they possessed the benefits of aristocracy – living without the encumbrances of its old form while drawing from the vestigial artifacts that remained advantageous.

> In the social world, an Englishman to-day has the best lot. He is a king in a plain coat. He goes with the most powerful protection, keeps the best company, is armed by the best education, is seconded by wealth; and his English name and accidents are like a flourish of trumpets announcing him. This, with his quiet style of manners, gives him the power of a sovereign, without the inconveniences which belong to that rank. I must prefer the condition of an English gentleman of the better class, to that of any potentate in Europe [...].[30]

Emerson's observation, and his stated preference, directs us to the genius or adaptive success of the mid-nineteenth century English bourgeoisie, the 'proudest result of this creation'.[31] Elsewhere in *English Traits* Emerson offers an illustrative contrast: 'The American system is more democratic, more humane; yet the American people do not yield better or more able men, or more inventions or books or benefits, than the English'.[32] Partly the English success is owing to the blend of inheritance ('his English name') with unpredictable vicissitudes ('and accidents'). In circumstances that acknowledge fate and freedom, one is grounded by tradition but liberated for invention.

In America we are perhaps given too much to creating names – for the nation, for its laws and for ourselves – making name-creation itself a site for invention. As such, names announce Americans differently: they signal a place of origin (when we let them reflect ethnic origins) or they suggest a destination (when origins are dropped or exchanged to favour another family or association); this is the alternation between where we are from and where we wish to be. A family name, then, merely conveys itself – not its bearers; there is no assurance that there is a family behind it. An invented first name – instead of some common John or Jane – almost insists on the lack of continuity to family and parentage, tradition and pedigree; it is a bid for radical, unimpeachable specificity. In both cases – of adopted surname or invented first name – we may come to know a person with these names, but the names do not divulge or describe where she is from. The new names obscure origins as much as they appear to invite our inquiry into them.

If the English are a family, then all English subjects are royal descendants. Though America is a child of England, she is also a child who rebelled against the family in order to declare that the bond between divine and royal descent and the natural state of the democratic individual was insolvent – and so she is a child without a claim to the king's crown. So much of Emerson's work in 1830s and 1840s is a study of the reason for this breach – between parent and child, country of origin and country of inhabitation – and the implications of this dissolution. The war for independence, the acts of resistance, the confirmation of separation all seem like destructive acts, and yet they are protestations motivated by a desire to form or formulate a new constitution, a new body, a new identity. Self-reliance, in Emerson's characterization of the term, suggests how one may rethink origins for the American context, at least within view of the country's founding and in the midst of the onrush of European Romanticism. This search for 'the aboriginal Self, on which a universal reliance may be grounded', provides a framework for shunning, turning away, abandoning and 'aversion' to conformity. These are moods and figures, gestures and habits, of the precocious child as much as the mature artist; they imply metaphysical varieties of definition and invention. Paradoxically, again, the achievement of being original, in this sense – free to seek the aboriginal Self, to have an original relation – demands a denial of origins.

15.   Sigmund Freud, *The Ego and the Id* (1923)

> [… W]e cannot in fact claim that there is a hereditary process operating directly within the ego. What we encounter here is the yawning gulf between actual individuals, and our notion of the species. […] The ego's experiences seem to be lost to heredity to begin with; however, if they recur often and strongly enough in numerous successive generations of individuals, they transform themselves so to speak into id experiences, and their impact is then preserved through heredity. The heritable id accordingly harbours within it remnants of countless numbers of previous egos, and when an individual ego evolves its super-ego from the id it is perhaps merely bringing older ego forms back to light, and back to life.[33]

What is this recovery or regeneration that Freud speaks of? The 'gulf' is not between individuals and the countries they come from, or currently inhabit. He addresses

the level of species in deep time. If there are traits that inhere in the British constitution, then would not the child of 'successive generations' of the English carry these
traits, and manifest them – even if on new terrain, in 'new conditions, more or less
propitious', or culminate – after Carlyle's phrase – in 'little more or little else' than
the parent country?[34] Is Emerson's New England, then, more truly English than we
know or recognize – more so, perhaps especially, than Emerson can observe and
attest to, or even would wish to? Has this successive, successful generation from
England – as America, as Emerson – shown itself a rightful heir with a legitimate
claim to succession, despite secession? If New England offers conditions that are not
definitively *more* propitious than Old England, then what accounts for the American
difference – could it be English traits? The Freudian intervention makes the political
achievements that resulted from declarations and proclamations seem fragile, even
feeble, compared with the enduring, directing forces present in one's veins.

16.   Nietzsche said of Emerson that '[H]e simply does not know how old he already is
and how young he will still be – he could say of himself, in the words of Lope de Vega,
'*yo me sucedo a mi mismo*' – 'I am my own successor'.[35] Could this mean that Emerson
gives birth to himself in yet another vision of fulfilled male pregnancy? Is he his own
parent and his own child? We can take a clue from the notion of succession – sharing
a characteristic that inheres in one instance after other; and, in both biological and
geological terms as they make evident the sequences of chronological inheritance, one
generation after another – in eons, erathems, periods and epochs. For Emerson to be
his own successor we might say that he follows after himself in some way. Succession
could also be described as a form of realization – of latencies made manifest – as in
'History' when he writes of the 'unattained but attainable self'.[36] One is not yet the
person one wishes to be, but in conceiving what it would mean to be that person,
one moves incrementally, successively toward what Stanley Cavell has described as a
'further, next [...] self.[37] This vision of the successive self – that it can succeed one's
present self and succeed as a self – lies at the core of Cavell's rendition of moral perfectionism, a path for perpetually onward conceptions of one's identity.
    Nietzsche's attribution of Lope de Vega's self-description knowingly reflects
Emerson's ambitions for rethinking both self-identity and self-creation – particularly
the way they appear to cohere as phenomena. And yet does not the proposition, or
even the speculation, of this relation intimate a metaphysical conceit? What sort
of self does one have, or have to have, that it can be concurrently fixed, stable and
unchanging (that is to say identifiable), and capable of undergoing transformation
from one successive version to another? How does one say who one is while also
remaining 'an endless seeker with no Past at my back', continually reforming the
content and character of his or her identity?[38] Nietzsche's promising, if provocative,
reply is to become one's own successor.

17.   The nature of human creation – whether through procreation or in writing
– makes a creator the very medium of his messages, perhaps even as the locus of
transmission for some divine message, the node through which God passes into

new forms. The writer, like the parent, then is simply *in medias res*. Using Aristotle's taxonomy of causes, the writer would be merely an efficient cause of his book – as if taking dictation from on high, from some divine muse; and parents would be the material causes of their children. The idea that animates a book, like the genes that form the zygote, makes it seem as if the author/parent is in a place where things are just passing through.

Yet are ideas really gene-like – discrete bits of information that together form an inheritable, embodied system of instructions? The discoveries of modern genetics postdate Emerson (and Darwin), yet the intuition that there is something in the blood goes back to the pre-Socratics. When Emerson's familiarity with ancient Greek and Roman philosophers is coupled with his first-hand experience of the burgeoning biological sciences of the nineteenth century, a nascent faith in ideas that pass through the blood should be forthcoming – a natural effect of such reading, such combinations of theories.

> All the admirable expedients or means hit upon in England, must be looked at as growths or irresistible offshoots of the expanding mind of the race. A man of that brain thinks and acts thus; and his neighbor, being afflicted with the same kind of brain, though he is rich, and called a baron, or a duke, thinks the same thing, and is ready to allow the justice of the thought and act in his retainer or tenant, though sorely against his baronial or ducal will.[39]

The sound and sentiment of an 'irresistible offshoot' from the 'mind of the race', reaches out to the opening remarks of Emerson's essay 'Fate' (1860): 'Tis fine for us to speculate and elect our course, if we must accept an irresistible dictation'.[40] Even if we can grow, or choose our action, there are already forces at work in us, compelling us – irresistibly – in the direction befitting the larger mind of which we are a part. If this account is accurate, then one does not think one's own thoughts: one thinks thoughts on behalf of some larger neural network.

18.   With this kind of 'irresistible' genetics at work in us, the idea of authorship demands another look. Let us say that writing is a manner of giving birth to something – a sequence of words and sentences in a specific order. Thinking in the terms of genetic chemistry, and the 'dictates' of biochemical replication, we can also say that a human birth is a mode of writing, since the child is the inscription of parental DNA in a sequence of chemicals in a specific order. In a literal sense, as Emerson writes, 'the child quotes his father', but figuratively, the child is also, in part, a quotation of the father.[41] The mother is the other accomplice from whom the child's being quotes itself into existence. The so-called alphabet of life, or Human Genome, is a book of letters. What are children – what we are – then but compositions made by conspiring authors?

19.   Authorship, we may presume, refers to the activity of creating something – causing it to come forth. But what is the meaning of CREATION in the present context: an emergent phenomena arising *ex nihilo* or one that develops from pre-existing conditions (namely, as a register of effects that culminates in a new thing)? Describing

an author's work as 'original' preserves a latent faith in the novelty of created things; to speak of it as 'seminal' points to its influence on other works. And yet, even as some may praise originality as a function of primordiality and apparent causelessness, others seek to trace the lineages that inform the creation of works. Context, influence and biographical detail are cited as evidence that suggests a pre-existing model – a source; yet an encounter with a work of art – literary, architectural or otherwise – can render such claims of causal influence specious, if also simultaneously captivating as imaginative explorations of the act of creation. Part of authorship's continuing aura involves the promise of a free application of ideas and instincts; being denied a claim to authorship then would seem no different than being told everything is fated, a matter of course, a function of particular events and effects – that such work must necessarily be appraised as an amalgamation, a collection of quotations. Likewise, even as we ponder the capacity for the authorship of art and other things, we acknowledge that we too are authored by forces beyond ourselves – neither self-created, nor self-made, we are the effect of another agent's mind and will or the indeterminate biological and material coursings of natural causation.

20.   Seneca, *Epistles*

> This is the law to which you were born; it was the lot of your father, your mother, your ancestors and of all who came before you as it will be of all who come after you. There is no means of altering the irresistible succession of events which carries all things along in its binding grip.[42]

21.   In *Nature* Emerson said that '[o]ur dealing with sensible objects is a constant exercise in the necessary lessons of difference, of likeness, of order, of being and seeming, of progressive arrangement; of ascent from particular to general; of combination to one end of manifold forces'.[43] Such an account would be as familiar to the florilegist as to the museum curator, and both roles require vigilant discernment of these tasks. But over time, as models and metaphors change, so will that 'dealing'. The contents of a commonplace book will be affected by the chosen categories, topics and terms, while a museum collection will undergo transformations of specimens, displays and commentaries, depending on its organizing principles. As such, curators – at least of the sort sympathetic to Emerson's approach – must be sensible to the world as both physician and metaphysician, as scientist and artist; so 'it is significant irony', claims John Dewey, 'that the old quarrel of philosopher and poet was brought off by one' – namely Emerson – 'who united in himself more than has another individual the qualities of both artist and metaphysician. At bottom the quarrel is not one of objectives nor yet of methods, but of the affections'.[44] The curator's work depends on discerning the features that unite things and distinguish them, and charting the courses and coordinates of these related objects and phenomena. Emerson recognized the power of perspicuity and placement when reading Carlyle's *Past and Present* (1843), and his remarks on its author stand for the effects such talents may afford: 'Truth is very old, but the merit of seers is not to invent but to dispose objects in their

right places, and he is the commander who is always in the mount, whose eye not only sees details, but throws crowds of details into their right arrangement and a larger and juster totality than any other'.[45] And as Emerson observed similarly in the first chapter of the *Natural History of Intellect*: 'to arrange general reflections in their natural order [...] – this is continuity for the great. [...] What we want is consecutiveness. 'Tis with us a flash of light, then a long darkness, then a flash again. Ah! could we turn these fugitive sparkles into an astronomy of Copernican worlds'.[46]

When Emerson visited the Jardin des Plantes and the other departments of the Muséum National d'Histoire Naturelle in 1833, he himself became sensible of not just the variety of specimens – and the awe they inspired in him – but the skills necessary to arrange them into effective curatorial schemes. His insights about the relationships and connections that pervade organic life were not made by encounters with inventions but with ancient samples ordered to prompt the visitor to recognize ancestry, and in that mood be 'moved by strange sympathies'.[47] Recalling his days at the museum Emerson noted: 'Ah said I this is philanthropy, wisdom, taste – to form a Cabinet of natural history'.[48] To initiate a collection that might inform and influence its viewers this way, a curator of organic specimens must try to make evident how these diverse, and perhaps at times unobvious or unintuitive, relationships might be displayed. An overarching metaphor can serve to frame not just the arrangement of a collection but the varied readings it may inspire.

Given the diversity of tropes in Darwin's *The Origin of Species*, it is noteworthy that the only illustration that appears in his lengthy, belated report is a 'tree of life' based on a sketch he made in 1837. The singularity and centrality of that image have shaped the conversation in evolutionary biology ever since. Likewise, the curatorial design of a museum collection may be defined and thereafter shaped by a trope with organizing force. When Emerson toured the Muséum National d'Histoire Naturelle he found collections arranged phenotypically, that is, by shared observable characteristics. Gathering specimens according to perceptible features can be traced back to Aristotle's taxonomies of sea life, but the Paris museum was in these years more overtly influenced by the ideas of biologists Carl Linnaeus and Georges Cuvier (the latter of whom was the director of the museum a few years prior to Emerson's arrival there). Linnaeus, for example, perceived continuity in the descent of organic creatures, and created a binomial nomenclature to reflect the similarities between related groups (the first of the two names identifying the genus).[49] The otherwise two-dimensional list of family, genus, species, etc. achieves physical embodiment in the galleries of paleontology and comparative anatomy where animal skeletons are arranged in formation, all facing in the same direction – a dramatic stampede of evolution. 'As Linnaeus made a dial of plants', noted Emerson, 'so shall you of all the objects that guide your walks'.[50] Here Emerson references an image from Linnaeus' *Philosophia Botanica* (1751) in which the Swedish scientist mapped an intricate *Horalogium Florae* (flower clock). Meanwhile, Linnaeus' diagram of nomenclature can be said to guide one's pathways in a museum, for example, where the design of exhibits corresponds to the principles and parameters of the sketch. A physical translation of a written taxonomy into the very floor plan of a museum is found at the American Museum of Natural History in

New York where a different, but related, design is the model for the halls of vertebrate origins, saurischian dinosaurs and ornithischian dinosaurs. The curators of these halls use individual skeletons and fossils to literalize the image known as a cladogram.

For curators, the tree-as-metaphor is attractive for its narrative potency, and the design of the fourth floor of the American Museum of Natural History – its Halls of Saurischian Dinosaurs – reflects their use of the story-like progression of descent. The 'branches' of the cladogram invite the visitor to follow a pathway in the narrative; the non-teleological form, however, also allows visitors to retrace their paths to common points of bi-section. Even more intriguingly, the curators also graft onto the exhibits an important aspect of the nineteenth-century cabinets in so far as the branches contain clustered glass-enclosed cases, for example with a representative species and its relatives. In this way the narrative features of the tree or cladogram are brought into concert with the collecting, arranging and editorial aspects of the traditional cabinet of natural history. These museum halls are themselves hybrids of two complementary strategies of display.

In the mid-twentieth century a model for understanding ancestral relationships among organisms was innovated based on the preceding century's dominant tree-of-life metaphor, now largely associated with the legacy of Darwin's evolution theory. Cladistics, the name itself acknowledging its continuity with the earlier tree-based trope (κλάδος, branch), became a promising method for classifying organisms based strictly on lineages of descent, and nothing else. The single branch, or monophyletic group, would include a founding ancestor, at the base of the limb, and its subsequent descendants. The design of cladograms is unlike the prior models, such as those offered by Linnaeus, in which morphology-oriented taxonomies grouped organisms by shared characteristics that were observable. Entomologist Willi Hennig, benefitting from advances in twentieth-century evolutionary biology, innovated cladograms to represent phylogenetic relations, thereby introducing a new level of accuracy into the arrangement of organisms, and enhancing precision in understanding the nature of descent from ancestors. The branching design of a tree of life diagram that relies primarily on the comparison of DNA sequences, for example, instead of physical characteristics, can take several forms, including a circular shape.[51] Cladistics does not displace or disprove the Linnaean taxonomy but recommends a different – and complementary – way of understanding the relationships between organisms; its organizing principle is genetic continuity rather than the identification and aggregation of observable traits.

When touring the Paris hall, with its rushing crowd of skeletons, one is overcome by the feeling of the strangely coordinated forces of nature. Organisms that may never have seen one another alive, much less existed at the same time, are here shown in a shared moment of tandem procession. The very manner in which the organisms are arranged suggests a fable or a theatrical intervention. Consequently the human hand and its attendant governing concepts becomes a prominent part of the display.

In the New York museum, the entire fourth floor is a physical instantiation of a cladogram, thereby enabling a visitor to navigate temporally and genetically by reference to discrete instances of varied species. In this exhibit, the continuities and relationships between species become evident according to one's appreciation of the cladogram. In both museums, though, the tree of life metaphor finds interpretation in the order and arrangement of organic specimens. Following the tree of life to its endpoint, a visitor wonders what lies below the roots.

22.   The visitor to a museum of natural history that achieves its design based on tree metaphors may be intrigued to read Gilles Deleuze and Félix Guattari describe their distrust of 'arborescence'. In 'Rhizome', the Introduction to their book *A Thousand Plateaus: Capitalism and Schizophrenia* (1980), they write: 'We're tired of trees'.

> We should stop believing in trees, roots, and radicles. They've made us suffer too much. All of arborescent culture is founded on them, from biology to linguistics. Nothing is beautiful or loving or political aside from underground stems and aerial roots, adventitious growths and rhizomes.[52]

They describe how a rhizome 'as subterranean stem is absolutely different from roots and radicles. Bulbs and tubers are rhizomes'.[53] And so the humble potato, crabgrass and rat are all habilitated by Deleuze and Guattari's anti-tree thesis. By his own account, Emerson would have welcomed the development of thinking on this often derided form of life. In the essay 'Beauty' he asked 'what does the botanist know of the virtues of his weeds?' and elsewhere, in answering the question 'What is a weed?' Emerson suggested: 'a plant whose virtues have not yet been discovered [...]'.[54] In the *Natural History of Intellect*, Emerson postulated the weed's promise even when set against the established wonders of nature and art: 'There are times when the cawing of a crow, a weed, a snow-flake, a boy's willow whistle, or a farmer planting in his field is more suggestive to the mind than the Yosemite gorge or the Vatican would be in another hour'.[55] Darwin, whose work is so often associated with the tree metaphor, may have proved sympathetic to the rhizome and the weed given his interest in the 'entangled bank, clothed with many plants of many kinds'.[56] As noted early on, Darwin wrote in *The Origin of Species* of an 'inextricable web of affinities' and 'a web of complex relations', metaphors that frustrate a quick or clichéd assessment of the tree in evolutionary thinking.

The image-fatigue described by Deleuze and Guattari may extend to a wide range of inherited tropes – namely, images that no longer appear to possess the explanatory power they once held. As the filmmaker – or imagemaker – Werner Herzog has claimed on our behalf, we are immersed in images that are degraded or no longer serve us, and we deserve new ones. Herzog glosses his much-quoted dictum about 'the inadequate imagery of today's civilization' by saying that he has 'the impression that the images that surround us today are worn out; they are abused and useless and exhausted. They are limping and dragging themselves behind the rest of our cultural evolution'. The rogue filmmaker further suggests that we are surrounded by worn out images because 'of the inability of too many people to seek out fresh ones'.[57] One way of seeking and finding novel images is not by inventing them but offering new interpretations of old, familiar, pervasive and 'worn out' pictures and modes of representation; the new reading can renew and reinvigorate the apparently worn out by recovering or reminding us what used to be interesting about the image and what might now be pertinent. Herzog's own *Cave of Forgotten Dreams* exemplifies how seeking out new images may culminate in finding 34 thousand year old images that are not at all worn out.

Still, disappointment or disillusionment with the abundance of well-worn, or perhaps worn out ('abused and useless and exhausted') metaphors does not make their replacement easy. Thomas Kuhn, who is very conscious of the presence of metaphor in the history of science, has shown how a paradigm grips the minds of intelligent people – until it does not. In *The Structure of Scientific Revolutions* (1962), Kuhn re-describes scientific 'discovery' (for which 'we need a new vocabulary and concepts') as dependent on the perception of anomaly – '[t]hat awareness of anomaly opens a period in which conceptual categories are adjusted until the initially anomalous has become the anticipated'.[58] And even then, or only then do we recognize how the displaced paradigm exists as a sort of relic drawn upon for illustration and reference. The model or metaphor may become antiquated but such maturity does not mean it becomes irrelevant; rather, its significance and credentials are incorporated anew into the history of thought. 'The world is flat' has been recovered as a motto – and metaphor – for the digital era of global cosmopolitanism and free market transnationalism, when not long ago it was a shorthand for ignorance, superstition and bad science. Like a weed, a metaphor cannot be eradicated but followed after (with new methods of investigation), directed when possible (with new modes of interpretation), and ultimately accepted as part of the structure and continuity of expression.

And yet Deleuze and Guattari attempt to displace the worn out image of the tree, of which they are 'tired', with an image they believe is more conceptually arresting, more vital and more philosophically responsible. The exchange they propose – the rhizome for the tree, one metaphor for another – reflects how prominently the weed is (in Emerson's word) 'suggestive' to their minds: how the weed-as-image, for instance, amplifies new or neglected conceptual and political values and virtues (among them a focus on connection and heterogeneity); embodies a principle of multiplicity that dissolves strict subject/object and dualistic relationships; references the continuous repair of networks despite ruptures; privileges maps over 'tracing' (of traits, for example); disallows the identification of a beginning or an end; and dismantles hierarchies that reinforce a focus on origins. 'There is always something genealogical about a tree', the authors note, whereas the rhizome – defined as it is by 'transversal communication' – is fundamentally opposed to that way of understanding relationships, connections and causes.[59] Instead of issuing a critique of metaphor per se, Deleuze and Guattari offer an alternative, competing metaphor – the rhizome – thereby showing that their disillusionment is not with the presence of metaphors in our language but the way we may either intentionally or inadvertently employ harmful, misleading, worn out and enervating tropes and analogies. Moreover, while still in the immediate presence of this book, and the works it draws from and references (many of them obviously partaking in a legacy of arborescence), the question nevertheless arises to what extent the *florilegium* and its several identified variants (*zibaldone*, etc.) may be fundamentally rhizomatic in form.

23.   What if Deleuze and Guattari, like so many inheritors (and critics) of tree-based imagery, emphasized certain features of the tree to the exclusion or diminishment of others? What if this happens with many readings and uses of Darwin's dominant tree of life metaphor? After all, as strong material and intellectual evidence suggests, and the later science of cladistics encodes in its etymology, Darwin himself was not so much championing trees as adopting an explanatory model that illustrated his principal interest in branches.

Darwin's sketch in *Notebook B* page 36 from 1837 is customarily viewed as a tree, as a sketch for the tree of life drawing that would become the only illustration in *The Origin of Species*.[60] But the most conspicuous feature of his abstract representation is not its tree-ness but its depiction of branching. The sketch, in other words, is not a picture of a tree but an image of the kinds of relationships branches make possible; for Darwin, it is a schematic for an idea of what a portion of a tree illustrates for evolutionary theory. And there are of course other life forms that can branch besides trees. In fact, only a few pages earlier in the same notebook, Darwin writes: 'The tree of life should perhaps be called the coral of life, base of branches dead; so that passages cannot be seen'.[61] In other words Darwin's interest in the tree metaphor was not primarily its qualities of rootedness, vertically, hierarchy or even its capacity to reflect insights about descent and sexual selection. Rather, Darwin was trying to find a metaphor to capture his interest in branching. Coral-as-metaphor is promising because it highlights asexual, rhizomatic relationships: a piece of coral, like a weed, can break away from its parent plant and continue to grow.

During the time when Darwin was composing *Notebook B* – which he titled *Zoonomia*, referencing the title of his grandfather Erasmus Darwin's book, *Zoonomia; or, The Laws of Organic Life* (1794) – he was reading *The Principles of Descriptive and Physiological Botany* (1835), a volume written by his mentor, John Stevens Henslow; and as the title promises, Henslow undertakes botanical investigations in this work, not the study of vertebrates as we see in Cuvier's research. Henslow's book was published in Dionysius Lardner's *Cabinet Cyclopedia*, the same series in which Emerson found John F. W. Herschel's *A Preliminary Discourse on the Study of Natural Philosophy* (1831) discussed earlier. In the year after returning from his voyage on the *Beagle*, and in the days and months in which he was adding to *Notebook B*, Darwin was reading Henslow's just-published book on the nature of plants, where Henslow writes:

Branches. – In very many plants, but more especially in dicotyledonous species, we find the stem furnished with 'branches'. [...] Branches have precisely the same organisation as the stem; and they may, in fact, be considered as so many partial stems engrafted into the main trunk. Originating, as we have stated, from buds, their disposition round the stem must depend upon the arrangement of the leaves, to which we shall allude when we treat of those organs. *We may, however, remark, that branches are never so symmetrically arranged as leaves; because a great many buds are never developed at all. This arises from the unfavourable circumstances under which many are placed, for receiving a sufficiency of air, of moisture, and more especially of light.* The consequence is, that those which originate on the lower parts of the stem, are either much stunted, or become abortive.[62]

Beside the italicized portion of Henslow's passage in Darwin's personal copy of the book, Darwin penciled in the margin 'tree of life'. Note that Henslow sets 'branches' off in quotation marks to emphasize it as a metaphor. When Darwin encountered the branch metaphor it, perhaps intuitively, naturally, logically suggested an association with a tree. Yet other kinds of plants – as well as corals and related rhizomatic forms – have branches. In *The Origin of Species* Darwin formalizes both the tree metaphor and the attribute of the tree's structure most relevant to his point:

> As buds give rise by growth to fresh buds, and these, if vigorous, branch out and overtop on all sides many a feebler branch, so by generation I believe it has been with the great Tree of Life, which fills with its dead and broken branches the crust of the earth, and covers the surface with its ever branching and beautiful ramifications.[63]

Branches, then, are things trees and rhizomes have in common, and this shared feature has led scholars and lay readers alike to associate Darwin's tree of life metaphor with other metaphorical aspects of trees – that is with traits that are not shared with rhizomatic life forms. Moreover, and perhaps even more dangerously, a trouble arises when inheritors of Darwin – again nonspecialist readers and scientists alike – treat the tree of life not as a metaphor at all, but as literal: as if any given tree were simply a literal manifestation of the mechanisms of evolution by natural selection. What happens in the light of Darwin's reading of Henslow, his marginalia in Henslow's *Botany*, and Darwin's writing in *Notebook B*, is that our appreciation for the metaphorical nature of his use of tree is re-habilitated and re-emphasized.

Adding further to the sense of what may be called a metaphorical milieu – or the imaginative space in which Darwin was working – we should remember that Darwin's father, Robert, was an avid gardener who experimented with ornamental trees and shrubs, and had particular success grafting varieties of fruit trees. In 1800, Robert's brother-in-law, John Wedgwood advocated the idea of a horticulture society and in 1804 became a founding member of the Royal Horticulture Society in London. Complementing this brief anecdotal list of prominent family practice in botany, there is Henslow, who recommended to Captain Fitzroy that Darwin take his spot on the *Beagle*, and who was the beneficiary of Darwin's collection of plant specimens while he was undertaking the nearly-five-year voyage. And to end at the beginning, consider afresh how Darwin begins *Notebook B* by summarizing Erasmus Darwin's *Zoonomia*, mentioning fruit trees on page one. In fact, in Darwin's personal copy of *Zoonomia*, the following passage is triple scored: '[…] buds and bulbs, [are] attended with a very curious circumstance; and that is, that they exactly resemble their parents, as is observable in grafting fruit trees, and in propagating flower-roots; whereas the seminal offspring of plants being supplied with nutriment by the mother, is liable to perpetual variation'.[64] That is to say, Darwin is very familiar with asexual reproduction (such as we find in rhizomes – in species of corals and weeds), and with the techniques of grafting.

As a kind of encomium to the foregoing aggregation of anecdotes from Darwin's personal and intellectual history, consider also how in 1868 (more than three decades after the composition of *Notebook B*) when schematizing an image for the descent of primates, Darwin remained more committed to the feature – and metaphor – of branching than to any other figurative aspect of trees.[65] Needless to say, this later drawing is most commonly referred to as a 'tree diagram', as the earlier one from 1837 is known as a 'tree of life' illustration. Even after 30 years, though, Darwin does not add or innovate: the central feature, the core metaphor that retains his interest – and is believed to possess the necessary representative power to illustrate his theory – is branching.

Moreover, when Darwin writes 'The tree of life should perhaps be called the coral of life', we are reminded that coral may be a more fitting over-all metaphor for natural selection, perhaps precisely because the 'base of branches [are] dead'.[66] Unlike seeded and seminal life forms that require the base to be alive in order to grow and procreate, rhizomatic species do not depend on this kind of life source or point of origin. When a rhizome breaks off it may continue to grow. Consequently it is worth considering that Darwin's attraction to Henslow's metaphor of branches – and his marginalia remark 'tree of life' – did not so much reflect his captivation with all tree-like features but rather quite specifically with the rhizomatic feature represented by the metaphor of branches. When we return to Darwin's tree of life sketch on page 36 of *Notebook B* in the light of the preceding contextualizing remarks, the abstractness of the drawing allows us to see it as also, or even primarily, as an illustration not of a tree at all, but of one trait of a tree, namely, its branches. Seeing the drawing under a different aspect, then, its branching qualities can seem quite overtly rhizomatic.

Adapting Some Secret of His Own Anatomy

1.   In *The Selfish Gene* (1976) Richard Dawkins wrote anthropomorphically of the eponymous molecular unit of heredity – a so-called 'selfish' gene – that uses humans as 'vehicles' to replicate itself.[1] Dawkins' imaginative, if at times ungenerous, reading of Darwinian evolution would have humans be little more than mobile information storage devices whose principal service is passing genetic material from one generation to the next. Running alongside this functionalist reading of genes, Dawkins also proposed a theory of memetics to account for cultural evolution. For this partner theory he innovated a metaphor to analogize the mechanisms of evolutionary biology as found in modern genetics: the unit of transmission here is not the gene, but the meme – the smallest unit of information or ideas. Memetics parallels (or we might say pictures or even caricatures) evolutionary thinking in so far as we imagine a meme – or 'unit of cultural transmission' – passing from one host to another in a series of inseminations or infections.[2] Dawkins also suggests, in another inflection of anthropomorphic description, that the meme may be a 'unit of imitation'.[3] This is perhaps most fitting to the etymology since meme is an abbreviation of the Greek *mimema* (μίμημα) meaning something imitated. As such the meme is Dawkins' assignation for 'the new replicator' of culture, or as he describes the analogy:

> Just as genes propagate themselves in the gene pool by leaping from body to body via sperms or eggs, so memes propagate themselves in the meme pool by leaping from brain to brain via a process which, in the broad sense, can be called imitation.[4]

Dawkins cautions, however, that his readers should not be distracted by the metaphorical language – such as we might be by words like 'leaping' – because his descriptions are meant to be literal, or in the account of Dawkins' research offered by his colleague N. K. Humphrey:

> memes should be regarded as living structures, not just metaphorically but technically. When you plant a fertile meme in my mind you literally parasitize my brain, turning it into a vehicle for the meme's propagation in just the way that a virus may parasitize the genetic mechanism of a host cell. And this isn't just a way of talking – the meme for, say, 'belief in life after death' is actually realized physically, millions of times over, as a structure in the nervous systems of individual men the world over.[5]

When selected from specific or representative passages, Emerson's mid-nineteenth century view seems a sibling (or at least a cousin) to Dawkins' contemporary mimetic theory in so far as Emerson is sympathetic to the notion that ideas appear to move – perhaps they leap – from one person to another in a cultural sense. Yet what about the passage of memes, not genes, from generation to generation – in the blood? Is there a biological, and not a metaphorical, mechanism for that process? Who goes further, then, Dawkins or Emerson, in speculating where the metaphorical ends and the literal begins? Perhaps because Dawkins is trying with memes to make an explicit analogue of Darwinian evolutionary thinking, and Emerson is writing *English Traits* in a pre-Darwinian era, there are explanatory memes – such as found in Lamarck's research – that continue to influence or infect Emerson's thinking, that make Emerson more susceptible to a belief in the transmission of ideas through successive generations.

Even while Emerson may remain fairly agnostic about, or leave inchoate, an explanatory mechanism for the biological transmission of acquired traits, he sustains a concentrated interest in the possibility. The degree to which such movement of ideas – in the blood – is metaphorical becomes part of the inheritance of reading his texts. For instance, if one were speaking figuratively, drawing from the tropes found in *English Traits*, one might be tempted to say, similar to Dawkins' view, that mimetic traits do in fact inhabit the blood – and pass through it to new offspring. But then such a speculation may be clarified or qualified by recalling that, as a close reader of Lamarck, Emerson would be aware of Lamarck's admonition at the outset of *Zoological Philosophy: An Exposition with Regard to the Natural History of Animals* (1809):

> It is true if this statement [viz., the environment affects the shape and organization of animals] were to be taken literally, I should be convicted of an error; for whatever the environment may do, it does not work any direct modification whatever in the shape and organization of animals.[6]

Following Lamarck, then, and still very close to Dawkins' mimetics, Emerson would take BLOOD as a synecdoche for the intellectual and cultural traits that are spread within a given generation and may be taught to subsequent ones. Such cultural traits would be acquired through imitation, that is, mimetically.

Concurrently, however, Lamarck did believe in the 'inheritance of acquired traits', which in the light of Dawkins sounds distinctly more like it should be a cultural theory instead of a genetic one, and therefore that 'inheritance' in this context should be understood as a descriptive rather than a constitutive fact of evolution. Reading terms like 'needs' and 'habits' in Lamarck while thinking of memes and blood-as-synecdoche, makes his early-nineteenth-century remarks resonate more with cultural anthropology than any theory of biological descent:

> But great alterations in the environment of animals lead to great alterations in their needs, and these alterations in their needs necessarily lead to others in their capacities. Now if the new needs become permanent, the animals then adopt new habits which last as long as the needs that evoked them. This is easy to demonstrate, and indeed requires no amplification.[7]

Reading this and other passages in Lamarck's philosophy of zoology shows that he did not always take his theory metaphorically. In the first of his two laws of evolution, as noted in the first chapter and repeated here with a different emphasis, he states: 'In every animal [...] a more frequent and continuous use of any organ gradually strengthens, develops and enlarges that organ [...] while the permanent disuse of any organ imperceptibly weakens and deteriorates it [...] until it finally disappears'.[8] But the specific character of his notions of development and disappearance are revealed more precisely in the second law:

> All the acquisitions or losses wrought by nature on individuals, through the influence of the environment in which their race has long been placed, and hence through the influence of the predominant use or permanent disuse of any organ; all these are preserved by reproduction to the new individuals which arise, provided that the acquired modifications are common to both sexes, or at least to the individuals which produce the young.[9]

Lamarck shifts his attention from the evolution of 'needs' and 'habits' (subject as they are to environmental influence) to the dissemination of traits through a biophysical process of reproduction. Scientifically speaking, then, Darwin directed attention away from the individual (phenotype) to the species (genotype). For Darwin evolutionary changes occur on the scale of whole species so any traits developed or lost by an individual would not get passed on to offspring in the way Lamarck describes descent. Once Darwin's theory became scientifically legitimate, Lamarck's theory became a literary interpretation of the physical evidence.

Emerson, for his part, appears skeptical of Lamarck's science while remaining compelled to use the theory in a figurative way, perhaps, as discussed in the first chapter, because the literary perceptions made possible by Lamarck's approach seem to inspire, even demand, further scientific investigation. The persistence of Lamarckian tropes in his work, aside from the scientific debate they motivated, suggests that Emerson continued to appreciate the poetical significance of Lamarck's interpretations, especially as they lent credence to ancient Greek accounts of the *daemon*, their more contemporary register in Goethe's understanding of genius and *bildung*, and Emerson's own deployment of the terms and tropes of mind, blood and traits. If it was no longer, or not yet, defensible natural science, Lamarckism could yet serve the ambitions of a natural history of intellect.

2. Emerson, again speaking metaphorically, uses Lamarckian thinking to explain how ideas are transmitted and how material (bodily or constitutional) elements are inherited as well. As we would say GENES are in the blood, so Emerson would say GENIUS is in the blood. Emerson who wrote, like Darwin, without knowledge of modern genetics, speaks in *English Traits* of the 'natural genius of the British mind', and how in its evolution from Norman origins, the English have benefitted 'from some effect of that powerful [French] soil on their blood and manners'.[10] Regarding another source of English stock, he speaks of 'the Saxon seed, with its instinct for liberty and law, for arts and for thought'.[11] The land creates the conditions for changes in blood; the blood in turn leads to changes in manner; and subsequently, according to Emerson, one stands in a position to catalogue the traits that persist because of

these combined influences. It sounds very Lamarckian; and it appears to be a constitutive part of Emerson's methodology in *English Traits*. But Emerson adds a twist, or invites a reorientation, since the attribution may go the other way too. A good man can create good conditions: 'If the race is good, so is the place'.[12] Emerson lauds Sir Kenelm Digby, a seventeenth-century council to Charles I, as someone who 'spoke the genius of the English people', when he said: 'syllogisms do breed or rather are all the variety of man's life. They are the steps by which we walk in all our businesses. Man, as he is man, doth nothing else but weave such chains'.[13] Of the Teutonic influence on English genius, Emerson says it can be seen in 'hereditary rectitude', and the way 'veracity derives from instinct'.[14] According to this logic, human mental and moral life is prominently shaped by the inner influences of genius – that is, by breeding instincts. And these forces in turn, in time, become the conditions for human effects on the environment: 'Man is a shrewd inventor, and is ever taking the hint of a new machine from his own structure, adapting some secret of his own anatomy in iron, wood, and leather, to some required function in the work of the world'.[15]

3.   The English attention (or it is contention?) with the origins of its blood – from the Angles, and the Saxons, from the Gauls and the Teutons, from unknown and unnamed tribes of Europe and Asia – appears sometimes as an anxiety about where things begin for the English. At other times we find, as in Elizabeth Gaskell's industrial novel *North and South* (published the year before *English Traits*) an identification with a strand of the English constitution, in this case used as an explanation for character, belief and conduct. Mr Thornton, the owner of a cotton factory talks with Mr Hale, a minister who abdicated his ecclesiastical role in much the same way Emerson did in 1832. Mr Thornton's remarks follow immediately after a disquisition on the meaning and nature of 'representative men'; whether and how the men speaking to one another – an industrialist, an ex-minister, and an Oxford don (Mr Bell) – qualify as representative is part of the tension and intrigue of the conversation.

> 'Wait a little while', said Mr Thornton. 'Remember, we are of a different race from the Greeks, to whom beauty was everything, and to whom Mr Bell might speak of a life of leisure and serene enjoyment, much of which entered in through their outward senses. I don't mean to despise them, any more than I would ape them. But I belong to Teutonic blood; it is little mingled in this part of England to what it is in others; we retain much of their language; we retain more of their spirit; we do not look upon life as a time for enjoyment, but as a time for action and exertion. Our glory and our beauty arise out of our inward strength, which makes us victorious over material resistance, and over greater difficulties still'.[16]

In *English Traits* Emerson registers the influence of Teutonic blood on the English character:

> The Teutonic tribes have a national singleness of heart, which contrasts with races. The German name has a proverbial significance of sincerity and honest meaning. The arts bear testimony to it. The faces of clergy and laity in old

sculptures and illuminated missals are charged with earnest belief. Add to this hereditary rectitude, the punctuality and precise dealing which commerce creates, and you have the English truth and credit.[17]

The scene above from *North and South* continues – in the presence of Mr Hale's daughter, Margaret, the object of Mr Thornton's affections – with Mr Thornton's invocation of a species of classical liberal philosophy defined by a desire for a small, non-interventionist government:

'We are Teutonic up here in Darkshire in another way. We hate to have laws made for us at a distance. We wish people would allow us to right ourselves, instead of continually meddling, with their imperfect legislation. We stand up for self-government, and oppose centralization'.[18]

Emerson continues his assessment of the German character in England with a description sustaining Mr Thornton's pride and enmity:

The government strictly performs its engagements. The subjects do not understand trifling on its part. When any breach of promise occurred, in the old days of prerogative, it was resented by the people as an intolerable grievance. And, in modern times, any slipperiness in the government in political faith, or any repudiation or crookedness in matters of finance, would bring the whole nation to a committee of inquiry and reform. Private men keep their promises, never so trivial. Down goes the flying word on the tablets, and is indelible as Domesday Book.[19]

Mr Bell's 'half testy condemnation of a town' provoked Mr Thornton's curt and commanding response about the nature of his *difference* from Mr Bell – the bold and undeniable trait of Teutonic blood. Mr Thornton tells Mr Bell:

'I don't set up Milton as a model of a town'.
'Not in architecture?' slyly asked Mr Bell.
'No! We've been too busy to attend to mere outward appearances'.
'Don't say *mere* outward appearances', said Mr Hale, gently. 'They impress us all, from childhood upward – every day of our life'.[20]

Mr Hale's correction, inspired by a defence for Lockean philosophy, does not offset the pertinence of Mr Thornton's point, which Emerson seems precisely attuned to when he further elaborates on the Teutons, who appear to live outwardly as Englishmen while inwardly remaining faithful to the traits and testaments of their Continental blood:

They love reality in wealth, power, hospitality, and do not easily learn to make a show, and take the world as it goes. They are not fond of ornaments, and if they wear them, they must be gems. They read gladly in old Fuller, that a lady, in the reign of Elizabeth, 'would have as patiently digested a lie, as the wearing of false stones or pendants of counterfeit pearl'. They have the earth-hunger, or preference for property in land, which is said to mark the Teutonic nations. They build of stone: public and private buildings are massive and durable: In comparing their ships, houses, and public offices with the American, it is commonly said, that they spend a pound, where we spend a dollar. Plain rich clothes, plain rich equipage, plain rich finish throughout their house and belongings, mark the English truth.[21]

The kind of truth for which Mr Thornton should be esteemed a representative man. Margaret Hale glosses the Emersonian sense of representative when she concludes: 'I don't know Oxford. But there is a difference between being representative of a city and the representative man of its inhabitants'.

4.   Robert Burton, *The Anatomy of Melancholy*

First Partition, Section II., Member I., Subsection VI.
Parents a Cause by Propagation

> That other inward, inbred cause of melancholy is our temperature, in whole or part, which we receive from our parents, which Fernelius calls *præter naturam*, or unnatural, it being an hereditary disease. […] *Et patrum in natos abeunt cum semine mores* [the character of the parents is transmitted to the children through the seed.] […]
>
> So many several ways are we plagued and punished for our fathers' defaults; insomuch that, as Fernelius truly saith, 'It is the greatest part of our felicity to be well born, and it were happy for humankind, if only such parents as are sound of body and mind should be suffered to marry'. [… W]e make choice of the best rams for our sheep, rear the neatest kine, and keep the best dogs, *quanto id diligentius in procreandis liberis observandum!* and how careful then should we be in begetting of our children! [… I]t comes to pass that our generation is corrupt, we have many weak persons, both in body and mind, many feral diseases raging amongst us, crazed families, *parentes peremptores* [our parents are our ruin], our fathers bad, and we are like to be worse. [22]

And sure, I think, it hath been ordered by God's especial providence, that in all ages there should be (as usually there is) once in six hundred years, a transmigration of nations, to amend and purify their blood, as we alter seed upon our land, and that there should be, as it were, an inundation of those northern Goths and Vandals, and many such-like people which came out of that continent of Scandia and Sarmatia (as some suppose) and overran, as a deluge, most part of Europe and Africa, to alter for our good our complexions, which were much defaced with hereditary infirmities, which by our lust and intemperance we had contracted.[23]

X

First Blood

1. The moment of conception is a moment of infection: a foreign substance invades and disseminates information. Once the zygote is formed, the impregnation is no longer akin to a disease (where germs spread), but similar to a parasite/host relationship. Yet this connection appears to lack symbiosis, and be sustained through a radical asymmetry; a mother does not seem to benefit from hosting the zygote, or its later form the fetus. Despite the unevenness and imbalance of relationship the gestation period gives way to a birth, a body constituted by its descent from its host body – a descent both from the maternal body and from parental DNA (the latter of which a contribution is drawn from the father, who is not involved as a somatic host – though he may support the mother's role, and thus host the host).

    The emergence of the infant is not, as the terms and tropes of religion and myth have articulated for millennia, the bringing forth of a pure being. There are exceptions to the narrative, as with Augustine who wrote bluntly but accurately *Inter faeces et urinam nascimur* ('We are born between excrement and urine'). Though the way into the world may be both graphic and humbling – soiled and blood spattered – the way in is also defined by the spiraling coils of DNA that come together in order to make a new identity. Whether the focus is on the conditions of entry or the conditions of creation, however, purity is a foreign notion – something that appears artificially imported as a function of narrative impact, not something that emerges naturally from phenomena.

    After all a child is living, embodied evidence of impurity, infection, parasitism and the commingling of foreign elements. Upon arrival a child betrays any sense of the parents' assumed privacy for their intimacy – admitting to all proof, once and forever, of their clandestine physical union. The child becomes at once a representative (or sign) of that connection, and thereafter a reminder that the child stands between the parents (as an intermediary who draws its wholeness from their separate selves – half of one and half of the other). As a collusion of their forces, however, the child also binds the parents together because she is the material result of their cooperative, conspiratorial engagement.

2. If one is compelled to seek purity – as a possible state of affairs – and reinforce and amplify variations on a myth of originlessness, perhaps quantum mechanics will pacify such longing, make it seem incoherent and unattractive (if only because it is also unintelligible). According to some accounts of quantum mechanics, one need not be preoccupied with the determination (or determinism) of origins but rather should become oriented to the expansiveness of possibilities that are within one's control, since

quantum mechanics gives imagined – even nearly empty – space a sense of energy, movement and consequence. The quantum physicist speaks of probabilities where we would describe conditions for the possibility of having an influence on the world – even one's own 'inner landscapes'.[1] 'I had fancied', wrote Emerson, 'that the value of life lay in its inscrutable possibilities; in the fact that I never know, in addressing myself to a new individual, what may befall me. I carry the keys of my castle in my hand, ready to throw them at the feet of my lord, whenever and in what disguise soever he shall appear'.[2] The interaction of probability with possibility suggests that one is able, if not entirely at least in some appreciable way, to rewrite one's somatic and neural constitution.

3. The growth of the zygote is a rapid process of writing, and with such haste in composition lends itself to the introduction of mistakes in replication. Errata in such writing may lead to birth defects but also contribute to changes that can be advantageous for survival, and for the emergence of new forms of life. Mutation is the condition for adaptation since replication errors create new possibilities for the development of a species and its offshoots.

At the genetic level writing is a process of replication not translation. The child is a (genetic) quotation of his parents, but in that combination of written things there is a new creation. This creation is dictated by God or DNA. In 'Experience' Emerson wrote 'It is very unhappy, but too late to be helped, the discovery we have made, that we exist'.[3] But having made the discovery we might as well see that:

> Human life is made up of the two elements, power and form, and the propo-
> sition must be invariably kept if we would have it sweet and sound. Each of these
> elements in excess makes a mischief as hurtful as its defect. Everything runs to
> excess; every good quality is noxious if unmixed, and to carry the danger to the
> edge of ruin, nature causes each man's peculiarity to superabound. Here, among
> the farms, we adduce the scholars as examples of this treachery. They are nature's
> victims of expression. [...] Irresistible nature made men such, and makes legions
> more of such, every day.[4]

The scholars are not the only 'victims of expression'. Everyone is. Long ago Manilius wrote: *Nascentes morimur, finisque ab origine pendet* ('Even as we are being born, we begin to die', or in an old English rendering: 'As soone as wee to bee begunne, We did beginne to be undone'.)[5] What else is a birth but an *ex*-pression – a pressing out – of some new dictation? Every child is a victim of expression, a mixture of mortal elements that make it peculiar, which is to say, unique. The 'irresistible offshoots' and 'irresistible dictation' are part and parcel of 'irresistible nature'.[6]

To be born is to be written by one's parents – caused and constrained by that inscription but also given the material conditions for growth and change. The principles that govern brain chemistry reveal that some neural pathways can be augmented even after they are initially established. The pliability of one's somatic and neural constitution suggests that there are freedoms encoded in fates. It must be counted an art to find the lines that can be re-written, since '[w]e are sure, that, though we know not how, necessity does comport with liberty'.[7]

4.   Memes replicate by means of imitation; their transmission is a function of individual and social action, not passive inheritance like genes. For this reason memes can spread fast – as with fashion trends and figures of speech – and die away just as quickly. And yet some memes can spread rapidly and endure. Asking why a meme persists – seeking the conditions and constituents that help it last – seems the greater part of our inquiries into intellectual influence. The scholar asks how an idea comes to prominence and then takes hold, affecting (infecting) generations of students and readers who, in turn, proliferate the idea in some version – or mutation – of it.

Imitation is a kind of interpretation so its quality is affected by the performance and capacities of an individual agent, and that action brings with it some degree of mutation – somewhere on the scale between innovation and degradation, between near-isomorphic replication and radically compromised deviant. The meme for building a campfire seems more easily transferable than ways for reading poetry. Once the basic principles of wood-burns-better-when-dry, oxygen-feeds-the-flame, etc., are understood, there is little more to say. Empirical success reinforces the meme further, and it can thereafter spread more adeptly. In this case the meme is easily intelligible, quickly transferable, and immensely useful. It is a meme with a strong likelihood of surviving over a long duration of time – and it has. Memes for teaching how to read poetry, on the contrary, have very little unified content. As a result memes for reading poetry are seldom easily intelligible, quickly transferable, and immensely useful. The widespread development of introductions and how-to books on poetry and other similarly difficult topics and fields can be regarded as attempts to create more easily replicable memes. Sometimes an innovation in content can lead to the spread of memes but more often the development of a methodology for understanding existing memes is the primary contribution an individual makes to their survival.

Since the transfer of memes is part of an active, interpretive process, memetic mutation reveals different costs depending on what one values: traditionalists reward a greater deal of isomorphism between the thoughts and practices of one generation as they are transferred to the next (Emerson calls this conformity); innovators risk that a change may lead to an improved state of affairs, and thus often bear the consequences – commonly levied by traditionalists – of mutating away from traditional forms, even as innovators also bear the risk of, and responsibility for, making things worse. 'For nonconformity', writes Emerson, 'the world whips you with its displeasure'.[8]

5.   In the gospel according to John, the grammatical and the somatic unite, the logos finds inhabitation as an existential predicate:

> And the Word was made flesh, and dwelt among us, (and we beheld his glory, the glory as of the only begotten of the Father,) full of grace and truth.[9]

Jesus was a man constituted by a divine grammar, as humans are made of a corporeal, genetic grammar. With the image of Jesus as word-made-flesh in mind, the transubstantiation takes on a new cast: and when the imagery of the Eucharist is literalized, drinking the blood and eating the flesh of Christ suggests a form of cannibalism – a ritual anathema to the intention of the parable and the wider Christian tradition.

However, if the bread and wine remain metonyms (or synecdoches) for body and blood – signs of Christ's offering – then reading the gospels is analogous to a diet in divinity. The faithful follower reads of this man constituted by words, or the Word, in a text that becomes his representative; and so the reader is nourished by the Gospels. When God is made flesh and that flesh becomes word then the reader takes God in through the mouth – later, in a reversal, speaking of faith embodies and enriches belief. In *The Confessions* Augustine recurrently described reading the Gospels as a process of ingestion and digestion.

In his youth Augustine was infatuated with Cicero's *Hortensius*, a passion that led him to say that even the Bible 'seemed to [him] unworthy of comparison with the grand style of Cicero'.[10] In time though Augustine began to feel that Cicero's words were insufficiently nutritive. Addressing God in *The Confessions* Augustine admits: 'I was hungry and thirsty [...] for you yourself'. By contrast, Cicero's writing and Augustine's many friends could not satisfy his somatic or spiritual desires.

> Nevertheless, since I thought that these were you, I fed on them, not with any great eagerness (for the taste in my mouth was not the real taste of you, just as you were not these empty fictions), and so far from being nourished by them, I became the weaker. The food we dream about is very like the food we see in waking life; yet in our dreams we are not fed; we are, in fact, asleep. [...]
>
> It was on such things as these that at this time I was fed – fed without being nourished.[11]

In his 20s, still under the influence of various false diets (including suspect friends, the art of rhetoric and non-scriptural texts), Augustine realized that he was trying to feed himself by feeding others, trying to redeem himself from malnutrition by contributing to the nutrition of sages and priests:

> On the one hand I and my friends would be hunting after the empty show of popularity – theatrical applause from the audience, verse competitions, contests for crowns of straw, the vanity of the stage, immoderate lusts – and on the other hand we would be trying to get clean of all this filth by carrying food to those people who were called 'the elect' and 'the holy ones', so that in the factory of their own stomachs they could turn this food into angels and gods, by whose aid we should be liberated.[12]

The transubstantiation of a text, whether as a volume of words such a holy scripture, or the body of Christ, involves an ontological change; it also requires a shift in perspective on these empirical phenomena. The book is not just a book, the body is no longer merely flesh. Augustine asks God about the origin of scripture, the appearance of Jesus, and the creation of man: 'What word, then, did you use in order to produce a bodily substance by means of which these words could be created?'[13] The divine Word is written as scripture, and the divine body is written in, or as, God's son. Scripture is the word of God, and Jesus is scripture embodied. *Ipsa philosophia Christus.* Jesus is 'the Wisdom itself of God incarnate'[14]

Anselm of Canterbury, the eleventh-century author of the *Proslogion* (1077–8), first advocate of the ontological argument for the existence of God (in which proof of God is given by reason alone), and the initial figure of medieval Scholasticism, implored others to feed on scripture:

> Taste the goodness of your Redeemer, burn with love for your Savior. Chew the honeycomb of his words, suck their flavor, which is more pleasing than honey, swallow their health-giving sweetness. Chew by thinking, suck by understanding, swallow by loving and rejoicing. Be happy in chewing, be grateful in sucking, delight in swallowing.[15]

Earlier than both Augustine and Anselm, the prophet Ezekiel reported on his 'visions of God':

> And he said to me, 'Son of man, eat what is offered to you; eat this scroll, and go, speak to the house of Israel'. So I opened my mouth, and he gave me the scroll to eat. And he said to me, 'Son of man, eat this scroll that I give you and fill your stomach with it'. Then I ate it; and it was in my mouth as sweet as honey.[16]

6.   John Stuart Mill, *On Liberty* (1859)

> To cite a rather trivial example, nothing in the creed or practice of Christians does more to envenom the hatred of Mohammedans against them, than the fact of their eating pork. There are few acts which Christians and Europeans regard with more unaffected disgust, than Mussulmans regard this particular mode of satisfying hunger. [...] Their aversion to the flesh of the 'unclean beast' is, on the contrary, of that peculiar character, resembling an instinctive antipathy, which the idea of uncleanness, when once it thoroughly sinks into the feelings, seems always to excite even in those whose personal habits are anything but scrupulously cleanly, and of which the sentiment of religious impurity, so intense in the Hindoos, is a remarkable example.[17]

7.   Narratives of ingestion and digestion share some features: entry of a substance into a receptive area (a mouth, a stomach, etc.); mastication of the substance (chewing); and catabolism (the sorting of nutrients and waste). With Augustine, and the other users of such metaphors, the literary vision of these literal analogues involves a different final step: excretion is sanitized, or rather, perhaps more strangely, reversed. Ingesting God's words results not in offensive defecation but in mellifluous speech – in words that convey back the nutriment that was once taken in. What comes out of one's mouth – not undigested regurgitation but steady, studied pulses of digested air – can be offered and shared as a form of sustenance to others; the speaker is now a medium or proxy for God's nourishing words. Sharing the word of the Lord – evangelizing – becomes an act of nutritive dissemination. Prayer would then be a practice of meditating on how to metamorphose what has been taken in so that something as sustaining can be sent out. Preaching would then follow only after a profound education in the art of ingesting and digesting scripture – another instance

when one would be called upon to reveal how, in Emerson's phrase, 'the inmost in due time becomes the outmost'.[18]

8.   Pregnancy is another somatic system that, under certain aspects, resembles ingestion and digestion, yet in Christian scripture the phenomenon of procreation is regarded as wholly foreign to the process of eating or consuming. While the process and aftermath of impregnation is sufficiently familiar, some analogical points of resemblance (and divergence) seem worth rehearsing. Pregnancy is caused by the entry of substances into a receptive area, followed by the mixture of these substances, and completed during a period (not of digestion) but gestation – when the fetus begins to feed on the host, and from the nutritional support of the host creates a miniature version of the host's process of ingestion and digestion. All parts of the newer body develop within the older body. And until the umbilical cord is cut these two systems are continuous – as the mother eats, so the child feeds. The same blood courses throughout them both. When the reader eats the Word of God – as scripture, or the transubstantiated flesh of Christ – there is only improvement, enrichment, nutritional benefit. The process strengthens the eater. With pregnancy, however, the same network of phenomena – consummation and consumption – engender an opposing conse-quence: not a consecration but the taint – or trait – of sin.

The First Epistle of Paul to the Corinthians

> But and if thou marry, thou hast not sinned; and if a virgin marry, she hath not sinned. Nevertheless such shall have trouble in the flesh: but I spare you.[19]

The Revelation of St John the Divine

> These are they which were not defiled with women; for they are virgins. These are they which follow the Lamb whithersoever he goeth. These were redeemed from among men, being the firstfruits unto God and to the Lamb.[20]

Jesus is born from a virgin, a status said to be without a trait or trace of sin. The central importance of the virgin birth to Jesus' identity – and his radical difference from the rest of humanity – suggests that causation is a sin. To be made of flesh by flesh is an abomination. The sin of causation is therefore the sin of nature, not God, because causation is nature's way of creating. Any human that is caused, born of the flesh, is not first from or of God but of continuity with nature. And all pregnancies – except Mary's – involve causes. A sinless birth is unnatural; it is a miracle.

The image of the virgin is imbued not just with the quality or attribute of purity; in this picture, she is also assumed to be fertile. Such a figure, however, may be pure in her barrenness; in this respect no seed could defile her. Purity without the power to procreate suggests some other metaphor. The virgin's metaphysical value lay, then, precisely – and perhaps fully – in the possibility that she is both pure (untouched) and fertile (capable of creating life and bringing it to term). The virgin's body is regarded as a site that is not contaminated but could be – call this impregnation. Once conceived, the child is the contaminant – a presence that at once dissolves the mother's virginal state and confirms that new life is possible only through an act of contagion – by breaching the pure and fertile body.

9.   Part of being BORN AGAIN in Jesus involves a ritualistic cleansing of sin. The new birth, or second birth, somehow re-writes the meaning of the first birth. There was an earthly creation – the child emergent from parents passing on the sin of embodiment – and then, in the rebirth, there is a divine re-creation. Is the new state an improvement or merely a mark of difference? After a second birth is one in a better position to judge oneself or others? Guarding against the righteousness that might result from feeling beyond reproach – as in the figure who believes he is in a state of purity and sinlessness – a parable is told of Jesus' response to the scribes and Pharisees who bring before him an adulterous woman who, according to Jewish law, should be stoned to death:

> So when they continued asking him, he lifted up himself, and said unto them, 'He that is without sin among you, let him first cast a stone at her'. And again he stooped down, and wrote on the ground. [...] When Jesus had lifted up himself, and saw none but the woman, he said unto her, 'Woman, where are those thine accusers? hath no man condemned thee?' She said, 'No man, Lord'. And Jesus said unto her, 'Neither do I condemn thee: go, and sin no more'.[21]

Here we find in Jesus' awareness of sin a recognition of how people believe it compromises them, for example, in the their capacity for faithfulness. Jesus neither condemns the adulterous woman nor does he castigate humanity for its sins. In a scene of purification, John was baptizing people with water, and identified Jesus as 'the lamb of God, which beareth [or taketh away] the sin of the world'.[22] Reference to a lamb for slaughter speaks to the religious tradition Jesus was born into – in which lamb's blood is understood as protection from the wrath of God. Moses said:

> And ye shall take a bunch of hyssop, and dip it in the blood that is in the bason, and strike the lintel and the two side posts with the blood that is in the bason [...]. For the LORD will pass through to smite the Egyptians; and when he seeth the blood upon the lintel, and on the two side posts, the LORD will pass over the door, and will not suffer the destroyer to come in unto your houses to smite you.[23]

In Leviticus it is said that a man should bring 'a female from the flock, a lamb or a kid of the goats, for a sin offering; and the priest shall make an atonement for him concerning his sin'.[24] As the lamb of God, Jesus is sacrificed for the atonement of all mankind. In the first epistle of Peter, it is written that humans are not 'redeemed with corruptible things', 'but with the precious blood of Christ, as of a lamb without blemish and without spot'.[25]

Instead of passing on the taint of sin to children, as the blood of parents must, Jesus' blood purifies. What John the Baptist says about Jesus' expiative act can be translated either as 'beareth' or 'taketh away', but whichever translation is preferred, Jesus takes responsibility for human sin. And whether one speaks of being born again in Jesus, of having him bear human sin (as a proxy, as a savior who 'taketh away the sin of the world' as if absorbing or curing a blood poisoning), we seem to encounter another story of male pregnancy.[26] In this case, though, being born of a man born without sin makes us also born (again) without sin – the virgin children of a virgin God. This logic would seem to invite a kind of transcendental deduction: if we are the children of Jesus, and Jesus is the son of a virgin mother, then those reborn in him also share in the state of living 'without blemish and without spot'. Living as if unborn, uncaused.

10.   Beginning definitively with the public expression of his theory of the Eucharist in 'The Lord's Supper' (1832), which rested on his claim that it was misplaced in contemporary Christian practice, Emerson registered his distance from the Pauline worldview. The imagery that Jesus used to narrate and conceptualize his last meal with disciples has, according to Emerson, been misinterpreted, or rather interpreted in ways that obscure the spirit in which the metaphors were deployed. A parable about the 'remission of sin' was transformed into a darkly literalized form of flesh eating and blood drinking, thereby disfiguring the original intent and context of Jesus' remarks.

> And as they were eating, Jesus took bread, and blessed it, and brake it, gave it to the disciples, and said, Take, eat: this is my body. And he took the cup, and gave thanks, and gave it to them, saying, Drink ye all of it; For this is my blood of the new testament, which is shed for many for the remission of sins.[27]

Eating the body and drinking the blood of Christ is meant to be a metaphor for the ingestion of words, or the spirit of the words followers find in the new testament. Yet the blood and body of Christ appear to exist on another level of ascription: namely as material forms that will be destroyed as proxies for human sin. Thus while the blood and body of Christ are sacrificed – displaced, in order to save man – the Eucharist *recovers* them in the form of wine and bread – to remember the material forms that were lost. But then the recovery is only fitting if the believer, or eater, remembers what the metonyms stand for: namely, the word-made-flesh in Jesus and his subsequent destruction – a sacrifice-as-substitution that makes a new kind of human life, without sin, possible.[28] Emerson writes that 'having recently paid particular attention to this subject, I was led to the conclusion that Jesus did not intend to establish an institution for perpetual observance when he ate the passover with his disciples'.[29] The institutional problems and controversies surrounding the Eucharist may be attributed, in this case at least, to the problem of literalizing something that was meant to remain a parable – a story full of figurative meaning that may become comical, confused and even dangerous without its literary context.

Emerson reminds his readers that the words 'Do this in remembrance of me' 'do not occur in Matthew, Mark, or John'; the sentiment is found in I Corinthians.[30] But to remember – to re-member – need not mean to re-create, as if staging the last supper again, iteratively, eternally. Moreover, Emerson cautions that the account of Jesus' last meal with followers does not show Jesus creating a novel ritual for them but reinforces 'that the leading circumstances in the gospel are only a faithful account of that ceremony' of Passover one would find practiced by ancient and modern Jews[31]: 'Jesus did not celebrate the passover and afterwards the supper, but the supper *was* the passover. He did with his disciples exactly what every master of a family in Jerusalem was doing at the same hour with his household'. As Jesus tends, on Emerson's reading, to 'spiritualize every occurrence', it should not surprise that Jesus added to the existing narrative and ritual with an invocation to drink his blood and eat his body: 'They are not extraordinary expressions for him. They were familiar in his mouth. He always taught by parable and symbols. [...]'[32]

> And when the Jews on that occasion complained that they did not comprehend what he meant, he added for their better understanding, and as if for our under-standing, that we might not think that this body was to be actually eaten, that he only meant that we should live by his commandment. He closed his discourse with these explanatory expressions: 'The flesh profiteth nothing; – the *words* that I speak to you, they are spirit and they are life'.[33]

Though the Eucharist is said by many to be a memorial – an act in remembrance of Christ – it is customarily forgotten, according to Emerson, that the ritual was local, familiar, and in Jesus' teaching, adapted through symbolical inflection to suit his emphasis on the new life he makes possible for his followers through words. Or more succinctly, as Emerson quotes from Romans: 'My friends, the Apostle well assures us that "the kingdom of God is not meat and drink".'[34]

11.   Nearly a decade after his career-ending remarks on the Eucharist, Emerson wrote in 'The Method of Nature' (1841) about his preoccupation with the legacy of sin – as a concept and as a metaphor: 'I will that we keep terms with sin and a sinful literature and society no longer [...]'.[35] The 'sinful literature' is compromised by an absence, not a presence; it is a lack not a taint that makes it unworthy. The 'sinful literature' embodies the 'adulterous divorce which the superstition of many ages has effected between the intellect and holiness'.[36] To create a literature of sin one must live in the sin – of an adulterous divorce – that falsely separates 'goodness' and 'wisdom', as Emerson says, 'as if either could exist in any purity without the other'.[37] It is precisely the miscegenation of goodness and wisdom that makes work holy and 'truth is always holy'. For his own work as one of the 'lowly ministers', Emerson states: 'I draw from nature the lesson of an intimate divinity', and in so doing, he assures his reader, 'will burn up all profane literature'.[38] In this asserveration, he will '[...] live a life of discovery and performance.'[39]

In the same lecture Emerson acknowledges the presence of sin – as one of several facts or factors that give shape to our embodied condition, and subsequently set limits to our capacity for action – but he eschews any sanctimony about sin's deleterious effects on our capacity to think, that is, to conceive.

> With this conception of the genius or method of nature, let us go back to man. It is true, he pretends to give account of himself to himself, but, at last, what has he to recite but the fact that there is a Life not to be described or known otherwise than by possession? What account can he give of his essence more than *so it was to be*? The *royal* reason, the Grace of God seems the only description of our multiform but ever identical fact. There is virtue, there is genius, there is success, or there is not. There is the incoming or the receding of God: that is all we can affirm; and we can show neither how nor why. Self-accusation, remorse, and the didactic morals

of self-denial and strife with sin, is a view we are constrained by our constitution to take of the fact seen from the platform of action; but seen from the platform of intellection, there is nothing for us but praise and wonder.[40]

Sin may remain an ineluctable feature of our constitution – a 'piece of nature and fate',[41] as Emerson says elsewhere – but it does not corrupt thinking, either in terms of inheriting what constrains us or in matters of self-conception (in the latter case, discovering how to think oneself into existence). The same year Emerson lectured on the method of nature he wrote in 'Spiritual Laws' of the antiquated, anachronistic, and foolish attention to sin, which in his view appears to be nothing else but a kind of intellectual disease – something we contract by negligent exposure, but something also that we are capable of curing:

> The intellectual life may be kept clean and healthful, if man will live the life of nature, and not import into his mind difficulties which are none of his. No man need be perplexed in his speculations. Let him do and say what strictly belongs to him, and, though very ignorant of books, his nature shall not yield him any intellectual obstructions and doubts. Our young people are diseased with the theological problems of original sin, origin of evil, predestination, and the like. These never presented a practical difficulty to any man, – never darkened across any man's road, who did not go out of his way to seek them. These are the soul's mumps, and measles, and whooping-coughs, and those who have not caught them cannot describe their health or prescribe the cure. A simple mind will not know these enemies. It is quite another thing that he should be able to give account of his faith, and expound to another the theory of his self-union and freedom. This requires rare gifts. Yet, without this self-knowledge, there may be a sylvan strength and integrity in that which he is. 'A few strong instincts and a few plain rules' suffice us.[42]

In 'Lecture on the Times', also from 1841, Emerson further validates the notion of sin as a kind of disease, a contagion that infects the better energies of human life, and though curable imperils its chances for flourishing. The present age – the 'times' of which he speaks – are beset not by the debility of faith but rather skepticism. But then such doubt has existed in tandem with the long history of creeds and dogmas. Diogenes and Porphyry were David Humes in their day, and we are not yet satisfied with philosophical rebuttals to their claims. The Pyrrhonism that threatens the times has more to do with an anxiety over idleness and vocation – expressed in terms of disorientation and inefficacy, restlessness and squandered potential – than a dread of damnation, and the inexorable mark of sin.

> A new disease has fallen on the life of man. Every Age, like every human body, has its own distemper. Other times have had war, or famine, or a barbarism domestic or bordering, as their antagonism. Our forefathers walked in the world and went to their graves, tormented with the fear of Sin, and the terror of the Day of Judgment. These terrors have lost their force, and our torment is Unbelief, the Uncertainty as to what we ought to do; the distrust of the value of what we do, and the distrust that the Necessity (which we all at last believe in) is fair and beneficent.

Our Religion assumes the negative form of rejection. Out of love of the true, we repudiate the false: and the Religion is an abolishing criticism. A great perplexity hangs like a cloud on the brow of all cultivated persons, a certain imbecility in the best spirits, which distinguishes the period. We do not find the same trait in the Arabian, in the Hebrew, in Greek, Roman, Norman, English periods; no, but in other men a natural firmness. The men did not see beyond the need of the hour. They planted their foot strong, and doubted nothing. We mistrust every step we take. We find it the worst thing about time, that we know not what to do with it. We are so sharp-sighted that we can neither work nor think, neither read Plato nor not read him.[43]

12.   Gillian Beer, *Darwin's Plots* (1983)

[I]n Darwinian myth, the history of man is of a difficult and extensive family network which takes in barnacles as well as bears, an extended family which will never permit the aspiring climber – man – quite to forget his lowly origins. One of the most disquieting aspects of Darwinian theory was that it muddied descent, and brought into question the privileged 'purity' of the 'great family'.[44]

Abbreviation can lead to misinterpretation; an ellipsis may abandon a crucial copula. Darwin's *The Origin of Species* apparently directs us to the importance of origins – beginnings, creation itself. But the full title of the work reads *On the Origin of Species by means of Natural Selection, or the Preservation of Favoured Races in the Struggle for Life*. Beer has pointed out how the abbreviated – now standard – title 'disguises the element of narrative' and transforms the meaning of 'origin' from 'a process into a place or substantive'.[45] In opposition to Robert Chambers' *Vestiges of the Natural History of Creation* (1844) – an unabridged title that announces its attention to remnants – Beer presents Darwin's project, which is about 'history, not cosmogony'. *The Origin of Species* is not about the origin of species but instead about the process of how species become themselves – and then die away.

13.   After Herman Melville finished writing *Moby-Dick; or, The Whale* he said to Nathaniel Hawthorne: 'I have written a wicked book, and feel spotless as the lamb'.[46] But does that purity – Christ-like as reflected in the figure of the metonymic lamb – mean that writing is a form of giving life to something impure that leaves the creator without taint (as a mode of expiation, as a way of shifting the locus of guilt from the man to his creation by means of a transfer, an insemination); or does it mean that the author is never compromised in the way his works must always be? Does Melville's novel take on the author's expurgated wretchedness or as created – by the hand of any man – did it have to be so, irrespective of Melville's private and particular condition? Such questions return us, in a different mood, to the proliferating narratives of male pregnancy. In this case Melville's remark to Hawthorne leaves us wondering if the wretchedness is transferred to the offspring – leaving the parent pure in heart and head – or whether the crux of the interpretation rests with Melville's sense of *feeling* spotless. Perhaps his state is just an impression, and though his creation – like a

child – is separate from him, alive unto itself after its birth, the two are nevertheless connected, marked as men of words must be.

Set to launch a harpoon at Moby-Dick, Captain Ahab anoints his weapon with pagan blood, drawn from the men on his ship.[47] Having figuratively instantiated this heretical baptism, Melville adopts an inversion of the Christian tradition that he read about in Francis Palgrave's 'Superstition and Knowledge' (1823): *Ego non baptizo te in nomine Patris et Filii et Spiritus Sancti – sed nomine Diaboli* ('I baptize you not in the name of the Father and the Holy Spirit, but in the name of the Devil.') Melville had written the Latin line on the recto of the last blank leaf of a volume of Shakespeare, and invoked the line again in a letter to his friend, Nathaniel Hawthorne.[48]

14.   A parent is prone to believe that since she created the child, the child is hers. The author of a book may feel similarly: that his writing is a kind of child – a possession owed from his labour to actualize; a being that is solely comprised of these little acts of will called writing; a result of thoughts matured after a period of gestation, finding their way into the word grammatically – for 'the inmost in due time becomes the outmost'.[49] Emerson learned tragically, terribly painfully, that a child is no such creation. Losing a toddling son to scarletina he writes: '[…] some thing that I fancied was a part of me, which could not be torn away without tearing me, nor enlarged without enriching me, falls off from me, and leaves no scar. It was caducous'.[50] Emerson has created a beautiful thing yet its loss 'leaves me as it found me'.

The term CADUCOUS is drawn from botanical science and Emerson, a gardener and arborist (particularly drawn, like Darwin, to the cultivation of fruit trees), registers the customary associations of the word when writing in his journal the year after Waldo's birth: 'These caducous relations are in the soul as leaves, flowers, & fruits are in the arboreous nature, and wherever it is put & how often soever they are lopped off, yet still it renews them ever'.[51]

Melville wrote his book. Emerson had his son. Both men, like women who give birth from their own bodies, discover they are not connected to their creations. The cord is cut, and the fate of books and boys is something beyond them, part of another life – leaving them as they found them. Unscarred. Spotless as a lamb.

15.   Seneca, *Epistles*

> Teach me instead what purity is, how much value there is in it, whether it lies in the body or in the mind.[52]

Since the first century of the common era when Seneca was writing, appreciable philosophical and religious debate – especially on the relationship between metaphysical, material and moral matters – has dwelled on the value and meaning of purity, and whether it is something physical or imaginary, an abiding attribute of extension or a mental ephemeron. Emerson says that religion – in the eponymous chapter of *English Traits* – is 'endogenous', meaning that it is something that has no apparent external cause, and originates from itself – is self-generating.[53] Based on his reading of Aristotle, the thirteenth-century theologian Thomas Aquinas developed a theory of an Uncaused Cause (part of the so-called cosmological argument for the existence of a first cause). Given the prevailing connection between purity, perfection and divinity – that these were unified virtues as well as values – it is intelligible why an Uncaused Cause would be understood as a synonym for God; it may also be a synecdoche for God since the term is described as one portion of a whole network of contiguous, defining features. Even though Jesus was born of a woman – and so originated from her – his conception was uncaused (making it possible for a virgin to bear a child). Jesus was the only endogenous human.

In the Pentateuch God is said to have issued Commandments – laws generated by performative speech, derived from divine origins, and given with divine authority. Transgressing such laws would doubtless be an affront to that divinity – its matchless perfection, its state without sin or blemish. In various works by Stoic philosophers in Greece and Rome, acts against natural law were treated as debasements and distortions since they violated the given order, which was understood to be coextensive with divine reason. Diogenes Laertius noted that '[T]he rational animal is corrupted, sometimes because of the persuasiveness of external activities and sometimes because of the influence of companions', but action that is 'perfectly in accord with nature' can only be good.[54] Accordingly 'God is an animal, immortal, rational, perfect in happiness, immune to everything bad, providentially [looking after] the cosmos and the things in the cosmos', and humans are good in so far as they abide by the laws of nature – an offshoot and continuation of God.[55]

Transgression against God's order – the natural order – introduces imperfection, impurity and action against the sanctity of a realm derived from divinity. SIN may be a euphemism for such transgression, a way to differentiate kinds of actions – making the metaphysical the ground for a moral judgement. Deviating from the assigned order would not compromise its perfection, then, but one's own; one would become a marked man. Unnatural action, then, pollutes the moral composition of individuals, introducing obscuring and dis-gracing elements. Yet when modern genetics confirmed that mutation is a deviation from inherited order and instruction, it dislocated the moral claim and gave credence to transgression as the necessary condition for the possibility of life. To survive in the order of nature a creature had to violate it. Evolutionary biology, by consequence and intention, is the study of such transgressions, successful and not.

16.   Selected remarks by Emerson on the legacy of sin, conceptually not chronologically arranged:

'Heroism' (1841)

> The violations of the laws of nature by our predecessors and our contemporaries are punished in us also. The disease and deformity around us certify the infraction of natural, intellectual and moral laws, and often violation on violation to breed such compounded misery. [...] Unhappily no man exists who has not in his own person become to some amount a stockholder in the sin, and so made himself liable to a share in the expiation.[56]

'The Method of Nature' (1841)

> Self-accusation, remorse, and the didactic morals of self-denial and strife with sin, are in the view we are constrained by our constitution to take of the fact seen from the platform of action; but seen from the platform of intellection there is nothing for us but praise and wonder.[57]

'Experience' (1844)

> We permit all things to ourselves, and that which we call sin in others is experiment for us.[58]

'The Tragic' (1838)

> If a man is centred, men and events appear to him a fair image or reflection of that which he knoweth beforehand in himself. If any perversity or profligacy break out in society, he will join with others to avert the mischief, but it will not arouse resentment or fear, because he discerns its impassable limits. He sees already in the ebullition of sin the simultaneous redress.[59]

'Circles' (1841)

> The only sin is limitation.[60]

The first remark reminds us of Emerson's intimacy with Calvinism – the predominant theology of his recent ancestors and a sufficient number of his contemporaries (including his influential, much-beloved aunt, Mary Moody) – and its doctrine of 'total depravity', which leaves all mankind guilty of Adam's original sin – 'constrained by our constitution', in Emerson's technical, poetic gloss. The only way to expiate this sin was by 'saving grace', a God-granted restoration, which no amount of prayer or good works could assure. In 'Uses of Great Men' (1850) Emerson imagines that 'Man is endogenous [...]' and if that is so, then an external savior is no longer necessary. He says a few lines later: 'I must absolve me to myself' – a notion carried over from 'Self-Reliance' a decade earlier.[61] For Emerson we sin when we are limited and constrained – principally in our cognitive conceptions – or impose restriction upon ourselves. Ideally – a word that connotes both promising conditions and the ideas that derive from them – *homo sapiens*, etymologically understood, is an agent of discernment (*sapiens*); he is *Man Thinking*. Action beyond the apparent law is not sin but experiment. In 'Self-Reliance' Emerson replies to the conservatives and traditionalists who are threatened, scandalized, confused or otherwise opposed to his critique of law:

> The populace think that your rejection of popular standards is a rejection of all standard, and mere antinomianism. [...] But the law of consciousness abides. There are two confessionals, in one or the other of which we must be shriven. You may fulfill your round of duties by clearing yourself in the *direct*, or in the *reflex* way. Consider whether you have satisfied your relations to father, mother, cousin, neighbour, town, cat, and dog; whether any of these can upbraid you. But

I may also neglect this reflex standard, and absolve me to myself. [...] If any one imagines that this law is lax, let him keep its commandment one day.

And truly it demands something godlike in him who has cast off the common motives of humanity, and has ventured to trust himself for a taskmaster.[62]

An individual is endogenous – 'godlike' – when she begins to write her own law (or establishes her own relation to discernable laws); absolves herself (instead of waiting to be shriven by a priest); and creates and keeps her own commandments (manifested as an active, thoughtful self-trust in lieu of a passive obeisance to an inherited, external authority).

17.   Sentimentality is an excessive preoccupation with attachment; it is a variety of anthropomorphic thinking. In matters of national and individual identity sentimental conceptualizations inflect the presence and value of causation, order and origins. The synecdoches of sin – the taint, the stain, the scar, the mark – inhere, often inadvertently, in the wider use and understanding of sentimentality.

With its attention to and allowances for causation, sentimentality stimulates superstition – what might be described as a faith or love of causation. Each instance of sentimentality admits an over-emotional involvement, attachment and valuation of causes – origins, beginnings, consequences – along with a desire for controlling the succession of events. Sentimentality, as this particular kind of excess, compromises the ability to appreciate phenomena in the present because it leaves one strictly focused on the causal progression of things (e.g., how an earlier state leads to a later one). Such movement can be usefully contrasted with Wittgenstein's notion of leading – how things should be said to appear in a 'natural order' and cannot be forced 'in any single direction against their natural inclination.'[63] Connections or causes are not, on this reading, essential and pre-existing but evolving, not linear but rhizomatic; the same arrangement or composition can reveal new things at different times. The sentimentalist, instead, seeks immutable traces of development from prior origins to the present – but then must discover that it is an evacuated present, an attenuated present in which value depends on antecedents not on emergent properties. By extension, one cannot be a sentimentalist about the future because its history of causes has not been disclosed.

To be original, strictly and paradoxically, requires the denial of origins. One must be one's own beginning. Acknowledging that one came from somewhere, from someone, means that one gives up one's claim to self-creation. The contested notion of ORIGIN in the case of America and England illustrates how descent became dissent: the bond was a necessary condition for severance.

A concern for origins leads to questions about the past: Where do we come from? If origins are ancillary – of debated and unfixed value – questions lead to the present, as with Emerson who asks: 'Where do we find ourselves?'[64] It is a speculative question that also has concrete answers: we find ourselves in a specific place, born of parents (known and unknown). Maturation often entails reformation – re-writing our cognitive inheritance anew. One drafts a new constitution, declares independence from the old, establishes a new life on foreign or familiar territory, by means of new terms and conditions. This is also America's story: a nation that did not define itself solely in reaction to the origins of its immigrants (once predominantly European, now decidedly global), but committed to a new founding according to principles established in the present that nevertheless make allowances for amendments in the future. Democracy, with its appeal to innovation, to hope, is structurally anti-sentimental; it is a political space for a present that leans into the future, the past kept near as a bulwark for novel initiatives and endeavours – inspiration for reforming and rethinking what has existed and what now exists.

18.   The sentimentalist's preoccupation with origins leaves him prone to a mood of fatalism. Continually dwelling on the influence of causes, determinism seems more and more compelling, perhaps, in time appearing as the only reasonable perspective from which to judge the organization of reality. From this mood or orientation there emerge at least three positions: a determinism thought to derive from an interested, intelligent, directive Godhead; from an unconscious, indiscriminate Fate; or from a force that does not reveal its characteristics – a force at once pervasive and indifferent. The positions may appear to reflect the rough outlines, respectively, of the theist, the atheist and the agnostic, but that impression leaves aside many subtle variations and versions of these three dominant – but easily caricatured – options for believing.

To initiate a consideration of the view that an intentional intelligence 'created man in his own image'[65] – as if a human were a picture, though partial, of its source – we read in the Gospel of John:

[God] was in the world, and the world was made by him, and the world knew
    him not.
He came unto his own, and his own received him not.
But as many as received him, to them have he power to become the sons of
    the God, even to them that believe on his name:
Which were born, not of blood, nor of the will of the flesh, nor of the will of
    man, but of God.[66]

From this initial view, being born again depends on one's faith in God. The influence of ancestral blood, the ritual power of blood (such as at Passover or during circumcision), the material fact of human conception, and the conscious intentions of humans are secondary – from a divine perspective perhaps irrelevant. The adduced facts of organic conception and procreation are corruptions – and sin begets sin. In order to become purified of these corruptions one must acquiesce fully to the will of God – born not from blood, not from one's fleshy will, not from one's cognitive will – and receive a transfusion of new blood – of God – from Jesus, which is a divinely imposed antiseptic – a cleansing – that takes away the sepsis of sin.

A second model transposes GOD with FATE so divine order is replaced with an impersonal order of necessary events. Sin in this context, as drawn by Diogenes above, is a violation of the natural-divine order.

Denis Diderot, who was familiar with the Stoic-inspired philosophy of Baruch Spinoza, wrote *Jacques, The Fatalist and his Master* (composed from 1765 to 1780; published posthumously, 1796), a work sufficiently agnostic that he withheld it from publication during his life fearing condemnation from a Christian audience. Travelling with his Master, Jacques frequently addresses the course of events with a fatalistic response. The Master's outlook is decidedly Christian and he finds unsettling Jacques' confident, often sardonic, rejoinders to his genuine questions. When asked by the Master how one squares fate with moral responsibility (for example, how one can hold a person responsible for a crime if the person was determined to commit the crime; or, how one can feel remorse after committing a crime if one was destined to do it), Jacques replies:

> The objection you raise has rattled my brains more than once. But for all that, however much I dislike the thought, I always come back to something my Captain used to say: 'Everything good or bad that happens to us here below is written on high'. Sir, do you know of some way of rubbing out what's written up there? Can I stop being me, or failing that, can I behave as though I were not me? Can I be both me and somebody else? And has there been a single instance since the time I came into the world when this was not the case? You can go on about it as much as you like and your arguments may be perfectly sound, but if it is written in me or up there that I shan't agree with them, there's not much I can do about it.[67]

The Master asks about the order of things – does one act because it was fated or was it fated because one acted in this way – and Jacques sagely says: 'Both were written side by side. Everything was written down at the same time. It's like a great scroll that unrolls a bit at a time'.[68] Jacques concedes to the literal dictates of fate, and accepts how troubling it is to feel like an actor reading lines written by some distant, cosmic author – yet that is the position he has resolved to believe in, and to live after. (Or Jacques might offer the rhetorical, self-reflexive riposte: was it not fated that I would believe in fate and not in some other view?)

Holding the third position entails commitment to the logic of either a divine order or a system of necessary causes and effects while remaining indifferent to the claim, or at a loss to decide, that one view is more correct than the other. For Marcus Aurelius and many other Stoics before and after him, living a good life becomes complicated and compromised when one is preoccupied with the difference; it is, on this view, not pertinent to discover or decide whether it is God or Fate that rules one's days.

> The revolutions of the cosmos are the same, up and down, through the ages. Either the mind of the Whole has an impulse which reaches to each individual – and if this be so, welcome that which it set in motion – or it had this impulse once, and the rest has followed in consequence. Why then are you anxious? The Whole either is a god, and all is well, or it is without plan – atoms somehow and indivisible particles – but you need not be without plan yourself.[69]

> Either a medley of entangled and dispersed atoms, or a unity of order and Providence. [...] The dispersal of atoms will come upon me whatever I do. If the latter, however, I worship and am content and derive courage from the governing Reason.[70]

> The nature of the Whole had an impulse to create the universe; now either all that comes to birth arises as a consequence of this, or even the most important

ends, toward which the ruling mind of the universe directs its own impulse, are irrational.[71]

For some, Aurelius' comfort with indeterminacy would be a cause for alarm, but he concludes soberly that '[r]emembering this will make you face many things more calmly'.[72] In other words we are not to confuse his openness to cosmological explanation as a confirmed acquiescence to relativism (anything goes) or to nihilism (nothing goes). Aurelius' view instead reflects a spirituality not given to extremes. He emphasizes neither finding a proof for a specific view nor explaining the causes underlying it. Rather, he directs attention to understanding how one's attitude toward one's adopted view affects the course of day-to-day affairs – and not in a practical or pragmatic sense but in a logical and moral sense; as a Stoic, the logical and moral cohere for him. Aurelius concludes that one's existence is better ordered, and more worthy because of the way one *thinks* about it.

19.   A sentimental reading of America takes the fact of achieved independence from England too far by distorting the nature of its hard-won originality. An unsentimental reading, however, bypasses concern with origins and instead provides an invitation to turn away from the determinative qualities of inherited forms – and toward the future, to the next and the new. Some of the defining tropes of American identity reinforce this kind of unsentimental orientation, often by reliance on appealing and enduring referents, contrasting and complementary features: the metropolis and the wilderness; the farm and the frontier; the cowboy and the rebel; the inventor and the entrepreneur; the highway and the marketplace. These are metaphors of freedom – all training attention on where one is going instead of where one is from – figures and places that emphasize qualities of mobility and independence, openness to risk and discovery; and the pursuit of innovation in a realm where genuine incentives drive authentic creativity.

   In so far as Americans are unsentimental they are free. Sentimentality about freedom is constraining, suffocating, debilitating – as it was in the immediate wake of 9/11. Sentimentality sets the conditions for poor judgement. Being sentimental one simply feels too much – an over-abundance of sensation and emotion that distorts, distracts and compromises creativity and moral reasoning. In those unprecedented days and years of aftermath, everywhere there were questions about the CAUSES of 9/11, the ORIGINS of terrorism, how to rally and root out the terrorists at their SOURCE, etc. Sentimentality always compels one to ask how something began, as if knowing its pedigree would bestow some secret knowledge. The search for origins makes one believe that if one were to eradicate origins – or originating conditions – one might *prevent* further unspeakable outgrowths and undesirable symptoms. This is history-as-etiology (αἰτιολογία, the giving of reasons by the finding of origins); the recurrent inclusion of Greek and Latin etymologies in this book is, admittedly, an appeal to the authority of origin-as-explanation, but it is made believing that roots are illuminative; such a practice – even if meant to emphasize the insights of a source – could be read, however, as a liability, a lapse, an irony – or it could be noted as another curious illustration of the pervasive, continuous – largely unconscious – habit of such entreaties. Since roots are rhizomatic – and in radical ways (from *radix* meaning ROOT) – there is reason to consider their powers of proliferation, their capacities for leading in many directions. Etymologies need not be etiologies. Yet so long as there persists a craving for a uniform, linear narrative of how-we-arrived-at-this-point, in etymology or elsewhere, the pursuit of origins – and the explanations for their effects – will endure. How odd, though, that one must speculate in reverse about how to go on. Such storytelling – for these histories are many times fabrications based on facts – often weakens and adulterates one's ability to perceive present circumstances in the light of future possibilities.

20. Though sentimental emotion is commonly depicted as unrestrained and overflowing, it makes emotional life stiffer and emptier. In this respect, sentimentality may be considered a sibling of certainty: one believes so strongly in something that one is torn to pieces by steadfastness; there is little skepticism and a lot of righteousness in it. The theatre director and performance theorist Anne Bogart has reflected on Don Saliers' notion that 'the silence that follows a violent event is similar in quality to the speechlessness of a powerful aesthetic experience'.[73] In the aftermath of such a moment, one is, as she says, in a state of *Betroffenheit* – literally 'having been met'.[74] But more specifically having entered a state of bewilderment, concernment, perplexity, even shock; it is a state of being without rules, sureness or certainty. Patriotism, for example, post-9/11, 'served as a way to replace disorientation and *Betroffenheit* with certainty. And certainty, if taken to its extreme, always ends in violence'.[75] Her commendation is for citizens to 'resist certainty', and yet to 'commit to things without or in-between certainties'. Ideally, she would have the populace 'act from uncertainty, with exactitude and clarity'.[76] Saying what one means is perhaps philosophically advisable, though politically irksome – as Emerson encouraged: 'Speak your latent conviction, and it shall be the universal sense; for the inmost in due time becomes the outmost'.[77] One nurtures a conviction as one would a child; here a man incubates an idea that will come forth from him, after its term, on his terms. Bogart says that '[o]ne of the most radical things you can do in this culture of the inexact is to finish a sentence. […] It takes effort and stubbornness to finish a sentence'.[78] The defeat of an ending – of the notion that one can complete a thought – is forestalled only when one can 'articulate in the face of uncertainty'. The alternative is to 'rely on how other people have said things', which gives the impression of sufficient articulation, and indulges one's comfort with inherited opinion – the repository for appeals to certainty.[79]

Just as sentimentality precludes the possibility of an authentic expression of love – because it corrupts emotion with clingy attachment and excessively self-indulgent understandings of the meaning of origins – so sentimentality corrupts political action and critique, making them nothing more than the fanfare of nostalgia. In these years after 9/11, pundits continue to describe America as having lost its innocence on that day of fiery death. Yet America as a place and as an idea began with an explosion – with conflagration and mortal loss. In 'The Concord Hymn' written to memorialize the inception of the American Revolution, Emerson wrote: 'By the rude bridge that arched the flood, Their flag to April's breeze unfurled; Here once the embattled farmers stood; And fired the shot heard round the world'.[80] America did not have innocence to lose because it was born from England, born out of protest, born in fire, born in blood shared and spilled.

21.   John Milton, *Areopagitica* (1644)

> I cannot praise a fugitive and cloister'd vertue, unexercis'd & unbreath'd, that never sallies out and sees her adversary, but slinks out of the race, where that immortall garland is to be run for, not without dust and heat. Assuredly we bring not innocence into the world, we bring impurity much rather: that which purifies us is triall, and triall is by what is contrary.

22.   Sin is a proxy slogan for error and wrongdoing, yet its counterforce is not the right but THE NEW. Understood as the sort of phenomenon that goes beyond the limits of its predecessor, the new cannot be explained reductively – retrospectively – but shows supervenient qualities on all sides, from all directions. The new is beyond total comprehension; it is essentially excessive. Emerson writes of the new as that which purifies the day so that it is no longer constrained by the spectre of past harm, by its connection to prior days – days of error, of misjudgement; days corrupted by the sin of others, and compromised by one's own misconceptions.

In the Introduction to *Nature* (1836) Emerson describes America as a new place – with 'new lands, new men, new thoughts'.[81] And of the land he writes in 'The Young American' (1844): 'I think we must regard the *land* as a commanding and increasing power on the citizen, the sanative and Americanizing influence, which promises to disclose new virtues for ages to come'.[82] The 'sanative influence' is one that heals or cures the condition of feeling beholden to history-as-etiology. 'The new man must feel that he is new', Emerson says as a claim and a commendation in 'Literary Ethics' (1838) 'and has not come into the world mortgaged to the opinions and usages of Europe, and Asia, and Egypt'.[83] And in 'The Method of Nature' (1841) Emerson is convinced that 'There is no attractiveness like that of a new man'.[84] Emerson does not embrace the fatalism of Diderot's Jacques: 'Our part is plainly not to throw ourselves across the track, to block improvement and sit till we are stone, but to watch the uprise of successive mornings and to conspire with the new works of new days'.[85] In 'Self-Reliance' (1841) Emerson fathoms that human will – he calls it 'power' – is 'new in nature'.[86] Furthermore, 'Power ceases in the instant of repose; it resides in the moment of transition from a past to a new state [...]. This one fact the world hates; that the soul *becomes*; for that forever degrades the past [...]'.[87] The sentimental thinker, by contrast, wishes to preserve the past for its formidable authority, and not to unsettle the tidy explanations already made by reference to causes and origins.

23.   'A *picture* held us captive', writes Wittgenstein in the *Philosophical Investigations*.[88] Sin is such a picture – an image in the mind, an apparition that haunts one's thoughts – and not traceable in any body; it is a metaphor that by means of use – in authoritative invocations of rhetorical force – appears to have transformed into literal fact. As if one could conjure physical realities by conceiving them.

24.   Having an origin, or believing in one, creates a hierarchy. Emerson observes the 'terrible aristocracy that is in Nature'.[89] In parallel fashion, God is sited at the beginning and so God is at the greatest height – or remove – from all that follows. Without origins, however, the centre can be anywhere or nowhere; the dispersion of central or vertical power is the promise of democracy, and as articulated by Plato in the *Republic*, democracy – as a political de-centreing – is the principal threat to the creation of decent men and the realization of justice. Using a sartorial trope, Socrates characterizes democracy as an alluring 'garment of many colors', 'embroidered with all kinds of hues', tempting us to like and wear it. But as a form of government democracy is 'anarchic and motley, assigning a kind of equality indiscriminately to equals and unequals alike!' Socrates, first ironically, then with a sincerity intended to mock and ridicule, describes the constitution of a democratic state:

> And the tolerance of democracy, its superiority to all our meticulous require-
> ments, its disdain for our solemn pronouncements made when we were founding
> our city, that except in the case of transcendent natural gifts no one could ever
> become a good man unless from childhood his play and all his pursuits were
> concerned with things fair and good – how superbly it tramples underfoot all such
> ideals, caring nothing from what practices and way of life a man turns to politics,
> but honoring him if only he says that he loves the people![90]

The absence of hierarchy, according to Plato, demands unique capacities for self-formation and self-direction, perhaps more than any well-ordered *polis* (πόλις) can expect from its citizens. No one is above the law – or below it – that is, unworthy of it, or deprived of a claim to it. What if aristocracy and its kind of descent were understood as paralleling the physical theories of the era in which Plato wrote? In this way an understanding of the ancient Greek universe was replicated on earth in the form of oligarchies, and retained traction through Ptolemy and long afterward into the middle ages. Only with Copernicus does the de-centred earth appear to summon a similar de-centring of the earthly governance of humans. What if democracy needed a new theory of the universe in order to fulfil its inherent, but not apparent, promise? With successive theories of cosmic evolution the very nature of the *demos* (δῆμος) is recalibrated. And though democracy's development keeps pace with the Enlightenment and the eighteenth-century political and scientific revolutions that bring it to prominence, perhaps it is the latest version of cosmology – as seen or found in quantum physics – that provides an even deeper sense of its potential. Democracy, as a model for the arrangement of elements, resembles theories in quantum physics in so far as one observes action happening from many points of reference, many perspectives, simultaneously. The subatomic realm itself appears to be an embroidered, many-coloured garment, a space defined by unfixity, by continual rearrangement. Each of these observations become happenings that affect the other positions: what they are, what can be known of them. In this context, evolution occurs sporadically, intermittently, and in different places all at once, instead of – as with classical and pre-Copernican ideas of origins – in a linear, consecutive or hierarchical fashion.

In Emerson's time, and long before it, America seemed an aberrant combination of the democratic and aristocratic, a creature that had not learned to distinguish what was elective and what was essential in its formation. Emerson was aware of Thomas Hamilton's critique of democracy in *Men and Manners in America* (1833) – that there is a class of men who though 'publicly advocating the broadest principles of democracy, are in private life aristocratic and exclusive'.[91] As Hamilton did, Emerson assessed the irony, hypocrisy and the distorting, destructive effect of slavery on a democratic country: '[...] in the Southern States, the tenure of land and the local laws, with slavery, give the social system not a democratic but an aristocratic complexion'.[92] The Civil War was, for Emerson, the very endeavour to dissolve the pernicious and ill-fitted comingling of aristocratic hierarchy and racial privilege (or liability) with the equalizing force of democratic laws and human rights: the war was meant to 'to break up the false combination of Southern society, to destroy the piratic feature in it which makes it our enemy only as it is the enemy of the human race'.[93]

25.   A belief in sin creates a desire for the originless – whether described as virginity, purity or freedom of the will. But the insistence on becoming free of sin contributes to its pervasiveness. Fighting against a fate of impurity and causation seems to increase anxiety about contamination and contagion, to make more pronounced a concern with the influence of external factors. Resistance and rebellion leads, in turn, to the development and proliferation of stories, myths and metaphors that will explain these conditions. The very narration of events – the rhythm of one thing after another, the pulse of history – seems to animate the presence of fate and causation. The protection of male children by the blood of slaughtered lambs (Leviticus and Exodus), and the birth of God-as-a-man by-way-of-a-virgin (John), are two – albeit ancient and prominent – stories that reinforce the narrative and emotional resonance of sin and sentimentality, and the implication that causes pervade existence. These are histories and parables, depictions and distortions, and they are likewise modes of self-image formation – since the stories we tell ourselves about the nature of the universe determine the degree of human power, and estimate the value of human existence.

Even as metaphors of blood dominate both Judaic and Christian accounts of human development and human status, such images – that carry with them so many aspects and allusions – can become confused, conflicted and conflated. Thus the paschal lamb of Leviticus, or the smearing of blood in Exodus, has nothing to do with virginal purity but instead with the protection of those who are already born – and obviously, not born of virgins. Narratives from the Christian tradition that draw their imagery from the Hebraic sacrificial system are therefore poised to be misunderstood and misapplied. As a result, the notion of degradation, for example, is part of the history of Christian influence and its contribution to asceticism – at least as interpreted by Nietzsche. By the time Emerson stands at the Unitarian pulpit, he is ready to shed the Calvinist doldrums, and remind us (as Nietzsche will soon after) of the metaphoric nature of religious texts and rituals that would otherwise confirm our depraved status.

But with quantum mechanics we are telling a different story, one that declares that we are, in fact, originless. That things do not evolve in a straight line but from many directions at once. There is no originary cause but multiple causes happening without a clear and predictable, which to say, controllable pattern. Moreover we are involved in the processes that affect us: we are not just acted upon, we also act upon ourselves. In *The Quest for Certainty* (1929) John Dewey accounted for this shift in perception when he contrasted the presumptions of Newtonian physics with the experiments of Werner Heisenberg:

> The basic philosophy of the Newtonian system of the universe is closely connected with what is termed the principle of canonic conjugates. The fundamental principle of the mechanical philosophy of nature is that it is possible to determine exactly (in principle if not in actual practice) both the position and the velocity of any body. Knowing this for each particle which enters into any change, as in motion, it is possible to calculate mathematically, that is exactly, just what will happen. [...]
>
> The philosophy in question assumed that these positions and velocities are there in nature independent of our knowing, of our experiments and observations [...]. The future and the past belong to the same completely determinate and fixed scheme. Observations, when correctly conducted, merely register this fixed state of changes according to laws of objects whose essential properties are fixed. [...] It is this philosophy which Heisenberg's principle has upset, a fact implied in calling it a principle of indeterminacy. [...]
>
> Heisenberg's principle compels a recognition of the fact that interaction prevents an accurate measurement of velocity and position for *any* body, the demonstration centering about the role of the interaction of the observer in determining what actually happens. [...]
>
> The element of indeterminateness is not connected with defect in the method of observation but is intrinsic. The particle observed does not *have* fixed position or velocity, for it is changing all the time because of interaction; specifically, in this case, interaction with the act of observing, or more strictly, with the conditions under which an observation is possible; for it is not the 'mental' phase of observation which makes the difference. [...]
>
> What is known is seen to be a product in which the act of observation plays a necessary role. Knowing is seen to be a participant in what is finally known. Moreover, the metaphysics of existence as something fixed and therefore capable of literally exact mathematical description and prediction is undermined. Knowing is, for philosophical theory, a case of specially directed activity instead of something isolated from practice. The quest for certainty by means of exact possession in mind of immutable reality is exchanged for the search for security by means of active control of the changing course of events. Intelligence in operation, another name for method, becomes the thing most worth winning.
>
> The principle of indeterminacy thus presents itself as the final step in the dislodgment of the old spectator theory of knowledge.[94]

Heisenberg's experiments are conducted at the subatomic level. At this scale the behaviour of particles – for example, exhibiting both wave and particle motion; or changing location based on human observation – creates new pictures of reality.

In such pictures causation is indeterminate and the postulation of an origin loses logical ground. But on the scale of the everyday, the plane on which we live, we do seem caused. One has parents, one is born in a specific location, and at the end of one's indefatigable struggle, one dies wherever one happens to be – also a particular site. Such lines and positions suggest origins and trajectories, pathways and traces. The levels of observation and encounter affect the parameters of explanation. As Lamarckian thinking may underwrite emerging theories of epigenetics (and perhaps ratify a version of the metaphorical meme's inheritance), so Newtonian physics retains an ongoing and immediate significance for everyday life (where gravity and inertia define the movements of the kinds of bodies we are). When accounting for evolutionary change on vast time scales across multiple species, Darwin's theories seem to obtain; and at the subatomic level Heisenberg's principle offers a compelling, if speculative, vision of that which eludes the naked eye.

At the level of the ordinary and everyday, assuming originlessness as a condition for freedom poses a dangerous fiction – harmful because it invites a pursuit of purity, the uncaused, the beginning of the beginning. There are grave theoretical and practical lengths one must go to achieve these states (that is, if they are achievable), especially if these circumstances are necessary preconditions for claiming action as one's own. By contrast, one could abandon the pursuit of some such absolute freedom – that privileges a wish to be uncaused – and seek instead an assessment of the LIMITATIONS that make freedom possible. Understanding freedom, in this mood, means not hoping for the absence of constraining conditions, but rather searching for them as the stipulations and shape-giving prompts for creativity. Freedom would flourish as a perpetual responsiveness to such constraints; these become the conditions on which to create on one's own terms. A self, a child, a book and a nation, are made through engagement with given circumstances, not *ex nihilo* and not in a vacuum. One is a 'piece of nature and fate', writes Emerson, and as such one must contend with that particularity and partiality – the limits that inscribe it and define it.[95]

While quantum mechanics often includes provoking theses – such as the proposition that matter is comprised mostly of empty space – one is left wondering what effect the truth of that notion has on one's life at the level where reality seems solid, material, and as such fragile and vulnerable to destruction. When considering the nature of causation, or non-causation, at the level of the everyday it seems that personal freedom intuitively makes sense: making discrete decisions, moving one's limbs, choosing one's words – they all appear to follow after cognitive intention. In ordinary human life one appears to exercise one's freedoms, as it were, naturally (or proximately) without much worry about the implications of far-off fate or a divine decree. At the extreme micro level, though, the robust physicality of the human condition would make it seem fully determined, or at least, out of one's control – that is, at the mercy of sequential causes, or utter randomness or perhaps an other-worldly intelligence. At the other extreme – the macro level – human life (even with its widespread and diversified presence on earth) appears to be too insignificant to be worth the concern of a godhead. Or in sheer physical and causal terms, the vastness of cosmic space suggests the entire existence of *homo sapiens* occupies but a breath (and at that, a shallow breath) in interstellar history; after the sun in our solar system, the nearest star – *Proxima Centauri* – is estimated to be 4.243 light years away, or nearly 2.5 trillion miles from earth; at the same scale, if the sun were an inch away from the earth, *Proxima Centauri* would be 4.2 miles in the distance. But on the scale of the human – of private thoughts and shared plans, of intimacies and aspirations – free will appears both intuitive and a faith that makes life worth living. Terrestrial freedom – despite that which is conscribed by gravity, biochemistry, the physical limits of the body, and contingencies beyond one's control – nevertheless lends a modest chance for self-appointed creation, for interpreting actions as part of an ongoing project of self-constitution and the development of personal identity.

While comforted by the impression of some degree of freedom, human life remains formed and defined by constraints; this accords with the laws of evolution, which suggest that development and mutation are the consequences of a continual engagement each species must make with the specific demands of its environment. With *homo sapiens* that engagement moves to the level of consciousness – the level at which attention and judgement form new kinds of interaction with surroundings. Dewey's idea of 'intelligence in operation' as a synonym for METHOD insightfully captures the link between mental and material life. Unfortunately Dewey's 'search for security by means of active control' seems less promising since the goal of this inter-action is not control but understanding. Often understanding yields some degree of control, but many times it importantly leaves one at a loss – feeling limited, pressed up against new boundaries, or deliriously incapable of discerning them. When this vertiginous feeling ceases to be regarded as a liability and is instead treated as part of one's creative potential, then the search for unbounded freedom will have lost its allure – and along with it, the desire for isolating origins and tracing causes will fade.

26.   In the film *The Five Obstructions* (2003), director Lars von Trier proposes to his filmic mentor and hero, Danish filmmaker, Jørgen Leth, that he re-make his short 1967 film *The Perfect Human* – but this time with obstacles – or OBSTRUCTIONS – both indiscriminately and artfully put in his way by Trier.[96] Trier's instructive sadism aside, the project is a study of how a creative person can flourish under constraining circumstances. CREATIVE need not necessarily mean artistic but rather generative of intelligent responses to assigned or found conditions; in this respect, a combatant who reacts to an enemy offensive by employing an innovative tactic is creative. Leth accepts Trier's offer, and goes off to re-make his film according to random, sometimes ambiguous rules, and returns again and again with arresting – often beautiful – revisions. Trier is not satisfied, though, since Leth seems pleased with the results of his efforts; Trier instead wants him to suffer because Trier believes that diminishing an artist's pride is necessary for truthful art. As 'punishment', Trier gives Leth a new assignment. This time there are not several, disparate rules (as there were on previous assignments) – just one: 'There are no rules'. Upon hearing this Leth recoils in panic, pleading: 'You can't do that to me'. Leth instantly understands the implication of Trier's obstruction: total freedom is utter cruelty for a creative person, a crippling injunction. The boundlessness leaves nothing to respond to, presents no points of resistance. Such

openness avails the artist to create in a void or a plenum – either way, an unwelcome prospect. And though it is possible to do so – Leth manages to make a splendid little film using the lack of obstruction as an invitation to invent and apply his own obstacles – it often does not yield the most felicitous outcomes, artistic or otherwise. Aesthetic and moral innovations seem to arise under compressed, constrained, even harsh circumstances.

Unlike Dewey's suggestion that one works to achieve security or perfection through control, the lesson learned from Trier's experiment is to develop judgement and responsiveness to encountered and imposed conditions. The concern then is less with the subject and object – as entities or forces that control and cause – than with the relationship one perceives between them. As Leth concludes, after thriving under one of Trier's most sinister filmic demands, the obstruction was 'a gift'.

27.   In *The Ignorant Schoolmaster* (1991) Jacques Rancière writes compelling about a lecturer in French literature, Joseph Jacotot, who found himself in 1818 needing to teach French to Flemish students. He knew no Flemish and they knew no French. 'There was thus no language in which he could teach them what they sought from him'.[97] In these limiting conditions, who is the ignorant and who is the master? What can be taught and who will learn it? Instead of Trier's five obstructions Rancière characterizes 'the power of the ignorant' as part of his illustration of *Five Lessons in Intellectual Emancipation*:

> This is the way the ignorant master can instruct the learned one as well as the ignorant one: by verifying that he is always searching. Whoever looks always finds. He doesn't necessarily find what he was looking for, and even less what he was supposed to find. But he finds something new to relate to the *thing* that he already knows. What is essential is the continuous vigilance, the attention that never subsides without irrationality setting in – something that the learned one, like the ignorant one, excels at. The master is he who keeps the researcher on his own route, the one that he alone is following and keeps following.[98]

28.   Leo Tolstoy, *A Confession*

> Now, looking back at that time, I can clearly see that the only real faith I had, apart from the animal instincts motivating my life, was a belief in perfection. [...] I tried to perfect myself intellectually and studied everything I came upon in life. I tried to perfect my will, setting myself rules I tried to follow. I perfected myself physically, practicing all kinds of exercises in order to develop my strength and dexterity, and I cultivated endurance and patience by undergoing all kinds of hardship. All this I regarded as perfection. The beginning of it all was, of course, moral perfection, but this was soon replaced by a belief in general perfection, that is a desire to be better not in my own eyes or before God but in the eyes of other people.[99]

Michael Wood, 'Why Praise Astaire?'

> Cavell recommends the Emersonian idea of 'perfectionism', which is oddly named
> precisely because it dispenses with the concept of the perfect.[100]

A perfectly reasonable and intuitive reading of perfectionism would have one understand
it as a moral philosophy that reflects the human attempt to get everything right. The
perfectionist imagines his life as an incremental triumph over errors – one at a time, one
after another; at its most extreme, such an understanding of perfectionism reveals a will
to control oneself in all aspects, to know and control the world and predict everything
that happens in it. To achieve such dominion, however, the spirit that animates such
perfectionism must be imbued with self-loathing, contempt for others, and frustration
with the ambiguity, dissipation and hindrances of the external world. Every moment is
spent being disaffected with the way things are, and struggling to achieve some measure
of amelioration. Notably, however, on this view there is no allowance for mutation or
innovation, and no tolerance for the unexpected – since such openness to contingency
would entail trusting the processes of change that dominate one's life. This kind of
perfectionism formalizes instincts from a range of categories – tradition, hierarchy,
paternalism, tyranny, myopia, order – instincts that appear threatened by difference and
diversity, and suspicious of development. Such instincts are fundamentally conservative
in nature. As Tolstoy notes, the changes he made were largely motivated by the hope of
creating favourable opinions of him by others; the objective was not improvement, just
the appearance of an uncommon rigor or discipline.

In *A Theory of Justice* (1972) John Rawls writes about the moral and political implications of another version of perfectionism, and criticizes Nietzsche for developing this
view, which Rawls believes to be deeply anti-democratic: 'At places he says that mankind
must continually strive to produce great individuals. We give value to our lives by working
for the good of the highest specimens'.[101] In this Rawlsian reading of Nietzschean perfectionism the goal of one's efforts is not to make oneself better but to make some 'great'
individual by means of one's sacrifice – unless, of course, you *are* that great individual.

Stanley Cavell develops a rival reading of perfectionism, one that is at odds with
Rawls' interpretation, and illustrates how Nietzsche's views – in part inspired by
Emerson's – are compatible with a robustly democratic position.

> [...] Emersonian perfectionism – place it as the thought that 'the main enterprise
> of the world for splendor, for extent, is the upbuilding of a man' – is not an elitist
> call to subject oneself to great individuals (to the 'one or two men' 'in a century, in
> a millennium') but to the greatness, the thing Emerson calls by the ancient name
> of the genius, in each of us; it is the quest he calls 'becoming what one is'. [...][102]

> [... I]f Emerson is right, his aversion [to conformity] provides for the democratic
> aspiration the only internal measure of its truth to itself – a voice only this
> aspiration could have inspired, and, if it is lucky, must inspire.[103]

The Tolstoyan perfectionist believes there is something inherently wrong with himself
– like the 'corrupt and corrupting sensualist in his degradation,' from Emerson's

sermon on Job[104] – and his work is to purify himself through various forms of self-punishment and self-denial. Rawls' reading of the Nietzschean perfectionist makes the purpose of common peoples' lives the creation of a few great individuals. Cavell's understanding of the Emersonian perfectionist, contrary to Rawls' position, suggests a model where every human possesses potential greatness; this view abandons a will-to-perfection that binds a person to various rituals of purification and self-mortification; and it dismisses the contention that the majority of human lives are the means for supporting the lives of a select group of elite human specimens. Conformity, as Emerson understood it, bears resemblance to ascetic self-punishment in so far as one wills to deny one's insight and impulses; it is functionally a form of self-denial or self-constraint that in its most extreme manifestations risks the diminishment or loss of one's fundamental identity. When Emerson writes that 'imitation is suicide' a reader must strain to keep in mind the metaphorical aspect of the claim.[105] In his address before the graduating students of Divinity at Harvard in 1838, Emerson said:

> But by this eastern monarchy of a Christianity, which indolence and fear have
> built, the friend of man is made the injurer of man. The manner in which his name
> [– Jesus –] is surrounded with expressions, which were once sallies of admiration
> and love, but are now petrified into official titles, kills all generous sympathy and
> liking. All who hear me, feel, that the language that describes Christ to Europe and
> America, is not the style of friendship and enthusiasm to a good and noble heart,
> but is appropriated and formal [...]. Accept the injurious impositions of our early
> catechetical instruction, and even honesty and self-denial were but splendid sins,
> if they did not wear the Christian name. One would rather be 'a pagan, suckled in
> a creed outworn', than to be defrauded of his manly right in coming into nature,
> and finding not names and places, not land and professions, but even virtue and
> truth foreclosed and monopolized. You shall not be a man even.[106]

Emerson is responsive to the ways that the 'style' of 'expressions' in language marks the difference between the ossified and the vital, between a life that is available to those who live it – and a life that is merely in the service of the afterlife. The admonition, then, is for any Christian teaching that is delivered ready-made, presented as categorically-fitted and eternally-fixed that leaves no space for the ongoing evolution of an interpreted, emergent Christian self – one readers could recognize in the style of expressions in Christ's teaching, in his language.

The interpretive shifts made possible in Emersonian perfectionism, a literary venture in contradistinction to Rawls' literalist reproach, enable one's passion for the incremental pursuit of one's own better self – not a perfect or finished self, not a pure or right self, but a self that is continually under negotiation – in language and action – a self that is sometimes beside itself, and at other times aware of the need for its development, a movement onward to a next version of itself. The hope is not to establish a terminal identity, but to embrace how identities have terms – and how one creates and inhabits them successively. Such an iterative approach underwrites a loyalty to the present, and reinforces an openness to the complexity of emerging phenomena, and the developing systems affected by mutation, innovation, and the dynamics of an evolving reality. For it is only in the present that any such negotiations of the self can take place; one's experience of the past and future occurs in the present through forms of remembering, expression and imagining – the present remaining perpetually the site of encounter. Regarding the spirit of his own perfectionism Emerson wrote: 'I unsettle all things. No facts are to me sacred; none are profane; I simply experiment, an endless seeker with no Past at my back'.[107]

XI

Second Selves

1. Emerson, *Journals* (1848)

> There are a great many talents in a drop of blood, and a little suppression or
> retardation would unchain & let out what horns & fangs, what manes & hoofs,
> what fins & flippers, what feathers & coats of mail which we are now subdued and
> refined into smooth & shapely limbs, into soft white skin, into the simple erect
> royal form of man.[1]

Emerson consolidates several theories in this brief passage: essence, inherency,
latency, mutation and the creative or constitutional effects of conditions. What is in
the blood that is not yet revealed or realized? What kinds of instructions are encoded
in the blood, and what remains to be written into it? How do environmental circumstances stimulate or inhibit the development of congenital or innate potential?

While the image of man with 'manes & hoofs' leaves one thinking of centaurs, there
is something of Emerson's idea of an intelligence in the blood that comes to light with
his remarks on horses, in particular, how the English breed horses: they 'boast that
they understand horses better than any other people in the world, and that their horses
are become their second selves'.[2] With Carlyle as a travelling companion, Emerson
visited the home of Philip Sidney at Wilton Hall – a house known to Shakespeare, and
the place where Sidney wrote *The Countess of Pembroke's Arcadia* in the late sixteenth
century. Emerson was much impressed with the gardens of this 'renowned seat of
the Earls of Pembroke', noting 'I had not seen more charming grounds'. But it is in a
moment of Sidney's *A Defence of Poesie* (1579) that we find an interlude of pertinent
lines relating a scene with Giovanni Pietro Pugliano, an equerry, who was teaching
Sidney (and his friend, Edward Wotton) about horsemanship at the Imperial Court
in Vienna: 'Then would he add certain praises by telling what a peerless beast the
horse was, the only serviceable courtier, without flattery, the beast of most beauty,
faithfulness, courage, and such more, that if I had not been a piece of a logician before
I came to him, I think he would have persuaded me to have wished myself a horse'.[3]

The English understanding of horses is more accurately described as a familiarity
with breeding, a familiarity one might say that begins not with the horses but with
themselves. The English, Emerson seems to suggest, believe that their horses, like
themselves, have two advantages: first, good stock and secondly, good training. '[I]t
is in the deep traits of race that the fortunes of nations are written', he writes, and in
England 'exists the best stock in the world'.[4] In a lecture presented in London during his
1848 tour, Emerson notes how 'the permanent traits of the Aristocracy' is 'an attractive

topic, which never goes out of vogue and is impertinent in no community'.[5] Part of the interest involves discerning not just the forms and effects but also the origins of aristocracy, perhaps how, as with the English, that '[a]ll nobility in its beginnings was somebody's natural superiority'.[6] For this reason, '[p]rimogeniture is a cardinal rule of English property and institutions. Laws, customs, manners, the very persons and faces, affirm it'.[7] When training horses, as when tutoring Englishmen, there must be a natural receptivity to indoctrination. The specimen's capacity to respond to training shows itself in manners and methods. The blood is stout and it is adaptable; the blood brings with it vigorous energy and yet it yields to instructions and the lessons of terrain.

As there are horses to train, and young men at universities in need of tutelage, so does British colonialism raise the spectre of impact and influence on realms of life beyond the immediate habitat of North Sea islands.

> The spawning force of the race has sufficed to the colonization of great parts of the world; yet it remains to be seen whether they can make good the exodus of millions from Great Britain, amounting, in 1852, to more than a thousand a day. They have assimilating force, since they are imitated by their foreign subjects; and they are still aggressive and propagandist, enlarging the dominion of their arts and liberty.[8]

Emerson invites readers to consider what precisely is or can be imitated by the colonized. If English moral wisdom, legal structure, scientific sophistication and manners can be assimilated – adopted into the flow of an existing civilization – that does not mean that 'foreign subjects' become Englishmen. Emerson asks rhetorically: 'It is race, is it not? that puts the hundred millions of India under the dominion of a remote island in the north of Europe'.[9] And he sketches how 'their colonization annexes archipelagoes and continents', drawing each new people and land into the commonwealth, while 'their speech seems destined to be the universal language'.[10] The English mode of colonization promotes influences to the level of 'dominion'; its presence is both suggestive and imposed. The colonists of New England – many of them of English descent – did not object to the cultural presence of England but bridled over England's legal, political, and economic impositions on them. The 'assimilation' of foreigners to English customs was supported by the English habit of bringing England wherever its emissaries went. Yet these representatives of the crown did not seek to make Englishmen of those over whom England claimed dominion, but rather aimed to convince (or insist when necessary) a culture to adopt ways sufficient for establishing a continuous order with Britain. Colonization, in this mode of fashioning, created islands of British presence and British identity in distant lands, among vast oceans of foreign people. The limits of the island do not mean the limits of the world; call this a picture of colonialism on British terms. 'If the race is good, so is the place', notes Emerson, so if the English traverse the globe, bringing their traits with them, then the places they invade or inhabit, colonize or conquer will be coextensive with the homeland. Still, such interventions in other races and lands may unsettle the blood of the colonists – leaving them infected and diseased, living with – or dying from

– the liabilities of adventitious sojourns; in this respect, the colonists were colonized – invaded internally by the races and lands they sought to outwardly command. Yet the colonizing instinct would prevail, despite losses and misprisions. As sailors and merchants aboard their ships were at home – the deck but an extension of native soil – the custom house, embassy and men's club was an instantiation of England. The ship itself was England: a sanctioned and sanctified domestic territory on which sails were raised and lowered. Consequently the seamen conducted themselves in accord with the laws and customs of their native island thousands of miles away.

> More intellectual than other races, when they live with other races, they do not take their language, but bestow their own. They subsidize other nations, and are not subsidized. They proselyte, and are not proselyted. They assimilate other races to themselves, and are not assimilated.[11]

The American experience of assimilation is defined by aggregation. As such the image of the melting pot is less apt – because it connotes dissolution of individual traits – than the intimations of *E pluribus unum* ('from many things emerge one thing'; or perhaps more precisely rendered: 'together, diverse elements constitute a whole'). The best attributes of an individual become more prominent, intelligible and useful because of her engagement with the best traits of others. We are back to Emerson standing before the Cabinets of Natural History: 'How much finer things are in composition than alone'.[12] But the pleasure and insight of the composition comes in part from being able to discern the discrete elements; they are not melted and homogenized but retain their distinctive contours and colours. As John Stuart Mill wrote in 1859: 'As it is useful that while mankind are imperfect there should be different opinions, so is it that there should be different experiments in life'.[13] Mill believed that 'the free development of individuality is one of the leading essentials of well-being', so a democratic assembly of many people ought to alternate between the power it draws from discontinuous individuals and the power it creates because of their alliance.[14]

The British, by contrast, did not colonize to discover the complementary powers of other races, but to constitute English traits abroad. Features of English life were commoditized and packaged, and packed on ships for export. Every colony, then, hosted a smaller England – or a layer of its sovereignty – on its familiar territory. Customs, manners and language were imposed; the local correlates of these were not drafted for their amplifying force, but quarantined (and if adopted occasionally, with circumspection, only to the limit of preserving the English forms). Such colonization draws its design from an aristocratic methodology that equates success with succession, and as such reflects a faith in the protection of inherited types and kinds, social propriety and linear descent. Leaving aside how the colonized might be affronted by British impositions, Emerson notes how the non-English marvel at the causes of the Englishman: 'Then first we care to examine the pedigree, and copy heedfully the training, – what food they ate, what nursing, school, and exercises they had, which resulted in this mother-wit, delicacy of thought, and robust wisdom'.[15] Acknowledging the accomplished specimens of English genius – 'King Alfred, and Roger Bacon, William of Wykeham, Walter Raleigh, Philip Sidney, Isaac

Newton, William Shakspeare, Francis Bacon, George Herbert, Henry Vane' – one wonders 'What made these delicate natures? was it the air? was it the sea? was it the parentage?'[16] The terrestrial conditions and the distinctive blood – all core traits of nationality – matter to the formation of individuals, and yet these factors are neither discretely traceable as the causes of their achievement nor do they set definite limits on what non-Englishmen can do once they assimilate English traits on their own terms, with the 'counteracting forces' that emerge from one's native culture.[17]

The American mode of colonization – carrying with it portions of capitalism, democracy, rule of law, scientism, consumerism and individualism – involves a democratic methodology based on the belief that success is unpredictable, follows spontaneously from many directions, and appears at an unreliable rhythm. Where British influence proceeds from the presence of habits, laws and customs derived from English 'stock', American influence happens when locals advance their own interpretations of American ideas and principles. While American political economy owes its origins to eighteenth-century English and Scottish thinkers (pre-eminently Adam Smith), the American model – as exemplified by a free market economy based on incentives for profit and productivity – is given to a reliance on spontaneous order (as opposed to the English imposition of order as coordinate with natural order). And so as the English would struggle to suppress any antagonisms with or deviations from imposed order, so must the American acknowledge the potential peril of spontaneous disorder.

Colonial influence is memetic: hosts are transformed through their imitative engagement with the customs, languages, laws and ideas of the outsider. Historically, the British stimulated local imitation by predicating genetic, political and social order worthy of their ambitions. The American turn, especially since the Great War, has been defined by a pronounced faith in democratic ideals that underwrite a free society; these are not somatic characteristics but cultivated concepts. There is nothing genetic, aristocratic or hereditary that supports these beliefs; they are available to all, and often adaptable to each. Liberty and democracy (commonly coupled with the promise of the marketplace) are said to be universal human truths (not American truths), which America merely advocates on behalf of. Yet the appeal of these forms often compels aggressive advocacy – even war – and leaves the skeptical wondering about such confident claims to universality.

The spread of American colonialism in the form of free markets and democracies tempts many to indulge a high-spirited patriotism (instead of say a stock-based nationalism or a traits-based racism – both of which are more historically a function of British colonialism and varieties of anglophilia). Yet the self-satisfaction and fanfare of both outlooks is misplaced: the aspirations embodied in American traits are circumstantial (not exclusively tied to place or pedigree); and the English boast is anachronistic (a cultural myth that nevertheless retains tremendous salience and prompts nostalgia). The English colonist discovers an 'easy pride when he finds every other countryman inferior to him as a man'.[18] Such presumptuousness works only so long as the 'inferior' men believe themselves inferior; if that belief is never held, or once it is broken, so is the 'easy pride'. For this reason, British colonialism 'necessitates a hopeless limitation'.[19] Believing that 'all men are created equal' requires a limitless vigilance; every new person demands a defence of his rights and liberties, beginning with an appeal to their reality. The American who believes he is specially – exceptionally – equipped for this defence should be faulted for a xenophobic patriotism. Yet when he takes that responsibility as part of finding terms for the 'rights of man' – a conversation for humanity – then one need not fear regression to jingoism.

> Patriotism is balderdash. Our side, our state, our town is boyish enough. But it is true that every foot of soil has its proper quality, that the grape on either side of the same fence has its own flavor, and so every acre on the globe, every group of people, every point of climate has its own moral meaning whereof it is the symbol. For such a patriotism let us stand.[20]

The aristocrat necessarily values origins and traits, blood and breeding, heredity and hierarchy, parentage and lineage, heraldry and the passing on of names; his power is inherited and preserved by a talent for tradition. The democrat, by contrast, wishes his power to appear without a source – as if it were an impersonal function of things as we find them, as if it were natural to be self-caused, as if freedom and equality were self-evident. The democrat's desire embodies a speculative faith in originlessness, self-creation, self-generation, merit, desert and parentlessness (under disparate banners: the orphan, the pilgrim, the wanderer, the homeless, the exile, the stranger, the loner, the cowboy, the entrepreneur, the travelling salesman and perhaps most conspicuously, the inventor). These nameless figures are fancies, are as much dreams as consequences; they shape one's personal identity, underwrite both reality and romance, and lend credence to the narrative and rhetoric of freedom.

> America is the idea of emancipation[.]
> [A]bolish kingcraft, Slavery, feudalism, blackletter monopoly, pull down gallows, explode priestcraft, tariff, open the doors of the sea to all emigrants. Extemporize government, California, Texas, Lynch Law. All this covers selfgovernment. All proceeds on the belief that as the people have made a gov.t they can make another[,] that their Union & law is not in their memory but in their blood. If they unmake the law they can easily make it again.[21]

Blood makes life possible and it is a mark human identity. Though blood may be instructive – teach beyond or above memory – it is also an inscription that can isolate one man from another; it may become the excuse for enslavement and the means of mutual destruction. Spilling blood on behalf of defending blood is an ancient ritual. War and murder are bloodlettings, attempts to destroy first what one imagines will destroy him. Ethnic cleansing is based on the grim fantasy that blood can be purified of its taint – reflecting the bivalent belief that the enemy's blood is corrupted and one's own is sanctified. Spilling another's blood is thought to compensate for blood already spilled – as if new blood (impure though it is) were the proper levy for the loss of old blood. The cleansing of blood is a passion based on a metaphysical presumption that some blood types contain undesirable origins and traits worthy of eradication. It is a fiction that causes realities of irremediable loss, incalculable pain, and interminable torment. As Jim Harrison writes in *Off to the Side*: 'There can be no allowable concept of ethnic or genetic virtue, inevitably the major source of human butchery'.[22]

2.   While touring England, Emerson heard that 'the upper classes have only birth'.[23] He does not report who said it but he does admire that the English 'have the sense of superiority, the absence of all the ambitious effort which disgusts in the aspiring classes, a pure tone of thought and feeling, and the power to command [...]'.[24] By definition, being born of aristocratic blood entails being aristocratic. So there is nothing to aspire to beyond one's class; having arrived already at one's destination, there is no need for ambition – for the kind of motivated action that would only befit a person who was not born physically and, as it were, metaphysically fully formed. As such, striving is indecorous – a trait of the lower classes; it is an energy that presumes the capacity and the desire for change. In a democratic state, where a faith in aristocracy has been shed (if still reluctantly admired by the bourgeoisie – because it is something that cannot be purchased or otherwise acquired), ambition becomes the means for postulating – if not establishing – self-worth, individual identity and the character of one's class. Worth and identity are no longer given in the blood; they have to be made in the course of daily life in and among a society of other strivers. Yet thinking of the American poet John Godfrey Saxe's line 'And born in Boston needs no second birth', there remain instances of residual belief that some families are naturally superior. For those without blue blood, however, there may be a perceived need for a second birth: either in the religious terms of being born again (into a self that relies on something outside the self); or in the secular ideology of self-creation (usually regarded as the phenomenon of being one's own cause – self-made), which supports the picture of an endogenously manifested self, in effect, a miracle of private will and imagination. The very notion of repetition is imbedded in the concept of a second birth and thus illustrates the preservation of faith in origins, and the felt need for a new beginning that requires a ritual of purification, or a renaming, or a new narrative of creation. Consequently, even the secular account depends on magic and myth.

3.   The secular ideology of self-creation is democratic; and it is highly complementary to the ideology of democracy. One who believes in self-creation disowns a faith in *fixed* origins, and counters with the possibility of a new beginning (a new founding). The ambition is not creation once and for all, but continual reformation of the given order of things – including one's own inner order; hence the relevance of Emersonian moral perfectionism to democracy. The new state of affairs – either in the rule of government or in the government of oneself – never achieves a foundational status, or the privilege of being the permanent source of a new line. Rather the reformed state and reforming self is continually under negotiation. Where the religious notion of the born again metaphorizes a natural birth (for example by claiming a new, pure beginning), self-creation is admittedly artificial. The reformation can be achieved in the re-writing of one's constitution (again both in terms of governments and individual men), or in renaming oneself.

But these new constitutions are not first or final points of origin; the whole history of one's evolutionary enterprise remains part of the ongoing project. '[E]very pumpkin in the field goes through every point of pumpkin history'.[25] And writing is often a means by which a democratic impulse of self-creation works its way through or against an inherited or an aristocratic or a tyrannical system. The image of the monster (such as Frankenstein), or more recent myriad versions of the robot, scandalizes the aspiration for self-creation because these are not creatures who can write themselves into existence (at least not yet). A robot, like a computer, is programmed; a code is written for it to execute; this is the very definition of exogenous creation. The familiar plot of robot rebellion – or re-programming – is usually a coupling of the robot's wish to know human emotions (such as love) and to possess self-directed freedom. But Emerson anticipates the robot's circumstance when he writes of human fate and its 'irresistible dictation'.[26] Like the child who is written by his parents' genetic code, each human is also programmed, and thereafter poised to question, contest and rewrite his condition.

The rhetoric of self-creation makes it incumbent that humans possess the power to dictate terms of their own accord. Such writing is the condition of endogeniety, and perhaps also betrays the attendant need to erase or occlude other writing – competing histories, conflicting myths and contradicting reports from empirical science. In this respect Emerson suggests that England may be a more fitting illustration than mid-nineteenth America for the reforming effect of words. While Emerson found that the 'power of the newspaper' in America is 'in accordance with our political system', he remarked that in England the power of such writing 'stands in antagonism with the feudal institutions'.[27] A nervous Lord Mansfield wrote to the Duke of Northumberland: 'So your grace likes the comfort of reading the newspapers, mark my words; you and I shall not live to see it, but this young gentleman (Lord Eldon) may, or it may be a little later; but a little sooner or later, these newspapers will most assuredly write the dukes of Northumberland out of their titles and possessions, and the country out of its king'.[28]

4. Class is an abbreviated form of classification. In Emerson's usage the scientific or biological sense of class (as persons or things that comprise a group by reference to common attributes) is often more prominent than the social and political intimation of the term (as a means for referencing socio-economic and educational strata or status). Yet whichever emphasis is detected, Emerson writes of class as a way of organizing, ordering, describing and arranging specimens according to traits – some inherited through the blood (race, parentage, family, physical constitution, physiognomy), and some drawn from cultural circumstance (language, education, institutional affilia-tions, tribal coalitions, habits of mind).

In *English Traits* we see Emerson explore the ways in which class is at once a natural form and a social construct. If the natural inheritance of class is a kind of fate, one is left to wonder what elements and characteristics are elective or freely-imposed but not necessary. What specifically about class is corrigible – and if change is possible, to some degree, is it strictly a change in one's non-genetic make-up? We cannot, it seems, speak of achieving a mutation of our corporeal composition at the level of genes – for example, by cognition or will; though epigenetics researchers conjecture that we may be able to alter the 'expression' of inherited genes. If one becomes oriented to changes that are possible in one's *cultural* context, however, how does one determine what should be retained and what discarded – for example, without going too far from the precinct of one's identity, that is, without giving up some essential aspect of one's own-most personhood? For instance, how much, or little, does a woman relinquish in changing from a maiden to a married name? Part of Emerson's diagnostic report of British society involves an examination of what may be permeable and mutable about class as we find it socially, educationally, linguistically, religiously and even biologically. One crucial result of Emerson's investigation is the taxonomical classification of class – in England; how he finds ways to parse the chosen from the given, the cultural bonds from the blood-ties, the superficial habits of persons from the 'deep traits of race'.[29]

An abiding theme of Emerson's reading of England is his emphasis on, and appreciation of, the English 'genius for freedom', an estimation that has been treated capably by other scholars.[30] To this conversation I wish to add attention to the natural scientific instincts apparent in Emerson's methodology – how, in particular, Emerson's account of the English elucidates his opinion of the forms and fashions of social class by deploying the scientist's approach to the classification of natural phenomena. In this move we again find Emerson working as an analogist – transferring and translating from one zone of experience to another.

After writing on some variation of the notion of the Anglo-Saxon race for decades, Emerson's finished book *English Traits* emerges as a field guide illustrated by nuanced attention to nomenclature and by the careful analysis – and synthesis – of aspects of the culture and the people who comprise the subject of his investigation, and importantly, the people from whom Emerson himself derived a legitimate lineage. In this respect, as a study of a race, *English Traits* is also the study of the men who live in and through that race – Emerson among them – and so, from a certain angle, *English Traits* possesses an inflection of Emerson's autobiography. The book does after all begin with two decidedly memoiristic chapters, then fades imperceptibly into a general, seemingly less personal discussion of the English, only to return just as subtly to the form of reminiscence and private account. And yet the work remains, page after page, a project with an intimate, frank and identifiable point of view. For this reason, among others, *English Traits* could never be mistaken for a work of sociology or cultural anthropology, much less social history or political theory; instead, it recommends itself as a report from the field notebooks of a natural historian of intellect – a proud and curious descendent of the race he studies.

5.   In the evolutionary terms of scientific discourse, descent is presented as a PROGRESSION from primitive to ever more elegant, sophisticated and HIGHER classes of forms. It is common to find evolutionary biologists, cultural anthropologists (and others similarly engaged in identifying causes for the development of forms), deploying the TREE OF LIFE schema as an explanatory icon or metaphor. In these cases the metaphor reinforces continuity and connection between generations, types and

classes; the superiority of later forms acknowledges its cohesion with earlier, lower forms (and when we learn that the whale descended from a diminutive, land-based ungulate [*Indohyus*], we are no longer sure of the hierarchy, rank or merit of one structure of life over or against another). By contrast the images that dominate social and political (that is, largely non-scientific) conceptions of class – while also still firmly rooted in cultural terms – presume fixed categories of separation that arrive in tandem with a hierarchy. In class theory as inherited by the nineteenth century, there is a clear designation of the 'higher' form, say, among aristocrats and intelligentsia; the 'upper' – of the upper class – becomes a metaphor for greater wealth, property, education and other manifestations of power (including political power). In this image of class, there is no indication that the higher/upper forms 'descend' (much less ascend) from the lower forms. These two levels appear to exist independently and in parallel – and decidedly without connection or transmission. (Emerson reports on the masses' disparaging opinion of the aristocracy: 'The upper classes have only birth, say the people here, and not thoughts'.)[31]

While the tree of life metaphor (as a graphic of the descent of hominid forms and kinds) reinforces how species are biologically linked, the difficulty of social movement from one class to another suggests that a permanent rupture between the two realms was historically prominent and profoundly felt, a feature that would find its way figuratively into the daily lives on both sides of the divide (for example, in the upstairs/downstairs scenarios of aristocrats and their servants). When there is social movement it would appear to go in one direction. For the wealthy aristocrat the spectre of impoverishment may only have been a threat (a nightmare of a mismatched marriage or a sudden death), and yet its possibility likely encouraged financial, legal, social and institutional protections to minimize its occurrence. Unless the aristocrat purposefully wagered his fortune and estate, he should not have had to expect the sudden, severe losses that are possible in highly leveraged capitalist ventures – likewise, without such risks he should also not anticipate sudden windfalls of expansive wealth. Emerson writes, 'The jealousy of every class to guard itself, is a testimony to the reality they have found in life'.[32] By contrast, for the lower class there was little chance of suddenly and accidentally becoming wealthy, educated and powerful – and no chance of becoming a bona fide aristocrat (since such a mantle is inherited passively, hereditarily); instead 'upward mobility' – with its sanguine faith in ASCENT – would become a phenomenon for generations to struggle with as they attempted to emerge slowly out of the lower class – as if making the transition from sea to land; certainly a kind of movement (escalating, accelerating, aggregating) that is part of the myth (and the reality) of capitalism. While the lower class is open to all, the upper class is structured to resist permeability by lower forms of life. The rigidity of class suggests there were very few amphibians. And what do we make of the descent of those cetaceans who left the bright land for the dark watery depths?

6. Melville, *Moby-Dick*, 'The Whiteness of the Whale' (1851)

It was the whiteness of the whale that above all things appalled me. [...]

Though in many natural objects, whiteness refiningly enhances beauty, as if imparting some special virtue of its own [...]; and though this pre-eminence in it applies to the human race itself, giving the white man ideal mastership over every dusky tribe [...]; and though in other mortal sympathies and symbolizings, this same hue is made the emblem of many touching, noble things – the innocence of brides, the benignity of age [...]; though even in the higher mysteries of the most august religions it has been made the symbol of the divine spotlessness and power [...] there yet lurks an elusive something in the innermost idea of this hue, which strikes more of panic to the soul than that redness which affrights in blood.

[... A]ll these are but subtile deceits, not actually inherent in substances, but only laid on from without [...].[33]

7.   Emerson, 'Aristocracy' (1848)

I observe the inextinguishable prejudice men have in favor of a hereditary trans-mission of qualities. It is in vain to remind them that Nature appears capricious. Some qualities she carefully fixes and transmits, but some, and those the finer, she exhales with the breath of the individual, as too costly to perpetuate. But I notice also that they may become fixed and permanent in any stock, by painting and re-painting them on every individual, until at last Nature adopts them and bakes them into her porcelain.[34]

8.   Recent developments in the field of epigenetics have revitalized portions of the Lamarckian conversation about the inheritance of acquired characteristics, and in the process transformed the long-standing Darwinian definitions and parameters of descent. At the heart of this investigation is the notion of the epigenome – namely, the environmental and natural history of *non-genetic* influences on gene expression. Or stated more elaborately and definitively by applied biological anthropologist Fatimah Jackson:

Epigenetic mechanisms are heritable and non-heritable modifications (or patterns) in gene expression that are transmitted by mechanisms other than changes in the DNA sequence. Chemicals surrounding specific gene sequences are able to influence the specific form of the protein coded for by the DNA sequence without changing the molecular sequence of the DNA.[35]

The epigeneticist seeks therefore to elucidate the molecular basis for the propa-gation of cellular traits instead of conducting the more customary search for genetic mechanisms – the latter tradition, one should acknowledge, beginning formally with Aristotle in his *On the Generation of Animals*.[36] While chemical modifications may regulate gene expression without affecting a DNA sequence, these changes can last for generations.[37] Prompted by the implications of this biological scenario, the epigenetic researcher asks how one's everyday, lived conditions affect chemical changes at the molecular level, which in turn influence the 'functional expression' of one's genes, and those of one's heirs.[38] Factors as diverse as *in utero* development, environmental chemicals, pharmaceuticals and diet may become epigenetic mechanisms that 'activate or repress' gene expression.[39] Researchers such as Fatimah Jackson suggest for example that a woman who smokes during pregnancy will likely change her epigenome and thereafter may pass on epigenomic traits – activated by her smoking – to her fetus and, if the fetus is female, even to her female grandchild; why the transmission appears laterally along gender lines is still under investigation.[40] As Jackson reflects on her empirical findings:

> The social phenomenon of smoking cigarettes has clear multigenerational corre-lations that go beyond transgenerational behavioral mimicry. A mother's active smoking during pregnancy has developmental ramifications for herself, her unborn female child and her grandchildren, even if her child and her grand-children do not smoke. [...] What emerges from these examples is the notion of genes and environments as malleable, dynamic, and coevolving. This contrasts sharply with the notion of genetic changes as solely a reflection of hard selective elements of the environment (as in the concept of 'nature tooth and claw'). Epigenetic effects counter the misconception of rigid biological determinism in disease onset and expression.[41]

Even in the momentum of articulating the pertinence of epigenetics research, the natural historian of metaphor is called to address the scientist's use of 'nature tooth and claw', an invocation of a phrase familiar in Emerson's day and an image employed to famous effect in Alfred Tennyson's *In Memoriam A. H. H.* (1850), in which he wrote:

Who trusted God was love indeed
And love Creation's final law
Tho' Nature, red in tooth and claw
With ravine, shriek'd against his creed.[42]

Tennyson's picture of 'Nature, red in tooth and claw' might call to mind a large felid on the savannah having swiped at the belly of an ungulate, its gaping mouth glimmering with the prey's fresh blood. Tennyson's visceral and visual trope became part of the emerging debates in evolutionary thinking in the 1850s – when there were attempts to harmonize a love of God (and God's love of man) with a respect for Nature's indif-ferent laws – and continues to be invoked, for example by Richard Dawkins in *The Selfish Gene*, for its resonance as an image of the survival of the fittest doctrine.[43] As a metaphor – 'Nature, red in tooth and claw' illustrates both Dawkins' theory of memes, and offers a linguistic analogue of Darwin's notion of a fit specimen, able to survive among many other competing and compelling metaphors. Whether a deep appreci-ation for Tennyson could become part of one's epigenome remains for future research.

Looking at the current empirical research in epigenetics, the suggestive Lamarckian shift in orientation comes when one recognizes that decisions and behaviours made in the course of one's own, individual life, or factors that occur unintentionally in the course of personal history – all part of one's phenotype – may change the constitution of the heritable epigenotype one may transmit to one's offspring. Thus for instance when Judith Shulevitz, who wrote a provocatively titled book review, 'Lamarck's

Revenge', attested to reasons 'Why Fathers Really Matter' – based on new research in epigenetics – she emphasized how stress and trauma may be passed on from fathers to sons and grandsons.[44] Think of the thousands of war veterans who return home with post-traumatic stress disorder; what if their pain is not just expressed in life – as anxiety and depression – but becomes part of their contribution to their children's epigenetic make-up? War stress may be epigenetically coded phenotypically and consequently revealed in the descendants of veterans – so people who never fought in a war may still experience aspects of its effects, emergent modifications in their own epigenomes.

In other words, in a surprisingly quasi-Lamarckian way, humans appear capable of inheriting epigenomes. In a process called 'direct mutation', the conditions grandparents live in can influence the patterns of gene expression in their grandchildren; such inheritance can be advantageous or not depending upon the degree of similarity between their respective environments.[45] 'Match' environments, as the term is used in epigenetics, can make these epigenetic changes adaptive and beneficial for grandchildren; significant environmental differences can result in a 'mismatch' and put grandchildren at a disadvantage.[46] Susceptibility to disease, for example, can be altered by the epigenome; in such cases, it appears natural conditions 'may prompt and shape variation'; as Shulevitz summarizes: 'Genes may turn off when traits prove non-adaptive, or turn on when they are helpful. [… S]ome form of variation, which was previously thought to be purely random, may turn out to be an evolved response to crisis that gives organisms a better chance of survival'.[47] When Emerson wrote 'Civilization is a re-agent, and eats away the old traits' we may glean both his appreciation for Lamarck and his anticipation of epigenetics.[48] A grandchild may possess immunity to a disease to which he was never exposed; in which case he likely inherited the immunity from a blood relative – perhaps a grandparent – a generation removed. Thus as Jackson notes: 'The ability of DNA to be subject to epigenetic changes revived Lamarck's theory of soft inheritance because it indicated that, indeed, the environment can impact upon gene expression in both direct and indirect ways and with both immediate and long term ramifications'.[49] So even the 'soft inheritance' suggests that 'a causal relationship exists between epigenetic modifications and early exposures to unpredictable environmental conditions'.[50] The soft/hard metaphor, used here and featured above in the citation from Peter Bowler (found in the introduction), may have useful associations with computer design and architecture: after all, one is resigned to the fixedness and planned obsolescence of one's computer hardware just as one expects continuous updates and adaptability to viruses from one's computer software. The softness – in both biological and micro-computing contexts – makes room for responsiveness to conditions through internal adaptation, the traits of which may be passed on through the affected/rewritten codes. After more than a century of dominance by Darwinian theories – often coupled with condescension to Lamarck's approach to the inheritance of acquired characteristics – Lamarck's premise seems partially vindicated by epigenetics: the phenotype is the object of selection. Genes are not destiny – not a hard and fast fate – but 'a flexible scaffolding'.[51] The environment gives shape to the scaffolding of the genome – allowing connections to be made, or not – and this genome (changed by its lived context) can be inherited by children and grandchildren.

In the light of epigenetics our myths and metaphors about inheritance are variously challenged and underwritten. As we have struggled to expurgate the notion that, say, a 'sin of the father' was something a child must be responsible for, epigenetics reinvigorates the idea that the child remains subject to its persistence – at the minimum, to the effect that 'sin' registers itself epigenetically. Phenotypical traits are, in this sense, modified as nature interacts with context and consciousness, and thereafter passed on. In another example of a genetically-inflected metaphor, those of noble birth or aristocratic descent have been called 'blue bloods' – yet, speaking more speculatively, what if the metaphor could be re-defined in a more literal sense, where epigenetic traits are passed on from one generation to the next?[52] Having been, we might say, exposed to wealth and privilege – to an environment that both creates and inhabits them as pervasive conditions – what if offspring were informed epigenetically by their effects? The term 'blue bloods' is said to derive from the Spanish *sangre azul* – likely a poetic description of the visible veins that appear through the translucent skin of fair complexioned aristocrats. In England Emerson seems to have encountered the 'red blooded', as he recounts: 'I found plenty of well-marked English types, the ruddy complexion fair and plump [...].[53] Yet while he noted how the 'old men are as red as roses', he also remarked how a 'clear skin, a peach-bloom complexion [...] are found all over the island.[54] In the light of epigenetics, the blue blood as a type – that is, as a class identifiable from a distance not just by conspicuous veins or by a regal name but by noting gestures, habits, and other phenotypical traits – may shift from a cultural metaphor (or epithet) of racial difference to a biological description of epigenetically modified, and modifiable, stock.

One of the contested implications of epigenetics is the possibility of inheriting behavioural traits.[55] Can blue bloods pass on more to their offspring than names and titles to land and property? What if instead of being passively acquired, attributes of one's biological constitution are performatively inscribed – both generated intentionally and decidedly mutable – and subject to lived conditions? Traits in this sense would be acquired actively in their responsiveness to one's activity. Such a description might sound familiar to one of the 'sixty-four students sitting in the auditorium during Lamarck's lecture in 1800 or those who read *Researches* after 1802 or *Zoological Philosophy (Philosophie zoologique)* after 1809'.[56] As Rebecca Stott notes in *Darwin's Ghosts: The Secret History of Evolution* (2012):

> The environment – changing temperatures, rising water levels, scarcity of food or water, or the spread of predators – caused animals to adopt new habits to survive. These new habits led infinitely slowly to the appearance of new structures through the inheritance of acquired characteristics: longer limbs for running, longer tongues for catching food, flat-topped teeth for chewing; other structures, if no longer needed or used, would gradually atrophy. It was a distinctive, simple, and radically new way of seeing the world. It was also, of course, deeply heretical to anyone of a religious disposition.[57]

Hence a genetic bestowal can be revealed differently depending on the conditions and actions of the inheritor – and in turn those circumstances and behaviours may become coded in the genes. This is remarkable and Lamarckian.

Yet, two centuries after Lamarck's lectures drew crowds, and in the wake of the long dominance of Darwinian theory that eclipsed Lamarck's popularity, aspects of Lamarck's notions – as featured in epigenetic research – have become 'deeply heretical' for some evolutionary scientists. Or one might say, more generously, but also more warily, 'this is not the part of Lamarckism that most scientists subscribe to'.[58] But does this rogue part of Lamarckism – when the metaphorical becomes literalized, that is, when the genotype has been affected in the lifespan of single specimen and achieves heritable transmission to offspring – tempt us to believe in, or to seek scientific proof for, these moments of evolutionary impact? To what extent does epigenetics intimate and invite – if not yet, or perhaps ever prove definitively – our conceptual shift from image and trope to chemical and physical property? That is, when the meme and the gene are truly empirical siblings, when the genome and the epigenome are part of an undeniable continuum?

The dawning impact of epigenetics may also stimulate interest in the environmental conditions in which science is formulated. Could it be that in Darwin we find an English approach to genetics and inheritance, and in Lamarck a French way? Or more narrowly, was Darwin's scientific work informed by the conditions and conditioning of his father and grandfather – the latter of whom was the legendary early evolutionist, Erasmus? To push the question even closer to the implications of historical Lamarckism (and admittedly, away from the mainstream of epigenetic research), could the young Charles be said to inherit genes from his grandfather that could or did affect his behaviour and his patterns of thought? The epigeneticist would urge caution in reply – seeking empirical evidence for a suggestion of *genotypical* change. If young Charles was more attracted to explanatory theories that emphasize categories and linear relationships, the epigeneticist would say, and therefore favour an evolutionary design that allows for change on the scale of species over vast spans of time – this might be an effect of a cultural circumstance and behaviour mimicry (since Charles grew up in an intellectual environment where scientific – evolutionary – ideas were openly discussed rather than repressed). Then we are returned to the terrain of Dawkins' meme – the 'unit of imitation'.[59] Meanwhile, one may be tempted to speculate – in heretical or disreputable Lamarckian terms – that Lamarck himself, on the other side of the Channel from young Charles, was inhabited by genes that allowed him to be more comfortable with theories featuring permeability, continuity and proximate influence. But then our investigation is suddenly beyond the scope of supportive empirical evidence. One could not, for example, extrapolate from differences between Darwin and Lamarck to differences in the respective genomes of the English and the French. If the data would suggest it, then perhaps one could discern contrasts in English and French modes of global colonization: where the English separate and quarantine within their sites of conquest (bringing England with them to the jungle and desert), the French integrate and blend into their conquered territories. Emerson writes of the 'unaccommodating manners' of the English, and their 'puissant nationality which makes their existence incompatible with all that is not English'.[60] But even setting aside these unempirical, heretical hunches, the *science* of epigenetics is poised to radically reorient our inherited notions of evolutionary theory. If we are not forced to choose between Darwinism and Lamarckism, but rather encouraged to find in the union of their distinctive – yet complementary – theoretical traits, we may possess a dialectically enriched view of genetic characteristics, both acquired in the blood and re-made through intentions, actions and the unseen bonds of culture. If it comes to term, this theory might be called their offspring.

XII

Genealogy and Guilt

1. Like Emerson's *English Traits*, Friedrich Nietzsche's *On the Genealogy of Morality* (1887) is replete with generative metaphors. Nietzsche, as befits his philosophical talents and as was customary to his literary style, wrote with tenacious self-awareness and self-reflexiveness about how metaphors are explanatory tools for understanding the origins of moral philosophy and human value. In fact, as Nietzsche points out many times, metaphors are linked to literal phenomena, and one finds that Nietzsche's own dramatic use of metaphor is mainly in the service of getting readers to think about the actual, that is literal, conditions of human lives. For example, when speaking of the origins of contract law Nietzsche says, 'the moral conceptual world "guilt", "conscience", "duty", "sacredness of duty" has its genesis – its beginning, like the beginning of everything great on earth, was thoroughly and prolongedly drenched in blood'.[1] Metaphors in this sense may become literary fictions but they are born of physical realities.

Nietzsche imagined that an understanding of guilt is based on the experience of having a beginning, which in turn reveals an abiding faith in a first cause – whether figured as God or as parents, as Nature or the morass of culture. He wonders: 'Have these previous genealogists of morality even remotely dreamt, for example, that that central moral concept "guilt" had its origins in the very material concept "debt"'.[2] Guilt then is the feeling of owing something to the past.

> The civil-law relationship of the debtor to his creditor [...] was [...] interpreted into a relationship [...] of *those presently living* to their *ancestors*. [...] What can one give back to them? Sacrifices [...] (the notorious sacrifice of the firstborn, for example; blood, human blood in any case) [... I]n the end the progenitor is necessarily transfigured into a *god*. This may even be the origin of the gods, an origin, that is, out of *fear*!*[3]

A debt to the past – to the dead, to the creators – is unrepayable, so the concept of guilt evolves into a form of practical use: it becomes a totem of that which one wishes to offload but cannot; it is all that one carries, irrevocably. In this mood – in the nature of this response – Nietzsche sees the origins of GOD as an idea (and as an imposition). He also reverses the assumed, acculturated value of the term and imagines that the end (or death) of God – the ultimate discharged debt – would mean the end of human feelings of guilt: '[T]he perfect and final victory of atheism might free humanity from this entire feeling of having debts to its beginnings, its *causa prima*. Atheism and a kind of *second innocence* belong together'.[4] Atheism could be understood as a response to origins, a sort of will to self-liberation from inherited debts. Nietzsche's notion of atheism granting a 'second innocence' references and recovers the assumed Fall of Man – that God's disappointment in mortal action left humans marked. The second innocence through atheism is an unmarking of man, removing sin as if from a new faith in God's nonexistence. Sin, like God's judgement, would then be another picture that 'held us captive'.[5] One belief is replaced by another, and in the process the blood is cleansed – the taint removed, man restored.

Yet any claim for a new purity – of blood without sin, of man without debt to God – creates an undesirable effect of a second innocence. In the new state, then, the human must go on mixing its blood to inoculate itself against the desire for a second purity, a revised culture of obsession with sin: '"The lords" are cast off; the morality of the common man has been victorious. One may take this victory to be at the same time a blood poisoning (it mixed the races together) – I won't contradict; in any event it is beyond doubt that this toxication *succeeded*'.[6] Miscegenation forever, gratefully, undermines any and all claims to purity. Hierarchies are flattened, categories are merged; debts to ancestors (and creators) are forgiven; the species becomes a network of blood relatives. Power and value cease to derive their significance from heredity.

2.   J. Hector St John de Crevecoeur, *Letters from an American Farmer*, 'What Is an American' (1782)

The next wish of this traveler will be to know whence came these people? they are a mixture of English, Scotch, Irish, French, Dutch, Germans, and Swedes. From this promiscuous breed, that race now called Americans have arisen.[7]

What attachment can a poor European emigrant have for a country where he had nothing? The knowledge of the language, the love of a few kindred as poor as himself, were the only cords that tied him: his country is now that which gives him land, bread, protection, and consequence: *Ubi panis ibi patria*, is the motto of all emigrants. What then is the American, this new man? He is either an European, or the descendent of an European, hence that strange mixture of blood, which you will find in no other country. [...] Here individuals of all nations are melted into a new race of men, whose labours and posterity will one day cause great changes in the world.[8]

3.   Nietzsche wrote about what he called 'the ascetic ideal' and how it had gradually developed in Western civilization to become the dominant view of life – or rather, a view of how to *deny* life. Like the Tostoyan perfectionist, the 'ascetic treats life as a wrong path that one must finally retrace back to the point where it begins; or as an error that one refutes through deeds [...]'.[9] This search for the beginning – for first causes and primal origins – creates an obsessive, ultimately unfulfillable goal: there is no end to searching for the beginning. As a result of this disappointment, this frustration, one's mood becomes self-hating; one joins the 'despisers of the body'.[10] One goes from attempting to 'retrace' a wrong path to wishing there was no path, no cause, no origin. The ascetic wants more than anything to control his life, and he

believes that if he could only know where things began he would know where things were going – perhaps even, garner or glimpse where they might end. Yet is not the desire to know the end blasphemy – a rebuke to the gift of existence itself? 'The ascetic priest is the incarnate wish for a different existence, an existence somewhere else, […] but the very *power* of his wishing is the shackle that binds him here'.[11] If he cannot know his origins, his beginning, he would rather look past them altogether and wish for a better life elsewhere: an uncaused life – after-the-end – an afterlife.

In their efforts at earthly restraint, in their fervor to control the world and their bodies, ascetics are not relatively devoid of emotion but, on the contrary according to Nietzsche, '[t]hey are all concerned with one thing: some kind of *excess of the emotions* […]'.[12] They are not just emotionally expressive, they are *excessively* emotionally expressive; hence their worry. Such excess emotion exacerbates the kinds of pictures an ascetic creates to explain his emotion, and his hope to constrain it – to give its denial meaning. The intensity of emotion can, in time, give the impression that such invented metaphors are somehow literal; and a will to sentimentality further colludes to cloud one's thinking about the origins of these pictures. As Nietzsche reminds us: '"[S]infulness" in humans is not a factual state but rather only the interpretation of a factual state […]'.[13] The ascetics tried to develop theories – based on pictures – to explain their condition, for instance, the feeling of being at a remove from God, or owing God penance, or being wretched and depraved by comparison to God, and so on. But being excessively emotional and sentimental compromised their explanatory powers. Again and again, according to Nietzsche, ascetics demonstrated their 'lack of measure, aversion to measure', when theorizing. Nietzsche described this immoderation as a '*non plus ultra*', something that is the ultimate or highest, at the extreme of possible options.[14] Thinking and theorizing at the extreme, with too much allowance for sentimentality, leads to the creation of extreme ideas – for example, where a *feeling* of indebtedness becomes a physical attribute of a human body, or a race of men, or the blood of all humanity. 'Only in the hands of the [ascetic] priest, this true artist of the feeling of guilt, did [guilt] take on form – oh what a form! "Sin"'.[15] The ascetics realized that 'reasons alleviate', that is, knowing why something happens provides a certain measure of peace, even an illusion of control (and certainly, though ironically, having created a controlling idea an ascetic might feel justified in having achieved some degree of control). But in the absence of a method for knowing – for example about origins – ascetics had to invent based on what they felt. And in feeling too much and in theorizing that excess into ruling pictures and ideas, the explanation they sought eluded them. This led, Nietzsche claimed, to a great deal of suffering in man: 'From his magician, the ascetic priest, he receives the *first* hint concerning the "cause" of his suffering: he is to seek it in *himself*, in a *guilt*, in a piece of the past, he is to understand his suffering itself as a *state of punishment*'.[16] Once the discovery – or invention – of an internal cause for suffering was made, we see '[e]verywhere the whip, the hair shirt, the starving body, contrition; everywhere the sinner breaking himself on the cruel wheel of a restless, diseased-lascivious conscience; everywhere mute torment, extreme fear, the agony of a tortured heart, the cramps of an unknown happiness, a cry for "redemption"'.[17] Does the ascetic wish to be saved from the misery he creates, and keeps innovating, or does the expansion of suffering reinforce his impression of progress toward God? The ascetic ideal '[…] brought new suffering with it, deeper, more inward, more poisonous, gnawing more at life: it brought suffering under the perspective of *guilt* … '.[18]

The ascetic believed, as Nietzsche wrote, that 'something was lacking, that an enormous void surrounded man – he did not know how to justify, to explain, to affirm himself; he suffered from the problem of his meaning'.[19] While reasons are supposed to 'alleviate', the development of an explanation for this meaning culminated in pain so that pain became a proof: both a syllogism and a piece of evidence. Somewhere in the search for insight about the meaning of suffering, pain itself – perhaps because it was so intense and so plentiful – replaced the pursuit of relief. As a result suffering became the meaning of life – sufficient and entire – and 'the enormous emptiness seemed filled'.[20]

4.   Though Emerson did not indulge a life-denying worldview or promote self-mortification, he did find reason to defend the intellectual and ethical gifts of ascetic rigor: 'The reason why an ingenious soul shuns society', he wrote in 'Literary Ethics', 'is to the end of finding society'.[21] To his audience at Dartmouth College in 1838 Emerson continued:

> You will pardon me, Gentlemen, if I say, I think that we have need of a more rigorous scholastic rule; such an asceticism, I mean, as only the hardihood and devotion of the scholar himself can enforce. We live in the sun and on the surface, – a thin, plausible, superficial existence, and talk of muse and prophet, of art and creation. But out of our shallow and frivolous way of life, how can greatness ever grow? Come now, let us go and be dumb. Let us sit with our hands on our mouths, a long, austere, Pythagorean lustrum. Let us live in corners, and do chores, and suffer, and weep, and drudge, with eyes and hearts that love the Lord. Silence, seclusion, austerity, may pierce deep into the grandeur and secret of our being, and so diving, bring up out of secular darkness, the sublimities of moral constitution.[22]

A few years later, in the chapter 'Prudence' from *Essays, First Series*, Emerson found reason to think that the life- or world-denying attributes of asceticism cloak its finer contribution to our thinking: namely, that in pairing things down and away, with a little less love of display, a scholar may be better able to reveal his or her best insights – as it stands, however, 'we call partial half-lights, by courtesy, genius; talent which converts itself to money; talent which glitters that it may dine and sleep well to-morrow; and society is officered by men of parts, as they are properly called, and not by divine men. They use their gifts to refine luxury, not to abolish it. Genius is always ascetic, and piety, and love'.[23]

Emerson's model of asceticism might be grasped by the notion of achieving solitude 'in the midst of the crowd', since he did also preach that scholars must not extricate themselves too severely from life, else they risk finding that 'the world revenges itself by exposing, at every turn, the folly of these incomplete, pedantic, useless, ghostly creatures'.[24] In the same spirit Emerson concluded:

The good scholar will not refuse to bear the yoke in his youth; to know, if he can, the uttermost secret of toil and endurance; to make his own hands acquainted with the soil by which he is fed, and the sweat that goes before comfort and luxury. [...] If he have this twofold goodness, – the drill and the inspiration, – then he has health; then he is a whole, and not a fragment; and the perfection of his endowment will appear in his compositions.[25]

XIII

The Pirate Baptized

1. Voltaire, *Letters Concerning the English Nation*

As trade enrich'd the Citizens in *England*, so it contributed to their Freedom, and this Freedom on the other side extended their Commerce, whence arose the Grandeur of the State. Trade rais'd by insensible Degrees the naval Power, which gives the *English* a Superiority over the Seas, and they now are Masters of very near two hundred Ships of War. Posterity will very possible be surpriz'd to hear that an Island whose only Produce is a little Lead, Tin, Fuller's Earth, and coarse Wool, should become so powerful by its Commerce, as to be able to send in 1723, three Fleets at the same Time to three different and far distanc'd Parts of the Globe.[1]

2. Emerson, 'Land'

England resembles a ship in its shape [...].[2]

3. In *English Traits* Emerson went beyond noting *avant le lettre* a certain Rorschach resemblance between the boundaries of England – and did he mean England and not the British Isles? – to suggest an analogical relationship between the English (sometimes 'these Britons') and the vessels they command: '[The English] are tenacious of their belief, and cannot easily change their opinions to suit the hour. They are like ships with too much head on to come quickly about, nor will prosperity or even adversity be allowed to shake their habitual view of conduct'.[3] Temperamentally, then, they need space to 'come about'. A change in conditions, for ill or favour, will not likely do much to diminish the inertia of inheritance and custom.

As Emerson took passage to the home of his ancestors, he noted that 'it is impossible not to personify a ship; every body does, in every thing they say: – she behaves well; she minds her rudder; she swims like a duck; she runs her nose into the water; she looks into a port'.[4] The ship is an Englishman too. And its membership in the citizenry reminds us of deeply veiled but persistent tribal habits – pathways of thinking that reveal preferences for the totemic, and perhaps also a vanity that justifies anthropomorphism: 'Then that wonderful *esprit du corps*', Emerson continues, 'by which we adopt into our self-love every thing we touch, makes us all champions of her sailing qualities'.[5] And as if to match our magical thinking with the perceived thoughts of the floating vessel, Emerson adds: 'The conscious ship hears all the praise'.[6]

Emerson drew another analogy, this one between the sailor and the curious and discerning mind that bespeaks their respective intelligences: 'A great mind is a good sailor, as a great heart is. And the sea is not slow in disclosing inestimable secrets to a good naturalist.[7] Any landlubber may be forgiven for thinking otherwise, but Emerson assures his readers, and skeptics of the ocean's revelations, that a certain cast of mind can read the signs made apparent on the open waters.

4.   Though islands do not navigate the water, they inhabit it like ships, they share a penetrating and undeniable isolation: cut off from other lands, constrained by water on all sides, islands are self-contained – or make their mates nervously aware of insufficiencies and emptying provisions. The idea of England (or more expansively and inclusively, Great Britain) as a ship seems especially appropriate given that it appears anchored off the coast of the European continent, and partly for that dislocation, possessed of a proud naval and maritime history – that as circumstance demanded, drew a line of connection for commerce and culture, or used the imposing waters as an allied agent in warfare. Emerson described the island's relation to and distance from the continent this way:

> The sea, which, according to Virgil's famous line, divided the poor Britons utterly from the world, proved to be the ring of marriage with all nations. It is not down in the books, – it is written only in the geological strata, – that fortunate day when a wave of the German Ocean burst the old isthmus which joined Kent and Cornwall to France, and gave to this fragment of Europe its impregnable sea wall, cutting off an island of eight hundred miles in length, with an irregular breadth reaching to three hundred miles; a territory large enough for independence enriched with every seed of national power [...].[8]

5.   Constructed islands, such as Manhattan – also anchored off the coast of a continent – write their biographies in stone and steel with the punctuation of bolt, rivet and frieze. So it does not surprise when architects and photographers – who create and transform space and its representation – should regard an island as a ship. Consider how architect Joseph Rykwert accounts for the symbolic effect of the 9/11 attacks: 'The skyline of New York lost one of its most prominent landmarks, since throughout the world [the Twin Towers of the World Trade Center] were seen as the masts of the good ship Manhattan – and with it, of Western economic domination.'[9] Within the city, certain pieces of architecture seemed to assume the character of a ship. The photographer, Alfred Stieglitz, who took the now iconic and ubiquitous black and white image of the Flatiron Building (at Broadway and 5th Avenue), said of his encounter with the edifice: 'It appeared to be moving towards me like the bow of a monster ocean steamer – a picture of a new America in the making.'[10] In these cases, the architect and the photographer see a connection between a building's monumentality and the nature of seacraft, but also capture something even more compelling, the idea of seacraft (here a city-as-an-island, or a building-as-a-ship – or a part of a ship: its mast, its rudder, its sail) as bound up with national identity. Rykwert writes of falling mastheads as the collapsing of an idea, the ceasing of forward movement – a sign of Manhattan's, and perhaps America's or capitalism's, demise. As the mastheads

of American or global capitalism, the towers formed a metonym; as the towers were perceived to be a continuous part of the great ship Manhattan, they signaled a synecdoche; however they are regarded, the visual and ideological richness of the towers doubtless contributed to their fate as targets. Even the destruction of the towers – the space that frames their absence – has achieved symbolic force as registered by the figurative trace of the uncanny 11 that marks the date: two vertical lines that mimic the silhouette of the lost skyline. For all the layering of metaphorical meaning, however, it remains of perennial interest how the critique of American empire was strikingly literalized on that September day. The mastheads that held the bannering sails of democracy, liberty – and perhaps most saliently – the promise and reality of wealth in the land of free, were felled before noon.

Stieglitz's awe-filled sense of an anchored building (in the middle of an island-city, a ship unto itself) somehow approaching him, gives one pause in thinking about what it means to pursue frontiers – and find them. In the American idiom new seas are not charted but instead the vast expanse of the American West. How does one explore this territory with its lakes and rivers, plains and mountains? The ship only takes one so far – the Hudson River and Erie Canal carried the seeker to the shores of Minnesota; the Mississippi River provided a north-south waterway into the middle of America, but the Western frontier always, inevitably, demanded a pull over land. Perhaps it had to be anticipated that when the coast of California and Oregon Territory was reached, the frontier suddenly became an idea. When the limits of the literal land were found, there was nowhere else for the frontier to go but into the mind – as a metaphor.

However, in the last century, the airplane provided the condition for entirely by-passing the overland trail. No more cliffs or ravines; no further fording or sallies. One can fly directly from John F. Kennedy Airport in New York to Los Angeles International Airport without touching the land in-between. If the airplane makes a unique kind of connection possible (where New York is connected to Los Angeles by the space of five hours in the air), does it also reinforce a dislocation (where the middle is lost, and Los Angeles feels like a suburb of Manhattan)? If England is a ship off the coast of Europe and New York is a ship off the coast of America, what kind of work can be done aboard such vessels, in such harbours? Are these ships docked for a departure or docked for display? Both ships have histories of global influence while remaining in port; their radiating force derives from the actions, people, events, institutions and embodied arts (art, architecture, literature, philosophy) of the crew. The countries become representative; the ships become the sites of realities and dreams. Their masts carry flags that reference both the observable and mythic content of nation-vessels – signaling the histories and the present-tense possibilities of anchored ships.

The metaphor suggests that a shipwreck figures the end of the empire. The falling mastheads of 9/11 literalized the collapse of an idea and an ambition while creating a haunting symbol of demise. With the 9/11 memorial and the emergence of 1 WTC (formerly, more politically known as the Freedom Tower) the ship may right itself. The new masthead, however, is not a replication of the old – the Twin Towers were not rebuilt – so the new building must innovate an identity for the forces it represents. As 1 WTC is slightly askew of the now hallowed ground of the lost towers, perhaps it will stand for something that allows for new definition but also always retains a view of the adjacent absences.

6.   If one regards a country as a ship, what is the nature of freedom on that ship? Is there a connection between the Englishman's experience of freedom at sea and his sense of freedom on his island? One might regard a ship as a moving island – fully braced by the constraints of the depths and distances that surround it in all directions. Such limitation appears to humble the ambitions of freedom both nautical and terrestrial.

Maybe the freedom of the ship is a positive freedom – the freedom to explore the world – even while the limits of the ship mean the limits of the sailor's world.[11] There is it seems very little negative freedom on a ship – precious little freedom from encumbrances – even for the captain. If one would be an explorer and experimenter, and dare to move, one must dare to be stilled. As when the wind dies so may you. A sailor can harness the wind but he cannot make it blow. And so the crew sits on the wide ocean waiting. What kind of freedom is that? Perhaps the freedom of a sailor to fathom ineluctable relations, to invite 'the blending cadence of waves with thoughts' so well-mixed 'that at last he loses his identity; takes the mystic ocean at his feet for the visible image of that deep, blue, bottomless soul, pervading mankind and nature'[12] The sailor, like the naturalist, would then perceive 'occult sympathies', as Emerson writes.[13] Just as a sailor cannot take flight from the deck or the crow's nest, he is gifted with a view of eternity above, laterally and into the deep. And thus from where he stands, or sits perched, as Emerson continues, he cannot occupy the site of such perceptions '[...] without feeling our family ties, and every rhomb, and vesicle, and spicule claiming old acquaintance, so neither can a tender Soul stand under the starry heaven, and explore the solar and stellar arrangements, without the wish to mix with them by knowledge. If men are analagons of acids and salts, and of beast and bird, so are they of geometric laws, and of astronomic galaxies'.[14]

7.   An island is an isolated thing, and so is a ship. But a ship can move and in that movement it can connect foreign elements and attributes. The British Empire was made by representative ships setting out from the island – their charted seaways like tentacles of influence and imposition that brought England to the world and the world to Piccadilly. One fathom at a time England linked itself to what else remained on the globe and by that reach made London the centre. 'Linnaeus like a naturalist', wrote Emerson, 'esteeming the globe a big egg, called London the punctum saliens in the yolk of the world'.[15]

8.   Aboard the brig *Jasper*, sailing east somewhere on the vast Atlantic, having had a week to observe the workings of the crew, Emerson wrote in his journal – still a month's worth of sea away from Malta:

> Thought again of the sailor & how superficial the differences – How shallow to make much of mere coat & hat distinctions. You can't get away from the radical,

uniform, interior experiences which peep out of the new faces identical with those of the old.[16]

Emerson looks past the clothes of the sailor to the universal quality of the human – to some shared characteristic that equalizes experience beneath surface attributes like clothes, like skin. Is this what a surgeon feels again and again when standing at the surgery table with a body opened up before him? The surgeon takes a good look at a man's guts. Knowing that blood's temperature holds fast in the healthy, and admitting that the veins and arteries have their proper lines of passage and connection, the challenge to mend the man comes out in full display. What else is this, the surgeon repeats to himself time and again, but God's view of man – seeing through, seeing past the superficial realm of human affairs, to the qualities that hold a man together within himself, and that link man with man. The body cut open for surgery may itself be, as Emerson says, 'an unavoidable acknowledgment of God' – of that which unifies and that which animates.[17] The surgeon as scientist might be content merely with a faith in the way things work; if he can get the belly back together again, and let the man breathe another day, then he should have his faith in full. Emerson says that his belief 'puts the soul in equilibrium'. Does not the good doctor pursue equilibrium based on his belief in the emerging laws of vascular science and physiology? Like Emerson, the surgeon could say: 'In this state the question whether your boat shall float in safety or go to the bottom is no more important than the flight of a snowflake'.[18]

And then Emerson looks the other way, or rather, looks at the surfaces, at the clothes that adorn the sailor – the lineaments that call forth his type, his trade, his rank and confirm that he is a small member of a large crew:

> Sailors are the best dressed of mankind. Convenience is studied from head to heel, & they have a change for every emergency. It seems to me they get more work out of the sailor than out of any other craftsman. His obedience is prompt as a soldier's & willing as a child's, & reconciles me to some dim remembrances of authority I wondered at. Thin skins do not believe in thick. Jack never looks an inch beyond his orders. 'Brace the yards', quoth the master; 'Ay Ay, sir', answers Jack, and never looks over the side at the squall or the sea that cometh as if it were no more to him than to the capstan.[19]

When Emerson looks at the seafarer's attire he gets a good sense of the way the life makes the clothes. In the sailor's day, as now one presumes, there was no patience for discomfort or the danger of a flapping cord or open cuff. The sailor had to have his pants on straight and tight or else more than the sail would go out.

The speaker can use words that cut like a knife. As such a thick skin is sometimes necessary to avoid polemical or grammatical injury; one tries to protect oneself from such dangerous words. But why should words cut so deeply? Why would an otherwise well-attired man fail to callous his mind and heart sufficient for such intrusions and abrasions? How many finely dressed men are at last insecure and exposed beneath the veneer of their woolen blazers? In surgery the razor must be sharp; a dull blade ensures a patient's pain. And so with words, they should be treated as the potentially sharp cutting implements they are – ready to make their marks, for treatment or torment. Political correctness censures sharp things – dulls them – perhaps true and intelligent ideas, to avoid harming sensitive souls. Yet censoring does not create thicker skin; rather it encourages the development of thinner and thinner skin, until the membrane has become transparent, without secret resources much less a sense of humour. With thin skin all around, a crowd of intelligent people is forced into silence for fear of scaring and scarring its members.

As Emerson said, 'our moods do not believe in each other', likewise '[t]hin skins do not believe in thick'. A good callus comes from use of skin, from interaction and engagement; for rough and uneven encounters find necessary points of counter-resistance. A callus, like a scar, is a reflection of life experience, a storytelling mark. But thick can be too thick, as thin too thin, so there must be a sense of where to make contact, and for how long. One neither wants to become dumb for insensitivity nor fragile for exposure. There are, as good lovers know, places to welcome the tentiginous and others to keep permeable and pliant.

9.   Still at sea in January 1833, Emerson wrote in his journal:

> We study the sailor, the man of his hands, man of all work; all eye, all finger, muscle, skill & endurance[;] a tailor, a carpenter, cooper, stevedore, & clerk & astronomer besides. He is a great saver, and a great quiddle by the necessity of his situation[.][20]

> I comfort the mate by assuring him that the sea life is excellent preparation for life ashore. No man well knows how many fingers he has got nor what are the faculties of a knife & a needle or the capabilities of a pine board until he has seen the expedients, & the ambidexterous invincibility of Jack Tar. Then he may buy an orchard or retreat to his paternal acres with a stock of thrifty science that will make him independent of all the village carpenters, masons, & wheelwrights & add withal an enchanting beauty to the waving of his yellow corn & sweetness to his shagbarks in his chimney corner. No squally Twelve o'clock Call the Watch shall break his dreams.[21]

Sea life forces a sailor to know the world by new categories. Assumptions are overturned, intuitions converted. When there are miles of water beneath the hull, another realm of habits and rules prevails on the oiled planks of the ship.

Sailors are poised to cross vast distances, but they do so from within extreme confinement. And whatever the sailor's rank or position, the required work is done atop the same watery surface – as able to drown a captain as a cook. If one navigates, one does so without reference to land; a wide sea like an open sky seem to be substances without context. If one cooks, plates and pans are bound to slide. And if one performs surgery, then the moment of incision must be quick and sure, or else the cut may be a fatal stab. Each sailor contributes to the health of the onboard community. The ship becomes an organism of organisms; a collective of agents attending to their respective duties, always under the duress of isolation at sea, unmatched physical restrictions, and the constant instability of the floor below. Getting sea legs means learning how to walk in a different world. Maybe to walk on water.

When the sailor returns to land, and tries to conduct his duties there, he finds his great antagonists are gone: there is terrestrial continuity, ground firmly under foot, and people in plenty. Is 'the sea life [...] excellent preparation for life ashore'? Is the sailor-surgeon a better surgeon for his training on the ship? If he is used to practicing his art on the shifting currents of a 'squally' sea, do his 'faculties of a knife & a needle' prove more delicate and 'ambidexterous' than those of his land-bound colleagues? A truth on land may be a falsehood at sea. Or the power of a sailor's refined sea-instincts may multiply when his feet step upon the good earth again.

10.   Emerson, *Journals* (1847)

> How often I have to remember the art of the surgeon, which, in replacing the broken bone, limits itself to relieving the dislocation, relieving the parts from their false position, putting them free, then they fly into place by the action of their own muscles.[22]

Interference must be not merely economical but deft. We want the surgeon to invade not just with the finest touch but the greatest positive effect. This kind of surgeon surveys a field of experience, studies the relationships between things, and then moves in to work on the misalignments and other damages. Healing then is a matter of subtle, knowing intervention and involvement. Compare this approach with the one Emerson criticizes in 'Experience' as 'manipular attempts to realize the world of thought'.[23] There he says: 'Many eager persons successively make an experiment in this way, and make themselves ridiculous'.[24] The surgeon enters the body in order to correct some fault; that invasion entails a presumption that the standing facts are known and can be changed. Deployed well, though, such interference should restore a system to equilibrium, bringing it back into accord with itself. In theoretical investigations – invasions of another sort – the goal might be similarly motivated. Thinking can be deliberate but not totalizing; thinking is necessarily partial, perspectival. One must remain open to shifting conditions while remaining responsive to them – as a sailor-surgeon on the high seas. With a moment-to-moment awareness, one is present to changing circumstances.

The purpose of training according to strict rules, and harsh discipline, is not to impose rigidity on the world, but just the opposite: to allow oneself to become and remain flexible and adaptable. Every kind of contemporary military training involves an extensive amount of simulated experience, such as virtual engagement with the enemy via digital software. But even actual field training is simulated – an analogical environment created to familiarize a soldier with possible future combat he or she may enter. '[A] voyage is one of the severest tests to try a man. A college examination is nothing to it'.[25]

College examinations, like simulated training, often reinforce the importance of rules (as recognized in custom, precedent and inherited forms of knowledge). Moral life is no different: rules are imposed for the purpose of governing human conduct and also, one hopes, to maximize human flourishing. Can such constraint be the cause of abundance? In everyday life, theoretically developed rules that are steadfastly adamantine and nonadaptive often become useless, vestigial or even harmful in their rigidity. We are tempted to amend them for our own perceived and chosen purposes, perhaps believing that human flourishing is hampered or occluded because of the rules that frame conduct. The perception that a rule or law is ineffective, inert or otherwise an imposition in a given context reflects the disjunction between theoretical and actual worlds; the former can match rules and responses, actions and events, but in lived experience there is much that lies beyond cognitive prediction and calculation. A moral precept or legal principle may function effectively in a thought experiment, it may even have worked in a prior lived circumstance, but in a new day it can seem irrelevant, the very condition and cause of ruin.

11.   In the following scene from Shakespeare's *Julius Caesar*, Brutus makes an appeal for reconciliation with Antony, but Antony spurns the overture and charges Brutus, along with Cassius, with murdering Caesar. Between the battlefield of Philippi and fresh blood on their blades, there is a brief interval for words between rivals.

BRUTUS	They stand, and would have parley.
CASSIUS	Stand fast, Titinius: we must out and talk.
OCTAVIUS	Mark Antony, shall we give sign of battle?
ANTONY	No, Caesar, we will answer on their charge.
	Make forth; the generals would have some words.
OCTAVIUS	Stir not until the signal.
BRUTUS	Words before blows: is it so, countrymen?
OCTAVIUS	Not that we love words better, as you do.
BRUTUS	Good words are better than bad strokes, Octavius.
ANTONY	In your bad strokes, Brutus, you give good words:
	Witness the hole you made in Caesar's heart,
	Crying 'Long live! hail, Caesar!'
CASSIUS	Antony,
	The posture of your blows are yet unknown;
	But for your words, they rob the Hybla bees,
	And leave them honeyless.
ANTONY	Not stingless too.
BRUTUS	O, yes, and soundless too;
	For you have stol'n their buzzing, Antony,
	And very wisely threat before you sting.[26]

These are metaphors of men at war, and their very acts of speech illustrate whether their words are sharp and cutting, stinging or without sweetness. But speech is the event – a scene of parley – an occasion where these leaders and rivals negotiate their way into or out of conflict. Whether they speak from precedent or pride, from hurt or hope, this platform supports their questions about how to proceed. Moral knowledge and political procedure are presented as much as the pain that would seek revenge – all of which invite consideration, and perhaps more troublingly, introduce ethical ambiguity, a skepticism about the very nature of right action (as it is sometimes spoken) and how to discern it.

12.   An ethics at sea – that is, a moral experience that is at once unmoored and onboard – demands recourse for speech, for the articulation of one's position in relation to an other's, for example, to another ship and its mates. A naval commander will need to address and perhaps negotiate with an unknown vessel, whether hostile or welcoming; and the pirate, likewise, may even find himself not unwilling to negotiate new terms. The grammar of *parlez* is at once an indicative and an imperative – you speak – and it sets the conditions for further conversation. How does an officer or a pirate make a claim to these conditions? By military imposition or by logic, by sabre or sober articulation? Historically a ship would fly a black flag if it wished to speak – a flag that lacks only the pirate's skull and crossbones; as such the flag for parley could be seen as the basis – the atramentous and nebulous conditions – for the pirate's flag. Moreover, the now familiar Jolly Roger was less frequently used by pirates in the seventeenth and eighteenth century than the sheer black flag – thus intriguingly conflating the signs for parley and for pirate.

As seen in Shakespeare's *Julius Caesar*, parley is a rule for the temporary suspension of threat or harm by one's enemy; it is a gentleman's recess from the sword – an invitation for the privilege to speak, and a confirmation of the privileging of speech.[27] 'They stand and would have parley', says Brutus, to which his accomplice Cassius says 'Stand fast, Titinius: we must out and talk'. In many cases the weaker party may appeal to parley as a way of achieving escape or deferring loss, even death; or signaling despair, the party may use the pause to find terms for surrender. A student of classical literature and military art, Montaigne wrote of the practice with circumspection but not cynicism in 'Parley Time is Dangerous', issuing a litany of historical cases when the gift of parley was employed disingenuously – tactically – as an invented opportunity for an offensive maneuver. The stronger party, perceived or not, is put in the awkward position of risking his advantage for the sake of honouring this principle. And yet if honour is the key to understanding how this rule is supposed to work, can one presume that a pirate relies on a code of honour as the naval officer does? If the stronger party ignores the weaker party's request for parley then he could be said to act dishonourably – as if ignoring a plea for mercy. Should the weaker party deceive the stronger by turning parley to his advantage, one might consider him lacking honour – using mercy as a weapon. 'Words before blows: is it so, countrymen?' 'Good words are better than bad strokes'. But then the very appeal to having words, as Montaigne writes, may be vile and duplicitous – a gimmick that trades on trust and clemency, and rewards it with the sting of defeat and death:

> […] I recently saw in my neighborhood at Mussidan that those who were forcibly driven out from there by our army, and others of their party, screamed as at treachery because during the discussion of terms, and while the treaty was still in effect, they had been surprised and cut to pieces.[28]

Perhaps it is more accurate to regard pirate moral philosophy as appealing to rules that cannot so much be broken as rewritten when conditions change. For is it not a piratical act to insist that a code of conduct is pliable rather than fixed – thereby making the invocation of parley another strategy to suit convenience and advantage? A pirate's code on this account resembles what some philosophers derogatorily call situational ethics – choosing moral principles as one goes, according to comfort, profit and other self-serving criteria; or more generously, as a strategy for creating consistency or harmony where there was conflict. Despite the disparaging charge of adding another line to the ledger of moral relativism or act utilitarianism, can one read the pirate's appeal – beyond rules – as an innovation in moral thinking?

Could a pirate's moral worth, such as it is, emerge against the grain of conventional morality, and yet illuminate something worthwhile for it? A good pirate would be someone who reads what is in front of him – the immediate, the proximate – instead of abiding by a set of abstract, *a priori* precepts; the argument of sharp swords at the neck outflanks the threat of moral outrage by others (often distant and dead), and even may outweigh omens of torment in the afterlife. The pirate would be a man of the moment, alive to the time, place, and people that surround him – be they princes or scoundrels, and occasionally both at once. Yet if outlaws are found to live by a code – seeming to inhabit a familiar universe of moral commitments – why does that faith appear to be a perversion of law, an affront to honour instead of its enactment and illustration? How is this rude contravention an innovative moral position and not just a confirmed relativism? The pirate's relationship to rules as inert and unresponsive to present experience justifies his desire to flout them when necessary. The pirate defers the moment of judgement until it is absolutely necessary to commit himself to a position; his danceable movements create a playful image of the man who uses subterfuge to distract others and evade capture.

An emphasis on the mutability of rules encourages adaptation and improvisation; the focus of one's judgement is immediate – the present and near future – and not the past or precedent. A rule by definition, or at least by convention, is thought to be definitive; it is stated categorically, and extends without limit until qualified. A rule-as-provisional, or as drawn speculatively, contrariwise, is approximate; it is suggestive of possible directions within a certain field of choices. To parallel this distinction in physics, we could say that there is a rule that reveals a TENDENCY (as in quantum mechanics), and a rule that declares a specific position or LAW of nature (as in Newtonian mechanics). 'We can point nowhere to anything final', writes Emerson in 'The Method of Nature', 'but tendency appears on all hands: planet, system, constellation, total Nature is growing like a field of maize in July; is becoming somewhat else; is in rapid metamorphosis'.[29] The agent of moral law knows where he will be before he has acted, whereas the pirate faces a new choice as contexts reveal themselves; the former depends on the mathematical, the latter on the grammatical.

The American Revolution – the turning around or turning over of British rule – was not a prediction but a predication; its calculations were made by men of speech, who gave words a clarifying and creative power. The founding fathers contested the notion and nature of divine right – that truth was a function of delivering a decree from on high. The American Revolution – its foment and fighting – was part of history's sequence of military conflicts, but it was the founding itself that was revolutionary since it introduced a piratical rethinking of the inherited terms of hierarchical, royal pronouncement. The speech of kings is not a recommendation but an edict, like that of popes, a dictation relayed from an even higher authority. The founding of the American Republic involved a radical revaluation, in Brutus' phrase, of 'good words' – what they are between men, what they mean for nations. And yet, Emerson also identified the 'piratic feature' in the 'false combination of Southern society', which makes that feature 'our enemy only as it is the enemy of the human race'.[30] The only fitting parley for slavery, then, are words spoken – declaratively, performatively – to assure its eradication.

A preference for capricious rules instead of eternal rules does not mean one advocates for piracy; the spectre of terrorism hampers any romance of moral standing for perpetrators of personal or anti-state violence. But then pirates, like colonial powers, are commonly not bent on destroying and disrupting persons or states (as terrorists are) but instead are focused more strictly on acquiring their property. 'Poverty makes pirates', Emerson noted in his journal.[31] Still, could moral reasoning benefit from a piratical tendency that promotes innovation or improvisation *based on rules*, while remaining open and responsive to the nuances of present experience? If not in terrorizing the state and its citizens – taunting their demise – by violence and insinuating weaknesses, can moral thinking under the guise of pirate logic lend support for the evolution of the current incarnations of the state and the rules that guide its citizens? If moral life demands more than arithmetic it must enable variation – even mutation; but where can it derive such reconstitution with moral clarity and legitimacy while evading relativism? The question and the concern is familiar from Christ to Kant.

In heralding that in 'all things whatsoever ye would that men should do to you, do ye even so to them: for this is the law and the prophets' (Matthew) and 'as ye would that men should do to you, do ye also to them likewise' (Luke), Jesus did not supply a concrete rule, but a method for generating a rule.[32] Each time one is faced with a moral decision, one has to determine the meaning of the ascriptions 'even so' (Matthew) and 'as' (Luke). That determination is not a reading by direct observation but a cipher enabling a moment of translation and interpretation. The challenge is to see one's action towards others as if it were an action – 'likewise' – by others toward oneself. In this respect the Golden Rule demands a perception of analogical connection between self and other; and therefore invites the mind to a magical act of mental and moral transposition. One must see oneself under the aspect of the other. This trade personalizes the other while it makes one *other* to oneself – estranged.

Though Immanuel Kant's Categorical Imperative – and its several sub-forms and supplemental variations – is stated in more densely phrased philosophical prose, it is a no less ethically sophisticated way of accounting for the inescapable ambition at the core of Jesus' homespun moral injunction.[33] While the rules for action, in Kant's view, remain constant and universal – categorical – the nature or kind of action undertaken in relation to any of these formulations requires an interpretation on the part of the agent. Kant distinguished the terms at issue: 'If I think of a hypothetical imperative as such, I do not know what it will contain until the condition is stated [under which it is an imperative]. But if I think of a categorical imperative, I know immediately what it will contain.'[34] What would it mean to will this particular action as a universal law (that is, as something everyone could formulate and follow)? How can one person, in this instance, treat another person as more than a means to an end? Would one be comfortable if the maxim of one's action were legislated into a kingdom of ends? In every case this kind of moral reasoning demands an engagement between the agent and her circumstances. The Categorical Imperative, like The Golden Rule, offers an adaptive framework for generating a possible moral command.

The reason why the foregoing does not amount to praise of pirate moral philosophy stems in part from a logical point Kant emphasized: that we violate moral reason when we generate a mode of conduct that is self-contradictory. And pirates are by definition involved in a contradiction. They value ownership of private property for themselves but not for others; what is mine is mine, and what is yours is mine. As a result, they cannot – consistently or logically – hold simultaneously a respect for ownership *and* stealing. That said, Hegel noted in his criticism of Kant that recourse to actual social and political conditions might reveal the absence of a contradiction. For example, a society without property rights is possible and in that society stealing would not be self-contradictory since there is no right to ownership of property. Taken as a limited case, some families might qualify for this description, that is, if a family is understood as a 'society' where each member has an equal claim to family possessions; what is mine is ours, and what is ours is mine.

Along with pirates, gangsters constitute another realm of suspect moral reasoners. Yet even a superficial review of gangster thought and behaviour reveals that within the system of morally profligate action there can be intensely severe codes of conduct. One might even go so far as to consider them *moral* codes, since they often – confined strictly to the realms they are meant to address and hold up under – form consistent, that is non-contradictory, standards for action. Regularly these codes – and their enforcement – amount to a practice, even a culture, of self-policing. Obeying a set of rules (many of them clearly stated: do not use the drugs you sell, do not kill 'made' men, make sure the boss is aware of all deals and is cut in on them, etc.) can lead to wealth, freedom and honour (at least among the members of the 'family'); and often violating such rules may sow the very conditions for one's undoing: transgressors are commonly ravaged by a radical inversion of their lives – left penniless, sent to penitentiary. After all, the gangster – however revered and powerful – is not a loner, but an integral part of a network, a syndicate, a cartel, a family. The principal virtue gangsters of this stripe can exhibit is loyalty: when that is lost, it would seem, all is lost.

A gangster world may be even more morally rigid than the pirate world. Adaptation or innovation of established rules, for gangsters, is tantamount to disloyalty. All moral reasoning issues from the boss – the don, the godfather, a kind of *pater familias* – as an edict, as a mandate, as if *ex cathedra*. If one would risk any change to the system, one would explain it to the godfather and hope for his approval. Yet for his agents, there is rarely an allowance – much less support – for an on-the-ground, in-the-moment, judgement or revaluation of values; instead such deviation invites punishment.

The gangster's moral code is austere and depends on a total acquiescence to its inherited design. The figure of the rat or snitch is commonly ridiculed and despised because each act of disloyalty puts everyone at risk. In an odd revision of the first formulation of Kant's Categorical Imperative, the gangster might say: 'Act only according to that maxim by which you can at the same time ensure that your action will not implicate any member of the family in criminal activity'.

Why does the pirate code appear to yield more flexibility than the gangster code? The ship of pirates is not less hierarchical, nor less of a family, than what we see in the lives of gangsters. The difference lies with the agents of moral adaptation: each pirate seems to confer upon himself the status of captain. The pirate ship then is a ship of captains, each man convinced he can lead the other men – a foolish conceit that threatens every mission (for a mutiny demands that established rank be contravened, whereas a pirate seems to create his rank by wits and wiles, by his capacity to convince, elude, and capture at the right times). Mob bosses can make adjustments like captains, but not their underlings. Pirates and gangsters reveal the humour and horror of a feudal system but also tease us with the poetry and power of a moral order that is adaptable to present conditions – again, a 'moral' order that obtains within the logic of their respective outlooks, obviously suspect to conventional ethical and legal reasoning. And yet the bona fide ship's captain, like pirate and the godfather, is in a position to make judgements, moment by moment, and rely on unarticulated beliefs derived from experience, intuition or an inherited code – and from that standpoint generate some new position. Where, then, is the seam between legitimate moral innovation and moral violation? Some critics might say that Kant's Categorical Imperative gives the common man – like the ship's captain, pirate and gangster – a similar chance for what appear to be self-generated and unimpeachable decrees; and yet the various formulations of the imperative can seem too theoretical for everyday use, and require too much forethought and knowledge of the future to be defensible. The limit of an inquiry into the notion or nature of moral innovation based on rules may simply rest with the fact that we cannot all be pirates and mobsters; it is crucial that for any law to achieve itself we must all stand under it. Even or as one wishes to speak – to find 'words before blows' – there may remain a desire to discover a moral art that, as Emerson wrote in his journal, 'limits itself to relieving the dislocation, relieving the parts from their false position, putting them free, then they fly into place'.[35]

13.   Nietzsche, *Beyond Good and Evil*, 'Natural History of Morals'

Even apart from the value of such claims as 'there is a categorical imperative in us', one can still always ask: what does such a claim tell us about the man who makes it?[36]

14.   Shakespeare, *Twelfth Night*

Notable Pyrate, thou salt-water Theefe.[37]

15.   Emerson, 'Race'

> As soon as the shores are sufficiently peopled to make piracy a losing business, the
> same skill and courage are ready for the service of trade.[38]

> As soon as this land, thus geographically posted, got a hardy people into
> it, they could not help becoming the sailors and factors of the globe. From
> childhood, they dabbled in water, they swum like fishes, their playthings were
> boats. In the case of the ship-money, the judges delivered it for law, that 'England
> being an island, the very midland shires therein are all to be accounted maritime:'
> and Fuller adds, 'the genius even of landlocked countries driving the natives with
> a maritime dexterity'. As early as the conquest, it is remarked in explanation of the
> wealth of England, that its merchants trade to all countries.[39]

The piratical nature of the English contributed to the two largest forces of the British
Empire: trade and colonialism. In the context of English influence and affluence it
is difficult to distinguish the two since they reinforced one another. Colonizing was
in large measure the creation of new markets; and it made them both wealthy and
well-known. A foreign country or country-as-condition was not conquered so that an
invader could drain it of its riches but instead was developed for its potential service
to a wider network of products and profits – the commonwealth of uncommon
wealth. The English enjoyed a 'sense of superiority', Emerson claims, 'founded on
habit of victory in labour and in war: and the appetite for superiority grows by
feeding'.[40] English colonialism destroyed its colonies only in so far as the colonies
resisted the expansion of English capital and custom. When a colony imagined its own
independence – and with it claims to equity in political, moral and economic terms –
conflict subsequently arose. In the chapter 'Result' Emerson writes:

> As they are many-headed, so they are many-nationed: their colonization annexes
> archipelagoes and continents, and their speech seems destined to be the universal
> language of men. I have noted the reserve of power in the English temperament.
> In the island, they never let out all the length of all the reins, there is no Berserkir
> rage, no abandonment or ecstasy of will or intellect, like that of the Arabs in the
> time of Mahomet, or like that which intoxicated France in 1789. But who would
> see the uncoiling of that tremendous spring, the explosion of their well-husbanded
> forces, must follow the swarms which pouring now for two hundred years from
> the British islands, have sailed, and rode, and traded, and planted, through all
> climates, mainly following the belt of empire, the temperate zones, carrying
> the Saxon seed, with its instinct for liberty and law, for arts and for thought, –
> acquiring under some skies a more electric energy than the native air allows, – to
> the conquest of the globe. Their colonial policy, obeying the necessities of a vast
> empire, has become liberal. Canada and Australia have been contented with
> substantial independence. They are expiating the wrongs of India, by benefits;
> first, in works for the irrigation of the peninsula, and roads and telegraphs; and
> secondly, in the instruction of the people, to qualify them for self-government,
> when the British power shall be finally called home.[41]

The English did not impose their language for aesthetic reasons; their language became the 'universal language of men' because it served commerce. Sharing a language was a mechanical, even artificial, method for Anglicizing the market, and word by word a *lingua franca* made London the centre of fiscal, political and cultural worlds.

Where the British Empire had to send out a naval fleet and establish islands of colonizing forces in order to effect influence on foreign territories, the American Empire – if it is not better to call it the American Idea – spreads in increasingly disembodied ways due to the prevalence of new media and the ubiquity of technologies of digital transportation. Satire and cultural criticism aid the widespread inheritance and integration of American culture – from its politics to its wars, from the manner of its celebrations to the protocols of response to its defeats. Cultural imperialism has usurped traditional military imperialism; wars are fought for hearts and minds, not territory and spoils. Even military aggression has become an excuse for conceptual persuasion. In the age of information it is no longer necessary to invade or occupy a nation in order to captivate its people; boots on the ground is a synecdoche for an invasion of memes. Unlike the colonial British, contemporary Americans do not have to be there in order to be there.

Every byte of media is embedded with its own allusions. Ideas, images, fantasies and hallucinations of America and Americans are displayed on screens then live on in the afterimages of influence and imitation. In song or speech, narrative or polemical node, the global audience is encouraged to consider the promise of freedom, the profitability of free markets, the logic of incentives and the sense of unlimited potential – in terms of domestic affluence, intellectual influence and personal improvement – so much so that this new 'speech' of the American vernacular 'seems destined to be the universal language of men'.[42] If it was destined, its status nevertheless may be provisional – and may have already declined or become augmented. In a transnational era of Web-based simultaneity, the notion that an idea would be linked to a physical terrain – to the political boundaries of a country or nation-state – is anachronistic. The American idiom has become instead a cognitive topography upon which a global community can create and contribute to.

16.   Melville, *Moby-Dick*, 'The Gam'

> Nor would difference of country make any very essential difference; that is, so long as both parties speak one language, as is the case with Americans and English. Though, to be sure, from the small number of English whalers, such meetings do not very often occur, and when they do occur there is too apt to be a sort of shyness between them; for your Englishman is rather reserved, and your Yankee, he does not fancy that sort of thing in anybody but himself. Besides, the English whalers sometimes affect a kind of metropolitan superiority over the American whalers; regarding the long, lean Nantucketer, with his nondescript provincialisms, as a sort of sea-peasant. But where this superiority in the English whalemen does really consist, it would be hard to say, seeing that the Yankees

in one day, collectively, kill more whales than all the English, collectively, in ten years. But this is a harmless little foible in the English whale-hunters, which the Nantucketer does not take much to heart; probably, because he knows that he has a few foibles himself.

XIV

My Giant Goes With Me

1. Emerson, 'Voyage to England'

   I am not a good traveller, nor have I found that long journeys yield a fair share of reasonable hours.[1]

2. Flying by airplane from Boston to Rome one could note the following approximate statistics for the transatlantic journey:

   DEPARTURE TIME: 6:00 PM (EST)
   ARRIVAL TIME: 10:40 AM (GMT +1)
   ELAPSED TIME: 10 hours 40 minutes
   DISTANCE TRAVELLED: 4,100 miles
   MAXIMAL AIR SPEED: 636 miles per hour
   HIGHEST ALTITUDE: 37,000 feet
   OUTSIDE AIR TEMPERATURE (at 37,000 feet): −70° F

During the flight, in a temperature-controlled air-pressurized environment, one can read by the light of a designated lamp, eat a hot three-course meal, drink from a glass of chilled sauvignon blanc, watch a film on a laptop computer, tablet, phone or built-in display, make a telephone call, connect to the Internet wirelessly, use a private bathroom, call for the service of a flight attendant from one's seat, and rest quietly with noise cancelling earphones. Of his experiences aboard the *Washington Irving* in 1847 Emerson wrote: 'The confinement, cold, motion, noise, and odor are not to be dispensed with. The floor of your room is sloped at an angle of twenty or thirty degrees, and I waked every morning with the belief that some one was tipping up my berth. Nobody likes to be treated ignominiously, upset, shoved against the side of the house, rolled over, suffocated with bilge, mephitis, and stewing oil'.[2] Based on his earlier times at sea, Emerson said the following in 'Experience': 'Every ship is a romantic object, except that we sail in. Embark, and the romance quits our vessel and hangs on every other sail in the horizon'.[3] (Meanwhile travel on land – by rail, for example – was similarly strenuous, risk inducing and time consuming. Before construction of the transcontinental railroad in 1869, it took as long to travel across the North American continent – 6 to 7 weeks – as it took to reach New York Harbour after disembarking from Southampton, England (3,091 nautical miles).[4] In 1854 the world record time – by sea – between New York and San Francisco was 80 days on the water.[5] After 1869, transcontinental rail-lines reduced travel duration between the East and West coasts to under a week.)

At the end of 1832 Emerson decided to sail for Europe for the first time. He boarded a ship in Boston Harbour – the brig *Jasper* – departing for Malta before the New Year. Here are some of the coordinates of his voyage across the Atlantic Ocean:

DEPARTURE TIME: 10:30 AM, 25 December 1832[6]
ARRIVAL AT PORT: 2 February 1833
LANDFALL: 15 February 1833
ELAPSED TIME: 53 days (40 days at sea plus an additional 13 days in ship-bound quarantine at Valletta, Malta)
DISTANCE TRAVELLED: 4,400 nautical miles

In Concord on 24 October 1847 Henry Thoreau wrote to his sister, Sophia, about Emerson's second voyage to Europe – including details of the physical realities on board as well as the opportunity costs of charting a sea-bound path from Boston to Liverpool. Thoreau had himself just recently stepped off the land at Walden Pond to lend aid to the Emerson family in Mr Emerson's absence, so his comparison – of life on the broad sea or in the midst of the local woods – was fresh in mind.

[…] I went to Boston the 5th of this month to see Mr Emerson off to Europe. He sailed in the *Washington Irving* packet ship; the same in which Mr [Frederick Henry] Hedge went before him. […] Mr Emerson's stateroom was like a carpeted dark closet, about six feet square, with a large keyhole for a window. The window was about as big as a saucer, and the glass two inches thick, not to mention another skylight overhead in the deck, the size of an oblong doughnut, and about as opaque. Of course it would be in vain to look up, if any contemplative prome-nader put his foot upon it. Such will be his lodgings for two or three weeks; and instead of a walk in Walden woods he will take a promenade on deck, where the few trees, you know, are stripped of their bark. The steam-tug carried the ship to sea against a head wind without a rag of sail being raised.[7]

DEPARTURE TIME: 5 October 1847
ARRIVAL TIME: 22 October 1847
ELAPSED TIME: 18 days
DISTANCE TRAVELLED IN THE FIRST 4 DAYS: 134 miles
DISTANCE TRAVELLED IN THE FOLLOWING 7 DAYS: 1,467 miles
DISTANCE TRAVELLED IN TOTAL: about 3,000 miles
LENGTH OF THE DECK, STERN TO STERN: 155 feet

Emerson drew a moral from his seafaring travels: 'The voyage of the best ship is a zigzag line of a hundred tacks. See the line from a sufficient distance, and it straightens itself to the average tendency'.[8] A sailing vessel must constantly adjust its sails and its course to utilize the wind. At a distance, at the perspective of a great length or from a great height, the tacking back and forth appears straight – a 'tendency' in one direction. Dodging and weaving, which comprise the art of good sailing, are deployed for the purpose of making the straightest course. In everyday life one may be discouraged by what feels like distractions and sallies, periods of maximum effort and minimal production, and by the contingencies that surprise with great demands on one's attention and siphon away from one's limited energies: births, deaths, romantic alliances and ruptures, vocational triumphs and upheavals, packing house and unpacking it, moving back and forth across countries and over seas, carrying beloved books read and unread (flourishing and suffering from the weight of these works – imposed or perceived), losing touch with old friends and making contact with new ones, becoming compelled by a prominent and uncommon idea while also feeling disillusioned by a familiar one.

> If any of us knew what we were doing, or where we are going, then when we think we best know! We do not know to-day whether we are busy or idle. In times when we thoughts ourselves indolent, we have afterwards discovered that much was accomplished and much was begun in us. All our days are so unprofitable while they pass, that 'tis wonderful where or when we ever got anything of this which we call wisdom, poetry, virtue. We never got it on any dated calendar day.[9]

With perspective, with some distance from the discrete hours as they pass, or at a remove from the particular struggles of ordinary life, general arcs of meaning appear. An education, for example, may be earned by writing so many thousands of words and by reading so many more. But what can be said in 10 or 20 year's time about those specific intimacies with texts? We are left with impressions – generally cleared of the daily crises that gave rise to them, crises that both presented intellectual frustration and occasionally yielded elation. At a distance, whether looking at the course charted by a ship or by a person, 'All the sallies of his will are rounded in by the law of his being, as the inequalities of Andes and Himmaleh are insignificant in the curve of the sphere'.[10]

3.   Travelling far from home one arrives in a new place only to realize that one has brought everything one tried to get away from. In flight one could not flee. So it is possible to go away from a place – one's home, a familiar site – but not away from oneself; and by equal compensation, one does not get nearer to oneself by returning to one's point of origin. It is a cliché to hear of travelling as a method of finding oneself – whether it entails fleeing an origin or finding it. Still, if the sentiment is genuine, if there are truths in these common notions, are not the findings rather less substantial than intimated? The self one leaves with is the self one arrives with; the self who discovers the site or source of conception must leave it to commence a new procession. If one aims to get away from one's self, or discover one's self when away, travel is a pretence. Emerson posted *Ne te quaesiveris extra* ('Do not seek yourself outside yourself') at the head of his seminal essay 'Self-Reliance', since external seeking does not reveal internal realities. Yet travel in the conventional imagination often seems predicated on just such a faith, as Emerson writes in 1841 after much sobering and instructive first-hand experience at sea and on rail:

> Travelling is a fool's paradise. Our first journeys discover to us the indifference of places. At home I dream that at Naples, at Rome, I can be intoxicated with beauty, and lose my sadness. I pack my trunk, embrace my friends, embark on the sea,

and at last wake up in Naples, and there beside me is the stern fact, the sad self, unrelenting, identical, that I fled from. I seek the Vatican, and the palaces. I affect to be intoxicated with sights and suggestions, but I am not intoxicated. My giant goes with me wherever I go.[11]

In his letters, Seneca quotes Socrates as saying: 'How can you wonder your travels do you no good, when you carry yourself around with you? You are saddled with the very thing that drove you away'.[12] In 1833 Emerson was, in significant measure, travelling to get away from himself – and the life he knew as his in Boston. During the previous year, he continued to languish over the death of his beloved first wife, Ellen, in 1831, and was tormented by a vocational crisis that led him ultimately to resign his prominent and coveted position as pastor of Boston's Second Church late in 1832. Additionally, he endured uneven health. There were many reasons to seek a change from his familiar life, a life at last undermined and upended by his resignation. When Emerson discovered in Italy that he had been followed, that a sea voyage across a tremendous ocean had not liberated him, he appeared defeated. Going away did not bring him anywhere new, except to a discovery that the foreign merely confirms how the familiar abides. Seneca's account of the disquieted soul travelling for relief applies well to Emerson in early 1833, here addressing himself in a letter to Lucilius, a Roman knight and procurator living in Sicily[13]: 'You are running away in your own company. You have to lay aside the load on your spirit. Until you do that, nowhere will satisfy you. [...] You rush hither and thither with the idea of dislodging a firmly seated weight when the very dashing about just adds to the trouble it causes you'.[14] A kindred sentiment appears earlier in Horace's *Epistles* where he wrote: 'they change their sky but not their soul, who run across the sea [*caelum, non animum mutant, qui trans mare currunt*]'.[15]

Awareness of a great weight – a conspicuous burden to one's movement of thought – often belies and exacerbates an inner restlessness. Sensitive to this pressure, one feels uneasy, perhaps claustrophobic: one perceives untoward limits. The weight – a depression upon the chest, or a dragging force hanging from the back – leaves one anxious, distracted and fatigued. In time, the doubtful and weary mind is compromised by an inability to concentrate even when not distracted. The present moment feels at once occupied with an awareness of the receding past (continually cast and re-cast according to some narrative imposition), and the expanding future that promises elastic possibilities, many of which will likely remain forever unrealized, unknown – private phantasms that stoke desire while leaving it unfulfilled. The restless mind is a wandering mind, trying to flee from the present – the undeniable here and the persistent now. While the wandering mind can be necessary for speculation about a wider world (for example, theorizing across time and space; challenging established histories and ideas; rethinking narratives and networks of explanation), it may be harmful to self-perception and the development of an abiding confidence about where one is, and what one is doing. The wandering mind wants to be elsewhere; it struggles to get a sense of anywhere but where it is. Merleau-Ponty seemed to think that the nature of mind was defined by an absence from itself: 'To be conscious is, among other things, to be somewhere else'.[16]

Emerson, 'Self-Reliance' (1841)

> [T]he rage of travelling is a symptom of a deeper unsoundness affecting the whole intellectual action. The intellect is vagabond, and our system of education fosters restlessness. Our minds travel when our bodies are forced to stay at home. We imitate; and what is imitation but the travelling of the mind? Our houses are built with foreign taste; our shelves are garnished with foreign ornaments; our opinions, our tastes, our faculties, lean, and follow the Past and the Distant. The soul created the arts wherever they have flourished.[17]

Emerson, 'Culture' (1860)

> I am not much an advocate for travelling, and I observe that men run away to other countries, because they are not good in their own, and run back to their own, because they pass for nothing in the new places. For the most part, only the light characters travel. Who are you that have no task to keep you at home? I have been quoted as saying captious things about travel; but I mean to do justice. I think, there is a restlessness in our people, which argues want of character.[18]

Such restlessness bespeaks a lack of commitment to oneself, one's state of affairs, and the power of the present; it signals a sense of inferiority to other people, other places and other times. The Americans of Emerson's day, including at various points Emerson himself, seemed prone to idolizing what lay elsewhere, often Greek and Roman antiquity, commonly the styles and sentiments of European capitals and culture. Like children standing in the wide shadow of a successful and domineering parent, Americans assumed a deferential status, and so they continually aspired to return to a place of primary – and primal – significance.

Emerson, 'Culture'

> All educated Americans, first or last, go to Europe; – perhaps, because it is their mental home, as the invalid habits of this country might suggest. An eminent teacher of girls said, 'the idea of a girl's education, is, whatever qualifies them for going to Europe'. Can we never extract this tape-worm of Europe from the brain of our countrymen? One sees very well what their fate must be. He that does not fill a place at home, cannot abroad. He only goes there to hide his insignificance in a larger crowd. You do not think you will find anything there which you have not seen at home? The stuff of all countries is just the same. Do you suppose, there is any country where they do not scald milkpans, and swaddle the infants, and burn the brushwood, and broil the fish? What is true anywhere is true everywhere. And let him go where he will, he can only find so much beauty or worth as he carries.[19]

Even as the child is being educated, she is aware that the training points her away from herself, away from where she lives. Such teaching makes the student skittish, unable to affirm her conviction or surmise without recourse to some external authority. Tutored to believe in her feebleness – to experience doubt as an aspect of instinct and intuition – she matures into a scholar or seeker who assumes that reality and truth and power lie beyond her purvey: 'The sinew and heart of man seem to be drawn out, and we are become timorous, desponding whimperers. We are afraid of truth, afraid of fortune, afraid of death, and afraid of each other'.[20] The whimperer cannot write *Whim*.

Emerson, 'Friendship' (1841)

> Let us feel, if we will, the absolute insulation of man. We are sure that we have all in us. We go to Europe, or we pursue persons, or we read books, in the instinctive faith that these will call it out and reveal us to ourselves. Beggars all. The persons are such as we; the Europe, an old faded garment of dead persons; the books their ghosts. Let us drop this idolatry. Let us give over this mendicancy.[21]

The fearful and insecure person travels to be transformed into someone brave and confident – someone other than oneself. But skating, much less studying, across Europe – touring museums, attending theatre and opera, skulking in the palaces and ruins – does not teach a new degree of self-assurance; it merely reinforces the poverty of one's situation, and confirms one's worst doubts. Not the poverty of the art, to be sure, or one's doubt of its achievement – but the way such touring mortifies the living by recommending obeisance in place of a willing and justified admiration. Touring diverse works, and the worlds they keep, should not level the visitor – wrecking her hope, confounding her ambitions – but allow for irritation and awe in alternation. Travelling should be a tumult of heart and brain, a quickening agent for one's pulse and one's nerve, and not a confirmation that all has been lived and achieved elsewhere and elsewhen – where one is not and will never be.

Emerson, 'Art' (1841)

> I remember, when in my younger days I had heard of the wonders of Italian painting, I fancied the great pictures would be great strangers; some surprising combination of color and form; a foreign wonder, barbaric pearl and gold, like the spontoons and standards of the militia, which play such pranks in the eyes and imaginations of school–boys. I was to see and acquire I knew not what. When I came at last to Rome, and saw with eyes the pictures, I found that genius left to novices the gay and fantastic and ostentatious, and itself pierced directly to the simple and true; that it was familiar and sincere; that it was the old, eternal fact I had met already in so many forms, – unto which I lived; that it was the plain *you and me* I knew so well, – had left at home in so many conversations. I had the same experience already in a church at Naples. There I saw that nothing was changed with me but the place, and said to myself, – 'Thou foolish child, hast thou come out hither, over four thousand miles of salt water, to find that which was perfect to thee there at home?' – that fact I saw again in the Academmia at Naples, in the chambers of sculpture, and yet again when I came to Rome, and to the paintings of Raphael, Angelo, Sacchi, Titian, and Leonardo da Vinci. 'What, old mole! workest thou in the earth so fast?' It had travelled by my side: that which I fancied I had left in Boston was here in the Vatican, and again at Milan, and at Paris, and made all travelling ridiculous as a treadmill.[22]

Seneca acknowledged this point in the first century: 'You do not tear from place to place and unsettle yourself with one move after another. Restlessness of that is symptomatic of a sick mind. Nothing, to my way of thinking, is better proof of a well ordered mind than a man's ability to stop just where he is and pass some time in his own company.'[23] Restlessness spurs travel, but once on the road there is no reason to expect peace – as if movement conveyed calm: 'What good has travel of itself ever been able to do to anyone? [...] All it has ever done is distract us for a little while, through novelty of our surroundings. [...] The instability, moreover, of a mind which is seriously unwell, is aggravated by it, the motion itself increasing the fitfulness and restlessness. [... T]ravel won't make a better or saner man of you.'[24]

Seneca also pre-dates Emerson's idea of the true and truthful residing in all places, even where one finds oneself: 'As it is, instead of travelling you are rambling and drifting, exchanging one place for another when the thing you are looking for, the good life, is available everywhere.'[25] Denying the promise of proximity leaves the traveller prone to disconnection from herself and others: 'To be everywhere is to be nowhere. People who spend their whole life travelling abroad end up having plenty of places where they can find hospitality but no real friendships.'[26] These are variations on the absent minded: at a distance when at home, and not at home when at a distance.

4.   Seneca and Emerson discern a connection between one's understanding of travel and one's mental health; everything from one's disposition to one's self-image is affected by the conception of travel's nature and utility. They worry that people are prone to travel for misbegotten reasons – perhaps most troubling among them, as noted, the bid to get away from, or to find, oneself. Yet despite their fervent declarations concerning the perils associated with an impoverished and misleading notion of what travelling entails (avoidance, faulty romanticism, restless searching), they also admit some of its positive aspects and potentially beneficial consequences. For instance, Seneca believed travelling is more likely to have favourable effects if it is conducted with a purpose, with established limits, under the auspices of a conscribed project. He objects, in short, to aimless travel – to endless roaming: 'When a person is following a track, there is an eventual end to it somewhere, but with wandering at large there is no limit. So give up pointless, empty journeys [...].'[27]

While travelling can lead to disturbing self-doubt – reinforcing one's already fragile state of searching or fleeing, it can also manifest a helpful degree of skepticism. Travelling can remonstrate long-held beliefs and therefore be a counterforce to dogmatism, and contrariwise: where skepticism once prevailed without objection, a first person encounter may confirm a new degree of faith. Travelling makes one see realities one could never imagine were real; it adds sensuous dimensions to things and people and places one had only a limited theoretical understanding of. The postcard picture made promises but come to life it complicates them, requiring the spectrum of one's instincts and learning – such as they are, not as they would ideally be.

The meaning of the given and established – even the sacred – is transformed, or at least put into question, before one's eyes – when one is sensuously present to these foreign facts, pressed up against them. The traveller is shocked into critical engagement with her core beliefs, forced to contend with all their often hidden nuances and oblique contours – often as if for the first time, since those details could not be gleaned without the benefit of contrast and comparison afforded by travel. Travel unsettles. 'People wish to be settled; only as far as they are unsettled is there any hope for them'.[28]

When one travels without aiming to escape or discover, novel opportunities emerge for experiencing the benefits of travelling: among them a sense of engaged interest in the foreignness of the foreign (for instance, how others undertake familiar tasks in unfamiliar ways), and a genuine intrigue about how the factors of a given social circumstance contribute to the development of a diverse range of personalities and beliefs. When one couples satisfaction with present conditions (including one's own private state) with an abiding eagerness to travel, there is less chance that one will end up being a restless, aimless traveller. Seneca says as much: 'Once you have rid yourself of the affliction there [within you], though, every change of scene will become a pleasure. [...] Where you arrive does not matter so much as what sort of person you are when you arrive there. [...] Whichever [place] you first came to would have satisfied you if you had believed you were at home in all'.[29] Travelling will be defined by awe not anxiety; it will afford its practitioner a wider and wilder view of the terms on which to take steps in one's experience.

Having travelled on trains and ships, Emerson saw first-hand how 'Of course, for some men, travel may be useful. Naturalists, discoverers and sailors are born. Some men are made for couriers, exchangers, envoys, missionaries, bearers of despatches, as others are for farmers and working-men'.[30] Just above Emerson seemed to condescend to the 'light characters' who are prone to travel – perhaps owing to some perceived insubstantiality in their form or lack of sense for where they reside – and yet such impulses and ephemerality may find their appointment, as he glosses the sentiment in a different mood: 'And if the man is of a light and social turn, and Nature has aimed to make a legged and winged creature, framed for locomotion, we must follow her hint, and furnish him with that breeding which gives currency, as sedulously as with that which gives worth'.[31] Emerson's remarks about the service of being – or remaining – unsettled suggest that someone with a light character is both prone to travel and also particularly capable of its demands, suited to them as if by nature: such a character does not think of having a single home somewhere, but encounters attributes of home wherever he goes. With such displacement – a comfort and solicitude in each new condition – this traveller will naturally avoid sentimentality about origins and therein find 'the journey's end in every step of the road', and during every undulating hour at sea.[32] In this mood, the naturalist and sailor are wiser for their talent at being present with themselves, and content where they are. And the same time, the steps they take are not settled in a place but taken ever onward – propelled by a latent inertia: 'For wherever the mind takes a step, it is to put itself at one with a larger class, discerned beyond the lesser class with which it has been conversant'.[33]

Emerson also considered the paradoxes of travel, the manner in which going away, on some occasions, somehow, brings us back to ourselves. Emerson ended the following passage by securing his thesis between square brackets – as if to state a very clear and direct thing in a clandestine whisper. Wittgenstein once asked rhetorically 'What can we [Europeans] give the Americans? Our half-decayed culture?'[34] In 'Culture', a chapter from *The Conduct of Life*, Emerson replies *avant le lettre* by stating that Europe offers 'some chance' – among other destinations – for deepening one's knowledge of the place for which one embarked.[35] Europe and Britain, in particular, may be possessed of a particularly potent effect on this turn since they are historically the places from which the New World disembarked. Taking steps away leads one back. Such travel is an exploration of what ancestors left behind – what they fathomed was worth leaving for a new and unknown world – the new and unknown world that is now familiar to the travelling American descendent.

> But let us not be pedantic, but allow to travel its full effect. The boy grown up on the farm, which he has never left, is said in the country to have had *no chance*, and boys and men of that condition look upon work on a railroad, or drudgery in a city, as opportunity. Poor country boys of Vermont and Connecticut formerly owed what knowledge they had, to their peddling trips to the Southern States. California and the Pacific Coast is now the university of this class, as Virginia was in old times. 'To have *some chance*' is their word. And the phrase 'to know the world', or to travel, is synonymous with all men's ideas of advantage and superiority. No doubt, to a man of sense, travel offers advantages. As many languages as he has, as many friends, as many arts and trades, so many times is he a man. A foreign country is a point of comparison, wherefrom to judge his own. One use of travel, is, to recommend the books and works of home; [we go to Europe to be Americanized;] and another, to find men.[36]

Emerson did not go to Europe to be Americanized but that is what happened. He did consciously set out to 'find men', though, as he recounts, 'Like most young men at that time, I was much indebted to the men of Edinburgh Review, [...] and my narrow and desultory reading had inspired the wish to see the faces of three or four writers, – Coleridge, Wordsworth, Landor, and De Quincey, and the latest and strongest contributor to the critical journals, Carlyle; and I suppose if I had sifted the reasons that led me to Europe, when I was ill and was advised to travel, it was mainly the attraction of these persons'.[37] If the ancient sites and cities of Europe left Emerson yearning for his young woodlands, he did find a measure of his capacities in speaking with the living heroes of English literature and philosophy. His adoration of Carlyle's work, read in Boston solitude, was overshadowed by the clarifying effect of spending time with Carlyle himself in Craigenputtock. A week from his visit to Scotland, back at sea on the ship *New York*, Emerson was summoning his forces and the effects of his abundant travel. Within a month of returning to Boston, as he commenced *pro tempore* preaching, Emerson presented 'The Uses of Natural History' before the Natural History Society. And he began the new year, 1834, with a lecture 'On the Relation of Man to the Globe'. But it was Emerson's reading of Carlyle's recently published *Sartor Resartus* and his newly established correspondence with its author – coupled with the award of his first wife's estate – that enabled Emerson to experiment with his unmoored, unaffiliated position as an itinerant man of letters. 'I please myself with contemplating the felicity of my present situation. May it last'.[38] A month later, Emerson's brother Charles wrote to their brother Edward Bliss:

> Natural history is the study now[.] We are all making catalogues of birds, reading memoirs of Cuvier, hearing lectures about Crustacea, Volcanoes, entymology & the like. Waldo is going to lecture day after tomorrow at the Mechan. Inst. on Water. […] If I were a rich man I would be a natural philosopher.[39]

XV

Corresponding Minds

1. Emerson, 'Culture' (1860)

> For, as Nature has put fruits apart in latitudes, a new fruit in every degree, so knowledge and fine moral quality she lodges in distant men. And thus, of the six or seven teachers whom each man wants among his contemporaries, it often happens that one or two of them live on the other side of the world.[1]

2.   After Emerson visited Thomas and Jane Carlyle at their home in Scotland in 1833 the young American admirer became a metonym for America in remote Craigenputtock. Half a decade after his visit to Scotland, Mrs. Carlyle wrote to Emerson from London: 'When I think of America, it is of you – neither Harriet Martineau nor any one else succeeds in giving me a more extended idea of it. When I wish to see America it is still you [...].'[2] Her husband was also as enamored with Emerson. The two began a lifelong correspondence that reflected their differing but complementary intelligences, their contrasting but sympathetic personalities, and the usual complexities of a long-distance relationship: there were passionate exchanges of ideas; periods of hurt, confusion and silence; and occasions of reconciliation and understanding. One of the topics that occupied their attention in the early years of writing was the relationship between England and America, often described as if they were speaking strictly of themselves – again with the men as metonyms for their nations. The year after Emerson's visit, Carlyle wrote: 'And so here, looking over the water, let me repeat once more what I believe is already simply the sentiment of all Englishmen, Cisoceanic and Transoceanic, that we and you are *not* two countries, and cannot for the life of us be; but only two *parishes* of one country [...].'[3] Years later, in protracted hope and negotiation to visit America, Carlyle told his American friend: 'I have not forgotten Concord or the West; no, it lies always beautiful in the blue of the horizon, afar off and yet attainable; it is a great possession to me, should it even never be attained. But I have got to consider lately that it is you who are coming hither first. That is the right way, is it not? New England is becoming more than ever part of Old England; why, you are nearer to us now than Yorkshire was a hundred years ago; this is literally a fact: you can come *without* making your will.'[4]

Concord River is Carlyle's West as the Mississippi River is Emerson's. In 1844 when Emerson accounts for America east of the Adirondacks, Alleghenies and Appalachians, he echoes Carlyle: 'I am ready to die out of nature, and be born again into this new yet unapproachable America I have found in the West'.[5] Both men are westward facing, and both appear preoccupied with the restorative, even regenerative ('born again'), possibilities of any movement that takes them further from the Thames. Remarkably, given a lifetime of longing, and Emerson's persistent and generous offers to host, Carlyle never made passage to the New World, to New England. And so his West remained 'afar off and yet attainable', as the self Emerson described in 'History' persisted: 'unattained but attainable'.[6]

Though Carlyle never closed the distance between England and America for himself, he was aware of how the space between these two lands was shrinking – how the otherwise vast ocean was acceding to steam, and land on the far side of the Atlantic was becoming 'nearer' than a place as close and familiar as Yorkshire. And while for Carlyle Emerson was metamorphosed into a mental representative of America – a cognitive mapping that compressed the psychological distance between friends – technologies of steam and sail were bringing New and Old England into a new physical intimacy, drawing down the temporal and constitutional demands of contact, which had hitherto been as grueling as seemingly necessary. Carlyle attributes a growing sense of America as 'more than ever' a part of England to this technological trend. And he sees other points of continuity as well:

> [...] I should rather fancy America mainly a new Commercial England, with a fuller pantry: little more or little else. The same unquenchable, almost frightfully unresting spirit of endeavor, directed (woe is me!) to the making of money, or money's worth, namely food finer and finer, and gigmanic renown higher and higher: nay must not your gigmanity be a *purse*-gigmanity, some half-shade worse than a purse-and-pedigree one? Or perhaps it is not a whit worse; only tougher, more substantial; on the whole better? At all events ours is fast becoming identical with it; for the pedigree ingredient is as near as may be gone: *Gagnez de l'argent, et ne vous faites pas pendre*, this is very nearly the whole Law, first Table and second. So that you see when I set foot on American land it will be on no Utopia; but on a *conditional* piece of ground, where some things are to be expected and other things not.[7]

Carlyle's neologisms can sometimes undermine readerly comprehension, yet he makes a rather intuitive, if playful and informative point: *gigmania* and its variants pervade American culture as in England; the continuity may also reveal Carlyle's hedge in having to visit America in order to discover the dystopia he assumes he will find there. Carlyle draws attention to America as 'a *conditional* piece of ground', that is, land that is subject to forces – the conspiring of native and foreign elements. Hence Carlyle's question about the 'pedigree ingredient' and whether it is present, prevails or has dissolved. Carlyle conjectures that in this land – with conditionality in place of utopia – little, perhaps nothing, is given except 'the whole Law' – namely gigmania – shorthand for all the constituent parts of a free market economy separated and liberated from church, state and heredity. Though the land is conditional, the gigmaniac is not called to account for origins, affiliations or allegiances. In America, gigmania is at best always and only a matter of one's experience with money. Everything else is open for experiment and evaluation.

A two-wheeled carriage drawn by a single horse was known as a gig. John Thurtell, the Mayor of Norwich's son, became involved in two of the most scandalous activities of early nineteenth century England: boxing and gambling. On the evening of 24 October 1823 Thurtell murdered his one-time friend William Weare and – as if it were a pertinent conjunction – was said to have driven a gig. Less than three months later, on 9 January 1824 Thurtell was hanged. During the trial a witness spoke of Thurtell: 'I always thought him a respectable man'. When the barrister asked 'What do you mean by 'respectable'?' the witness replied 'He kept a gig'. Based on the implications of owing a gig in the testimony, Carlyle began using gigman, gigmanity, gigmania, & co. as synonyms for the respectability of the bourgeoisie, and further, the philistine. In his book *The Diamond Necklace* (1837) he wrote: 'a Princess of the Blood, yet whose father had sold his inexpressibles [...] in a word, *Gigmanity disgigged*'.[8]

In his letter to Emerson, Carlyle repeated a sentiment that had arisen many times between the correspondents, namely that America is truly, or literally, a New England. Here, though, Carlyle emphasizes the extent to which that identity is economic in nature: he distinguishes the purse-gigmanity of America with the purse-and-pedigree-gigmanity of England, concluding that the former is perhaps a better form of respectability than the latter, especially since pedigree (or aristocracy) 'is as near as may be gone'. In England, wealth and family status were forever coordinated; in America wealth could be accumulated by, as one might say, a man without a name. In fact the very activity of wealth accumulation became a means for making a name for oneself. In America, profit was a reflection of one's talent (or luck) in the marketplace, and so wealth was no longer a simple sign of family inheritance or influence. When Carlyle reflects on what it might mean for the 'pedigree ingredient' to be lost he uses a French phrase that translates as 'Earn money, and don't get yourself hanged' [*Gagnez de l'argent, et ne vous faites pas pendre*].[9] That is, do not emulate the gig-driving murderer John Thurtell. Emerson, bringing himself in for a bit of self-mocking – while aiming to secure Carlyle profitable conditions for the publication of the Scotsman's work in the States – would later say that 'my vulgar hope of dollars' (even if for his friend's benefit) is an 'innate idea of the American mind', something inescapably part of the outlook and values of life in the New World.[10] Given money's essential role in American life, the challenge, for some, is how to make a killing in the market without committing murder.

3.   D. Q. McInerny, *Being Logical*

> We all tend to favor our own ideas, which is natural enough. They are, after all, in a sense our very own babies, the conceptions of our minds.[11]

4.   In their conversational correspondence, Emerson and Carlyle recurred regularly to the relationship that obtained between their works and themselves. How were agent and authored to stand – for themselves separately, for one another? Who was conceiving and what was conceived? In one letter Carlyle wrote: 'But to speak candidly, I do feel sometimes as if another Book were growing in me, – tho' I almost tremble to think it'.[12] The following year he wrote to his friend in Concord:

Rudiments of a new Book (thank Heaven!) do sometimes disclose themselves to me. *Festinare lente* [*Make haste slowly*]. It ought to be better than F.[rench] Rev[olution]; I mean better written. The greater part of that Book, as I read proof-sheets of it in these weeks, does nothing but *disgust* me. And yet it was, as nearly as was good, the utmost that lay in me. I should not like to be nearer killed with any other Book![13]

The 'utmost' that lay in Carlyle was not a child but an idea – his most pronounced conception. As with a difficult pregnancy, though, giving birth to a book can be perilous, a fatal undertaking. For those familiar with his labour, it is not surprising to learn that Carlyle might be 'nearer killed' with his celebrated two-volume *French Revolution*, since he had to conceive of it and birth it *twice*. Carlyle's friend, the renowned philosopher John Stuart Mill borrowed the only manuscript copy of *French Revolution* and not long after had to return to his friend's house on Cheyne Row in London to confess where it lay. Mill's maid had accidentally burned the entire manuscript. Like a beautiful child stolen early by a fatal disease, the book was consumed and taken away in its infancy. It is a measure of Carlyle's temperament that he was not himself overcome by grief at his loss, or disconsolate anger at Mill – both of which could likely sustain a long-standing paranoia about whether Mill had a hand in destroying a competing work of world philosophy. Carlyle returned to his upstairs sound-proof study and picked up his pen. That *The French Revolution, a History* appeared in 1837 to high acclaim, perhaps does not offset Carlyle's trial in re-creating it. His 'disgust' with the work may reside in his impression that the first edition – the first manuscript – was a fairer conception, and this later effort – robust as it was – could only be at a remove, a secondary re-telling of the luminous initial creation. Did the fire confirm Carlyle of the beauty of his first offspring or did it protect him from having to find words to give expression to another such admirable sequences of words?

There were also conceptions, we are told, that did not come to life – even once. Of these mis-conceptions, Carlyle lamented to Emerson: 'My other Manuscripts are scratchings and scrawlings, – children's IN*fant* souls weeping, because they never could be born, but were left there whimpering *in limine primo* [*at the outer threshold*]!'[14] And Emerson wrote to Carlyle about books that made it to press but seem threatened with extinction: 'Since the little Nature book [that is *Nature* (1836)] is not quite dead, I have sent you a few copies and wish you would offer one to Mr Milnes with my respects'.[15] When one of their books becomes the subject of praise, it seems like an adored family member deserving respect and attention, as when Emerson commends Carlyle on his *Sartor Resartus* as if he were praising a nephew: 'The book is welcome & awakens a sort of nepotism in me – my brother's child'.[16] Famously David Hume wrote with honesty, and perhaps a tinge of vanity, that his book *A Treatise of Human Nature* (1739–40) 'fell deadborn from the press'. In these accounts of men giving birth to books, one can muster a typology for understanding a written work in terms of male creativity: it is a creation that grows within the creator until it is ripe for emission; is so difficult to release into the world that it threatens the life of its creator; is mired in the purgatory of failed completion; is so endearing that it seems a living part of an already established community; or issues from its creator only to languish or perish once given over to the world.

In a letter to Emerson from 1839, Carlyle anticipated ideas that would be popularized by J. L. Austin in the 1950s – so-called performative utterances or speech acts – while concomitantly depicting a scene of male creation. Carlyle implored Emerson to create a 'symbolic' work that is composed of speech, but has the effect of an action. The form of this work, according to Carlyle's description, resembles a child: it originates with Emerson, is imbued with his life, and goes out from him – into an independent existence.

> Speak, therefore, while you feel called to do it, and when you feel called. But for yourself, my friend, I prophecy it will not do always, a faculty is in you for a *sort* of speech which is itself *action*, an artistic sort. You *tell* us with piercing emphasis that man's soul is great; *show* us a great soul of a man, in some work symbolic of such: this is the seal of such a message, and you will feel by and by that you are called to this. I long to see some concrete Thing, some Event, Man's Life, American Forest, or piece of Creation, which this Emerson loves and wonders at, well *Emersonized*: depictured by Emerson, filled with the life of Emerson, and cast forth from him then to live by itself.[17]

XVI

Titles Manifold

1.   William Wordsworth (1802/7)

– In everything we are
sprung
of Earth's first blood, have titles manifold.[1]

2.   Emerson, 'Aristocracy'

The names are excellent, – an atmosphere of legendary melody spread over the
land. Older than all epics and histories, which clothe a nation, this undershirt sits
close to the body. What history too, and what stores of primitive and savage observation it infolds! Cambridge is the bridge of the Cam; Sheffield the field of the river
Sheaf; Leicester the *castra* or camp of the Lear or Leir (now Soar); Rochdale, of the
Roch; Exeter or Excester, the *castra* of the Ex; Exmouth, Dartmouth, Sidmouth,
Teignmouth, the mouths of the Ex, Dart, Sid, and Teign rivers. Waltham is strong
town; Radcliffe is red cliff; and so on: – a sincerity and use in naming very striking
to an American, whose country is whitewashed all over by unmeaning names,
the cast-off clothes of the country from which its emigrants came; or, named at a
pinch from a psalm-tune.[2]

In England names stood for their proximate referents; the name itself – born from
the land or river – seemed native, definitively English. In New England, however,
these familiar English names – carried over the sea like so much cultural chattel –
remained English but were used to stand for American places. New England is a land
of borrowed titles, imported names employed derivatively. Such usage, one could say,
has the effect of confusing a name with the thing named. As Emerson wrote in 1836:
'new imagery ceases to be created, and old words are perverted to stand for things
which are not; a paper currency is employed, when there is no bullion in the vaults'.[3]
America's Cambridge is not beside the River Cam, but beside a river – the Charles –
given its name by the English King, Charles I, himself (when invited by Captain John
Smith to substitute English names for 'barbarous' ones[4]). Americans, especially in
New England, lived with these transatlantic names affixed like badges from another
place – and in some cases, as with the Charles River, the title was a royal decree. A
name was chosen to befit the sentiments of founders and locals, or used as a sign of
reference and remembrance, or as a testament to a beloved hometown or homeland.
Just as a son might be named after his father, so the land and waters were often named

after the cities and citizens once familiar in the fatherland; keeping the parallel, one might suspect that the new place – the newly named place with the old name – is also a lesser place, a junior, a second; it certainly can be said that it derived its existence from a parental source. Yet peculiarly, these sons were naming themselves after the father-names of England and Europe; the sons did not, in these cases, break the line between old and new, established and innovating, but reached for known, traditional, distinguished, pedigreed names. And even after generations, when New England is not so new, the names continually remind and reinforce this derivativeness – this birth borrowed from ancient fathers and their cities. Any American traveller in Britain today will be amused to enter Boston and Manchester, Plymouth and Southampton.

English place-names are complemented by the names of royal persons – their heraldry and estates – another set of which identify American towns, for example in New York State, where kings, dukes and lords yield their titles to Albany (after King James VII of Scotland, *Alba* being Gaelic for Scotland) and the city of (New) York – renamed from New Amsterdam by King Charles II as a gift to his brother, the Duke of York. Meanwhile, names of ostensibly English origin are made native before they are adopted, as with the city of Rochester, which takes its name from a Virginia-born Revolutionary War soldier, and the city of Binghamton, which derives its name from a delegate to the Continental Congress, William Bingham. Rochester, though, was first the name of a town in Kent (notably, where Charles Dickens is said to have drawn inspiration for some of his novels), and Bingham is a town in Nottinghamshire. Still in the state of New York one finds a different cycle of names imported from ancient lands – from Greece and Italy (Ithaca, Athens, Sparta; Syracuse, Palermo, Naples, Florence, Rome (and its founder, Romulus), Genoa, Verona and Venice) – along with selected authors (Homer, Solon, Ovid, Virgil, Cato, Cicero, Cincinnatus and Scipio). More remotely one finds Jerusalem, Lebanon, Hebron, Cairo, Babylon and Eden. European sites were chosen as well: Amsterdam, Belfast, Dresden, Geneva, Ghent, Hanover, Lisle, Lyons (an English spelling of the French city), Paris and Waterloo. As American boundaries widened beyond New England and New York, the same rubric of naming practices were applied from other cultural predecessors. Native American tribal names (prevalent in New England and New York) – or Anglicized versions of them – were used from Niagara to the Natchez Trace and westward from Chicago (*Shikaakwa*) to Seattle (*Si'ahl*). French influence gave rise to New Orleans, and Spanish pedigree revealed a crescent of names along the west coast from San Francisco to San Diego, and eastward to Santa Fe and San Antonio.

All of these names – English and not – reference points and places of origin, if not for the founders, then for some other distant kin. One does not have to be a child of Rome, Italy to name a town in New York State, Rome or Romulus or even Italy. Unlike the English names that Emerson describes in 'Aristocracy' above, these New York State habits of naming – whether drawing from English lords or European capitals of culture – replicate a title without copying its referents. Naming a place Venice or Paris does not make it so. Are the names honourific – used to acknowledge and celebrate England and Europe?; aspirational – a reminder of what a city can become?; or a bid for continuity – established to draw some measure of the source city's grandness by quoted affiliation?

Emerson writes of the 'long descent of families and this cleaving through the ages to the same spot of ground' as creating the conditions for 'responsibleness'.[5] The English derive a moral norm from the relationship between names and places. In this respect, naming is an ethical act. The act involves recognizing – even creating – a connection between a place and a person, the way a human comes to life from the land as he does from his parents: emerging out of a native soil, forever marked by the place, inscribed by the particularity of the context. Naming in this sense is a performative act and summons a metaphysical transformation: the thing is named and then it exists. When a place is named it marks thereafter all who are born there; and where a person is born – and named – becomes a site sacred to the named. When the English speak of a man *from* Devonshire they could mean it literally, as Emerson writes suggestively in 'Aristocracy':

> The English lords do not call their lands after their own names, but call themselves after their lands; as if the man represented the country that bred him; and they rightly wear the token of the glebe that gave them birth; suggesting that the tie is not cut, but that there in London, – the crags of Argyle, the kail of Cornwall, the downs of Devon, the iron of Wales, the clays of Stafford, are neither forgetting nor forgotten, but know the man who was born by them, and who, like the long line of his fathers, has carried that crag, that shore, dale, fen, or woodland, in his blood and manners.[6]

The metaphorical 'tie' – a sort of perpetual umbilical connection – makes a child as beholden to the land as to his parents ('the long line of his father'; or his mother, as the child's blood is continually nourished by her). 'A susceptible man could not wear a name which represented in a strict sense a city or a county of England, without hearing in it a challenge to duty and honor'.[7] Attuned to his origins, the way he came from this or that place, makes the Englishman receptive – or perhaps vulnerable – to equivocating a town's name with his surname, assuming the literal senses of emerging from one's land of birth and thereafter carrying its traits and features in his 'blood and manners'. The idea of a hometown never seemed so intimate, reflecting its knowledge of bodies, its role as a telluric precondition for life, and its conjuring of the arterial relations between land, name, stock and familial blood. And so Mr Radcliffe will not just explain and defend himself, but his family's title, and the pride of the Red Cliffs where his whole clan claims its origins. Naming in this context is an act of continuity-making – from land to parent to child, in a 'long line of fathers', where 'the tie is not cut'. Naming is a way of identifying the bond that links these distinct manifestations of terrestrial and somatic life. The name forms a metaphysical amalgamation in the way blood forms a physical union.

3.   Emerson, 'Wealth'

   [...] and his English name and accidents are like a flourish of trumpets announcing him.[8]

4.   The English 'call themselves after their lands' whereas Americans borrow names from other places – import and apply them as so many de-contextualized labels. This

is not Ithaca, not Syracuse, until the name is naturalized – de-historicized – and finds its fashion after local custom.

England might be said to have a Wittgensteinian notion of naming since names emerge as if from the land; they are part of the surroundings and what it means to be involved in a form of life; names are habitations, and are used organically – continuously – to refer to the land and the people who live upon it. America, then, might be regarded as holding an Augustinian approach to naming, where names are words with their own realities. Borrowed from the English – and Native Americans, Spanish and French – names are affixed to places and persons without reference to source or generation. The English town of Waltham reflects its Saxon origins – *Walt Ham*, or woodland village – and was predated by Roman settlements; The American town of Waltham, outside Boston, neighbour to Cambridge, was named by people who remember England's Waltham. The nature of that naming holds its own intrigue: are the namers trying to create an unmistakable link with or lineage from a homeland (as one might in using a family name for one's newborn child)? Are they hoping to re-create a known place in an unknown land, for instance, to make the foreign America familiar by giving it familiar (English) names? Does this mean one could be from two Walthams? – the (English) Waltham of one's birth or ancestry and the (American) Waltham of one's lived experience? Are they borrowing some pedigree or prestige in order to make a new place attractive and substantial – as in Rome, New York; Paris, Texas; Cambridge, Massachusetts; or, Oxford, Mississippi?

As Augustine writes in the *Confessions* (and Wittgenstein quotes at the outset of the *Philosophical Investigations*): '[… A]s I heard words repeatedly used in their proper places in various sentences, I gradually learned to understand what objects they signified'.[9] Augustine's 'picture of language', as Wittgenstein understood it, reinforces the idea that 'Every word has a meaning. This meaning is correlated with the word. [And the meaning] is the object for which the words stands'. When someone asked Wittgenstein what the meaning of word is he would reply '– No such thing is in question here, only how the word […] is used'.[10]

The illustration of English versus American habits of naming places creates an occasion to reflect on Augustine's account and Wittgenstein's reading of it. It is, for example, eminently useful to refer to the land where a bridge strides the river Cam as Cambridge. And if a man should hail from a town named after its red cliffs, why not call him Mr Radcliffe? And so on. There is a practicality, a naturalness – even a literalness – in this approach to naming. Names are not artificially imposed on people, invented to represent an idea, or enlisted to acknowledge or honour an ancestor; rather names are expressed by the place, and then described by the observant in the course of everyday affairs. In England, one would be less likely to be embarrassed by an invented name since names appear to invent the people who use them. The Duke of Devonshire identifies both an aristocratic role and a geographical location; the man born to the title inhabits the name, like the land. He is a representative of the name – live in it and as it – until it is inherited by a further son of Devonshire. Individual personality may emerge from the context of the name, but the name awaits its representative.

In America individual personality and preference were founding values and as such informed the Founders' decision to write heraldry away – to disown it as an institution for the new land. Despite the novelty of this anti-aristocratic gesture, Wittgenstein might say it is Augustinian in nature, and for that reason 'primitive'.[11] America is not a place whose origins recede beyond the horizon of history. It is a land that is discovered and also invented. All inhabitants of the New World are immigrants; even natives arrived at some point; the myth of being first as being purer is undermined if there is no pre-eminence of stock, no hierarchy of inheritance. Finding a place is one thing and founding it is another; and in order to found a place one needs names – for orientation, for property, for institutions. The naming habits of seventeenth-century New England seem to reflect the immediate needs and exigencies of the community coupled with their imported vocabulary. Calling the place New England was the first indication that the place was seen as a child – as an intentional replication of the mother- and fatherland. Discovered places – often regardless of their actual characteristics of type and terrain – were treated as analogues to familiar places left behind. Naming this way proved a comfort, even as it might seem variously sentimental or braggadocious, and at times, ironical. The educated men of Cambridge University built homes and tilled fields on the banks of Charles River (drawing its name from an English king) as they founded Harvard College (named for an English alumnus of Emmanuel College at Cambridge University), and felt at ease naming their new American university town, Cambridge. The American practice of naming has been, and to a large extent still is, 'primitive' in this way: referential, treating names as legitimizing and explanatory labels drawn from other, more natural and established contexts.

Have these long-standing habits of naming made Americans more prone to what Wittgenstein called 'picture thinking'? In America the 'ostensive teaching of words' can be said to establish an association between the word and the thing'.[12] Among other effects, this may mean that when a word is uttered 'a picture of the object' may come to mind. For those founding a nation, or making claim to a new identity, an 'association' with something that is already well-founded, well-known, well-regarded and the like, may greatly aid one's ambitions for a creation that will survive, and perhaps flourish. Borrowing a name such as 'Cambridge' gives a place instant credibility well before the appearance of any bona fide credentials; it may also establish the conditions for embarrassment if the experiment falters or fails. In America, it would seem that the name comes first and the thing it represents second; a constitution is written for a nation that does not exist, then leaves us to learn how to live after the spirit and letter of the inscribed laws and legislations. In England, contrariwise, there is precedent enough to say that the place – and its name – is initial and the people derive themselves from it subsequently. The English live, notes Emerson, 'as if the man represented the country that bred him'.[13] Americans live as if the country represented the man who created it by naming it.

5.   Montaigne, *Of Names* (1580)

> Item, there is a saying that it is a good thing to have a good name, that is to say credit and reputation. But also, in truth, it is advantageous to have a handsome name and one that is easy to pronounce and retain, for thereby kings and grandees recognize us more easily and are less apt to forget us; and even with our own

servants, we more ordinarily call on and employ those whose names come easiest to the tongue.[14]

6.   Thinking further about the relationship, as Emerson puts it, between 'name and blood', one can ask what constitutes that bond, and whether, or how, it can be annulled or dissolved.[15] On the one hand, the English traditions of pedigree make it seem that a name and a family bloodline cohere naturally, as if logically suited to forming a mutually reinforcing pair. On the other hand, the American interruption of aristocratic culture – the insistence that 'all men are created equal' and have a 'unalienable right to life, liberty, and the pursuit of happiness' – makes it seem as if names can be *only* labels, things affixed or removed for the purposes of a dynamic democratic experience.

   In England, historically, one might say that blood is fate, and a name is a sign of that fate. Knowing a family name means knowing a lot. In America, by contrast, blood cannot be a source of knowledge beyond biographical interest. Blood may be a topic of historical interest, may orient readers to narratives and tropes that inform personal and familial identity, but it is not a category for moral determination or legal restriction. Blood cannot, for example, be used as evidence for anything that would count against a citizen's equal standing before or under the law, or his free and responsible pursuit of happiness. Blood as symbol, used in sober hours, has achieved a prevailing metaphorical status; when invoked as an excuse for literalism, remarks on blood are usually directed appropriately to the annals of gossip and rant.

7.   The practice of name-changing reflects habits and prejudices of both English and American cultures. In England one's title expands around the family name – encompassing it, not displacing it. A man of noble birth, in time, may become a Baron or a Duke or an Earl. And he is known as a Baron from some particular locale – a habit, as noted, that links the person with the place. Names such as Baron Chetwode, Duke of Northumberland and Earl of Pembroke, among many others, announce a rank and a location in each title. When knighted by royalty, a man's given name was sanctified by the authority of the church and the state. Though any free man could become a knight, elevated training expenses nearly insured that the honour would go to wealthy candidates. And since the wealthy tended to be from strong family lines – with distinguished names, titles and heraldry – the connection between a person and his land was arguably as strong as the connection between a person's name and his bloodline. In fact, historically when knights were paid for their services the remuneration came in the form of land, not currency.

   In America naming-giving and name-changing operate primarily on a criterion of choice and conception not descent from prior models and molds. Name-giving, for instance, can be disposed of honourifically as with Jefferson City, Missouri; Lincoln, Nebraska (which was renamed, albeit with considerable political contestation, after the President's assassination); or the nation's capital. Contrary to what Emerson observed – that 'The English lords do not call their lands after their own names, but call themselves after their lands' – these cities and lands are called after the names of men.[16] And if popular opinion or political will should have it, such places can be renamed: Lancaster becomes Lincoln, New Amsterdam cedes to New York. Columbus seeds the New World and afterwards we call it Columbia. These lands are anointed, as if in prayer, *in nomine Patris*... .

Furthermore, still in contrast with English custom, name-changing by persons in America is not delineated by the prerequisites of wealth and nobility: adopting a name may have little or nothing to do with the status of one's personal finances, and still less with one's relation to ancestry or real estate. One of the most prevalent narratives of name-changing (and name-creating) in America derives from accounts of the way names were handled, or mishandled, at Ellis Island during pronounced waves of immigration in the late nineteenth and early twentieth centuries. A name misheard was misspelled. By virtue of poor translation or transcription, a family just arrived in America would begin legal status as Americans under a new name – perhaps sonically similar but graphically distinct from the name carried at sea, and from the homeland. If the ancestral name survived intact, however, it might later be changed for other reasons: to improve the chances of assimilation and expand opportunities for education; to make the daily experience of using one's name more efficient, more intelligible, or a practical asset for business (in the spirit of Montaigne's remark that 'it is advantageous to have a handsome name and one that is easy to pronounce and retain'); and even to create or capture some new aesthetic significance (such as when actors, artists and musicians take on a stage name). In some cases, a changed surname might reflect a person's faith in a mythical notion of a neutral American identity – a name that does not immediately or overwhelming proclaim one's origins with every invocation; aiming for a kind of originless position, the practice might involve adopting a popular, well-known name (that hides its origins because of its prevalence), or Anglicizing a name imported from some land beyond the British Isles. Such stresses and strains at harmonizing one's immigrant self to the perceived archetypes of a new land highlight how the very notion – or fantasy – of assimilation may indicate that one possesses a preformed idea of a standard or an identity one wants to be aligned with, known by, or recognized as. But such standards change. And the group one desires to join – to be taken for – may slip out of power or favour or influence. To assimilate, then, always requires a bold commitment to affiliate. The achievement of assimilation is not a uniform good yielding a fixed identity; rather, it is a status that demands vigilant, endless reassessment.

The names and name-changes of film actors provide a clinic on aspects of immigrancy, association, affiliation, assimilation and the aspiration for 'a good name', in Montaigne's rendering, 'a handsome name and one that is easy to pronounce and retain', that 'comes easiest to the tongue'.[17] The motivations that animate an actor's decision to change his or her name are varied and complex, but there are some shared *effects* of such reconfigurations: a newly created or chosen name may have pleasing aesthetic resonances or cultural references; it may improve the actor's alliances with other admired figures. The contemporary prevalence of names of international origin suggests that we would be equally compelled by the acting of Walter Matuschanskayasky, Issur Danielovitch Demsky, Thomas Mapother IV, Ramon Estevez, Marion Morrison,

Allan Konigsberg and Archibald Leach, but before we could be, they changed their names to Walter Matthau, Kirk Douglas, Tom Cruise, Martin Sheen, John Wayne, Woody Allen and Cary Grant. The threat of racism (including anti-Semitism) inspired some actors to change their names, while aspirations, admiration, shame or vanity seem to have driven others (for example, Cary Grant is said to have invented his name by beginning with the initials of marquee actors Clark Gable and Gary Cooper). We are not in a position to say *a priori* if a given or a stage name will prove more advantageous; cultural norms and circumstances, as the brief list above attests, appear to greatly inform one's chances and one's choices. We would likely be as engaged by Ruby Stevens as Barbara Stanwyck, or by Gladys Greene as Jean Arthur.

While the foregoing is meant to be a partial and provisional query into the phenomenon of the names one chooses to replace given names, the prior – maybe even the primary – interest here is in the mere fact, or act, of changing the name: what it says about who one is (ethically, epistemically, ontologically); what one thinks one does or achieves by making this change (does the self survive a name-change or is it changed as well?); and in consequence, what name-changing entails for self-understanding and for being known by others.

The display of ethnicity and racial origins in one's name has, in the course of cultural liberalization, become a point of pride in tandem with its diminution as a liability. A more widespread loyalty to the original spelling of traditional ethnic names has the effect of collectively shifting attention away from the national (with its specific histories of founding, origins and mythic incarnations of primogeniture) and toward the international, thereby reinforcing the virtues of the transnational, and even instigating consideration of the post-national. The evolution of ethnic and racial identity implied by names continues to interact with shifting cultural norms, and naming trends suggest that the proliferation – and emphasis – of ethnic and racial difference has undermined long-standing habits of perceiving inherent value in names. Consequently, hierarchies and lineages are increasingly discredited as the basis for legitimate appeals to authority.

8.   William Shakespeare, *Coriolanus*

> COMINIUS: Yet one time he did call me by my name:
> I urged our old acquaintance, and the drops
> That we have bled together. Coriolanus
> He would not answer to: forbad all names;
> He was a king of nothing, titleless,
> Till he had forged himself a name o' the fire
> Of burning Rome.[18]

9.   Can we go so far as to say that a name-change bespeaks a metaphysical change for the attributed object – be it land or a person? Is this a kind of divination suggesting – or confirming – that a name has an *effect* on the named? Already at work is the long-standing practice of passing on a surname from father to child. The anointed name

marks the child, partly, as a confirmation of paternity: this is the child of this father. As part of the sweep of this nomination, a family is generated by or coalesces around the shared name, and over time a faith develops that the name holds the family together – ties the child to the parent, perhaps especially to the *pater familias*. What happens, then, when a child changes his or her surname? Is the daughter newly married less bound or beholden to her family or father because she replaced her maiden name with the surname of her husband? Is the son who changes his surname somehow detached from his father as if the name-change also signaled a change in blood – a switch in heredity, a shift in paternity? In both cases, the name-change is a function of choice: the child has the freedom to decide what to do with the surname – to retain, alter or expunge it. The choice is fundamentally about the idea of creating a new life; at certain angles, this form of self-nomination could be listed as a type of performative utterance – an act of speech that generates a new set of conditions and relations. Still, the child may debate: What is the significance of one's given – that is, inherited – surname? Does one need a new name in order to metamorphose into a new person? What exactly would a new name be a sign of? If it is a sign for someone other than oneself, is the new name a metonym or a pseudonym for the former name/identity? Or is one's identity consistent from name to name – thereby suggesting that such surnames (given and chosen) are synonymous? Is taking on a new name – for whatever reason, for stage and screen, at the Port Authority, on the occasion of a marriage – part of a faith in a more evolved version of oneself, or perhaps another life altogether (variously in terms of being reborn, or born again)? People sometimes say of their youth: I was a different person then. Is a new birth possible because of a new name, or does blood ensure that continuity prevails? What is the significance of one's claim to a new life (for oneself) – by way of a new name – if one remains bound by blood to one's former self?

The person who has changed his or her name wonders and worries about the status of what was done before the name change. How does the person with the new name have a claim to the thoughts and actions of the former life – the life lived under the banner of a different, now absent, title? Why is one inclined to say 'former' here instead of the same life under a different name? Changing one's name can seem an act of dispossession: a denial of one's family, of one's conduct, of one's education, of the various acts that together helped one comprehend the meaning and continuity of personal identity; in some contexts, a change of name may appear to be a fugitive act – an attempt to flee from one's history, or even the law or debts. Still, for some agents, the radical quality of the act of name-changing may be the very point, even if it is legally sanctioned or culturally expected: at its extreme, displacing the given name may be an act of willful aggression against a former self, or a family – a desire to be cleared (cleaned, absolved, exculpated, exonerated; made blameless and pure; rendered unblemished, uncensurable, and beyond reproach), to achieve dissociation, to be guiltless and without stain or defilement or sin. With a new name, the person can feel as distant from the life under the former name as from another person; yet even in, or perhaps understandably because of, such liberation, one may register a kind of trauma of separation and loss. One risks becoming unknown to oneself because all that was familiar, all that felt permanently self-possessed, seems abandoned; and since most legal barriers to name-changing are superficial, the name-change itself can feel nonchalant – a relinquishment of something so dear, so essential, yet given up with such ease. And in the new state one has a new name but nothing to claim *for* it or *from* it. In this respect the person with a new name resembles an infant: a new being in the world, freshly named, and presented to human experience anew.

Taking on a new name can make one feel that one has created a ghost, given birth to a ghost of his or her former self. One might think of the discharged name as the name one used to use to know oneself as one's own; it was the name that all experience referenced and fell under. Now that one does not claim that name, the things one knew as one's own seem foreign, part of the experience of some other person – seemingly the ghost of oneself – a spectre, who identifies with the name, as if animated in parallel, haunting the fringes of consciousness and the very precincts of personal identity.

10.   Yet does not the life and work of someone who has changed her name remain tied – inexorably – to her despite her name-change, just as the blood of the father flows in the daughter who has changed her name upon marrying? Is there a fitting analogy to be considered in cases of geographical re-description and the processes involved in nation-building by acts of nation-naming?

With examples such as the creation or invention of the modern Italian Republic – aggregated by Garibaldi from disparate provinces on the Italian peninsula and islands off its coast – and the Union of Soviet Socialistic Republics, we find name attribution that is part of a process of political ascription, an effort to re-conceive a land and its people. But in these two cases the ethnic, religious and linguistic composition of these republics is, even while acknowledging points of regional distinction, comparatively homogeneous when contrasted with the more extreme religious, linguistic and ethnic differences found in Bosnia, Iraq, Israel and Sudan. In the later cases, drawing up new maps, declaring political alliances and framing novel topographical unions can matter little to centuries-old prejudices, abiding religious incompatibilities and other conceptual antagonisms. In cases where religious, ethnic and linguistic differences are more pronounced – seemingly permanent, ossified by years of conflict that reinforce differences – the notion that a new name has the power to confer a metaphysical trans-formation appears a naïve prospect. In effect, in such cases, the new name would seem but a metaphor for an aspiration of something like, for example, political coherency, religious toleration and mutual empowerment. Can the same be said for the individual who drafts a new name for herself upon emigrating to a new land, or adopts one for himself upon marrying? Is self-naming a reflection of hope – a way of creating a space where a new kind of life might emerge and be referred to? In this way, the naming and re-naming of nations, families, and persons are coordinate enterprises of imagination.

In the geopolitical definitions of Italy and Russia, we see that what we *call* a thing and what a thing *is* are both under negotiation, and depend on the assent of language users and their allegiances. In this fashion, objective or material or topographical status and identity are often understood in terms of names. Geographical boundaries and political federations provide ample evidence of the creative and affective force of naming as a constitutive (and destructive) phenomenon. In America each state that joined or was added to the union demanded geographical definition and a name; boundaries became a condition for the identity of statehood. Naturally space-defining topographical features were enlisted – rivers, bays, mountains, forests – as were the political and historical claims that gave shape to open prairies and vast wildernesses. Meanwhile the union absorbed each new-state-as-political-entity and consolidated the evolving amalgamation under a single, unchanging name: the United States of America. As the naming of countries, states and cities illustrates, at any a given moment what we call a thing and what a thing is can be understood as unified and stable, and yet at some other time, we seem capable of amending our judgement about what a thing is by calling it by some other name – as if a mental or metaphysical decision could transform material reality, as if an act of nomination can issue a new state of affairs: a place known anew under a new name.

One seems to know what the shape of a thing is, what name it has, and what its limits are. But then something stirs – an inner or outer revolution, a momentum for reform, an idea that demands a political or material response – and then, somewhere between a slow transformation and a sudden revolt, the shape is different, the name is different, and once known and familiar limits become historical facts, displaced by newly reformed realities. Such an account seems equally applicable to countries as persons. A name is a phenomenon that holds reality together until one decides to change reality.

11.   Henry David Thoreau, *Journal* (1851)

> I am pleased to read in Stoever's Life of Linnæus (Trapp's translation) that his father, being the first learned man of his family, changed his family name and borrowed that of Linnæus (Linden-tree-man) from a lofty linden tree which stood near his native place, – 'a custom', he says, 'not unfrequent in Sweden, to take fresh appelations from natural objects'. What more fit than that the advent of a new man into a family should acquire for it, and transmit to his posterity, a new patronymic? It is refreshing to get to a man whom you will not be satisfied to call John's son or Johnson's son, but a new name applicable to himself alone, he being the first of his kind. Get yourself therefore a name, and better a nickname than none at all. There was one enterprising boy came to school to me whose name was 'Buster', and an honorable name it was. He was the only boy in the school, to my knowledge, who was named.[19]

12.   The American philosopher Stanley Cavell has written, in maturity, of his experience changing his surname when he was 16. Training early as a musician, and only later coming to professional philosophy, Cavell's account of his name-changing instantiates a rare opportunity to hear someone philosophize about the transformation – or is it translation? – from one appellation to another.

After graduating from high school, Cavell, then known by his birth name Stanley Goldstein, was in a music band that allowed him, as he relates in *A Pitch of Philosophy: Autobiographical Exercises* (1994), to 'experiment with giving myself stage names'.[20] The effect of the experimentation was that 'sometimes the change of name felt like wanting to know what difference it would make if I did not simply announce my Jewishness by my name. Sometimes, and increasingly, it felt like a desire to know anonymity […]'.[21] In his diaristic memoir *Little Did I Know: Excerpts from Memory* (2010), Cavell reflects (parenthetically) on how the means by which he achieved anonymity 'was to change my name'.[22] In the following case, as for so many others in *Little Did I Know*, Cavell allows – and occasionally invites – a personal, autobiographical moment to rise to the level of philosophical significance; and in this elevation gives a private anecdote credence for public thinking about names and naming, the nature of mind and action, and the quality of identity and ascription:

> (The classical empiricists pictured the newly born mind as a tabula rasa, a blank slate thereupon to be filled with impressions. If you think further of the mind as perpetually yet incompletely being erased or as shedding or shunning impressions, say, as becoming modified by what it is you are impressed by or unimpressed by, you may picture it not as the latest in a succession of states expanding upon following the one you are born with but as one you may be reborn into, a set not of facts but of acts.)[23]

Cavell's self-described 'search for a life I could want, not merely endure' was registered in this act of effacement – an act that also perhaps registers a wish for self-generated renewal. Decades after the fact – or act – of renaming himself, and following nearly a lifetime lived under a stage name, Cavell says it achieved 'for me, the experience of reentering the world unknown to the world, the freedom to perceive without position, as if behind the mask of rebirth'.[24] Despite their differences and disagreements, Cavell remarks laconically that his name change became 'a mark of sameness' between him and his father, 'since now, like him, I would bear a name I was not born with'.[25] And so both men – Kavelieruskii become Goldstein, and Goldstein become Cavell – lived under self-appointed names, names that inscribed aspects of their constituted and contingent self-creation.[26]

13.   In changing his name, Cavell did not want to achieve mere neutrality, but a kind of invisibility. The desire to avoid announcing or declaring one's race (often coupled with ethnicity and religion) by saying one's name could only be addressed as Cavell did, as so many others, because of the capacity of words – and perhaps especially names – to distinctively possess and perspicuous display (the apparent) traits of race. The name comes attached with its inherited referents, and reaches out to lands, peoples and their histories. The linguistic marking of a racially identifiable name, then, must be distinguished from the ineluctable biological traits of race at the level of cartilage and skin, and at the level of genetic encoding. The name, like skin pigment, carries culture and value – referents that may transform or disturb one's everyday experience – but the name can be changed in a way that biological attributes cannot. The invisibility Cavell sought was not the sort suffered, for example, by the protagonist of Ralph Ellison's most celebrated novel.

For architect Frank Gehry something summoned him in 1952 aged 23 – we may presume something more than his then-wife's insistence – to change his surname from Goldberg to Gehry. Was Gehry's motivation, like Cavell's, part of a desire for the sort of racial elision 'Gehry' achieved in place of 'Goldberg' – as 'Cavell' eclipsed 'Goldstein'?[27] For German filmmaker Werner Herzog, his decision for a self-appointed name-change seems more lyrical than Gehry's – even though it entailed recovering his father's name and displacing his mother's maiden name. As Herzog tells it: 'Herzog means "duke" in German and I thought there should be someone like Count Basie or Duke Ellington making films' – and so Werner Stipetić, then a 16–year old Bavarian teenager, became Werner Herzog.[28] (At the time, did young Werner know that Duke Ellington changed his name from Edward Kennedy?)

Another scenario of name-changing might find a teenager or young adult trying to deny or flee the associations of his inherited name as a means of subverting or overcoming his normalcy – absorbed in a fantasy that an invented or newly assigned name might launch him from anonymity to fame; might enable a way to use the name for greater prominence or control – not less, that is, not for anonymity and other forms of oblivion; might register a distinctive difference from homogenizing norms and patterns of names and their connotations. The English photographer Edward Muybridge said as much when he told his grandmother of his plans to emigrate to America: 'I'm going to make a name for myself. If I fail, you will never hear of me again'.[29] And make a name he did – in a double sense – since Muybridge was born Muggeridge, changed it to Muygridge in the 1850s upon emigrating to the United States and settled on the name Muybridge in the 1860s.[30] As Rebecca Solnit has said: 'his several rearrangements of his own name suggest how consciously he was crafting a self, how ardently desiring to be someone'.[31] And as Edward became Eadweard late in life, so the renaming persisted posthumously, for his tombstone reads Maybridge. The teenager or young adult who awkwardly flails about trying desperately to know himself, perhaps countermanding the authority of parents and mentors as part of such an experiment, might assume a new (or provocative) name as a bid for enhanced power – maybe even as a penalty against the name-givers who have defined him, however innocently; the teenager or young adult aims to exhibit some control over a life that he so anxiously wants to know as his own – and be known for. Cavell's discovery is different.

Cavell relates a story his father told him about the day he arrived at Ellis Island. 'Goldstein was not the family's proper name but was dealt it by an immigration officer on their arrival in New York in 1905'.[32] Cavell's father was 16 when he arrived in America, and once Cavell asked him how he knew his date of birth (since records in his European shtetl could be imprecise): 'He told me that when the immigration officer asked him for his birth date, he replied that it happened to be that very day'.[33] When the widespread practice of immigrants receiving new – or distorted – names at Ellis Island is not told with an air of patriotic or aspirational sentimentality, it is often underwritten by regret, even injustice – as if something important was lost in the transition from the old world, wherever it might be, to the new. In the case of Cavell's father, we hear an apocryphal story where the immigrant seems to understand the stakes of what is happening to him, and involves himself in the creative moment he has submitted himself to. The immigration officer, perhaps without the intent to dissolve a family name, makes and marks the origin of this man in his newly adopted country; and yet by assigning the name Goldstein, the officer, identifies the man racially, ethnically, religiously – though one may assume that Goldstein announced its Jewishness more or less as much as the name the father arrived with. In this scene of bureaucratic gestation and linguistic labour, the officer acts with authority and definitiveness – as a man, seemingly, with the power to create men. There is no consultation or negotiation with the immigrant, just a declaration. We seem to be witnessing a site of birthing, the officer acting as a parent to the infant American. How better to acknowledge one's self-consciousness at this transformative moment than to declare it one's day of birth? This fact alone can distinguish the immigrant from the babe: the immigrant knows what day it is, and is present for the beginning of his (new) existence, his rebirth under a new name.

One day in 1935 the young Stanley Goldstein was walking with his father in Sacramento when his father 'cried out with astonishment, "That's our name! Cavalier!"'[34] The name was painted on a large plate-glass window of his brother's pawn shop. The father explained that the name derived from Cavalerskii (or Cavaleriiskii) – in *Little Did I Know*, further obscuring clarity of precise origins, at least as they are rendered by names, Cavell writes Kavelieruskii (or Kavelieriskii)[35] – and appeared to be so delighted with seeing the family name prominently displayed that he said: 'It's the same'. As proud and knowing as father Goldstein was upon arriving in America, here he is overwhelmed by an occluding sentimentality, unwilling or unable to recognize the way an immigrant name was made to fit an American idiom. But then the father's perception of synonymity grants its own, distinctive, insight – namely that he experienced his wide and disparate experience as continuous, as part of an identifiable progression from Eastern European to American Southerner to Californian. Privately, in his own eyes, given his own capacities for translation, the names were his own – despite their variant spellings.

And one could hardly hope for a name that so evocatively announced its relation to the icon of the American West – the horse – in every instantiation. 'A man must ride alternately on the horses of his private and his public nature', Emerson writes in 'Fate'.[36] (Years earlier, in 'The Poet', Emerson remarked: '[I]n every word he speaks he rides on them as the horses of thought'.[37]) Emerson's image is an analogy drawn from Plato's *Phaedrus* where the allegory of the chariot characterizes the nature of the human soul. Socrates says the soul is comprised of 'the natural union of a team of winged horses and their charioteer'. The gods have two good and beautiful horses, while the rest of us have but one good and beautiful horse, and another that is neither.[38] And yet Cavell's writing – to reference another family name he might have adopted – is cavalier only in so far as it measures his faith in intellectual adventure. The work avoids being haughty or supercilious because it is motivated by gallant aspirations for philosophical prose, in part, a project that demands a person's (a writer's, a citizen's) awareness and acknowledgment of another person – both in speech and in action. One sub-definition of the word suggests that a cavalier may also be a man acting as a partner in dancing; given Cavell's commitment to the legacy of Fred Astaire for the history of philosophy, the etymological trace serves up an unexpectedly fitting association.

The name Cavell, admittedly, also bears a graphic resemblance and sonic resonance with cavil – the making of petty or unnecessary objections – and as such the latter name might be taken as a humorous, ironic gloss on the seriousness, personal investment and consequentiality of Cavell's prose. Cavil features prominently in Burton's *The Anatomy of Melancholy*, and is defined by the *OED* as 'a captious, quibbling, frivolous objection', 'a flout, gibe, jeer', and speech aimed 'to mock, jest, rail'.[39] These definitions suggest that the meaning of cavil is precisely at odds with the kind of writing – the tone and pitch of his work – Cavell has created. Cavil and Cavell are antonyms. Meanwhile, an account should be given – or added – for the relation of the name Cavell to the Yiddish kvelling – the present particle of kvell – which is defined as an expression of happiness and pride. Perhaps cavil and kvell, in their differences, in their antagonisms and oppositions, are horses upon which the name Cavell – and its name-bearer – can ride upon alternately.

Cavell chose neither to reclaim Cavalerskii, or its several variants, from his father and European ancestors, nor to appropriate the current family usage at the pawn shop, Cavalier. Instead, he says: 'In my later ecstatic improvisation, erasing and transfiguring my identity, I took the first two syllables as more fittingly reticent than, and again different from, the first three (which was the form adopted by those other family members). Whatever escapes I was frantically contriving, I have from then on taken it as an obligation with each new acquaintance to let my origins show [...]'.[40] Cavell depicts the radical contingency of how he came to his new name, not just the chance that his family would visit Sacramento at this point in his life and discover therein a lost or translated family name, but also the deliberateness of his creative emendation of the names he had before him. In this moment of 'improvisation' (a fitting activity for a jazz musician) we find Cavell riffing on names, perhaps studying variations on them, and judging them for their rhythm, associations and typographical styles. Importantly, too, the achievement of the name that offered some anonymity, some effacement (of his Jewish roots), also created the conditions for his need to confess – to announce – his origins. Now that his ethnicity was not evident in his name, he felt compelled to share and show it.

Cavell's 'escapes', as he put it, had to do primarily with the perennial phenomenon of children leaving home after graduation from high school, and the variety of options any given American teenager might have (or, at least, entertain). In 1942 the young Cavell considered joining a travelling band, or joining the navy in order to attend college. Yet even as Cavell had chosen, or achieved for himself, a name that did not (or did not seem to him) to disclose his racial or ethnic origins, he relates that he felt an obligation to let his origins show in some other way – by describing experience, say, or invoking other names that cue or configure his relatedness to a people and a history.

Choosing the name Cavell, while sudden, still contains an evolution, a process that reflects the movement away from explicit racial identification to seeming racial anonymity. How does one find or make such a name? In this case, Cavell jettisoned the name of his immediate family, Goldstein – the name his father was given upon arriving in America, and the name his parents thereafter bore and passed on to the infant Stanley. And the 16-year old Cavell (or, more precisely, Goldstein) is not moved by nostalgia to adopt the earlier version of the European family name (Cavalerskii) or the form used by the California family (Cavalier) – as a bid for recovering family roots in the distant past or the shared present – but instead determines to render his own name, his own syllables, his own spelling: Cavell.

In letting go of Goldstein and improvising on Cavalerskii and Cavalier, Cavell achieves multiple and conflicting things: he denies his association with the Jewish name his parents were assigned upon their arrival in America; he acknowledges his European heritage, and the name of his distant Jewish ancestors, by inventing or improvising a name based on the etymology of a name used by kin of preceding generations; he parallels the actions of his California relatives (his uncle, for example) by dropping Goldstein in favour of a name that derives, if obliquely, from the European family – instead of asking for or adopting a name arbitrarily generated by government or immigration; and also, Cavell parallels the act of transforming the European family name to his specific preference (as his uncle did in conjuring Cavalier out of Cavalerskii).

In the context of his autobiographical exercises, Cavell means to claim or imply that with a name such as Cavell he does not announce his Jewish origins the way he might with a name such as Goldstein or Cavalerskii. And yet, arguably, given the unique history of his appropriation of the European family name, he announces his Jewish origins more with the name Cavell than with the name Goldstein – as the act of suppression or repression may call attention to itself. What sort of name is Cavell anyway? Goldstein might be taken as a vestige – a remnant name that retains its Jewish resonance without confirming that one is solely or strictly Jewish; after all, unless the mother is Jewish, the child is not.

Though Cavell did not fully reclaim one of the European spellings of the family name, just as his uncle did not, Cavell's improvisation can seem like an homage to distant Eastern European ancestors, and in that respect read as a particularly American way of preserving and honouring the traditions one has left behind – or that one never knew. Such reclamation and revision is an imaginative act of continuity-making between ancestor and inheritor – but after an American fashion that resists pure or undiluted adoption in favour of radical transformation informed by personal idiosyncrasies, political and social context, and the need – since the scene of American Independence and up to the innovations of jazz – to rethink the structure, method and content of inherited forms.

Cavell's improvisation on a European pedigree seems part of the history of American invention – its reliance on tradition while remaking it. And yet, though the spirit of that double-movement may instantiate a natural and self-evident truth for any American identity – like an unalienable right or feature – it can also seem like a transgression of some profound, unassumed, unknown law. On the occasion of legally changing his name from Goldstein to Cavell, he reports: 'I was soon to discover that judges, not alone parents, need a reason to grant the petition to change your name, and a reason for the name you wish to change it to'.[41] While a reason needs to be presented for the consideration of the court, one's current name is published in a newspaper for several weeks prior to the proceeding, alongside one's proposed name, listed as a petition, and submitted to the wider knowledge of the public. The petition accompanies a notice alerting the public to the 'jeopardized' name in case there are any outstanding debts that the person might have incurred and owe. (Commonly there are addenda making sure the petitioner is not attempting to escape liabilities such as loans or injunctions on conduct, such as an assigned prison sentence). Cavell says of himself, on the verge of submitting his petition to the court: 'I began to know or know that I knew that the deed of declaring a name, or making a name, or any questioning of your identity, was being linked with criminality, forged together with it'.[42] One is not born with a name but it feels that way. A 'given' name, after years of use, feels natural, and so any plan or pledge to replace it seems a violation of a natural law or a natural order. Cavell's petition, while free of pecuniary or penitential debts, still felt wrong – like an elision of a reality or a duty. The court seems to say one *can* change one's name, but why. Coming up with a reason to accompany one's right can be unnerving, unsettling, as if one were asked to account for something as essential – as familiar and yet as indescribable – as one's identity. As Cavell notes in *A Pitch of Philosophy*: 'The first guilt is being the one you are'.[43] In *Little Did I Know*, Cavell returns to the newspaper scene and the question of how one might enumerate sufficient and legitimate claims for the right to disown or displace one name in order to take on a new one: 'I don't know when I came to sense that a reasonably accurate account of such causes would have, or should have, filled the columns and sections of a major Sunday newspaper every day for ninety days, proposing an absolute autobiography'.[44]

In passing one's petition, the court does not seem to liberate – or forgive – but rather to make one's apparent violation a matter of legal fact. 'Quite as if the reason for being singled out with a name were not just to be traceable in case of wrongdoing', Cavell writes, 'but before that, as its ground, to serve notice that identifiable actions, deeds, the works of human beings, are the source of identity, and consequently constitute identity through accusation – all doing known as wrongdoing. [...] So we are originally sinners'.[45] Changing one's name reminds us of the fact that a sinner goes up to the limit of the law, and then goes past it. When the gavel slams down and the judgement permitting the change is ratified, one cannot help but feel beholden to the newly appointed laws governing one's being, whether they are understood as contingent or not. A nervous shock spreads, and one believes some kind of miracle has been enacted – as if having transgressed natural laws while remaining intact, upright. Standing alone (anew) and standing for oneself; being a representative on one's own behalf. If one's name was not, after all, a sign of a natural fact, then what else can be changed? How much more can one do to become oneself? Do these speech acts – that performatively constitute new facts – name the world differently so that it may be lived differently? In that moment one may feel as Emerson did standing in front of the Cabinets of Natural History in Paris: 'The limits of the possible are enlarged, & the real is stranger than the imaginary'. When he came to incorporate this journal passage into the public lecture 'The Uses of Natural History' (1833) Emerson added a response to feeling 'moved by strange sympathies': 'I say I will listen to this invitation'.[46] What does that cabinet of specimens – all of them with assigned names – summon in us? Is their display an invitation to imagine one's own placement in a similar arrangement?

Perhaps the encounter occasions an awareness of one's own strange status as a future member of the cabinet – and for the time being, as an agent who can perceive relations, who – in the spirit and practice of the naturalist – can name things. Even oneself.

Changing one's given name to one's declared name inaugurates the conditions for feeling that one no longer really knows the line between the natural and the divine, the necessary and the contingent; the cues of transgression move or perish; sin becomes an undisclosed variable. A threshold appears to have been crossed, prompting an anxiety, as Cavell describes it, 'marked by the seam across my life figured in my change of name'.[47] Unlike many life-defining, identity-making moments, this threshold is peculiar because it is made by choice, not by parental or divine intervention: calling oneself by a name feels different than being given or bestowed a name (or existence) by another. One feels simultaneously empowered by the fact that a name can be changed (self-chosen, self-appointed) and distraught that what one believed was so stable, so real – perhaps even natural – was in fact a matter of little more than the effect of habit: something held together by a private and collective activity, an effect of intentional application instead of assured by some existential condition or metaphysical reality. Names are customarily, understandably, felt and believed to be fixed because they are given (granted, confirmed, consecrated, christened, anointed), and thereafter, so often, retain a presence or pretense of indissoluble permanency; but the givenness of the name is, under a different aspect, the very clue to the provisionality of names – that since they are assigned they can be decommissioned, replaced or reconfigured.

Once a new name is declared, and made legal, it is hard to predict how the unsettling of one's given name for the imposition of another (chosen name) will affect the agent (who is at once the instigator of the change, and the subject of its effect). Perhaps she will revel in her anonymity and attempt to sustain the oblivion of the just-birthed signifier as long as she can; not forgetting, though, that her physical form remains prominent evidence indifferent to the name-change; she may be recognized by her face without any knowledge of a shift in appellation. Or perhaps she will scramble to find some way of stabilizing the adopted name, as if its survival or her own depended on a new, conscious effort at publicity – a novel and notorious anointing that will reinforce the fixedness of the freshly engraved title. In this tremulous transition – a liminal phase in which she appears to move from one life to another – anonymity (in the form of the unknownness or unfamiliarity of her new name) can make her feel altogether nameless: not just newly named, but without one. And namelessness, in the wake of her replacement of the established name, amounts to nothing less than nonexistence. Or rather, in a braver moment, new existence; like a baby, she has to do everything for the first time. Yet being born anew in her new name suggests a difference: that she does everything for the first time *again*.

For some, the sheer written and spoken repetition of a birth-name naturalizes it, makes it invisible – an unseen condition of identity. The forgetfulness that given names are in fact given, however, prompts consideration of how being newly named, or renamed, charges the occasion with the significance of choosing a suitable metaphor for oneself. A new surname, for instance, may function as a conduit for bringing things – attributes, qualities, associations – to the person, as if by a self-generated (endogenous) or privately engineered inheritance. Even as the birth name is under threat and eventually displaced, one feels compelled to create promising conditions for the power and authority of the new surname, as Cavell writes: 'My choice [of name] has more than a touch in it of the myth of the secret name – even of radical propriety, of the name owned before the name is given [...]'.[48] That propriety, though, was initially 'a furtive legitimacy', as one might expect it must be.[49] In the days and weeks leading up to the court hearing, the claimant (or is it defendant?) may ask whether in disowning one's given name one is not somehow killing oneself off. What sort of identity can one have after one's name is gone? Is the act of name-changing a manifestation of self-loathing, shame, trauma, in brief, a metaphysical form of suicide? When one reports to others on the name-change, will they – like the judge – ask for a reason; and if given one, will they also judge, perhaps preternaturally convinced that one must be guilty for such a breach of what seems natural. Trends of reception alter this narrative; the bride who is not given but *takes* her bridegroom's name as her own is part of an undulating history of valuation. Yet Cavell – as a teenager inventing and claiming a name, however much a name may reference a bona fide ancestry – would be likely to experience his legitimacy as furtive, since the authority of the new name is not inherited, not evident, and thus a kind of secret. The name-changer may be emboldened by the need or purpose of a new name aside from any tradition or social expectation, such as with the regularly displaced maiden name of the bride, and yet – when pressed for reasons, when asked to give an account for the change – the name-changer may feel guilt that his stipulation sounds rather more like a confession of wrongdoing – intimating a sin, a transgression of nature – than a narration of self-constitution.

14.   In his final year at Harvard College, 1821, Emerson chose to be known by his middle name, Waldo. Joel Porte suggests a practical explanation for the decision: that since 'there were so many Ralphs in his family' he needed a more distinctive moniker.[50] Yet there were several Waldos in the family line dating back centuries, instances when Waldo is the first name or the surname: Edward Emerson Waldo was the grandfather of Joseph Emerson, born in 1700, who sired a son named Waldo in 1735.[51] Regardless of uniqueness or repetitions, the name Waldo announces its associations and resonances, those that would be especially well-known to the son and grandson of Protestant ministers. The name cascaded through generations, finding a conspicuous heir in Peter Waldo, the twelfth-century founder of an early pre-Protestant sect – the Waldensians – a group that, according to some, derived its name from him as well. Though Peter Waldo met with Pope Alexander III, and made a defence of his and his followers' faith, the sect was condemned by Pope Lucius III and spent centuries being persecuted before joining the Genevan branch of the Protestant Reformation. As Emerson knew these names and influences, and as he prepared for his own part in the ecclesiastical history of the family, he returned to Ralph – lecturing and then publishing under his full tripartite name. Yet in the month after the publication of *Nature*, October 1836, his first child was born, and for his first son he chose the name Waldo.

15.   Melville, *Moby-Dick*, 'The Masthead' (1851)

> He called it the SLEET's CROW's-NEST, in honour of himself; he being the original
> inventor and patentee, and free from all ridiculous false delicacy, and holding that
> if we call our own children after our own names (we fathers being the original
> inventors and patentees), so likewise should we denominate after ourselves any
> other apparatus we may beget.[52]

16.   Boris Pasternak, *Dr Zhivago* (1957)

> For an instant the meaning of existence was again revealed to Lara. She was here
> – so she conceived – in order to see into the mad enchantment of the earth, and
> to call everything by name, and if that was beyond her strength, then, out of love
> for life, to give birth to her successors, who would do it in her place.[53]

17.   Cavell's experience of self-appointed naming affords the generous conditions
for thinking further about ways in which one takes on a name, for example, when an
adopted name is a cover – a means of hiding – or otherwise divides authority between
the name and named. Some of the rituals and practices employed to establish, and
occasionally mask, personal identity reveal our tacit acceptance that what a thing is
bears a deep relation to what a thing is called; but in Cavell's case such nominations
complicate our sense of the relationship between a work of art (as a thing) and its
author: what if the author is also a work of art? Not just where one's life is a work of art
in a Nietzschean sense, but where authorship itself is distinguished from the author, as
with Kierkegaard's deliberate use of pseudonyms, and the authors those pseudonyms
are said to represent?

Names, metonyms, metaphors and pseudonyms are signs that may contain, or
connote, a wide variety of intellectual and emotional associations, and so often they
coalesce into symbols of remarkable sentimental power. Simply seeing a name can
unleash an intensely affective reaction, at different turns full of attraction or repulsion.
At such times one wants to say that hearing, seeing or inscribing a name casts a spell –
as if summoning forces in speech or print. And since, or while, beholden to the occult
influence of names, one's effort to account for that presence often eludes satisfying
description. The very thing one wishes to speak of, to write about, leaves one wordless.

Cavell's autobiographical account of his name-change elucidates how a court may
be a forum in which a name can achieve legitimacy, even while it may also serve as
a context for inducing skepticism about proffered justifications. The recognition of a
court may not satisfy one's sense that the name is sufficiently real – either in terms
of self-possession (as a name of one's own) or in terms of metaphysical and episte-
mological fixity (as a name that is known, as it were, naturally). Perhaps, however,
the scene of a legal proceeding reminds us that the condition for legitimation is the
person's insistence on the name as a new sign of signification. The petition after all is
brought by the claimant seeking to name or rename herself; the court hears the appeal,
and judges the claim. But who was making that claim for Cavell? Was it the young
Stanley Goldstein on behalf of himself, or some kind of nameless intermediary that

was lobbying for his next – successive – self as Stanley Cavell? According to one of the four central principles of logic – the so-called Principle of the Excluded Middle – there is no middle state between being and non-being. As D. Q. McInerny writes, 'There is no such thing as becoming; there are only *things that become*. The state of becoming is already within the realm of existence'.[54] A present self must therefore always be regarded as the proper source for creating some future state of affairs; through his or her own agency – complemented by laws and language – one may bring about these new, subsequent conditions. Outside of court, legitimacy for a name derives from a self-generated insistence on its reality coupled with a recurrent, even perpetual, interest in the meaning of that action. Here again, a man, as much as a woman, can be said to sire successive selves – first conceived and thereafter achieved through labour.

18.   Plato, *Sophist*

> Well, when we speak of a man we give him many additional names – we attribute to him colors and shapes and sizes and defects and good qualities, and in all these countless other statements we say he is not merely a 'man' but also 'good' and any number of other things.[55]

19.   The nineteenth-century Danish philosopher, Søren Kierkegaard famously employed pseudonyms for most of his published works, including *Fear and Trembling* by Johannes de Silentio, *Repetition* by Constantin Constantius, *Either/Or* by Victor Eremita, *The Concept of Anxiety* by Vigilius Haufniensis, *Prefaces* by Nicholaus Notabene, *Stages on Life's Way* by Hilarius Bookbinder and *Concluding Unscientific Postscript to the Philosophical Fragments* by Johannes Climacus. Kierkegaard himself was clear to distinguish between work he published under his name and work published under one of many pseudonyms; typically philosophical writing was claimed by a pseudonymous author, while Kierkegaard signed his own name to Christian devotional writing.[56] When a critic would assume that he could treat one of the pseudonymous writers as Kierkegaard, Kierkegaard was dismayed. In 1846, in the last pages of *Concluding Unscientific Postscript*, he wrote 'A First and Last Declaration', in which he stated: 'Formally and for the sake of regularity I acknowledge herewith (what in fact hardly anyone can be interested in *knowing*) that I am the author, as people would call it, […]' of the books noted above.[57] The confession that ties Kierkegaard to these various pseudonymous authors is not nearly as interesting as his own sense of distance from those authors. He continues: 'What is written therefore is in fact mine, but only in so far as I put into the mouth of the poetically actual individuality whom I *produced*, his life-view expressed in audible lines'.[58] As Jonathan Lear has commented, Kierkegaard 'takes himself to be the author of the authors who then go on to express their own life-views'.[59] Kierkegaard, then, gives birth to sovereign authors – not his representatives but rather his offspring. Kierkegaard says more about how such a 'poetically actual individuality' should be understood in relation to him, as its author:

> For I am impersonal, or am personal in the second person, a *souffleur* who has poetically produced the *authors*, whose preface in turn is their own production,

as are even their own names. So in the pseudonymous work there is not a single word which is mine, I have no opinion about these works except as a third person, no knowledge of their meaning except as a reader, not the remotest private relation to them [...].[60]

Despite seeing that the authorship of *Fear and Trembling* is claimed by Johannes de Silentio, a reader is still likely to quote from the work as if it were written by Kierkegaard. Such attribution seems to miss something important about Kierkegaard's use of pseudonyms, and betrays his own desire for how we should understand the nature of these pseudonymous authors. 'My wish, my prayer', confides Kierkegaard, 'is that, if it might occur to anyone to quote a particular saying from the books, he would do me the favour to cite the name of the respective pseudonymous author'. The favour inherent in Kierkegaard's solicitude conveys his hope that readers – and critics – can imagine neglecting to cite Kierkegaard (as the author of pseudonymous work) as a first step in reading those works and their authors on their appointed terms. Instead of authorship 'as people would call it', readers have authorship – the creation of authors – as Kierkegaard would, and did, call it.

Kierkegaard provided a metaphysical reason for his distinction: that in the pseudonymous writing 'there is not a single word' that is his. It could seem that Kierkegaard believes he is merely taking dictation from a coterie of pseudonymous authors who are independent, 'poetically actual subjective thinker[s]'; or that having conceived the pseudonymous authors, they are sufficiently independent to compose their own work – at a remove from him, in positions from which he has 'not the remotest private relation to them'. At one point he describes his role as that of a 'secretary', and as already seen, he calls himself a *souffleur* – literally a 'blower', one who pushes something from one place to another, perhaps a blower of life into new creations. Perhaps he is a conduit for the air, or maybe he is its source, but the image – and its attendant action – call to mind the giving, putting, or sending of life into inanimate forms. As an author, Kierkegaard choses or invents a name and then breathes – blows – life into the name, culminating in a pseudonymous author. This is another parable of male pregnancy, though here coupled with parenting: the begetting of offspring who may, in turn, (pro)create.

And Kierkegaard offered a psychological reason why we should believe in this theory of authorship: an extreme self-deprecation incited by a palpable shame. 'From the beginning', Kierkegaard says, 'I perceived very clearly and do still perceive that my personal reality is an embarrassment which the pseudonyms with pathetic self-assertion might wish to be rid of, the sooner the better, or to have reduced to the least possible significance, and yet again with ironic courtesy might wish to have in their company as a repellent contrast'.[61]

To some extent Kierkegaard's shame about his 'personal reality' is not just the cause of writing with pseudonyms, but more extremely, the cause of writing with the belief that he is not writing at all. Of himself he says that he is 'one who has contributed to bring it about that the pseudonyms could become authors'. Oddly, though, if it was shame that drove him to hide behind a fictitious name, it might be false modesty coupled with false pretence that enabled him to go further than merely obscuring his presence as an author: that is, to pursue the further frontier of insisting on the distinct, independent existence of the pseudonymous authors. Such a seminal thought makes Kierkegaard a demiurge of authors. The *souffleur* takes on the guise of a god or a pregnant parent who breathes life into new creations. When he says, 'I am acquainted with [the pseudonymous authors] indeed through familiar discourse', we suspect Kierkegaard is not merely hearing voices in his head, but experiencing something external, something more substantial than a thought but the very presence of 'poetically actual subjective thinker[s]'. Thinkers, that is, who are outside him, or who have come out from inside him – having been made by him. Kierkegaard writes about his relationship to the pseudonymous authors with a self-conscious declaration of invention – he says he has 'produced the authors' – and yet he writes also with an unequivocal emotional dissociation – emphasizing that he has 'not the remotest private relation' to them. As a result, the parable of Kierkegaard as a creative force may resemble the position of a god more than a parent. If this is another story of male pregnancy and a man giving birth, it is about a man who wants no credit for his creation, and no responsibility for it either. Yet even if his paternity is acknowledged as genuine (and he has attested to his complicity in the creation of these authors), his relation to and responsibility for his creations is disowned. Kierkegaard is the father of foundlings. Readers are left, then, to consider the intellectual traits that nevertheless inhere in his sired pseudonymous authors.

Is Kierkegaard genuine in his insistence that he is not, and should not be regarded as, the author of the work 'written' by the pseudonymous authors? A biographer of Kierkegaard, Joakim Garff, contends that Kierkegaard's insistence on the separation is 'literary smoke and mirrors', 'a dose of deceit', and part of a 'massive marketing campaign': '[P]seudonymity came close to being an unspoken aesthetic requirement, and this sort of literary mystification held great appeal for Kierkegaard'.[62] Garff's condescension to the notion that Kierkegaard humbly and truly wished to be discounted as the author of his work is countered by Jonathan Lear who says that 'one cannot give the pseudonymous works a serious reading unless one takes seriously the literary reality of the pseudonyms'.[63] Lear explains that the pseudonymous authors have 'extreme personalit[ies]' and each is 'the working-out-to-the-limit of a certain (confused) life-view'. Lear believes that readers are aided in realizing their own 'distortions' about such views because of the pseudonymous nature of the work. In this way, reading Kierkegaard strongly resembles, according to Lear, psychoanalytic therapy: 'Every reader of the pseudonymous works is invited to take up the role of analyst – not ultimately to analyze the 'patient' so as much as to develop oneself'. Lear argues that it is Kierkegaard's inspired use of pseudonymity that makes possible a 'therapeutic function for the reader', but that we can only benefit from that function if we take seriously the 'literary reality' of the pseudonymous authors.

Consequently, some measure of the philosophical pertinence of Kierkegaard's invention of pseudonymous authors depends on a reader's capacity to fathom their 'literary reality'. Despite admitting that he is the author of the pseudonymous authors, Kierkegaard clearly wants his readers to deny that he is the author of the pseudonymous *writings*. Kierkegaard's sincerity about his metaphysical isolation from the pseudonymous works may, for some critics, transform a commonplace literary device from an innocuous, distracting pretence into something truly consequential for thinking about the authorship of authors and the authorship of works; or if it must remain pretence, then perhaps it can be a guise that reveals some genuine philosophical insight about how worlds are made, and how men are made of words. Such is the always alarming power of an author to name reality – to give it form as if by an utterance, as if by breathing or blowing. For Kierkegaard, being the author of authors involves an application of literary imagination that resembles the divinity who calls forth beings, and the human who knows his world by naming it. Kierkegaard creates poetically actual subjective thinkers by giving them names, names under which they may, in turn, create realities of their own.

20.   Genesis

> And God said, Let there be light: and there was light. […]
> And God called the light Day, and the darkness he called Night. […]
> And God called the firmament Heaven. […]
> And God called the dry land Earth; and the gathering together of the waters called he Seas. […]
> And out of the ground the LORD God formed every beast of the field, and every fowl of the air; and brought them unto Adam to see what he would call them: and whatsoever Adam called every living creature, that was the name thereof.[64]

21.   Twice in print we find Emerson say 'We do what we must, and call it by the best names we can'.[65] On the first occasion, in 1844, he continued: 'and would fain have the praise of having intended the result which ensues. I cannot recall any form of man who is not superfluous sometimes'.[66] Kierkegaard may have felt that he was superfluous to the literary reality of his pseudonymous authors. The impression that authorship causes a seam in reality appears relevant to the consideration of any work of imaginative literature: either the pseudonymous author becomes a literary reality unto itself, in the way that characters in novels and films have an ongoing reality beyond their animation by readers and viewers; or the pseudonymous author is an 'aesthetic requirement' or novelistic convention a reader submits to as part of the willing suspension of disbelief adopted when approaching a work for which the author has obscured, or complicated, his presence as the author. Kierkegaard's postulated relationship to his pseudonymous authors and their works may have attributes of both aspects. Like a parent, and perhaps like a god, however, Kierkegaard did not wish to be superfluous to his creations. He gave them life and then he granted them independence.

22.   'Swifter than light the world converts itself into that thing you name', wrote Emerson in his journal, 'and all things find their right place under this new and capricious classification'.[67] Much has been made by critics of Emerson writing *Whim* on

the lintel of his door-post, and his hope that 'it is somewhat better than whim at last', but the act or art of naming is always, it seems, caught up in the condition of being a 'new and capricious classification'. Non-human, animals, by contrast do not have individual names; domesticated animals and pets are given names, thus separating them from the unnamed masses of their respective species (alive, dead and extinct). Animals beyond the farm and field, outside the kennel and cage, are named primarily as a function of classification with descending specificity (life, domain, kingdom, phylum, class, order, family, genus, species) and yet never reach the individual specimen. Once membership in the taxonomic family *hominidae* is established, the being is parsed as a creature belonging to the genus *homo*, and further as a part of the only surviving species of the genus, *homo sapiens*. These classifications differentiate one creature from another, but only generally; humans, contrariwise, use naming for radical, literalized individuation. Not this member of a species or genus or family, but this child, born on this day, in this location (a site that includes one's 'birthplace', one's country of origin – the land from and to which one will be granted citizenship), of these two progenitors (who are in turn, befitting their involvement, newly named in the classification parents – respectively, mother and father). It is not enough to be one among many *homo sapiens*; instead one is highlighted and heralded by a 'first name'. Naming, for the human community, is the beginning of being a person – an entity distinguishable from others by means of a linguistic referent. Though an infant is already born, already present as a bona fide entity in the species *homo sapiens*, she exists generically; she is not granted the conditions for partial individuation and personal identity until she is named. With her first breath of oxygen the fetus becomes a child; but it is only with the further act of assigning the first name – by parents, likely, perhaps necessarily according to a 'new and capricious classification' – that the child is created.

23.   In 1721 Montesquieu wrote a preface to a work entitled *The Persian Letters*, which was published anonymously:

> I have issued these first letters to gauge public taste; I have many more in my portfolio which I may release later.
>
> This, however, is only on condition that I remain unknown; I shall be silent the moment my name becomes public. [...] Were I known, it would be said, 'His book is inconsistent with his character; he ought to occupy his time to better purpose; this is not worthy of a serious man'. [...]
>
> The Persians who write here were lodged in my home, and we spent time together. [...] They would show me most of their letters; I copied them. [...]
>
> I am, then, only a translator. [...]⁶⁸

Montesquieu wrote this preface as a pretence: to illustrate, by way of masquerade, that his relationship to the text was intended to contribute literary value to his work, not to protect his literary reputation. The 'literary mystification' that he created becomes then a sign of his talent, not a reason to ridicule it; in fact, on the basis of *The Persian Letters*, Montesquieu's reputation was made; the work's merits led to his acceptance into the Académie française, the premier learned institution on matters of the French language.

Since the book was published anonymously by the author of the preface, and the letters contained therein were reputedly written by two Persian brothers visiting Paris from 1711 to 1720, *The Persian Letters* is an anonymous *and* a pseudonymous work. Instead of writing a satire in his own voice, under his own name, Montesquieu gave his readers the chance to see themselves as if from the outside, from the perspective of a foreigner who analyzes life in France. And for this externalized position, informed by intimate knowledge, Montesquieu's anonymous/pseudonymous writing seems to achieve precisely that 'therapeutic function' that Jonathan Lear describes as a quality and consequence of Kierkegaard's work on account of the literary reality of his pseudonymous authors. The comparison of the French and Danish authors, then, usefully suggests that the therapeutic effects of distancing – estranging the text in some fashion from its author, or its author's author – are inherent in literary techniques such as pseudonymous authorship. Charged with obvious deceit (like Montesquieu) or weighted with overt sincerity (like Kierkegaard), pseudonymity yields an unlikely and substantive denouement: enhancing a reader's perception of her own command of reality by means of naming it, that is, discovering her own capacity to author the world.

24.   Emerson, 'Eloquence' (1847)

> A crowd of men go up to Faneuil Hall; they are all pretty well acquainted with the object of the meeting; they have all read the facts in the same newspapers. The orator possesses no information which his hearers have not, yet he teaches them to see the thing with his eyes. By the new placing, the circumstances acquire new solidity and worth. Every fact gains consequence by his naming it, and trifles become important.[69]

By presenting established facts in a new way the orator reveals the artistry of his thinking. Because he has made plain things strange again one cannot leave Faneuil Hall and enter the same world. The orator shows that by his 'new placing' he has created something unknown or unseen before – though all the facts lay in the open. By the orator's 'naming it' – a reality, a relationship, a phenomenon, a mystery – we understand what to call it. The listener is struck at once both by the invention of his assemblage and the authority of his presentation. As Kierkegaard and Montesquieu exemplify, writing pseudonymously adds another dimension to our appreciation of such artistry and authority: writing under a fictitious name gives the reader a chance to encounter reality anew. The *souffleur* creates with each word, reminding readers – who are as such also writers – of their share in the divine action of shaping mental action and material form. We too create by naming the world – one thing in it, one person in it, one idea in it after another.

Acknowledgments

'The guiding star to the arrangement & use of facts,' wrote Emerson, 'is in your leading thought.'[1] And I have been fortunate to have received much support and guidance in the course of writing this book – while trying to suss out and sustain its 'leading thought' – a process for which I began research more than a decade ago. During that long period of active gestation and formation, the work accrued a number of genetic and environmental influences, personal debts and allowances that I am here grateful to acknowledge with thanks, directly and publically.

This book was not the sort I could sit down and write, even when moved by the spur of interest or occasion, but was instead a project that required incremental development over many years, while in conversation with disparate scholars, under the auspices of organizations and invigorated by colloquia in several countries. As part of the work's maturation, and my own, I continually benefitted from generative engagements with brilliant thinkers and the knowledgeable agents of supportive institutions.

Relatedly, I could not, when I began the project, have anticipated that my reading and research would so closely befit (or at least analogize) methods familiar to the naturalist and natural scientist, especially in a nineteenth century mode or frame of mind: travelling at home and abroad, taking notes and making sketches based on observations in the field, collecting varied specimens, grafting together unexpected and multifarious discoveries, spending years trying to achieve artfully affecting and conceptually coherent displays of findings in a cabinet, and devoting time to reflecting and revising the terms and conditions of arrangement. As for any scientist, so for any scholar, artist and critic, it emerges that these varied and variable undertakings reveal some measure of the way miscegenation and mutation, anomaly and deviation, transmission and circulation, composition and compensation, are the animating forces of life – its experiments, its trials, its essaying. Not surprisingly, these excursions and expropriations prompt questions of legitimacy and consequence; also not surprisingly, they were very often made possible by the generosity, intellectual and otherwise, shown to me by others. Thus, while bracketing concerns about the effect of adopted and adapted methods, I wish to recognize and express my gratitude to the people, institutions and events adduced below: some of the most conspicuous 'origins,' 'causes,' conditions, traces, palimpsests and influences that helped constitute the present work.

I begin at the end this time with sincerest thanks to Haaris Naqvi – a visionary editor, whose masterful capacities as facilitator, guide and collaborator continue to

---

[1] Ralph Waldo Emerson, *PH* ['Philosophy'], *The Topical Notebooks of Ralph Waldo Emerson*, ed. Ronald A. Bosco (Columbia: University of Missouri Press, 1993), Vol. II, 341. See also Emerson, 'Fortune of the Republic' (1863), *Emerson's Antislavery Writings*, 153.

astonish me. As was the case with our previous collaboration, *Estimating Emerson: An Anthology of Criticism from Carlyle to Cavell* (Bloomsbury Academic, 2013), I am immensely grateful for his attention, judgement and inventiveness on this book – a work that is significantly better for his crucial and inspired input.

The principal institutions that offered auspicious conditions for writing and research include: Harvard University, where the Committee on General Scholarships appointed me the Sinclair Kennedy Traveling Fellow for study in the United Kingdom (2003–4); Liberty Fund, Inc. where I held the position of Scholar-in-Residence (2005–6); and The New York Public Library, which granted me a multi-year term as Writer-in-Residence in the Frederick Lewis Allen Room at the Stephen A. Schwarzman Building (2010–13). In particular, I thank Jay Barksdale of the General Research Division and Study Rooms Liaison for his ongoing assistance – including hosting talks in the South Court and facilitating the Manhattan Research Libraries Initiative.

I continue with further thanks to the Harvard community:

At the Houghton Library of the Harvard College Library: Leslie Morris, Elizabeth Falsey, Susan Halpert, Tom Ford and other curators and staff at the library.

At Harvard Divinity School: David D. Hall, Stephanie Paulsell, David C. Lamberth, Kimberley C. Patton, Helmut Koester and the late Peter J. Gomes.

In Harvard's Department of Visual and Environmental Studies: Giuliana Bruno, Elizabeth Grosz and Peggy Phelan.

Faculty and staff at The Harvard Museum of Natural History, The Peabody Museum of Archeology and Ethnology, and The Louis Agassiz Museum of Comparative Zoology at Harvard – with special thanks to the late Stephen Jay Gould for his paradigm altering remarks on cladogenesis.

For instruction in the work of Wittgenstein: Newton Garver, Caleb Thompson, Michael Hodges, the late Gordon D. Kaufman, Liam Hughes and Mario von der Ruhr.

For instruction in the aesthetics of metaphor in language: J. M. Bernstein, Gregg Horowitz, Anthony Cascardi and Michael Mascuch. Relatedly, the usefulness and insight of work on the nature of metaphorical expression by Richard Lanham and Bernard Harrison has been matched by their generosity and thoughtfulness in person.

The National Endowment for the Humanities Summer Institute on Emerson, 'Literature, Philosophy, Democracy,' convened in Santa Fe, New Mexico (2003), with specific thanks to Steven Affeldt, Ronald Bosco, Stanley Cavell, William Day, Richard Deming, Thomas Dumm, K. L. Evans, Andrew Fiala, Erin Flynn, Russell Goodman, Timothy Gould, Maurice Lee, John Lysaker, Joel Myerson, the late Barbara Packer, Lawrence Rhu, William Rothman and Cornel West.

M. Jane Evans of London, formerly of the BBC, currently with the National Trust. Her lifetime knowledge of London was invaluable during my year-long residency in the city; she made possible a meaningful research life in and among the area institutions that were most pertinent to my inquiry – helping me do much more than merely catch a tourist's glimpse of the places Emerson visited.

Librarians and staff in England: at The London Library, The British Library, The Bodleian Library at Oxford University and the University Library at Cambridge. In the United States, I am especially grateful for resources at the following libraries, and for librarians and staff whose assistance made those resources more easily accessible and beneficial to research: The Library of Congress, The New York Society Library, The New York Public Library, The New-York Historical Society and The Morgan Library & Museum; the Widener, Houghton, Andover-Harvard Theological, History of Science, Fine Arts, Lamont, Hilles, Grossman, Loeb Design and Robbins libraries at Harvard University; the Heard Library at Vanderbilt University; the Bancroft Library at UC Berkeley; the Bobst Library at New York University; and the Butler and Rare Books and Manuscripts libraries at Columbia University.

Curators and staff at The Ashmolean Museum at Oxford University, The Sedgwick Museum of Geology at The University of Cambridge, The American Museum of Natural History in New York, The Exploratorium in San Francisco; and in London: The National Gallery, The National Portrait Gallery, The Tate Museum, The British Museum and The Victoria and Albert Museum.

Docents at Thomas Carlyle's house, 24 Cheyne Row, Chelsea, London; at The Old Manse on Monument Street; and at Emerson's house, 28 Cambridge Turnpike, Concord, Massachusetts.

Laura K. O'Keefe, Head of Cataloging and Special Collections; Erin Schreiner, Special Collections Librarian; and their colleagues at The New York Society Library.

Kyle R. Triplett and associates at The Brooke Russell Astor Reading Room for Rare Books and Manuscripts at The New York Public Library.

R. R. Rockingham Gill of the University of Wales, Trinity Saint David for directing me to work on philosophy and autobiography by Peter Suber at Earlham College.

David Kohn of the American Museum of Natural History and the Director and General Editor of the Darwin Manuscripts Project, who offered generous curatorial and bibliographic input that deeply informed and enriched my remarks on Darwin's use of organic metaphors.

Fatimah Jackson, Professor of Applied Biological Anthropology at the University of Maryland in College Park (Emeritus), Professor of Anthropology at the University of North Carolina and Director of UNC's Institute of African American Research, who has undertaken original empirical research in epigenetics. I benefited from her presentation on epigenetics given at a Content Seminar conducted at the American Museum of Natural History (2012), during which time she clarified many of the central definitions of the subfield, along with its claims and manifold implications; and subsequently, I am especially grateful to her for a close analysis of, and commentary on, an earlier draft of my comments on epigenetics in this manuscript.

The Ralph Waldo Emerson Society for a Community Project Award (2008) for the development of a colloquium on Emerson and Nietzsche I directed in Big Sky, Montana (2009).

The conferees at 'Shakespeare and Cavell' (Loránd Eötvös University: Budapest, 2004), 'Stanley Cavell and Literary Criticism' (University of Edinburgh, 2008), 'Cavelleria Siracusa' (Le Moyne College, 2009), 'Stanley Cavell and Literary Studies: Consequences of Skepticism' (The Humanities Center at Harvard, 2010) and 'Stanley Cavell's *Little Did I Know: Excerpts from Memory* Symposium' (The Johns Hopkins Humanities Center, 2011).

Liberty Fund, Inc. for specific conferences that stimulated research during my year in residence (2005–2006): 'Revolution, Secession, and Liberty: American Independence, The Civil War, and Beyond' (Big Sky); 'Liberty and Virtue in the Stoic Tradition' (San Francisco); and 'Inner Liberty, Self-Mastery, and Transcendence' (San Diego). And later, the conferees at 'Liberty, Language, and The Origins of American Intellectual Identity,' a colloquium I directed in San Diego (2007) and for which I served as discussion leader in Louisville (2008); 'Individual Liberty, Self-Reliance, and Private Property in Emerson and Mill,' a colloquium for which I led discussion in San Diego (2009); and 'Liberty and Necessity in Emerson and Nietzsche,' a colloquium I directed in Big Sky, Montana (2009). Also, my research for this book benefitted from conversations at Liberty Fund conferences on Emerson's *Essays* (Miami), Anthony Trollope and Elizabeth Gaskell (Cambridge, England), John Locke and Algernon Sydney (Portland, Maine), Roman Stoicism (Palo Alto), Emerson and John Stuart Mill (San Diego), Neo-Calvinism (La Jolla), Lord Kames and Adam Smith (San Francisco), Alexis de Tocqueville and Edith Wharton (Charleston) and Henry Fielding (Toronto).

To the community of scholars, friends and visitors who gathered for tea at Sparks House on Wednesday afternoons (with special gratitude to our late, self-described 'Afro-Saxon' host), and those who assembled at table and tea at The Signet Society.

From Memphis to Budapest, Cambridge, Massachusetts to Edinburgh, Santa Fe to Gregynog, and of course on many occasions in Syracuse, I have appreciated the comments and company of William Day. And I will retain perpetual thanks for the summoning power of the *Moonstruck* essay.

For a sustaining year of collaboration in San Francisco, and meaningful conversations in Switzerland and Italy before and since, Alessandro Subrizi.

For sharing substantive thoughts on his native England, life in British colonies and the wider Commonwealth, all drawn from first-hand experience; for remarks on the psychology of metaphor use; and for alimentary accommodation in New Zealand and New York, Ian M. Evans.

For being an ever onward source of expertise, reinforcement and cheer, Richard Deming.

For indispensible scholarly and editorial guidance in the final stages of revision, David Mikics.

For conducive reflections on the wily nuances of grammar, Lorna K. Hershinow.

At Bloomsbury, I benefited from comments by anonymous readers for the press, and offer sincere thanks for their generous and incisive input. For attention to marketing the present book I thank Laura Murray, and I add (unintentionally delayed) thanks to Ally Jane Grossan for marketing initiatives and permissions assistance on the last one, *Estimating Emerson*. For helpful communication and liaising, I thank Claire Henry at Bloomsbury Academic. And for editorial support in the last phase of development, I am exceedingly grateful to Robert Bullard and Kim Storry at Fakenham Prepress Solutions for their meticulous preparation of the final manuscript during the pre-production process.

For intellectual, moral, social, technical, practical and other forms of support in New York City, Buffalo, Ithaca, Syracuse, Boston, Cambridge, Baltimore, Bellingham,

Whidbey Island, Portland, San Francisco, Berkeley, Redlands, Indianapolis, Nashville, Hawaii, Swansea, London and the Isle of Arran, as well as in various locales of Great Britain, New Zealand, Italy, Switzerland, Sweden and elsewhere, I thank: Gigi Barlowe, Roberto Berardi, Joel Bettridge, Graham and Alexa Bodel, Jane Brady, Michael Brodrick, Elisabeth Bronfen, Rebecca M. Brown, Geri and Philip Burke, Eduardo Cadava, Cathleen Cavell, Elisabeth Ceppi, Samuel A. Chambers, Henry C. Clark, Ruth Cohen, Jeremy Colvin, Mark T. Conard, Paul Cronin, Brunello Cucinelli, Julia Cumes, Jigme and Haven Sarah Ripley Daniels, Kenneth Dauber, Catharina De Geer, Giorgio Dell'Acqua, Douglas J. Den Uyl, Bella Desai, Douglas P. Drake, Andrew Duncan, Joshua Edelstein, Henry T. Edmondson III, Richard Eldridge, Robert Elfstrom, Drew and Menna Etheridge, Gil Even-Tsur, Shana Fisher, Nayia Frangouli, Talia Gad, William H. Gass, Ian and Jane Gillespie, Tarleton and Jenna Lahmann Gillespie, Jonathan Glick, Nathan Goldberg, Daniel Austin Green, Lisa Gugenheim, Jennifer Gurley, Robert D. Habich, Garry L. Hagberg, the late Peter H. Hare, David M. Hart, David Harvey, David and Stephanie Hershinow, Sheldon Hershinow, Julian Hibbard, Lucy Hilmer, Angela V. McGuth Hodge, Hi-Jin and David Nassea Hodge, Kirsten FitzGerald Hodge, Jack Howard, Susan Howe, William Jersey, Brian Jones, Shirley Kessler, Will Knapp, John and Shirley Lachs, Frances LaRocca, Lavonne Leong, Paola Macrí, Giorgiana Magnolfi, Victoria Malkin, John Marsh, Daniel and Josephine Masiello, John Masters, John J. McDermott, Peter Mentzel, Horst Mewes, Luanna Meyer, Ricardo Miguel-Alfonso, Ray Monk, Edward F. Mooney, Rita Mullaney, Mihai Nadin, Jamesa Noelle, Andrew Norris, John Opera, Cine Ostrow, Sandra de Ovando, Joni Papp, Lynn Parr, Daniel and Kelly Ramot, Kathy Ray, Bernie Rhie, Lawrence Rhu, Daniella Rilov, Michael Alec Rose, Brad Rothschild, Michele Sachar, Anne and Michael Shaw, Helen Shaw, Jane Shaw, Mark Siddall, Kristen Steslow, Garrett Stewart, Roselle Sweeney, Barry Tharaud, Mario von der Ruhr, Andrew and Sarah Walston, Jonathan Walston, Stephanie Werner, Katja Wessling, Cornel West, Thomas Wood and Tom Wood.

For putting a copy of Darwin's *Voyage of the Beagle* and Irving Stone's *The Origin* in my hands during those formative years of early adolescence, the late Richard Machelor.

For conversations about Virgil, and prompting pathways of rogue reading, Werner Herzog.

For expansive intellectual generosity, exemplary provocations in prose and in person, and lasting guidance, Stanley Cavell.

My inspiration for trying to make things clearer, better and truer – my beloved daughters, Ruby and Star.

And the *sine qua non* – K. L. Evans – wife, help-meet and intellectual lodestar.

Notes

Prefatory Notes

1 Ludwig Wittgenstein, *Philosophical Investigations*, tr. G. E. M. Anscombe (New York: The Macmillan Company, 1953), §415.
2 D. Q. McInerny, *Being Logical: A Guide to Good Thinking* (New York: Random House, 2004), x.
3 Ralph Waldo Emerson, 'Spiritual Laws' (1841), *Essays, First Series*, *The Complete Works of Ralph Waldo Emerson*, Concord Edition (Boston: Houghton, Mifflin and Company, 1903–4), Vol. 2, 146–7. Henceforth, material drawn from the Concord Edition will be preceded by the abbreviation *Works* and followed by the volume number (in Roman) and page number (in Arabic), e.g. *Works*, II.146–7. Also, all citations of Emerson's *English Traits* (1856) derive from volume V of the *Works*. Unless otherwise indicated, all italics – in Emerson's work and elsewhere – are original to the source text.
4 Wittgenstein, *Philosophical Investigations*, §127.
5 Emerson, 'The American Scholar' (1837), *Works*, I.100.
6 McInerny, *Being Logical*, 8.
7 Friedrich Nietzsche, *Twilight of the Idols; Or How to Philosophize with a Hammer*, tr. Richard Polt (Indianapolis: Hackett Publishing Company, Inc., 1997), §4, 19–20.
8 Gertrude Stein, *Narration: Four Lectures* (Chicago: University of Chicago Press, 1969/1935), 46.
9 Virgil, *Georgics*, tr. Janet Lembke (New Haven: Yale University Press, 2005), Book I, 14.

Introduction: Some Traits of *English Traits*

1 Cornel West, 'The Emersonian Prehistory of American Pragmatism', *Estimating Emerson: An Anthology of Criticism from Carlyle to Cavell*, ed. David LaRocca (New York: Bloomsbury, 2013), 639.
2 Emerson, 'Land', *Works*, V.35. For earlier reflections on *English Traits*, and a brief intellectual biography of Emerson, see David Justin Hodge, *On Emerson* (Belmont, California: Wadsworth, 2003).
3 Ralph Waldo Emerson, *The Journals and Miscellaneous Notebooks of Ralph Waldo Emerson*, 16 vols, ed. William H. Gilman, et al. (Cambridge: Harvard University Press, 1960–82), XIII.270.
4 Walt Whitman, 'How I Still Get Around and Take Notes (No. 5)', *Estimating Emerson*, 180.
5 Emerson, *Journals* (25 November 1842), VII.222.
6 Charles Dickens, 'Boston', *Estimating Emerson*, 47.

7   Philip Nicoloff, *Emerson on Race and History: A Study of* English Traits (New York: Columbia University Press, 1961), 39.

8   Moncure Daniel Conway, *Emerson at Home and Abroad* (Boston: James R. Osgood, 1882), 242; Len Gougeon, *Virtue's Hero: Emerson, Antislavery, and Reform* (Athens: University of Georgia Press, 1990), 4.

9   Emerson, 'Man the Reformer' (1841), *Works*, I.232. For more on Emerson and reform see David Justin Hodge, 'Reforming Emerson: A Review of Recent Scholarship', *Transactions of the Charles S. Peirce Society: A Quarterly Journal in American Philosophy*, Vol. XXXVII, No. 4 (Fall 2001), 537–53.

10 Ralph Waldo Emerson, *Emerson's Antislavery Writings*, ed. Len Gougeon and Joel Myerson (New Haven: Yale University Press, 1995), 26.

11 Joseph Blau, 'Emerson's Transcendentalist Individualism as a Social Philosophy', *Estimating Emerson*, 489. Blau's quotation from Emerson appears in 'American Civilization' (1862), *Works*, XI.302. See also Emerson, 'Permanent Traits of the English National Genius' (1835), 'Genius of the Anglo-Saxon Race' (1843), and *English Traits*, where, among scores of invocations of the word 'genius', Emerson writes of 'the Saxon seed, with its instinct for liberty and law, for arts and for thought'. 'Result', *Works*, V.303.

12 For more on mark-making, see David LaRocca, 'Out of Nowhere: Remarks on Julian Hibbard's Existential Graphs', in Julian Hibbard, *Schematics: A Love Story*, (New York: Mark Batty, 2011); and David Justin Hodge, 'The Grammar of Origin', *John Opera: SOUP* (Buffalo: Burchfield Penney Art Center, 2003).

13 *The Compact Edition of the Oxford English Dictionary* (Oxford: Oxford University Press, 1971), Vol. II, 3375; 241 of the quarto page.

14 Emerson, 'Behavior', *Works,* VI.181.

15 'The modern and medieval word *species* is a Latin translation of the classical Greek word *eidos*, sometimes translated as 'idea' or 'form.' [...] Liddell and Scott (1888) tell us that *eidos* means 'form,' and is derived from the root word 'to see' [...]. We still find these senses in the English words *specify, special, spectacle* [...].' John S. Wilkins, *Species: A History of the Idea* (Berkeley: University of California Press, 2009), 10, 10–22 *passim*.

16 West, 'The Emersonian Prehistory of American Pragmatism', *Estimating Emerson*, 639.

17 In addition to Philip Nicoloff's *Emerson on Race and History* (1961) and *English Traits* with historical notes by Nicoloff (Cambridge: Harvard University Press, 1994), see, for example, *English Traits* edited and with an introduction by Howard Mumford Jones (Cambridge: Harvard University Press, 1966); Stephen L. Tanner, 'The Theme of Mind in Emerson's *English Traits*' and T. S. McMillin, 'Beauty Meets Beast: Emerson's *English Traits*' in *Emerson for the Twenty-First Century*, ed. Barry Tharaud (Newark: University of Delaware Press, 2010); Nell Irvin Painter, *The History of White People* (New York: W. W. Norton, 2010); *English Traits*, foreword by Phillip Lopate (London: Tauris Parke, 2011); and Marek Paryż, *The Postcolonial and Imperial Experience in American Transcendentalism* (New York: Palgrave, 2012).

18 Elizabeth A. Dant, 'Composing the World: Emerson and the Cabinet of Natural History', *Nineteenth-Century Literature*, Vol. 44, No. 1 (June 1989), 19.

19 For more on Nietzsche's reading of Emerson, see David Justin Hodge, 'Una traduzione transatlantica: Fato e libertà in Emerson e nel giovane Nietzsche' ['Transatlantic Translation: Young Nietzsche Writing Toward Emerson'], *Nietzsche e*

l'America, ed. and tr. Sergio Franzese (Pisa: Edizioni ETS, 2005), Nietzsceana Saggi 2, 83–105.

20 Friedrich Nietzsche, 'Natural History of Morals', *Beyond Good and Evil: Prelude to a Philosophy of the Future*, tr. Walter Kaufmann (New York: Vintage, 1989/1966), §186, §200, §202.

21 Nietzsche, *Beyond Good and Evil*, §186.

22 Ralph Waldo Emerson, *The Selected Lectures of Ralph Waldo Emerson*, ed. Ronald A. Bosco and Joel Myerson (Athens: University of Georgia Press, 2005), 16.

23 Ralph Waldo Emerson, *The Complete Sermons of Ralph Waldo Emerson*, ed. Albert von Frank (Columbia: University of Missouri Press, 1989), Sermon XXXIX, I.299.

24 Laura Dassow Walls, *Emerson's Life in Science: The Culture of Truth* (Ithaca: Cornell University Press, 2003), 167.

25 Moncure Daniel Conway, *Autobiography: Memories and Experiences*, 2 vols (Boston and New York: Houghton Mifflin and Company, 1904), Ch. XIX, I.281.

26 Conway, *Emerson at Home and Abroad*, 124.

27 Emerson, 'The Method of Nature' (1841), *Works*, I.203.

28 James Elliot Cabot, *A Memoir of Ralph Waldo Emerson*, 2 vols (Boston and New York: Houghton and Mifflin Company, 1887), I.224. See also Ralph Waldo Emerson, 'On the Relation of Man to the Globe', *Early Lectures of Ralph Waldo Emerson*, Vol. I (1833–6), ed. Stephen Whicher and Robert Spiller (Cambridge: Harvard University Press, 1959), 29, 32.

29 Emerson, 'Works and Days' (1857), *Works*, VII.171.

30 Emerson, 'Fate' (1860), *Works*, VI.49.

31 Emerson, *Journals* (1836), V.137.

32 Joseph Warren Beach, 'Emerson and Evolution' *University of Toronto Quarterly*, Vol. 3, (1934), 474–97.

33 Ralph Waldo Emerson, 'The Natural Method of Mental Philosophy', *The Later Lectures of Ralph Waldo Emerson*, ed. Ronald A. Bosco and Joel Myerson (Athens, Georgia and London, 2001), Vol. II, 97–8.

34 Harold Fromm, 'Overcoming the Oversoul: Emerson's Evolutionary Existentialism' *The Hudson Review*, Vol. LVII, No. 1 (Spring 2004).

35 Barbara Packer, *Emerson's Fall: A New Interpretation of the Major Essays* (New York: Continuum, 1982); David Robinson, *Apostle of Culture: Emerson as Preacher and Lecturer* (Philadelphia: University of Pennsylvania Press, 1982); Robert D. Richardson, *Emerson: The Mind on Fire* (Berkeley: University of California Press, 1996); Lee Rust Brown, *The Emerson Museum: Practical Romanticism and the Pursuit of the Whole* (Cambridge: Harvard University Press, 1997); Eduardo Cadava, *Emerson and the Climates of History* (Stanford: Stanford University Press, 1997); Eric Wilson, *Emerson's Sublime Science* (New York: St Martin's Press, 1999); Peter Obuchoswki, *Emerson and Science: Goethe, Monism, and the Search for Unity* (Great Barrington, MA: Lindisfarne Books, 2005); Christopher Windolph, *Emerson's Nonlinear Nature* (Columbia: University of Missouri Press, 2007); David Greenham, *Emerson's Transatlantic Romanticism* (New York: Palgrave MacMillan, 2012); and Daniel Koch, *Ralph Waldo Emerson in Europe: Class, Race, and Revolution in the Making of an American Thinker* (New York: I. B. Tauris, 2012).

36 Harry Hayden Clark, 'Emerson and Science', *Philological Quarterly* 10 (1931), Bliss Perry, *Emerson Today* (Princeton: Princeton University Press, 1931), and Ralph Rusk, *The Life of Ralph Waldo Emerson* (New York: Charles Scribner's Sons, 1949).

37   John Jay Chapman, 'Emerson', *Estimating Emerson*, 254.

38   Charles William Eliot, 'Emerson', *Estimating Emerson*, 330.

39   Lewis Mumford, 'The Morning Star', *Estimating Emerson*, 407.

40   Ray Monk, *Ludwig Wittgenstein: The Duty of Genius* (New York: Penguin, 1991), 536.

41   Monk, *Ludwig Wittgenstein: The Duty of Genius*, 536.

42   Monk, *Ludwig Wittgenstein: The Duty of Genius*, 537.

43   Maurice O'C. Drury, 'Conversations with Wittgenstein', ed. Rush Rhees, *Recollections of Wittgenstein* (Oxford: Oxford University Press, 1984), 157; William Shakespeare, *King Lear*, Act I, Sc. IV.

44   Monk, *Ludwig Wittgenstein: The Duty of Genius*, 536–7.

45   Elizabeth A. Dant notes that the cabinet of natural history is 'both the dominant symbol' and an 'ordering principle for Emerson's thought and writing.' 'Composing the World: Emerson and the Cabinet of Natural History', *Nineteenth-Century Literature*, Vol. 44, No. 1 (June 1989), 19.

46   Emerson, 'Discipline', *Nature*, *Works*, I.43.

47   Orestes Augustus Brownson, 'Emerson's *Essays*', *Estimating Emerson*, 67.

48   William Henry Channing, 'Emerson's Phi Beta Kappa Oration', *Estimating Emerson*, 76.

49   Amos Bronson Alcott, 'Essay', *Estimating Emerson*, 95.

50   Alcott, 'Essay', *Estimating Emerson*, 95.

51   Augustine Birrell, 'Emerson', *Estimating Emerson*, 216.

52   Theodore Parker, 'The Writings of Ralph Waldo Emerson', *Estimating Emerson*, 112.

53   Emerson, *Journals* (6 July 1841), VIII.8. See David Jacobson, 'Introduction: The Joyous Science of Power', *Emerson's Pragmatic Vision: The Dance of the Eye* (University Park: Pennsylvania State University Press, 1993), 1–26.

54   John Dewey, 'Emerson – Philosopher of Democracy', *Estimating Emerson*, 294.

55   William James, 'Address at the Emerson Centenary in Concord', *Estimating Emerson*, 289.

56   George Santayana, 'Emerson', *Estimating Emerson*, 304.

57   Lewis Mumford, 'The Morning Star', *Estimating Emerson*, 406.

58   Emerson, *Works*: 'Beauty', *Nature*, I.23; see also 'Discipline', *Nature*, I.42, 'all organizations are radically alike.'

59   Emerson, 'The American Scholar', *Works*, I.86.

60   Charles Ives, 'Essays Before a Sonata (Emerson)', *Estimating Emerson*, 385. The original text by Emerson is 'Nature loves analogies, but not repetitions.' 'Education' (1863–4), *Works*, X.143.

61   Emerson, *Journals* (1836), V.146; and cf. 'Language', *Works*, I.27. See also *Journals*, V.138: 'Man is an analogist. And therefore no man loses any time or any means who studies that one thing that is before him, though a log or a snail.'

62   Emerson, 'Poetry and Imagination' (1841–72), *Works*, VIII.15; See also David LaRocca, 'Seeing Metaphors', *Emerson for the Twenty-First Century: Global Perspectives on an American Icon*, ed. Barry Tharaud (Newark: University of Delaware Press, 2010), 331–48.

63   Emerson, *Journals* (December 1841), VIII.148; Emerson adapts these lines in 'Inspiration', *Works*, VIII.294.

64   Emerson, 'Montaigne; or, the Skeptic', *Representative Men* (1850), *Works*, IV.168.

65   As quoted in William H. Gass, 'Emerson and the Essay', *Estimating Emerson*, 582–3.

66 Chapman, 'Emerson', *Estimating Emerson*, 246.

67 Emerson, *Journals* (1841), VIII.23.

68 Emerson, 'Culture' (1860), *Works*, VI.137.

69 Walls, *Emerson's Life in Science*, 5.

70 Walls, *Emerson's Life in Science*, 5.

71 Walls, *Emerson's Life in Science*, 5.

72 Walls, *Emerson's Life in Science*, 12.

73 Walls, *Emerson's Life in Science*, 12–13.

74 Emerson, 'Nature', *Nature, Works*, I.10.

75 Walls, *Emerson's Life in Science*, 14.

76 Walls, *Emerson's Life in Science*, 14.

77 Chapman, 'Emerson', *Estimating Emerson*, 249.

78 Emerson, *Journals* (1824), II.224.

79 Walls, *Emerson's Life in Science*, 25.

80 See, for example, Donald Pease, *Visionary Compacts: American Renaissance Writings in Cultural Context* (Madison: University of Wisconsin Press, 1987), 226, 231.

81 Walls, *Emerson's Life in Science*, 26.

82 Walls, *Emerson's Life in Science*, 27.

83 Emerson, 'Nature' (1844), *Works*, III.196.

84 Emerson, 'Language', *Nature, Works*, I.33.

85 Michel Foucault, *The Order of Things: An Archaeology of the Human Sciences* (New York: Pantheon Books, 1971; Vintage Books, 1994), 125.

86 Foucault, *The Order of Things*, 159.

87 Foucault, *The Order of Things*, 161. Foucault quotes from Linnaeus' *Systema Naturae* (1735).

88 Foucault, *The Order of Things*, 158.

89 Foucault, *The Order of Things*, 132.

90 Foucault, *The Order of Things*, 130.

91 Foucault, *The Order of Things*, 161.

92 Foucault, *The Order of Things*, 132.

93 Foucault, *The Order of Things*, 129.

94 Foucault, *The Order of Things*, 135; Foucault references Linnaeus' *Philosophia Botanica* (1751), Sec. 328–9.

95 Henry David Thoreau, *The Writings of Henry David Thoreau: Journal, 1852–1853*, ed. Patrick F. O'Connell (Princeton: Princeton University Press, 1997), Vol. V, 19 June 1852, 112.

96 Foucault, *The Order of Things*, 135.

97 Foucault, *The Order of Things*, 160.

98 As quoted in Foucault, *The Order of Things*, 139n16, referencing Joseph Pitton de Tournefort, *Éléments de Botanique, ou Méthode pour reconnaître les Plantes* (1694), 1–2.

99 Foucault, *The Order of Things*, 139.

100 Foucault, *The Order of Things*, 146.

101 Charles Dickens, 'Nature's Greatness in Small Things', *Household Words: A Weekly Journal* (London: Bradbury and Evans, 1857), Vol. XVI, 513.

102 Richard Owen, *Richard Owen's Hunterian Lectures at the Royal College of Physicians, May–June 1837*, ed. Phillip R. Sloan (Chicago: The University of Chicago Press, 1992), 32.

103 Owen, *Richard Owen's Hunterian Lectures*, 32.
104 Peter J. Bowler, *Evolution: The History of an Idea* (Berkeley: University of California Press, 2003/1984), 227–8.
105 Bowler, *Evolution: The History of an Idea*, 227–8.
106 Charles Darwin, *Voyage of the Beagle* (20 March 1835), ed. Janet Browne and Michael Neve (New York: Penguin, 1989), 244–5. Darwin's account was published under a variety of titles after initially appearing in four volumes in May 1838. For example, it was issued in three volumes by Henry Colburn (London 1839) as *Narrative of the Surveying Voyages of His Majesty's Ships Adventure and Beagle between the years 1826 and 1836, Describing their Examination of the Southern Shores of South America and The Beagle's Circumnavigation of the Globe*. The title of John Murray's 1845 edition, published at London, was *Journal of Researches into the Natural History and Geology of the Countries Visited During the Voyage of the H.M.S. 'Beagle' Round the World Under the Command of Capt. FitzRoy*; the spine read *A Naturalist's Voyage Round the World*.
107 Emerson, 'Experience', *Works*, III.70.
108 Emerson, 'Experience', *Works*, III.72.
109 Owen, *Richard Owen's Hunterian Lectures*, 72.
110 Emerson, 'Experience', *Works*, III.70.
111 Emerson, 'Fate', *Works*, VI.49.
112 West, 'The Emersonian Prehistory of American Pragmatism', *Estimating Emerson*, 642.
113 Robert Knox, *The Races of Men: A Fragment* (Philadelphia: Lea and Blanchard, 1850), 151.
114 Knox, *The Races of Men*, 152–3.
115 Knox, *The Races of Men*, 147.
116 Knox, *The Races of Men*, 153–4.
117 Laura Dassow Walls, '"If Body Can Sing": Emerson and Victorian Science', *Emerson Bicentennial Essays*, ed. Ronald A. Bosco and Joel Myerson (Boston: Massachusetts Historical Society/University of Virginia Press, 2006), 334–66.
118 Joseph Warren Beach, 'Emerson and Evolution', *University of Toronto Quarterly*, Vol. 3 (1934), 494. See Harold Fromm, *The Nature of Being Human: From Environmentalism to Consciousness* (Baltimore: The Johns Hopkins University Press, 2009), 215–16.
119 Fromm, *The Nature of Being Human*, 216.
120 Beach, 'Emerson and Evolution', 496.
121 Ralph Waldo Emerson, *The Letters of Ralph Waldo Emerson*, 5 vols, ed. Ralph L. Rusk (New York: Columbia University Press, 1939), I.435.
122 Emerson, *Works*: 'Language', *Nature*, I.25; 'The Transcendentalist' I.335 and I.339.
123 F. O. Matthiessen, 'In the Optative Mood', *Estimating Emerson*, 439.
124 Emerson, 'Self-Reliance', *Works*, II.45.
125 Emerson, 'Education' (1863–4), *Works*, X.132.
126 Emerson, 'The Poet', *Works*, III.18.
127 D. H. Lawrence, '*Americans*', *Estimating Emerson*, 398.
128 George Santayana, 'The Genteel Tradition in American Philosophy', *Estimating Emerson*, 309.
129 Santayana, 'The Genteel Tradition in American Philosophy', *Estimating Emerson*, 311.

130 Santayana, 'The Genteel Tradition in American Philosophy', *Estimating Emerson*, 310.

131 Santayana, 'The Genteel Tradition in American Philosophy', *Estimating Emerson*, 310.

132 Richard Rorty, 'Professional Philosophy and Transcendentalist Culture', *Estimating Emerson*, 525.

133 *Literature and Science in the Nineteenth Century: An Anthology*, ed. Laura Otis (Oxford: Oxford University Press, 2002), xvii, xxv.

134 Otis, ed. *Literature and Science in the Nineteenth Century*, xvii; see also Richard Yeo, *Defining Science: William Whewell, Natural Knowledge and Public Debate in Early Victorian Britain* (Cambridge: Cambridge University Press, 1993), 10–11. For more on Emerson's contributions and challenges to the practices, definitions, and disciplinary boundaries of literature, science and philosophy, see David LaRocca 'Not Following Emerson: Intelligibility and Identity in the Authorship of Literature, Science, and Philosophy', *The Midwest Quarterly: A Journal of Contemporary Thought*, Vol. LIV, No. 2 (Winter 2013), 115–35.

135 Otis, ed. *Literature and Science in the Nineteenth Century*, xix.

136 Otis, ed. *Literature and Science in the Nineteenth Century*, xxiii.

137 Otis, ed. *Literature and Science in the Nineteenth Century*, xxiv.

138 Otis, ed. *Literature and Science in the Nineteenth Century*, xxii.

139 Otis, ed. *Literature and Science in the Nineteenth Century*, xxv.

140 Emerson, 'Race', *Works*, V.50.

141 Otis, ed. *Literature and Science in the Nineteenth Century*, xxi; Gillian Beer, *Darwin's Plots: Evolutionary Narrative in Darwin, George Eliot, and Nineteenth-Century Fiction* (London: Routledge and Kegan Paul, 1983), 3, 14.

142 Otis, ed. *Literature and Science in the Nineteenth Century*, xx.

143 Otis, ed. *Literature and Science in the Nineteenth Century*, xxvi.

144 M. H. Abrams, from the Preface to *The Mirror and the Lamp: Romantic Theory and the Critical Tradition* (Oxford: Oxford University Press, 1971/1953).

145 Abrams, *The Mirror and the Lamp*, Preface.

146 Abrams, *The Mirror and the Lamp*, 57.

147 David Lodge, 'Metaphor and Metonymy', *The Modes of Modern Writing: Metaphor, Metonymy, and the Typology of Modern Literature* (Ithaca: Cornell University Press, 1977), 75.

148 Lodge, *The Modes of Modern Writing*, 77.

149 Lodge, *The Modes of Modern Writing*, 76.

150 Lodge, *The Modes of Modern Writing*, 76.

151 Emerson, 'Quotation and Originality', *Works*, VIII.178.

152 Emerson, 'The Relation of Intellect to Natural Science', *Later Lectures*, I.161–2.

153 Bernard Harrison, 'The Truth about Metaphor', *Inconvenient Fictions: Literature and the Limits of Theory* (New Haven: Yale University Press, 1991), 262.

154 Stanley Cavell, 'Aversive Thinking: Emersonian Representations' and the Introduction, *Emerson's Transcendental Etudes*, ed. David Justin Hodge (Stanford: Stanford University Press, 2003), 147, 4.

155 Cavell, 'Old and New in Emerson and Nietzsche', *Emerson's Transcendental Etudes*, 231.

156 Donald Davidson, 'What Metaphors Mean', *Critical Inquiry*, Vol. 5, No. 1 (Autumn 1978), 47.

157 Hugh Bredin, 'Roman Jakobson on Metaphor and Metonymy', *Philosophy and Literature*, Vol. 8, No. 1 (1984), 101.
158 Neal Dolan, *Emerson's Liberalism* (Madison: University of Wisconsin Press, 2009), 3.
159 Dolan, *Emerson's Liberalism*, 15.
160 West, 'The Emersonian Prehistory of American Pragmatism', *Estimating Emerson*, 644.
161 Cavell, 'What's the Use of Calling Emerson's a Pragmatist?' *Estimating Emerson*, 689.
162 Dolan, *Emerson's Liberalism*, 4–5.
163 Dolan, *Emerson's Liberalism*, 256.
164 Ralph Waldo Emerson, *English Traits*, *The Collected Works of Ralph Waldo Emerson*, Vol. 5 (Cambridge: Harvard University Press, 1994), historical notes by Philip Nicoloff, xxi; see also Nicoloff, *Emerson on Race and History* (1961), 36.
165 In the years following his return to America in 1848, Emerson delivered a series of lectures based on his travels and research: between 1848 and 1852 he presented 'England' dozens of times throughout New York State and New England, as far west as Cincinnati and as far north as Montreal; and then between 1852 and 1856, leading up to the publication of *English Traits*, he gave lectures entitled 'Characteristics of the English', 'English Character and Influence', 'English Influence on Modern Civilization', and 'English Civilization' (Emerson, *Selected Lectures*, 152).
166 Nicoloff, *Collected Works*, Vol. 5 (1994), xliii.
167 Dolan, *Emerson's Liberalism*, 265.
168 Emerson, 'Speech at Manchester', *Works*, V.309.
169 Emerson, 'Speech at Manchester', *Works*, V.310.
170 Emerson, *Works*: 'Speech at Manchester', V.311; 'Result', V.302.
171 Emerson, 'Speech at Manchester', *Works*, V.311.
172 Emerson, 'Speech at Manchester', *Works*, V.312.
173 Emerson, 'Speech at Manchester', *Works*, V.313.
174 Emerson, 'Speech at Manchester', *Works*, V.313.
175 Emerson, 'Personal', *Works*, V.294.
176 Emerson, 'Personal', *Works*, V.295.
177 Emerson, 'Personal', *Works*, V.294.
178 Emerson, 'Personal', *Works*, V.294.
179 Emerson, 'Personal', *Works*, V.295.
180 Emerson, 'Personal', *Works*, V.295.
181 Emerson, 'Result', *Works*, V.302.
182 Emerson, 'Personal', *Works*, V.291.
183 Dolan, *Emerson's Liberalism*, 4.
184 Nicoloff, *Collected Works*, Vol. 5 (1994), xxii.
185 Nicoloff, *Emerson on Race and History*, 108.
186 Dolan, *Emerson's Liberalism*, 265.
187 Gougeon, *Virtue's Hero*, 15.
188 Gougeon, *Virtue's Hero*, 15.
189 Gougeon, *Virtue's Hero*, 12.
190 Emerson, 'Theodore Parker', *Works*, XI.285.
191 Ralph Waldo Emerson, *Emerson's Antislavery Writings*, ed. Len Gougeon and Joel Myerson (New Haven: Yale University Press, 1995); *A Political Companion to Ralph Waldo Emerson*, ed. Alan M. Levine and Daniel S. Malachuk (Lexington: University

Press of Kentucky, 2011); and Robert Habich, *Building Their Own Waldos: Emerson's First Biographers and the Politics of Life-Writing in the Gilded Age* (Iowa City: University of Iowa Press, 2011).

192 Gougeon, *Virtue's Hero*, 17.
193 Nicoloff, *Emerson on Race and History*, 151.
194 Dolan, *Emerson's Liberalism*, 265; Emerson, 'Race', *Works*, V.48.
195 Emerson, 'Race', *Works*, V.50.
196 Dolan, *Emerson's Liberalism*, 266.
197 Emerson, 'Race', *Works*, V.50.
198 Emerson, 'Race', *Works*, V.52.
199 Emerson, 'Race', *Works*, V.50.
200 Dolan, *Emerson's Liberalism*, 266.
201 Emerson, 'Ability', *Works*, V.74; Dolan, *Emerson's Liberalism*, 266.
202 Dolan, *Emerson's Liberalism*, 266–7.
203 Dolan, *Emerson's Liberalism*, 3.
204 Beer, *Darwin's Plots*, xxv.
205 Beer, *Darwin's Plots*, xviii.
206 Beer, *Darwin's Plots*, xxv.
207 Beer, *Darwin's Plots*, xxv.
208 Beer, *Darwin's Plots*, 89.
209 Beer, *Darwin's Plots*, xxx
210 Beer, *Darwin's Plots*, 5.
211 Beer, *Darwin's Plots*, 5.
212 Beer, *Darwin's Plots*, 7.
213 Beer, *Darwin's Plots*, 7.
214 Beer, *Darwin's Plots*, 10.
215 Beer, *Darwin's Plots*, 85.
216 George Levine, *Darwin and the Novelists: Patterns of Science in Victorian Fiction* (Cambridge: Harvard University Press, 1988), 1.
217 Levine, *Darwin and the Novelists*, 3.
218 Beer, *Darwin's Plots*, 6; Levine, *Darwin and the Novelists*, 3.
219 Levine, *Darwin and the Novelists*, 3.
220 Robert William Mackay, *The Progress of the Intellect: As Exemplified in the Religious Development of the Greeks and Hebrews* (London: J. Chapman, 1850), 172.
221 Immanuel Kant, *Critique of Judgment* (1790), ed. J. C. Meredith (Oxford: Oxford University Press, 1911), 168–9.
222 1 John 1.7. All quotations from the Bible are from the King James Version, unless otherwise cited.
223 Emerson, 'The Sovereignty of Ethics' (1878), *Works*, X.201. William James paraphrased this passage in his 'Address at the Emerson Centenary in Concord' (1903): 'If anyone would lay an axe to your tree with a text from I John, vs. 7, or a sentence from Saint Paul, say to him', Emerson wrote, 'My tree is Yggdrasil, the tree of life.' *Estimating Emerson*, 287. See also *Journals* (1847): Yggdrasil, X.103; Ygdrasil, X.163. Cf. *The Poetic Edda*, tr. Lee M. Hollander (Austin: University of Texas Press, 2008/1962).
224 Thomas Carlyle, *On Heroes, Hero-Worship, and the Heroic in History*, Lecture I, 'The Hero as Divinity', ed. Archibald MacMechan (Boston: The Athenæum Press, 1902), 23.
225 Charles Darwin, *The Origin of Species by Means of Natural Selection, or the*

Preservation of Favoured Races in the Struggle for Life (New York: D. Appleton and Company, 1864), Ch. IV. Natural Selection, 77–8.

226 Darwin, *The Origin of Species*, Ch. VI, 168.
227 Nicoloff, *Emerson on Race and History*, viii.
228 Robert Chambers, *Vestiges of the Natural History of Creation and other Evolutionary Writings* (1844), ed. James Secord (Chicago: The University of Chicago Press, 1994), 350.
229 Emerson, 'Fate', *Works*, VI.9.
230 Nicoloff, *Emerson on Race and History*, 111.
231 Nicoloff, *Emerson on Race and History*, 111.
232 Chambers, *Vestiges of the Natural History of Creation*, 198–9.
233 Nicoloff, *Emerson on Race and History*, 113.
234 Emerson, 'Civilization' (1861), *Works*, VII.25; Nicoloff, *Emerson on Race and History*, 114.
235 Nicoloff, *Emerson on Race and History*, 114–15.
236 See for example 'Pedigree of Man' (1874), an illustration by Ernst Haeckel in *The Evolution of Man: A Popular Exposition of the Principal Points of Human Ontogeny and Phylogeny*, Vol. II (New York: D. Appleton and Co., 1896), Plate XV; reprinted in Stephen G. Alter, *Darwin and the Linguistic Image: Language, Race, and Natural Theology in the Nineteenth Century* (Baltimore: Johns Hopkins University Press, 1999), fig. 5.3, 113.
237 Emerson, 'Ability', *Works*, V.97.
238 Emerson, 'Aristocracy', *Works*, V.186.
239 Emerson, 'Character', *Works*, V.130.
240 Emerson, 'Aristocracy', *Works*, V.197.
241 Emerson, 'Aristocracy', *Works*, V.197.
242 Emerson, 'Wealth', *Works*, V.166.
243 Bowler, *Evolution: The History of an Idea*, 298.
244 Harriet Ritvo, *The Platypus and the Mermaid and Other Figments of the Classifying Imagination* (Cambridge: Harvard University Press, 1997), 130.
245 Alter, *Darwin and the Linguistic Image*, xi.
246 Alter, *Darwin and the Linguistic Image*, xi.
247 Alter, *Darwin and the Linguistic Image*, xii.
248 For illustrations from Haeckel's *The Evolution of Man* (1874), see Alter, *Darwin and the Linguistic Image*, 'Pedigree of the Twelve Species of Men', fig. 5.8, 120; 'Pedigree of the Indo-Germanic Languages', fig 5.6, 118.
249 Alter, *Darwin and the Linguistic Image*, 1.
250 Alter, *Darwin and the Linguistic Image*, 2.
251 Alter, *Darwin and the Linguistic Image*, 2.
252 Beer, *Darwin's Plots*, 85–6.
253 Darwin, *The Origin of Species*, Ch. XIII, 377.
254 Darwin, *The Origin of Species*, Ch. IV, 118.
255 Darwin, *The Origin of Species*, Ch. IV, 71.
256 Emerson, *Journals* (1836), V.168.
257 Emerson, 'Humanity of Science' (1836–48), *Selected Lectures*, 19.
258 Emerson, *Selected Lectures*, 21.
259 Emerson, *Selected Lectures*, 19–20; Emerson, *Early Lectures*, 23.
260 Emerson, *Selected Lectures*, 19.

261 Emerson, 'Demonology', *Early Lectures*, III.158.

262 Emerson, 'Language', *Nature*, *Works*, I.35.

263 Emerson, 'Language', *Nature*, *Works*, I.35.

264 Emerson, *Journals* (1836), V.146.

265 Emerson, *Journals*, V.221–2.

266 Emerson, *Selected Lectures*, 19.

267 Emerson, *Journals* (1840), VII.540.

268 Emerson, *Journals*, V.137.

269 Emerson, 'Poetry and Imagination' (1841–1872), *Works*, VIII.15.

270 Alexis de Tocqueville, *Democracy in America*, forward by Harold Laski (New York: A. A. Knopf, 1957/1945).

271 Ralph Waldo Emerson, *English Traits*, ed. Howard Mumford Jones (Cambridge: Harvard University Press, 1966), ix.

272 Emerson, *Letters* (10 September 1856), V.30.

273 John Jay Chapman, 'Emerson, Sixty Years After', *The Atlantic Monthly*, Vol. LXXIX, (Boston: Houghton, Mifflin, and Company, 1897), 38; a selection from Chapman's essay appears in *Estimating Emerson*, 245–56.

274 Amos Bronson Alcott, 'Essay', *Estimating Emerson*, 94.

275 Theodore Parker, 'The Writings of Ralph Waldo Emerson', *Estimating Emerson*, 109.

276 *The Correspondence of Thomas Carlyle and Ralph Waldo Emerson*, ed. Charles Eliot Norton (Rockville, MD: Arc Manor, 2009; Boston: James R. Osgood, 1883), (28 August 1856), II.146.

277 *Correspondence of Carlyle and Emerson* (2 December 1856), II.147.

278 *Correspondence of Carlyle and Emerson* (27 January 1867), II.552–3. See David LaRocca, 'The Education of Grown-ups: An Aesthetics of Reading Cavell', *The Journal of Aesthetic Education*, Vol. 47, No. 2 (Summer 2013).

279 Walter Savage Landor, *Landor's Letter to Emerson*, ed. Samuel Arthur Jones (Cleveland: The Rowfant Club, 1895), 11. Landor's letter appears in *Estimating Emerson*, 116–27.

280 Landor, *Landor's Letter to Emerson*, 31.

281 Emerson, 'First Visit to England', V.8; Landor, '*Landor's Letter to Emerson*,' *Estimating Emerson*, 124.

282 Landor, *Landor's Letter to Emerson*, 70, 73.

283 Nicoloff, *Collected Works*, Vol. 5 (1994), *l*; see also Nicoloff, *Emerson on Race and History*, appendix.

284 *The Rambler* (October 1856).

285 Matthew Arnold, 'Emerson', *Estimating Emerson*, 205.

286 Arnold, *Estimating Emerson*, 205; see also David LaRocca, 'A Conversation Among Critics', *Estimating Emerson*, 11–12.

287 Arnold, 'Emerson', *Estimating Emerson*, 205.

288 Parker, 'The Writings of Ralph Waldo Emerson', *Estimating Emerson*, 111.

289 Emerson, 'The Anglo-American', *Later Lectures*, I.279, I.293, I.283.

290 Emerson, *Later Lectures*, I.295.

291 Emerson, *Later Lectures*, I.295.

292 Emerson, *Later Lectures*, I.282–3.

293 Emerson, *Later Lectures*, I.287.

294 Emerson, *Later Lectures*, I.291.

295 Emerson, *Later Lectures*, I.294, I.290.

296 Emerson, *Letters* (20 April 1853), IV.352.
297 Hugo Münsterberg, *American Traits from the Point of View of a German* (Boston: Houghton Mifflin and Company, 1901), vii.
298 Parke Godwin, *Putnam's Monthly Magazine* (October 1856); Noah Porter, Jr., *The New Englander* (November 1856).
299 *Westminster Review* (October 1856).
300 Alexis de Tocqueville, *Democracy in America*, ed. and tr. Harvey Mansfield and Delba Winthrop (Chicago: The University of Chicago Press, 2000), Vol. II, Pt. I, Ch. 3 and 4.
301 Emerson, *English Traits*, ed. H. M. Jones, xvii.
302 Emerson, *English Traits*, ed. H. M. Jones, xvii-xviii.
303 Emerson, 'Character', *Works*, V.134.
304 Emerson, 'First Visit to England', *Works*, V.5.
305 Emerson, 'First Visit to England', *Works*, V.5.
306 Emerson, *Later Lectures*, I.191.
307 Voltaire, *Letters Concerning the English Nation*, ed. Nicholas Cronk (Oxford: Oxford University Press, 1994), Preface.
308 Voltaire, *Letters Concerning the English Nation*, 5–6.
309 Voltaire, *Letters Concerning the English Nation*, Letter XX, 'On such of the Nobility as cultivate the Belles Lettres', 98.
310 Emerson, 'Race', *Works*, V.46.
311 George Santayana, 'The Genteel Tradition in American Philosophy', *Estimating Emerson*, 307–8.
312 *English Traits*, ed. H. M. Jones, xvii.
313 Emerson, 'The Naturalist' (1834), *Early Lectures*, 75.
314 Emerson, *Early Lectures*, 74–5.
315 Emerson, *Early Lectures*, 80.
316 Emerson, *Selected Lectures*, 70–1.
317 Emerson, *Selected Lectures*, 74.
318 Emerson, *Selected Lectures*, 74.
319 Emerson, *Journals* (May 26, 1837), V.336.
320 Emerson, 'Circles', *Works*, II.307.
321 Stanley Cavell, 'In the Place of the Classroom', *Estimating Emerson*, 709.
322 West, 'The Emersonian Prehistory of American Pragmatism', *Estimating Emerson*, 621.
323 Emerson, 'The Method of Nature' (1841), *Works*, II.210.
324 Emerson, *Works*: 'The Method of Nature', II.210; 'Self-Reliance', II.53.
325 Harold Bloom, 'Emerson and Influence', *Estimating Emerson*, 508–9.
326 Bloom, 'Emerson and Influence', *Estimating Emerson*, 511.
327 Emerson, 'The American Scholar', *Works*, I.91.
328 Emerson, *Journals* (1839), VII.326.
329 Harold Bloom, 'Mr America', *Estimating Emerson*, 499.
330 Emerson, 'Man the Reformer' *Works*, I.231.
331 George Herbert Mead, *Selected Writings*, ed. Andrew J. Reck (Indianapolis: Bobb-Merrill, 1964), 377.
332 West, 'The Emersonian Prehistory of American Pragmatism', *Estimating Emerson*, 646.
333 Emerson, *Nature*, *Works*, I.3.

334 Emerson, 'Fate', *Works*, VI.37.
335 Emerson, 'Fate', *Works*, VI.3.
336 West, 'The Emersonian Prehistory of American Pragmatism', *Estimating Emerson*, 640.
337 West, 'The Emersonian Prehistory of American Pragmatism', *Estimating Emerson*, 642.
338 Emerson, 'Theodore Parker', *Works*, XI.285.
339 West, 'The Emersonian Prehistory of American Pragmatism', *Estimating Emerson*, 647.
340 Emerson, 'Truth', *Works*, V.123.
341 Emerson, 'An Address … on … the Emancipation of the Negroes in the British West Indies', *Emerson's Antislavery Writings*, 31.
342 Emerson, 'Wealth', *Works*, V.164.
343 Emerson, 'Wealth', *Works*, V.164.
344 Cabot, *A Memoir of Ralph Waldo Emerson*, Vol. II, 633.
345 Emerson, 'Nature' (1844), *Works*, III.180.
346 Emerson, 'Poetry and Imagination', *Works*, VIII.5.
347 Cavell, *Emerson's Transcendental Etudes*, 120.
348 Emerson, 'Cockayne', *Works*, V.152.
349 Cavell, *Emerson's Transcendental Etudes*, 120.
350 Emerson, *Journals*, V.217.

I More Prone to Melancholy

1 Emerson, 'Quotation and Originality', *Works*, VIII.196.
2 Robert Burton, *The Anatomy of Melancholy* (New York: New York Review of Books, 2001), 15.
3 Burton, *The Anatomy of Melancholy*, 17–8.
4 Emerson, *Journals* (13 July 1833), IV.198.
5 Burton, *The Anatomy of Melancholy*, 17.
6 For more on autobiography, see David LaRocca, 'Rethinking the First Person: Autobiography, Authorship, and the Contested Self in *Malcolm X*', *The Philosophy of Spike Lee*, ed. Mark T. Conard (Lexington: The University Press of Kentucky, 2011), 215–41; and 'Unauthorized Autobiography: Truth and Fact in *Confessions of a Dangerous Mind*', *The Philosophy of Charlie Kaufman* (Lexington: The University Press of Kentucky, 2011), 89–110.
7 Thomas Warton, *The Poetical Works of John Milton with Notes of Various Authors, Principally from the Editions of Thomas Newton, Charles Dunster, and Thomas Warton*, ed. Edward Hawkins (Oxford: W. Baxter, 1824), Vol. III, 437.
8 Burton, *The Anatomy of Melancholy*, 20–1.
9 Burton, *The Anatomy of Melancholy*, 22.
10 Burton, *The Anatomy of Melancholy*, 21.
11 Emerson, 'Personal', *Works*, V.295.
12 Walter Benjamin, *Illuminations: Essays and Reflections*, ed. Hannah Arendt, tr. Harry Zohn (New York: Schocken Books, 1968), 59–61.
13 Wittgenstein, *Philosophical Investigations*, Pt. II, Sec. vi, 181.

14 Wittgenstein, *Philosophical Investigations*, Pt. II, Sec. xi, 218.
15 Emerson, *Works*: 'Self-Reliance', II.45; 'History', II.3.
16 Burton, *The Anatomy of Melancholy*, 15; Michel de Montaigne, *The Complete Essays of Montaigne*, tr. Donald Frame (Stanford: Stanford University Press, 1958), 2.
17 Emerson, *Journals* (July–August, 1841), VIII.26.
18 Emerson, 'Montaigne; or, the Skeptic', *Works*, IV.168.
19 Samuel Taylor Coleridge, *The Complete Works of Samuel Taylor Coleridge*, ed. W. G. T. Shedd (New York: Harper & Brothers, 1884), Vol. III: *Biographia Literaria; or Biographical Sketches of My Literary Life and Opinions*, 149.
20 Chapman, 'Emerson', *Estimating Emerson*, 251.
21 Emerson, 'Montaigne; or, the Skeptic', IV.177.
22 Emerson, 'Montaigne; or, the Skeptic', IV.178.
23 Emerson, 'Montaigne; or, the Skeptic', IV.183.
24 Emerson, 'Montaigne; or, the Skeptic', IV.183.
25 Emerson, 'Montaigne; or, the Skeptic', IV.178.
26 Emerson, 'Montaigne; or, the Skeptic', IV.179.
27 Colin Burrow, 'A Towering Intellect', *London Review of Books* (6 November 2003), 21.
28 Maurice Merleau-Ponty, *Signs*, tr. Richard C. McCleary (Evanston: Northwestern University Press, 1964), 203.
29 Burrow, 'A Towering Intellect', 21.
30 Emerson, 'History', *Works*, II.23.
31 Emerson, 'Beauty', VI.293–4.
32 Montaigne, 'Of Friendship', *Essays*, tr. M. A. Screech (New York: Penguin, 2005), 41.
33 Burton, *The Anatomy of Melancholy*, the 1628 frontispiece, 9.
34 Emerson, 'Race', *Works*, V.48.
35 Emerson, *Journals* (May 15, 1842), VIII.173.
36 Emerson, 'Experience', *Works*, III.51.
37 Emerson, 'Fate', *Works*, VI.9–11.
38 Emerson, 'Literary Ethics', *Works*, I.187.
39 Emerson, 'Spiritual Laws', *Works*, II.159.
40 Emerson, 'Worship', *Works*, VI.223.
41 Emerson, *Journals* (*Encyclopedia*, 1824–36), VI.115.
42 Montaigne, 'Of Physiognomy', *Essays*, tr. D. Frame, Book III, Ch. 12, 811.
43 John Webster, *The Dutchess of Malfi* (1612–13), ed. C. Vaughan (London: J. M. Dent and Co., 1896), 11.
44 Pliny the Elder, *Natural History: A Selection*, tr. John F. Healy (New York: Penguin, 2004), Book VII, 75.
45 George Combe, *Elements of Phrenology*, 7th Edition (Edinburgh: Maclachlan and Stewart, 1850), 17–18; the selected passage is from the original 1824 edition (See Otis, ed., 377).
46 Johann Gaspar Spurzheim, *Phrenology in Connection with the Study of Physiognomy* (London: Treuttel, Wurtz, and Richter, 1826), 7–8.
47 Melville, *Moby-Dick; or, The Whale* (New York: Harper and Brothers Publishers, 1851), 'The Prairie', Ch. 79.
48 Emerson, 'Domestic Life' (1859), *Works*, VII.108.
49 Emerson, *Journals* (1838), VII.43.
50 Nietzsche, 'The Free Spirit', *Beyond Good and Evil*, §24.
51 Nietzsche, *Beyond Good and Evil*, §34.

52 Nietzsche, *Beyond Good and Evil*, §28.

53 Emerson, *Journals* (2 September 1849), XI.152.

54 Emerson, 'Character', *Works*, V.130.

55 Emerson, 'Character', *Works*, V.130.

56 Emerson, 'Character', *Works*, V.133.

57 Emerson, 'Character', *Works*, V.135.

58 Emerson, 'Character', *Works*, V.128.

59 Emerson, 'Works and Days' (1857), *Works*, VII.163.

60 Mark Twain, *The Innocents Abroad, or, The New Pilgrim's Progress*, afterword by Leslie Fiedler (New York: Signet Classic, 1966), 493.

61 Harold Bloom, 'Mr America', *Estimating Emerson*, 498–9.

62 Emerson, 'Self-Reliance', *Works*, II.69.

63 Harold Bloom, 'Mr America', *Estimating Emerson*, 499. For more on Emerson's remarks on transition, thresholds and liminal spaces, see David LaRocca, 'Emerson at *The Gates*', *New Morning: Emerson in the Twenty-First Century*, ed. Arthur Lothstein and Michael Brodrick (Albany: State University of New York Press, 2008), 101–21.

64 Emerson, *Nature*, *Works*, I.3.

65 Emerson, 'Plato; or, the Philosopher', *Works*, IV.41–2.

66 Nietzsche, 'The Wanderer and His Shadow', *Human, All Too Human: A Book of Free Spirits*, tr. R. J. Hollingdale (Cambridge: Cambridge University Press, 1986), §302, 386.

67 Emerson, 'Manners', *Works*, V.104.

68 Emerson, 'Manners', *Works*, V.105.

69 Emerson, 'Behavior', *Works*, VI.176.

70 Emerson, 'The Over-Soul', *Works*, II.294.

71 Emerson, 'Literary Ethics', *Works*, I.171.

72 Emerson, 'Race', *Works*, V.62.

73 Emerson, *Works*: 'Race', V.50; 'Poetry and Imagination', VIII.5.

74 Emerson, 'Self-Reliance', *Works*, II.48.

75 Emerson, 'Self-Reliance', *Works*, II.48.

76 *The American Heritage Dictionary of the English Language*, 4th Edition (New York: Houghton Mifflin Company, 2003).

77 Emerson, 'Race', *Works*, V.46, 49.

78 See John D. Gartner, *The Hypomanic Edge* (New York: Simon & Schuster, 2005), and Peter C. Whybrow, *American Mania* (New York: W. W. Norton, 2005).

79 Whybrow, *American Mania*, 98.

80 Whybrow, *American Mania*, 8–14 and Pt. I *passim*.

81 See Joseph Blau, 'Emerson's Transcendentalist Individualism as a Social Philosophy', *Estimating Emerson*, 484–94.

82 Emerson, 'Self-Reliance', *Works*, II.49.

83 Daniel K. Campbell-Meiklejohn, et al., 'Structure of Orbitofrontal Cortex Predicts Social Influence', *Current Biology*, Vol. 22, No. 4 (2012).

84 Emerson, 'Ability', *Works*, V.101.

85 Gertrude Stein, 'Lecture I', *Narration: Four Lectures* (1969/1935).

86 Emerson, 'Cockayne', *Works*, V.148.

87 Montaigne, 'Of Friendship', *Essays of Michael Seigneur de Montaigne in Three Books with Marginal Notes and Quotations and an Account of the Author's Life with a Short*

Character of the Author and Translator, by a Person of Honour. Made English by Charles Cotton, Esq., 4th Edition (London: Printed for Daniel Brown, et al., 1711), Ch. 27, 253.

88 Coleridge, *Biographia Literaria*, Ch. XII.

89 Stanley Cavell, *The Claim of Reason: Wittgenstein, Skepticism, Morality, and Tragedy* (Oxford: Oxford University Press, 1999/1979). See especially Pt. IV. 'Skepticism and the Problem of Others', 397–496.

90 Emerson, 'Beauty', *Works*, VI.299; for 'shreds and patches' see also 'The Over-Soul', *Works*, II.297 and 'Plato; or, the Philosopher', *Works*, IV.77.

91 Herman Melville, *Mardi and a Voyage Thither*, ed. Harrison Hayford, Hershel Parker and G. Thomas Tanselle (Evanston: Northwestern University Press, 1998), Ch. 124, 387.

92 *Correspondence of Carlyle and Emerson* (12 August 1834), I.21. See also *Estimating Emerson*, 31.

93 *Correspondence of Carlyle and Emerson* (16 March 1838), I.80.

94 Montaigne, 'Of Physiognomy', *Essays*, tr. D. Frame, 809.

95 Montaigne, 'Of Physiognomy', *Essays*, tr. D. Frame, 809.

96 Emerson, *Works*: 'Quotation and Originality', VIII.178 (and see also VIII.190); 'Race', V.56; 'Culture', VI.142; and 'Address at the Opening of the Concord Free Public Library', VIII.178.

97 Emerson, *Works*, 'Quotation and Originality', VIII.188.

98 Emerson, *Works*, 'Quotation and Originality', VIII.188.

99 Emerson, *Works*, 'Quotation and Originality', VIII.189.

100 Emerson, *Works*, 'Quotation and Originality', VIII.191.

101 Emerson, *Works*, 'Quotation and Originality', VIII.189.

II With Muffins and Not the Promise of Muffins

1 Pliny the Elder, *Natural History*, Book XII, 164; cf. Books XII-XIII: Trees.

2 Thomas Carlyle, *On Heroes, Hero-Worship, and the Heroic in History*, Lecture III, 'The Hero as Poet', ed. A. MacMechan, 117.

3 Emerson, 'Literature', *Works*, V.251.

4 Lionel Trilling, 'Society and Authenticity' (1972), *Estimating Emerson*, 471.

5 Emerson, 'Land', *Works*, V.34.

6 Emerson, 'Literature', *Works*, V.252.

7 Emerson, 'Stonehenge', *Works*, V.288.

8 Emerson, 'Stonehenge', *Works*, V.276.

9 Emerson, 'Religion', *Works*, V.216.

10 Virgil, *Georgics*, Book II, 27.

11 Emerson, 'Personal', *Works*, V.291.

12 Emerson, 'Literature', *Works*, V.255–6.

13 J. Hector St John de Crevecoeur, *Letters from an American Farmer Describing Certain Provincial Situations, Manners, and Customs not Generally Known; and Conveying Some Idea of the Late and Present Interior Circumstances of the British Colonies in North America*, Letter III, 'What Is an American', (Mineola, NY: Dover, 2005/1912), 25.

14   Crevecoeur, *Letters from an American Farmer*, 27.
15   Crevecoeur, *Letters from an American Farmer*, 34.
16   John Stuart Mill, 'Of Individuality, As One of the Elements of Well-Being', *On Liberty and Other Essays*, ed. John Gray (Oxford: Oxford University Press, 1991), Ch. III, 66.
17   Mill, *On Liberty*, III.69.
18   Mill, *On Liberty*, III.72.
19   Coleridge, *Biographia Literaria*, Ch. XII.
20   Emerson, *Letters* (to William Emerson, 13 and 29 September 1826), I.173 and I.176.
21   Sampson Reed, *Observations on the Growth of the Mind* (1826), 5th Edition (Boston: T. H. Carter and Company, 1865), 39–40.
22   Reed, *Observations on the Growth of the Mind*, 40.
23   Reed, *Observations on the Growth of the Mind*, 41.
24   Reed, *Observations on the Growth of the Mind*, 43.
25   Reed, *Observations on the Growth of the Mind*, 48–9.
26   Reed, *Observations on the Growth of the Mind*, 45.
27   Walls, *Emerson's Life in Science*, 16.
28   Walls, *Emerson's Life in Science*, 16.
29   Walls, *Emerson's Life in Science*, 16.
30   Walls, *Emerson's Life in Science*, 16.
31   See Stanley Cavell, *Emerson's Transcendental Etudes*, ed. David Justin Hodge (Stanford: Stanford University Press, 2003); *Cities of Words: Pedagogical Letters on a Register of the Moral Life* (Cambridge: Harvard University Press, 2005); and *Estimating Emerson: An Anthology of Criticism from Carlyle to Cavell*, ed. David LaRocca (New York: Bloomsbury, 2013).
32   Walls, *Emerson's Life in Science*, 16.
33   Walls, *Emerson's Life in Science*, 17.
34   Emerson, 'Goethe; or, the Writer', *Works*, IV.275.
35   Emerson, 'The Powers and Laws of Thought', *Works*, XII.24–5.
36   Emerson, 'The Powers and Laws of Thought', *Later Lectures*, I.148.
37   Abrams, *The Mirror and the Lamp*, 204.
38   Abrams, *The Mirror and the Lamp*, 219.
39   Abrams, *The Mirror and the Lamp*, 219.
40   Johann Gottfried von Herder, 'On the Knowing and Feeling of the Human Soul' (1778), *Sämtliche Werke*, Vol. VIII (Hildesheim: Georg Olms, 1967–8). See also Abrams, *The Mirror and the Lamp*, 236.
41   Samuel Taylor Coleridge, *S. T. Coleridge's Treatise on Method, as published in the Encyclopædia metropolitana*, ed. A. D. Snyder (London: Constable & Co., 1934), 7.
42   Samuel Taylor Coleridge, *The Statesman's Manual; or the Bible the Best Guide to Political Skill and Foresight: A Lay Sermon, Addressed to the Higher Classes of Society, with an Appendix, Containing Comments and Essays Connected with the Study of Inspired Writings* (London: Gale and Fenner, 1816), xiv-xv; see also *Lay Sermons*, ed. Derwent Coleridge, 3rd Edition (London: Edward Moxon, 1852), 75–7.
43   Emerson, 'Ability', *Works*, V.88.
44   Emerson, 'Wealth', *Works*, V.169–70.
45   Emerson, 'Ability', *Works*, V.93.
46   Emerson, 'Ability', *Works*, V.93–6.
47   Emerson, 'Result', *Works*, V.303.
48   Emerson, 'Literature', *Works*, V.232.

49 Emerson, 'Experience', *Works*, III.385.
50 Emerson, 'Experience', *Works*, III.385.
51 Emerson, 'Circles', II.318.
52 Emerson, 'Experience', *Works*, III.386.
53 Voltaire, *Letters Concerning the English Nation*, Letter XXIII. 'On the Regard that Ought to be Shown to Men of Letters', 112–3.

III The Lively Traits of Criticism

1 Emerson, *Journals* (1847), X.171.
2 Emerson, 'The Poet', *Works*, III.15.
3 Emerson, 'The Poet', *Works*, III.20.
4 Emerson, 'History', *Works*, II.9.
5 Friedrich Nietzsche, *Human, All Too Human: A Book for Free Spirits*, tr. Marion Faber with Stephen Lehmann (Lincoln: University of Nebraska Press, 1996/1984), §513, 238.
6 Emerson, 'History', *Works*, II.17, 21, 30.
7 William James, 'The Present Dilemma in Philosophy' (Lecture I), *Pragmatism: A New Name for Some Old Ways of Thinking* (1907), *Writings 1902–10* (New York: The Library of America, 1987), 488–9.
8 David Hume, *A Treatise of Human Nature*, Pt. IV, Sec. III, *The Philosophical Works of David Hume*, Vol. I (London: Black and Tait, 1825/1739), 282.
9 Ludwig Wittgenstein, *Culture and Value*, tr. Peter Winch, ed. G. H. von Wright (Chicago: The University of Chicago Press, 1980), 1931, 20.
10 Carl Gustav Jung, 'Letter to Arnold Künzli' (28 February 1943), *Letters*, Vol. I, 1906–50, ed. Gerhard Adler, tr. R. F. C. Hull (Princeton: Princeton University Press, 1973).
11 Emerson, 'Behavior', *Works*, VI.176.
12 Johann Gottlieb Fichte, *The Science of Knowledge (Wissenshaftslehre) with First and Second Introductions*, ed. and tr. Peter Heath and John Lachs (New York: Appleton-Century-Croft, 1970), 16.
13 Ferdinand Canning Scott Schiller, 'Must Philosophy be Dull?', *Our Human Truths* (New York: Columbia University Press, 1939), 98.
14 Nietzsche, 'On the Prejudices of Philosophers', *Beyond Good and Evil*, §6.
15 Miguel de Unamuno, *The Tragic Sense of Life*, tr., J. E. C. Flitch (New York: Dover Publications, 1953/1921), 2.
16 John Oulton Wisdom, *The Metamorphosis of Philosophy* (UMI, 1998). Late in the composition of this chapter I was directed to Peter Suber's 'Philosophy as Autobiography: Psychologistic, Reductive, and Non-Immanent Readings of Philosophy' (available online), and found in it many passages that overlapped with my own research, and a few additional excerpts that amplify the inductive report underway. I am indebted to R. R. Rockingham Gill (University of Wales, Trinity Saint David) for bringing Suber's compendium to my attention.
17 Stanley Cavell, 'What's the Use of Calling Emerson a Pragmatist?' *Estimating Emerson*, 689; 'Must We Mean What We Say?', *Must We Mean What We Say?: A Book of Essays* (New York: Scribner, 1969), 36n10. See also Timothy Gould, *Hearing*

Things: Voice and Method in the Writing of Stanley Cavell (Chicago: The University of Chicago Press, 1998), and my review of Gould's book: *The Review of Metaphysics*, Vol. LIII, No. 4 (June 2000), 931–3.

18 Emerson, 'Ability', *Works*, V.79.
19 Emerson, 'Ability', *Works*, V.80.
20 Emerson, 'Ability', *Works*, V.82.
21 Emerson, 'Ability', *Works*, V.84.
22 Emerson, 'Ability', *Works*, V.84.
23 *The Compact Edition of the Oxford English Dictionary* (Oxford: Oxford University Press, 1971), Vol. I, 361; 204 of the quarto page.
24 Emerson, *Journals* (11 January 1841), VII.547.
25 Emerson, 'Literature', *Works*, V.235.
26 Emerson, 'Literature', *Works*, V.234.
27 Emerson, 'Literature', *Works*, V.236.
28 Emerson, 'Literature', *Works*, V.238.
29 Emerson, 'Literature', *Works*, V.239.
30 Emerson, 'Literature', *Works*, V.239.
31 David Hume, 'Of the Origin of Ideas', *An Enquiry Concerning Human Understanding* (1748) (Chicago: The Open Court Publishing Co., 1907), Sec. II, 16.
32 Emerson, 'Language', *Nature*, *Works*, I.34.
33 Emerson, 'Language', *Nature*, *Works*, I.35.
34 Emerson, 'Idealism', *Nature*, *Works*, I.47.
35 Emerson, 'Idealism', *Nature*, *Works*, I.48.
36 Emerson, 'Idealism', *Nature*, *Works*, I.50.
37 Herman Melville, *Moby-Dick*, 'The Sphinx', Ch. 70.
38 See anonymous editor's postscript 'About this Compact Edition', *Moby-Dick in Half the Time* (London: Orion Books, 2007), 315.
39 Damion Searls, *; or The Whale*, *The Review of Contemporary Fiction*, Vol. XXIX (Summer 2009).
40 Emerson, 'The Lord's Supper', *Selected Writings*, 107.
41 Emerson, 'The Lord's Supper', *Selected Writings*, 107.
42 Emerson, *Nature*, *Works*, I.3.
43 Emerson, *Journals* (13 July 1833), IV.200.
44 Emerson, occult harmonies, *Journals*, VIII.8; occult sympathy/ies, *Works*, I.67, II.107, XII.22, and *Later Lectures*, I.161; occult symmetries, X.262; occult power, *Works*, III.94; occult facts, *Works*, X.24; occult mutual attractions, III.238; occult resemblances, *Selected Lectures*, 20; occult relation/s, *Works*, I.10, and *Journals*, IV.200.
45 Emerson, 'Experience', *Works*, III.85.
46 Emerson, *Journals*, XVI.281.
47 Emerson, 'Fate', *Works*, VI.44.
48 Emerson, 'Poetry and Imagination', *Works*, VIII.13.
49 Emerson, 'Poetry and Imagination', *Works*, VIII.13.
50 Emerson, *Letters* (25 December 1831), I.342–3.
51 John Frederick William Herschel, *A Preliminary Discourse on the Study of Natural Philosophy* (London: Longman, Brown, Green, 1845/1831), Ch. II, Sec. 95, 102–3.
52 Emerson, 'Self-Reliance', *Works*, II.57.

53   Emerson, 'Intellect', *Works*, II.331.
54   Emerson, 'Fate', *Works*, VI.22.
55   Emerson, 'Fate', *Works*, VI.22.
56   Emerson, *Journals* (1847), X.171.

IV The Cabman is Phrenologist So Far

 1   Barry Smith, 'Bosnia: The Cognitive Geometry of War', Department of Philosophy,
     University at Buffalo, February 1996.
 2   Emerson, 'Compensation', *Works*, II.98.
 3   Friedrich Nietzsche, 'On the Truth and Lies in a Nonmoral Sense' (1873),
     Philosophy and Truth: Selections from Nietzsche's Notebooks from the Early 1870s, ed.
     and tr. Daniel Breazeale (Atlantic Highlands, NJ: Humanities Press, 1997/1979).
 4   Wittgenstein, *Philosophical Investigations*, §115.
 5   Nietzsche, 'The Free Spirit', *Beyond Good and Evil*, §32.
 6   Emerson, *Journals* (13 July 1833), IV.198.
 7   See for example *Seeing Wittgenstein Anew: New Essays on Aspect-Seeing*, ed. William
     Day and Victor Krebs (Cambridge: Cambridge University Press, 2010), and David
     LaRocca, 'Seeing Metaphors', *Emerson for the Twenty-First Century*, ed. Barry
     Tharaud (Newark: University of Delaware Press, 2010), 331–48; and 'The False
     Pretender: Deleuze, Sherman, and the Space of Simulacra', *The Journal of Aesthetics
     and Art Criticism*, Vol. 69, No. 3 (Summer 2011), 321–29.
 8   Emerson, 'Experience', *Works*, III.75.
 9   Wittgenstein, *Philosophical Investigations*, §127.
10   Emerson, 'Fate', *Works*, VI.9.
11   Emerson, 'Fate', *Works*, VI.29.
12   Emerson, 'Fate', *Works*, VI.39.
13   Emerson, 'Fate', *Works*, VI.39.
14   W. James, 'The Present Dilemma in Philosophy', *Pragmatism* (1907), 489.
15   Emerson, 'Fate', *Works*, VI.40.
16   Galatians 6:7–9.
17   Emerson, 'Fate', *Works*, VI.41.
18   Emerson, 'Fate', *Works*, VI.42.
19   Emerson, 'Fate', *Works*, VI.43.
20   Emerson, 'Fate', *Works*, VI.42.
21   Emerson, 'Discipline', *Nature*, *Works*, I.42.
22   Emerson, 'Discipline', *Nature*, Works, I.42. See David LaRocca, 'Performative
     Inferentialism: A Semiotic Ethics', *Liminalities: A Journal of Performance Studies*, Vol.
     9, No. 1 (February 2013), 1–26.
23   Emerson, 'Perpetual Forces', *Works*, X.86.
24   Emerson, 'Fate', *Works*, VI.45.
25   Emerson, 'Fate', *Works*, VI.45.
26   Emerson, 'Fate', *Works*, VI.24.
27   Emerson, 'Fate', *Works*, VI.25.
28   Emerson, 'Fate', *Works*, VI.31.

V The Florilegium and the Cabinets of Natural History

1 Pliny the Elder, *Natural History*, Book VII, 74.
2 Thomas Carlyle, *Sartor Resartus: The Life and Opinions of Herr Diogenes Teufelsdröckh* (London: Chapman & Hall, 1891), 18–19; 22–3.
3 Arthur Hugh Clough, *Emerson-Clough Letters*, ed. Howard F. Lowry and Ralph Leslie Rusk (Cleveland, The Rowfant Club, 1934), Letter #29 (12 September 1856).
4 Emerson, 'Success', *Works*, VII.296.
5 Aristotle, *The Art of Rhetoric*, tr. H. C. Lawson-Tancred (New York: Penguin, 2004/1991), 'Enthymeme', Pt. II, Sec. 8, Ch. 2.22, 195.
6 Emerson, 'Experience', *Works*, III.83.
7 Wittgenstein, *Philosophical Investigations*, ix.
8 Wittgenstein, *Philosophical Investigations*, §415.
9 Wittgenstein, *Philosophical Investigations*, §127.
10 Emerson, *Journals* (13 July 1833), IV.200.
11 Emerson, 'Intellect', *Works*, II.325.
12 Thomas Hamilton, *Men and Manners in America* (Edinburgh: Blackwood, 1833), Vol. II, 4.
13 Hamilton, *Men and Manners in America*, Vol. II, 283.
14 Emerson, *Later Lectures*, I.137.
15 Wittgenstein, *Philosophical Investigations*, 'remarks', §415; 'natural order', v; 'reminders', §127.
16 Wittgenstein, *Philosophical Investigations*, v.
17 Wittgenstein, *Philosophical Investigations*, v.
18 Wittgenstein, *Philosophical Investigations*, vi.
19 For more on Wittgenstein, Aurelius, and autobiographical writing see David LaRocca, 'Note to Self: Learn to Write Autobiographical Remarks from Wittgenstein', *Wittgenstein Reading*, ed. Sascha Bru, Daniel Steuer, and Wolfgang Huemer (Berlin: De Gruyter, 2013).
20 Emerson, 'Preface to *Parnassus*', *Emerson's Literary Criticism*, ed. Eric W. Carlson (Lincoln: University of Nebraska Press, 1995/1979), 144.
21 Wittgenstein, *Philosophical Investigations*, v.
22 Emerson, 'Preface to *Parnassus*', *Emerson's Literary Criticism*, 144.
23 Emerson, *Journals* (13 July 1833), IV.198.
24 Burton, *The Anatomy of Melancholy*, 32–3.
25 Burton, *The Anatomy of Melancholy*, 24–5.
26 Burton, *The Anatomy of Melancholy*, 25.
27 Burton, *The Anatomy of Melancholy*, 25.
28 Burton, *The Anatomy of Melancholy*, 23.
29 See David LaRocca 'The Unseen Site of Plato's Biography', *Platonic Traditions in American Thought*, ed. Jay Bregman and Melanie B. Mineo (New Orleans: University Press of the South, 2008), 77–93.
30 Emerson, 'Plato; or, the Philosopher', *Works*, IV.42.
31 Wittgenstein, *Philosophical Investigations*, §415.
32 Wittgenstein, *Philosophical Investigations*, §415.
33 See David LaRocca, 'Changing the Subject: The Auto/biographical as the Philosophical in Wittgenstein', *Epoché: A Journal for the History of Philosophy*, Vol. 12, No. 1 (Fall 2007), 169–84.

34 Emerson, *Journals* (1835), V.71.
35 Coleridge, *Biographia Literaria*, Ch. IX.
36 Ray Monk, 'Philosophical Biography: The Very Idea', *Wittgenstein: Biography and Philosophy*, ed. James C. Klagge (Cambridge: Cambridge University Press, 2001), 5.
37 Coleridge, *Biographia Literaria*, Chapter XII.
38 Wittgenstein, *Philosophical Investigations*, v.
39 Melville, *Moby-Dick*, 'Extracts (Supplied by a Sub-Sub-Librarian).'
40 Dale V. Kent, *Cosimo de' Medici and the Florentine Renaissance: The Patron's Oeuvre* (New Haven and London: Yale University Press, 2000), 69.
41 Armando Petrucci, *Writers and Readers in Medieval Italy*, tr. Charles M. Radding (New Haven: Yale University Press, 1995), 187.
42 D. Graham Burnett, *A Little Common Place Book* (Brooklyn: Cabinet Books & Proteotypes, 2010), Introduction.
43 John Locke, *Letters on Study*, as quoted in the printed introduction to *Bell's Common-Place Book, Formed Generally upon the Principles Recommended and Practiced by Mr Locke* (London: John Bell, 1770), 5.
44 Emerson, *Journals* (1845), IX.341.
45 Emerson, 'An Address', *Works*, I.127.
46 Michael Ondaatje, *The English Patient* (London: Bloomsbury, 1992), Ch. II, 58; Ch. III, 96.
47 Herodotus, *The History of Herodotus*, tr. G. C. Macaulay (New York: Macmillan and Company, 1890), Vol. I, Book I.
48 John Randolph, *Commonplace Book* (1680), The Library of Congress, *The Thomas Jefferson Papers*, Series 8, Virginia Records Manuscripts (1606–1737). Sir John Randolph (1693–1736) was Speaker of the House of Burgesses and the King's Attorney in Virginia; Peyton Randolph (1721–75), his son, who also held those offices, was Thomas Jefferson's mentor in the House of Burgesses in the 1760s and 1770s.
49 See David LaRocca, 'Note to Self: Learn to Write Autobiographical Remarks from Wittgenstein', *Wittgenstein Reading* (2013).
50 Michel Foucault, *The Hermeneutics of the Subject: Lectures at the Collège de France 1981–2*, tr. Graham Burchell (New York: Picador, 2005), 500.
51 Pierre Hadot, *Philosophy as a Way of Life*, ed. Arnold I. Davidson, tr. Michael Chase (Oxford: Blackwell Publishing, 1995), 179.
52 Hadot, *Philosophy as a Way of Life*, 13.
53 Hadot, *Philosophy as a Way of Life*, 163.
54 Hadot, *Philosophy as a Way of Life*, 130, 134.
55 Hadot, *Philosophy as a Way of Life*, 136.
56 Hadot, *Philosophy as a Way of Life*, 179.
57 Lee Rust Brown, *The Emerson Museum*, 77.
58 Brown, *The Emerson Museum*, 77.
59 Stanley Cavell, 'The World as Things: Collecting Thoughts on Collecting' (1998), *Cavell on Film*, ed. William Rothman (Albany: State University of New York Press, 2005), 268. Cf. Cavell, *Philosophy the Day After Tomorrow* (Cambridge: Harvard University Press, 2005), 270.
60 Cavell, 'The World as Things', *Cavell on Film*, 268.
61 Cavell, 'The World as Things', *Cavell on Film*, 268. For more on the nature of philosophical writing, and by relation, philosophical reading, see David LaRocca, 'Reading Cavell Reading', *Stanley Cavell, Literature, and Film: The Idea of America*,

ed. Andrew Taylor and Áine Kelly (New York: Routledge, 2013), 26–41; and 'The Education of Grown-ups: An Aesthetics of Reading Cavell', *The Journal of Aesthetic Education*, Vol. 47, No. 2 (Summer 2013).

62 Cavell, 'The World as Things', *Cavell on Film*, 268.
63 Brown, *The Emerson Museum*, 78.
64 Elizabeth A. Dant, 'Composing the World: Emerson and the Cabinet of Natural History', *Nineteenth-Century Literature*, Vol. 44, No. 1 (June 1989), 19.
65 Dant, 'Composing the World', 19.
66 Emerson, 'Race', *Works*, V.54.
67 Emerson, 'Self-Reliance', *Works*, II.50.
68 See P. F. Strawson, *Individuals: An Essay in Descriptive Metaphysics* (London: Methuen, 1959), 168ff; and Gerald Vision, 'Essentialism and the Senses of Proper Names', *American Philosophical Quarterly*, Vol. 7, No. 4 (October 1970).
69 Emerson, 'The Poet', *Works*, III.34.
70 David Punter, *Metaphor* (London: Routledge, 2007), 13; see also 3, 102, 132, 138, 140, and especially Ch. 1 'The Classical Problem: Figurative Language.'
71 Emerson, *Journals* (1824), II.224.
72 Carl Schmitt, *The Concept of the Political*, Expanded Edition, tr. George Schwab (Chicago: The University of Chicago Press, 2007), 26.
73 Emerson, *Journals* (13 July 1833), IV.200.
74 Emerson, *Journals* (13 July 1833), IV.200.
75 Carlyle, *Sartor Resartus*, Book I, 50.
76 Emerson, 'The Poet', *Works*, III.21.
77 Nietzsche, 'On the Truth and Lies in a Nonmoral Sense', 85.
78 Wittgenstein, *Philosophical Investigations*, §112.
79 Wittgenstein, *Philosophical Investigations*, §114.
80 Wittgenstein, *Philosophical Investigations*, §115.
81 Derrida, *Margins of Philosophy*, 209.
82 Cavell, *The Claim of Reason*, 496.
83 Emerson, 'The Relation of Intellect to Natural Science', *Later Lectures*, I.156.
84 Cavell, *Little Did I Know: Excerpts from Memory* (Stanford: Stanford University Press, 2010), 491.
85 George Lakoff and Mark Johnson, *Philosophy in the Flesh: The Embodied Mind and Its Challenge to Western Thought* (New York: Basic Books, 1999), 7.
86 Emerson, 'Blight', *Works*, IX.140.
87 Emerson, 'Thoreau', *Works*, X.471–2.
88 Charles Butler, *The Feminine Monarchie* (Oxford: Joseph Barnes, 1609).
89 Charles Butler, *The Feminine Monarchie* (London: John Haviland, 1623).
90 Virgil, *Georgics*, Book IV, 60, 67, 78.
91 Emerson, 'History', *Works*, II.9.
92 Emerson, 'History', *Works*, II.40.
93 Emerson, 'History', *Works*, II.17.
94 Emerson, 'History', *Works*, II.21.
95 Emerson, 'History', *Works*, II.29.
96 Emerson, *Journals* (1845), IX.299–300.
97 Emerson, *Journals* (1846), IX.365.
98 Emerson, 'Works and Days', *Works*, VII.162.
99 Emerson, 'The Powers and Laws of Thought', XII.25–6.

100   Emerson, 'The Relation of Intellect to Natural Science', *Later Lectures*, I.155.
101   Melville, *Moby-Dick*, 'The Affidavit', Ch. 45.
102   Emerson, 'The Poet', *Works*, III.22.
103   Emerson, 'Personal', *Works*, V.291.
104   Cadava, *Emerson and the Climates of History*, 11.
105   Frederic Jameson, *The Political Unconscious: Narrative as Socially Symbolic Act* (Ithaca: Cornell University Press, 1981), 61.
106   Friedrich Nietzsche, *Basic Writings of Nietzsche*, tr. Walter Kaufmann (New York: Modern Library, 1968), 175 n6.
107   Plato, *Sophist*, *The Collected Dialogues of Plato*, tr. Edith Hamilton and Huntington Cairns (Princeton: Princeton University Press, 1961), 251a, 996.
108   Jacques Derrida, 'White Mythology: Metaphor in the Text of Philosophy', *Margins of Philosophy*, tr. Alan Bass (Chicago: The University of Chicago Press, 1982), 209.

VI Founding Thoughts

1   Emerson, 'Land', *Works*, V.36.
2   John Locke, *Two Treatises of Government*, ed. Peter Laslett (Cambridge: Cambridge University Press, 1988), 9.
3   Robert Filmer, *Patriarcha, or the Natural Power of Kings* (1680). See *Patriarcha and other Writings*, ed. Johann P. Sommerville (Cambridge: Cambridge University Press, 1991).
4   Algernon Sidney, *Discourses Concerning Government* (1698), ed. Thomas G. West (Indianapolis: Liberty Classics, 1990), Sec. 1.
5   John Locke, *Second Treatise on Government*, Ch. VI. Of Paternal Power, §57.
6   *The American Republic: Primary Sources*, ed. Bruce Frohnen (Indianapolis: Liberty Fund, Inc., 2002), 140.
7   Frohnen, ed. *The American Republic*, 141.
8   Frohnen, ed. *The American Republic*, 143.
9   Frohnen, ed. *The American Republic*, 143.
10   Frohnen, ed. *The American Republic*, 143.
11   Frohnen, ed. *The American Republic*, 145.
12   Frohnen, ed. *The American Republic*, 145.
13   Emerson, 'Historical Discourse at Concord', *Works*, XI.68.
14   Frohnen, ed. *The American Republic*, 144–5.
15   Frohnen, ed. *The American Republic*, 182.
16   Frohnen, ed. *The American Republic*, 182.
17   Frohnen, ed. *The American Republic*, 182–3.
18   Frohnen, ed. *The American Republic*, 185.
19   Frohnen, ed. *The American Republic*, 190–1.
20   Frohnen, ed. *The American Republic*, 200.
21   *Correspondence of Carlyle and Emerson* (May 18, 1847), II.85.
22   Ferdinand Canning Scott Schiller, *Must Philosophers Disagree?: And Other Essays in Popular Philosophy* (London: Macmillan, 1934), 10.
23   Hannah Arendt, *On Revolution* (New York: Viking Press, 1963), 40.
24   Cavell, *Emerson's Transcendental Etudes*, 129.

25 Thomas Jefferson wrote in 1825, the year before his death: 'Neither aiming at originality of principle or sentiment, nor yet copied from any particular and previous writing, [the Declaration of Independence] was intended to be an expression of the American mind, and to give to that expression the proper tone and spirit called for by the occasion.' *The Essential Thomas Jefferson*, ed. John Dewey (New York: Longmans, Green and Co., 1940), 32.

26 Carlyle, *On Heroes, Hero-Worship, and the Heroic in History*, Lecture I, 'The Hero as Divinity', 23.

27 Emerson, 'Literary Ethics', *Works*, I.162.

28 William H. Gass, 'Emerson and the Essay', *Estimating Emerson*, 566.

29 Emerson, *Journals* (28 May 1839), VII.202.

30 Gass, 'Emerson and the Essay', *Estimating Emerson*, 579.

31 Melville, Letter to Evert A. Duyckinck (3 March 1849), *Estimating Emerson*, 103.

32 Gass, 'Emerson and the Essay', *Estimating Emerson*, 575.

33 Jorge Luis Borges, 'Pierre Menard, Author of the *Quixote*', *Collected Fictions* (New York: Penguin Books, 1998), 93.

34 Borges, *Collected Fictions*, 94.

35 Emerson, 'Education', *Works*, X.143.

36 Emerson, 'Self-Reliance', *Works*, II.45.

37 Gass, 'Emerson and the Essay', *Estimating Emerson*, 578.

38 See John Updike, 'Emersonianism' and 'Big Dead White Male', *Estimating Emerson*, 530–46 and 547–54.

39 Emerson, 'Self-Reliance', *Works*, II.69.

40 Emerson, 'Self-Reliance', *Works*, II.69.

41 Frederick Douglass, 'Self-Made Men', *Estimating Emerson*, 162–3.

42 Douglass, 'Self-Made Men', *Estimating Emerson*, 156.

43 Douglass, 'Self-Made Men', *Estimating Emerson*, 156–7.

44 Douglass, 'Self-Made Men', *Estimating Emerson*, 156.

45 Douglass, 'Self-Made Men', *Estimating Emerson*, 157.

46 Douglass, 'Self-Made Men', *Estimating Emerson*, 171.

47 Douglass, 'Self-Made Men', *Estimating Emerson*, 171–2.

48 Douglass, 'Self-Made Men', *Estimating Emerson*, 173.

49 Douglass, 'Self-Made Men', *Estimating Emerson*, 173.

50 Virgil, *Georgics*, Book II, 22.

51 Andrea Wulf, *Founding Gardeners: The Revolutionary Generation, Nature, and the Shaping of the American Nation* (New York: Knopf, 2011), 4.

52 Thomas Jefferson, *Notes on the State of Virginia* (London: John Stockdale, 1787), 62.

53 Wulf, *Founding Gardeners*, 15.

54 Wulf, *Founding Gardeners*, 52.

55 Wulf, *Founding Gardeners*, 62.

56 Angela Lucas, *Anglo-Irish Poems of the Middle Ages* (Dublin: Columba Press, 1995).

57 Thomas Jefferson, *The Works of Thomas Jefferson*, Federal Edition, ed. Paul Leicester Ford (New York: G. P. Putnam's and Sons, 1904–5), Vol. 4, *Notes on Virginia II*, Query XXII.

58 Jefferson, *The Works of Thomas Jefferson*, Vol. 4, Query XXII.

59 Abraham Lincoln, 'The Gettysburg Address', *Abraham Lincoln: Complete Works, Comprising his Speeches, Letters, State Papers, and Miscellaneous Writings*, ed. John G. Nicolay and John Hay (New York: The Century Co., 1907).

60 Abraham Lincoln, 'The Emancipation Proclamation', *Abraham Lincoln: Complete Works*.
61 Emerson, 'The Emancipation Proclamation', *Works*, XI.320.
62 Emerson, 'The Emancipation Proclamation', *Works*, XI.315.
63 Emerson, 'Lincoln', *Works*, XI.329.
64 Emerson, 'Lincoln', *Works*, XI.337.
65 Emerson, 'Lincoln', *Works*, XI.330.
66 Emerson, 'The Emancipation Proclamation', *Works*, XI.318.
67 Emerson, 'Lincoln', *Works*, XI.334–5.
68 'Declaration of Independence', *The American Republic*, ed. Frohnen, 189.
69 Abraham Lincoln, *The Collected Works of Abraham Lincoln*, ed. Roy P. Basler (New Brunswick: Rutgers University Press, 1953), Vol. V, 388–9. The full sequence of Lincoln's considered options was expressed to Horace Greeley this way: 'My paramount object in this struggle is to save the Union, and is not either to save or to destroy slavery. If I could save the Union without freeing any slave I would do it, and if I could save it by freeing all the slaves I would do it; and if I could save it by freeing some and leaving others alone I could also do that. What I do about slavery, and the colored race, I do because I believe it helps to save the Union.' And Lincoln concluded the letter by stating 'I intend no modification of my oft-expressed personal wish that all men everywhere could be free' (22 August 1862).
70 Emerson, 'The American Scholar', *Works*, I.81.
71 Emerson, 'The American Scholar', *Works*, I.114.
72 Emerson, 'The Young American', *Works*, I.363.
73 Emerson, *Nature*, *Works*, I.3.
74 Emerson, *Nature*, *Works*, I.3.
75 Emerson, 'The American Scholar', *Works*, I.81.
76 Emerson, 'The American Scholar', *Works*, I.81.
77 Emerson, 'The Young American', I.368.
78 Stanley Cavell, 'Declining Decline: Wittgenstein as a Philosopher of Culture', *This New Yet Unapproachable America: Lectures after Emerson after Wittgenstein* (Albuquerque: Living Batch Press, 1989), 70.
79 Alexis de Tocqueville, *Democracy in America* (1840), Vol. II, First Book, Ch. 1, 170.

VII A Child of the Saxon Race

1 Emerson, 'Race', *Works*, V.48.
2 West, 'The Emersonian Prehistory of American Pragmatism', *Estimating Emerson*, 640–1.
3 Emerson, 'Race', *Works*, V.48.
4 Emerson, 'Aristocracy', *Works*, V.180.
5 Emerson, 'Character', *Works*, V.130.
6 Emerson, 'Character', *Works*, V.130.
7 West, 'The Emersonian Prehistory of American Pragmatism', *Estimating Emerson*, 642.
8 Emerson, 'Speech at Manchester', *Works*, V.312.
9 Emerson, 'Speech at Manchester', *Works*, V.311.
10 Emerson, 'Speech at Manchester', *Works*, V.311.
11 Emerson, 'Speech at Manchester', *Works*, V.311.

VIII Living Without a Cause

1   Ludwig Wittgenstein, *On Certainty*, ed. G. E. M. Anscombe and G. H. von Wright, tr. Denis Paul and G. E. M. Anscombe (New York: Harper, 1969), §471.

2   Virgil, *Georgics*, Book II, 32.

3   John 1:3.

4   Virgil, *Georgics*, Book III, 49.

5   J. L. Austin, *How To Do Things With Words* (Cambridge: Harvard University Press, 1962), 1.

6   Austin, *How To Do Things With Words*, 5.

7   Austin, *How To Do Things With Words*, 6.

8   'Naturalization Oath of Allegiance to the United States of America', Code of Federal Regulations Sec. 337.1 based on codification in Sec. 337(a) of the Immigration and Nationality Act (INA).

9   Brother Lawrence, *The Practice of the Presence of God the best rule of a Holy Life, Being Conversations and Letters of Nicholas Herman of Lorraine, Brother Lawrence* (New York: Fleming H. Revell Company, 1895), 12–13.

10   St Francis of Assisi, *Letter to All the Friars* (New York: Classic Books International, 2010), 76.

11   Sophocles, *Oedipus the King*, tr. David Grene (Chicago: The University of Chicago Press, 2010), 14–15.

12   Still, this may be an American notion of the foundling – someone inspired, as Emerson's experimenter, to be 'an endless seeker, with no Past at my back'. Whereas an assessment of foundling figures in European culture, including Carlyle's Diogenes Teufelsdröckh, might reveal, as Robert Milder notes, how '[t]he foundling was a favorite Romantic image for humanity, children of high lineage abandoned on the threshold of the world. […] Unless he can establish paternity and thereby identity, the Romantic foundling is condemned to be a wanderer'. Thus despite a conspicuous example such as Billy Budd (a foundling whose '[n]oble descent was as evident in him as in a blood horse'), it would seem that being (or figuring oneself as) a foundling is a condition for identity as lived and known in America (Cf. also the figure of the foundling as it resonates from the last line of *Moby-Dick*, where Ishmael characterizes himself as 'another orphan.' Further enriching the recursion of genealogical, maeutic and anthropomorphic metaphors in the American literary, political and moral imagination, the image of the approaching *Rachael*'s 'search after her missing children' suggests that sailors, and castaways such as Ishmael, are not solely parented — and sometimes abandoned — by men (call them captains and mates) but also by the ship that carries them, by the country whose flag they sail beneath.) Emerson, 'Circles', *Works*, II.318; Robert Milder, *Exiled Royalites: Melville and the Life We Imagine* (Oxford: Oxford University Press, 2006), 101; Herman Melville, *Billy Budd, Sailor*, ed. Harrison Hayford and Merton M. Sealts, Jr. (Chicago: The University of Chicago Press, 1962), 52.

13   E. B. White, 'Here is New York', *Essays of E. B. White* (New York: Perennial Classics 1977), 150.

14   Emerson, *Journals* (6 September 1833), IV.237.

15   Emerson, 'Experience', *Works*, III.35.

16   Friedrich Nietzsche, *On the Genealogy of Morals: A Polemic*, *Basic Writings of Nietzsche*, tr. Walter Kaufman, Preface, Sec. 1, 451.

17   Henry David Thoreau, *Walden, or, Life in the Woods* (New York: The Library of America, 1991), 139. See also David LaRocca, 'In the Place of Mourning: Questioning the Privations of the Private', *Nineteenth-Century Prose*, Vol. 40, No. 2 (Fall 2013), and 'A Desperate Education: Reading Thoreau's *Walden* in Douglas Sirk's *All That Heaven Allows*', *Film and Philosophy*, Vol. 8 (2004), 1–16.

18   Jonathan Franzen, 'First City', *How to Be Alone: Essays* (New York: Farrar, Straus and Giroux, 2002), 187.

19   Emerson, 'Circles', *Works*, II.318.

20   Emerson, 'Land', *Works*, V.35.

21   Emerson, 'Fate', *Works*, VI.3.

22   Emerson, 'Land', *Works*, V.37.

23   Emerson, 'Land', *Works*, V.37.

24   Emerson, 'Land', *Works*, V.37.

25   Emerson, 'Race', *Works*, V.52.

26   Emerson, 'Self-Reliance', *Works*, II.51.

27   Emerson, 'Self-Reliance', *Works*, II.66. See also Emerson, *Journals* (1838), VII.149.

28   Emerson, 'Education' (1863–4), *Works*, X.136.

29   Emerson, 'Fate', *Works*, VI.3.

30   Emerson, 'Wealth', *Works*, V.166.

31   Emerson, 'Wealth', *Works*, V.165.

32   Emerson, 'Result', *Works*, V.307.

33   Sigmund Freud, 'The Ego and the Super Ego', *The Ego and the Id* (1923; first English publication 1927), Ch. III. Cf. also the Standard Edition, ed. Peter Gay, tr. James Strachey (New York: W. W. Norton & Company, Inc., 1989/1960), 35: 'Nevertheless it is not possible to speak of direct inheritance in the ego. It is here that the gulf between an actual individual and the concept of a species becomes evident. Moreover, one must not take the difference between the ego and id in too hard-and-fast a sense, nor forget that the ego is a specially differentiated part of the id. The experiences of the ego seem at first to be lost for inheritance; but when they have been repeated often enough and with sufficient strength in many individuals in successive generations, they transform themselves, so to say, into experiences of the id, the impressions of which are preserved by heredity. Thus in the id, which is capable of being inherited, are harboured residues of the existences of countless egos; and, when the ego forms its super-ego out of the id, it may perhaps only be reviving shapes of former egos and be bringing them to resurrection.

34   *Correspondence of Carlyle and Emerson* (3 February 1835), I.32.

35   Nietzsche, 'Raids of an Untimely Man', *Twilight of the Idols*, Sec. 13, 58. See also *Estimating Emerson*, 284.

36   Emerson, 'History', *Works*, II.7.

37   Cavell, *Emerson's Transcendental Etudes*, 164.

38   Emerson, 'Circles', *Works*, II.318.

39   Emerson, 'Ability', *Works*, V.77.

40   Emerson, 'Fate', *Works*, VI.3.

41   Emerson, 'Quotation and Originality', *Works*, VIII.190.

42   Seneca, *Epistles 66–92*, tr. Richard M. Gummere (Cambridge: Harvard University Press, 1920), Loeb No. 76, Letter LXXVII, 128.

43   Emerson, 'Discipline', *Nature*, *Works*, I.36.

44   Dewey, 'Emerson – The Philosopher of Democracy', *Estimating Emerson*, 293.

45   Emerson, 'Past and Present' (the *Dial*, July 1843), *Works*, XII.380.

46 Emerson, 'Powers and Laws of Thought', *Works*, XII.52–3.

47 Emerson, *Journals* (13 July 1833), IV.200.

48 Emerson, *Journals* (13 July 1833), IV.199.

49 See for example Linnaeus' extensive chart illustration '*Caroli Linnæi Regnum Animale*' from the first edition of *Systema Naturae* (1735).

50 Emerson, 'Concord Walks' (1867) *Works*, XII.174.

51 See for example a circular cladogram on display in The Hall of Human Origins at The American Museum of Natural History in New York (2012).

52 Gilles Deleuze and Félix Guattari, *A Thousand Plateaus: Capitalism and Schizophrenia*, tr. Brian Massumi (Minneapolis: University of Minnesota Press, 1987), 17.

53 Deleuze and Guattari, *A Thousand Plateaus*, 7.

54 Emerson, *Works*: 'Beauty', VI.281; 'The Fortune of the Republic', XI.512.

55 Emerson, 'The Powers and Laws of Thought', *Works*, XII.43. The inclusion of the snowflake in this context also bears relation to the theory (and metaphor) of fractals and fractal geometry as innovated by mathematician Benoit Mandelbrot. See *Fractals: Hunting the Hidden Dimension* (2008; *Nova*, S36:E4), dir. Michael Schwarz and Bill Jersey. For more on the semiotics of the farm and work of the farmer, see David LaRocca, 'Performative Inferentialism: A Semiotic Ethics', *Liminalities: A Journal of Performance Studies*, Vol. 9, No. 1 (February 2013), 1–26.

56 Darwin, *The Origin of Species*, Ch. XIV, 425. Cf. also Ch. III, 72.

57 Werner Herzog, *Herzog on Herzog*, ed. Paul Cronin (New York: Faber and Faber, 2002), 66.

58 Thomas Kuhn, *The Structure of Scientific Revolutions*, Third Edition (Chicago: The University of Chicago Press, 1996/1962), 55, 64.

59 Deleuze and Guattari, *A Thousand Plateaus*, 8, 12.

60 Throughout this section, I am especially indebted to David Kohn of the American Museum of Natural History and the Director and General Editor of the Darwin Manuscripts Project for his generous and informed remarks about Darwin's notebooks and Darwin's reading at the time of composing them.

61 Darwin, *Notebook B* (1837), 36. Cf. *The Origin of Species*, Ch. IV, 119. See also an early tree of life diagram featuring prominent branching in *Charles Darwin's Notebooks, 1836–44*, ed. Paul H. Barrett, et al. (Ithaca: Cornell University Press), fig. 2, 177.

62 John Stevens Henslow, *The Principles of Descriptive and Physiological Botany* (London: Longman, 1836/1835), Pt. I, Ch. II, Sec. 1, No. 59, 51–2.

63 Charles Darwin, *The Origin of Species*, Ch. IV, 119.

64 Erasmus Darwin, *Zoonomia; or, The Laws of Organic Life* (1794–6), 4 vols (London: J. Johnson, 1801), Vol I, 487.

65 See Darwin's notebook sketch from 21 April 1868.

66 Darwin, *Notebook B* (1837). See Justin Prystash, 'Zoomorphizing the Human: How to Use Darwin's Coral and Barnacles', *Rhizomes*, No. 24 (2012).

IX Adapting Some Secret of His Own Anatomy

1 Richard Dawkins, *The Selfish Gene* (Oxford: Oxford University press, 2006/1976), 47, 256, 265. See also Richard Dawkins, 'Replicators and Vehicles', *Current Problems*

in *Sociobiology*, ed. King's College Sociobiology Group (Cambridge: Cambridge University Press, 1982), 45–64.

2 Dawkins, *The Selfish Gene*, 192.
3 Dawkins, *The Selfish Gene*, 192.
4 Dawkins, *The Selfish Gene*, 192.
5 Dawkins, *The Selfish Gene*, 192.
6 Jean-Baptiste de Lamarck, *Zoological Philosophy: An Exposition with Regard to the Natural History of Animals*, tr. Hugh Elliot (London: Macmillan and Company, 1809), 107.
7 Lamarck, *Zoological Philosophy*, 107.
8 Lamarck, *Zoological Philosophy*, 113.
9 Lamarck, *Zoological Philosophy*, 113.
10 Emerson, *Works*: 'Land', V.36; 'Ability', V.74.
11 Emerson, 'Result', *Works*, V.303.
12 Emerson, 'Ability', *Works*, V.77.
13 Emerson, 'Ability', *Works*, V.79.
14 Emerson, 'Truth', *Works*, V.117.
15 Emerson, 'Wealth', *Works*, V.166.
16 Elizabeth Gaskell, *North and South* (Leipzig: Bernhard Tauchnitz, 1855), Ch. XL, 328.
17 Emerson, 'Truth', *English Traits*, *Works*, V.116.
18 Gaskell, *North and South*, 328.
19 Emerson, 'Truth', *Works*, V.116.
20 Gaskell, *North and South*, 328.
21 Emerson, 'Truth', *Works*, V.119.
22 Burton, *The Anatomy of Melancholy*, 211–16.
23 Burton, *The Anatomy of Melancholy*, 212–13.

X First Blood

1 Herzog, *Herzog on Herzog*, 81, 136.
2 Emerson, 'Experience', *Works*, III.53.
3 Emerson, 'Experience', *Works*, III.75.
4 Emerson, 'Experience', *Works*, III.65–6.
5 Frederick Parkes Weber, *Aspects of Death and Correlated Aspects of Life in Art, Epigram, and Poetry: Contributions Towards an Anthology and Iconography of the Subject*, Third Edition (New York: Paul B. Hoeber, 1918), 166.
6 Emerson, *Works*: 'irresistible offshoots', 'Ability', V.77; 'irresistible dictation', 'Fate', VI.3–4; 'irresistible nature', 'Experience', III.66.
7 Emerson, 'Fate', *Works*, VI.4.
8 Emerson, 'Self-Reliance', *Works*, II.55.
9 John 1:14.
10 Augustine, *The Confessions*, tr. Rex Warner (New York: New American Library of Penguin Putnam, 2001), 43.
11 Augustine, *The Confessions*, 45.
12 Augustine, *The Confessions*, 56.
13 Augustine, *The Confessions*, 257.

14 Jean Leclercq, *The Love of Learning and the Desire For God: A Study of Monastic Culture* (New York: Fordham University Press, 1982), 101.

15 Paul J. Griffiths, *Religious Reading: The Place of Reading in the Practice of Religion* (Oxford: Oxford University Press, 1999), 43.

16 Griffiths, *Religious Reading*, 46. Ezekiel, 3.1–3; translation from *The New Oxford Annotated Bible*, ed. Herbert G. May and Bruce M. Metzger (Oxford: Oxford University Press, 1977).

17 Mill, 'Of the Limits to the Authority of Society Over the Individual', *On Liberty*, IV.94.

18 Emerson, 'Self-Reliance', *Works*, II.45.

19 I Corinthians, 7.28.

20 Revelation, 14.4.

21 John, 8.7–8, 10–11.

22 John, 1.29.

23 Exodus, 12.22–3.

24 Leviticus, 5.6.

25 1 Peter, 1.18–19.

26 John, 1.29.

27 Matthew, 26.26.

28 John, 1.29.

29 Emerson, 'The Lord's Supper', *Works*, XI.4.

30 I Corinthians, 11.24–5.

31 Emerson, 'The Lord's Supper', *Works*, XI.8.

32 Emerson, 'The Lord's Supper', *Works*, XI.9.

33 Emerson, 'The Lord's Supper', *Works*, XI.9; John 6.63.

34 Emerson, 'The Lord's Supper', *Works*, XI.3, 20; Romans, 14.17.

35 Emerson, 'The Method of Nature', *Works*, I.221.

36 Emerson, 'The Method of Nature', *Works*, I.221.

37 Emerson, 'The Method of Nature', *Works*, I.221.

38 Emerson, 'The Method of Nature', *Works*, I.221.

39 Emerson, 'The Method of Nature', *Works*, I.221.

40 Emerson, 'The Method of Nature', *Works*, I.204.

41 Emerson, 'Nominalist and Realist', *Works*, III.233.

42 Emerson, 'Spiritual Laws', *Works*, II.132.

43 Emerson, 'Lecture on the Times', *Works*, I.281–2.

44 Beer, *Darwin's Plots*, 57.

45 Beer, *Darwin's Plots*, 58.

46 Melville, *The Writings of Herman Melville*, The Northwestern-Newberry Edition, *Moby-Dick; or, The Whale*, ed. Harrison Hayford, Hershel Parker and G. Thomas Tanselle (Evanston: Northwestern University Press, 1988), Vol. VI, 970.

47 Melville, *Moby-Dick*, 'The Forge', Ch. 113.

48 Melville, *The Writings of Herman Melville*, Vol. VI, 970. See also Hershel Parker, *Herman Melville: A Biography* (Baltimore: The Johns Hopkins University Press, 2002), Vol. II, 15–16.

49 Emerson, 'Self-Reliance', *Works*, II.45.

50 Emerson, 'Experience', *Works*, III.49.

51 Emerson, *Journals* (17 August 1837), III.363.

52 Seneca, *Epistles*, LXXXVIII.

53 Emerson, 'Religion', *Works*, V.225.

54 Diogenes Laertius, *Hellenistic Philosophy*, tr. Brad Inwood and Lloyd P. Gerson (Indianapolis: Hackett Publishing Co. Inc., 1997/1988), Sec. 89 and 94, 192–3. See also *The Stoics Reader: Selected Writings and Testimonia*, tr. Inwood and Gerson (Hackett Publishing Company, Inc., 2008).
55 Diogenes Laertius, *Hellenistic Philosophy*, Sec. 147, 136.
56 Emerson, 'Heroism', *Works*, II.249.
57 Emerson, 'The Method of Nature', *Works*, I.204.
58 Emerson, 'Experience', *Works*, III.78.
59 Emerson, 'The Tragic', *Works*, XII.414.
60 Emerson, 'Circles', *Works*, II.308.
61 Emerson, *Works*: 'The Uses of Great Men', IV.8; 'Self-Reliance', II.74.
62 Emerson, 'Self-Reliance', *Works*, II.74.
63 Wittgenstein, *Philosophical Investigations*, v.
64 Emerson, 'Experience', *Works*, III.35.
65 Genesis, 1.27.
66 John, 1.10–14.
67 Denis Diderot, *Jacques, The Fatalist and his Master*, tr. David Coward (Oxford: Oxford University Press, 1999), 7.
68 Diderot, *Jacques, The Fatalist and his Master*, 7.
69 Marcus Aurelius, *The Meditations*, tr. G. M. A. Grube (Indianapolis: Hackett Publishing Company, Inc., 1983), IX.28.
70 Aurelius, *The Meditations*, VI.10.
71 Aurelius, *The Meditations*, VII.75.
72 Aurelius, *The Meditations*, VII.75.
73 Anne Bogart, *And Then, You Act: Making Art in An Unpredictable World* (New York: Routledge, 2007), 2.
74 Bogart, *And Then, You Act*, 2.
75 Bogart, *And Then, You Act*, 3.
76 From an earlier version of Bogart's Introduction to *And Then, You Act*.
77 Emerson, 'Self-Reliance', *Works*, II.45.
78 Bogart, *And Then, You Act*, 17.
79 From an earlier version of Bogart's Introduction to *And Then, You Act*.
80 Emerson, 'The Concord Hymn' (4 July 1837), *Works*, IX.158.
81 Emerson, *Nature*, *Works*, I.3.
82 Emerson, 'The Young American', *Works*, I.370.
83 Emerson, 'Literary Ethics', *Works*, I.159.
84 Emerson, 'The Method of Nature', *Works*, I.206.
85 Emerson, 'The Young American', *Works*, I.379.
86 Emerson, 'Self-Reliance', *Works*, II.46.
87 Emerson, 'Self-Reliance', *Works*, II.69.
88 Wittgenstein, *Philosophical Investigations*, §115.
89 Emerson, 'Aristocracy' (1848), *Works*, X.33.
90 Plato, *Republic*, tr. Hamilton and Cairns, Book VIII, 558b, 786.
91 Hamilton, *Men and Manners in America*, Vol. II, 283.
92 Emerson, 'The Emancipation Proclamation', *Works*, XI.324–5.
93 Emerson, 'The Emancipation Proclamation', *Works*, XI.325.
94 John Dewey, *The Quest for Certainty*, ed. Jo Ann Boydston (Carbondale: Southern Illinois University Press, 1988), *The Later Works, 1925–53*, Vol. IV (1929), 161–3.

95 Emerson, 'Nominalist and Realist', *Works*, III.233.

96 See David LaRocca, 'The Limits of Instruction' (pedagogical remarks on Lars von Trier's *The Five Obstructions*), *Film and Philosophy*, Vol. 13 (2009), 35–50.

97 Jacques Rancière, *The Ignorant Schoolmaster: Five Lessons in Intellectual Emancipation*, tr. Kristin Ross (Stanford: Stanford University Press, 1991), 1.

98 Rancière, *The Ignorant Schoolmaster*, 33.

99 Leo Tolstoy, *A Confession and other Religious Writings*, tr. Jane Kentish (New York: Viking Penguin, 1987), 21.

100 Michael Wood, 'Why Praise Astaire?' (a review of Stanley Cavell, *Philosophy the Day After Tomorrow* [Cambridge: Harvard University Press, 2005]), *The London Review of Books* (20 October 2005), 14.

101 John Rawls, *A Theory of Justice* (Cambridge: Belknap Press of Harvard University Press, 1971), Sec. 50, 325. See Nietzsche's 'Schopenhauer as Educator', *Untimely Meditations*, ed. Daniel Breazeale, tr. R. J. Hollingdale (Cambridge: Cambridge University Press, 1997), Sec. 6, 161–2: 'Sometimes it is harder to accede to a thing than it is to see its truth; and that is how most people may feel when they reflect on the proposition: 'Mankind must work continually at the production of individual great men – that and nothing else is its task.' [...] For the question is this: how can your life, the individual life, retain the highest value, the deepest significance? How can it be least squandered? Certainly only by your living for the good of the rarest and most valuable exemplars, and not for the good of the majority [...].' The phrase 'most valuable exemplars', has also been translated as 'most valuable types' (tr. Anthony M. Ludovici and Adrian Collins, 2009), and elsewhere by Hollingdale, whom Rawls cites (325n51), as 'most valuable specimens' (R. J. Hollingdale, *Nietzsche: The Man and His Philosophy*, Revised Edition [Cambridge: Cambridge University Press, 1999/1965], 104).

102 Cavell, 'What is the Emersonian Event?' *Emerson's Transcendental Etudes*, 184; see also *Etudes*, Ch. 9, note 2, 258; and Emerson, 'Considerations by the Way' (1860), *Works*, VI.278.

103 Cavell, *Emerson's Transcendental Etudes*, 166.

104 Emerson, *Complete Sermons*, Sermon LXVII, II.145.

105 Emerson, 'Self-Reliance', *Works*, II.46.

106 Emerson, 'An Address', *Works*, I.130–1. Emerson quotes from Wordsworth, *Miscellaneous Sonnets*, 'The World is Too Much with Us.'

107 Emerson, 'Circles', *Works*, II.318.

XI Second Selves

1 Emerson, *Journals* (1848), X.197.

2 Emerson, 'Race', *Works*, V.72.

3 Philip Sidney, Introduction 'An Apologie for Poetrie', *A Defence of Poesie* (1579).

4 Emerson, 'Character', *Works*, V.134.

5 Emerson, 'Aristocracy' (1848), *Works*, X.31.

6 Emerson, 'Aristocracy', *Works*, V.174.

7 Emerson, 'Aristocracy', *Works*, V.172.

8 Emerson, 'Race', *Works*, V.45.

9   Emerson, 'Race', *Works*, V.47.

10 Emerson, 'Result', *Works*, V.303.

11 Emerson, 'Character', *Works*, V.137.

12 Emerson, *Journals* (13 July 1833), IV.198.

13 Mill, *On Liberty*, III.63.

14 Mill, *On Liberty*, III.63. For more on Emerson and Mill on the self and individuality,
    see David LaRocca, 'The Opacity of the Initial: Deciphering the Terms of Agency and
    Identity in 'Self-Reliance', and *On Liberty*', *Ralph Waldo Emerson: Bicentennial Appraisals*,
    ed. Barry Tharaud (Trier, Germany: Wissenshaftlicher Verlag, 2007), 297–324.

15 Emerson, 'Race', *Works*, V.47.

16 Emerson, 'Race', *Works*, V.47.

17 Emerson, 'Race', *Works*, V.49.

18 Emerson, *Journals* (1847), X.168

19 Emerson, *Journals* (1847), X.168.

20 Emerson, *Journals* (1847), X.161.

21 Emerson, *Journals* (1851), XI.406. Cf. 'Moral Forces' (1862), *Later Lectures*, II.284–5.

22 Jim Harrison, *Off to the Side: A Memoir* (New York: Atlantic Monthly Press, 2002), 160.

23 Emerson, 'Aristocracy', *Works*, V.186.

24 Emerson, 'Aristocracy', *Works*, V.186.

25 Emerson, 'Nominalist and Realist', *Works*, III.246.

26 Emerson, 'Fate', *Works*, VI.3.

27 Emerson, 'The Times', *Works*, V.261.

28 Emerson, 'The Times', *Works*, V.262.

29 Emerson, 'Character', *Works*, V.134. Emerson's broad exploration of English traits
    is conducted as an alternation between an immersive study of history, philosophy,
    literature, and religion (in books and the material artifacts of culture), and a series
    of contingent encounters with particular, embodied Englishmen and women.
    This twofold engagement engenders an intuitive and proximate concern with the
    extent to which individual traits (of a person, of his or her personality) are, in
    fact, manifestations of the 'deep traits of race', and to what degree those traits find
    expression in the particularities of individual persons. Consequently, Emerson
    studies culture but also what he and his German guides call 'self-culture' – that
    sphere of individuated experience in which one's own efforts at *bildung*, at moral
    perfectionism, are articulated (See Emerson, *Works*: 'Self-Reliance', II.80; 'Goethe; or,
    the Writer', IV.288).

30 See, for example, Nicoloff, *Emerson on Race and History*, and Dolan, *Emerson's Liberalism*.

31 Emerson, 'Aristocracy', *Works*, V.186.

32 Emerson, 'Aristocracy', *Works*, V.187.

33 Melville, *Moby-Dick*, 'The Whiteness of the Whale', Ch. 42.

34 Emerson, 'Aristocracy' (1848), *Works*, X.33–4.

35 A definition of epigenetics written by Fatimah Jackson from an unpublished manuscript.

36 A. Eccleston, N. DeWitt, C. Gunter, B. Marte, and D. Nath, *Nature Insight:
    Epigenetics*, Vol. 447, No. 7143 (May 2007), 396–440.

37 A. Bird 'Perceptions of Epigenetics', *Nature*, Vol. 447, No. 7143 (May 2007), 396–8.

38 F. Jackson, M. Niculescu, and R. Jackson, 'Conceptual shifts needed to understand
    the dynamic interactions of genes, environment, epigenetics, social processes, and
    behavioral choices' (2012, an unpublished manuscript).

39 F. Jackson, et al., 'Conceptual shifts ...'.

40 F. Jackson, et al., 'Conceptual shifts …'.
41 Fatimah Jackson, 'Maternal Cigarette Smoking During Pregnancy' (2012, an unpublished manuscript).
42 Alfred Lord Tennyson, *In Memoriam A. H. H.* (Boston: Knight & Millet, 1901), Canto LVI, 68. A tribute to Arthur Henry Hallam (1850).
43 Dawkins, *The Selfish Gene*, 2, 233.
44 Judith Shulevitz, 'Lamarck's Revenge', (review of Richard C. Francis, *Epigenetics: The Ultimate Mystery of Inheritance* [New York: W. W. Norton & Company, 2011]), *The New Republic* (18 August 2001); 'Why Fathers Really Matter', *The New York Times* (8 September 2012).
45 Shulevitz, 'Lamarck's Revenge.'
46 F. Jackson, et al., 'Conceptual shifts …'.
47 Shulevitz, 'Lamarck's Revenge.'
48 Emerson, 'Race', *Works*, V.48.
49 F. Jackson, et al., 'Conceptual shifts …'.
50 F. Jackson, et al., 'Conceptual shifts …'.
51 Fatimah Jackson, 'Epigenetics', presented at a Content Seminar at the American Museum of Natural History in New York (2 April 2012).
52 I emphasize the speculative nature of this question as a way of acknowledging that it takes us beyond the scope of epigenetics as it is currently understood. As Fatimah Jackson noted after reading this passage in manuscript form, epigenetics does not involve changes to the genotype: 'only the epigenome is modified by heritable and non-heritable environmental influences. Wealth and privilege may indeed modify the epigenome since these are associated with consistently good nutrition, access to health care, etc.' Correspondence, F. Jackson to D. LaRocca (2 November 2012).
53 Emerson, 'Race', *Works*, V.54.
54 Emerson, 'Race', *Works*, V.69.
55 Hugh Raffles, 'Revolutionary Theory' (review of Rebecca Stott, *Darwin's Ghosts: The Secret History of Evolution* [New York: Spiegel & Grau, 2012]), *The New York Times Book Review* (15 July 2012), 15.
56 Stott, *Darwin's Ghosts*, 192.
57 Stott, *Darwin's Ghosts*, 192.
58 Correspondence, F. Jackson to D. LaRocca (2 November 2012).
59 Dawkins, *The Selfish Gene*, 192.
60 Emerson, 'Result', *Works*, V.302.

XII Genealogy and Guilt

1 Nietzsche, *On the Genealogy of Morality: A Polemic*, tr. Maudemarie Clark and Alan J. Swensen (Indianapolis: Hackett Publishing Company, Inc., 1998), II.6, 41.
2 Nietzsche, *On the Genealogy of Morality*, II.4, 39.
3 Nietzsche, *On the Genealogy of Morality*, II.19, 60–1.
4 Nietzsche, *On the Genealogy of Morality*, II.20, 62.
5 Wittgenstein, *Philosophical Investigations*, §115.
6 Nietzsche, *On the Genealogy of Morality*, I.9, 18.

7   Crevecoeur, *Letters from an American Farmer*, 22.
8   Crevecoeur, *Letters from an American Farmer*, 26.
9   Nietzsche, *On the Genealogy of Morality*, III.11, 83
10 See Nietzsche, 'On the Despisers of the Body', *Thus Spoke Zarathustra: A Book for All and None*, ed. Robert Pippin, tr. Adrian Del Caro (Cambridge: Cambridge University Press, 2006), First Part, 22–4.
11 Nietzsche, *On the Genealogy of Morality*, III.13, 86.
12 Nietzsche, *On the Genealogy of Morality*, III.19, 99.
13 Nietzsche, *On the Genealogy of Morality*, III.16, 92–3.
14 Nietzsche, *On the Genealogy of Morality*, III.22, 106.
15 Nietzsche, *On the Genealogy of Morality*, III.20, 102.
16 Nietzsche, *On the Genealogy of Morality*, III.20, 102.
17 Nietzsche, *On the Genealogy of Morality*, III.20, 102.
18 Nietzsche, *On the Genealogy of Morality*, III.28, 118.
19 Nietzsche, *On the Genealogy of Morality*, III.28, 118.
20 Nietzsche, *On the Genealogy of Morality*, III.28, 118.
21 Emerson, 'Literary Ethics', *Works*, I.175.
22 Emerson, 'Literary Ethics', *Works*, I.176.
23 Emerson, 'Prudence', *Works*, II.231.
24 Emerson, 'Literary Ethics', *Works*, I.177.
25 Emerson, 'Literary Ethics', *Works*, I.181–2.

XIII The Pirate Baptized

1   Voltaire, *Letters Concerning the English Nation*, Letter X. 'On Trade', 42.
2   Emerson, 'Land', *Works*, V.40.
3   Emerson, 'Truth', *Works*, V.121.
4   Emerson, 'Voyage to England', *Works*, V.28.
5   Emerson, 'Voyage to England', *Works*, V.28.
6   Emerson, 'Voyage to England', *Works*, V.28.
7   Emerson, 'Voyage to England', *Works*, V.31.
8   Emerson, 'Land', *Works*, V.41.
9   Joseph Rykwert, *Harvard Design Magazine*, No. 19 (Fall 2003/Winter 2004), 86.
10 Dorothy Norman, *Alfred Stieglitz: An American Seer* (New York: Random House/ Aperture, 1973), 45.
11 Ludwig Wittgenstein, *Tractatus Logico-Philosophicus*, tr. D. F. Pears and B. F. McGuinness (New York: Routledge, 1995/1961), §5.6.
12 Melville, *Moby-Dick*, 'The Mast-Head', Ch. 35.
13 Emerson, 'The Relation of Intellect to Natural Science', *Later Lectures*, I.161; 'Powers and Laws of Thought', *Works*, XII.22; *Journals* (1848), X.317.
14 Emerson, *Later Lectures*, I.162.
15 Emerson, 'Boston', Works, XII.188.
16 Emerson, *Journals* (2 January 1833), IV.103.
17 Emerson, *Journals* (2 January 1833), IV.104.
18 Emerson, *Journals* (2 January 1833), IV.104.
19 Emerson, *Journals* (7 January 1833), IV.107.

20 Emerson, *Journals* (2 January 1833), IV.103.

21 Emerson, *Journals* (14 January 1833), IV.109–10.

22 Emerson, *Journals* (1847), X.163.

23 Emerson, 'Experience', *Works*, III.83.

24 Emerson, 'Experience', *Works*, III.85.

25 Emerson, 'Voyage to England', *Works*, V.32.

26 William Shakespeare, *Julius Caesar*, Act V, Sc. I.

27 Shakespeare, *Julius Caesar*, Act V, Sc. I.

28 Montaigne, 'Parley Time is Dangerous', *Essays*, tr. D. Frame, 18.

29 Emerson, 'The Method of Nature', *Works*, I.203.

30 Emerson, 'The Emancipation Proclamation', *Works*, XI.325.

31 Emerson, *Journals* (1838), VII.43.

32 Matthew 7.12; Luke 6.31.

33 For the delineation of the formulations of the Categorical Imperative and its related principles in deontological ethics, see Immanuel Kant, *Foundations of the Metaphysics of Morals* (1785), tr. Lewis White Beck (Upper Saddle River, NJ: Prentice Hall, 1995/1959), Second Section, 38, 46. Cf. *Grounding of the Metaphysics of Morals*, tr. James W. Ellington (Indianapolis: Hackett Publishing Company, 1993/1981). The standard 3 formulations may be described as deriving from (1) the law of nature, or the 'categorical imperative', (2) the end itself, or the 'practical imperative', and (3) the kingdom of ends. All three forms presume the autonomy of the will, where the will can regard itself as creating universal law through its maxims.

34 Kant, *Foundations of the Metaphysics of Morals*, 37.

35 Shakespeare, *Julius Caesar*, Act V, Sc. I; Emerson, *Journals*, X.163.

36 Nietzsche, 'Natural History of Morals', *Beyond Good and Evil*, §187.

37 Shakespeare, *Twelfth Night*, Act V, Sc. I.

38 Emerson, 'Race' *Works*, V.56.

39 Emerson, 'Race', *Works*, V.64–5.

40 Emerson, 'Race', *Works*, V.49.

41 Emerson, 'Result', *Works*, V.931.

42 Emerson, 'Result', Works, V.303.

XIV My Giant Goes With Me

1 Emerson, 'Voyage to England', *Works*, V.25.

2 Emerson, 'Voyage to England', *Works*, V.28.

3 Emerson, 'Experience', *Works*, III.46.

4 Rebecca Solnit, *River of Shadows: Eadweard Muybridge and the Technological Wild West* (New York: Viking, 2003), 5.

5 Solnit, *River of Shadows*, 29.

6 Emerson, *Letters* (25 December 1832), I.360n.

7 Henry David Thoreau, *The Writings of Henry David Thoreau*, VI. Familiar Letters (H. D. Thoreau to Sofia Thoreau, 24 October 1847), ed. F. B. Sanborn (Boston: Houghton Mifflin and Company, 1906), 132–3.

8 Emerson, 'Self-Reliance', *Works*, II.59.

9 Emerson, 'Experience', *Works*, III.46.

10 Emerson, 'Self-Reliance', *Works*, II.58.

11 Emerson, 'Self-Reliance', *Works*, II.81.

12 Seneca, *Epistles*, Letter XXVIII, 75.

13 Seneca, *Epistles* (tr. R. M. Gummere), ix.

14 Seneca, *Epistles*, Letter XXVIII, 76.

15 Horace, *Epistles*, ed. Roland Mayer (Cambridge: University of Cambridge Press, 1994), Book I, Sec. XI, line 27, 71.

16 Merleau-Ponty, *Signs*, 200.

17 Emerson, 'Self-Reliance', *Works*, II.82.

18 Emerson, 'Culture', *Works*, VI.145.

19 Emerson, 'Culture', *Works*, VI.145–6.

20 Emerson, 'Self-Reliance', *Works*, II.75.

21 Emerson, 'Friendship', *Works*, II.214.

22 Emerson, 'Art', *Works*, II.360–2.

23 Seneca, *Epistles 1–65*, tr. Richard M. Gummere (Cambridge: Harvard University Press, 1996/1917), Loeb No. 75, Letter II, 33.

24 Seneca, *Epistles*, Letter CIV, 188–9.

25 Seneca, *Epistles*, Letter XXVIII, 77.

26 Seneca, *Epistles*, Letter II, 33.

27 Seneca, *Epistles*, Letter XVI, 65.

28 Emerson, 'Circles', *Works*, II.320.

29 Seneca, *Epistles*, Letter XXVIII, 76–7.

30 Emerson, 'Culture', *Works*, VI.146.

31 Emerson, 'Culture', *Works*, VI.146.

32 Emerson, 'Experience', *Works*, III.60.

33 Emerson, 'Literature', V.239.

34 Rush Rhees, 'Postscript', *Recollections of Wittgenstein*, 205.

35 Emerson, 'Culture', *Works*, VI.146.

36 Emerson, 'Culture', *Works*, VI.146–7.

37 Emerson, 'First Visit to England', *Works*, V.3.

38 Emerson, *Journals* (14 December 1833), IV.253.

39 From a manuscript owned by the Ralph Waldo Emerson Memorial Association, cited in *An Emerson Chronology* (15 January 1834), 88.

XV Corresponding Minds

1 Emerson, 'Culture', *Works*, VI.147.

2 *Correspondence of Carlyle and Emerson* (7 November 1838), Carlyle to Emerson with a postscript by Jane Carlyle, I.98.

3 *Correspondence of Carlyle and Emerson* (12 August 1834), I.21. See also *Estimating Emerson*, 31.

4 *Correspondence of Carlyle and Emerson* (15 November 1838), I.100–1.

5 Emerson, 'Experience', *Works*, III.72.

6 Emerson, 'History', *Works*, II.7.

7 *Correspondence of Carlyle and Emerson* (3 February 1835), I.35.

8 Thomas Carlyle, *The Diamond Necklace* (Boston: Houghton Mifflin, 1913), Ch. V, 63.

9 Translation by J. Kathleen Wine (Dartmouth College) and Henry C. Clark (Clemson University).

10 *Correspondence of Carlyle and Emerson* (12 March 1838), I.79.

11 McInerny, *Being Logical*, 7–8.

12 *Correspondence of Carlyle and Emerson* (15 November 1838), I.100.

13 *Correspondence of Carlyle and Emerson* (29 May 1839), I.125.

14 *Correspondence of Carlyle and Emerson* (17 April 1839), I.116; Carlyle's reference is to Virgil, *Aeneid*, XI.

15 *Correspondence of Carlyle and Emerson* (15 May 1839), I.124. Richard Monckton Milnes (1809–85), 1st Baron Houghton, English poet and essayist, member of Apostles Club, and supporter of Emerson in Great Britain.

16 *Correspondence of Carlyle and Emerson* (15 March 1839), I.112.

17 *Correspondence of Carlyle and Emerson* (8 February 1839), I.108–9.

XVI Titles Manifold

1 William Wordsworth, 'It is Not to be Thought of', *The Complete Poetical Works of William Wordsworth*, ed. Andrew J. George (Cambridge: The Riverside Press, 1904), 288.

2 Emerson, 'Aristocracy', *Works*, V.179.

3 Emerson, 'Language', *Nature*, *Works*, I.30.

4 George R. Stewart, *Names on the Land: A Historical Account of Place-Naming in the United States*, 3rd Edition (Boston: Houghton Mifflin, 1967), 38.

5 Emerson, *Works*: 'Aristocracy', V.178; responsibleness, 'Ability', V.99 and 'Aristocracy', V.180.

6 Emerson, 'Aristocracy', *Works*, V.179.

7 Emerson, 'Aristocracy', *Works*, V.180.

8 Emerson, 'Wealth', *Works*, V.165.

9 Wittgenstein, *Philosophical Investigations*, §1.

10 Wittgenstein, *Philosophical Investigations*, §1.

11 Wittgenstein, *Philosophical Investigations*, §7.

12 Wittgenstein, *Philosophical Investigations*, §6.

13 Emerson, 'Aristocracy', *Works*, V.180.

14 Montaigne, *Essays*, tr. D. Frame, Sec. 46, 202.

15 Emerson, *Works*: 'Manners', V.110; 'Aristocracy', V.178.

16 Emerson, 'Aristocracy', *Works*, V.180.

17 Montaigne, *Essays*, tr. D. Frame, Sec. 46, 202.

18 Shakespeare, *Coriolanus*, Act V, Sc. I.

19 Henry David Thoreau, *The Journals, 1837–61* (15 November 1851), ed. Damion Searls (New York: New York Review of Books, 2009), 96.

20 Stanley Cavell, *A Pitch of Philosophy: Autobiographical Exercises* (Cambridge: Harvard University Press, 1994), 24.

21 Cavell, *A Pitch of Philosophy*, 24.

22 Stanley Cavell, *Little Did I Know: Excerpts from Memory* (Stanford: Stanford University Press, 2010), 199.

23 Cavell, *Little Did I Know*, 199.

Notes

24 Cavell, *Little Did I Know*, 201.
25 Cavell, *Little Did I Know*, 202.
26 Cavell, *Little Did I Know*, 10.
27 *Sketches of Frank Gehry*, dir. Sydney Pollack (2006), *American Masters* (S20:E7).
28 Herzog, *Herzog on Herzog*, 8.
29 Solnit, *River of Shadows*, 27.
30 Solnit, *River of Shadows*, 271–2, endnote for page 3.
31 Solnit, *River of Shadows*, 37.
32 Cavell, *A Pitch of Philosophy*, 27.
33 Cavell, *A Pitch of Philosophy*, 27.
34 Cavell, *A Pitch of Philosophy*, 28.
35 Cavell, *A Pitch of Philosophy*, 28; Cavell, *Little Did I Know*, 10.
36 Emerson, 'Fate', *Works*, VI.47. For more on this line, and 'riding alternately the horses of human nature', see Cavell, 'Emerson's Constitutional Amending: Reading 'Fate', *Emerson's Transcendental Etudes*, 3, 198–200.
37 Emerson, 'The Poet', *Works*, III.21. For more on this line, and 'words as horses', see Stanley Cavell, 'Staying the Course', *Conditions Handsome and Unhandsome: The Constitution of Emersonian Perfectionism*, The Carus Lectures (Chicago: The University of Chicago Press, 1990), 22.
38 Plato, *Phaedrus*, tr. and ed. R. Hackforth (Cambridge: Cambridge University Press, 1972/1952), 246a-b.
39 *The Compact Edition of the Oxford English Dictionary* (Oxford: Oxford University Press, 1971), Vol. I, 361; 204 of the quarto page.
40 Cavell, *A Pitch of Philosophy*, 28–9.
41 Cavell, *A Pitch of Philosophy*, 25.
42 Cavell, *A Pitch of Philosophy*, 26.
43 Cavell, *A Pitch of Philosophy*, 26.
44 Cavell, *Little Did I Know*, 203.
45 Cavell, *A Pitch of Philosophy*, 26.
46 Emerson, 'The Uses of Natural History', *Selected Lectures*, 5.
47 Cavell, *Little Did I Know*, 206.
48 Cavell, *A Pitch of Philosophy*, 27.
49 Cavell, *A Pitch of Philosophy*, 28.
50 Ralph Waldo Emerson, *Emerson in His Journals*, ed. Joel Porte (Cambridge: Belknap Press of Harvard University Press, 1982), 1.
51 Emerson, *Journals* (1847), X.186.
52 Melville, *Moby-Dick*, 'The Masthead', Ch. 35.
53 Boris Pasternak, *Dr Zhivago* (1957), tr. Richard Pevear and Larissa Volokhonsky (New York: Pantheon Books, 2010), 87–8.
54 McInerny, *Being Logical*, 26.
55 Plato, *Sophist*, 251b.
56 See David LaRocca, 'Inconclusive Unscientific Postscript: Late Remarks on Kierkegaard and Kaufman', *The Philosophy of Charlie Kaufman* (Lexington: The University Press of Kentucky, 2011), 269–94.
57 Søren Kierkegaard, 'A First and Last Declaration', *Concluding Unscientific Postscript*, tr. David F. Swenson and Walter Lowrie (Princeton: Princeton University Press, 1968/1941), 551.
58 Kierkegaard, 'A First and Last Declaration', *Concluding Unscientific Postscript*, 551.

59 Jonathan Lear, 'Author of Authors', (a review of *Søren Kierkegaard: A Biography*, Joakim Garff, tr. Bruce H. Kirmmse [Princeton: Princeton University Press, 2005]), *The Times Literary Supplement* (28 January 2005), 3.
60 Kierkegaard, 'A First and Last Declaration', *Concluding Unscientific Postscript*, 551.
61 Kierkegaard, 'A First and Last Declaration', *Concluding Unscientific Postscript*, 552.
62 Garff, *Søren Kierkegaard: A Biography*, 214, 216.
63 Garff, *Søren Kierkegaard: A Biography*, 214; Lear, 'Author of Authors', *The Times Literary Supplement* (28 January 2005), 4.
64 Genesis, 1.3, 1.5, 1.8, 1.10, 2.19.
65 Emerson, *Works*: 'Experience', III.57; 'Considerations by the Way', VI.246.
66 Emerson, 'Experience', *Works*, III.57.
67 Emerson, *Journals* (1841), VIII.23.
68 Charles-Louis de Secondat, baron de La Brède et de Montesquieu, *The Persian Letters* (1721), tr. George R. Healy (Indianapolis: Hackett Publishing Company, Inc., 1964), 7.
69 Emerson, 'Eloquence', *Works*, VII.89.

Index

Bacon, Francis 42, 61, 109, 118, 141, 148, 254
Beach, Joseph Warren: 'Emerson and Evolution' 10, 25
Beer, Gillian 29
  Darwin's Plots 30, Int.24–5, Int.36, X.12
bees 117, 136, 142–3, V.21–2, 166, XIII.11
  see also Burton; Butler
beginning XI.2–3, XII.1
  beginning of the 244
  ending and VIII.9
  God and X.24
  immigrancy and 318
  origin and 107, X.1, X.17
  search for XII.2
  the word and VIII.3
  see also birth; blood; causation; conception; origins
Benjamin, Walter: 'Unpacking My Library' I.3
bildung *see* self-culture
biography 38, 59, Int.42, 113–15, V.23, 180
  philosophical 144
  see also autobiography
biology Int.10–11, 41, Int.35, II.8, 209
  biologism and II.8–10
  evolutionary 207–8, IX.1, X.16
  see also evolution; transcendental biology
Birrell, Augustine: 'Emerson' 12–13
birth
  American 65, I.29, XVI.6
  aristocratic I.29, VII.2, X.24, XI.2, XVI.7
  of books I.1, I.27, XV.4
  English upper class and 47–8, 256, 259
  second birth X.9, XI *passim*
  virgin 226
  see also beginning; class; causation; conception; epigenetics; rebirth; born again
Blau, Joseph: 'Emerson's Transcendentalist Individualism as a Social Philosophy' 4, 94
blood VI.20, X *passim*
  aristocracy and XI.2, XI.4
  culture in the I.29–30, IX.1

descent and 5
  epigenetics and XI.8
  equality and 90
  inheritance of VI.2
  land and XVI.2
  language and 133, III.13, VI.10
  is moral Int.45, 128
  name and XVI.6
  origins and 194
  purity and impurity of 165, VIII.8, 227
  race and I.32
  sacrifice and X.9–10, X.18, X.25
  see also children; DNA; miscegenation; origins; parent; pedigree; sin
Bloom, Harold: 'Emerson and Influence' 64–5
  'Mr. America' I.26, 87
Bogart, Anne: *And Then, You Act* X.20
Borges, Jorge Luis: 'Pierre Menard' 180
born again 188, VIII.5, X.9, 236, XI.2–3, 299–300, 313, 322 *see also* birth; rebirth
Bowler, Peter, J.: *Evolution* 21–2, 48, 262
branch 49–50, 208, VIII.23, 365n. 61 *see also* cladistics; topiary; tree; web
Bredin, Hugh 32
Brown, Lee Rust: *The Emerson Museum* V.16–17
Brownson, Orestes Augustus 12
Burnett, D. Graham 147
Burrow, Colin 79
Burton, Robert: *The Anatomy of Melancholy* I.1–5, V.9, IX.4, 319 *see also* melancholy
Butler, Charles: *The Feminine Monarchie*, viii, 163 *see also* bees

cabinets of natural history 122–3, 133, V *passim*, 253, 321 *see also* analogy; combination; composition; curation; metaphor
Cabot, James Elliot 69, 137
Cadava, Eduardo: *Emerson and the Climates of History* 16, 169
Calvinism 63–4, I.7, 161, 181, 234, 242
Carlyle, Thomas
  correspondence with Emerson i, 54, 70, 98, VI.11, 204, XV *passim*

Deleuze, Gilles and Félix Guattari: *A Thousand Plateaus* VIII.22–3

democracy Int.38, I.24, 88, 139, 174, 184, X.17, X.24, 254, XI.3 *see also* aristocracy; Plato; self-created; Tocqueville

Democritus 73 *see also* Burton, I.1

De Quincy, Thomas 59, 297

Derrida, Jacques: *Margins of Philosophy* vii, 160, 169

descent 5–6, Int.23–4, Int.31–3, Int.35–6, Int.52–3, II.7, 139, 161, VI.2, 190, 194, VIII.9, VIII.14, VIII.21, VIII.23, IX.1, X.1, X.12, X.17, X.24, XI.1, XI.5, XI.8, XVI.2, XVI.7, 363n. 12 *see also* ascent; birth; blood; class; pedigree

Dewey, John: 'Emerson – Philosopher of Democracy' 13, 206

Quest for Certainty, The 243–6

Dickens, Charles: *American Notes for Circulation* 2–3

'Nature's Greatness in Small Things' Int.9

dictation 32, 205, 222, 283, 326

irresistible 66, 96, 199, VIII.13, VIII.17, X.3, XI.3

see also blood; fate; language; originality; quotation

Digby, Kenelm III.13, 218

digestion 78, 144, X.5, X.7–8, X.10 *see also* Augustine; Burton; Eucharist

Diderot, Denis: *Encyclopédie* 147

Jacques, The Fatalist and his Master 236–7, 240

Diogenes Laertius 141, 230, 233, 236

Diogenes Teufelsdröckh *see* Carlyle: *Sartor Resartus*

divorce VI.9, VI.26, X.11 *see also* children; colonies

DNA 31, 92–3, 97, 222

American I.33

conceptual 137

epigenetics and 260, 262

genetic language (ATCG) and 116

mitosis and 179

parental 176, 205, X.1

tree of life and 208

see also blood; the hybrid; grammar

Dolan, Neal: *Emerson's Liberalism* Int.21, Int.23, 55

double-helix 31, 90, 92–3, 176 *see also* DNA; the hybrid

Douglass, Frederick: 'Self-Made Men' VI.19 *see also* self-created; self-made; self-reliance

Downer, Silas: 'A Son of Liberty' VI.3, VI.5, 175, 186

Drury, Maurice O'C. Int.4

Eliot, Charles William 11

Eliot, George 28, 30

Emancipation Proclamation Int.44, 184, 188 *see also* Lincoln

Emerson, Charles 298

Emerson, Ralph Waldo:

'Address to the Divinity School' 65

'Address … on … the Emancipation of the Negroes in the British West Indies, An' 4, Int.45

'Address at the Opening of the Concord Free Public Library' 99

'American Scholar, The' Pre.2, 14, 64–5, 88, 191

'Anglo-American, The' 56–8

'Aristocracy' (1848) 34, 241, 251–2, XI.7

'Aristocracy' (*English Traits* Ch. XI) 34, 48, XVI.2

'Art' 294

'Blight' 162

'Circles' 64, 234

'Characteristics of the English' 344n. 154

'Cockayne' (*English Traits* Ch. IX) Int.52, VI.23

'Compensation' 128

'Culture' 99, 293, 297, XV.1

'Demonology' 52

'Domestic Life' I.19

'Education', Int.14, 201, 340n. 60

'Eloquence' XVI.24

Encyclopedia I.13

'England' 34, 344n. 165

'England' (notebook *ED*) I.22

'English Character and Influence' 344n. 154

evolution 9–11, Int.10–13, Int.32–5,
    VIII.21, IX.2, X.24
  cultural Int.23, II.11, VIII.22, IX.1
  of identity XVI.7, XVI.13
  mental II.10, X.17
  see also Darwin; Lamarck
exogeneity and exogenous creation Int.54,
    111, 257 see also father; imitation;
    mother; parent; quotation

facts Int.14, 28, 30, 38, 44, 51, 62–3, 84,
    113, III.12, 129, V.10, 179, 249, 279,
    321, XVI.24
  acts and XVI.12
  analogy and III.17
  beliefs and 78, 127
  collect 3
  constitutional 52
  history and III.2, V.23, X.19, XVI.10
  interpretations and 28, 127
  laws and 52, 140
  material 18
  natural 19, 25, 28
  public and private III.2, V.23
  spiritual 12, 25, 110
  symbols and V.23
  use of 331
Faraday, Michael 69, 140
fate 15, 45, 109, 131, VI.10, 182, VIII.13,
    X.18, 293
  of books Int.76, X.14
  causation and 78, 197, X.25
  class and XI.4
  of embodiment 133
  epigenetics and XI.8
  genetics and 66
  geography and 128
  history and VII.1
  of metaphor 154
  names and XVI.6
  as natural history 125
  race and Int.42, Int.47
  sin and 230
  temperament and I.9
  see also dictation; Diderot: *Jacques,
    The Fatalist and his Master*;
    Emerson: 'Fate'; epigenetics;
    quotation

father 81, 87, 92, VI.2, VI.5, 188–9,
    VIII.2–4, 200, IX.4, X.1, XI.8, 329
  anonymous 184
  debt and the 180–2
  fore- 35, VII.2, 230
  of foundlings 197, 327, 363n. 12
  god- 284–5
  heavenly 105, X.5
  intellectual VI.18
  names from the XVI.2, XVI.9, XVI.11,
    XVI.13, XVI.15
  a nation VI.16
  as origin 180–1, VIII.18, VIII.20
  a people 175
  sin of the 263
  tongue 64
  writer- VI.15
  see also blood; children; mother;
    parent
fathered
  being 181–2, VI.20
  lands 189
  refusal of being 66
  see also causa sui; constitution; male
    pregnancy; originless
fatherless 181–2, 185, VI.20, 197 *see also*
    foundling; orphan; parent
fatherland (father country), 181–2, 196,
    XVI.2, 309 *see also* motherland
Fathers, Founding 41, 90, 173, VI.10,
    VI.14, VI.16, VI.22, 189–90,
    VIII.3–5, 282–3
Fichte, J. G.: *The Science of Knowledge*
    III.8
Fiedler, Leslie I.24, I.27
Filmer, Robert: *Patriarcha* VI.2
first cause 233, 267–8 *see also* causa
    prima
florilegium 73, IV.5, V *passim*, 141–2,
    144, 146–7, 167, 169 *see also*
    commonplace book, compendium;
    zibaldone
Foucault, Michel
  archaeology and 162
  on classifying Int.7
  Hermeneutics of the Subject, The 150
  Order of Things, The Int.7–8
foundationalism 33

guiltless 313 *see also* sinless

Hadot, Pierre: *Philosophy as a Way of Life*
    V.15
Haeckel, Ernst: *The History of Creation*
    Int.35
Hamilton, Thomas: *Men and Manners in*
    America V.6, 242
Harrison, Bernard: *Inconvenient Fictions*,
    Int.20
Harrison, Jim: *Off to the Side* 256
Harvey, Christopher: *The Synagogue* V.8,
    V.12
Hawthorne, Nathaniel 61, X.13
    on *English Traits* 53
Hegel, G. W. F. 12, 284
Heisenberg, Werner X.25
Henslow, John Stevens: *The Principles*
    of Descriptive and Physiological
    Botany VIII.23
Heraclitus 141
heraldry 48, 113, 164, 181, 197, 199, 255,
    306, 308, 310 *see also* land; names;
    pedigree
Herder, J. G.: 'On the Knowing and
    Feeling of the Human Soul' II.8–10
heredity 5, 48, VIII.9, VIII.15, IX.1, 255,
    XII.1, 300, 313, 364n. 33 *see also*
    blood; descent; pedigree
Herodotus: *Histories* V.14–15, V.23
Herschel, John F. W. 41
    Preliminary Discourse on the Study of
    Natural Philosophy, A III.21, 211
Herzog, Werner 209–10, 317
hierarchy 64, 211
    aristocracy and X.24, 255
    class and 259
    evolution and 46
    perfectionism and 247
    origins and X.24, XVI.4
    trees and Int.36, XI.5
    of values 33
    see also aristocracy; class; rhizome;
    tree
history, as biography III.2, V.23 *see also*
    biography
Horace: *Epistles* 292
horses 132, 251–2, 301

as second selves XI.1
of thought 318–19, 376nn. 36, 37
human body, the I.5, 133
    books and V.5
    expressiveness of III.7
    indebtedness of 269
    parts and laws of 140
    as visible garment 158
    see also dictation; fate; physiognomy;
    quotation
Hume, David 119
    On Human Understanding III.18
    skepticism and 230
    Treatise of Human Nature, A III.4, 302
humours, doctrine of I.9, 92 *see also*
    Burton; melancholy; temperaments
Hunterian Museum (London) 21
Huxley, Thomas Henry 22
hybrid, the Int.33, 121
    analogy and III.17
    English success and 39
    English Traits and 1–3
    museum design and 208
    Ritvo on Int.34
    transcendental biology and 21, 28
    see also combination; cross-breeding;
    cross-pollination; miscegenation
hypomnemata 144, V.15 *see also* Aurelius

imitation 66, 97, 99, 180, 254, 293
    memes and X.1, X.4, 264, 287
    as suicide 248
    quotation and 64
    as vice of our times 63
    see also authorship; memes; quotation
immigrants I.33, V.24, 184, VIII.5,
    VIII.9–12, 235–6, 309, 311
    names and XVI.13
    see also foundlings; orphans
individualism 38, I.34, 254
    'rugged' 183
    see also self-reliance
inductive reasoning Int.3, Int.8, Int.25,
    I.16, III.21, 145, V.18 *see also*
    enthymeme
inheritance 48, 86, 91, 133, 171, 176, 181,
    VI.22, 200, 202, 204, 216, X.4, 264,
    XIII.3, 287, 301, 309, 323